Design and Deploy a Secure Azure Environment

Mapping the NIST Cybersecurity Framework to Azure Services

Puthiyavan Udayakumar

Apress®

Design and Deploy a Secure Azure Environment: Mapping the NIST Cybersecurity Framework to Azure Services

Puthiyavan Udayakumar
Abu Dhabi, Abu Dhabi, United Arab Emirates

ISBN-13 (pbk): 978-1-4842-9677-6
https://doi.org/10.1007/978-1-4842-9678-3

ISBN-13 (electronic): 978-1-4842-9678-3

Managing Director, Apress Media LLC: Welmoed Spahr
Acquisitions Editor: Smriti Srivastava
Development Editor: Laura Berendson
Editorial Project Manager: Mark Powers
Copyeditor: Kim Wimpsett

Cover designed by eStudioCalamar

Cover image by Steve Buissinne on Pixabay (www.pixabay.com)

Distributed to the book trade worldwide by Apress Media, LLC, 1 New York Plaza, New York, NY 10004, U.S.A. Phone 1-800-SPRINGER, fax (201) 348-4505, e-mail orders-ny@springer-sbm.com, or visit www.springeronline.com. Apress Media, LLC is a California LLC and the sole member (owner) is Springer Science + Business Media Finance Inc (SSBM Finance Inc). SSBM Finance Inc is a Delaware corporation.

For information on translations, please e-mail booktranslations@springernature.com; for reprint, paperback, or audio rights, please e-mail bookpermissions@springernature.com.

Apress titles may be purchased in bulk for academic, corporate, or promotional use. eBook versions and licenses are also available for most titles. For more information, reference our Print and eBook Bulk Sales web page at www.apress.com/bulk-sales.

Any source code or other supplementary material referenced by the author in this book is available to readers on GitHub (https://github.com/Apress). For more detailed information, please visit https://www.apress.com/gp/services/source-code.

Paper in this product is recyclable

To the Apress team for supporting the publication of this book

Table of Contents

About the Author

Puthiyavan Udayakumar is an infrastructure architect with more than 15 years of experience in modernizing and securing IT infrastructure, including in the cloud. He has been writing technical books for more than 10 years on various infrastructure and cybersecurity domains. He has designed, deployed, and secured IT infrastructure on premises and in the cloud, including virtual servers, networks, storage, and desktops for various industries (such as pharmaceutical, banking, healthcare, aviation, and federal entities). He also earned the Master Certified Architect certification from Open Group.

About the Technical Reviewer

 **Kalyan Chanumolu** is a senior technical program manager at Microsoft. He works on building the engineering systems that power the world's computers. He has been a technical reviewer for books on ASP.NET, Blazor, microservices, and more, and is passionate about distributed systems and cloud computing. He has vast experience in software development, consulting, and migrating large customer workloads to the cloud. He loves cycling, swimming, and reading books.

Acknowledgments

Thanks to Smriti Srivastava for your invaluable support and guidance throughout the publication process of this book. Your role as an acquisitions editor was instrumental in bringing this book to fruition, and I am truly grateful for your expertise and dedication.

To Kalyan Chanumolu, I appreciate your time and effort in reviewing my work, providing detailed feedback, and assisting with the necessary revisions. Your professional approach, prompt communication, and attention to detail have made the publishing journey smoother and more fulfilling.

Special thanks to Shonmirin P. A for your tireless efforts in publishing this book.

Thanks to all the Apress production team members.

Introduction

The rapid growth and adoption of cloud computing technologies have revolutionized how organizations manage and deploy their information systems. However, with this technological advancement comes an increased risk of cyber threats and security breaches. Organizations need comprehensive frameworks and guidelines to address these concerns and to establish robust cybersecurity practices. One such framework that has gained significant traction in recent years is the National Institute of Standards and Technology (NIST) Cybersecurity Framework (CSF).

In this book, we will explore the implementation of the NIST CSF within an Azure cloud environment. This book provides a 360-degree view of the NIST CSF in line with Microsoft Azure Services.

In alignment with industry best practices, the NIST CSF provides a structure for organizations to assess and enhance their cybersecurity posture. This book shows how to leverage Azure's security features with the NIST CSF, enabling organizations to strengthen their cloud security and protect their valuable assets. Specifically, the book's chapters cover the following:

Chapter 1: Get Started with Azure Security

Chapter 1 is an introductory guide to Azure and the NIST CSF, providing essential knowledge to understand the subsequent chapters. The chapter covers the following key topics:

- Introduction to cybersecurity

- Getting started with cloud computing and Azure

- Microsoft Azure security capabilities

- The foundation of the NIST CSF

By the end of this chapter, you will have a clear understanding of the basic concepts of cybersecurity, cloud computing, and Microsoft Azure's security capabilities. You will also gain familiarity with the NIST CSF and its functions. This foundation sets the stage for the subsequent chapters, which map the Azure security controls to the framework and guide you on implementing effective cybersecurity practices within the Azure environment.

Chapter 2: Design and Deploy Security for Infrastructure, Data, and Applications

Chapter 2 focuses on designing and deploying effective security strategies in Azure, covering three key areas: securing infrastructure and platform components, securing identify, and securing apps and data. Additionally, the chapter introduces the concept of Microsoft SecOps, which integrates security and operations to enable proactive security practices. The chapter provides key insights for the following:

- Designing and deploying a strategy for securing infrastructure and platform components

- Designing and deploying a strategy for securing identify

- Designing and deploying a strategy for securing apps and data

- Getting started with Microsoft SecOps

By the end of this chapter, you will have a comprehensive understanding of designing and deploying security strategies in Azure. The chapter provides insights into securing infrastructure and platform components, implementing robust identify management, and safeguarding applications and data. Additionally, the chapter introduces you to the concept of Microsoft SecOps and the significance of integrating security and operations in Azure environments. This knowledge equips you with the foundation to implement adequate security practices in subsequent chapters.

Chapter 3: Design and Deploy an Identify Solution

Chapter 3 introduces Azure's identify security services and their alignment with the NIST CSF's Identify functions. It explores vital Azure services that support asset management, business environment analysis, governance, and risk assessment. The chapter offers key insights about the following topics:

- Introduction to Azure identify security services

- Asset Management (ID.AM)

- Business Environment (ID.BE)

- Governance (ID.GV)

- Risk Assessment (ID.RA)

By the end of this chapter, you will have a solid understanding of Azure's identify security services and their alignment with the NIST CSF's Identify functions. You will gain insights into asset management, business environment analysis, governance, and risk assessment within Azure. This knowledge will lay the foundation for implementing effective identify security strategies in subsequent chapters, strengthening the overall security posture of Azure environments.

Chapter 4: Design and Deploy a Protect Solution – Part 01

Chapter 4 introduces Azure's protect security services and their alignment with the NIST Cybersecurity Framework's Protect functions. It explores vital Azure services that support identify management, authentication, access control, awareness and training.

- Introduction to Azure protect security services

- PR.AC: Identify Management, Authentication and Access Control

- PR.AT: Awareness and Training

By the end of this chapter, readers will have a solid understanding of Azure's protect security services and their alignment with the NIST Cybersecurity Framework's Protect functions. They will gain insights into identify management, authentication, access control, awareness and training within Azure.

Chapter 5: Design and Deploy a Protect Solution – Part 02

Chapter 5 introduces Azure's protect security services and their alignment with the NIST Cybersecurity Framework's Protect functions. It explores vital Azure services that align with data security.

- PR.DS: Data Security

By the end of this chapter, readers will have a solid understanding of Azure's protect security services and their alignment with the NIST Cybersecurity Framework's Protect functions. They will gain insights into ata security, within Azure. This knowledge will enable readers to implement adequate security measures in Azure environments, safeguarding data against security threats.

Chapter 6: Design and Deploy a Protect Solution – Part 03

Chapter 6 introduces Azure's protect security services and their alignment with the NIST Cybersecurity Framework's Protect functions. It explores vital Azure services that align with Information Protection Processes and Procedures and Protective Technology.

- PR.IP: Information Protection Processes and Procedures

- PR.PT: Protective Technology

By the end of this chapter, readers will have a solid understanding of Azure's protect security services and their alignment with the NIST Cybersecurity Framework's Protect functions. They will gain insights into information protection processes and procedures, and protective technology within Azure. This knowledge will enable readers to implement adequate security measures in Azure environments.

Chapter 7: Design and Deploy a Detect Solution

Chapter 7 introduces Azure's detect security services and their alignment with the NIST Cybersecurity Framework's Detect functions. It explores critical Azure services that support the detection of anomalies, events, and security incidents, as well as continuous monitoring and detection processes.

- Introduction to Azure detect security services

- DE.AE: Anomalies and Events

- DE.CM: Security Continuous Monitoring

- DE. DP: Detection Processes

By the end of this chapter, readers will have a solid understanding of Azure's detect security services and their alignment with the NIST Cybersecurity Framework's Detect functions. They will gain insights into detecting anomalies, events, and security incidents within Azure environments and the importance of continuous monitoring and efficient detection processes. This knowledge will equip readers with the tools and techniques to implement effective threat detection and incident response strategies in Azure, enhancing the overall security posture of their environments.

Chapter 8: Design and Deploy Respond Solution

Chapter 8 introduces Azure's response security services and their alignment with the NIST Cybersecurity Framework's Respond functions. It explores critical Azure services that support response planning, communications, analysis, and mitigation during security incidents. The chapter offers the following key insights:

- Introduction to Azure respond security services

- RS.RP: Response Planning

- RS.CO: Communications

- RS.AN: Analysis

- RS.MI: Mitigation

By the end of this chapter, readers will have a solid understanding of Azure's respond security services and their alignment with the NIST Cybersecurity Framework's Respond functions. They will gain insights into response planning, effective communications, incident analysis, and mitigation strategies within Azure environments. This knowledge will equip readers with the tools and techniques to develop robust incident response capabilities in Azure, minimizing the impact of security incidents and facilitating a swift and effective response.

Chapter 9: Design and Deploy Recover Solution

Chapter 9 introduces NIST recovery principles and explores Azure's recovery services that align with these principles. It focuses on Azure Recovery Services Mapping, Azure Backup, and Azure Site Recovery, which are integral components of Azure's robust recovery capabilities.

- Introduction to NIST recovery

- Azure Recovery Services Mapping

- Azure Backup

- Azure Site Recovery

By the end of this chapter, readers will have a solid understanding of NIST recovery principles and how Azure's recovery services align with these principles. They will gain insights into Azure Recovery Services Mapping, Azure Backup, and Azure Site Recovery and their role in facilitating efficient and reliable recovery in Azure environments. This knowledge will enable readers to develop robust recovery strategies, implement appropriate backup mechanisms, and leverage Azure's recovery services to minimize downtime and ensure the resiliency of their systems and data.

CHAPTER 1

Get Started with Azure Security

Since the dawn of the Internet, people, organizations, and governments have fallen victim to cyberattacks. Cybersecurity, cyberattacks, cybercriminals, and more have been frequently discussed in the IT and business world. You'll need a basic understanding of these concepts to protect yourself and those around you.

Cybersecurity aims to prevent attacks, damage, and unauthorized access to networks, programs, and data. In computing, security includes both cyber and physical security—organizations use both to prevent unauthorized access to data centers and other computerized systems.

Data security, which maintains data confidentiality, integrity, and availability, is a subset of cybersecurity. *Cybersecurity* refers to techniques and practices designed to secure digital data. Organizations and individuals are protected from the unauthorized exploitation of systems, networks, and technologies when organizations and individuals have effective cybersecurity.

This chapter explains the fundamentals of cybersecurity and the key terminology you will need to understand to implement Azure security and the National Institute of Standards and Technology (NIST) Cybersecurity Framework (CSF).

Specifically, in this chapter, we will cover the following:

- Introduction to cybersecurity

- Getting started with cloud computing and Azure

- Microsoft Azure security capabilities

- Foundation of the NIST CSF

1

© Puthiyavan Udayakumar 2023
P. Udayakumar, *Design and Deploy a Secure Azure Environment*,
https://doi.org/10.1007/978-1-4842-9678-3_1

Introduction to Cybersecurity

In this section, we'll get started by understanding what cybersecurity is.

In a nutshell, *cybersecurity* is the practice of protecting systems, networks, and programs from digital attacks. These attacks usually aim to access, change, or destroy sensitive information, extort money from users, or interrupt normal business processes. It is an essential part of any organization's IT strategy. Cybersecurity is critical because cybercriminals are constantly developing new methods to attack systems, networks, and programs. Without proper security measures, organizations risk losing data, which can be costly and can damage their reputation. It is, therefore, essential for organizations to invest in cybersecurity to protect their data and systems. For example, organizations should invest in cybersecurity for the following reasons:

- *Protect sensitive data*: One of the main reasons to invest in cybersecurity is to protect sensitive data, such as financial information, customer data, and intellectual property. A data breach can have serious financial and reputational consequences for an organization, and investing in cybersecurity can help prevent such breaches.

- *Comply with regulations*: Many industries have regulations that require organizations to have certain cybersecurity measures in place. Failure to comply with these regulations can result in fines and legal action. Investing in cybersecurity can help organizations stay compliant with these regulations.

- *Maintain customer trust*: Customers expect organizations to keep their data safe, and a data breach can erode trust in an organization. By investing in cybersecurity, organizations can demonstrate their commitment to protecting customer data and maintaining customer trust.

- *Prevent business disruption*: Cyberattacks can disrupt business operations, causing downtime and lost productivity. Investing in cybersecurity can help prevent such disruptions and ensure that business operations continue smoothly.

- *Stay ahead of evolving threats*: Cybersecurity threats are constantly changing, and investing in cybersecurity can help organizations stay ahead of these threats. This may involve investing in new technologies, training employees on cybersecurity best practices, and regularly updating cybersecurity measures to keep current with the latest threats.

What Is a Cybersecurity Attack?

A *cybersecurity attack* is a malicious attempt to compromise a computer system, website, or other digital platform, usually to steal data or disrupt operations. Cybersecurity attacks can take many forms, such as phishing, malware, ransomware, and distributed denial-of-service (DDoS) attacks.

The most notable cyberattacks in history have been in the last five years.

Atlanta Ransomware Attack (2018): In March 2018, the city of Atlanta, Georgia, in the United States, fell victim to a ransomware attack. City services and systems were widely affected. The attackers demanded a payment in Bitcoin to restore the systems, but the city refused to pay.

VPNFilter (2018): A sophisticated malware campaign that targeted routers and network-attached storage (NAS) devices. It is believed to have affected over half a million devices. The FBI attributed the campaign to a group known as APT 28, which is thought to have ties to Russia.

British Airways Data Breach (2018): Between August and September 2018, British Airways reported a significant data breach that affected around 380,000 transactions. Credit card information, names, addresses, and travel booking details were exposed.

Marriott Data Breach (2018): In November 2018, Marriott International announced that the Starwood guest reservation database had been breached, exposing the personal information of approximately 500 million guests.

Capital One Data Breach (2019): In July 2019, Capital One Financial Corporation announced a significant data breach affecting over 100 million customers in the United States and 6 million in Canada. Personal information was exposed, including names, addresses, credit scores, and social security numbers.

Maze Ransomware Attacks (2019-2020): Maze was a prominent ransomware strain known for encrypting victims' files and exfiltrating data, and threatening to make it public if the ransom wasn't paid. It targeted a wide range of industries and organizations.

SolarWinds Cyberattack (2020): In late 2020, a large-scale, sophisticated supply chain attack was uncovered. It was initiated by compromising the infrastructure of SolarWinds, a company that creates software for managing and monitoring computer networks. The attackers were able to insert a vulnerability into SolarWinds' Orion product, and this compromised software update was subsequently distributed to thousands of SolarWinds' customers. The U.S. government and many other organizations worldwide were affected. This attack is attributed to a state-sponsored actor suspected to be Russian.

Microsoft Exchange Server Attacks (2021): In early 2021, multiple zero-day vulnerabilities in Microsoft Exchange Server were exploited in a widespread campaign. Tens of thousands of organizations around the world were affected. Microsoft attributed the attack to a group it calls HAFNIUM, which it believes to be state-sponsored and operating out of China.

Colonial Pipeline Ransomware Attack (2021): In May 2021, a major U.S. fuel pipeline operator, Colonial Pipeline, was hit by a ransomware attack attributed to a criminal group known as DarkSide. The attack forced the company to shut down its fuel distribution network, leading to fuel shortages in parts of the U.S. Eastern Seaboard.

Kaseya Ransomware Attack (2021): In July 2021, a ransomware attack targeted Kaseya, a company that provides software tools to IT outsourcing shops. The attack propagated through Kaseya's software to the systems of companies that use Kaseya's products, resulting in one of the most widespread ransomware attacks on record.

Here are some of history's other significant cyberattacks:

- The Melissa virus

- NASA cyberattack

- The 2007 Estonia cyberattack

- A cyberattack on Sony's PlayStation Network

- Adobe cyberattack

- The 2014 cyberattack on Yahoo

- Ukraine's power grid attack

Why Are Cyberattacks Executed?

Malicious actors carry out cyberattacks to steal data or disrupt operations. Cybercriminals may have financial motives, such as extorting money from users or being motivated by political or ideological reasons. Cyberattacks can also be used to gain access to sensitive data, disrupt services, or damage an organization's reputation.

A Closer Look at Cybersecurity

Enterprises must invest in cybersecurity and protect themselves against threats such as hacking, data compromise, and identify theft, especially as more and more companies switch to remote/hybrid working models and the online space expands. With technology getting more innovative, cybercriminals are getting smarter. Cybercrimes include cyberextortion, ransomware attacks, identify fraud, Internet of Things (IoT) hacking, malware, and phishing scams.

As cyber threats and attacks increase, cybersecurity is of utmost concern. Cyberattackers now use sophisticated techniques to target systems, impacting individuals, small businesses, and large organizations. As a result, these IT or non-IT firms are taking measures to combat cyber threats and understand the importance of cybersecurity. There is a shortage of cybersecurity workers, even when cyberattacks are happening constantly. Now is the time to start a career in cybersecurity.

To meet the growing demands of today's businesses, we need 65 percent more cybersecurity professionals, according to the (ISC)[2] Cybersecurity Workforce Study.

Cybersecurity consists of techniques to safeguard the integrity of users, applications, infrastructure, and data from attack damage and unauthorized access. It focuses on organizational information security management and addresses business objectives and IT security interdependence.

The benefits of cybersecurity programs include protecting the system from viruses, worms, spyware, and other unwanted programs; minimizing computer crashes and freezing; preventing hackers from hacking the system; and increasing cyber defense. Cybersecurity aims to protect systems against digital attacks, damage, and unauthorized access.

Information systems must be protected from unauthorized access, integrity, and availability by cybersecurity analysts. Information security must be viewed from a defense-in-depth perspective that utilizes multiple, overlapping security controls to accomplish every cybersecurity objective. For analysts to develop controls capable of rising to the occasion and responding to threats, they need to understand their organization's threat environment.

Cybersecurity Risk Analysis

The cornerstone of any information security program is cybersecurity risk analysis. Analysts must thoroughly understand their technology environments and the external threats that threaten them. Cybersecurity risk assessments combine information about internal and external factors to understand the threats their organization faces and design controls that address them. To communicate clearly with other risk analysts, you must understand three critical terms: vulnerabilities, threats, and risks.

- A *vulnerability* is a weakness in a device, system, application, or process that might allow an attacker to occur. Cybersecurity professionals can protect vulnerabilities. An attacker can, for example, conduct a denial-of-service (DoS) attack against the websites hosted on an outdated version of the Apache web server by exploiting a vulnerability. A DoS attack can be mitigated by upgrading the Apache service within the organization to the most recent version that is not susceptible to this vulnerability.

- When it comes to cybersecurity, a *threat* is any outside force that might exploit a vulnerability, such as a hacker who wants to attack a website with a DoS attack and knows about an Apache vulnerability. Many threats are malicious, but this is only sometimes the case. For example, earthquakes may damage the data center containing the web servers, causing the website to be unavailable. Earthquakes have no malicious intent at all. In most cases, cybersecurity professionals cannot do much to eliminate a threat. Hackers will hack, and earthquakes will strike whether we like it or not.

- There must be a combination of a threat and a vulnerability to pose a security *risk* to an organization. In the example of a hacker targeting a web server for a DoS attack, say the server is patched so that it cannot be attacked; in that case, there is no risk because even though a threat is present (the hacker), there is no vulnerability. Similarly, a data center may be vulnerable to earthquakes because the walls are not built to withstand the extreme movements present during an earthquake. However, it may be located in an area that does not experience earthquakes. It may be vulnerable to earthquakes, but its location does not threaten an earthquake, so no risk exists.

According to the Federal Information Processing Standards (FIPS), there are three core security principles that guide the information security area: confidentiality, integrity, and availability.

The three together make up the CIA triad, as shown in Figure 1-1.

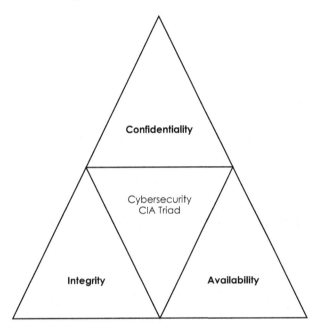

Figure 1-1. *FIPS CIA triad*

The role of the cybersecurity architect is to ensure that the built systems or solutions will meet the three principles.

- *Confidentiality*: A cybersecurity architect wants to preserve the access control and disclosure restrictions on information. It guarantees that no one will be able to break the rules of personal privacy and proprietary information.

- *Integrity*: A cybersecurity architect wants to avoid improper (unauthorized) information modification or destruction. Here we ensure nonrepudiation and information authenticity.

7

- *Availability*: The information must be available to access and use all the time and with reliable access. Certainly, this must be true for those who have the proper rights of access.

Cyberattacks and their ramifications are everywhere these days. Global supply chains are being attacked, resulting in significant economic consequences. It seems like almost daily we hear about cybercriminals stealing the personal information of millions of consumers from e-commerce sites. Government and health services are sometimes blocked and extorted for ransom.

As cyberattacks evolve, they become more sophisticated. An organization or institution can be targeted by cybercriminals from anywhere, including from inside an organization.

Threat Landscape

Cyberattacks can exploit the entire digital landscape in which an organization interacts, whether large or small. The following are key areas of the threat landscape: email accounts, social media accounts, mobile devices, the organization's technology infrastructure, cloud services, and people.

Besides computers and mobile phones, threat landscapes can encompass any element owned or managed by an organization and some that are not. Criminals use any method to mount and carry out attacks, as you will learn next.

Threat modeling is an approach for analyzing the security of an application. In this method, security risks are identified, quantified, and addressed in a structured manner. It should be noted that a threat is not a vulnerability, as mentioned earlier. Threats can exist even if there are no vulnerabilities.

Attack Vectors

Assailants access a system through an *attack vector*.

For example, cybercriminals can use email as a vector to attack users. These emails may appear legitimate but ultimately result in a user downloading files or clicking links that compromise their devices. Wireless networks are another common attack vector. Bad actors in airports and coffee shops often exploit vulnerabilities in people's devices by accessing unsecured wireless networks. Another common way for cyberattacks to take advantage of a system is by gaining access to unsecured Internet of Things (IoT) devices.

However, it is essential to know that attackers do not have to use any of these. They can use a variety of less obvious attack vectors. Figure 1-2 shows some key attack vectors.

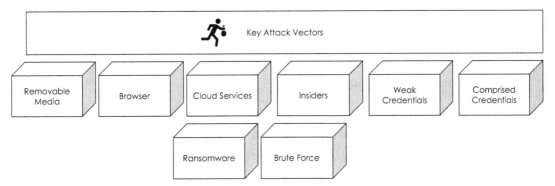

Figure 1-2. *Key attack vectors*

These are the attack vectors shown in the figure:

- *Removable media*: Media such as USB drives, smart cables, storage cards, and more can be used by attackers to compromise a device. As an example, hackers might load malicious code into USB devices that are given to users as gifts or left in public spaces to be found.

- *Browser*: By using malicious websites or browser extensions, attackers can install malicious software on their devices or change the settings of their browsers. This allows access to a broader system or network.

- *Cloud services*: In today's world, organizations are increasingly dependent on cloud services to conduct their business. An attacker can compromise a poorly secured cloud resource or service or an account in a cloud service, gaining control over all the resources and services accessible to that account. They can also gain access to another account with even more permissions.

- *Insider threats*: An organization's employees can be an attack vector in a cyberattack, intentionally or unintentionally. An employee might become the victim of a cybercriminal who impersonates them as a person of authority to gain unauthorized access to a system. This type of attack is called *social engineering*. Although the employee may act unintentionally as an attack vector in this scenario, employees with authorized access can also use it to steal or harm others.

- *Weak credentials*: A data breach caused by a weak password can lead to many more due to reused and weak passwords.

- *Compromised credentials*: In data leaks, phishing scams, and malware, usernames and passwords continue to be exposed as access credentials. When lost, stolen, or exposed, credentials allow attackers unfettered access.

- *Ransomware*: Ransomware is malicious software (malware) that blocks access to a system or data until a ransom is paid. This attack is typically carried out by encrypting the victim's files and demanding payment in exchange for the decryption key. Ransomware attacks can be delivered through various methods, including phishing emails, infected websites, or exploiting software or systems vulnerabilities. The impact of ransomware attacks can be severe, with victims potentially losing access to essential data or systems and facing significant financial losses.

- *Brute force*: Attackers may try to access your organization in a brute-force attack until one attack succeeds. This may include phishing emails, infected attachments, or weak passwords or encryption.

Security Breaches

It is a security breach when someone gains unauthorized access to devices, services, or networks. This is similar to an intruder (attacker) successfully breaking into a building (a device, application, or network).

The following are forms of security breaches:

- *Social engineering attacks*: There is a common misconception that security breaches occur when a flaw or vulnerability in a technology service or equipment is exploited or that security breaches can happen only when technology is vulnerable. That's only sometimes true. Attackers can exploit or manipulate users into granting them unauthorized access to a system through social engineering attacks.

- *Browser attacks*: Browser attacks are a type of cyberattack that targets vulnerabilities in web browsers to compromise user data and systems. These attacks can take many forms, including phishing, malvertising, and drive-by downloads.

Phishing attacks involve tricking users into clicking malicious links or downloading malware disguised as legitimate software. Malvertising involves injecting malicious code into online advertisements, which can compromise the user's browser when clicked. Drive-by downloads involve automatically downloading malware onto the user's system when they visit a compromised website.

Browser attacks can have serious consequences, including data theft, system compromise, and financial loss. To protect against these attacks, users should keep their browsers and plugins up-to-date, use strong and unique passwords, and avoid clicking suspicious links or downloading unknown software. Additionally, businesses should employ security measures such as web filters, intrusion detection, and prevention systems to detect and block these attacks.

- *Password attacks*: During a password attack, someone tries to gain access to a device or system by using authentication for a password-protected account. For example, suppose an attacker has somehow discovered someone's work account username. They often use software to speed up cracking and guessing passwords.

  This is known as a *brute-force attack*, and it involves trying many different password combinations to gain access to a user's account. The password must be correct only once for the attacker to gain access.

Data Breaches

Data breaches occur when an attacker successfully gets access to someone's data. This can lead to severe consequences for the victim, whether that is a person, an organization, or even a government. This is because the victim's data could be abused in many ways. For example, it can be held as ransom or used to cause financial or reputational harm.

Malware

Cybercriminals use malware to infect systems and carry out actions that cause harm, such as stealing data or disrupting normal operations. A malware program consists of two main components: the propagation mechanism and the payload.

Propagation is how the malware spreads itself across one or more systems. Here are a few examples of standard propagation techniques:

- *Virus*: In biology, a virus enters the human body and can spread once it has caused harm. We are already familiar with the term. A technology-based virus enters a system through a means of entry, a user action. For example, a user might download a file or plug in a USB device that contains the virus, contaminating the system. A security breach has occurred.

- *Worm*: Once a worm has infected the system, it can spread to other computers connected to it, and it does not require any action from the user to apply itself across systems like viruses do. Worms can infect a device by exploiting a vulnerability in an application, and they cause damage by finding vulnerable systems they can exploit. A worm can spread to other devices on the same network or connected networks once it has infected one.

- *Trojan*: Trojan horses are malware that mimics real software. They got their name from soldiers hiding inside the wooden horse given by the Trojans to soldiers. After installation, the program performs malicious actions, including stealing information.

The *payload* is a malware action on an infected device or system. Here are some common types of payloads:

- A *ransomware payload* locks down systems or data until a ransom is paid. Cybercriminals can exploit an unknown vulnerability in a network of connected devices to access all files across this network and encrypt them. The attacker then demands a ransom for decrypting the files. They may threaten to remove the files if the ransom is not paid by a deadline.

- A *malware payload* installs spyware on a device or system. For instance, the malware installs keyboard scanner software, collects password information, and transmits it to the attacker without the user's knowledge.

  It is the payload that enables a cybercriminal to bypass existing security measures and cause harm to a system or device by exploiting a vulnerability in the system or device. Cybercriminals leave some code behind after infiltrating a software development company and carrying out attacks on the company. A cybercriminal can use this backdoor to hack into the application, the device it runs on, and even the network and systems of an organization or customer.

- As a payload, *botnets* link computers, servers, and other devices to a network of infected devices that can be remotely controlled to carry out malicious activities. Crypto-mining (often referred to as *crypto-mining malware*) is one of the most common applications of botnet malware. A device is connected to a botnet that mines or generates cryptocurrencies with the device's computing power. Users might notice their computers running slower than normal and getting worse daily.

Known Mitigation Strategies

Cyberattacks come in many forms. But how can you protect your organization against them?

Organizations can keep cyberattackers at bay in several ways, from multifactor authentication to improved browser security to advising and educating end users.

An organization's mitigation strategy consists of steps to prevent or defend against a cyberattack. Attacks are usually controlled by implementing technological and organizational policies and processes. The following are some of the numerous additional mitigation strategies.

Multifactor Authentication

Cybercriminals can access an account if a password or username is compromised, but multifactor authentication prevents this.

It is common for users to provide more than one form of identification during multifactor authentication. A password, which the user understands, is one of the most common forms of identification.

A phone, hardware key, or another trusted device can also be used for authentication, as can fingerprints or retinal scans (biometric authentication). The purpose of multifactor authentication is to verify the identify of a user using two or more of these forms of verification.

When accessing an online account, a bank might require users to enter security codes received on their mobile device and their username and password.

Browser Security

As you have already seen, our Internet access can be compromised by attackers compromising poorly secured browsers. By downloading malicious files or installing malicious add-ons, users can compromise their browsers, devices, and even their organizations' systems by compromising them. Organizations can prevent attacks of this type by implementing these security policies:

- You should avoid installing unauthorized browser extensions and add-ons.

- Allow only permitted browsers to be installed on devices.

- Block specific sites from using web content filters.

- Keep browsers up-to-date.

- Educate users.

Educating your staff about social engineering attacks can help organizations defend themselves. Social engineering attacks aim to exploit human vulnerabilities to harm individuals. Organizations can teach users how to recognize malicious content they receive or encounter and act when they see something suspicious.

- Recognize suspicious elements in a message.

- Never respond to external requests for personal information.

- Lock devices when they're not in use.

- Store, share, and remove data according to the organization's policies only.

Threat Intelligence

It is not uncommon for cybercriminals to target organizations via a wide range of attack vectors, and the threat landscape can be vast. As a result, organizations need to monitor, prevent, defend against, and even identify potential vulnerabilities before cybercriminals use them to conduct attacks.

Organizations can use threat intelligence to gather information about their systems, vulnerabilities, and attacks. As a result of its understanding of this information, the organization will be able to develop policies that protect against cyberattacks, including those for security, devices, and user access. Threat intelligence collects information that enables a company to gain insights into cyberattacks and respond accordingly.

Organizations can use technological solutions to implement threat intelligence across their systems. These are often threat-intelligent solutions that automatically collect information and even hunt and respond to attacks and vulnerabilities.

These are just some mitigation strategies organizations can take to protect against cyberattacks. Mitigation strategies enable an organization to take a robust approach to cybersecurity, ultimately preserving confidentiality, integrity, and availability.

Cryptography

Cryptography and encryption may conjure up visions of spies and covert operations or hackers sitting in windowless rooms. Yet much of today's modern online world is possible only with these two techniques. In fact, cryptography and encryption are the cornerstones of any good cybersecurity solution. For example, they help to keep your emails safe from prying eyes and protect online payments. As you continue your journey into cybersecurity, you'll see how we use cryptography and encryption to protect ourselves in day-to-day activities.

Information confidentiality, integrity, and availability are protected by cryptography, which also protects against cyberattacks. Derived from the Greek word *kryptos*, which means "hidden" or "secret," cryptography is the application of secure communication between a sender and a recipient. Cryptography is typically used to obscure a written message's meaning, but it can also be applied to images.

The first known use of cryptography can be traced back to ancient Egypt and the use of complex hieroglyphics. One of the first ciphers ever used to secure military communications came from the Roman emperor Julius Caesar.

These two examples make clear that cryptography has many uses and isn't limited to the digital world. However, from those humble origins, one thing is sure: cryptography is now a fundamental requirement in helping secure our digitally connected planet.

- Each time you use a browser to access, for example, an HTTPS address, an online retail store, or your bank, elements of cryptography keep your interactions confidential and secure.

- Whenever you wirelessly connect a device to a router to access the Internet, cryptography helps make it secure.

- You can use cryptography to secure and protect external and internal storage files.

- Smartphones have changed communication, from video and audio calls to text messaging. Cryptography is used to maintain the confidentiality and integrity of these communications.

As with all systems, cryptography has its own language; two important ones are *plaintext* and *ciphertext*.

- The term *plaintext* represents any message, including documents, music, pictures, movies, data, and computer programs, waiting to be cryptographically transformed.

- When the plaintext has been turned into a secret message, it's called *ciphertext*. This term represents the encrypted/secured data.

Authentication and Authorization

Protecting against cybersecurity threats begins with secure authentication and authorization. Discover how to prevent unauthorized access and identify identify-based attacks.

Good cybersecurity relies on several factors to provide confidence and assurance that your data is safe and being used as expected. For authentication to be effective, it must be robust and straightforward, and it provides the mechanism by which you know someone is who they claim to be.

As a rule, users should be given just enough permission to access the resources they need once they have been authenticated. Authorization grants the user access to the appropriate data and assets.

For example, when you go to the airport to board a flight, you must validate your identify before receiving the boarding pass. You present yourself and your passport; if they match, you are granted the boarding pass. Your boarding pass is your authorization, allowing you to board the aircraft only for the booked flight.

Threats to Network Security

Protecting your network is essential in today's modern online world, where information is a valuable currency. Every day, networks are bombarded by thousands of cyberattacks. Mostly, these attacks are thwarted, but occasionally, the news headlines will report on the theft of data.

Here you'll discover the different types of networks, how you connect with them, and how data moves around a network. You'll get an idea of the types of attacks cybercriminals use to break into a network and the tools available to help you stop them.

Our modern world is built on networks, allowing us to communicate, shop, play, and work from anywhere. This makes networks a prime target for cybercriminals who see information as the new currency. They allow us access to a vast amount of information not only about ourselves but also about businesses. A weak network security system may compromise critical data's confidentiality, availability, and integrity.

A robust security network requires an understanding of threats.

Attacks on networks can take the following forms:

- *Active*: The attacker gains unauthorized access to the network and then compromises data (say, by encrypting it) to compromise its usability and value.

- *Passive*: Cybercriminals attack networks to collect and monitor data without altering it.

The following are common attacks on networks:

- *Distributed denial-of-service attack*: Malicious actors deploy botnets to redirect high volumes of false traffic to enterprise networks via large networks of malware-compromised devices. An organization's entire IT infrastructure can be crippled by DDoS attacks, which overwhelm servers, prevent legitimate users from accessing a website, and cause crashes.

- *Man-in-the-middle attack*: During a man-in-the-middle attack, an attacker intercepts legitimate data traffic between a network and an external data source (like a website) or within the network. Generally, weak security protocols allow bad actors to steal credit card numbers, usernames, and sessions from real-time transactions.

- *Unauthorized access*: In unauthorized network access attacks, attackers often use weak passwords to guess legitimate users' passwords and log in under false pretenses.

  The following are the most common causes:

  - Unencrypted networks or data

  - Previously compromised accounts

  - Insider threats

  - Accounts with misused administrator rights

  - Social engineering

  - Phishing or spear-phishing attacks

  Because social engineering attacks rely on human weaknesses, they are notoriously difficult to prevent. Stronger cybersecurity protections can better address technical vulnerabilities.

- *Insider threats*: There was a 47 percent increase in insider threat–related incidents between 2018 and 2020 and an $11.45 million increase in the total cost of insider threats.

Any individual with access to an organization's computer systems and data increases the risk of a network attack, whether employees, vendors, contractors, or partners. It is difficult to detect and prevent such attacks because the attacker already has access to the network's systems and data.

- *Privilege escalation*: Cleverly, attackers use privilege escalation to expand their reach within a target system or network. In horizontal attacks, they gain access to adjacent systems; in vertical attacks, they gain high privileges within the target system.

  Organizations must strictly adhere to the principle of least privilege (PoLP) to prevent privilege escalation and protect high-value data from unauthorized access. All users, whether employees, third parties, applications, systems, or connected IoT devices, are granted only the access levels necessary to perform their job functions.

- *SQL injection attacks*: Less mature websites accept user input without validating or moderating it, exposing their networks to SQL injection attacks.

  The attacker may submit malicious code instead of the expected data values by filling out a support request form, leaving a comment, or calling an API. Upon execution of this code, a hacker can compromise the network and gain access to sensitive information.

  SQL injection attacks are more likely to occur on websites and web applications using SQL-based databases.

- *Bluetooth attacks*: Bluetooth devices, such as smartwatches and audio devices, have made communication more common. Although Bluetooth networks are less common than wireless networks, they are still suitable attack vectors. However, the criminal must be within your device's range. In *bluejacking* attacks, criminals send unsolicited messages to Bluetooth-enabled devices. They are similar to how someone rings your doorbell and runs away before you can answer, and it's mostly an annoyance.

- *Wireless attacks*: We can connect to networks anywhere in the world seamlessly using wireless networks. Using a wireless network at home, your smartphone and always-on IoT devices can connect to the Internet. Cybercriminals use these networks to commit crimes since they are widely available. Wardriving and spoofing Wi-Fi hotspots are common wireless attacks.

- *DNS attacks*: A DNS server is designed for efficiency and usability rather than security, so DNS attacks aim to exploit its weaknesses. For example, DNS poisoning is one of the most common DNS attacks. This is when a bad site redirects traffic from a legitimate site to a bad site containing malicious links or malware by changing the IP addresses in DNS lookup tables.

Threats to Application Security

There are applications for nearly everything in today's digitally connected world, from how we interact with friends to how we work, what we buy and purchase, and how we learn. As a result, cybercriminals have increased opportunities to wreak havoc.

Protecting your data is essential whether you're a small business or a big corporation. Understanding how applications can be compromised and where these threats come from will enhance your application security and the confidentiality of any stored or accessed data.

Applications with Untrustworthy Origins

In recent years, downloading applications has become easier, regardless of whether you use a computer, smartphone, or tablet. Almost all of us use the more significant, well-established app stores. Some of these will verify the authenticity of applications before listing them and will prohibit certain types from being sold.

However, some app stores have few restrictions and minimal verification of an app's authenticity. Only some of the apps available in these stores are good. It is possible, however, for cybercriminals to package source code, give it the name of a legitimate application that users might be familiar with, and upload it along with legitimate applications to a hosting site.

It is therefore possible to become a cyberattack victim if you install or run applications from untrustworthy sources.

Vulnerabilities in Embedded Applications

Even though developers strive to keep their apps secure, it is impossible to guarantee 100 percent protection. Cybercriminals will inevitably try to exploit any vulnerability they can find, and open-source and zero-day vulnerabilities are among the most common application vulnerabilities.

Open-Source Vulnerabilities

The source code of open-source libraries is usually freely available, so anyone can access it when they need to solve a specific problem. Developers will always check for open-source solutions when solving a particular problem.

In addition to being publicly developed, open-source libraries can be used by cybercriminals who try to exploit them. If a developer uses open-source libraries as part of their application, they need to stay current on the latest versions to prevent cyberattacks.

Zero-Day Vulnerabilities

When cybercriminals find a zero-day vulnerability, they won't publicize it but will take full advantage of it. A cybercriminal conducts detailed reconnaissance of applications, looking for vulnerabilities. By definition, the application owner was previously unaware of zero-day vulnerabilities and has not patched them.

A cybercriminal might have noticed that a banking app has a zero-day vulnerability and use this to steal money and information from application users. The *zero days* refers to the number of days between discovering a vulnerability and releasing a fix.

Browser-Based Threats

In addition to serving as our gateway to the Internet, browsers play a key role in our daily lives. The following are two more common browser-based threats to look out for.

Cookie-Based Attacks

You have probably heard about cookies, but do you actually know what they are? Cookies are plaintext files containing small bits of data, such as your user credentials, the last search you made, the last time you bought something, etc. By simplifying the need to constantly log in to the site, cookies enhance your browser experience and make browsing easier.

In a session replay attack, the cybercriminal intercepts your communication, eavesdrops on your login details, and then steals the cookie data to access the website posing as you.

Typosquatting

A typosquatting attack involves a cybercriminal obtaining a domain name that is mistakenly spelled, putting malicious code on it, and disguising it as a legitimate website.

It is possible for users to confuse the malicious website for the legitimate one they intended to visit.

Threats to Device Security

Every aspect of our daily lives and business relies on Internet-connected devices. In our modern world, people and organizations depend on connected devices to meet their most vital day-to-day needs. Devices access, store, and continuously collect information about us while accessing and storing important business and personal data. Therefore, cybercriminals target devices for unauthorized access and control of valuable data, causing havoc for users and organizations alike.

Everyday life is reliant on devices in so many ways. All kinds of sensitive information about us must be captured, stored, and shared by devices to do their jobs effectively. Some devices may be almost invisible to us; we don't realize how often we use them.

Device Threat Vectors

Cybercriminals can use devices to carry out attacks, such as the following, while using them to do their work and go about their daily lives.

Phone, Laptop, or Tablet

Malicious apps can contaminate devices with malware that can exfiltrate sensitive data from local storage without the user's knowledge, compromising confidentiality and integrity.

USB Drives

In the case of ransomware, the data has been compromised because it's locked in exchange for a ransom. Cybercriminals can, for instance, load malicious software or files onto USB drives and insert them into laptops.

Always-On Home Assistant Devices

Cybercriminals can add malicious software to app stores for these devices, so they can always be listening or watching. Cybercriminals can, for instance, secretly attack the device with spyware to record information and compromise data confidentiality if a user installs it. The data could be compromised laterally by moving from one home device to another.

Device Vulnerabilities

Devices can be compromised when they lack the latest security updates or strong authentication. Attackers know the common vulnerabilities of devices and applications and how to gain unauthorized access. If a device is connected to a Wi-Fi hotspot—in an airport, for instance—it's a prime target for attackers.

In most cases, malware such as backdoors and botnets can persist on a device even after being updated, causing further damage when connected to a network.

Jailbreaking is when users find unofficial ways to get full access to their devices' core systems to customize them or to achieve other purposes. As a result, the device becomes vulnerable because it might circumvent security measures. Cybercriminals can provide false instructions or software that compromises the device.

When connected devices are not adequately secured, they can represent a threat vector. Having learned this, we will now look at ways to keep them safe with cloud computing.

Getting Started with Cloud Computing

In this section, we'll start by understanding what cloud computing is.

A cloud computing service delivers IT resources and applications via the Internet with pay-per-use pricing on a pay-as-you-go basis. Suppose cloud consumers need to share photos with millions of mobile users or provide services that help enterprises run effectively and efficiently. In that case, the cloud offers rapid access to flexible and low-cost IT resources.

Cloud computing delivers computing functions such as compute, network, storage, database, software, analytics, artificial intelligence, and other IT functions to businesses and consumers through a secured network, thus achieving economies of scale.

The concept of cloud computing has evolved enormously from a confusing and highly insecure concept to one that IT consumers widely embrace. Whether the cloud consumer's business is large, medium, or small, cloud computing is now a crucial part of an IT strategy.

Providers such as Microsoft Azure, Amazon Web Services, Google Cloud, and others own the network-connected devices required for cloud services and allow consumers to utilize cloud services as needed.

The following are the key characteristics of cloud computing:

1. **Self Service**: Once deployed, method of the self-provisioned IT functions can be automated, requiring no further IT administrator's involvement by the cloud consumer or cloud provider.

2. **Flexibility**: Cloud hosting provides businesses with more flexibility than on-premises hosting. Furthermore, if cloud consumers need extra bandwidth, a cloud-based service can deliver it instantly.

3. **Pooled resource**: Cloud to transparently scale IT resources, as required in response to runtime conditions or as pre-determined by the cloud consumer or cloud provider.

4. **Measured Service**: Measured usage characteristic represents a cloud platform's ability to keep track of the usage of its IT resources, primarily by cloud consumers.

5. **Rapid elasticity**: Different virtual and container resources are dynamically provisioned and deprovisioned according to cloud consumer demand, typically followed by execution through auto scaling.

6. **Broad Network Access**: Broad network access includes private clouds that operate within a company's firewall, public clouds, or a hybrid deployment.

7. **Automation**: Automation is an essential characteristic of cloud computing. Automating a cloud service is the process by which it can be installed, configured, and maintained automatically. In other words, it reduces manual effort by maximizing the use of technology.

8. **Security**: As one of the best features of Cloud Computing, data security is one of its best features. Cloud services make a copy of the data they store so that it cannot be lost. If one server fails the data, the copy version can be restored from the other server.

Consumers of cloud computing don't have to make significant up-front investments in hardware or spend a great deal of time managing their networks. Cloud consumers can select the exact type and size of computing resources they need. Using cloud computing, cloud consumers can access as many resources as they need almost instantly.

In a nutshell, cloud computing enables you to access servers, storage, databases, and a wide range of application services over the Internet. Cloud computing service providers such as Microsoft own and maintain the network-connected hardware necessary for these application services while also providing and using the computing resources required by cloud consumers.

Cloud computing introduces a paradigm shift in how businesses obtain, use, and manage their technology and how they budget and pay for technology services. Adapting the computing environment quickly to changing business requirements enables organizations to optimize spending. As usage patterns fluctuate, capacity can be automatically scaled up or down, and services can be temporarily taken down or shut down permanently as needed. In addition, Azure cloud services become operational (opex) rather than capital expenses (capex) with pay-per-use billing.

Top Benefits of Cloud Computing

Both small and large organizations use cloud computing technology to store information in the cloud and access it from anywhere using an Internet connection. The benefits of moving to the cloud vary based on the organization, but as illustrated in Figure 1-3, several advantages are consistent.

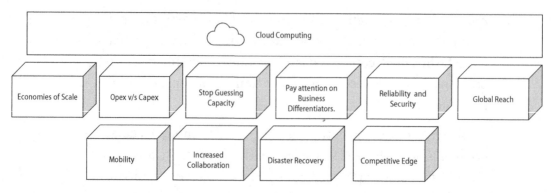

Figure 1-3. *Benefits of cloud computing*

Cloud computing offers economies of scale. Cloud computing is available in both global or local availability to meet security, regulation, and compliance requirements.

Enterprises can lower their variable costs compared to private cloud consumers. Azure, for example, can achieve economies of scale by aggregating usage from hundreds of thousands of customers, which translates into lower prices.

The second benefit is the opex versus capex—cloud computing eliminates the need for capital expenditures such as hardware and software running in on-prem data centers, round-the-clock power and cooling, and subject-matter experts in managing complex components 24/7. Cloud service providers run on a consumption-based model, which means no up-front costs or capex. Companies pay for additional resources only when needed and stop paying when they're no longer needed.

The third benefit is the ability to stop guessing about capacity. Consumers of cloud services often end up with either expensive idle resources or limited capacity when making a capacity decision before deploying any applications. Cloud computing allows organizations to stop guessing about their infrastructure requirements for meeting their business needs. With a few minutes' notice, cloud consumers can scale up or down as necessary based on what is required.

Another benefit is being able to pay attention to business differentiators. Instead of spending time racking, stacking, and powering servers, organizations can focus on their business priorities with cloud computing. This paradigm shift can free organizations from spending money on maintaining and running data centers. By using cloud computing, businesses can concentrate on projects that differentiate them from competitors, such as analyzing petabytes of data, delivering video content, creating mobile applications, or exploring Mars.

Cloud computing offers companies reliability and security. Cloud computing makes data backup, business continuity, and disaster recovery significantly less expensive with availability zones. Cloud computing also has site-level redundancy. Data and applications are replicated and mirrored across the redundant sites as per subscriptions.

In addition, modern-day cloud service providers offer unlimited security components, controls, policies, compliance needs, and regulations standards, which heavily increase a security posture from end to end. As a result, application infrastructure data is highly secure against potential vulnerabilities and threats.

Global reach is another benefit. Cloud computing provides the advantage of going global in minutes and in just a few clicks. Organizations can use this technology to provide redundancy across the globe and provide lower latency and better experiences to their customers at a minimal cost. Cloud computing makes it possible for any organization to go global, which was previously available only to the biggest corporations.

Mobility, increased collaboration, disaster recovery, and competitive edge are other key benefits of cloud computing.

Three Delivery Models of Cloud Computing

Today IT infrastructure must meet growing client expectations for speedy, secure, and stable services. As companies strive to develop their IT systems' processing, compute, and storage abilities, they often find that improving and managing a hardy, scalable, and secure IT foundation is prohibitively high-priced.

Cloud computing equips DevOps, DevSecOps, and SRE engineers with the ability to converge on what matters most and avoid unnecessary procurement, support, and retention planning. As cloud computing has increased in prevalence, numerous distinct models and deployment strategies have emerged to improve the specific needs of other users. Each cloud service and deployment organization provides consumers with diverse control, flexibility, and management levels.

Cloud-native and hybrid cloud deployment models are the two available cloud computing deployment models that enterprises focus on, as shown in Figure 1-4. Understanding how each strategy applies to architectural decisions and options is crucial.

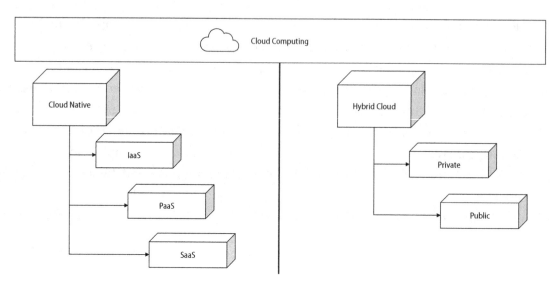

Figure 1-4. *Cloud computing deployment types*

Cloud native refers to all application components running on the cloud, with the cloud-based application is fully deployed in the cloud. Applications in the cloud have been either developed using cloud technology or migrated from conventional infrastructure to take advantage of its benefits. In cloud-based applications, low-level infrastructure pieces or higher-level services can be used, abstracting away the management, scalability, and architecture requirements of the core infrastructure.

Cloud hybridization refers to workloads run on-premises, on co-located infrastructure, and on infrastructure that the cloud provider hosts. A hybrid cloud environment enables cloud consumers to maximize the agility and flexibility of a public cloud environment while taking advantage of their existing investments.

Imagine using the same tools cloud consumers have used for years to manage all these resources. Cloud consumers can extend VMware infrastructure to the Azure cloud using a hybrid cloud. The hybrid cloud can quickly and securely expand or consolidate data centers, build disaster recovery environments, and modernize applications to meet urgent security and compliance goals.

The cloud-native delivery model depicts a specific flow of IT resources offered by a cloud provider. This terminology is typically linked with cloud computing and is commonly used to represent a remote environment and administration level.

Cloud computing has three distinct delivery models: infrastructure as a service, platform as a service, and software as a service, as depicted in Figure 1-5.

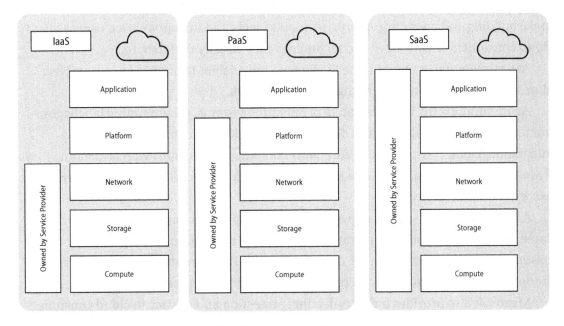

Figure 1-5. *Cloud computing deployment models*

Here are more details about the three types:

- *Infrastructure as a service* (IaaS) is about delivering compute, network, storage, and backup as a service that can be consumed either yearly, monthly, or hourly. Resource units and their prices are provided as a catalog.

- *Platform as a service* (PaaS) is all about IaaS with an integrated set of middleware functions. Software development and deployment tools allow a consistent way to create, modify, update, and deploy an application on the cloud environment.

- *Software as a service* (SaaS) is all about the application hosted on top of PaaS or IaaS, either dedicated or shared. In this deployment model, cloud consumers pay based on the app's consumption. The cloud service provider fully manages the underlying infrastructure and platform.

Now let's explore the Azure cloud.

Microsoft Azure Overview

The integrated tools, prebuilt templates, and managed services from Microsoft Azure make building and operating enterprise, mobile, web, and IoT apps easier, using skills cloud consumers already have and technology they already understand.

Azure offers 200 or more online IT services and enables businesses to accomplish almost all their needs in modern digital environments.

Azure supports the broadest range of operating systems, programming languages, frameworks, tools, databases, and devices of any cloud provider. With Docker integration, cloud consumers can run Linux containers; build apps with JavaScript, Python, .NET, PHP, Java, and Node.js; and create back ends for any device. Millions of users trust Azure services.

Azure has features such as networks with secure private connections, hybrid databases, storage solutions, and data residency and encryption to integrate with existing IT environments. With the Azure stack, cloud consumers can bring the Azure model of app development and deployment into their data centers.

Microsoft also provides industry-leading protection and privacy to cloud consumers. The European Union's data protection authorities have recognized Microsoft for its commitment to strict EU privacy laws. Microsoft was also the first global cloud provider to adopt the new ISO 27018 international privacy standard.

Cloud consumers pay only for what they use with Azure's pay-as-you-go services. Microsoft can guarantee unbeatable performance prices by offering per-minute billing and comparing competitor prices for popular infrastructure services such as compute storage and bandwidth.

At the time of writing this book, Microsoft manages Azure's worldwide network of data centers in 26 regions—more than Amazon Web Services and Google Cloud combined. With this fast-growing global footprint, cloud consumers can run apps and ensure excellent performance for cloud consumers.

Azure's predictive analytics services redefine business intelligence, including machine learning, Cortana analytics, and stream analytics. By analyzing cloud consumers' structured, unstructured, and streaming IoT data, cloud consumers can improve customer service and uncover new business opportunities.

No workload is too big or too small for Azure. At the time of writing this book, Azure is used by more than 66 percent of Fortune 500 companies because it offers enterprise-grade service-level agreements, 24/7 tech support, and round-the-clock service monitoring.

Generally, large businesses integrate Azure into their existing environments by migrating from a lower one. Cloud computing is not just about moving workloads to the cloud, though; with constant improvements and new features, it is much more.

Cloud consumers access Azure services in many ways, such as Azure CLI, Azure Mobile App, Azure PowerShell, Azure REST API, Azure Storage Explorer, and the Azure Portal.

The Azure Portal can be used by businesses to manage Azure tenant subscriptions, and IT can deploy, manage, and monitor all subscribed IT services. Customized IT dashboards can be created in the Azure Portal so that cloud consumers can see structured views of the IT services they consume. Azure Portal users can also customize accessibility options for a better experience.

The Azure cloud offers cloud high availability, scalability, reliability, elasticity, agility, geo-distribution, resiliency, security, and edge to provide end users with the maximum uptime. The following are the nine critical concepts associated with the Azure cloud.

1. **High availability**: Azure wide variety of service-level agreements (SLA) to choose from; Cloud consumer cloud-based applications can implement continuous user action without possible downtime.

2. **Reliability**: Azure is in a stable position; Azure offers an IT services workload to perform its intended function accurately and consistently when demanded. Offer a wide variety of auto-recovery from failure.

3. **Scalability**: Application in the cloud can scale both formats such as vertically and horizontally: Scale vertical add compute capacity by adding vCPU or vRAM to a virtual machine. Scaling horizontal add compute capacity by adding instances of resources, such as adding VMs.

4. **Elasticity**: Cloud consumers can configure cloud-based applications to take advantage of autoscaling, so cloud consumers' applications forever have the resources on demand.

5. **Agility**: Deploy and configure cloud-based resources promptly as cloud consumers' app requirements demands.

6. **Geo-distribution**: Cloud consumers can deploy applications and data to regional data centers around the globe. Efficiently deploy cloud consumer applications in multiple regions throughout the world.

7. **Resiliency**: By taking advantage of cloud-based backup services, data replication, and geo-distribution, Cloud consumers have a fallback solution whenever disaster kicks in.

8. **Security**: Azure security is the highest priority. Azure cloud consumers benefit from a cloud architecture developed to meet the obligations of the standard security-sensitive businesses.

9. **Edge**: Azure IoT Edge is a fully managed Microsoft service built on Azure IoT Hub. Deploy cloud consumers workloads artificial intelligence, Azure services, 3rd party services, and cloud consumer business logic to operate on Internet of Things edge devices.

An Azure global infrastructure is developed with two key elements: physical infrastructure and connective network components. The physical infrastructure comprises 200+ physical data centers, organized into regions and connected by one of the most extensive interconnected networks.

An Azure global infrastructure is classified into the following: regions, geographies, availability zones, and availability sets, as shown in Figure 1-6.

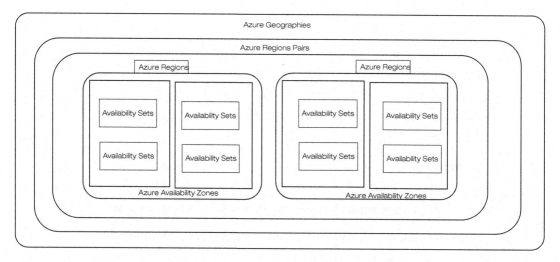

Figure 1-6. *Microsoft Azure global infrastructure logical view*

Azure Regions

Azure regions are a collection of physical data centers installed within a security and latency-defined network perimeter and connected via a dedicated, in part secure, low-latency network.

Dedicated regional low-latency networks connect each region's data centers within a latency-defined perimeter. Azure's design ensures optimal performance and security for all regions.

With Microsoft Azure, cloud consumers have the freedom to install and configure applications on demand. Each Azure region is equipped with a variety of IT services and pricing. A pair of regions is what Azure calls a *logical boundary*, and regional teams contain two geographically defined regions. Azure regions are defined by a specific geographical boundary, typically hundreds of miles apart.

There are more Azure regions globally than any other cloud provider. Azure architects can bring cloud consumer applications close by putting them in these regions no matter where cloud consumer end users are. The global regions provide better scalability and redundancy, and cloud consumers can also maintain data residency.

Azure Geography

Azure geography is composed of regions that meet various compliance and data residency requirements. As much as possible, Azure geography enables cloud consumers to keep their apps and data close to their business. Azure geography is fault-tolerant to withstand region failure via the dedicated high-capacity networking elements of Azure.

By utilizing the dedicated high-capacity networking elements, Azure geography is fault tolerant to withstand region failures. There are at least two regions separated by a considerable physical distance in each geography, which is vital to the Azure cloud. This pattern allows Azure to achieve disaster recovery in each region.

Microsoft encourages customers to replicate their data across multiple Azure regions. Microsoft promises network performance between regions of 2 milliseconds or less.

Azure Availability Zones

Microsoft Azure developed a cloud pattern named *availability zones* to achieve maximum availability for IT services that demand maximum uptime.

Availability zones are physically separate locations within a region that can withstand local failures, including software and hardware failures, earthquakes, floods, and fires. Because of Azure's redundancy and logical isolation, it has a high degree of fault tolerance. Each availability zone-enabled region has a minimum of three availability zones for resiliency.

Availability zones enable the cloud to consume data with high availability and fault tolerance. Figure 1-7 shows an Azure availability zone logical view. Availability zones apply only to the available services and not all services offered by Azure.

By deploying IT services to two or more availability zones, the business achieves maximum availability. Microsoft Azure offers a service-level agreement of 99.99 percent uptime for virtual machines provided that two or more VMs are deployed into two or more zones.

For the first-time user, it isn't easy to differentiate between availability zones and availability sets. *Availability sets* allow an IT service to create two or more virtual machines in different physical server racks in an Azure DataCenter (DC). Microsoft Azure offers a service-level agreement of 99.95 percent for availability sets, while Microsoft Azure provides a service-level agreement of a 99.99 percent for availability zones.

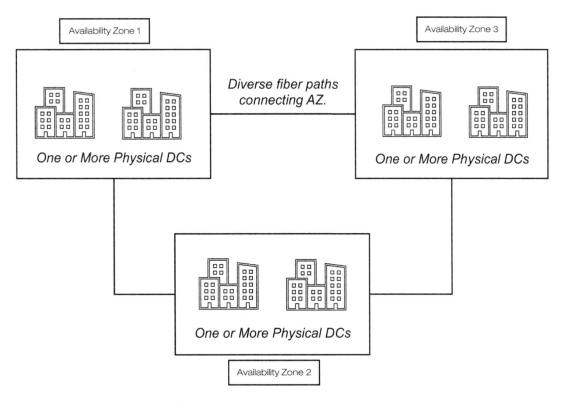

Figure 1-7. *Azure availability zone*

Microsoft Azure offers three types of availability zones: zonal services, zone-redundant services, and zone nonregional services. Figure 1-10 shows a logical view of three availability zones.

Microsoft Azure zonal services are IT services such as VMs, managed disks used in VMs, and public IP addresses used in VMs. To achieve the high availability (HA) design pattern, the IT function must explicitly install zonal services into two or more zones.

Microsoft Azure zone-redundant services are services such as zone-redundant storage and SQL databases. To use the availability zones with ZRS and SQL DB services, we need to specify the option to make them zone redundant during the deployment.

Microsoft Azure nonregional services are Azure services that are constantly ready from Azure geographies and are resilient to zone-wide blackouts and region-wide blackouts.

Azure services enabled by availability zones are designed to offer the right reliability and flexibility. They can be configured in two ways. Depending on the configuration, they can be zone redundant, with automatic replication across zones, or zonal, with instances pinned to specific zones. Clients can combine these patterns.

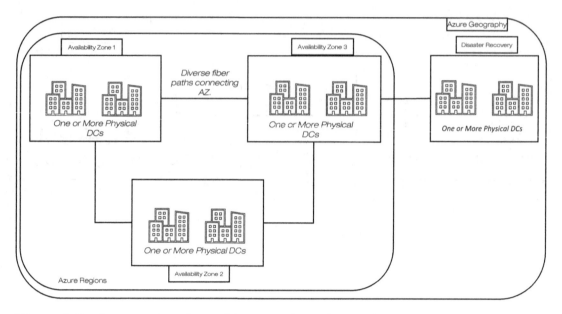

Figure 1-8. *Azure regions by making use of another region*

It is important to understand the FinTech management choices offered by Azure. By grouping your Azure subscriptions, you can take bulk actions on them. You can manage your subscriptions and resources efficiently by creating an Azure management group hierarchy tailored to your business needs. You can apply governance conditions to any Azure service, such as policies, access controls, or full-fledged blueprints, using the full platform integration. You can manage resources better and get visibility into all your resources. Using a single dashboard, you can monitor costs and usage.

Microsoft Azure requires you to assign Azure services to Azure resource groups when you create them. Even though this grouping structure may seem like just another form of administration, cloud consumers will use it for better infrastructure governance and cost management. Figure 1-9 shows logical view of the Azure infrastructure governance and cost management.

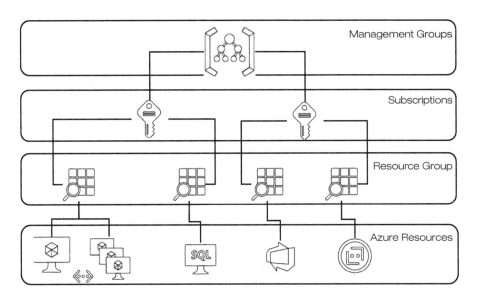

Figure 1-9. *Azure infrastructure governance and cost management*

Let's walk through each level of organization from the bottom up.

- A *resource* is an instance of a service cloud that consumers create, such as a virtual machine, storage, or SQL database.

- *Resource groups* act as logical containers that Azure uses to deploy and manage resources, such as web apps, databases, and storage accounts.

- An *account subscription* is a grouping of user accounts and the resources they create. A certain number of resources can be created and used per subscription. Organizations can use subscribers to manage costs and the resources that users, teams, and projects create.

- You can manage access, policy, and compliance across multiple subscriptions with *management groups*. All subscriptions inherit the conditions applied to the management group in a management group.

Let's look at these in more detail.

Azure Management Groups

Management groups are an efficient way to enforce policies and privilege control to Azure cloud resources. Like a resource group, a management group is a logical container for structuring Azure resources. However, management groups can hold a single Azure subscription or a nested management group. An Azure management group hierarchy supports up to six levels. It is impossible to have multiple parents on a single management group or a single subscription.

Here are a few facts about management groups:

- It is possible to support 10,000 management groups in one directory.

- It is possible to have a depth of six levels in a management group tree. Subscription and root levels are excluded.

- There can be only one parent for each management group and subscription.

- There can be many children for each management group.

- All subscriptions and management groups are grouped into a single hierarchy in each directory.

Azure Subscriptions

Azure subscriptions are automatically initiated as soon as you sign up for the Azure cloud, and all the resources are created within the subscription. However, a business can create additional subscriptions that are tied to the Azure account. Other subscriptions are applicable whenever companies want to have logical groupings for Azure resources, especially for reports on resources consumed by departments.

Microsoft Azure subscriptions are offered in the following three categories:

- *Free trial*: This offers completely free access for a limited time per account for limited resources; expired accounts cannot be reused.

- *Pay-as-you-go*: Pay only for resources consumed in Azure. No capex is involved, and cancellation is possible at any time.

- *Pay-as-you-go dev/test*: A subscription for Visual Studio can be used for dev and testing. This offers no production usage.

Each Microsoft Azure subscription has a unique identifier called a *subscription ID*. Microsoft recommends using the subscription ID to recognize the subscription.

Azure Resource Groups

A resource group is a logical collection of virtual machines, containers, storage accounts, virtual networks, web apps, databases, and dedicated servers. Users typically group related resources for an application, divided into production and nonproduction, but you may decide to further subdivide them on demand.

Admins can deploy and run all services integrated with a specific app by grouping them. Maintaining an enterprise array of services within a silo is now unnecessary.

It is impossible to attach an Azure resource to more than one resource group. You can also move resources from one group to another whenever you delete a resource group. All resources associated with a resource group are deleted when the resource group is deleted.

Azure Resource Manager

Azure Resource Manager (ARM) is a crucial component for managing the underlying IT resources and avoiding the operational overhead when managing all Azure services separately.

Both the Azure Portal and the Azure command-line tools work by using ARM, which permits cloud consumers to deploy multiple Azure resources on the go quickly. ARM makes it possible to reproduce any redeployment with a consistent outcome after a failure of an existing build.

Here are the most popular Azure resources and services:

- Azure virtual machines are an IaaS from Microsoft, and Microsoft manages the underlying physical compute, network, and storage. Cloud consumers manage the operating system, apps, and data that run on top of the VM.

- Availability sets protect VMs with fault domains. Fault domains protect VMs from hardware failures in a hardware rack.

- Scale sets allow the business to set up autoscale rules to scale horizontally when needed.

- Azure App Service makes it easy to host web apps in the cloud because it's a PaaS service that removes the management burden from the user.

- Azure App Service apps run inside an App Service plan that specifies the number of VMs and the configuration of those VMs.

- Containers allow cloud consumers to create an image of an application and everything needed to run it.

- Azure Container Instances (ACI) allows cloud consumers to run containers for a minimal cost.

- Azure Container Apps simplifies the deployment of containerized applications in the cloud. It enables developers to package their applications into containers, deploy them to Azure, and manage them using familiar tools and workflows.

- Azure Kubernetes Service (AKS) is a managed service that makes it easy to host Kubernetes clusters in the cloud.

- Azure Cosmos DB is a NoSQL database for unstructured data.

- Azure SQL Database is a Microsoft-managed relational database.

- Azure Database is a Microsoft-managed MySQL.

- An Azure virtual network provides Azure services to communicate with several others and the Internet.

- Azure Load Balancer can distribute traffic from the Internet across various VMs in a dedicated VNet.

- ExpressRoute allows cloud consumers to have a high-bandwidth connection to Azure of up to 10 Gbps by attaching to a Microsoft Enterprise Edge router.

- Azure DNS accommodates fast DNS responses and high domain availability.

- Azure Disk Storage is virtual disk storage specific to Azure VMs. Managed disks remove the operation burden of disks.

- Azure Files allows cloud consumers to have disk space in the cloud to map to a drive on-premises.

- Azure Blob Storage offers hot, cool, and archive storage tiers based on how long cloud consumers intend to store the data, whereby usually the data is accessed.

- Azure DevOps uses development collaboration tools such as pipelines, Kanban boards, Git repositories, and comprehensive automated and cloud-based nonfunctional testing.

- Azure Virtual Desktop makes apps and desktop readily available to multiple users from almost any device anywhere.

Azure Management Offerings

Management in Azure is the foundational building block for deploying and supporting resources in Azure. Management tools can be divided into visual and code-based tools at a high level, as shown in Figure 1-10.

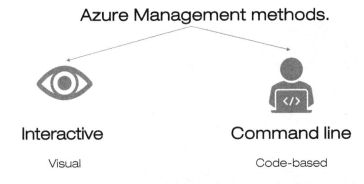

Figure 1-10. *Azure management methods*

Azure's visual tools provide full access to all functionality in a visually friendly manner. It may be less valuable to use visual tools when you're trying to deploy a large number of interdependent resources and have multiple configuration options.

In most cases, a code-based tool is the better choice when configuring Azure resources quickly. The correct commands and parameters may take some time to understand, but they can be saved into files and used repeatedly. Setup and configuration code can also be stored, versioned, and maintained in a source code management tool such as Git. When developers write application code, they use this approach to manage hardware and cloud resources. It is called *infrastructure as code*.

In infrastructure as code, two approaches are available: imperative and declarative. The *imperative code* details each step required to achieve the desired result. Contrary to declarative code, the *declarative code* specifies only the desired outcome, and it allows an interpreter to determine how to achieve it. It is crucial to distinguish declarative code tools from those based on logic, as declarative code tools provide a more robust way of deploying dozens or hundreds of resources simultaneously and reliably.

To manage your cloud environment, Microsoft offers a variety of tools and services, each geared toward a different scenario and user.

Management refers to the assignments and methods required to maintain IT applications and the resources supporting the organization's business. Azure has several services and tools that operate together to give complete management tools to cloud consumers, as shown in Figure 1-11.

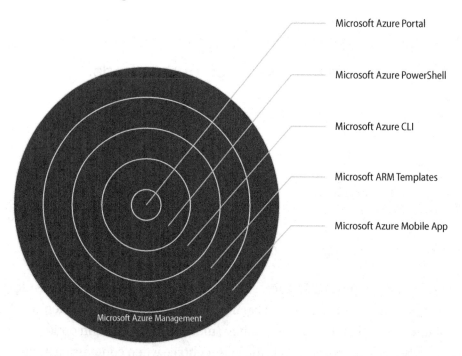

Figure 1-11. *Microsoft Azure management methods*

Microsoft Azure Portal

Use the Azure Portal to deploy, run, and monitor everything via a single management plane from web apps, databases, virtual machines, virtual networks, storage, and Visual Studio team projects to the aggregate cloud-native application from a unified console.

The first time you sign up for the Azure Portal, you'll be given a choice to take a tour of it. If you are not familiar with it, take the time to see how the Azure Portal works.

The Azure Portal provides a web-based interface that accesses almost all of the Azure features. The Azure Portal provides an intuitive graphical user interface to view all of the services you are using, create new services, and configure them. This is how most people engage with Azure for the first time. As your Azure usage grows, cloud consumers are more likely to choose a more repeatable, code-centric approach to managing cloud consumers' Azure resources.

Figure 1-12 shows the first view of the Azure Portal.

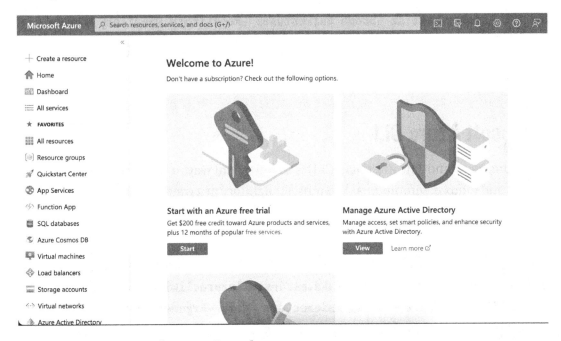

Figure 1-12. *Microsoft Azure Portal*

Microsoft Azure PowerShell

Azure PowerShell is a kit of cmdlets for operating Azure resources that can be used from the PowerShell command-line interface. Microsoft developed Azure PowerShell to make it easy to read, write, and execute the code to provide powerful automation features for IT support functions. AVD cloud administrators can use Azure PowerShell when they want to automate.

Microsoft PowerShell 7.x and higher are the Microsoft Azure Az PowerShell module's recommended PowerShell module on all platforms.

Use the following command to check the PowerShell version:

```
$PSVersionTable.PSVersion
```

Use the following command to install the Azure PowerShell Module (Az PowerShell module):

```
Install-Module -Name Az -Scope CurrentUser -Repository PSGallery -Force
```

Use the following command to connect to an Azure account (Az PowerShell module):

```
Connect-AzAccount
```

Microsoft Azure CLI

The Azure command-line interface (CLI) is a convenient way to deploy in Windows, macOS, and Linux environments. The most straightforward way to begin with Azure PowerShell is by trying it in an Azure Cloud Shell environment.

Use the following command to install the Azure CLI on Windows or to download and deploy the latest release of the Azure CLI:

```
Invoke-WebRequest -Uri https://aka.ms/installazurecliwindows -OutFile
.\AzureCLI.msi; Start-Process msiexec.exe -Wait -ArgumentList
'/I AzureCLI.msi /quiet'; rm .\AzureCLI.msi
```

Use the following command to log in with cloud consumer account credentials in the browser:

```
az login
```

Microsoft Azure Cloud Shell

The Azure Cloud Shell is a completely online version; there's no need for any deployment.

To reach the Azure Cloud Shell, click the Cloud Shell button in the Microsoft Azure Portal. When you first launch the Cloud Shell, you choose the environment to be used. The Cloud Shell is presented with two choices, Bash and PowerShell, as shown in Figure 1-13; cloud consumers can change this if they want.

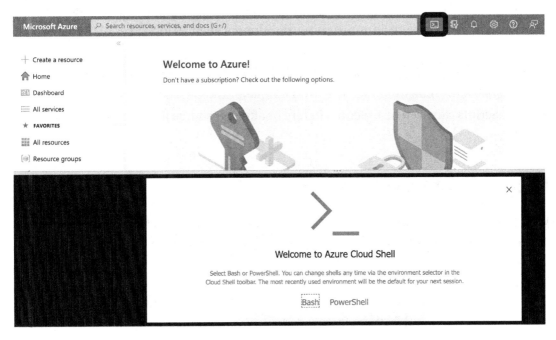

Figure 1-13. *Azure Cloud Shell*

Upon clicking, the console loads, and you can then create an Azure storage account; however, you need an active subscription.

Type the following command to get knowledge about PowerShell in the Azure Cloud Shell:

```
Get-Help.
```

Microsoft ARM Templates

The Azure CLI and Azure PowerShell both allow Azure administrators/developers to set up and tear down one Azure resource or orchestrate an infrastructure comprised of hundreds of resources; however, there's a better way to do this.

Azure Resource Manager templates (ARM templates) allow Azure administrators/developers to describe resources in a declarative JSON format. As a result, the entire ARM template is verified before any code is executed, ensuring that the resources are correctly created and connected. The template then orchestrates parallel creation.

Consequently, if Azure administrators/developers need 50 instances of the same resource, all will be created simultaneously.

Developers, DevOps professionals, or IT professionals specify each resource's desired state and configuration in the ARM template, and the template takes care of the rest. Scripts can even be executed before or after a resource has been set up using templates.

Microsoft Azure Mobile App

While users are away from their computers, they can still access Azure resources via the Azure mobile app. Consumers can use the app to do the following:

- Monitor the Azure resource's health and status.

- Restart a web app or virtual machine to catch alerts, diagnose problems, and fix them fast.

- Manage Azure resources for cloud consumers using the Azure CLI and Azure PowerShell commands.

Azure Monitoring Offerings

Azure Monitor allows cloud consumers to maximize the functional and nonfunctional KPIs of applications and services. It gives an end-to-end solution for gathering, interpreting, and acting on data from the Azure tenant cloud and for integrating it with on-premises environments. In addition, it offers golden signals to identify issues affecting KPIs proactively.

Azure Monitor can perform the following tasks such as gathering metrics, storing logs, and providing insights:

- *Metrics*: The Azure service automatically gathers metrics (defined as key performance indicators) and puts them in Azure Monitor metrics.

- *Logs*: The Azure service maintains diagnostic configurations, collecting platform logs and key performance indicators for Azure Monitor logs.

- *Application Insights*: Azure Application Insights is available and presents a well-defined monitoring experience for the consuming service.

- *Service health (complementary services)*: Microsoft runs an Azure Status web page where cloud consumers can observe Azure services' status in each region where Azure runs. While it is a healthy aspect of overall Azure health, the immense complexity of the web page doesn't make it a common way to get an overview of the health of cloud consumer-specific services. Instead, Azure Service Health can provide cloud consumers with a picture of the consumed resources.

To reach Azure Monitor, click the Monitor button in the Microsoft Azure Portal. Figure 1-14 shows the Azure Monitor dashboard.

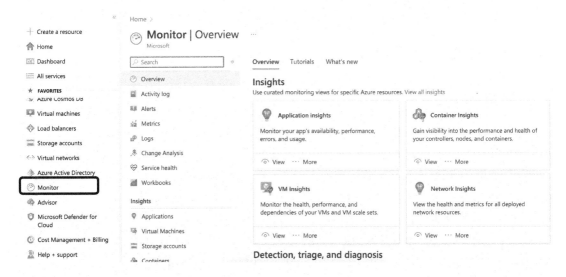

Figure 1-14. *Azure Monitor*

Microsoft Azure Advisor

Microsoft Azure Advisor offers recommendations and impacts of services against cost, security, reliability, performance, and operational excellence. It also guarantees that cloud consumer resources are configured accurately for availability and efficiency. In addition, Microsoft Azure Advisor can inform cloud consumers about predicaments in an Azure services configuration to avoid troubles.

To reach Azure Advisor, click the Advisor button in the Microsoft Azure Portal; Figure 1-15 shows the Azure Advisor dashboard.

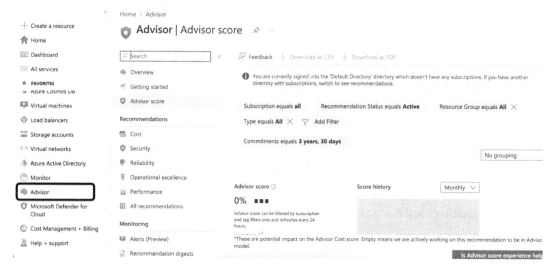

Figure 1-15. *Azure Advisor overview*

Microsoft Azure Security Capabilities

In this section, we'll look at the Azure security offerings.

Obviously, you need accurate and timely information about Azure security since security is job one in the cloud. Azure's wide range of security tools and capabilities is one of the best reasons to use it for your applications and services. Through these tools and capabilities, it is possible to build secure solutions on Azure's platform. Using Microsoft Azure, customers can access confidential, secure, and reliable data while maintaining transparency and accountability.

Computer attacks are commonly defined as attempts to gain illegal access to computers or computer systems to damage or harm them. But thinking only about computers or computer systems is limiting, as virtually any modern digital device can be a target for a cyberattack. As covered earlier in the chapter, they can range in severity from a minor inconvenience to a global disruption of economic and social systems.

A cloud service model determines who manages the application or service's security. As part of the Azure platform, built-in features and partner solutions can be deployed within a subscription to assist you with meeting these responsibilities.

The Azure platform has six distinct functional areas: operations, applications, storage, networking, compute, and identify, as shown in Figure 1-16.

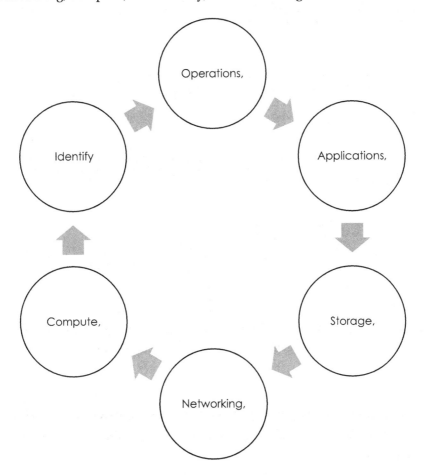

Figure 1-16. *Azure security functional areas*

The following are the key features in security operations.

Microsoft Sentinel

With Microsoft Sentinel, you can manage security information and events online, as well as automate security orchestration, automation, and response (SOAR). As a threat intelligence and security analytics solution, Sentinel allows organizations to detect, visualize, respond to, and monitor attacks in one place.

Microsoft Defender for Cloud

Thanks to Microsoft Defender for Cloud, Azure resources can be protected, detected, and responded to with more visibility and control. Integrated security monitoring and policy management across Azure subscriptions help detect threats that might otherwise go unnoticed; it also integrates with a broad ecosystem of security products.

Additionally, Defender for Cloud helps you manage security operations by providing a single dashboard that surfaces alerts and recommendations for immediate action. Many issues can be resolved with just a single click within the console.

Azure Resource Manager

As mentioned earlier, with Azure Resource Manager, your solution resources can be deployed, updated, or deleted in a single, coordinated operation. You can deploy, update, or delete all the resources at once. Azure Resource Manager templates are used for deployments, which can be used for testing, staging, and production environments. When you deploy your resources, Resource Manager provides security, auditing, and tagging features to make them easier to manage.

By integrating standard security control settings into standardized template-based deployments, ARM template-based deployments improve the security of Azure solutions because manual implementations are more likely to result in security configuration errors.

Application Insights

With Application Insights, web developers can monitor live web applications and detect performance anomalies automatically. The service provides extensible application performance management (APM). It monitors your application constantly as it runs during testing and after deployment.

Charts and tables generated by Application Insights show you, for example, when you get the most users, how responsive the app is, and how well it interacts with external services.

When your app becomes available or performs poorly, the service sends you an email notification. In the case of crashes, failures, or performance issues, you can examine telemetry data in detail to determine what's causing them. Application Insights ensures confidentiality, integrity, and availability, making it an effective security tool.

Azure Monitor

Both the Azure subscription (activity log) and individual Azure resources (resource logs) can be visualized, queried, routed, alerted, autoscaled, and automated using Azure Monitor. Azure Monitor alerts you to Azure logs that contain security-related events.

Azure Monitor Logs

With Azure Monitor logs, you can manage Azure resources and third-party cloud infrastructure (such as Amazon Web Services). With Azure Monitor logs, you can view metrics and logs for your entire environment in one place because data from Azure Monitor can be routed directly there.

As the tool enables you to quickly search through large amounts of security-related entries with a flexible query approach, Azure Monitor logs can be helpful in forensic and other security analyses.

Azure Advisor

Azure Advisor is a customized cloud consultant that helps you optimize your Azure deployments by analyzing your resource configuration and usage telemetry. After analyzing your resources, it recommends ways to improve their performance, security, and reliability and reduce the costs of Azure. With Azure Advisor, your security posture can be significantly improved for the Azure solutions you deploy by providing security recommendations. Microsoft Defender for Cloud generates these recommendations based on its security analysis.

Azure-Based Application Security Capabilities

A summary of key features in application security is provided in the following sections.

Penetration Testing

Microsoft is not responsible for performing penetration testing on your application, but we understand you would like to do so yourself. As a result, you contribute to the security of the entire Azure ecosystem by enhancing your applications' security. Although notifying Microsoft of pen testing activities is no longer required, customers must still follow Microsoft Cloud Penetration Testing Rules of Engagement.

Web Application Firewall

Web application firewalls (WAFs) are part of Azure Application Gateway, which help protect web applications from common web-based attacks like SQL injection, cross-site scripting, and session hijacking. OWASP's top 10 vulnerabilities are preconfigured into the system so it defends against them automatically.

Authentication and Authorization in Azure App Service

App Service authentication/authorization allows you to protect your application and work with per-user data without changing your back-end code.

Layered Security Architecture

Using App Service environments, developers can create layered security architectures that grant each application tier different levels of access to the network because they provide an isolated runtime environment deployed within an Azure Virtual Network (VNet). There is a common desire to hide API back ends from general Internet access and allow only upstream web applications to use APIs. Azure VNet subnets containing App Service environments can be configured with network security groups (NSGs) to restrict public access to API applications.

Web Server Diagnostics and Application Diagnostics

Diagnostic capabilities are provided by App Service web apps, which log information from both the web server and the web application. Web server and application diagnostics are logically separated. There are two significant advances in diagnosing and troubleshooting sites and applications on the web server.

In addition, the tracing events track requests throughout the entire request-and-response cycle, providing real-time information about application pools, worker processes, sites, and domains.

Using elapsed time or error codes, IIS 7 can automatically capture full trace logs for any specific request in XML format.

Azure-Based Storage Security Capabilities

The following are the key features of Azure storage security.

Azure Role-Based Access Control (Azure RBAC)

Azure RBAC can be configured to secure your storage account. For organizations that want to enforce security policies for data access, it is imperative to restrict access according to the need-to-know and least-privilege security principles. The Azure roles you assign to groups and applications at a certain scope allow you to grant access rights to users and groups.

In addition to built-in roles in Azure, such as Storage Account Contributor, Azure RBAC can also be used to secure your storage account.

Shared Access Signature

Delegating access to resources in your storage account is possible with shared access signatures. You can grant limited permissions to objects in your storage account using SAS for a specific period of time and with a specific set of permissions. You do not need to share your account access keys to grant these limited permissions.

Encryption in Transit

With Azure Storage, you can secure data when it is transmitted across networks using encryption in transit.

- When transferring data into or out of Azure Storage, you should use transport-level encryption, such as HTTPS.

- SMB 3.0 encryption for Azure File shares provides wire encryption.

- Data is encrypted before being transferred into storage and decrypted after being transferred out.

Encryption at Rest

Three Azure storage security features provide encryption of data that is "at rest" to ensure data privacy, compliance, and data sovereignty.

- When you write data to Azure Storage, storage service encryption automatically encrypts it.

- The feature of encryption at rest is also provided by client-side encryption.

- Azure Disk Encryption for Linux VMs and Azure Disk Encryption for Windows VMs allow you to encrypt the OS disk and data disks used by an IaaS virtual machine.

Storage Analytics

For a storage account, Azure Storage Analytics provides logging and metrics data. Storage Analytics records detailed information about successful and failed requests to a storage service so that you can trace requests, analyze usage trends, and diagnose storage account issues. You can monitor individual requests and diagnose storage service problems using this information. Requests are logged based on best efforts. Authenticated requests are logged in the following ways:

- Requests that were successful

- Requests that failed due to timeouts, throttling, network issues, or authorization issues

- The success and failure of propositions that use a Shared Access Signature (SAS)

- Analytical requests

Enabling Browser-Based Clients Using CORS

The user-agent sends extra headers to ensure that JavaScript code loaded from one domain can access resources located in another using cross-origin resource sharing (CORS). Afterward, the latter domain replies with extra headers that allow the original domain to access its resources or deny access.

When you set the CORS rules for Azure storage services, a properly authenticated request from a different domain will be evaluated to determine if it is allowed.

Azure Network Security Capabilities

This section highlights key features of Azure network security.

An Azure VNet is the fundamental building block for a private network. VNets provide a secure communication channel between Azure resources, such as virtual machines (VMs). VNets are like traditional data centers but have the advantage of Azure's infrastructure, such as scalability, availability, reliability, broad network access, hybrid connectivity, segmentation, isolation, and security.

An Azure VNet is the representations of your own network in the cloud. The Azure cloud is logically isolated and dedicated to your subscription. VNets can be used to provision and manage virtual private networks (VPNs) in Azure. Alternatively, they can be linked to other VNets in Azure or your on-premises IT infrastructure to create hybrid or hybrid cross-premises solutions. You can link each VNet you make with another VNet and an on-premises network if the CIDR blocks don't overlap. The administrator can also control VNet settings, and subnets can be segmented.

In Azure, resources communicate securely with each other, the Internet, and on-premises networks. With a virtual network, it's possible to use Azure resources to communicate with the Internet, communicate between your own Azure resources, communicate with on-premises resources, filter network traffic, route network traffic, and integrate Azure services.

Azure Network Communication with the Internet

A VNet's outbound communications are enabled by default for all resources. You can share and manage an inbound connection to a resource by assigning a public IP address or using a public load balancer.

Azure Communication Between Azure Resources

Azure resources are used in three main ways: by virtual network, VNet peering, and virtual network service endpoint.

Azure VNets and Azure Kubernetes Service are also available for connections between VMs and Azure resources, including the App Service environment.

Azure resources like Azure SQL databases and storage accounts can be accessed via service endpoints. As soon as you create a VNet, your services and virtual machines will be able to work together directly in the cloud.

The following methods are used by Azure resources to communicate securely with each other:

- *By a virtual network*: Azure public virtual networks are used to deploy virtual machines, as well as Azure App Service environments, Azure Kubernetes Services (AKS), and Azure Virtual Machine Scale Sets.

- *By VNet peering*: Virtual networks can be connected, allowing resources to communicate with another using virtual network peering. Connecting virtual networks in different Azure regions is possible.

- *By a virtual network service endpoint*: Directly connect your virtual network server with Azure services, such as Azure Storage and Azure SQL Database, so your virtual network can access their private address space and identify. You can secure Azure service resources to just a virtual network using service endpoints.

Azure Network Communication with the Private Cloud

Protect your data center by extending it securely. With Azure ExpressRoute, your on-premises computers and networks can be connected to a virtual network via a point-to-site VPN, site-to-site VPN, or Microsoft VPN. Connecting your on-premises computers and network to a virtual network may be accomplished through any of the following options:

- *Azure ExpressRoute*: This establishes a connection between your network and Azure via an ExpressRoute partner. It is a private connection. Traffic does not go over the Internet.

- *Point-to-site VPN*: This is an Internet-based VPN between a virtual network and a single computer in your network. Those who want to establish connections to virtual networks must configure their computers to do so. You can use this connection type if you're a first-time Azure user, work on a Proof of concept (POC), or are a developer. A virtual network's communication with your computer is done over the Internet using an encrypted tunnel.

- *Site-to-site VPN*: A site-to-site VPN creates a virtual network connection between your corporate VPN device and the Azure VPN gateway. Access to a virtual network is enabled through this connection type for any resource on-premises you authorize. An encrypted tunnel connects your VPN device on-premises with the Azure VPN gateway.

Filter Network Traffic

Using firewalls, gateways, proxies, and network address translation (NAT) services, you can filter network traffic between subnets while maintaining network security. There are two options for filtering network traffic between subnets.

- *Network virtual appliances*: Virtual network appliances perform network functions such as firewalls, WAN optimization, or other functions using virtual machines.

- *Network security sets*: Network security sets and application security sets allow you to filter network traffic entering and leaving resources by IP and protocol addresses, ports, and sources.

Route Network Traffic

Azure routes traffic between subnets, connected virtual networks, on-premises networks, and the Internet. To override Azure's default routes, implement one of these two options:

- *Route tables*: It is possible to create custom route tables with routes that control where traffic is routed for each subnet.

- *Border Gateway Protocol (BGP) routes*: By connecting your virtual network to your on-premises network using an Azure VPN Gateway or ExpressRoute connection, you can propagate your on-premises BGP routes to your virtual network.

Integrate Azure Services

Virtual machines or compute resources in an Azure virtual network can access Azure services privately when they are integrated into the virtual network. Your virtual network can be integrated into several ways with Azure services.

- You can virtualize the service by creating dedicated instances. The services can then be accessed privately within the virtual network and from the on-premises network.

- From your virtual network and on-premises networks, you can access a specific service instance using Private Link.

- Similarly, it is possible to connect to the service through service endpoints by building a virtual network. The virtual network can be protected with service endpoints.

Other Network Services

The following are other Azure network services that help to strengthen Azure networking:

- *Azure Firewall*: Azure Firewall protects your Azure VNet resources by providing managed, cloud-based network security. You can create, enforce, and log policies across subscriptions and virtual networks by using Azure Firewall.

- *Azure Bastion*: Azure Bastion is a fully managed service that delivers more secured and seamless Remote Desktop Protocol and SSH access to VMs without any exposure to public IP addresses. It provides the service instantly in your local or peered virtual network to get support for all the VMs within it.

- *Azure Peering Services*: By using Azure Peering, customers can connect to Microsoft cloud services such as Microsoft 365, Dynamics 365, SaaS services, Azure, and any other Microsoft service accessible on the Internet.

- *Azure DDoS Protection*: Azure DDoS Protection provides countermeasures for the most sophisticated DDoS attacks. You can use the service to enhance the mitigation of DDoS attacks on your virtual network resources and applications.

  Customers that move their applications to the cloud face a number of security and availability concerns due to DDoS attacks. In a DDoS attack, the application's resources are exhausted, preventing legitimate users from accessing the application. The attack can be targeted at any Internet-accessible endpoint.

- *Azure Private Link*: Azure Private Link lets you connect to Azure PaaS services (Azure Storage and SQL Database) and Azure-hosted, customer-owned, and partner services over a private network connection.

- *Virtual private network*: the Internet makes it possible to connect separate LANs while maintaining privacy. A VPN connects remote systems as if they were on a local network, often for security reasons.

- *Virtual Network NAT*: Gateway NAT simplifies outbound-only Internet connectivity for virtual networks. When configured on a subnet, a static public IP address is used for all outbound connections.

- *ExpressRoute*: You can extend your on-premises networks into the Microsoft cloud with ExpressRoute over a private connection through a connectivity provider.

- *ExpressRoute circuits*: You can deploy an ExpressRoute circuit either through a connectivity provider or through ExpressRoute Direct. If you want to use ExpressRoute with any combination of ExpressRoute offerings, you must use an ExpressRoute circuit.

- *ExpressRoute Direct*: With ExpressRoute Direct, you can connect directly to the global Microsoft network. It is available in 10 Gbps and 100 Gbps dedicated capacity. ExpressRoute Direct supports massive data ingestion into services such as Cosmos DB, physical isolation for regulated industries, and control over circuit distribution by business unit.

- *ExpressRoute FastPath*: FastPath is an ExpressRoute circuit configuration designed to improve the performance of data paths from the on-premises network to the virtual network in Azure. By enabling FastPath, network traffic is sent directly to virtual machines in the virtual network, bypassing the host.

- *ExpressRoute Gateway*: The ExpressRoute virtual network gateway allows you to exchange IP routes and route network traffic between your Azure and on-premises networks. ExpressRoute requires you to create a virtual network gateway to connect to virtual networks in Azure.

- *ExpressRoute Global Reach*: ExpressRoute Global Reach lets you connect your on-premises networks by linking circuits together. You can establish connections between your branch offices and Microsoft that allow them to exchange data directly if you have multiple circuits linking them.

- *ExpressRoute Monitor*: ExpressRoute Monitor lets you view ExpressRoute circuit metrics, resource logs, and alerts.

- *Web Application Firewall*: Azure WAF protects your web applications against common exploits and vulnerabilities. Malicious attacks using known vulnerabilities are increasingly targeting web applications. Cross-site scripting attacks, for example, and SQL injection are common.

- *Azure Application Gateway*: Azure Application Gateway manages traffic to your web applications with a load balancer. It offers a variety of load-balancing capabilities for Layer 7 as an Application Delivery Controller (ADC) as a service.

- *Azure Traffic Manager*: Azure Traffic Manager is a DNS-based network load balancer that provides high availability and responsiveness while distributing traffic optimally to services across global Azure regions.

- *Azure Load Balancer*: Azure Load Balancer provides high availability and network performance to your applications. Incoming traffic is distributed among healthy instances of services within a load-balanced set using a layer 4 (TCP, UDP) load balancer.

Azure Compute Security Capabilities

The following are the key features in Azure compute security.

Azure Confidential Computing

As the final piece of the data protection puzzle, Azure confidential computing allows you to protect your data at all times, including while it is at rest, while it is being transferred over the network, or when it is in memory or being used. As well as being able to cryptographically verify that the virtual machine you provision has booted securely and is configured correctly, remote attestation allows you to unlock your data securely.

You can enable "lift-and-shift" scenarios of existing applications or control security features completely. In IaaS, you can use AMD SEV-SNP virtual machines or Intel Software Guard Extensions (SGX) virtual machines with confidential application enclaves. Microsoft has several container-based PaaS options, including Azure Kubernetes Service (AKS).

Anti-malware and Antivirus

As part of Azure IaaS, you can protect your virtual machines from malicious files, adware, and other threats by using antimalware software from Microsoft, Symantec, Trend Micro, McAfee, and Kaspersky. Microsoft Antimalware for Azure Cloud Services and virtual machines helps protect your cloud services by identifying and removing viruses, spyware, and other malicious software. Using Microsoft Defender for Cloud or Microsoft Antimalware, Microsoft Antimalware can alert you when known malicious or unwanted software attempts to install or run on your Azure systems.

Hardware Security Module

To improve security, encryption and authentication must be protected. In Azure Key Vault, you can store your critical secrets and keys in hardware security modules (HSMs) that meet FIPS 140-2 Level 2 standards. You can store your keys in Key Vault along with any keys or secrets from your applications to simplify the management and security of your critical secrets. Azure Active Directory manages permissions and access to these protected items.

Virtual Machine Backup

With Azure Backup, you can protect your application data for free, with minimal operating costs and no capital investment. Your virtual machines running Windows and Linux can be protected from application errors and human error, which can lead to security issues. Azure Backup protects your virtual machines from these errors and from human errors.

Azure Site Recovery

You must identify how to keep your business continuity/disaster recovery (BCDR) strategy up and running during planned and unplanned outages. Azure Site Recovery makes your workloads and apps available if your primary location fails by orchestrating replication, failover, and recovery.

SQL VM TDE

CLE and TDE are SQL server encryption features that require customers to manage and store their cryptographic keys. Azure Key Vault (AKV) improves the security of these keys and allows them to be managed in a highly available, secure environment. SQL Server can use these keys through the Azure Key Vault connector.

For SQL Server in Azure VMs, you can use the Azure Key Vault Integration feature to save time accessing Azure Key Vault from your on-premises SQL Server instance. The configuration required for a SQL VM to access your key vault can be automated with a few Azure PowerShell cmdlets.

VM Disk Encryption

Your IaaS virtual machine disks can be encrypted using Azure Disk Encryption for Linux and Windows VMs. To offer volume encryption for the operating system and data disks, it uses Windows BitLocker and Linux DM-Crypt. To manage and control the disk-encryption keys and secrets of your Key Vault subscription, the solution is integrated with Azure Key Vault. Your Azure storage account encrypts all data on virtual machine disks at rest as part of the solution.

Virtual Networking

Virtual machines must have network connectivity in Azure to support that requirement. To keep an Azure VNet, virtual machines must be connected to it. A VNet is a logical construct built on the Azure network fabric. This ensures that other Azure customers cannot access your deployments by isolating them from all other VNets.

Patch Updates

Using patch updates simplifies the process of finding and fixing potential problems and simplifies the management of software updates by reducing the number of updates you need to deploy in your enterprise and improving compliance monitoring.

Security Policy Management and Reporting

In addition to increasing visibility and control over your Azure resources' security, Defender for Cloud helps you prevent, detect, and respond to threats. Security monitoring and policy management are integrated across your Azure subscriptions, allowing you to detect threats that could otherwise go undetected. It works with a wide range of security solutions.

Azure Identify Security Capabilities

Microsoft manages identify and access across its products and services using multiple security practices and technologies.

Azure Active Directory (Azure AD)

Authentication by multifactor authentication and Conditional Access are some of the features available with Azure Active Directory (Azure AD), part of Microsoft Entra.

- The multifactor authentication process requires users to use multiple authentication methods, both on-premises and in the cloud. It provides strong authentication while accommodating users through simple sign-in options.

- With Microsoft Authenticator, you get multifactor authentication for your Microsoft Azure Active Directory and Microsoft account and support for wearables and fingerprint authentication.

Azure Active Directory External Identities

A highly secure digital experience with customized controls is available for partners, customers, and anyone else outside your organization with Azure Active Directory External Identities, part of Microsoft Entra. Manage access across an organization seamlessly with one portal that combines external identities and user directories.

Azure Active Directory Domain Services

By using Azure Active Directory Domain Services (Azure AD DS), you can deploy, maintain, and patch a domain controller without deploying, managing, or patching managed domain services such as Windows Domain Join, group policy, and LDAP.

- Through password policy enforcement, long and complex passwords are enforced, periodic password rotation is enforced, and accounts are locked out after failed authentication attempts.

- Authentication via Azure Active Directory is supported by token-based authentication.

- Users are given only the access they need to perform their job duties when they use Azure RBAC based on their assigned roles. Azure RBAC can be customized based on your organization's risk tolerance and business model.

- You can control user access to data centers and cloud platforms by using integrated identify management (hybrid identify), which creates a single user identify across both.

Azure Apps and Data Security Capabilities

By integrating Microsoft Active Directory with applications on-site and in the cloud, Azure Active Directory secures data access and simplifies user and group management. Developers can easily integrate policy-based identify management into their apps thanks to its combination of core directory services, advanced identify governance, security, and application access management. You can use the Azure Active Directory Basic, Premium P1, and Premium P2 editions to enhance Azure Active Directory.

- With Cloud App Discovery, a premium feature in Azure Active Directory, you can identify cloud applications that your employees use.

- With Azure Active Directory Identify Protection, you can gain an overview of risk detections and potential vulnerabilities that could affect your organization's identities from a consolidated view.

- By deploying Azure Active Directory Domain Services, you can join Azure virtual machines to a domain without deploying domain controllers. Users can access resources within the domain using their corporate Active Directory credentials.

- Designed for consumer-facing applications, Azure Active Directory B2C is a globally available, highly available identify management service that can scale to hundreds of millions of identities and integrate across mobile and web platforms. Customers can sign in to all your apps using existing social media accounts or creating new stand-alone credentials.

- Azure Active Directory B2B Collaboration is a secure partner integration solution that supports cross-company relationships. It enables partners to access your corporate applications and data selectively using their self-managed identities.

- Integrating Azure Active Directory with Windows 10 devices allows you to extend cloud capabilities to centralized management, simplifying access to apps and resources and connecting users to corporate or organizational clouds.

- The Azure Active Directory Application Proxy provides secure remote access to on-premises web applications.

Overview of the NIST CSF

Cybersecurity threats exploit essential infrastructure systems' increased complexity and connectivity, putting the nation's security, economy, and public safety and health at risk. In the same way that financial and reputational risks affect a company's bottom line, cybersecurity risks can drive up costs and impact revenue. They can harm an organization's ability to innovate and gain and maintain customers. The management of risk in an organization can be amplified by cybersecurity.

To better address cybersecurity risks, the Cybersecurity Enhancement Act updated the National Institute of Standards and Technology (NIST) role to include identifying and developing cybersecurity risk frameworks for voluntary use by critical infrastructure owners and operators. The CEA states that NIST must identify a prioritized, flexible, repeatable, performance-based, and cost-effective approach, including information security measures and controls that owners and operators of critical infrastructure may voluntarily adopt to help them identify, assess, and manage cyber risks.

Organizations should consider cybersecurity risks as part of their risk management processes, using business drivers to guide cybersecurity activities.

The framework has three features: the framework core, the implementation tiers, and the framework profiles.

The framework core comprises cybersecurity activities, desired outcomes, and applicable reference standards across critical infrastructure sectors. From executive to implementation/operations, the core provides industry standards, guidelines, and practices for communicating cybersecurity activities and products across the organization. Five concurrent and continuous functions comprise the framework core—identifying, protecting, detecting, responding, and recovering. An organization's cybersecurity risk management life cycle can be viewed from a high-level, strategic perspective when these functions are considered together. Based on the framework core, key categories and subcategories are identified—discrete outcomes—for each function. For each subcategory, NIST identifies relevant informative references such as standards, guidelines, and practices.

The following are the five framework core functions. As a result, these functions aren't intended to form a serial path or lead to a static desired outcome. They should be performed concurrently and continuously to create an operational culture that addresses the dynamic cybersecurity risk.

- *Identify*: An organization needs to proactively understand cybersecurity risks to people, systems, data, and processes via the Identify function. When prioritizing and focusing efforts, it is vital to be aware of the business context, the resources supporting critical functions, and cybersecurity risks. This function includes the following outcome categories: asset management, business environment, governance, risk assessment, and risk management strategies.

- *Protect*: The identify management and access control function ensures potential cyberattacks are contained or limited. By supporting the Protect function, critical services can be delivered while limiting or containing the impact of a potential cyberattack. It consists of several outcome categories: awareness and training, data security, processes and procedures for information protection, maintenance, and protective technology.

- *Detect*: Cybersecurity events can be discovered in real time through the Detect function to identify cybersecurity events and develop and implement appropriate activities. Anomalies and events, continuous security monitoring, and detection processes are examples of outcome categories within this function.

- *Respond*: In response to a detected cybersecurity incident, the Respond function develops and implements appropriate responses to contain the impact of the incident. Examples of outcome categories are response planning, communication, analysis, mitigation, and improvement.

- *Recover*: The Recovery function supports timely recovery to normal operations during cybersecurity incidents by maintaining resilience plans and restoring any capabilities or services impaired because of a cybersecurity incident. Recovery planning, improvements, and communications are examples of outcome categories within this function.

An organization's framework implementation tiers provide insights into how it views and manages cybersecurity risk. Cybersecurity risk management practices are assessed according to whether they exhibit the characteristics described in the framework (e.g., awareness of risks and threats, repeatability, and adaptability). Tiers are categorized based on a company's practices, ranging from partial to adaptive. These tiers are progressing from informal, reactive responses to agile and risk-informed approaches. When selecting tiers, organizations should consider their current risk management practices, their threats, their legal and regulatory requirements, as well as their business objectives, and organizational constraints.

The framework profiles represent the outcomes chosen by an organization based on its business needs. A profile aligns standards, guidelines, and practices with the framework core in a particular implementation scenario. A "current" profile can be compared to a "target" profile (the "to be" state), and cybersecurity posture can be identified as opportunity for improvement. Organizations can define a profile by reviewing all categories and subcategories and determining which are most important based on their business/mission drivers and risk assessments; categories and subcategories can be added as appropriate. The current profile can support prioritization and measuring progress toward the target profile by factoring in other business needs, including cost-effectiveness and innovation. Self-assessments and communication between organizations can be conducted using profiles.

As part of FedRAMP, cloud computing products and services are evaluated, monitored, and authorized based on standardized procedures. The FedRAMP Joint Authorization Board (JAB) has granted Azure and Azure Government the High Provisional Authorization to Operate (P-ATO), which augments FedRAMP controls. Using Azure FedRAMP High authorizations, customers are assured that FedRAMP audit scope Azure services align with NIST CSF risk management practices.

Microsoft Azure cloud services have been attested to comply with NIST CSF risk management practices according to NIST CSF, Version 1.0, dated February 12, 2014. Azure NIST CSF control mapping demonstrates alignment between Azure FedRAMP authorized services and CSF Core. Further, three supply chain risk management subcategories are included in NIST CSF Draft Version 1.1.

In addition, Microsoft has developed a NIST CSF customer responsibility matrix (CRM) that outlines all control requirements dependent on customer implementation and shared responsibility controls and control implementation details for Microsoft-owned controls. NIST CSF CRM can be downloaded from the Service Trust Portal Blueprints section under NIST CSF Blueprints.

Azure Policy regulatory compliance built-in initiatives provide additional customer assistance, mapping to the NIST SP 800-53 compliance domains and controls.

- *Azure*: Azure regulatory compliance built-in to NIST SP 800-53 Rev. 4

- *Azure Government*: A regulatory compliance initiative built into Azure Government based on NIST SP 800-53 Rev. 4

Azure Policy provides built-in initiative definitions for regulatory compliance based on responsibility: customer, Microsoft, and shared. Microsoft can use third-party attestations and control implementation details to ensure control compliance with NIST SP 800-53. Azure Policy definitions are associated with each NIST SP 800-53 control. Compliance with these controls can be assessed using Azure Policy; however, compliance is only one part of the overall compliance picture. As an organizational standard enforcer and compliance assessor, Azure Policy provides users with aggregated view and drill-down capabilities.

Table 1-1 describes specific cybersecurity activities common to all critical infrastructure sectors using functions, categories, subcategories, and informative references. The framework core presentation format does not imply a particular order of implementation or a degree of importance for categories, subcategories, and informative references. The framework is not exhaustive but is extensible, enabling organizations, sectors, and other entities to manage their cybersecurity risk efficiently and cost-effectively using subcategories and informative references.

During the profile creation process, activities from the framework core can be selected, and additional categories, subcategories, and informative references can be added. During profile creation, these activities are selected based on the organizational constraints, risk management processes, legal/regulatory requirements, and business/mission objectives of an organization. Personal information is considered part of the data or assets described in the categories when assessing security risks and protections.

Despite the similarities between the functions, categories, and subcategories of IT and Industrial Control Systems (ICS), they operate in different operational environments and require additional considerations. In addition to affecting the physical world directly, ICS can also pose risks to people's health and safety. Additionally, ICS has unique performance and reliability requirements compared with IT, and cybersecurity measures must consider safety and efficiency.

Functions and categories have unique alphabetic identifiers, according to Table 1-1, which makes it easier for users to use the framework core.

Table 1-1. *Function and Category Unique Identifiers*

SI.No	Function	Category Unique Identifier	Category
1	Identify	ID.AM	Asset Management
		ID.BE	Business Environment
		ID.GV	Governance
		ID.RA	Risk Assessment
		ID.RM	Risk Management Strategy
		ID.SC	Supply Chain Risk Management
2	Protect	PR.AC	Identify Management and Access Control
		PR.AT	Awareness and Training
		PR.DS	Data Security
		PR.IP	Information Protection Processes and Procedures
		PR.MA	Maintenance
		PR.PT	Protective Technology
3	Detect	DE.AE	Anomalies and Events
		DE.CM	Security Continuous Monitoring
		DE.DP	Detection Processes

(*continued*)

Table 1-1. (*continued*)

Sl.No	Function	Category Unique Identifier	Category
4	Respond	RS.RP	Response Planning
		RS.CO	Communications
		RS.AN	Analysis
		RS.MI	Mitigation
		RS.IM	Improvements
5	Recover	RC.RP	Recovery Planning
		RC.IM	Improvements
		RC.CO	Communications

Microsoft cyber offerings can meet many security functions described in these frameworks. Microsoft cyber offerings can assist with five NIST CSF core functions (Identify, Protect, Detect, Respond, and Recover).

Table 1-2 maps the NIST CSF core functions (Identify, Protect, Detect, Respond, and Recover) to Azure Services.

Table 1-2. *Function and Azure Services Mapping*

Function	Azure Services Mapping
Identify	Azure AD
	Azure AD Identify protection
	Azure AD Privileged Identify Management
	Azure Policy
	Azure IOT Hub
	Microsoft Intune
	Azure Network Watcher
	Azure Automation
	Azure Information Protection
	Service Map
	Microsoft Threat Modeling Tool
	Privileged Access Workstation
	Microsoft Compliance Manager
	Azure Security Center
Protect	Azure Application Gateway
	Azure WAF
	Azure AD
	Azure Firewall
	Azure AD Identify Protection
	Azure Advanced Threat Protection
	Office ATP
	Azure Key Vault
	Azure DDoS
	Azure VPN Gateway
	Network Security Groups
	Azure Bastion
	Azure Encryption

(continued)

Table 1-2. (*continued*)

Function	Azure Services Mapping
Detect	Azure Firewall
	Azure Monitor
	Azure Intelligent Security Graph
	Azure Sentinel
	Azure Security Center
	Microsoft for Cloud
	Azure DDoS Protection
	Azure Rights Management Service (RMS)
	Microsoft Purview Information Protection
	Azure Network Security Group (NSG)
Respond	Azure AD Identify Protection
	Azure Advanced Threat Protection
	Office ATP
	Azure Logic App
	Microsoft Threat Experts
Recover	Azure Backup
	Azure Site Recovery

Summary

This chapter covered the fundamentals of cybersecurity, cloud computing, and Microsoft Azure. It gave you a broad understanding of essential Microsoft Azure security capabilities and insights into the NIST CSF.

In the next chapter of the book, you will learn about designing and deploying security for infrastructure, data, and apps.

CHAPTER 2

Design and Deploy Security for Infrastructure, Data, and Applications

Cybersecurity is essential in protecting systems from malicious attacks and unauthorized access. It also helps to ensure that data is kept safe and secure and that applications remain available and reliable. Without proper cybersecurity measures in place, organizations can be exposed to costly data breaches and other security incidents. Cybersecurity should be a top priority for any organization, and companies should invest in measures to detect and prevent security threats and vulnerabilities, as well as to respond quickly and effectively when incidents occur.

Without appropriate cybersecurity measures, organizations can be left vulnerable to malicious actors who can exploit their systems to access confidential information or damage their networks. Investing in cybersecurity measures can help protect companies from these threats, as well as the financial impacts of data breaches and other security incidents, such as loss of customers, reputational damage, legal costs, and regulatory fines. The first cybersecurity measures were introduced in 1972 with a research project on ARPANET. (ARPANET was a precursor to the Internet and developed protocols for remote computer networking.)

Cloud security is critical for protecting critical data and applications from cyber threats. Cloud providers must have robust security measures in place to ensure the safety of their customers' data. Companies should also take steps to ensure their own data is secure by implementing the proper security protocols.

Since cybersecurity is integrated into cloud platforms, customers often let their guard down and take cloud security for granted. Microsoft Azure's shared responsibility model can help you overcome these challenges.

© Puthiyavan Udayakumar 2023
P. Udayakumar, *Design and Deploy a Secure Azure Environment*,
https://doi.org/10.1007/978-1-4842-9678-3_2

With Azure's built-in controls, data, networking, and app services, you can protect your workloads quickly. In this chapter, you'll read about strategically designing and deploying security for infrastructure, data, and applications using the Microsoft cloud security benchmarks.

By the end of this chapter, you will understand the following:

- Designing and deploying a strategy for securing infrastructure and platform components

- Designing and deploying a strategy for securing identify

- Designing and deploying a strategy for securing apps and data

- Getting started with Microsoft SecOps

Design and Deploy a Strategy for Securing Infrastructure Components

In this section, we'll look at Microsoft Azure data centers. Microsoft Azure data centers house a global network of computer servers.

The Microsoft Azure global infrastructure is divided into two major components: physical infrastructure and connective network components. Physical data centers are arranged into regions and connected through one of the largest interconnected networks in the world.

The Microsoft Azure global network provides high availability, low latency, scalability, and cutting-edge technology in a cloud infrastructure, all using the Azure platform. This way, IP traffic never reaches the public Internet because all the data is kept entirely in the trustworthy Microsoft network.

More than 200 cloud services are offered by Microsoft Azure to customers on a 24/7/365 basis, including enterprise services like Microsoft Azure, Microsoft 365, and Microsoft Dynamics 365. These services are hosted on Microsoft's cloud infrastructure, which consists of globally distributed data centers, edge computing nodes, and service operations centers. The extensive fiber footprint connects them to one of the world's largest global networks.

To provide a trustworthy online experience for customers and partners worldwide, the data centers that power the Microsoft cloud offerings focus on high reliability, operational excellence, environmental sustainability, and cost-effectiveness. In addition, Microsoft regularly conducts internal and third-party security audits of its data centers. Its cloud services are trusted by the world's most highly regulated organizations.

With the most comprehensive set of compliance offerings available from any cloud service provider, Microsoft infrastructure and cloud services meet its customers' strict privacy and security requirements. By providing the most comprehensive set of compliance offerings available to any cloud service provider, Microsoft helps customers comply with national, regional, and industry-specific regulations governing the collection and use of individuals' data.

Besides meeting ISO, HIPAA, FedRAMP, and SOC standards, Microsoft's cloud infrastructure and offerings meet country-specific standards such as Australia's IRAP, the UK's G-Cloud, and Singapore's MTCS. Rigorous, third-party audits verify its adherence to the strict security controls these standards mandate, and the Microsoft Service Trust Portal provides audit reports for data center infrastructure and cloud services.

Microsoft Azure operates in data centers built and managed by Microsoft. To ensure security and reliability, Microsoft operations staff members manage, monitor, and administer the data centers, which comply with essential industry standards, such as ISO/IEC 27001:2013 and NIST SP 800-53. These employees have years of experience delivering 24/7 continuity of the world's most extensive online services.

Azure Data Centers and Network

The Microsoft Cloud Infrastructure and Operations (MCIO) team manages the physical infrastructure and data centers of all Microsoft online services. In addition to managing and supporting internal perimeter network devices (such as edge routers and data center routers), the MCIO is also responsible for managing and maintaining physical and environmental controls within the data centers. In addition, the MCIO is accountable for setting up the data center racks with a bare minimum of server hardware. There is no direct interaction between Azure data centers and customers.

Cloud-scale traffic can be handled effectively by a data center network, which is a modified version of a Clos network. The network is constructed with many commodity devices to minimize the impact of individual hardware failure. Separate power and cooling domains are located in different physical locations to reduce the impact of environmental events. All network devices are running on the control plane in the OSI model's layer 3 routing mode, eradicating the historical traffic loop issue. With Equal-Cost Multi-Path (ECMP) routing, all paths between diverse tiers are active to provide high redundancy and bandwidth.

Combined with multiple primary and secondary DNS server clusters, Azure Domain Name Service (DNS) infrastructure provides fault tolerance on an internal and external level. Additionally, Azure network security controls, such as NetScaler, protect Azure DNS services from distributed denial-of-service (DDoS) attacks.

The Microsoft network, which connects Microsoft data centers and customers globally over 165,000 miles, is one of the largest backbone networks in the world.

At the time of writing, an excellent cloud experience is delivered through Microsoft's global network (WAN). With a global network of Microsoft data centers distributed across 61 Azure regions and edge nodes strategically placed worldwide, Microsoft can meet any demand with availability, capacity, and flexibility.

Figure 2-1 shows the Microsoft global network.

Figure 2-1. *Microsoft global network*

A secondary and primary DNS server hierarchy resolves Azure customer domain names in multiple data centers. Azure DNS servers are located in various data centers. Usually, the domain names are resolved to CloudApp.net addresses, which wrap the virtual IP (VIP) address for the customer's service. Microsoft load balancers translate the VIP to an internal dedicated IP (DIP) address for Azure tenants.

Azure is hosted in geographically dispersed data centers within the United States and is built on the latest routing platforms that implement scalable, robust architectural standards.

- Traffic engineering based on Multiprotocol Label Switching (MPLS) provides efficient link utilization and graceful service degradation in the event of an outage.

- A "need plus one" (N+1) redundancy architecture is used when implementing networks.

- In addition to redundantly connecting properties with more than 1,200 Internet service providers globally at multiple peering points, data centers are served by dedicated, high-bandwidth network circuits. With this connection, the edge capacity is more than 2,000 gigabytes per second (Gbps).

Because Microsoft owns its network circuits between data centers, these attributes help Azure achieve 99.9+ percent network availability without needing traditional third-party Internet service providers.

A Microsoft Azure network Internet traffic flow policy directs traffic to the nearest regional data centers for Azure production networks. All Azure production data centers share the same network architecture and hardware, so the following traffic flow description applies consistently.

As soon as Azure Internet traffic is routed to the nearest data center, a connection is established between Azure nodes and customer-instantiated VMs. Network infrastructure devices serve as boundary points for ingress and egress filters at the access and edge locations. These routers isolate traffic between Azure nodes and customer-instantiated VMs. Filtering unwanted network traffic and limiting traffic speed is possible using a tiered access control list (ACL) on these routers. In addition to allowing only IP addresses that Microsoft approves, distribution routers provide anti-spoofing and ACLs for TCP connections.

In addition to performing network address translation (NAT) from Internet-routable IP addresses to Azure internal IP addresses, external load-balancing devices are located behind the access routers. Additionally, the devices route packets to valid production internal IP addresses and ports. They serve as a protection mechanism to keep the internal production network address space from being exposed.

All traffic transmitted to a customer's web browser, including sign-in and afterward, is encrypted with Hypertext Transfer Protocol Secure (HTTPS). The use of TLS v1.2 enables a secure tunnel for traffic to flow through. Access and core router ACLs ensure that the source of the traffic is consistent with what is expected.

The significant difference between this and traditional security architecture is that it does not require dedicated hardware firewalls, specialized intrusion detection and prevention systems, or other security appliances before connecting to Azure's production environment. In contrast to what customers would expect in Azure, Azure does not employ these hardware firewalls. Security features, including firewall capabilities, are almost exclusively built into the Azure environment's software.

Within the Azure environment, several core security and firewall features reflect a defense-in-depth strategy, including host-based software firewalls.

As a relational database service, Azure SQL Database provides customers with the robust security features they expect from a relational database service. SQL Database has its security capabilities to protect customer data and provide robust security features. The controls inherited from Azure are built upon these capabilities.

Data center regions are accessible across the world, so customers can deploy applications anywhere in the world.

There are dedicated regional low-latency networks connecting data centers within a latency-defined perimeter. There are regions with different pricing and service availability for Microsoft 365 and Dynamics 365, as opposed to geographies for Microsoft 365 and Dynamics 365.

Availability zones provide resiliency and options for high availability, and data center failures can be prevented by implementing availability zones.

For added resilience, high availability, and confidence that data traversing between availability zones is always encrypted, Azure availability zones, consisting of at least three zones, allow customers to spread their infrastructure and applications across discrete and dispersed data centers.

Microsoft evaluates each availability zones' placement using more than 30 viability and risk-based criteria, identifying both significant individual risks and collective and shared risks between availability zones without compromising their low-latency perimeter.

Every country in which Microsoft operates a data center region has an Azure availability zone.

Azure Data Center Physical Security

Across more than 100 highly secure facilities worldwide, Azure hosts thousands of online services.

As the infrastructure is designed to bring applications closer to users worldwide, it preserves data residency and offers customers comprehensive compliance and resilience options. Azure is available in 140 countries and regions around the world.

Data centers are connected through a massive and resilient network to form regions. All Azure traffic within a region or between regions is protected by default by content distribution, load balancing, redundancy, and data-link layer encryption. Azure offers more global regions than any other cloud provider, so you can deploy applications wherever needed.

Azure regions are organized into geopolitical regions. Geopolitical regions ensure that data residency, sovereignty, compliance, and resilience requirements are met.

Microsoft Azure's shared responsibility model can help you overcome these challenges. The dedicated, high-capacity network infrastructure enables customers with specific data residency and compliance requirements to keep their data and applications close to the source. Azure geographies are fault tolerant to withstand Azure region failure.

Within an Azure region, availability zones are physically separated.

You can run mission-critical applications with high availability and low-latency replication in availability zones. Availability zones comprise one or more data centers with independent power, cooling, and networking.

Microsoft designed, built, and operates data centers in a way that strictly restricts access to data storage areas. Microsoft's goal is to help secure the data centers containing your data, as it understands the importance of protecting your data. Dedicated to maintaining state-of-the-art physical security, Microsoft has an entire division devoted to designing, deploying, and managing Azure's physical data center facilities.

To reduce the impact of unauthorized access to data center resources and information hosted within DC, Microsoft adopts a layered approach to physical security. The Microsoft data centers have multiple layers of protection: access approval at the facility's perimeter, the building's perimeter, the building's interior, and the data center's floor.

Azure Infrastructure Availability

As part of Microsoft's commitment to high availability, the company monitors and responds to incidents, provides service support, and helps with backup failover. It is one of the largest networks in the world. Microsoft has geographically distributed operations centers operating 24/7/365. A fiber-optic and content distribution network connects data centers and edge nodes to ensure high performance and reliability.

Data is kept in two locations by Azure. You can choose where your backup site is; in the primary location, three copies of your data are continuously maintained.

Active databases are monitored every five minutes to determine their health and status. Azure ensures that a database accesses the Internet via an Internet gateway, maintaining database availability.

By providing connectivity endpoints, Azure delivers highly scalable and durable storage. Applications can therefore access the storage service directly. The storage service processes incoming requests efficiently and with transactional integrity.

Cloud Security Shared Responsibility Model

Cloud security is an essential consideration for any organization that stores data in the cloud. It is important to ensure that the cloud provider has the necessary security measures in place to protect data from potential threats such as hackers and malware. Additionally, organizations should also have their own security strategies in place to further protect their data.

In an enterprise, security is your responsibility in a traditional data center model across all areas of your operation, including your applications, servers, user controls, and even the security of your building. By taking on many operational burdens, including security, your cloud provider provides valuable relief to your teams. Regarding public clouds such as Azure, cloud security is defined as a shared responsibility model, and security ownership must be clearly understood, with each party maintaining complete control over those assets, processes, and functions they own. Working with your cloud provider and sharing some security responsibilities can help you maintain a secure environment with less operational overhead.

Security responsibilities shift as organizations move workloads to Azure cloud-based infrastructure from their on-premises data centers. As a result, you (as an organization) are now solely responsible for all security aspects, as you would be in a traditional environment. All cloud providers, including Microsoft's competitors such as AWS and GCP, follow the cloud security shared responsibility model.

As you evaluate and consider public cloud services such as Microsoft Azure, you must know the shared responsibility model, which security tasks the cloud service provider is responsible for, and which are your responsibility as the consumer.

Depending on the Azure service model, your security responsibility differs. The following is a high-level summary:

- All aspects of security and operations are the customer's responsibility for on-premises solutions.

- The platform vendor should manage the elements such as buildings, servers, networking hardware, and the hypervisor for IaaS solutions.

- Operating systems, networks, applications, identities, clients, and data are the customer's responsibilities or are shared with them.

- IaaS solutions build on IaaS deployments, and the provider manages and secures the network controls, but applications, identify, clients, and data are still the customer's responsibility.

- A vendor provides the application for SaaS solutions and abstracts customers from the underlying components. However, the customer is still responsible for ensuring that data is classified correctly and is managing endpoint devices and users.

In the case of an IaaS service like Azure Virtual Machines, you have more security responsibilities to take care of. For example, you need to patch the operating system of your virtual machines hosted on Azure.

With an IaaS service model, for capabilities such as virtual machines, storage, and networking, it is the customer's responsibility to configure and protect the stored and transmitted data. When using an IaaS-based solution, data classification must be considered at all layers of the solution. Figure 2-2 shows a logical view of the cloud security shared responsibility.

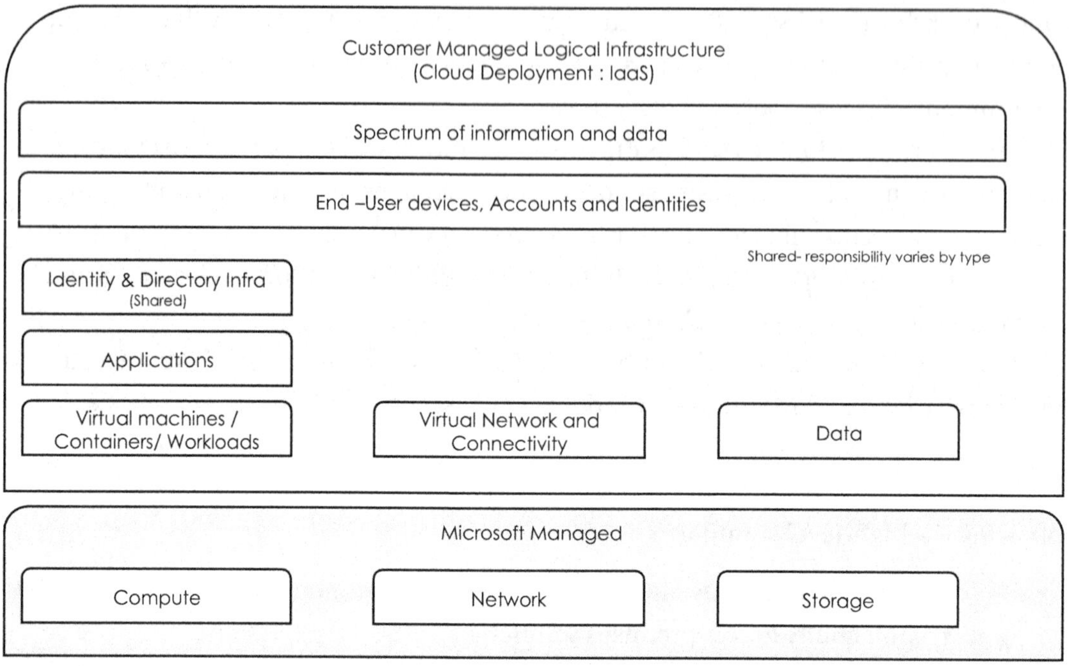

Figure 2-2. *Cloud deployment: IaaS with cloud security shared responsibility view*

A PaaS such as Azure App Service has fewer security responsibilities than a traditional service. You're not responsible for patching the operating system used by the service. However, you're still responsible for configuring the service and controlling access to it.

In PaaS solutions, the customers' responsibility for data classification and management should be recognized during the planning process. To ensure data protection, customers must configure and establish a process for protecting both the data and the solution. Azure Rights Management (ARM) services provide customer data protection capabilities and integrate into many Microsoft SaaS products. Figure 2-3 shows the cloud security shared responsibility from a PaaS logical view.

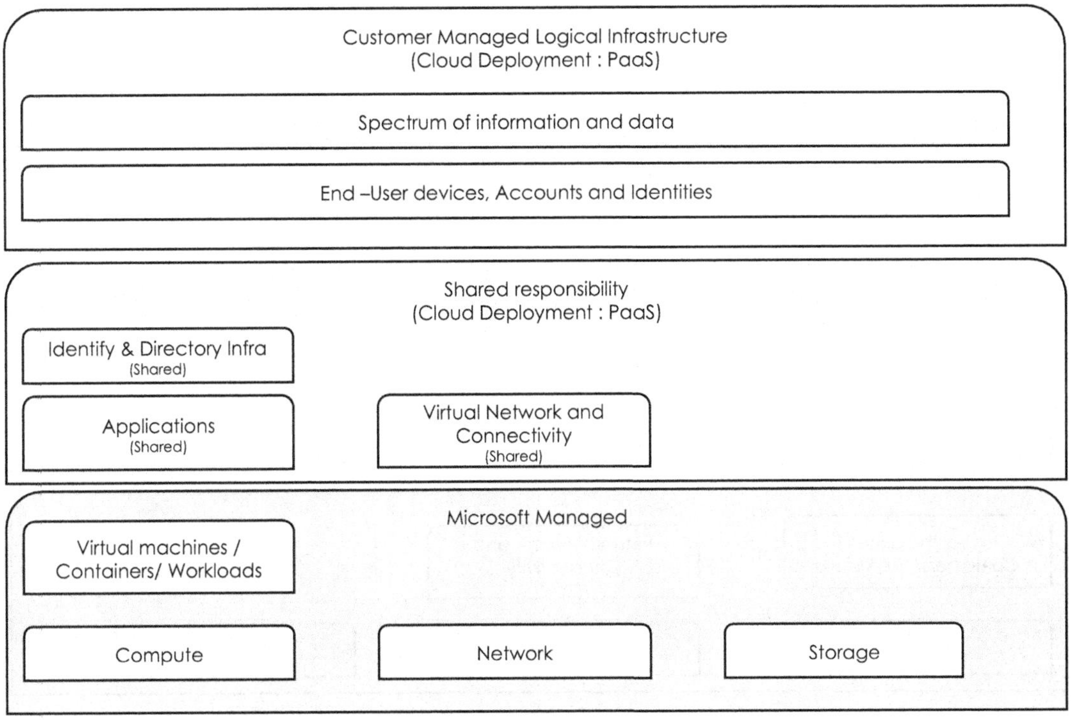

Figure 2-3. *Cloud deployment: PaaS with cloud security shared responsibility view*

With a SaaS service like Azure Search, you have even fewer security responsibilities, but you should still control access to your data.

In SaaS solutions like Office 365 and Dynamics 365, customer data can be protected with features such as Office Lockbox and data loss prevention. Still, customers must ultimately configure, classify, and manage these solutions to meet their unique compliance and security requirements. Figure 2-4 shows the cloud security shared responsibility from a SaaS logical view.

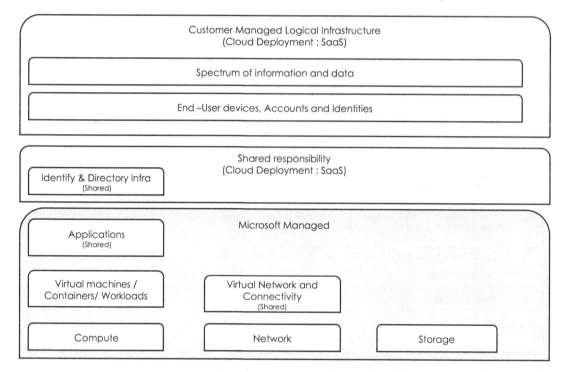

Figure 2-4. *Cloud deployment: SaaS with cloud security shared responsibility view*

Foundation of Cloud Infrastructure and Endpoint Security

A cloud security team provides security protections, detective functions, and response procedures for infrastructure and network components used by enterprise applications and users.

Data centers enabled by software-defined technologies are aiding in the security of infrastructure and endpoints in several ways, including the following:

- Inventory and configuration error discovery for cloud-hosted assets is much more reliable since they are all immediately visible (versus a physical data center).

- Vulnerability management has become an integral part of managing overall security posture.

- The addition of container technologies should be managed and secured by infrastructure and network teams as this technology is widely adopted throughout the organization.

- Security agent consolidation and tool simplification will reduce maintenance and performance overhead for security agents and tools.

- Allow-listing of applications and internal network filtering is becoming more accessible and easier to implement on cloud-hosted servers (using machine learning rule sets).

- Cloud-based software-defined data centers are much easier to manage with automated templates for configuring infrastructure and security. Azure Blueprints are an example.

- For privileged access on servers and endpoints, just in time (JIT) and just enough access (JEA) enable the practical application of least privilege principles.

- Since endpoint devices are increasingly available for purchase or choice, user experience becomes increasingly critical.

- In addition to ensuring that all endpoint devices, including traditional PCs and mobile devices, are managed securely, unified endpoint management provides critical device integrity signals for zero-trust access control.

- With the shift to cloud application architectures, network security architectures and controls are somewhat diminished, but they remain a primary security measure.

Securing Virtual Machines

Virtual machines can be used to deploy a variety of computing solutions in an agile way with Azure. With Azure BizTalk Services, you can deploy any workload and language on nearly any operating system, including Microsoft Windows, Linux, Microsoft SQL Server, Oracle, IBM, SAP, and Microsoft BizTalk Services.

With Azure virtual machines, you don't need to buy and maintain physical hardware to run them. In highly secure data centers, your data is protected and safe so that you can build and deploy your applications with peace of mind.

The Azure platform enables you to build security-enhanced, compliant solutions that do the following:

- Make sure your virtual machines are protected from viruses and malware

- Protect sensitive information by encrypting it

- Ensure the security of network traffic

- Detect and identify threats

- Comply with regulations

Antimalware

You can use antimalware software from Microsoft, Symantec, Trend Micro, McAfee, and Kaspersky to protect your virtual machines from malicious files, adware, and other threats. You can deploy, configure, and maintain antimalware solutions remotely using Azure PowerShell, the Azure Portal, and the command line.

Protect Sensitive Data

Microsoft monitors your data 24/7 and has built data centers to safeguard your data and services from unauthorized access. It also offers industry-leading encryption solutions from CloudLink and Trend Micro for your virtual machines and their data for extra protection. A transparent data encryption feature is also available in Microsoft SQL Server for real-time application security.

Organize Your Keys and Secrets with Key Vault

You can simplify management and security by storing your critical secrets and keys in Azure Key Vault. Key Vault stores your keys in hardware security modules (HSMs) certified to FIPS 140-2 Level 2. In Key Vault, you can store your SQL Server encryption keys, CloudLink SecureVM keys, and any other keys or secrets you have created. You can manage permissions and access to these protected items through Azure Active Directory.

Virtual Machine Disks for Linux and Windows Can Be Encrypted

Using Azure Disk Encryption, you can encrypt your virtual machine disks with keys and policies that you control in Azure Key Vault, meeting organizational security and compliance requirements. In Azure Disk Encryption, you can encrypt both your virtual machine's boot and data disks. You can protect your disk encryption keys, manage access policies, and audit the usage of your keys with Key Vault.

Azure Key Vault is available for both Linux and Windows operating systems. In Azure Storage accounts, all the data on your virtual machine disks are encrypted at rest using industry-standard encryption technology. Microsoft BitLocker Drive Encryption is used for Azure Disk Encryption for Windows, while dm-crypt is used for Linux.

Azure Disk Encryption (premium storage tier) does not support virtual machines with DS-Series storage.

Build More Compliant Solutions

As an authorized partner with Federal Information Security Modernization Act (FISMA), Federal Risk and Authorization Management Program (FedRAMP), HIPAA, PCI DSS Level 1, and other critical compliance programs, Azure Virtual Machines is certified to comply with these requirements, allowing your Azure applications to meet compliance requirements and your business to comply with domestic and international regulatory requirements.

Shield Network Traffic from Threats

You can create a highly secure VPN connection between your virtual machines using Azure Virtual Network or bypass the Internet completely with Azure ExpressRoute. As well as isolating network traffic between applications, Virtual Network allows you to control the configuration of your network, including subnets and preferred DNS addresses. Secure your endpoints with access control controls and deploy a web application firewall with aiScaler, Alert Logic, Barracuda Networks, Check Point, and Cohesive Networks from the Azure Marketplace.

Securing Containers

An application runs in a container in a lightweight, isolated silo on the host system. On top of the kernel of the host operating system (which can be viewed as the buried plumbing of the OS), containers contain only apps and lightweight APIs and services from the operating system. Containers share the kernel of the host operating system, but their access is limited. Instead, the container gets an isolated—and sometimes virtualized—view of the system. The container can, for example, access a virtualized version of the file system and registry, but the changes affect only it and are discarded when it stops. The container can mount persistent storage, such as Azure Disks or file shares (including Azure Files) to save data.

The kernel is the base of a container, but it does not provide all of the APIs and services an app needs to run—most of these are provided by system files (libraries) executed in user mode above the kernel. The container needs a copy of these user-mode system files packaged into a base image because it is isolated from the host's user-mode environment. As the foundation for your container, the base image provides operating system services not provided by the kernel.

Containers are easy to deploy and start fast because they utilize fewer resources (for example, they do not require an entire operating system).

The concept of a container group is similar to a pod in Kubernetes, a collection of containers scheduled on the same machine. The containers in a container group share a lifecycle, resources, local network, and storage volumes.

Use a Private Registry

An image container is built from an image stored in a repository. These repositories may belong to a public registry, such as Docker Hub, or they may belong to a private registry. The Docker Trusted Registry, an example of a private registry, can be installed on-premises or in a virtual private cloud. Azure Container Registry, for example, can also be used as a private container registry service in the cloud.

A Publicly Available Container Image Does Not Guarantee Security

Each software layer in container images might have a vulnerability. It is advisable to store and retrieve images from a private registry, such as Azure Container Registry or Docker Trusted Registry, to help reduce the threat of attacks. Through Azure Active Directory, Azure Container Registry provides a managed private registry and service principal–based authentication. Users can be granted read-only (pull), write-only (push), and other permissions based on their role.

Monitor and Scan Container Images

To identify potential vulnerabilities, utilize solutions that scan container images in a private registry. Understanding how each solution detects threats is critical to choosing the right solution.

Azure Container Registry can be integrated with Microsoft Defender for Cloud to scan all Linux images pushed to a registry automatically. Qualys, a scanning tool integrated into Microsoft Defender for Cloud, detects image vulnerabilities, classifies them, and provides remediation advice.

Through Azure Marketplace, you can also find solutions such as Twistlock and Aqua Security for security monitoring and image scanning.

Protect Credentials

As containers are distributed across several clusters and Azure regions, credentials such as passwords or tokens for logging in or accessing APIs must be secured. Only privileged users should be able to access these containers in transit and at rest. Inventory all credential secrets and then require developers to use tools designed to manage secrets for container platforms. Ensure your solution includes the following:

- Encrypted databases

- TLS encryption for secret data in transit

- Azure role-based access control (RBAC)

Containerized applications can be protected with Azure Key Vault's encryption keys and secrets (such as certificates, connections, and passwords). Secure access to your key vaults so only authorized applications and users can access them since this data is sensitive and business-critical.

Securing Hosts

You must lock down the host machines where your applications run. Installing updates, using jump boxes to only access servers, and following Microsoft Defender for Cloud recommendations are great ways to keep your hosts secure.

An endpoint system interacts directly with users. Devices made up of computers, laptops, smartphones, tablets, and other computing devices need to be protected against security attacks on the networked systems of an organization.

Microsoft Defender for Cloud provides tools for hardening your network, securing your services, and maintaining your security posture.

Use Microsoft Antimalware or an endpoint protection solution from a Microsoft partner to help identify and remove viruses, spyware, and other malicious software.

Security Center reports antimalware status on the "Endpoint protection issues" blade after integrating your antimalware solution with Microsoft Defender for Cloud.

You can plan to address any identified issues by using the information provided by the Security Center, such as detected threats and insufficient protection.

Providing RDP/SSH connectivity directly to your virtual machines via TLS in the Azure Portal, Azure Bastion is a fully platform-managed PaaS service you provision inside your virtual network. Azure Bastion doesn't require a public IP address to connect to your virtual machines.

All VMs in a virtual network that Bastion is a part of are connected securely using RDP and SSH.

Azure Bastion protects your VM from disclosing RDP/SSH ports to the outside world while providing secure access using RDP/SSH. With Azure Bastion, you connect to the VM straight from the Azure Portal.

To have a secured host, you need to ensure the following security components are contained on the device Trusted Platform Module (TPM) 2.0, BitLocker Drive Encryption, UEFI Secure Boot, Drivers, and Firmware Distributed through Windows Update, Virtualization and HVCI Enabled, Drivers and Apps HVCI-Ready, Windows Hello, DMA I/O Protection, System Guard, and Modern Standby.

Securing Networks

Protect your information technology assets by controlling traffic that originates in Azure, traffic to and from Azure, and traffic between on-premises and Azure resources. In the absence of security measures, attackers can, for example, scan public IP ranges to gain access. Proper network security controls can deliver defense-in-depth components that detect, control, and prevent attackers who acquire access to your cloud deployments.

As in your on-premises network, Azure virtual networks are similar to LANs. They allow you to place all your virtual machines on a single private IP address space. By placing Azure virtual machines (VMs) and appliances on Azure virtual networks, you can connect them to other networked devices. Connect virtual network interface cards (NICs) to a virtual network to allow TCP/IP-based communications between network-enabled devices. Employees can access a company's resources from anywhere, on various devices and apps, making perimeter security controls irrelevant.

A virtual network access control system limits connectivity to and from specific devices and subnets. Access controls allow or deny connections to your virtual machines and services based on your decisions about allowing or denying connections. Network access controls limit access to your virtual machines and services to approved users and devices.

Microsoft Defender for Cloud can manage the network security groups (NSGs) on virtual machines and protect access to the virtual machine until a user with the authorized Azure role-based access control Azure RBAC permissions requests access.

With Azure Firewall, you get a fully stateful, highly available, unrestricted cloud scalability firewall security service that provides threat protection for your Azure cloud workloads.

The following are key strategies to be adopted:

- Align the network segmentation with the overall enterprise segmentation strategy by segmenting your network footprint and creating secure communication paths between segments.

- Develop security controls to identify and permit or deny traffic, access requests, and application communication between segments.

- Azure Front Door, Application Gateway, Azure Firewall, and Azure DDoS Protection protect all public endpoints.

- Protect critical workloads from DDoS attacks with Azure DDoS Protection.

- Virtual machines can stay private and secure online using Azure Virtual Network NAT (NAT gateway).

- Interconnect application tiers (north-south) and subnets (east-west).

- Cover from data exfiltration attacks via a defense-in-depth strategy with management at each layer.

Microsoft Cloud Security Benchmark for Network Security

Various aspects of network security contribute to the security and protection of networks, including securing virtual networks, establishing private connections, controlling and mitigating external attacks, and securing DNS.

Figure 2-5 provides high-level insights into the Microsoft cloud security benchmark.

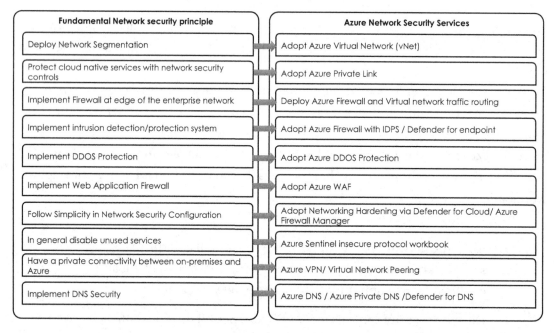

Figure 2-5. *Microsoft cloud security benchmark for network security*

Deploy Network Segmentation

Implement your enterprise segmentation strategy in your virtual network deployment and isolate any workload that could pose a higher risk to the organization.

Examples of high-risk workloads include the following:

- Sensitive data was stored or processed by an application.

- Public or external users can access external network-facing applications.

- An application has insecure architecture or vulnerabilities that are difficult to fix.

Enhance your enterprise segmentation strategy by restricting or monitoring traffic between internal resources. This highly secure "deny by default, permit by exception" approach determines the traffic's ports, protocols, source, and destination IP addresses for specific, well-defined applications (such as a three-tier app). If you have many applications and endpoints interacting, blocking traffic may not scale well, and you may only be able to monitor traffic.

As a fundamental segmentation approach in Azure, Microsoft suggests creating a virtual network (VNet) so resources such as VMs can be deployed within a network boundary within the VNet. To more precisely segment the network, you can deploy subnetworks for smaller subnetworks within a VNet.

Azure network engineers can restrict or monitor traffic by port, protocol, source IP address, or destination IP address using NSGs.

Organizations can also use application security groups (ASGs) to simplify complex configurations. Defining a policy based on explicit IP addresses in NSGs and ASGs enables you to configure network security as a natural extension of an application's structure, allowing you to group virtual machines and define network security policies based on those groups.

Protect Cloud Native Services with Network Security Controls

Secure cloud services by setting up a private access point and disabling or restricting public network access.

When implementing Private Link, the private connection will not be routed through the public network for all Azure resources that support it.

VNet integration for certain services allows you to create a private access point by restricting the VNET.

The service native network ACL rules can also be configured to block access from public networks, such as Azure SQL.

For Azure VMs, unless there is an assertive use case, you should avoid allocating public IPs/subnets straight to the VM NIC interface but utilize gateway or load balancer services as the front end for entry by the public network.

Implement a Firewall at the Edge of the Enterprise Network

Firewalls can be used to filter network traffic from and to external networks, as well as between internal segments to support a segmentation strategy. When you need network traffic to go through a network appliance for security control reasons, use custom routes for your subnet to override the system route.

Be sure to block known bad IP addresses and high-risk protocols, like remote management (such as RDP and SSH) and intranet access (such as SMB and Kerberos).

For example, URL filtering can be managed centrally using hub-spoke configurations.

Utilize Azure Firewall to control application-layer traffic (such as URL filtering) and centrally manage many enterprise segments or spokes (in a hub-and-spoke configuration).

Creating user-defined routes (UDRs) may be necessary if your network topology is complex, such as a hub-spoke configuration. For example, Azure Firewall or a virtual network appliance can be used to redirect egress Internet traffic through a UDR.

Implement Intrusion Detection/Protection System

Ensure your network intrusion detection and intrusion prevention system (IDS/IPS) provides high-quality alerts to your SIEM solution anytime there is network or payload traffic to or from your workload.

A host-based IDS/IPS or endpoint detection and response (EDR) solution coupled with a network-based IDS/IPS provides a deeper level of detection and prevention at the host level.

Using Azure Firewall's IDPS capability, you can detect and block traffic from and to known malicious IP addresses and domains.

VM-level IDS/IPS can be combined with network-level IDS/IPS for a more comprehensive host-level detection and prevention capability. One example of this is Microsoft Defender for Endpoint.

Implement DDOS Protection

Your network and applications can be protected from attacks with distributed denial-of-service (DDoS) protection.

In Azure, DDoS Protection Basic automatically protects the underlying platform infrastructure (such as Azure DNS) and does not require user configuration.

To protect resources exposed to public networks, enable the DDoS standard protection plan on your VNet for higher-level protection from application layer (layer 7) attacks such as HTTP.

Implement Web Application Firewall

Ensure your web applications and APIs are protected from application-specific attacks using a web application firewall (WAF).

Azure Application Gateway, Front Door, and Content Delivery Network (CDN) provide WAF capabilities to protect applications, services, and APIs from application-layer attacks.

Depending on your needs and threat landscape, you can set your WAF in "detection" or "prevention" mode.

You can choose one of the built-in rulesets, such as the OWASP Top 10 vulnerabilities, and customize it based on your application's needs.

Follow Simplicity in Network Security Configuration

You can manage network security using tools that simplify, centralize, and enhance the process. Implement and manage virtual networks, NSG rules, and Azure Firewall rules more efficiently with these features:

- Virtual networks can be grouped, configured, deployed, and managed across regions and subscriptions using Azure Virtual Network Manager.

- Microsoft Defender can recommend NSG hardening rules for cloud adaptive network hardening based on threat intelligence and traffic analysis results.

- The Azure Firewall Manager ARM (Azure Resource Manager) templates simplify the implementation of firewall rules and network security groups.

In General, Disable Unused Services

Implement compensatory controls if disabling insecure services and protocols is not possible. Detect and disable insecure protocols, services, and applications at the OS and application layers.

To identify insecure services and protocols such as SSL/TLSv1, SSHv1, SMBv1, LM/NTLMv1, wDigest, Unsigned LDAP Binds, and weak ciphers in Kerberos, use Microsoft Sentinel's built-in Insecure Protocol Workbook. Disable insecure services and protocols that fail to meet the appropriate security standards.

Note If disabling insecure services or protocols is unattainable, use compensating controls such as stopping resource access to reduce the attack surface via Azure security services such as network security groups, Azure Firewall, or Azure Web Application Firewall.

Have a Private Connectivity Between On-Premises and Azure

Colocation environments, such as cloud service providers' data centers and on-premises infrastructure, can be made more secure using private connections.

Connect your on-premises site or end-user device to the Azure virtual network using a VPN for lightweight site-to-site or point-to-site connectivity.

Colocation environments can benefit from enterprise-level high-performance connectivity through Azure ExpressRoute (or virtual WAN).

When integrating two or more Azure virtual networks, use virtual network peering. Network traffic flows between peered virtual networks are private, as is network traffic placed on the Azure global backbone network.

Implement DNS Security

Security configurations for DNS should protect against the following threats:

- Ensure your cloud environment uses authoritative and recursive DNS services to ensure clients (operating systems and applications) receive the correct results.

- To isolate the private network's DNS resolution process from the public network's DNS resolution process, separate the public and private DNS resolution processes.

- DNS security strategies should also protect against common attacks such as dangling DNS, DNS amplification attacks, DNS poisoning, and spoofing.

When setting up recursive DNS in a workload, such as an OS or an app, use Azure recursive DNS or an external DNS server you trust.

You can use Azure Private DNS to set up a private DNS zone and run the DNS resolution process within the virtual network. You can use a custom DNS to restrict the DNS resolution process only to allow trusted resolutions for your clients.

Using Microsoft Defender for DNS can expose your workload or DNS service to the following security threats:

- Data exfiltration from your Azure resources using DNS tunneling

- Malware communicating with a command-and-control server

- Communication with malicious domains such as phishing and crypto mining

- DNS attacks in communication with malicious DNS resolvers

Adopt Microsoft Defender for App Service to detect dangling DNS records if you decommission an App Service website without dragging its custom domain from your DNS registrar.

Securing Storage

Regardless of location, every organization has data that needs to be protected at rest, in transit, and within applications. Azure provides security features to protect your data.

A data sovereignty concept holds that information stored in binary digital form is subject to the laws of the country or region in which it is located after it has been converted and stored. A significant concern around data sovereignty is enforcing privacy regulations and preventing foreign governments from subpoenaing data stored in foreign countries or regions.

In Azure, customer data might be replicated within a specified geographic area for improved data durability during a major data center disaster. In some cases, it will not be replicated outside it.

Deploy Shared Access Signatures

To keep your data safe, you should never share storage account keys with external third-party applications. If these apps need access to your data, they must secure their connections without using storage account keys.

A shared access signature (SAS) can be attached to a URI to be used with untrusted clients. A shared access signature contains a security token. Using a shared access signature, you can delegate access to storage objects and specify constraints, including permissions and time ranges.

Customers can upload pictures to Blob storage using a shared access signature token, and web applications can also read those pictures if they have permission. In both cases, you only grant the application the necessary access to perform the task.

Govern Azure AD Storage Authentication

Azure Storage supports the authorization of blob data requests using Azure Active Directory (Azure AD) and shared keys and access signatures. Through Azure AD, you can grant permissions to a security principal, a user, a group, or an application service principal by using Azure RBAC. Azure AD authenticates the security principle and returns an OAuth 2.0 token, which can then be used to authorize a request to the Blob service.

Azure Storage Encryption for Data at Rest

By persisting your data to the cloud, Azure Storage automatically encrypts it, protecting your data and helping you meet your organization's compliance and security obligations. Azure Storage encryption is similar to BitLocker encryption on Windows, and 256-bit AES encryption is used to encrypt and decrypt data transparently. Azure Storage encryption is compliant with FIPS 140-2.

To use Azure Storage encryption, your code or applications do not need to be modified. Because your data is secured by default, you can't disable it.

No matter which redundancy option a storage account uses (standard or premium), all copies are encrypted. All Azure Storage resources, including blobs, disks, files, queues, and tables, are encrypted, as are all copies of a storage account. Metadata for objects can also be encrypted.

It is free to encrypt Azure Storage. Azure Storage encryption does not affect performance.

Securing Endpoints

To ensure servers and client endpoints are protected and to constantly assess their security posture to ensure they are up-to-date, a security strategy needs to be established along with tools for obtaining enterprise-wide visibility into attack dynamics.

Microsoft Windows Client and Windows Server are designed to be secure, but many organizations prefer more control over their security configurations. Microsoft shows how to configure various security features in security baselines to assist organizations in navigating many controls.

Security baselines are preconfigured Windows settings that help you apply and enforce granular security settings recommended by the relevant security teams. Intune allows you to create a security baseline profile composed of multiple device configuration profiles, which can be customized to enforce only the settings and values you need.

To increase flexibility and reduce costs, Microsoft recommends implementing an industry-standard, widely known, and well-tested configuration, such as Microsoft security baselines.

Understanding the operating system for which the security baseline is to be applied is the first step in choosing the appropriate security baseline. Windows clients and servers come in many versions, and you may need multiple baselines to address the

101

requirements of each operating system in a heterogeneous environment. You can choose which tool to use to deploy these baselines once you have an inventory of the operating systems and their versions.

Enterprise security administrators can use a set of tools called the Security Compliance Toolkit (SCT) to download, analyze, test, edit, and store Microsoft-recommended security configuration baselines for Windows and other Microsoft products. Using the SCT, administrators can efficiently manage Group Policy Objects (GPOs) for their enterprises.

It lets administrators compare their current GPOs with Microsoft-recommended GPO baselines or other baselines, edit them, and store them in GPO backup files for use in Active Directory and local policies.

There are also security baselines for Windows and Linux servers under Azure Security Benchmark (ASB). The ASB has guidance for OS hardening, resulting in security baseline documents.

In October 2022, Microsoft rebranded the Azure Security Benchmark (ASB) as Microsoft Cloud Security Benchmark. This new benchmark is in public preview when writing this book.

However, if your security baseline focuses on configuring the endpoint (Windows Client), you can use Intune to automate the deployment and configuration. With Intune capabilities, users and devices can be securely protected by quickly deploying Windows security baselines. Intune allows you to deploy security baselines to groups of users or devices, and these settings apply to Windows 10/11 as well. It automatically activates BitLocker for removable drives, requires a password to unlock a device, disables basic authentication, and more with the MDM security baseline. Customize the baseline to apply the necessary settings if a default value does not work for your environment.

You need to understand the default values in the baselines you use and modify each baseline to fit your organization's needs. Baselines can include the same settings but use different default values.

It's important to stress that Microsoft Intune security baselines do not align with CIS or NIST standards. While Microsoft consults with organizations, such as CIS, when compiling security recommendations, Microsoft baselines differ from CIS-compliant.

In creating these baselines, Microsoft's security team consulted enterprise customers and external agencies, including the Department of Defense (DoD), the National Institute of Standards and Technology (NIST), and others. These organizations share Microsoft's recommendations and baselines, as well as their suggestions that are similar to Microsoft's. Microsoft created equivalent MDM recommendations of these group policy baselines as MDM expanded into the cloud. Microsoft Intune provides compliance reports on users, groups, and devices that follow (or do not follow) these additional baselines.

Let's do a deep dive into the Microsoft cloud security benchmark.

The Azure and cloud service provider platforms release new services and features daily, developers publish new cloud applications built on these platforms, and attackers are constantly looking for new ways to exploit misconfigured resources. Developers and the cloud move fast, and attackers move fast as well.

- What measures do you take to ensure your cloud deployments are secure?

- What are the differences between cloud security practices and those used by on-premises systems?

- Do you monitor your workload across multiple cloud platforms to ensure consistency?

As stated by Microsoft, security benchmarks can help you secure cloud deployments quickly. Using a comprehensive security best-practice framework provided by cloud service providers, you can select specific security configuration settings in your cloud environment and monitor these settings from a single perspective.

The Microsoft cloud security benchmark (MCSB) includes a series of high-impact security recommendations to help you secure cloud services in a single or multicloud environment. These recommendations include the following:

- *Controls for security*: These recommendations can be applied irrespective of your cloud workloads. They include a list of stakeholders typically planning, approving, or implementing the benchmark.

- *Cloud service baselines*: These provide recommendations for the security configuration of individual cloud services. Only Azure service baselines are currently available.

Microsoft Cloud Security Benchmark for Endpoint Security

The Microsoft cloud security benchmark for endpoint security contains three essential recommendations: using endpoint detection and response (EDR) controls for endpoints in cloud environments, using anti-malware services, and making sure anti-malware software and signatures are updated.

Figure 2-6 provides some high-level insights into the Microsoft cloud security benchmark.

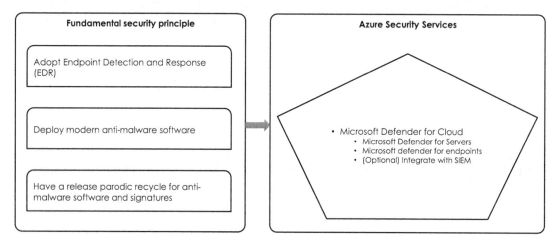

Figure 2-6. *Microsoft cloud security benchmark for endpoint security*

Adopt Endpoint Detection and Response (EDR)

Microsoft recommends EDR capabilities be enabled for VMs and that SIEM and security operations processes be integrated.

Microsoft Defender can provide EDR capability for advanced threats for servers (with Microsoft Defender for Endpoint integrated). Integrate your SIEM solution, such as Microsoft Sentinel, with Microsoft Defender for Cloud to deploy Microsoft Defender for Servers for your endpoints.

Windows and Linux servers running on Microsoft Azure, Amazon Web Services (AWS), Google Cloud Platform (GCP), or on-premises are protected by Microsoft Defender for Servers.

You can defend against advanced threats by monitoring, detecting, investigating, and responding to them with Microsoft Defender for Endpoint. To deliver EDR and other threat protection features, Microsoft Defender for Servers integrates with Microsoft Defender for Endpoint. At the time of writing this book, Microsoft Defender for Cloud is free for the first 30 days, and any usage beyond 30 days will be automatically charged based on the use and services adopted.

Deploy Modern Anti-malware Software

In Azure ARC-configured virtual machines and on-premises machines running Microsoft Defender for Cloud, the software can automatically identify and report the status of the endpoint protection solution.

Windows servers 2016 and higher come with Microsoft Defender Antivirus as their default antimalware solution. In Windows Server 2012 R2, enable System Center Endpoint Protection (SCEP) using the Microsoft Antimalware extension. For Linux virtual machines, use Microsoft Defender for Endpoint on Linux.

Antimalware solutions can be discovered and assessed using Microsoft Defender for Cloud for Windows and Linux.

You can also consider Defender for Storage, another choice that detects malware uploaded to Azure Storage accounts using Defender for Storage.

Have a Release Parodic Recycle for Anti-Malware Software and Signatures

T3o keep endpoints up-to-date with the latest signatures, Microsoft recommends using Microsof3t Defender for Cloud. Microsoft Antimalware for Windows and Microsoft Defender for Endpoint for Linux will automatically update signatures and engines.

Securing Backup and Recovery

Using Azure Backup, you can back up and recover your data from the cloud in a straightforward, secure, and cost-effective manner.

Azure Backup allows protecting your crucial business systems and backup data against a ransomware attack by deploying defensive measures and offering tools that shield your enterprise from each step attackers take to compromise your systems.

Backups are stored in a Recovery Services vault with built-in management of recovery points to protect your VMs from unintended data destruction. Backups are isolated and independent. Scaling and configuration are simple, backups are optimized, and quick reinstallation is possible.

A snapshot of the production workload is taken during backup and transferred to the Recovery Services vault with no impact on production workloads.

Microsoft Cloud Security Benchmark for Backup and Recovery

Azure backup and Recovery Strategy should aim to manage to ensure that data and configuration backups at the various service tiers are performed, verified, and protected.

Figure 2-7 provides high-level insights into the Microsoft cloud security benchmark specific to backup and recovery.

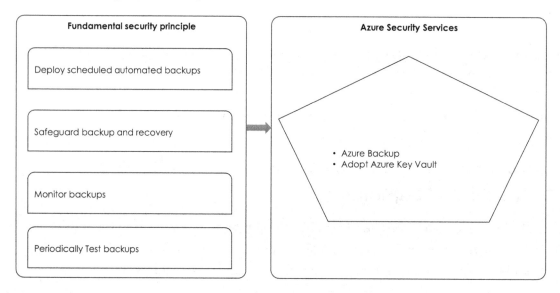

Figure 2-7. *Microsoft cloud security benchmark for backup*

Deploy Scheduled Automated Backups

You should ensure backups of business-critical resources are enforced through policies during resource creation or as part of existing resource creation.

On Azure Backup–supported resources, Azure Backup can be enabled, and the backup source can be Azure VMs, SQL Server, HANA databases, Azure PostgreSQL databases, File Shares, Blobs, or Disks with the desired frequency and retention period. Backup on Azure VMs can be enabled automatically with Azure Policy.

You can use the native backup capabilities the resource or service provides if Azure Backup doesn't support in taking backup of the services or resource. For example, Azure Key Vault provides native backup capabilities.

If your resources/services do not support Azure Backup or do not have native backup capabilities, you can create your own backup and disaster recovery mechanism. Without native backup capability on your resources/services, you can create a disaster recovery mechanism.

- Data stored in Azure Storage blobs can be preserved, retrieved, and restored anytime.

- Service configuration settings can usually be exported to Azure Resource Manager templates.

Safeguard Backup and Recovery

It is imperative to protect backup data and operations against data exfiltration, data compromise, ransomware/malware, and malicious insiders. Data encryption and user and network access controls should be employed at rest and in transit.

To secure critical Azure Backup operations (such as deleting, changing retention, and updating backup configuration), use multifactor authentication and Azure RBAC. Create private endpoints in your Azure Virtual Network for backup and restoration of data from your Recovery Services vaults by using Azure RBAC.

256-bit AES encryption is automatically applied to backup data for Azure Backup resources. As an alternative, you can encrypt backups with a customer-managed key. Be sure this customer-managed key in Azure Key Vault is also included in the backup scope. Azure Key Vault offers soft delete and purge protection so that keys cannot be accidentally or maliciously deleted if you use customer-managed vital options. Azure Backup provides encryption at rest based on the passphrase you supply.

Backup data should be protected against accidental or malicious deletion due to ransomware attacks or attempts to encrypt or alter backup data.

When Azure Backup supports it, you can enable soft delete to ensure that data is not lost during recovery for up to 14 days following an unauthorized deletion. You can also use multifactor authentication with a PIN. Enable georedundant storage or cross-region recovery to ensure backup data can be restored if a disaster occurs in the primary region. Zone-redundant storage (ZRS) will provide restorable backups in the event of zone failures.

Note   If you use the resource's native backup feature or backup services other than Azure Backup, refer to the Microsoft cloud security benchmark (and service baselines) to implement these controls.

Monitor Backups

Compliance with the defined backup policy and standard should be ensured for all business-critical protectable resources.

For Azure Backup supported resources, Backup Center helps you centrally govern your backup estate. Use Azure Policies for Backup to audit and enforce such controls.

Ensure critical backup operations (deleting, changing retention, updating the backup configuration) are monitored and audited and alerts are set up. Monitor backup health, receive alerts for critical backup incidents, and audit user-triggered vault actions.

Note: Use built-in policies (Azure Policy) where appropriate to guarantee that your Azure resources are configured for Backup.

Periodically Test Backups

Test the recovery of your backup data periodically to ensure that the backup configuration and availability meet the recovery requirements defined in the recovery time objective (RPO) and recovery point objective (RTO).

Periodically test your backups for data recovery to ensure they meet the recovery requirements defined in the RTO and RPO.

You may need to determine your backup recovery test strategy, including the test area, commonness, and techniques, as performing the full recovery test each time can be challenging.

Design and Deploy a Strategy for Securing Identify

Using Azure Identify and Access Management solutions, you can secure access to your resources and protect your applications and data from malicious login attempts. Protect credentials with risk-based access controls, identify protection tools, and robust authentication options—without disrupting business operations.

Consider the following three critical services in your securing identify:

- Azure Active Directory (Azure AD) provides identify and access management for cloud and hybrid environments.

- Azure Active Directory External Identities manage consumer identities and access in the cloud.

- Virtual machines in Azure can be joined to a domain without deploying domain controllers using Azure Active Directory Domain Services.

Microsoft's Azure Active Directory

Azure AD is a cloud-based identify and directory service for multitenants. In addition to providing single sign-on (SSO) access to thousands of cloud SaaS applications, Azure AD is an affordable and easy-to-use solution for IT administrators to give employees and business partners.

The Azure AD identify management solution makes it easy for developers to integrate their applications with a world-class solution.

A full range of identify management features is also included in Azure AD, including multifactor authentication, device registration, self-service password management, self-service group management, privileged account management, role-based access control, application usage monitoring, auditing and security monitoring, and alerting. Cloud-based applications can be secured, IT processes can be streamlined, costs can be reduced, and compliance goals can be met.

Additionally, Azure AD can be integrated with an existing Windows Server Active Directory, enabling organizations to manage SaaS access from their existing on-premises identify investments.

There are four editions of Azure Active Directory: Free, Microsoft 365 Apps, Premium P1, and Premium P2. As part of an Azure subscription, the Free edition is included. Azure and Microsoft 365 subscribers may purchase Azure Active Directory Premium P1 and P2 online through a Microsoft Enterprise Agreement, Open Volume License Program, or Cloud Solution Providers program.

- *Azure Active Directory Free*: Manage users and groups, synchronize on-premises directories, generate basic reports, and provide single sign-on across Azure, Microsoft 365, and many popular SaaS apps.

- *Azure Active Directory Microsoft 365 Apps*: This edition is part of Microsoft Office 365. In addition to the Free features, this edition provides Identify and Access Management for Microsoft 365 apps including branding, MFA, group access management, and self-service password reset for cloud users.

- *With Microsoft Active Directory Premium P1*: Hybrid users can access both on-premises and cloud resources and its free features. Additionally, it offers advanced administration features, including dynamic groups, self-service group management, Microsoft Identify Manager (on-premises identify management suite), and cloud write-back capabilities, allowing users on-premises to reset their passwords themselves.

- *Azure Active Directory Premium P2*: P2 provides Conditional Access to your apps and critical company data based on risk-based identify protection and Free and P1 features. In addition to providing just-in-time access to resources, privileged identify management enables administrators to discover, restrict, and monitor their access.

Authentication Choices

Organizations wanting to move their apps to the cloud must choose the correct authentication method. Don't take this decision lightly for these reasons:

- This is the first decision for an organization looking to move to the cloud.

- It controls access to all cloud data and resources. The authentication method is critical to an organization's presence in the cloud.

- Azure AD's advanced security and user experience features are built on this foundation.

An organization needs an identify control plane that strengthens its security and keeps its cloud apps safe from intruders in the new cloud world. Authentication is the new control plane of IT security. Thus, authentication is the company's access guard in the cloud.

The foundation of cloud access is authentication when Azure AD hybrid identify is your new control plane. Choosing the correct authentication method for Azure AD hybrid identify is crucial. Using Azure AD Connect, which also provides cloud users, implement the authentication method configured.

For hybrid identify solutions, Azure AD supports the following authentication methods.

Cloud Authentication

With cloud authentication, you can choose one of two options: either Azure AD manages user sign-in or you can enable seamless single sign-on (SSO) so that users don't have to reenter their credentials every time they sign in.

- A simple method of enabling authentication for on-premises directory objects in Azure AD is synchronizing password hashes. Users can use the same username and password on-premises without deploying additional infrastructure. No matter the authentication method used to access Azure AD, some premium features, such as Domain Services and Identify Protection, require synchronization of password hashes.

- Using a software agent on one or more on-premises servers, Azure AD Pass-through Authentication provides simple password validation for Azure AD authentication services. Using the server, users are validated directly with your on-premises Active Directory, so passwords are not validated in the cloud.

An organization might use this authentication method to immediately enforce password policies, sign-in hours, or user account states.

Federated Authentication

To validate the password of an Azure AD user, federated authentication transfers the authentication process to a trusted authentication system, such as Active Directory Federation Services (AD FS) on-premises.

The authentication system, such as smartcard-based or multifactor authentication by third parties, can provide advanced authentication requirements.

Three essential tasks can be accomplished using Azure Identify Protection.

- Risks associated with identify can be detected and remedied automatically.

- You can utilize the portal data to investigate risks.

- Data from risk detection can be exported to third-party utilities for further analysis.

Azure AD Identify Protection

With Identify Protection, Microsoft takes the learnings from its position in organizations with Azure AD, in the consumer space with Microsoft Accounts, and in gaming with Xbox and uses them to protect your users. To identify and protect customers from threats, Microsoft analyzes 6.5 trillion signals every day.

Risk detection is triggered by suspicious actions associated with an Azure AD Identify Protection user account. Based on your organization's enforced policies, the signals generated by Identify Protection can be fed into tools such as Conditional Access to make access decisions or fed back into a SIEM tool for further investigation.

Identify Protection provides organizations with powerful resources to respond quickly to suspicious activities.

Azure AD Privileged Identify Protection

It is possible to give users just-in-time access and just-enough access to the most important resources in your organization with Azure Active Directory Privileged Identify Management (PIM).

With Azure Active Directory, you can manage, control, and monitor access to essential resources within your organization using Privileged Identify Management (PIM). These resources include Azure AD, Azure, and Microsoft Online Services like Microsoft 365 and Microsoft Intune.

Azure Active Directory Privileged Identify Management (PIM) needs Azure AD Premium P2 licenses

Privileged Identify Management provides time-based and approval-based role activation to mitigate the risks of excessive, unnecessary, or misused access permissions on resources that you care about.

The following are key use cases Azure AD PIM provides solutions for.

Information or resources that are secure should be accessible to the fewest people possible since this reduces the chance of unauthorized disclosure.

- Malicious actors gain access.

- An authorized user inadvertently impacts a sensitive resource.

As a result, users can use Azure AD, Azure, Microsoft 365, or SaaS apps to perform privileged operations. Organizations can provide users with just-in-time privileged access to Azure and Azure AD resources, which allows them to monitor what those users are doing.

Microsoft Cloud Security Benchmark for Identify

Microsoft Cloud Security Benchmark for Identify Management security controls are used to establish a secure identify and access control system, including the use of single sign-on, strong authentication, managed identities (and service principals) for applications, Conditional Access, and monitoring for anomalies in accounts.

Figure 2-8 provides high-level insights into the Microsoft cloud security benchmark specific to identify.

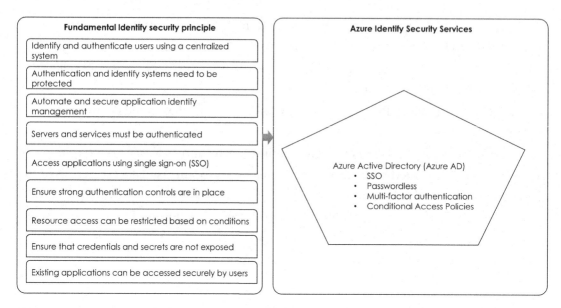

Figure 2-8. *Microsoft cloud security benchmark for Azure identify*

Identify and Authenticate Users Using a Centralized System

Use a centralized identify and authentication system to manage the identities and authentications of your organization's cloud and noncloud resources.

Your organization will benefit from standardized identify and authentication policies governed by Azure AD.

- Identify and authentication policies governed by Azure Active Directory can be used to protect Microsoft Cloud resources, including Azure Storage, Azure Virtual Machines (Windows and Linux), Azure Key Vault, and PaaS and SaaS applications.

- Resources that belong to your organization include Azure applications, third-party applications running on your corporate network, and SaaS apps belonging to third parties.

- To ensure a consistent and centrally managed identify strategy, synchronize Active Directory identities with Azure AD.

Note   It is best to migrate on-premises Active Directory–based applications to Azure AD as soon as it is technically feasible. This can be done via Azure AD Enterprise Directory, a business-to-business configuration, or business-to-consumer configuration.

Authentication and Identify Systems Need to Be Protected

Ensure that your organization's cloud security practice prioritizes identify and authentication. Common security controls include the following:

- Accounts and roles with privileged access should be restricted.

- All privileged access should require strong authentication.

- High-risk activities should be monitored and audited.

Azure AD Identify Secure Score evaluates Azure AD identify security posture and allows you to remediate gaps in security and configuration.

- Don't use too many administrative roles.

- Make sure the user risk policy is enabled.

- A global administrator should be nominated by more than one organization.

- Block legacy authentication.

- For secure access, ensure that all users can complete multifactor authentication.

- For administrative roles, MFA should be required.

- Self-service password reset is available.

- Keep your passwords up-to-date.

- A sign-in risk policy should be enabled.

- Users should not be allowed to grant consent to unmanaged applications.

Note   Active Directory and third-party services, as well as operating systems, networks, and databases, should be configured in accordance with published best practices.

Automate and Secure Application Identify Management

Use managed application identities rather than creating human accounts when applying code and accessing resources. As a result of managed application identities, credentials are less exposed and are rotated automatically to ensure identify security.

Microsoft Azure AD authentication can be used with Azure managed identities to access Azure services and resources. The platform manages, rotates, and protects managed identify credentials, so they aren't hard-coded in source code or configuration files.

Service principals without managed identities can be created using Azure AD. Certificate credentials are recommended for service principals; client secrets are recommended for services without managed identities.

Servers and Services Must Be Authenticated

Connect to trusted servers and services by authenticating them from your client side. An authentication protocol most commonly used for servers is Transport Layer Security (TLS). The client (often the browser or client device) verifies the server by verifying that a trusted authority issued the server's certificate.

Note   Server and client authentication can be mutual.

The default authentication method for many Azure services is TLS. If the service supports a TLS enable/disable switch, ensure that it is always enabled so that the server/service authentication can be supported. The handshake stage of your client application should also verify the identify of the server/service (by confirming the certificate issued by a trusted certificate authority).

Note   Some API management and API gateway services support TLS mutual authentication.

Access Applications Using Single Sign-On (SSO)

SSO simplifies the authentication process for cloud services and on-premises resources, including applications and data. SSO simplifies the authentication process for cloud services and on-premises resources, including applications and data.

Reduce the need for duplicate accounts by using Azure AD SSO for workload application (customer-facing) access. In addition to managing identify and access to Azure resources (management plane including CLI, PowerShell, and the Azure Portal), Azure AD also manages cloud apps and on-premises applications.

As well as enterprise identities and external identities from trusted third parties and the public, Azure AD supports single sign-on for enterprise identities.

Ensure Strong Authentication Controls Are in Place

Secure all resource access through your centralized identify management system by implementing strong authentication controls (strong passwordless or multifactor authentication). Password credentials alone are insecure and cannot withstand popular attack methods, so they are considered legacy authentication.

Configure administrators and privileged users first to ensure the highest level of strong authentication, and then roll out the appropriate strong authentication policy to all users.

Ensure password complexity requirements are followed if legacy password-based authentication is required for legacy applications and scenarios.

Azure AD supports strong authentication controls through passwordless methods and multifactor authentication (MFA).

- As a default authentication method, use passwordless authentication. Microsoft Authenticator app phone sign-in, Windows Hello for Business, and FIDO 2Keys are all available for passwordless authentication. In addition, customers can use on-premises authentication methods such as smart cards to log in.

- Authenticate users with multiple factors based on their sign-in conditions and risk factors. Azure MFA can be enabled for all users, selected users, or per user based on their sign-in conditions and risk factors.

Azure AD legacy password-based authentication has a default baseline password policy for cloud-only accounts (users created directly in Azure). Hybrid accounts (users whose accounts are based on Active Directory on-premises) have the same password policies as those for on-premises users.

When you set up the service, it would be helpful if you disabled or changed the default IDs and passwords.

Resource Access Can Be Restricted Based on Conditions

A zero-trust access model requires explicitly validating trusted signals to grant or deny access to resources. Strong authentication of user accounts, behavioral analytics of user accounts, device trustworthiness, member or group membership, location, etc., should all be validated.

You can use Azure AD Conditional Access to restrict access based on user-defined conditions, such as requiring users to use MFA if they log in from a certain IP range (or device). You can control access to your organization's apps using Azure AD Conditional Access based on specific conditions.

Consider the following common use cases when defining the Azure AD Conditional Access criteria:

- Users with administrative roles should be required to use multifactor authentication.

- For Azure management tasks, multifactor authentication is required.

- Use legacy authentication protocols to block sign-ins.

- Registration for Azure AD multifactor authentication requires trusted locations.

- Access from specific locations can be blocked or granted.

- Prevent risky sign-in behaviors.

- Require organization-managed devices for specific applications.

Note   A granular authentication session management can also be used via Azure AD Conditional Access policy for management such as sign-in commonness and continuous browser session.

Ensure That Credentials and Secrets Are Not Exposed

Credentials and secrets should be handled securely by application developers:

- Code and configuration files should not contain credentials and secrets.

- To store credentials and secrets, use a Key Vault or secure key store service.

- Look for credentials in source code.

Secure software development life cycles (SDLCs) and DevOps security processes are often used to govern and enforce this.

Rather than embedding credentials and secrets into code and configuration files, ensure they are stored securely, such as Azure Key Vault.

Your code management platform should be Azure DevOps and GitHub.

- Identify credentials within the code using Azure DevOps Credential Scanner.

- When scanning GitHub code for credentials or other secrets, use the native secret scanning feature.

A managed identify can securely access Azure Key Vault through Azure Functions, Azure Apps, and VMs.

The Azure Key Vault rotates secrets automatically for services that are supported. If secrets cannot be rotated automatically, they should be rotated periodically and purged when no longer needed.

Existing Applications Can Be Accessed Securely by Users

Consider cloud access security brokers (CASBs), application proxies, or SSO solutions to govern the access to non-native and on-premise applications using legacy authentication. These solutions provide the following benefits:

- Enforce a strong centralized authentication

- End-user activities that pose a risk should be monitored and controlled

- Risky legacy application activities should be monitored and remedied

- Detect and prevent sensitive data transmission

Protect your on-premises and non-native cloud applications using legacy authentication by connecting them to do the following:

- Azure AD Application Proxy combined with header-based authentication for publishing legacy on-premises applications to remote users with SSO. At the same time, Azure AD Conditional Access explicitly validates the trustworthiness of remote users and devices. You can use a third-party software-defined perimeter (SDP) solution if needed.

- To monitor and block access to unapproved third-party SaaS applications, Microsoft Defender for Cloud Apps is used as a CASB.

- Third parties provide networks and application delivery controllers.

Note   VPNs are commonly used to access legacy applications; they usually have a limited level of session monitoring and a little group of access control.

Microsoft Cloud Security Benchmark for Privileged Access

A range of controls against deliberate and unintentional risk protects your privileged access model, administrative accounts, and workstations.

Figure 2-9 provides high-level insights into the Microsoft cloud security benchmark specific to privileged access.

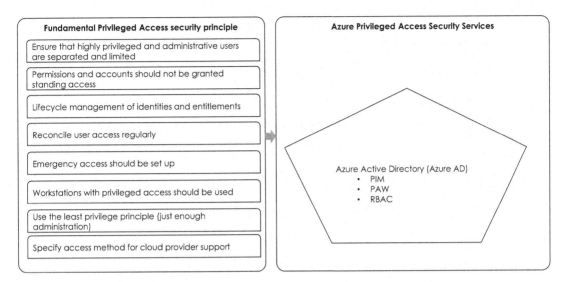

Figure 2-9. *Microsoft cloud security benchmark for privileged access*

Your cloud's control, management, and data/workload planes should be designed to limit the number of privileged or administrative accounts.

Ensure That Highly Privileged and Administrative Users Are Separated and Limited

Identities and access are managed by Azure Active Directory. Since users assigned to these two roles can delegate administrator roles, Azure AD has two critical built-in roles: Global Administrator and Privileged Role Administrator. With these privileges, users can read and modify all of the resources in your Azure environment directly or indirectly.

- The global administrator/company administrator role allows users to access all Azure AD administrative features and services.

- With this role, users can manage roles within Azure AD and within Azure AD Privileged Identify Management (PIM). In addition, they can manage all aspects of PIM and administrative units within AD.

Additionally, Azure has built-in roles that can be critical for privileged access at the resource level outside of Azure AD.

- Owners can assign roles in Azure RBAC and manage all resources.

- Manages all resources but does not permit assigning roles in Azure RBAC, managing assignments in Azure Blueprints, or sharing image galleries.

- Manage user access to Azure resources with User Access Administrator.

Note   Custom roles in Azure AD or resources with specific privileged permissions may have other essential roles that must be governed.

It is also essential to restrict privileged accounts with administrative access to your critical business assets in other management, identify, and security systems, including Active Directory Domain Controllers (DCs), security tools, and system management tools installed on business-critical systems. Attackers can immediately weaponize these management and security systems to compromise critical business assets once compromised.

Permissions and Accounts Should Not Be Granted Standing Access

Assign privileged access to the different resource tiers using just-in-time (JIT) mechanisms instead of standing privileges.

With Azure AD Privileged Identify Management, you can access Azure resources and Azure AD just in time. In JIT, users receive temporary permissions for privileged tasks, so malicious or unauthorized users cannot gain access after the permissions expire. PIM can also generate security alerts if suspicious or unsafe activity occurs in your Azure AD organization. Access is granted only when users need it.

JIT for VM access from Microsoft Defender for Cloud lets you control inbound traffic to your sensitive VM management ports.

Life-Cycle Management of Identities and Entitlements

Ensure the identify and access life cycle is managed through an automated process or technical control, including requests, reviews, approvals, provisioning, and deprovisioning.

Azure AD entitlement management allows you to automate access request workflows for Azure resource groups. Workflows for Azure resource groups can manage access assignments, reviews, expirations, and dual or multistage approval processes.

Reconcile User Access Regularly

Regularly review privileged account entitlements. Ensure the accounts can administer control planes, management planes, and workloads.

Examine all privileged accounts and access entitlements in Azure, including Azure tenants, Azure services, VMs, IaaS, and CI/CD processes.

Review Azure AD roles, Azure resource access roles, group memberships, and enterprise application access with Azure AD access reviews. Azure AD reporting can also help find stale accounts that have not been used for a period of time.

Additionally, administrator accounts that are stale or improperly configured can be identified by Azure AD Privileged Identify Management if an excessive number of them are created for a specific role.

Emergency Access Should Be Set Up

Establish emergency access to your cloud infrastructure (such as your identify and access management system) to avoid being shut out in an emergency.

Although emergency access accounts should be used only rarely and can cause severe damage to the organization if compromised, their availability is also crucial for the few scenarios when they are required.

Whenever normal administrative accounts cannot be used, create an emergency access account (e.g., with a Global Administrator role) to prevent being locked out of your Azure AD organization. When an emergency or "break glass" scenario occurs where normal administrative accounts cannot be used, emergency access accounts are highly privileged and should not be assigned to specific individuals.

It is important to keep all credentials (such as passwords, certificates, and smart cards) secure and available only to individuals who need them for emergency access. Using dual controls (e.g., splitting the credential into two pieces and giving them to two separate individuals) can also enhance the security of this process. Monitor the logs of sign-ins and audits to ensure emergency access accounts are used only when authorized.

Workstations with Privileged Access Should Be Used

Admins, developers, and operators of critical services require secure, isolated workstations. Private access workstations (PAWs) can be deployed on-premises or in Azure using Azure Active Directory, Microsoft Defender, and Microsoft Intune. A secure configuration, including strong authentication, software and hardware baselines, and restricted logical and network access, should be enforced centrally by the PAW.

As another option, Azure Bastion is a fully platform-managed solution that can be provisioned directly within your virtual network. With Azure Bastion, you can connect directly from your browser to your virtual machines via RDP/SSH.

Use the Least Privilege Principle (Just-Enough Administration)

Implement features like role-based access control (RBAC) to manage resource access at a fine-grained level by following the just-enough administration (least privilege) principle.

Manage Azure resource access using Azure RBAC. Users can be assigned roles, service principals can be grouped, and identities can be managed. You can inventory and query the built-in roles for specific resources through tools such as Azure CLI, Azure PowerShell, and the Azure Portal.

When you assign Azure RBAC privileges to resources, they should always be limited to the role requirements. Azure AD Privileged Identify Management (PIM) will complement just-in-time (JIT) with limited privileges, and those privileges should be reviewed periodically. In addition to specifying the time-length (time-bound-assignment) condition in role assignment, you can also set the end and start dates for a user to activate or use the role.

Note   Create custom roles only when necessary, as Azure built-in roles can be used to assign permissions.

Specify Access Method for Cloud Provider Support

Request and approve vendor support requests and temporary access to your data via a secure channel through an approval process and access path.

You can review and approve or reject each Microsoft data access request using Customer Lockbox when Microsoft needs access to your data for support.

Design and Deploy a Strategy for Securing Apps and Data

Many services in Azure can assist you in securing your application in the cloud, which is one of the most important aspects of any application. Fortunately, Azure offers many services to help you secure your application in the cloud. You can implement Azure services and activities at each stage of your software development life cycle to develop more secure code and deploy a more secure cloud application.

The following resources can be used for developing and deploying secure applications on Azure:

- *Microsoft Security Development Lifecycle (SDL)*: Using SDL, developers can build more secure software while reducing development costs and meeting security compliance requirements.

  For more info, see: `https://www.microsoft.com/en-us/securityengineering/sdl/`

- *Open Web Application Security Project (OWASP)*: An online community of web application security experts, OWASP publishes free articles, methodologies, documentation, tools, and technologies.

  For more info, see: `https://owasp.org/`

- *Pushing left, like boss*: To create more secure code, developers should complete different application security activities outlined in `wehackpurple.com`.

  For more info, see: `https://wehackpurple.com/pushing-left-like-a-boss-part-1/`

- *Microsoft identify platform*: Microsoft's identify platform evolved from Azure AD's identify service and developer platform. It has an authentication service, open-source libraries, application registration and configuration, complete developer documentation, code samples, and other developer resources. OAuth 2.0 and OpenID Connect are industry-standard protocols that the Microsoft identify platform supports.

  For more info, see: `https://learn.microsoft.com/en-us/azure/active-directory/develop/`

- *Security best practices for Azure solutions*: Use Azure security best practices to design, deploy, and manage cloud solutions using security best practices.

  For more info, see: `https://azure.microsoft.com/en-gb/resources/security-best-practices-for-azure-solutions/`

- *Security and compliance blueprints on Azure*: Complying with stringent regulations and standards can be complex, but Azure Security and Compliance Blueprints help.

  For more info, see: `https://learn.microsoft.com/en-us/azure/governance/blueprints/samples/azure-security-benchmark-foundation/`

An essential part of the design phase is establishing best practices for the design and functionality of the project as well as performing risk analyses to mitigate security and privacy risks.

You can minimize the chances of security flaws and use secure design concepts when you have security requirements. When an application has been released, a security flaw can allow a user to perform malicious or unexpected actions due to an oversight in its design.

It would be best to consider applying layers of security during the development phase. What happens if an attacker gets past your web application firewall? You will need another security control to prevent this from happening.

With this in mind, the following are vital controls to consider:

- Use software frameworks and secure coding libraries.

- Conduct a vulnerability scan.

- When designing an application, use threat modeling.

- Keep your attack surface as small as possible.

- Identify identify as the primary security perimeter.

- For important transactions, require reauthentication.

- Ensure the security of keys, credentials, and other secrets by using a key management solution.

- Make sure sensitive data is protected.

- Make sure fail-safe measures are in place.

- Ensure that errors and exceptions are handled correctly.

- Use alerts and logging.

- Modernize.

The following sections break these rules down.

Software Frameworks and Secure Coding Libraries Should Be Used

When developing software, you should use a software framework with embedded security and a secure coding library. Instead of creating security controls from scratch, developers can use existing, proven features (encryption, input sanitation, output encoding, keys, connection strings, etc.). Design and implementation flaws can be prevented this way.

Use the latest version of your framework and all security features available. Developing cloud applications on any platform or language is possible with Microsoft's comprehensive development tools. You can choose from various SDKs depending on the language you prefer. A full-featured integrated development environment (IDE) and the editor can be used with Azure support and advanced debugging capabilities.

Conduct a Vulnerability Scan

A continuous inventory of your client- and server-side components and their dependencies is essential to preventing vulnerabilities. New vulnerabilities and updated software versions are released continuously. Monitor, triage, and update your libraries and details continually.

When Designing an Application, Use Threat Modeling

Threat modeling aims to identify potential security threats to your business and application so that proper mitigations can be implemented. It is recommended that teams use threat modeling during the design phase when resolving potential issues is relatively simple and cost-effective. Your total development costs can be significantly reduced by using threat modeling during the design phase.

The SDL Threat Modeling Tool was designed with nonsecurity experts in mind. This tool guides developers through creating and analyzing threat models clearly and concisely.

Keep Your Attack Surface as Small as Possible

As the name implies, an attack surface is a sum of where potential vulnerabilities might occur. This paper discusses how an application can be protected from attacks. Removing unused code and resources from your application can quickly reduce your attack surface. The smaller your application, the smaller it is.

Identify Identify as the Primary Security Perimeter

As you design cloud applications, you must change your security perimeter focus from a network-centric approach to an identify-centric one. Most on-premises security designs use the network as the primary security pivot, as it was historically the primary security perimeter on-premises. Consider identify as the immediate security perimeter for cloud applications.

For Important Transactions, Reauthentication Should Be Required

The current standard for authentication and authorization is two-factor authentication, which avoids the security vulnerabilities inherent in usernames and passwords. A multifactor authentication method for access to Azure management interfaces (Azure Portal/remote PowerShell) and customer-facing services should be designed and configured.

Ensure the Security of Keys, Credentials, and Other Secrets by Using a Key Management Solution

Losing keys and credentials is a common problem; the only thing worse than losing them is having an unauthorized party gain access to them. Attackers can use automated and manual techniques to find keys and secrets stored in code repositories like GitHub. Don't put keys and secrets in these public code repositories or on any other server.

The best way to manage your keys, certificates, secrets, and connection strings is to use a centralized solution with hardware security modules (HSM). Azure offers an HSM in the cloud with Azure Key Vault.

Make Sure Sensitive Data Is Protected

To design your app with data security in mind, it is important to classify your data and identify your data protection needs. Developers can determine the risks associated with stored data by categorizing it by sensitivity and business impact.

Make Sure Fail-Safe Measures Are in Place

During execution, your application must be able to handle errors consistently, and it must catch all errors and either fail-safe or close when they occur.

Errors should also be logged with sufficient user context to identify malicious or suspicious behavior. Logs should be retained for enough time to allow delayed forensic analysis. Logs should be in a format easily consumed by log management solutions. Make sure security-related errors are notified. By logging and monitoring insufficiently, attackers can continue to attack systems and maintain persistence.

Ensure That Errors and Exceptions Are Handled Correctly

For a system to be reliable and secure, it must be able to handle errors and exceptions correctly. Error and exception handling are essential parts of defensive coding. When errors are made in error handling, they can lead to security vulnerabilities, such as leaks of information to attackers and the ability to learn more about your platform.

Alerts and Logging Should Be Used

Ensure you log security issues for security investigations and trigger alerts so that people are informed of problems immediately. Logging and auditing should be enabled on all components, and audit logs should record user context and identify all critical events.

Modernize

DevOps team models, rapid release cadences, and cloud services and APIs are all being reshaped simultaneously as the application development process undergoes rapid changes. To understand these changes, see how the cloud changes security relationships and responsibilities.

In addition to modernizing antiquated development models, DevSecOps can be viewed as securing applications and development processes. DevSecOps drives such changes as the following:

- Since application development is evolving rapidly, traditional approaches to scanning and reporting still need to be available. Security is integrated, not outside approval. Legacy approaches can keep up with releases only by grinding development to a halt, resulting in delays in time-to-market, developer underutilization, and a growing backlog of issues.

  - During application development processes, shift left to engage security earlier to fix issues faster, cheaper, and more effectively. If you wait until after the cake has been baked, it is hard to change it.

  - Security practices must be integrated seamlessly to prevent unhealthy friction in development workflows and continuous integration/continuous deployment (CI/CD) processes.

- • Security must provide high-quality findings and guidance that help developers fix issues quickly and avoid false positives.

- • A shared culture shared values, and shared goals and accountabilities should result from a converged culture among security, development, and operations roles.

- • Implement an agile security approach that starts with minimum viable security for applications (and for developing processes) and continuously improves it.

- • Simplify development processes by integrating cloud-native infrastructure and security features.

- • Ensure that open-source software (OSS) and third-party components are updated and bug-fixed and take a zero-trust approach to them.

- • As developer services, sometimes called *platform as a service (PaaS)* services, and applications change in composition, developers, operations, and security team members will constantly learn new technologies.

- • Application security programmatically to ensure continuous improvement of agile approaches.

Microsoft Cloud Security Benchmark for DevOps

Generally, DevOps security focuses on the security engineering and operations involved in DevOps processes, including the deployment of critical security checks (such as static application security testing and vulnerability management) before deployment to ensure the security of the entire DevOps process; threat modeling and software supply security are also covered.

Figure 2-10 provides high-level insights into the Microsoft cloud security benchmark specific to DevOps.

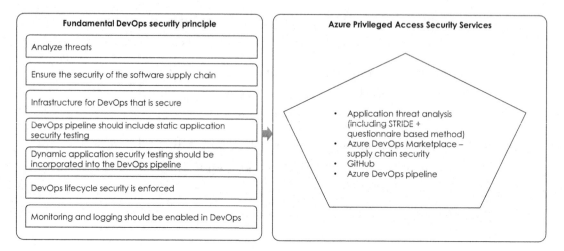

Figure 2-10. *Microsoft cloud security benchmark for DevOps*

Analyze Threats

Ensure your threat modeling serves the following purposes:

- Identify threats and enumerate mitigating controls.

- In the runtime production stage, secure your applications and services.

- Threat modeling should at least consider the following aspects to secure build, test, and deployment artifacts, pipelines, and tooling environments:

  - Make sure the threat modeling satisfies the application's security requirements.

  - Ensure you analyze the upstream and downstream connections outside your application scope and the application components and data connections.

  - Determine which of your application components, data connections, and upstream and downstream services are at risk of potential threats and attack vectors.

- Assess the appropriate security controls that can mitigate the threats mentioned and identify any gaps in those controls (e.g., security vulnerabilities) that may need to be addressed.

- Identify the vulnerabilities and design controls that can mitigate them.

The following are the high-level recommendations for Microsoft Azure:

- You can drive your threat modeling process with tools like the Microsoft threat modeling tool with the embedded Azure threat model template.

- Using the STRIDE model, identify the appropriate controls and enumerate the internal and external threats.

- Incorporate threats in DevOps processes, such as malicious code injection through an insecure artifacts repository that is misconfigured for access control.

To identify threats, at the least, you should use a questionnaire-based threat modeling process if your organization does not have access to a threat modeling tool.

If your application or threat landscape undergoes a significant security-impact change, update the threat modeling or analysis results.

Ensure the Security of the Software Supply Chain

Your enterprise needs to ensure that it is SDLC or process includes security controls to govern the in-house and third-party software components that depend on your application (proprietary and open-source). Prevent vulnerable or malicious components from being integrated and deployed into the environment by defining gate criteria.

The following aspects should be included in software supply chain security controls at the least:

- Determine the dependencies for the development phase, build, integrate, and deploy the service/resource in a software bill of materials (SBOM).

- Ensure in-house and third-party software components are accounted for when there is a known vulnerability and a fix is available.

- Static and dynamic application testing can be used to identify unknown vulnerabilities in software components.

- If direct mitigation is unavailable, well defined security elements to compensate controls for mitigating the vulnerabilities. Mitigation approaches may include local and upstream source code fixes, feature exclusions, and compensating controls.

You may need to learn how secure it is when you use closed-source third-party components in your production environment. The impact of malicious activity or a vulnerability associated with the element can be minimized by adding additional security controls such as access control, network isolation, and endpoint security.

Here is some Azure guidance: Ensure the software supply chain is secure using the following capabilities or tools provided by GitHub Advanced Security or by GitHub native features. Through Advisory Database, find all your project's dependencies and vulnerabilities by scanning, inventorying, and identifying them.

- Use Dependabot to ensure that the vulnerable dependency is tracked and remediated and provide your repository automatically keeps up with the latest releases of the packages and applications it depends on.

- Use the GitHub native code scanning capability to scan the source code when sourcing the code from external sources.

- Use Microsoft Defender for Cloud to integrate vulnerability assessment for your container image in the CI/CD workflow.

Azure DevOps can be extended with third-party extensions to inventory, analyze, and remediate third-party software components and their vulnerabilities.

Infrastructure for DevOps That Is Secure

Incorporate security best practices into the DevOps pipeline and infrastructure across environments, including build, test, and production stages, such as the following controls:

- A repository for storing source code, built packages, images, project artifacts, and business data

- CI/CD pipeline hosting servers, tools, and services

- Configuration of CI/CD pipelines

The following controls should be prioritized in your DevOps infrastructure security controls for the Microsoft cloud security benchmark:

- Protect artifacts and underlying environments to prevent malicious code from being inserted into CI/CD pipelines. Identify any misconfiguration in the core areas of Azure DevOps, such as Organization, Projects, Users, Pipelines (Build & Release), Connections, or Build Agent, in your CI/CD pipeline, including open access, weak authentication, insecure connection setup, etc. Use similar controls to secure GitHub's Organization permissions.

- Consistent deployment of DevOps infrastructure across development projects is essential. With Microsoft Defender for Cloud (such as Compliance Dashboard, Azure Policy, or Cloud Posture Management) or your own compliance monitoring tools, you can monitor compliance across your DevOps infrastructure at scale.

- Make sure CI/CD tools, Azure AD, and native services are configured with access permissions and entitlement policies to ensure that changes to pipelines are authorized.

- Just-in-time access to Azure-managed identities can prevent permanent "standing" privileges from being granted to human accounts, such as developers and testers.

- Code and scripts used in CI/CD workflow jobs should not contain keys, credentials, or secrets. Store them in key stores or Azure Key Vaults instead.

- For self-hosted build/deployment agents, your environment should be secured by following Microsoft Cloud Security Benchmark controls such as network security, posture and vulnerability management, and endpoint security.

To enable governance, compliance, operational auditing, and risk auditing for your DevOps infrastructure, refer to the Logging and Threat Detection and DS-7 Posture and Vulnerability Management sections.

DevOps Pipeline Should Include Static Application Security Testing

Test static, fuzzy, interactive, and mobile applications as part of the CI/CD workflow with gating controls. Depending on the test results, gates can be set so vulnerable packages are not committed, built into the packages, or deployed to production.

The Azure DevOps Pipeline and GitHub can integrate with tools such as Checkmarx, Fortify, Veracode, SonarQube and much more into your CI/CD workflow to automatically scan and analyze your source code.

- Perform source code analysis using GitHub CodeQL.

- Analyze binary files on Windows and Linux with Microsoft BinSkim.

- For credential scanning in the source code, Azure DevOps Credential Scanner (Microsoft Security DevOps extension) and GitHub native secret scanning are used.

Dynamic Application Security Testing Should Be Incorporated Into the DevOps Pipeline

Including dynamic application security testing (DAST) as a gating control in the CI/CD workflow is important, because it prevents vulnerabilities from being incorporated into packages or deployed into production.

DAST should be integrated into your pipeline so the runtime application can be tested automatically within your CI/CD pipeline through Azure DevOps or GitHub. Automated penetration testing (and manual validation) should also be implemented.

CI/CD workflows can be integrated with third-party DAST tools via Azure DevOps Pipeline or GitHub.

DevOps Life-Cycle Security Is Enforced

Through development, testing, and deployment, ensure the workload is securely managed. The Microsoft cloud security benchmark can be used by evaluating controls (such as network security, identify management, privileged access, etc.) that can be set as guardrails by default or shifted left before deployment. Ensure your DevOps process includes these controls:

- Automate deployment using Azure or third-party tooling for the CI/CD workflow, infrastructure management (infrastructure as code), and testing to reduce human error and attack surfaces.

- Prevent malicious manipulation of virtual machines, container images, and other artifacts.

- Perform a SAST and DAST scan on the workload artifacts before CI/CD deployment (e.g., container images, dependencies, SASTs, etc.).

- Use threat detection and vulnerability assessment capabilities continuously in the production environment.

Here is some guidance for Azure virtual machines:

- Use the Azure Shared Image Gallery to share and control access to your custom images with your users, service principals, or AD groups. Make sure only authorized users can access your custom images using Azure RBAC.

- Create custom images, Azure Resource Manager templates, and Azure Policy guest configurations to define the secure configuration baselines for the VMs to eliminate unnecessary credentials, permissions, and packages.

Here is some Azure container services guidance:

- Create your private container registry using Azure Container Registry (ACR). With Azure RBAC, you can configure restricted access so only authorized accounts and services can access the containers.

- You can use Microsoft Defender for Azure Containers to assess the vulnerability of the images within your private Azure Container Registry. You can also use Microsoft Defender for Cloud to integrate container image scanning into your continuous integration and delivery process.

In Azure serverless services, adopt similar controls to ensure that security controls are shifted to the pre-deployment stage.

Monitoring and Logging Should Be Enabled in DevOps

Ensure your logging and monitoring scope includes nonproduction environments and CI/CD workflow elements used in DevOps (and any other development process). If not adequately monitored, vulnerabilities and threats targeting these environments can pose significant risks to your production environment. To identify deviations in the CI/CD workflow jobs, monitoring the events from the build, test, and deployment workflows is essential.

To implement your logging and monitoring controls for workloads, follow the Microsoft cloud security benchmark for logging and threat detection.

Ensure audit logging is enabled and configured in nonproduction and CI/CD tooling environments (such as Azure DevOps and GitHub).

To identify any exception results in the CI/CD jobs, the Azure DevOps and GitHub CI/CD events should also be monitored.

To ensure security incidents are correctly monitored and handled, ingesting these logs and events into Microsoft Sentinel or other SIEM tools is recommended.

Getting Started with Microsoft SecOps

Let's get started with the basics of security operation strategy.

A security operations center (SOC) aims to address organizational and technological security challenges. SOC analysts manage and improve security across the three pillars of an organization: people, processes, and technology.

A SOC can be a team within your organization or outsourced to a third-party specializing in managed detection and response.

Although *SOC* is used interchangeably to describe in-house and outsourced teams, the correct abbreviation for outsourced teams is *SOC as a service* (SOCaaS). Since this article is primarily about SOCaaS, we'll refer to both as a SOC.

Organizations rely on specialized IT security teams to monitor and respond to cybersecurity events in real-time, whether in-house or outsourced. A SOC is sometimes called an *information security operations center* (ISOC).

In addition, SOCs select, operate, maintain, and analyze threat data to improve the security posture of organizations.

In most small or midsize data centers, a centralized facility will continuously monitor network performance and security controls. Network operations centers (or similar terms) are also known as *security operations centers*. Security personnel and administrators typically have access to live and historical feeds from security devices and agents placed throughout the IT environment. Security operations centers will receive logs and reports from DLP, anti-malware, SIEM/SEM/SIM, firewalls, and IDS/IPS for analysis and real-time response.

The SOC can be physically located within the data center. The security operations center of an enterprise with many branches and offices may be operated remotely, allowing remote monitoring. Third parties, meaning vendors with the tools, knowledge, and personnel to provide security as a core competency, can often handle security operations and continuous monitoring.

Organizations can sometimes synchronize their security tools, practices, and responses to security incidents when a SOC is operated or outsourced. By improving preventative measures and security policies, detecting security threats more quickly, and responding more effectively and efficiently to them, security threats can usually be reduced. Furthermore, SOCs can simplify and strengthen compliance with industry, national, and international privacy laws.

Traditionally, you had to keep track of each level. The good news about cloud providers is that they are responsible for intrusion detection and response in their areas of responsibility, just like other controls. A provider breach could affect you, in which case you will be notified and may have to perform response and recovery activities specific to the services you use. However, in most cases, all your detection, response, and recovery activities will be in the areas marked by consumer responsibility.

Depending on the service and deployment model, the cloud provider will have a security operations center overseeing the various cloud data centers, underlying infrastructure, platforms, and applications. However, cloud customers may also have their security operations monitoring their users and accounts. The provider and customer may share responsibilities and activities for detection, reporting, investigation, and response actions; all of these must be included in the contract.

SOC teams vary according to the organization's size and the industry, but most share similar roles and responsibilities. Typically, a SOC is a centralized function that monitors and improves an organization's cybersecurity posture by preventing, detecting, analyzing, and responding to cybersecurity incidents.

As far as cybersecurity is concerned, prevention always outweighs reaction. A SOC monitors the network around the clock rather than responding to threats as they occur. Detecting malicious activities and preventing them before they cause damage is possible with the SOC team.

When SOC analysts witness something suspicious, they assemble as many details as possible for a deeper analysis.

An analyst performs a threat analysis at the investigation stage to determine whether and to what extent a threat has penetrated the system. By viewing the network and operations of the organization from an attacker's perspective, the security analyst searches for crucial indicators and vulnerabilities before they can be exploited.

By identifying and triaging various security incidents, the analyst understands how attacks unfold and how to respond before things get out of hand. The SOC analyst incorporates the most up-to-date global threat intelligence for a successful triage, including details on attacker tools, methods, and movements.

The SOC team coordinates a response following the investigation. Immediately after an incident's confirmation, the SOC isolates endpoints, terminates harmful processes, prevents them from executing, deletes files, etc.

The SOC works to restore systems and recover data after an incident. To counter ransomware attacks, you may need to wipe and restart endpoints, reconfigure systems, or deploy viable backups to circumvent the ransomware.

The IT environment does not have durable security controls. For a control to be considered complete (and the associated risk to be permanently mitigated), it cannot be purchased, implemented, and regarded as complete. You must monitor IT resources continuously to ensure that controls are adequate, operating as intended, and addressing the risks or vulnerabilities they are supposed to mitigate. Furthermore, new or emerging threats or hazards must be monitored continuously to ensure they are handled appropriately.

The key difference between NOCs and SOCs is that NOCs monitor the network proactively for issues that could slow traffic and respond to outages when necessary. In addition to monitoring the network and other environments, a SOC is looking for evidence of cyberattacks. NOCs and SOCs need to coordinate activities to prevent network performance disruptions. Some organizations house their SOC within their NOCs to encourage collaboration.

SOC teams use real-time security monitoring to identify potential threats on servers, devices, databases, network applications, websites, and other systems. Additionally, they do proactive security work by staying on top of the latest threats and identifying and addressing system or process vulnerabilities before attackers can exploit them. If a successful attack occurs, the SOC team is responsible for removing the threat and restoring backups and systems.

An IT environment could be protected for a particular period if the study was successful or did not show significant results under older security paradigms. It is recommended that continuous monitoring be used in accordance with current industry guidance and best practices. It is a central principle of protecting an IT environment that NIST (in the Risk Management Framework), ISO (in the 27000 series of IT security standards), and the CIS (formerly SANS Top 20 security controls guidance) emphasize continuous monitoring.

In general, traditional environments categorize SOC activities and responsibilities into three categories.

- *Category 1*: Preparation, planning, and prevention

- *Category 2*: Monitoring, detection, and response

- *Category 3*: Recovery, refinement, and compliance

Let's understand in depth each of the categories.

Category 1: Preparation, Planning, and Prevention

The following list is focused on the majority of the organization.

- *Asset Inventory*: Data center protection includes application, database, server, cloud service, and endpoint protection, along with security tools (firewalls, antivirus/anti-malware/anti-ransomware tools, monitoring software, etc.). Asset discovery solutions are often used to do this.

- *Regular maintenance and preparation*: The SOC performs preventive maintenance, including software patches and upgrades, firewalls, allow lists and blocklists, and security policies and procedures to maximize the effectiveness of security tools. The SOC may develop backup policies and procedures to ensure business continuity in data breaches, ransomware attacks, or other cybersecurity incidents.

- *Incident response planning*: An organization's SOC develops its incident response plan, which defines activities, responsibilities, and metrics for assessing response effectiveness during a threat or incident.

- *Continuous testing*: A SOC team performs comprehensive assessments to determine the risks and costs associated with each resource. Penetration tests are also conducted to simulate specific attacks on a system. Based on the results of these tests, the team remediates or refines applications, security policies, and best practices.

- *Staying current*: SOC must keep up-to-date with the latest security solutions and technologies and threat intelligence as well as news and information on cyberattacks and their perpetrators gathered from social media, industry sources, and the dark web.

Category 2: Monitoring, Detection, and Response

The following list is focused on the majority of the organization:

- *Continuous, around-the-clock security monitoring*: The SOC monitors all IT infrastructure 24/7/365 for signs of known exploits and suspicious activity, including applications, servers, system software, computing devices, cloud workloads, and the network.

- *Security information and event management*: SIEM has been the core monitoring, detection, and response technology for many SOCs. To identify potential threats, SIEM monitors and aggregates real-time alerts and telemetry from software and hardware on the network. A recent development is the adoption of XDR technology, which provides detailed telemetry and monitoring and can automatically detect and respond to incidents.

- *Log management*: Every networking event generates log data that needs to be collected and analyzed; log management is an essential subset of monitoring. Most IT departments contain log data, but their analysis determines regular activity and identifies anomalies that indicate suspicious activity. Many hackers take advantage of companies not constantly analyzing log data, enabling their malware and viruses to run undetected for long periods. SIEM solutions generally include log management capabilities.

- *Threat detection*: After sorting the noise from the signals, the SOC team triages threats by severity based on the indications of actual cyber threats and hacker exploits. Artificial intelligence (AI) is incorporated into modern SIEM solutions to automate these processes and to detect suspicious activity more accurately over time.

- *Incident response*: The SOC responds to threats or actual incidents to limit the damage. Actions can include the following:

  - An investigation of the incident's root cause is necessary to determine the technical vulnerabilities that allowed hackers to gain access to the system, as well as other factors (such as poor password hygiene or a lack of enforcement of policies) that contributed to the attack.

  - Endpoints that have been compromised should be shut down or disconnected from the network.

  - Isolating and rerouting compromised network traffic.

  - Apps or processes that are compromised should be paused or stopped.

  - Files that are damaged or infected should be deleted.

  - Running antivirus or anti-malware software.

  - Internally and externally decommissioning passwords.

In addition to automating and accelerating these responses, many SOCs can use XDR solutions.

Category 3: Recovery, Refinement, and Compliance

The following list is focused on the majority of the organization:

- *Recovery and remediation*: The SOC eradicates a threat once an incident has been contained and then works to restore the impacted assets to their original state (e.g., wiping, restoring, and reconnecting disks, end-user devices, and other endpoints; restoring network traffic; restarting applications and processes). In a ransomware attack or data breach, recovery may require switching to backup systems and resetting passwords.

- *Post-mortem and refinement*: As part of the incident response plan, the SOC may choose to update processes and policies, choose new cybersecurity tools, or revise the incident response plan to prevent a recurrence. In addition to assessing whether the incident has revealed a new or changing cybersecurity trend, the SOC team may also determine how to prepare for it.

- *Compliance management*: The SOC ensures all applications, systems, and security tools and processes comply with data privacy regulations. This includes the GDPR, the CCPA, and Payment Card Industry Data Security Standard (PCI DSS). SOCs ensure that regulations notify users, regulators, law enforcement, and other parties after an incident and retain critical incident data for evidence and auditing.

In summary, the SOC team monitors detect, contains, and remediates IT threats across applications, devices, systems, networks, and locations. To determine whether a threat is active, what the impact is, and what measures are needed, SOC teams use various technologies and processes (e.g., indicators, artifacts, and other evidence) in conjunction with the latest threat intelligence (e.g., indicators, artifacts, and other evidence). The increasing frequency and severity of incidents have altered the roles and responsibilities of security operations centers.

SOCs help organizations prevent cyberattacks by combining people, tools, and processes. Among its functions are inventorying assets and technology, routine maintenance, continuous monitoring, threat detection, threat intelligence, log management, incident response, recovery and remediation, root-cause investigations, security refinement, and compliance management, all of which contribute to achieving its goals.

By unifying defenders, threat detection tools, and security processes, a strong SOC helps organizations manage security more efficiently and effectively. With a SOC, companies can manage compliance better, respond faster to threats, and improve security processes.

Microsoft SOC Function for Azure Cloud

Detecting, prioritizing, and potentially triaging attacks is the responsibility of the security operation team. By eliminating false positives and focusing on actual attacks, the central SecOps team reduces the time it takes to remedy actual attacks. Communication, investigation, and hunting activities must be aligned with the application team so that false positives are eliminated, and actual attacks are focused on.

Microsoft defines that SOC functions need to address three critical objectives: incident management, incident preparation, and threat intelligence. Let's take a high-level view of each one of them.

- *Incident management*: Protect the environment from active attacks, including the following:

    - Responding to detected attacks in a reactive manner

    - Identifying attacks that proactively slipped through traditional threat detections

    - Coordinating legal, communications, and other business implications of security incidents

- *Incident preparation*: The organization should undertake preparation for future attacks. It is a broader set of activities designed to build muscle memory and context at all levels of the organization. As a result of this strategy, people will be better prepared to handle significant attacks, and insights will be gained on improving security processes.

- *Threat intelligence*: Providing security operations, security teams, business leadership stakeholders, and security leadership with threat intelligence collected processed, and disseminated solution.

It is critical for security operations teams to focus on essential outcomes to achieve these outcomes. It is common for SecOps teams to break the outcome into subteams in larger organizations.

Now, let us explore each level. Let us start with Tier 0.

Tier 0 is the ultimate efficiency to automate and optimize your security posture through SOC Automation. Detection and remediation of threats can be sped up with SOC automation.

You manage threats and vulnerabilities, respond to incidents, and automate security operations. Automating processes allows them to be handled automatically, such as scanning for vulnerabilities or searching for logs or resolving well known attacks.

Tier 1 is a security incident's first point of contact. In triage, alerts are generated by automation, and tools are processed at high volumes. Most of the common incident types are resolved within the team through triage. A tier 2 incident should be escalated if it is more complex or has not been seen before.

In Tier 2, the SOC should focus on incidents requiring further investigation, often requiring data points from various sources to be correlated. Tier 2 investigates escalated issues to provide repeatable solutions, so Tier 1 can address similar problems in the future. A business-critical system alert will also be handled by Tier 2, which will reflect the severity of the risk and the need for immediate action.

In Tier 3, the SOC should focus primarily on proactively hunting for highly sophisticated attack processes and developing guidance for the broader teams for maturing security controls. Tier 3 provides forensic analysis and response support for significant incidents.

Microsoft Azure Security Operations Center

In cloud security operations (SecOps), active attacks on enterprise assets are detected, responded to, and recovered from.

Security operations teams (SOCs, SecOps, and Security Operations Centers) detect, prioritize, and potentially triage attacks in real time. The SecOps team eliminates false positives and reduces the time to remediate actual incidents by monitoring security-related telemetry data and investigating security breaches. Whenever possible, communication, investigation, and hunting activities should be coordinated with the team working on the application.

SecOps should mature as follows:

- Responding reactively to tool-detected attacks

- Detecting attacks before they slip through reactive detections by being proactive

Generally, these are the best practices to follow when conducting security operations:

- Operate according to the NIST Cybersecurity Framework (CSF).

  - *Detect*: Analyze the system for adversaries.

  - *Respond*: Investigate the situation quickly to determine whether it's a false alarm or an actual attack.

  - *Recover:* Assure that the workload is secure, reliable, and available during and after an attack.

- Alerts must be acknowledged quickly. Defenders must not ignore a detected adversary while triaging false positives.

- Reduce the opportunities for an adversary to conduct an attack and reach sensitive systems by reducing the time it takes to remediate a detected adversary.

- Make security investments in systems with high intrinsic value, such as administrator accounts.

- Detect adversaries proactively as your system matures. This will reduce the time a more sophisticated adversary can operate in the environment.

SecOps Tools

An Azure SOC team can use SecOps tools to investigate and remediate incidents.

A cloud-based SIEM solution is one of the most important tools in a SOC. It aggregates data from multiple security solutions and log files to detect emerging threats, expedite an incident response, and keep up with attackers.

With SOAR, recurring and predictable enrichment, response, and remediation tasks can be automated, allowing more time and resources for investigations and hunting.

Microsoft Sentinel is a SIEM tool for enterprise-wide log monitoring. With Microsoft Sentinel, you can easily integrate any product or service in your environment with Microsoft Sentinel's playbooks and connectors for security orchestration, automation, and response (SOAR).

By integrating security products and data into simplified solutions, XDR provides holistic, optimized security through software as a service. Multicloud and hybrid environments require organizations to use these solutions to address evolving threats and complex security challenges proactively and efficiently. Unlike systems like endpoint detection and response (EDR), XDR covers a broader range of security products, including endpoints, servers, cloud applications, and emails, all protected with XDR. As a result, XDR provides visibility, analytics, correlated alerts, and automated responses to protect data and combat threats by combining prevention, detection, investigation, and response.

You can also use Microsoft Defender for Cloud to respond to an alert using a security playbook. The Microsoft Defender software provides an end-to-end solution for threat detection and response on-prem, in the cloud, and other clouds across your Microsoft estate. Cloud telemetry and on-premises telemetry must be collected, analyzed, and responded to with comprehensive monitoring solutions.

Or, you can use Azure Monitor to create Azure application and service event logs. With Azure Monitor, you can aggregate all the data from your system into one platform. It combines data from multiple Azure subscriptions and tenants and hosts data for other Azure services.

You can use an Azure NSG to monitor network activity or use Azure Information Protection to protect sensitive data, such as emails, documents, and files, outside of your organization.

Summary

In this chapter, you read about methods to design and deploy a strategy for securing infrastructure and platform components, design and deploy a strategy for securing identify, and design and deploy a strategy for securing apps and data. You also learned about Microsoft SecOps.

In the next chapter of the book, you will read about designing and deploying identify solutions in alignment with the NIST CSF.

CHAPTER 3

Design and Deploy an Identify Solution

Throughout history, people, organizations, and governments have fallen victim to cyberattacks. Cybersecurity, cyberattacks, cybercriminals, and more have been frequently discussed in the IT and business world. You'll need a basic understanding of these concepts to protect yourself and those around you.

Microsoft Cybersecurity NIST Identify is an identification and authentication framework designed to help organizations secure their data and systems. It enables organizations to create a secure identify ecosystem and protect against malicious actors, and it also provides guidance on best practices for authentication and identify management.

Microsoft Cybersecurity NIST Identify creates a secure and trusted identify environment that is reliable and easy to use. It also helps organizations protect their networks and data from unauthorized access and provides consistent security requirements and policies. This allows organizations to meet compliance and regulatory standards while increasing productivity and user experience. It also reduces operational costs and improves the organization's overall security posture.

Microsoft Cybersecurity NIST Identify also provides a comprehensive dashboard to monitor the system's performance, allowing organizations to identify and address any potential security issues quickly and efficiently. Additionally, it supports multiple authentication methods, allowing organizations to customize their authentication process easily.

Microsoft Cybersecurity NIST Identify also supports automated compliance reporting, allowing organizations to easily demonstrate compliance with industry standards. This assures organizations that their security measures are up-to-date and effective. It also puts less burden on IT staff, freeing them up to focus on more critical tasks.

© Puthiyavan Udayakumar 2023
P. Udayakumar, *Design and Deploy a Secure Azure Environment*,
https://doi.org/10.1007/978-1-4842-9678-3_3

This chapter provides the fundamentals of Microsoft Cybersecurity NIST Identify. By the end of this chapter, you should be able to understand the following:

- Azure identify security services

- ID.AM: Asset Management

- ID.BE: Business Environment

- ID.GV: Governance

- ID.RA: Risk Assessment

Introduction to NIST Identify

In this section, let's get started by understanding what NIST Identify is.

The Identify function assists in developing an organizational understanding of managing cybersecurity risk to systems, people, assets, data, and capabilities.

An organization's understanding of managing cybersecurity risk to systems, people, assets, data, and capabilities can be developed through the Identify function. An organization's risk management strategy and business needs can be aligned with the business context, the resources supporting critical functions, and the cybersecurity risks related to these functions.

Within this function, there are the following outcomes categories:

- Establishing the basis of an asset management program by identifying and evaluating physical and software assets in the organization

- Establishing the organization's place in the critical infrastructure sector and its role in the supply chain must be identified.

- Identifying policies and legal and regulatory requirements regarding cybersecurity capability within the organization to define the Governance program.

- Assessing the risk associated with an organization's assets, threats, and risk response activities

- Establishing the organization's risk tolerances and developing a risk management strategy

- Identifying a supply chain risk management strategy, which includes priorities, constraints, risk tolerances, and assumptions used to support risk determinations associated with handling supply chain risks

The activities in the Identify function are critical for effectively using the NIST CSF framework. Develop an organizational understanding of cybersecurity risk to systems, people, assets, data, and capabilities. Based on its risk management strategy and business needs, an organization can prioritize its cybersecurity efforts based on understanding the business context, the resources supporting critical functions, and the cybersecurity risks. The outcome categories included in this function are Asset Management, Business Environment, Governance, Risk Assessment, Risk Management Strategy, and Supply Chain Risk Management. Figure 3-1 depicts the classification.

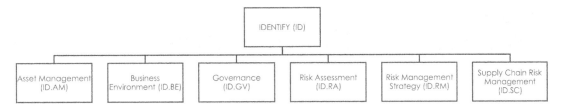

Figure 3-1. *NIST Identify categories*

Asset Management (ID.AM)

Asset management is the process of managing and preserving the value of an asset over its life cycle. It involves assessing and understanding the risks associated with an asset, monitoring its performance, and taking corrective action when necessary. Asset management helps to optimize the utilization of resources and maximize returns. It helps ensure that assets are properly maintained and updated and that any potential risks are identified and mitigated. It is important to have an effective asset management system in place to ensure that resources are used efficiently and risks are minimized. This will help to maximize returns and ensure the long-term success of the organization.

Asset management tracks and manages the hardware, software, and other physical assets used in an organization's cloud infrastructure. It is essential for maintaining an effective cybersecurity strategy since it helps to identify and monitor the security risks associated with each asset.

Asset management enables organizations to identify potential threats and take the necessary steps to mitigate them. It also helps organizations identify areas where additional security measures can be implemented. By comprehensively understanding their assets, organizations can ensure that their IT infrastructure remains secure.

Asset management provides organizations with visibility into their IT infrastructure and an understanding of its use. It allows organizations to identify and categorize their assets and track them over time to detect any infrastructure changes. This visibility helps organizations identify potential vulnerabilities and take steps to mitigate the risks associated with them.

Asset management also helps organizations identify areas where additional security measures can be implemented, allowing them to protect their assets from potential threats proactively.

Organizations identify and manage the data, personnel, devices, systems, and facilities appropriate to their relative importance to business objectives and risk management plans. Figure 3-2 depicts the Identify categories.

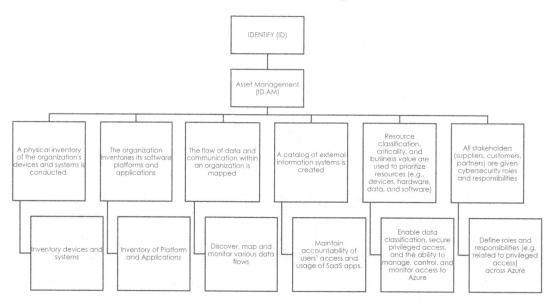

Figure 3-2. *NIST Identify asset management categories*

The NIST control statement recommends the following:

- A system component inventory should be developed and documented that

    - Ensures that the system is accurately reflected

- The entire system is included

- Components that are assigned to other systems are not duplicated in this accounting

- Tracks and reports at the appropriate level of granularity

- Information necessary to achieve effective system component accountability

- Update the inventory of system components

Azure Mapping for Asset Management (ID.AM)

Microsoft Azure asset management capabilities via various services and products enables organizations to manage their assets and resources more efficiently. It provides a centralized platform to track, monitor, and manage assets, as well as insights into their performance. It also helps to reduce costs and maximize productivity.

A key component of asset management is the implementation of controls for securing Azure resources, including recommendations about permissions for security personnel, access to asset inventory, and managing approvals for services and resources (inventory, tracking, and correcting).

Security posture can be accurately assessed only by identifying a system's assets and value. Assets include tangible elements such as information or equipment and abstract ones such as reputation. It is essential to quantify the impact of these assets. Every organization must identify its digital assets and determine what level of protection they require.

Here are the Microsoft Azure guidelines for asset management:

- Discover all your cloud resources by querying your asset inventory. Tagging and grouping your assets according to their service nature, location, or other characteristics will help you organize them logically. Maintain a continuously updated asset inventory for your security organization. By aggregating security insights and risks centrally, you can ensure your security organization can monitor risks to cloud assets.

- Audit and restrict user access to cloud services to ensure only approved cloud services can be used.

- Maintain security attributes and configurations of assets throughout their life cycles.

- Your cloud assets should be protected from accidental or malicious modifications by limiting access to asset management features.

- Create an allow list and block unauthorized software from executing in your environment by ensuring that only authorized software is executed.

Let's now to explore the Azure NIST Identify mapping for asset management and Microsoft's outlined responsibility classification among Microsoft and customers, which matches up with cloud security shared responsibility models.

Figure 3-3 depicts the subcategories of Azure mapping against the Identify module of the NIST CSF.

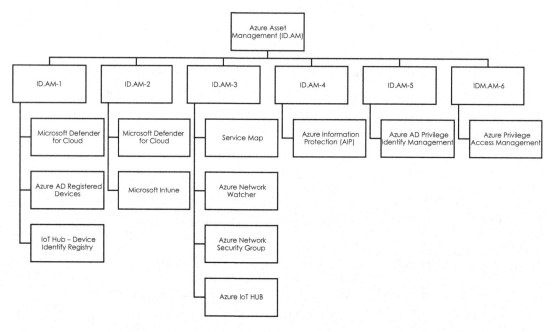

Figure 3-3. *NIST Identify asset management categories and subcategories*

As part of the Azure cloud shared responsibility model, the NIST CSF security functions are provided in Table 3-1 with respect to ID.AM.

Table 3-1. *ID.AM Responsibility Matrix*

Category	Subcategory	Informative References	Responsibility	Customer Responsibility	Microsoft Azure Responsibility
Asset Management (ID.AM): Data, personnel, devices, systems, and facilities that enable the organization to meet its business objectives are identified and managed in accordance with the risk strategy of the organization.	ID.AM-1: A physical inventory of the organization's devices and systems is conducted.	NIST SP 800-53 Rev. 4 CM-8	Shared	All external information systems interconnected with the Azure subscription must be catalogued and documented by the customer.	Microsoft Azure maintains an inventory of information system components. Keeping the inventory up to date with new installations and decommissioning of devices is done with an inventory database system, which keeps it accurate and up to date. A security group must establish standards based on which assets are classified. The inventory must identify the owner, current location, and classification of each asset. All asset types are kept up-to-date with new installations and decommissionings.

(*continued*)

Table 3-1. (*continued*)

Category	Subcategory	Informative References	Responsibility	Customer Responsibility	Microsoft Azure Responsibility
	ID.AM-2: The organization inventories its software platforms and applications	NIST SP 800-53 Rev. 4 CM-8	Shared	Customers are responsible for identifying and inventorying applications and platforms critical to their business objectives. A Microsoft Azure subscription may include the following: an operating system, an application, or software, but customers are still responsible for inventorying these items.	As part of maintaining fleet health, Microsoft Azure maintains a list of information system components, including software platforms and applications.

ID.AM-3: The flow of data and communication within an organization is mapped	NIST SP 800-53 Rev. 4 AC-4, CA-3, CA-9, PL-8	Shared	Customers are responsible for managing communication and data between their applications and between them and external systems. The customer is responsible for authorizing connections to external and internal information systems and documenting these connections.	To protect internal data flows, Microsoft Azure employs and enforces approved authorizations to control information flow both within the system and between interconnected systems and encrypt all data in transit.
ID.AM-4: A catalog of external information systems is created	NIST SP 800-53 Rev. 4 AC-20, SA-9	Customer	All external information systems interconnected with the Azure subscription must be catalogued and documented by the customer.	N/A

(continued)

157

Table 3-1. (*continued*)

Category	Subcategory	Informative References	Responsibility	Customer Responsibility	Microsoft Azure Responsibility
	ID.AM-5: Resource classification, criticality, and business value are used to prioritize resources (e.g., devices, hardware, data, and software)	NIST SP 800-53 Rev. 4 CP-2, RA-2, SA-14	Customer	The customer prioritizes resources (such as hardware, devices, data, time, and software) according to their classification, criticality, and business value. The customer will define the priority of Microsoft Azure based on the criteria listed, but it will be listed as a resource.	N/A
	ID.AM-6: All stakeholders (suppliers, customers, partners) are given cybersecurity roles and responsibilities	NIST SP 800-53 Rev. 4 CP-2, PS-7, PM-11	Customer	Customers are responsible for identifying cybersecurity roles and responsibilities within their companies.	N/A

Microsoft Defender for Cloud

Microsoft Defender for Cloud is a cloud-native cybersecurity platform that provides advanced protection for cloud workloads, data, applications, and networks. It offers threat detection and protection against advanced persistent threats, zero-day vulnerabilities, and automated incident response capabilities.

Microsoft Defender for Cloud is a cloud-native application protection platform (CNAPP), it offers tools and practices to secure cloud-based applications against cyber threatsCyber threats and vulnerabilitiesVulnerabilities. As part of Microsoft Defender for Cloud is a cloud-native application protection platform (CNAPP), you will be able to do the following:

- You can unify security management at the code level across multicloud and multi-pipeline environments with development security operations (DevSecOps).

- CSPM provides actionable guidance on how to prevent breaches in the cloud.

- Workloads such as virtual machines, containers, storage, databases, and other workloads can be protected with a cloud workload protection platform (CWPP).

Developer security operations, or DevSecOps, are incorporated into DevSecOps with Defender for Cloud. From a single location, you can protect your code management environments and pipelines and monitor your development environments' security posture. There is currently a Defender for DevOps included in Defender for Cloud.

These are the key capabilities of Microsoft Defender for Cloud:

- Improve your cloud security posture proactively with free continuous assessment, benchmarks, and Azure, AWS, and Google Cloud recommendations.

- Utilize contextual threat analysis to prioritize remediation of critical risks. Discover high-priority risks by analyzing attack paths.

- With insights from industry-leading security intelligence, secure virtual machines, containers, databases, and storage.

- Scan with an agentless or agent-based approach for flexibility and comprehensive workload protection.

- Visualize DevOps security posture across multi-cloud and multi-pipeline environments.

- Gain visibility into DevOps inventory, application code, and configuration security posture.

- Remediate critical code issues faster by prioritizing and providing remediation guidance natively in developer tools.

- Our controls are mapped to major regulatory industry benchmarks for multicloud security compliance by default.

Security awareness is required at the code, infrastructure, and runtime levels of today's applications to ensure they are hardened against attacks. Configuring and deploying your cloud and on-premises resources correctly is critical to ensuring their security. You can secure your environment using Defender for Cloud recommendations.

With Defender for Cloud, you can access free Foundational CSPM capabilities. By enabling paid Defender plans, you can also enable advanced CSPM capabilities. Taking proactive measures to protect your workload from threats requires implementing security practices. By recommending the proper security controls for your workload, cloud workload protection (CWP) surfaces workload-specific recommendations.

What Is a Hybrid Cloud?   Organizations can use a hybrid cloud to orchestrate, manage, and port their applications across public, private, and on-premises infrastructures. It creates a unified, flexible, distributed computing environment where traditional or cloud-native workloads can be scaled according to the most appropriate computing model. Using multiple providers of public cloud services as part of a hybrid multicloud is called a *hybrid multicloud*.

Security alerts immediately inform you of the nature and severity of threats to your environment so you can prepare to respond. After you identify a threat in your environment, you need to respond to limit the risk to your resources quickly.

In a hybrid and multicloud environment, you need to protect your resources. Microsoft Defender for Cloud, Microsoft Entra Permissions Management, Azure Network Security, GitHub Advanced Security, and Microsoft Defender External Attack Surface Management work together to provide comprehensive cloud security.

For protection against attacks that exploit today's multicloud, multiplatform environment, combine the breadth of a security information and event management (SIEM) solution with the depth of extended detection and response (XDR). As part of Microsoft's SIEM and XDR solution, Microsoft Defender for Cloud is a key component.

Figure 3-4 shows Microsoft Azure for Defender.

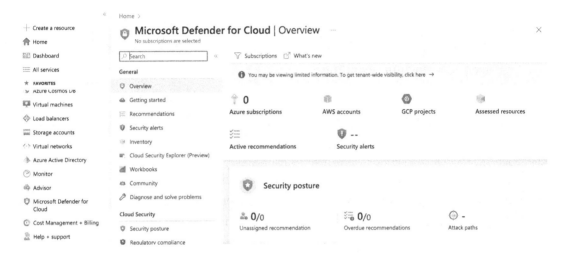

Figure 3-4. *Microsoft Defender for Cloud*

Asset Inventory

An IT asset inventory is a systematic process of gathering, recording, and maintaining information about all an organization's hardware and software IT assets. This process helps ensure that IT resources are used efficiently and that all assets are accounted for and properly maintained.

A security posture view of your connected resources is available on the asset inventory page of Microsoft Defender for Cloud. Regular security checks by Defender for Cloud identify potential security issues and provide actionable recommendations. A security posture can be improved by resolving functional requests.

As part of Defender for Cloud's asset inventory, you can query Defender for Cloud's security posture across multiple subscriptions using Azure Resource Graph (ARG).

ARG provides efficient resource exploration and scalable querying capabilities. It allows users to explore resources efficiently and to query them in a scalable manner.

Cross-referencing Defender for Cloud data with other resource properties can quickly provide deep insights using Kusto Query Language (KQL).

Software Inventory

Defender for Cloud's Software Inventory helps organizations better manage, track, and secure their software assets. It provides a secure, centralized repository to store, track and report on software inventory. It also helps organizations ensure compliance with software licensing regulations.

One of these paid solutions is required to access the software inventory:

- The Defender Cloud Security Posture Management (CSPM) offers agentless machine scanning.

- Defender for Servers P2 provides agentless machine scanning.

- Microsoft Offers Integration capability for Microsoft Defender for Endpoints with Microsoft Defender for Servers.

You can access the software inventory if you have already enabled Microsoft Defender for Endpoints and Microsoft Defender for Servers integrations.

Here are the key Microsoft Defender for cloud identify capabilities:

- Malware can be identified even if antimalware solutions fail to detect it.

- Ensure that licensed software is used following local security policies.

- Identify applications that are outdated or unsupported.

- Find out what software is running on your machines that your organization has banned.

- Apps that access sensitive data should be closely monitored.

- Rapidly changing workloads like virtual machines, SQL, and AKS require identifying security vulnerabilities quickly, especially those that can be exploited.

- Detect identify/access-based attacks on virtual machines, containers, Azure Storage, Key Vault, and Resource Manager (privilege escalation, credential access, initial access).

How to Enable It

Whenever you turn on a Defender plan, monitoring extensions are automatically deployed to collect data from your resources. It is necessary to enable the Defender plans that cover each workload that you want to protect in order to get Defender for Cloud's full protections. The following is the process to turn on Microsoft Defender for Cloud:

1. Log in to the Azure Portal.

2. You can search for and choose *Microsoft Defender for Cloud.*

3. In the Defender for Cloud menu, choose "Environment settings."

4. Choose the subscription or workspace you want to protect.

5. Click "Enable all" to enable all Defender for Cloud plans.

6. Click Save.

Azure AD Registered Devices

Microsoft Entra, which is a new family of solutions for multicloud identify and access management, includes Azure AD.

Azure AD registered devices are used for single sign-on authentication to access cloud applications. This feature enables users to connect to their corporate environment from any device securely. It also simplifies the management of user access rights. This helps ensure the corporate environment's security while providing users with a seamless experience when accessing cloud applications. It also allows IT admins to manage user access rights and permissions easily.

Furthermore, this feature provides end-to-end encryption, allowing secure communication and data transfer while keeping corporate data safe. It also offers two-factor authentication, which adds an extra layer of security to the user authentication process. This helps protect corporate data from cyber threats and unauthorized access. It also increases the overall security of the corporate network. This helps protect corporate data from cyber threats and unauthorized access and provides peace of mind to users. It also helps reduce IT costs by eliminating the need for manual user authentication processes.

Additionally, two-factor authentication can significantly reduce the risk of data breaches and ensure that only authorized personnel can access sensitive information. This helps to ensure compliance with data privacy regulations and enhances the security of the company's network. This can help protect the company's reputation, credibility, and financial assets. It also helps protect the personal data of employees and customers. In addition, two-factor authentication can help protect the company from costly legal fees and penalties.

Figure 3-5 depicts the Azure AD registered devices screen.

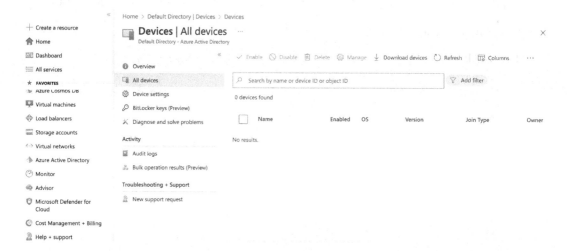

Figure 3-5. *Azure AD registered devices*

Windows 10 or newer devices with Azure AD registered accounts are signed in with a Microsoft account. For access to organizational resources, these devices have an Azure AD account. Azure AD accounts and Conditional Access policies applied to device identities can limit access to resources within an organization.

By using mobile device management (MDM) tools like Microsoft Intune, administrators can further secure and control these Azure AD-registered devices. By implementing MDM, organizations can enforce policies such as requiring encrypted storage and complex passwords and keeping their security software up-to-date.

Using the Windows 10 or Windows 11 Settings menu, you can manually register Azure AD when accessing a work application for the first time.

A primary refresh token (PRT) is issued to registered and joined devices, which can serve as a primary authentication artifact and a multifactor authentication artifact in some cases. Attackers can register their devices, use PRTs to access business data, steal PRT-based tokens from legitimate user devices, or find misconfigurations in Azure Active Directory controls. Administrators initiate and control the hybrid Azure AD joining process, reducing attack methods.

Identify-based attacks do not commonly target devices, but they can be used to fool security controls or impersonate users. Devices can have one of four relationships with Azure AD as Unregistered, Azure Active Directory (Azure AD) registered, Azure AD joined, and Hybrid Azure AD joined.

Keep an eye on your devices so that bad actors cannot access your infrastructure through them.

- Registration and integration with Azure AD

- Devices accessing noncompliant applications

- The retrieval of BitLocker keys

- Administrator roles for devices

- Logging on to virtual machines

Azure AD audit logs can be viewed and downloaded as CSV or JSON files from the Azure Portal. A variety of tools can be integrated with Azure AD logs via the Azure Portal, including Microsoft Sentinel, Sigma rules, Azure Monitor, Azure Event Hubs, and Microsoft Defender for Cloud Apps. You can also secure workload identities with Identify Protection Preview, enabling improved monitoring and alerting.

How to Enable It

In addition to domain join, group policy, LDAP, and Kerberos/NTLM authentication, Azure Active Directory Domain Services (Azure AD DS) is fully compatible with Windows Server Active Directory. Azure AD DS integrates with your existing Azure AD tenant, so you don't have to deploy, manage, and patch domain controllers yourself. Using this integration, users can log in using corporate credentials, and you can secure access to resources using existing groups and user accounts.

It is important to define a unique namespace for an Azure AD DS managed domain when you create one. A replica set is a deployment of two Windows Server domain controllers (DCs) into your selected Azure region.

You will need to complete the following steps to launch the Enable Azure AD Domain Services wizard:

1. Log in to the Azure Portal.

2. Choose "Create a resource" from the Azure Portal menu or the Home page.

3. Choose Azure AD Domain Services from the search suggestions after entering **Domain Services** in the search bar.

4. Select Enable Azure AD Domain Services from the Azure AD Domain Services page.

5. Choose the Azure Subscription in which you want to create the managed domain.

6. Select the resource group to which the managed domain belongs. Create a new resource group or select an existing one.

IoT Hub Identify Registry

IoT Hub Identify Registry is a secure cloud-based service used to create, manage, and store the identities of Internet-connected devices. It keeps track of device metadata such as name, type, and capabilities to make it easier to manage many devices. It also allows developers to set up and control access control policies easily.

What Is IOT?   The Internet of Things (IoT) is a network of physical devices, vehicles, home appliances, and other items embedded with electronics, software, sensors, actuators, and network connectivity, which enable these objects to collect and exchange data. This data is then used to automate processes and make better decisions. This technology has the potential to revolutionize how we interact with our environment and how businesses operate. It can automate processes, increase efficiency, and reduce costs. IoT also enables companies to gain valuable insights from data collected from connected devices.

IoT Hub Identify Registry helps developers securely manage device identities, enabling them to control access to the devices and their data securely. It also helps reduce the complexity of managing large, connected devices. It also provides a secure way to manage device certificates and allows for the revocation of certificates when needed. IoT Hub Identify Registry is designed to simplify the process of managing device identities and access control policies, allowing developers to quickly and securely set up and manage many connected devices. IoT Hub Identify Registry also provides a secure way to store device data, ensuring it is accessible only to authenticated users. It also enables device authentication and authorization, allowing developers to control access to their devices and manage user permissions.

IoT Hub Identify Registry also provides tools for monitoring device activity and managing device updates, making it easier for developers to manage connected devices. It also enables users to configure devices easily, allowing them to control how they interact with each other.

IoT Hub Identify Registry also provides secure storage of device credentials, which helps to protect user data and prevent unauthorized access. IoT Hub Identify Registry helps maintain a secure and reliable network of connected devices, ensuring that data is protected and that devices can communicate securely with each other. It also helps to reduce the time and effort required to manage and maintain devices, allowing developers to focus on the development process.

Device and back-end developers can build robust device management solutions with Azure IoT Hub thanks to its features and extensibility model. Sensors and microcontrollers with limited functionality can be paired with robust gateways that route communications for groups of devices. In addition, IoT operators' use cases and requirements vary widely by industry. Despite this variation, device management with IoT Hub can accommodate a wide range of end users and devices.

Identities of devices and modules connected to IoT hubs are stored in identify registries. IoT hubs require that devices and modules have entries in their identify registries before they can connect. Credentials stored in the identify registry must also be used to authenticate devices or modules with the IoT hub.

A case-sensitive requirement for the device or module ID is stored in the identify registry.

REST-capable identify resources are collected in the identify registry at a high level. The IoT Hub creates per-device resources when you add an entry to the identify registry, such as the queue for cloud-to-device messages.

When you need to use the identify registry, do the following:

1. Connect your IoT hub to devices or modules.

2. Access your hub's device and module-facing endpoints per device or module.

There are several operations available through the IoT Hub identify registry.

- Identify creation for devices and modules.

- Identify updates for devices or modules.

- IDs of devices or modules can be retrieved.

- The identify of a device or module can be deleted.

- A maximum of 1,000 identities can be listed.

- Azure blob storage for device identities.

- The Azure blob storage can be used to import device identities.

Microsoft Intune

Microsoft Intune is a cloud-based service that helps organizations to manage their mobile devices and apps. It enables administrators to set up device policies and restrictions, manage applications, and control access to corporate resources. It also provides users with a secure and productive experience on their devices.

What Is MDM and MAM?   Mobile device management (MDM) is a technology that allows IT administrators to manage, secure, and monitor mobile devices within the organization. Mobile application management (MAM) is a technology that allows IT administrators to control and manage the applications used on mobile devices. MDM and MAM together provide a comprehensive solution for organizations to manage and secure their mobile devices and applications. This helps organizations ensure that their data is secure and that devices are used in accordance with the organization's policies.

Microsoft Intune also helps organizations to protect their data and ensure compliance with security and privacy regulations. Intune makes managing and securing mobile devices, apps, and corporate data easier. It also helps to ensure that only approved apps are installed on company-owned mobile devices. Intune provides detailed reports and analytics about device usage for greater visibility and control. Intune helps ensure that devices and apps are updated with the latest security patches.

This helps to lower the risk of unauthorized access to company data, malicious code execution, and other security threats. It also helps organizations meet regulatory compliance requirements and enforce data protection policies across devices.

Intune also provides secure access to corporate resources, such as email and other applications, while ensuring that corporate data remains safe. It also allows for remote lock and wipe of devices if they are lost or stolen. Finally, it helps to enforce security policies, such as requiring a secure password or biometric authentication.

Organizations are challenged to manage the devices to access organization resources as they support hybrid and remote workers. Collaborating across locations, working from anywhere, and securely connecting to these resources are essential for employees and students. Data must be protected, access managed, and support provided from anywhere by administrators.

With Microsoft Intune, you can manage your endpoints from the cloud. Mobile devices, desktop computers, and virtual endpoints can all be managed with it, including user access and app and device management.

Figure 3-6 shows the Microsoft Intune interface.

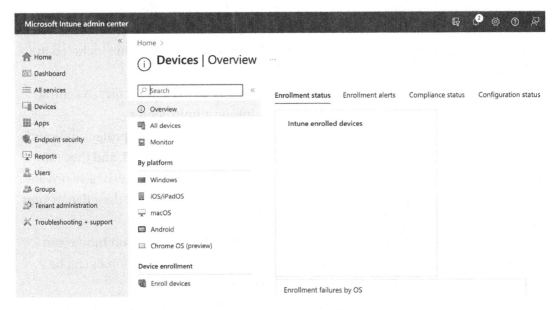

Figure 3-6. *Microsoft Intune admin center*

On both company-owned and user-owned devices, access and data can be protected. Additionally, Intune offers compliance and reporting features that support zero-trust security. Any endpoint management strategy and solution must manage and protect user identities. User accounts and groups control access to your organization's resources.

Users' identities must be secured and protected from malicious intent, as well as account membership, authorization, and authentication. Microsoft Intune can handle all of these tasks. User identities can be managed through Intune policies, including security and authentication.

As part of Intune's identify and permission management, Azure Active Directory is used. Intune's admin center provides a central place for managing endpoints. In addition to managing endpoints, endpoint management solutions include device management. Organizers manage more devices, including laptops, tablets, mobile phones, and wearables. It can be a huge undertaking if you need assistance figuring out where to begin.

Therefore, let's take a look at Microsoft Intune. It is a cloud-based service that can control devices through policies, including security policies. Managing devices and protecting their data is a top priority for any organization. Devices that access your organization's company-owned and personally owned resources are included in this task.

For device storage and permissions, Intune uses Azure Active Directory. A central location for managing endpoints is the Microsoft Intune admin center.

Endpoint management strategies and solutions must manage and protect apps and their data. Public retail apps are usually available for users to download, and they may be able to access organization data through these apps. Organizations also have private and line-of-business apps they need to deploy and manage and ensure their data is kept within the organization.

Intune can make app management easier. The cloud-based Microsoft Intune can manage a wide range of apps. Apps that access your organization's resources can be deployed, configured, protected, and updated using Intune.

Client devices running Android, iOS/iPadOS, macOS, and Windows are supported by Microsoft Intune. Therefore, you can manage apps across multiple devices using Intune.

How to Enable It

With Microsoft Intune, you have easy access to mobile device management and client app management from the cloud. It ensures secure productivity across all of your devices, including Windows, iOS, macOS, and Android.

- Device enrollment and configuration.

- You can upload and distribute your apps.

- Data protection for your organization.

- ConfigMgr-enrolled cloud-enabled computers.

- Make sure your deployments are monitored and troubleshooted.

Prior to signing up for Intune, check if you already have a Microsoft Online Services, Enterprise Agreement, or equivalent volume licensing agreement. Microsoft volume licensing agreements or Microsoft Azure services subscriptions like Microsoft 365 typically include a work or school account.

For your organization, you can sign up for a new account if you already have a work or school account.

The following is the process to get started:

1. Log in to the Azure Portal.

After signing up for Intune, you can manage the service using any device with a supported browser.

By default, Azure AD requires you to have one of these permissions: Global Administrator or Intune Service Administrator.

Allowing users with other permissions to administer the service

Azure Service Map

Azure Service Map helps customers to gain insights into their physical and virtual networks. It provides visibility into the relationships between applications, processes, and network infrastructure, enabling customers to identify and understand how their applications are connected. It also helps customers to detect and troubleshoot network issues. Service Map helps customers identify and address security threats such as open ports or weak authentication methods.

Azure Monitor   The Azure Monitor is critical for monitoring our services. It collects and analyzes two fundamental types of data: metrics and logs. Monitoring in Azure consists of three key types of data: metrics, activity logs, and resource logs. Without raw information from services, systems, and applications, you cannot analyze insights and issues.

Furthermore, it can be used to identify resources that can be optimized, helping customers reduce their cloud costs. Service Maps can also monitor network performance, assisting customers in quickly identifying and resolving performance issues. It can be used to gather insights into network usage, allowing customers to make informed decisions about their network infrastructure. Service Maps can also be used for security, helping customers detect and respond to threats.

Additionally, it can be used to troubleshoot customer issues, helping them quickly identify and resolve any problems. Service Maps can also be used to optimize network performance, as customers can use them to identify areas of over-utilization and congestion. This allows them to adjust and increase the speed and reliability of their network. Service Map can also be used for compliance and audit purposes, helping customers ensure their network operates within local regulations.

Service Maps can also be used to detect security threats, such as malicious activity or cyberattacks, by providing insights into network traffic patterns. Finally, the Service Maps service can troubleshoot network issues and diagnose problems quickly.

A feature of Azure Monitor is called Service Map. Service Map maps the communication between services on Windows and Linux systems using Service Map. Your servers are interconnected systems that provide critical services with Service Map. Across any TCP-connected architecture, Service Map displays connections between servers, processes, and latency. Installation of an agent is the only configuration required.

Figure 3-7 depicts the Map tab via Azure Monitor in the Azure Portal.

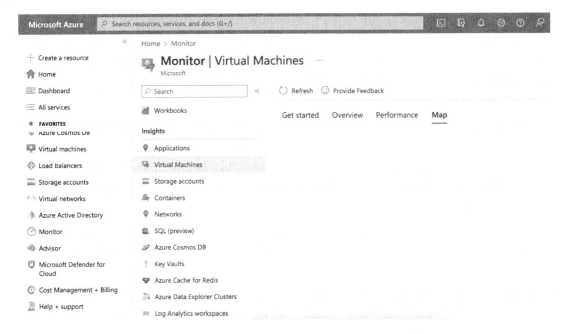

Figure 3-7. Azure Monitor's Maps tab

Service Map creates a standard reference map by automatically mapping dependencies across your servers, processes, and third-party services. All TCP dependencies are discovered and mapped. Managed systems attempt to make failed network connections using Service Map. A server misconfiguration, a service outage, or a network problem could be identified using this information.

Service Map helps eliminate the guesswork of problem isolation by showing you how systems are connected and affect each other. Along with identifying failed connections, it helps identify misconfigured load balancers, surprising or excessive load on critical services, and rogue clients, such as developer machines talking to production systems. Using integrated workflows with change tracking, you can also see whether a change event on a back-end machine or service explains the root cause of an incident.

On the server where they are installed, Service Map agents collect information about all TCP-connected processes. Additionally, they collect information about inbound and outbound connections.

You can visualize the dependencies between machines or groups that have Service Map agents in the left pane by selecting them from the list. There is a focus on a specific machine in machine dependency maps. A direct TCP client or server of that machine is shown. A machine group map shows the dependencies between sets of servers.

On the map, you can expand machines to show running process groups and processes with active network connections. Agentless front-end machines are connected to the focus machine via the left side of their processes. A server port group is created when a focus machine connects to a back-end machine without an agent. Other connections to the same port number are also included in this group.

Service Map shows dependency information for the last 30 minutes by default. Using the time controls at the upper left, you can view historical dependencies for a time range of up to one hour. If you want to see what they looked like before or after an incident, for example. Paid workspaces store Service Map data for 30 days, while free workspaces store it for 7 days.

A process group consists of processes associated with the same product or service. Expanding a machine node will display stand-alone processes as well as groups of processes. The connection to a process within a process group is marked as failed if it fails either inbound or outbound.

Rather than just seeing maps of one server, machine groups allow you to see maps of multiple servers. Multitier applications and server clusters can be visualized this way. Each server is assigned a name and a group is created by the user. After that, you can choose to view all the processes and connections of the group. The group can also be viewed with only the processes and connections pertaining to its members.

How to Enable It

The Azure Monitor can collect data from multiple sources, including your application, the platform, the operating systems, and the services it uses.

As soon as you create an Azure resource that supports metrics, this data is collected and sent into the Azure Monitor metrics data store by the Azure platform.

Almost all Azure resources emit metrics every minute, but a few metrics are emitted every five minutes.

You can export metrics to a third-party service for longer retention periods. Azure Monitor's metrics data store retains metrics for 93 days for free.

Azure Network Watcher and Network Security Group

Azure Network Watcher is a service that provides network monitoring and diagnostics for Azure virtual networks. It gives users visibility into their network performance, security, and network topology.

Azure Network Watcher can help detect, diagnose, and resolve network issues quickly and efficiently. It also provides powerful analytics to help improve network performance. It helps assess network security, troubleshoot network issues, and optimize network performance. Network Watcher is an invaluable resource for Azure users, as it helps keep their networks running smoothly and securely. It is an essential tool for managing and optimizing Azure networks.

Azure Network Watcher offers advanced monitoring and analytics capabilities. It can detect suspicious activity, alert users to potential security threats, and identify and troubleshoot network issues. Network Watcher also provides insights into traffic patterns and performance metrics that can help Azure users optimize their networks for maximum efficiency. It is an invaluable tool for managing and protecting Azure networks.

Azure Network Watcher is easy to use and helps users quickly detect and respond to security threats. It also reduces the need for manual intervention, making it an efficient and cost-effective solution for managing Azure networks.

Azure Network Watcher provides tools for monitoring, diagnosing, viewing metrics, and enabling or disabling logs for Azure virtual networks. As an infrastructure-as-a-service (IaaS) product, Network Watcher monitors and fixes the network health of virtual machines (VMs), virtual networks (VNets), application gateways, load balancers, etc.

Virtual machines, fully qualified domain names (FQDNs), uniform resource identifiers (URIs), and IPv4 addresses can all be used as endpoints. Monitoring communication between the VM and the endpoint regularly provides information on reachability, latency, and changes in the network topology. For example, you might have a database server VM communicating with a web server VM. Someone in your organization may change the web server, database server VM, or subnet without your knowledge.

The connection troubleshooting feature informs you of unreachable endpoints. VMs may experience DNS name resolution problems, CPU problems, memory problems, firewall issues, hop types of custom routes, or security rules for the VM or subnet.

Figure 3-8 depicts the Network Watcher.

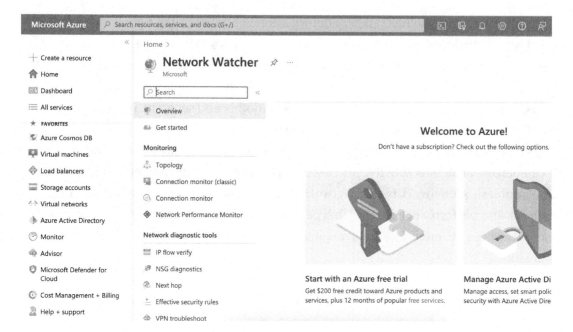

Figure 3-8. *Azure Network Watcher*

Furthermore, the connection monitor displays the minimum, average, and maximum latency observed over time. You may reduce the latency for a connection by moving your Azure resources to different Azure regions after learning the latency for a connection. Instead of monitoring the connection over time as you would with a connected monitor, you can use connection troubleshooting if you would rather test the connection at a specific point in time.

You can monitor network performance between different points in your network infrastructure with Network Performance Monitor, a cloud-based hybrid network monitoring solution. As well as monitoring network connectivity to application and service endpoints, Azure ExpressRoute's performance can also be monitored. Traditional network monitoring methods cannot detect traffic blackholing, routing errors, and network performance issues. When a threshold for a network link is breached, the solution generates alerts and notifies you. Furthermore, it ensures the timely detection of network performance problems and pinpoints the source of the problem to a specific device or network segment.

Adding resources to a virtual network can make it difficult to understand how they are related and what resources are in the network. Topology allows you to visualize the resources in a virtual network and their relationships.

VM network interfaces are protected by network security groups (NSGs).

An NSG is a network-level firewall that controls traffic in and out of a virtual network. It allows you to create rules that filter traffic based on port, protocol, and source and destination IP addresses. This helps to protect against malicious activity and ensure that only the desired traffic has access to the network. NSGs can be used to segment traffic within a virtual network, allowing for greater control over data flow. This ensures that only the necessary traffic is allowed in and out, helping to protect the network from malicious activity.

Additionally, the rules can be configured to allow for different levels of access based on the type of traffic, ensuring that only the desired traffic is allowed into the network. By setting up rules within the NSGs, administrators can control the traffic flow within the network and keep it secure. This will enable them to block traffic from malicious sources and limit access to only authorized ones. Additionally, the rules within an NSG can be configured to prioritize certain types of traffic over others, ensuring that the most critical traffic is given priority and passes through the network quickly and securely.

An NSG protects the organization's digital assets from cyber security threats. They develop and implement security policies, procedures, and technologies to ensure the safety of the network. They also investigate and respond to security incidents. The NSG monitors traffic to detect suspicious activities and potential threats. They regularly review system logs and assess vulnerabilities to identify and address security risks. They also provide training and guidance to users on security best practices and advice on security strategies. They ensure that all security systems are up-to-date and working correctly. Finally, they work closely with other IT teams to ensure the network's security.

You can log the IP address, port number, protocol, and whether traffic was approved or denied using the NSG flow log capability. Power BI and traffic analytics are tools you can use to analyze logs. Data written to NSG flow logs can be visualized using traffic analytics.

Various Azure networking resources can be configured to log diagnostic information, including network security groups, public IP addresses, load balancers, virtual network gateways, and application gateways. Any existing network resource that generates a diagnostic log can be enabled and disabled using the diagnostic logs capability. Microsoft Power BI and Azure Monitor logs can be used to view diagnostic logs.

How to Enable It

You must have an existing Network Watcher instance or enable Network Watcher in each region where you have NSGs that you want to analyze traffic for. The traffic analytics feature can be enabled for any region where NSGs are hosted.

A network security group must be created before NSG flow logging can be enabled. If you don't have one, create one.

You will need to complete the following steps to turn on Network Watcher:

1. Log in to the Azure Portal.

2. Go to Network Watcher and then choose NSG Flow.

Azure Information Protection

You can securely share sensitive data outside your company, such as emails, documents, and documents. With Azure Information Protection, you can enhance data protection no matter where it's stored or who it's shared with—with easy classification, embedded labels, and permissions. You can also track and revoke access if needed, as well as detect any unauthorized access attempts. Azure Information Protection is designed to keep your data secure, no matter where it is or who it's shared with. It ensures that only the right people have access to the right data.

Azure Information Protection is a data classification and protection solution that helps organizations securely share data with their customers and partners. It uses encryption, identify, and access management to identify, classify, and protect sensitive data. The solution enables organizations to classify and protect data based on its sensitivity and relevance to the organization and its stakeholders.

Azure Information Protection also provides detailed reporting and auditing capabilities, allowing organizations to monitor and track data usage, detect anomalies, and ensure compliance with regulatory requirements. It also provides the ability to revoke access to shared data at any time. It also provides granular control over who can access the data, ensuring only authorized users can access it.

Azure Information Protection helps organizations maintain data security and protect sensitive information from unauthorized access. It enables organizations to control their data and monitor its usage. It also helps organizations to comply with data privacy regulations by providing a secure environment to store, process, and access data. This, in turn, allows organizations to protect their data and reduce the risk of data breaches.

Azure Information Protection also provides an extra layer of security by encrypting data stored in the cloud. It also uses machine learning to identify and classify sensitive data, making it easier for organizations to manage and protect their data.

Azure Information Protection (AIP) is part of Microsoft Purview Information Protection, previously known as Microsoft Information Protection (MIP). Regardless of where sensitive information lives or travels, Microsoft Purview Information Protection helps you discover, classify, protect, and govern it.

Azure Information Protection offers the following:

- Data sensitivity can be classified, labeled, and protected using policies. Azure Information Protection provides fully automatic, user-driven, and recommendation-based classification.

- Protect your data no matter where it's stored or with whom it's shared by adding classification and protection information.

- Ensure that shared data is being tracked and revoked as needed. Monitoring, analyzing, and reasoning over data can be done with powerful logging and reporting tools.

- Ensure that your co-workers, customers, and partners have access to your data safely. Allow users to view and edit files but not print or forward them. Define who can access data and what they can do with it.

- You can secure the data you're working on with one click in Microsoft Office and most typical applications. A recommended classification notification in the product assists users in making the right decisions.

- Whether your data is stored on-premises or in the cloud, we can help protect it. Bring your own key (BYOK) and hold your own key (HYOK) are two ways to manage encryption keys.

AIP classifies and protects information by applying labels to documents and emails. The AIP client must be installed on all machines you want to use AIP features. A plan for classifying, labeling, and protecting information using the Azure Information Protection scanner or client would be helpful.

AIP uses Azure Rights Management (Azure RMS) to protect your data. It can be used with other Microsoft Azure applications and services, such as Office 365 and Azure Active Directory, as well as with your applications and other information security solutions. Azure RMS supports cloud and on-premises solutions. Using Azure RMS, you can encrypt, identify, and authorize users. In the same way as AIP labels, Azure RMS ensures that your content is protected even when it is shared, regardless of where the documents or emails are located.

You can restrict data access to users within your organization once the Azure Rights Management service is activated. Apply more restrictive controls to new templates by configuring your protection settings. The Azure Rights Management templates can be used with applications and services that support the service.

How to Enable It

Azure Information Protection requires that your organization have a service plan that includes Azure Rights Management.

All users in your organization can apply protection to their documents and emails when the protection service has been activated, and all users can open (consume) protected documents and emails. Alternatively, you can use onboarding controls to phase out the deployment of information protection if you prefer.

PowerShell is now the only way to activate or deactivate Azure RMS.

1. Configure and manage the protection service by installing the AIPService module.

2. Connect-AIPService should be run from a PowerShell session, and you should provide the Global Administrator account details for your Azure Information Protection tenant when prompted.

3. You can check whether the protection service is active by running Get-AIPService. If the status is Enabled, the service is active; if it is Disabled, the service is deactivated.

4. Activate the service by running Enable-AIPService.

Azure AD Privilege Identify Management

Azure AD Privilege Identify Management is a cloud-based service that helps organizations manage access to privileged accounts and resources. It provides visibility into who has access to what and additional security features like multifactor authentication and Conditional Access policies.

Importance of Privilege Identify Management   Privilege Identify Management helps organizations protect their data and systems from malicious actors. It allows organizations to create and enforce privileges for users and applications, ensuring that only authorized personnel can access sensitive data and resources. This helps organizations maintain compliance with data privacy regulations and minimize the risk of a security breach.

AD Privilege Identify Management allows organizations to reduce the risk of unauthorized access to privileged accounts, improve audibility, and maintain compliance with various regulations. Azure AD Privilege Identify Management also provides detailed reporting capabilities to give organizations further insights into their privileged access.

Azure AD Privilege Identify Management uses an automated, policy-driven approach to secure and manage privileged accounts, which helps to ensure that only authorized users can access the accounts. This helps reduce the risk of malicious actors gaining access to the accounts and makes it easier to audit and keep track of who has access to the accounts. Additionally, the detailed reporting capabilities provide organizations with greater visibility into the access granted to privileged accounts, which helps to maintain compliance with various regulations.

AD Privilege Identify Management helps ensure that only the right people have access to the accounts and that access is used appropriately. Additionally, it can help to detect potential suspicious activity and security breaches. This, in turn, reduces the risk of a data breach, providing organizations with peace of mind.

Furthermore, it can help organizations identify weaknesses in their security policies and make necessary changes. This can help protect an organization's data and reputation and reduce its liability. Regular monitoring of access can also help organizations comply with data privacy regulations.

The Privileged Identify Management (PIM) service works with Azure AD to allow you to manage, control, and monitor access to vital resources within your organization. Azure AD, Azure, and other Microsoft Online Services, such as Microsoft 365 or Microsoft Intune, are among these resources.

A company wants to limit the number of people who have access to secure information or resources because that reduces the risk of the following:

- Malicious actors gaining access

- Authorized users using sensitive resources inadvertently

It is still necessary for users to perform privileged operations within Azure AD, Azure, Microsoft 365, or SaaS apps. By granting just-in-time access to Azure and Azure AD resources, organizations can keep tabs on how their privileged users use them.

Privileged Identify Management provides time-based and approval-based role activation to mitigate the risk of excessive, unnecessary, or misused access permissions on resources you care about. Privileged Identify Management provides the following key features:

- Azure AD and Azure resources can be accessed just-in-time.

- By assigning start and end dates to resources, you can limit access to resources for a defined time bound.

- Activating privileged roles requires approval.

- To activate any role, multifactor authentication must be enabled.

- Use it to understand why users activate can be accomplished by using justification.

- PIM activates privileged roles and receive notifications.

- PIM makes sure roles are still needed by conducting access reviews.

- Internal or external audit history can be downloaded.

- PIM protects the last active role assignment for Global Administrators and Privileged Role Administrators.

Upon setting up Privileged Identify Management, you'll see the Tasks, Manage, and Activity options in the navigation menu on the left. Administrators can choose between managing Azure AD roles, Azure resource roles, or PIM for groups. You will see the appropriate options depending on what you want to manage.

Users can only manage assignments for other administrators with the privileged role of Administrator or Global Administrator role in Privileged Identify Management. Privileged Identify Management also allows the Global Administrators, Security Administrators, Global Readers, and Security Readers roles to view Azure AD roles.

Subscription administrators can manage assignments for Azure resource roles, resource owners, or resource user access administrators in Privileged Identify Management. Assignments to Azure resource roles in Privileged Identify Management are not accessible by default to Privileged Role Administrators, Security Administrators, or Security Readers.

How to Enable It

Licenses required for Privileged Identify Management include Azure AD Premium P2 and Enterprise Mobility + Security (EMS) E5.

With PIM, roles can be activated based on time and approval, reducing the chances of excessive, unnecessary, or misused access permissions. These resources include Microsoft Azure Active Directory (Azure AD), Azure, and Microsoft Online Services like Microsoft 365 or Microsoft Intune.

You will need to complete the following steps to turn on Azure PIM:

1. Log in to the Azure Portal.

2. Choose "All services" and locate the Azure AD Privileged Identify Management service.

3. Click Privileged Identify Management QuickStart.

Privilege Access Management

Privileged access management (PAM) is an identify security solution that monitors, detects, and prevents unauthorized access to critical resources to protect organizations from cyber threats. As a result of a combination of people, processes, and technology,

PAM provides visibility into who is using privileged accounts and what they are doing. Additional layers of protection mitigate data breaches by threat actors by limiting the number of users with access to administrative functions.

Privilege Access Management   Privilege Access Management ensures that only authorized users can access an organization's critical resources while protecting those resources from malicious actors. It also allows organizations to monitor and audit user access, ensuring compliance with all applicable regulations. Privilege Access Management also helps to detect and prevent unauthorized access attempts and any attempts to misuse privileged access. It also provides a secure platform for users to access and manage critical resources without compromising security.

Privilege Access Management also simplifies the process of monitoring user activities and helps organizations comply with security policies. It can be used to automatically revoke access when users leave the organization or change roles, ensuring that access is always secure. It also helps detect and respond to potential threats quickly, making it easier for organizations to protect their data and maintain their security posture. Azure Privilege Access Management is an essential tool for organizations looking to secure their data and maintain compliance.

It is also cost-effective and easy to deploy, making it a great tool for organizations of any size. Azure Privilege Access Management is a powerful tool for keeping organizations secure and compliant. In addition, Azure Privilege Access Management provides peace of mind with its comprehensive security and compliance features.

Using PAM, organizations can prevent unauthorized access to critical resources by monitoring, detecting, and preventing privileged access. It is possible to track who uses privileged accounts and what they do while logged in with PAM by combining people, processes, and technology. Limiting the number of users with access to administrative functions is essential, as this increases the system's security while adding additional layers of protection mitigates the risk of data breaches.

PAM solutions identify the people, processes, and technology requiring privileged access and define their policies. Account creation, amendments, and deletion should be automated in your PAM solution (for example, automated password management and multifactor authentication). Your PAM solution should continuously monitor sessions to identify anomalies and investigate them.

Credential theft prevention and compliance are two primary uses of privileged access management.

For example, say an attacker steals a user's login information to access their account. The ability to log in allows them to access organizational data and install malware on devices. All admin identities and accounts can be accessed just-in-time and just enough with PAM solutions.

Protecting sensitive data, such as payment or health information, may require a least-privilege policy if your organization must comply with compliance standards. Using a PAM solution, you can generate reports showing which data is accessed by which users.

In addition, users may be automatically created, provisioned, and decommissioned, privileged accounts can be monitored, remote access can be secured, and third-party access can be controlled. PAM solutions can also manage DevOps projects, devices (the Internet of Things), and cloud environments.

Cybersecurity threats can cause serious and extensive damage to organizations when privileged access is misused. Keeping ahead of this risk is easier with a PAM solution.

- Ensure critical resources are accessible just-in-time.

- Passwords can be replaced with encrypted gateways for secure remote access.

- Support investigative audits by monitoring privileged sessions.

- Identify an unusual privileged activity that could harm your organization.

- To audit compliance, capture events related to privileged accounts.

- Produce reports on the action and access of privileged users.

- Implement password security for DevOps.

Privileged accounts pose a significant risk to your organization because humans control them. As a result of PAM, security teams can identify malicious activities resulting from privilege abuse and take immediate actions to remediate the risks. A PAM solution can provide employees only the access they need.

Your organization can also benefit from a PAM solution by identifying malicious activities linked to privilege abuse.

- Keep security breaches to a minimum. PAM solutions help limit the impact of violations if they do occur.

- Threat actors need fewer entry points and pathways. People, processes, and applications have limited privileges to protect themselves from internal and external threats.

- You can defend against malware attacks. Remove excessive privileges if malware gains a foothold.

- You can make the environment more audit-friendly. Monitor and detect suspicious activity with activity logs to achieve a comprehensive security and risk management strategy.

How to Enable It

For your organization's security and risk mitigation, you should follow best practices when planning for and implementing a PAM solution.

- *Implement multifactor authentication*: Adding multifactor authentication to the sign-in process ensures that users are authenticated through another verified device when accessing accounts or apps.

- *Automate your security*: You can improve your security environment by automating it, for example, by restricting privileges and preventing unsafe or unauthorized actions when a threat is detected.

- *Remove endpoint users*: It is essential to remove unnecessary endpoint users from local admin groups on IT Windows workstations. Threat actors can use these accounts to leap between workstations, steal other credentials, and elevate their privileges to move through the network.

- *Establish baselines and monitor variations*: Knowing the baseline for acceptable activity in your system helps you spot deviations that may compromise your system. Looking at privileged access activity lets you see who is doing what in the design and how privileged passwords are used.

- *Equip just-in-time access*: Applying the least-privilege principle to every system and network is essential. This will help you segment systems and networks according to levels of trust, needs, and privileges.

- *Get rid of perpetual privileged access*: Instead of perpetual privileged access, consider temporary just-in-time access and just-enough access, ensuring that users only need such access for a limited time.

- *Use activity-based access control*: The gap between privileges granted and those users should be minimized by granting privileges only to resources a person uses.

It would be best if you had the plan to get started with privileged access management.

- You should be able to see all privileges used by humans and workloads using your PAM solution. Once you have this visibility, you should remove default admin accounts and apply the least privilege principle.

- Stay current on privileged access and control privilege elevation to prevent it from getting out of hand and compromising your organization's cybersecurity.

- Establish policies that define acceptable behavior for privileged users and identify any actions that violate those policies. Monitor and audit privileged activities.

- With automated PAM solutions, you can scale across millions of users, assets, and privileged accounts to improve your security and compliance. You can automate discovery, management, and monitoring to simplify your administration.

Depending on your IT department, you can use your PAM solution immediately and then gradually add modules to increase functionality and help you meet compliance requirements.

Business Environment (ID.BE)

Cybersecurity roles, responsibilities, and risk management decisions are informed by understanding the organization's mission, objectives, stakeholders, and activities.

Let's now to explore the Azure NIST Identify mapping for a business environment and Microsoft's outlined responsibility classification among Microsoft and customers, which is in line with the cloud security shared responsibility models.

Figure 3-9 depicts the subcategories of the Azure mapping against the Identify module of the NIST CSF.

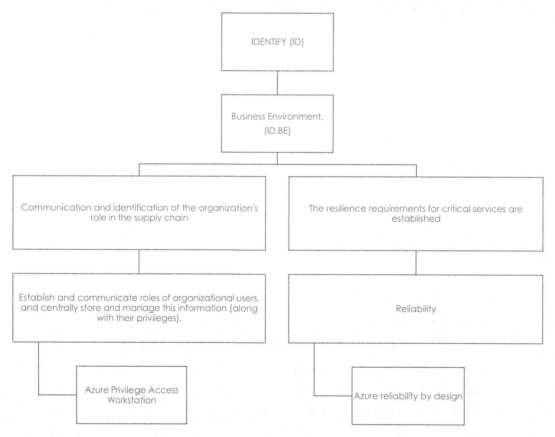

Figure 3-9. *NIST Identify business environment*

As part of the Azure cloud shared responsibility model, the NIST Cybersecurity Framework security functions are provided in Table 3-2 with respect to ID.BE.

Table 3-2. *Business Environment Responsibility Matrix*

Category	Subcategory	Informative References	Responsibility	Customer Responsibility	Microsoft Azure Responsibility
Business Environment (ID. BE): Defining cybersecurity roles and responsibilities and managing risks is based on the organization's mission, objectives, stakeholders, and activities.	ID.BE-1: Communication and identification of the organization's role in the supply chain	NIST SP 800-53 Rev. 4 CP-2, SA-12	Customer	Supply chain roles must be identified, documented, and communicated by customers.	N/A

(continued)

Table 3-2. (*continued*)

Category	Subcategory	Informative References	Responsibility	Customer Responsibility	Microsoft Azure Responsibility
	ID.BE-2: A description of the organization's role in critical infrastructure and its industry sector is provided	NIST SP 800-53 Rev. 4 PM-8	Customer	The customer must identify, document, and communicate all critical infrastructure used by the system. The customer's critical infrastructure includes but is not limited to Virtual Machines hosted by Azure subscriptions and virtual networks connecting Azure Virtual Machines.	N/A
	ID.BE-3: Establishing and communicating organizational mission, objectives, and activities	NIST SP 800-53 Rev. 4 PM-11, SA-14	Customer	Organization missions and business objectives must be identified, documented, and communicated by the customer.	N/A

ID.BE-4: Delivering critical services requires dependencies and critical functions.	NIST SP 800-53 Rev. 4 CP-8, PE-9, PE-11, PM-8, SA-14	Customer	A critical service provider must identify, document, and communicate dependencies.	N/A
ID.BE-5: The resilience requirements for critical services are established	NIST SP 800-53 Rev. 4 CP-2, CP-11, SA-14	Customer	The customer must identify and document resilience requirements for all operating states to ensure the delivery of critical services. The customer is responsible for enabling and documenting many services related to system resiliency (e.g., alternate processing location, alternate storage location) despite Microsoft Azure facilitating many solutions.	N/A

Privilege Access Workstation

Administrators, developers, and critical service operators require secure, isolated workstations for their security. Privileged access workstations should be kept up-to-date with the latest security patches and protections. They should also be monitored and audited regularly to detect and address any vulnerabilities quickly. Access to privileged workstations should be strictly limited and monitored, and any changes to the system should be documented and approved. Finally, privileged workstations should be regularly tested for vulnerabilities and integrity.

Privilege Access Workstation is a security solution designed to protect privileged accounts from potential threats. It provides advanced security protection and continuous monitoring to help protect against malicious attacks. It also helps reduce the risk of data breaches and other security incidents.

Importance of Privilege Access Workstation   PAWs are physical or virtual systems that access privileged accounts. These systems are isolated from other networks and must be closely monitored to prevent unauthorized access. PAWs are a crucial part of any organization's cybersecurity strategy, and they allow privileged users to access sensitive networks and data without risk of compromise. As a result, PAWs have become an essential tool for protecting an organization's data and systems from malicious actors.

A PAW can be deployed on-premises or in Azure using Azure Active Directory, Microsoft Defender, or Microsoft Intune. Secure configuration, including strong authentication, software and hardware baselines, and restricted logical and network access, should be managed centrally in the PAW. Regular monitoring and auditing should be done to ensure the PAW is secure and compliant with security policies. Any detected violations should be documented and addressed immediately. Furthermore, all users should be trained in the importance of security and the proper usage of the PAW. Security policies should be reviewed periodically, and any changes should be applied immediately. Systems and applications should be regularly patched to ensure the latest security updates are used. Access to the PAW should be revoked for any users who no longer require it.

Additionally, Azure Bastion can be provisioned within your virtual network as a fully platform-managed service that allows direct RDP/SSH access from the Azure portal. This service provides secure, seamless connectivity to virtual machines over the Internet without exposing the virtual machine to public IP addresses. Azure Bastion is also highly available, with built-in redundancy to protect against service outages. This makes it an excellent choice for organizations that need secure remote access to their virtual machines. Azure Bastion is also easily configurable and requires minimal maintenance. It provides an additional layer of security by securely connecting users to their virtual machines through the Azure Portal, utilizing encryption protocols such as SSL/TLS. It also helps protect against malicious attacks by ensuring that virtual machines are not exposed to public IP addresses. It also offers secure access to virtual machines for users with limited privileges, as it does not require them to have administrative credentials. This allows organizations to grant secure access to users without sacrificing security.

Microsoft Azure Bastion

Azure Bastion is designed to protect your virtual machines by providing private and secure access from the public Internet without exposing your virtual machines directly to the internet. It provides secure access to your virtual machines by using SSL encryption with no exposure of the private IP address. Additionally, it provides an easy-to-use web-based interface, allowing users to easily access their virtual machines without configuring any additional software or hardware. It also provides other security measures such as IP allow listing and two-factor authentication, ensuring that only authorized users can access your virtual machines. It also allows for easy management of user access permissions.

Furthermore, it allows for automated backups and disaster recovery, ensuring that all data is secure and easily recoverable in an emergency. Additionally, it provides granular control over user access, allowing for faster access management. It also provides detailed audit logs to monitor user activity and detect any suspicious activity. This makes it an ideal solution for businesses looking to ensure their data is secure and readily available.

By using a Bastion host, you'll be protected from port scanning, malware, and other threats targeting your VMs. It's not necessary to harden each one separately.

You can eliminate the need to manually deploy your own jump box by using Azure Bastion. It's cost-effective because it charges on a per-hour basis, plus charges for sending data out of the platform.

Azure Reliability by Design

The reliability of Azure helps keep businesses running smoothly, offering a 99.9 percent uptime guarantee on its services. It also provides proactive monitoring, backup, and data recovery capabilities that help ensure data is secure and available. Additionally, it offers disaster recovery solutions to help protect against potential outages.

"Azure reliability by design" is a set of technologies and best practices integrated into the development process to ensure that cloud applications and services are reliable and resilient. This includes the use of automation, monitoring, and proactive management of the system. This allows Azure to provide a reliable and secure environment for its customers. In addition, it also helps customers to reduce the cost and complexity of managing their cloud environment.

The Importance of Reliability   Cloud system reliability by design is an approach that focuses on making reliability a fundamental component of the cloud system from the very beginning of the development process. It includes techniques such as fault-tolerant design, redundancy, and error recovery. These techniques increase the reliability of the system, ensuring that it is able to handle any potential issues. This approach ensures that the system is built with reliability in mind from the ground up, rather than attempting to add reliability features onto an existing system. This helps to minimize the amount of time and resources needed to ensure the system is reliable, resulting in a more cost-effective and efficient system.

Reliability ensures that your application can meet your customers' expectations. You can provide the availability of your workloads and the ability to recover from failures at any scale by architecting resiliency into your application framework.

Reliability is built by doing the following:

- Creating a highly available architecture

- Recuperating from events such as data loss, significant downtime, or ransomware incidents

There are many built-in resilience features in Azure.

- You can automatically replicate data across availability zones and regions using Azure Storage, Azure SQL Database, or Azure Cosmos DB.

- Azure-managed disks are automatically placed in different storage scale units to limit the effects of hardware failures.

- An availability set consists of several fault domains for virtual machines (VMs). Fault domains consist of VMs with a standard power source and network switch. Physical hardware failures, network outages, and power outages can be minimized by spreading VMs across fault domains.

In addition, high availability needs to be balanced with high resiliency, low latency, and low cost. It is equally important for applications to recover from failures (resiliency).

Multitenant environments such as Azure are highly distributed and prone to failure. By anticipating failures from particular elements to entire Azure regions, you can design a solution in a resilient way to enhance reliability. The concept of reliability is subjective. For an application to be suitably reliable, it must echo the business requirements covering it.

To mitigate issues impacting application reliability, you must first detect them. Reliability issues can be detected and predicted by monitoring the application's operation compared to its healthy state. Taking swift and remedial action is possible with monitoring.

A system that self-heals can deal with failures automatically. Predefined remediation protocols are used to handle failures, and these protocols connect to failure modes within the solution. To achieve this level of maturity, the system must be monitored and automated to a high degree. Aiming to maximize reliability should be the goal of self-healing from the start.

Azure services offer a wide range of cloud-native services to support reliability such as Azure Front Door, Azure Traffic Manager, Azure Load Balancer, Azure Virtual Network NAT, Service Fabric, Kubernetes Service (AKS), and Azure Site Recovery.

During the architectural phase, Microsoft recommends implementing practices that meet your business requirements, identifying failure points, and minimizing the scope of failures.

Reliability by design means the following:

- *Establish recovery and availability targets that meet the needs of the business*: SLAs are availability targets that represent a commitment to performance and availability. To define reliability targets, it is crucial to understand each component's service level agreement (SLA). In a disaster, recovery targets determine the duration of the workload's unavailability and the amount of data that can be lost. Identify critical scenarios and target reports for the application. Penalties, such as finance charges, may apply if an SLA is not met. The consequences of not moving availability targets should be fully understood.

- *Platforms and applications must meet your reliability requirements*: Designing application and data platform resiliency and availability are essential to securing overall application reliability.

- *Promote availability by configuring connection paths*: For improving Azure service reliability and connection availability, Microsoft recommends the following:

  - Use a global load balancer for traffic distribution and failover across regions.

  - Ensure there are redundant connections from different locations for cross-premises connectivity (ExpressRoute or VPN).

  - To ensure connectivity over alternative paths, simulate a failure path.

  - Eradicate all single points of failure from the data path between on-premises and Azure.

- *To improve reliability and reduce costs, use availability zones where possible*: When failure scenarios affect regional data centers, zone-aware services can help improve availability and reliability. They can also deploy gateway instances across zones for enhanced reliability and availability during delinquency strategies concerning a regional data center.

- *Build a resilient application architecture*: A critical application scenario or function should be able to operate even when affected by regional or zonal failures of services or components. Application operations may encounter diminished functionality or degraded arrangement during an outage.

- *Understand the consequences of not meeting service level agreements*: Early in the design process, FMA incorporates resilience into applications. Using it will allow you to identify the types of failures your application might experience, their potential effects, and possible recovery strategies. With its help, you can identify how your application might fail, its potential effects, and what recovery strategies you can use in the event of a failure. The single point of failure is a fault point in an application that would bring it down if it were to fail. When a single component fails, an application will be unavailable, presenting a significant risk. Are every fault point and fault mode identified? In an application architecture, fault points represent elements that may fail, while fault modes represent how fault points may fall. All fault points and ways must be apprehended and operationalized to confirm an application is resilient to end-to-end failures.

- *Build resilience in the system by identifying possible failure points*: Dependencies play a critical role in the functionality and availability of an application. Strong dependencies will affect overall availability, whereas weak dependencies may affect only specific features. An application can be classified as strong or weak based on its ability to continue functioning even without its dependencies.

- *Assure applications can work in the lack of their dependencies*: The cloud application must be able to scale as usage changes. Design the application so that it automatically responds to changes in load when they occur. Uphold scaling limits in mind during design so you can grow smoothly in the future.

Governance (ID.GV)

Cybersecurity governance establishes and enforces policies, standards, and procedures designed to protect your organization's digital assets and information systems. It is an integral part of any organization's risk management strategy and helps to ensure compliance with relevant regulations. It is essential to have a comprehensive cybersecurity governance program in place to protect the organization from cyber-attacks, data breaches, and other security incidents. Regular program reviews are essential to ensure its effectiveness and compliance with industry standards. Regular training of staff is also essential to ensure they are aware of the latest security protocols and best practices.

Additionally, organizations should invest in the latest cybersecurity technologies to further protect their data and systems. Organizations should also regularly update their security policies to reflect the latest threats and risks. Regular audits should also be conducted to identify potential risks or vulnerabilities. Finally, organizations should ensure all employees know their responsibilities and adhere to security policies.

The policies, procedures, and processes to control and monitor the community's regulatory, legal, risk, ecological, and operational requirements are understood and inform cybersecurity risk management.

Let's now explore the Azure NIST Identify mapping for governance and Microsoft's outlined responsibility classification among Microsoft and customers, which is in line with the cloud security shared responsibility models.

Figure 3-10 depicts the NIST Identify mapping for governance.

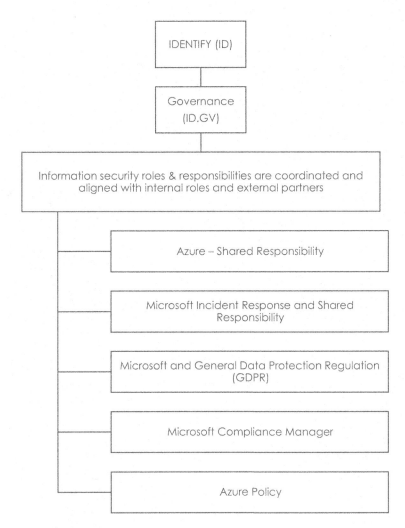

Figure 3-10. *NIST Identify governance*

As part of the Azure cloud shared responsibility model, the NIST CSF security functions are provided in Table 3-3 with respect to ID.GV.

Table 3-3. *ID.GV Responsibility Matrix*

Category	Subcategory	Informative References	Responsibility	Customer Responsibility	Microsoft Azure Responsibility
Governance (ID. GV): Organizational policies, procedures, and processes govern the management of cybersecurity risks, including regulations, legal requirements, risk management, environmental management, and operational management.	ID.GV-1: The organization establishes an information security policy.	NIST SP 800-53 Rev. 4 -1 controls from all families	Shared	Organizations are responsible for establishing information security policies and procedures to manage and monitor regulatory, legal, risk, environmental, and operational requirements and inform themselves about cybersecurity risks.	As part of Microsoft Azure Compliance, all Azure assets are subject to the Microsoft Security Policy. Among the items included in the policy are the roles and requirements of applicable personnel, the scope covering properties and services, and the roles and responsibilities of those involved.
	ID.GV-2: Coordination and alignment of information security roles and responsibilities with internal and external partners	NIST SP 800-53 Rev. 4 PM-1, PS-7	Customer	The customer is responsible for identifying and documenting information security roles and responsibilities. Microsoft Azure positions must align with internal roles under the customer's internal policies.	N/A

ID.GV-3: Understanding and managing cybersecurity legal and regulatory obligations, such as privacy and civil liberties	NIST SP 800-53 Rev. 4 -1 controls from all families (except PM-1)	Customer	The customer must develop, document, and disseminate regulatory and legal requirements concerning cybersecurity.	N/A
ID.GV-4: Risk management and governance processes address cybersecurity issues	NIST SP 800-53 Rev. 4 PM-9, PM-11	Customer	The customer is responsible for developing, documenting, and disseminating cybersecurity risk management policies and procedures.	N/A

Microsoft Incident Response and Shared Responsibility

Microsoft provides tools and services to help customers detect, investigate, and respond to security incidents. Customers have a shared responsibility to ensure the security and compliance of their environment. Microsoft provides guidance and recommended best practices to help customers meet security objectives. Regularly monitoring security logs and analytics can help customers detect suspicious activity and take action quickly. Customers should also ensure they have the appropriate personnel and processes in place to respond to security incidents should they arise. Microsoft supports customers in all security aspects, from training to incident response. Microsoft also offers a wide range of security products, such as its Azure Security Center, to help customers protect their data and systems.

Additionally, Microsoft provides security awareness training to help customers stay up-to-date with the latest security threats. Microsoft also provides security consulting services to help customers identify, assess, and mitigate risks. The company also offers a variety of tools and services to help customers detect, investigate, and respond to security incidents. Finally, Microsoft works closely with customers to help them develop secure development practices.

Key Points   Microsoft Incident Response provides an array of services to help organizations respond to security incidents. These services include incident analysis, malware investigation and analysis, and forensic analysis. Microsoft also provides a wide range of resources for incident response teams. Microsoft also offers specialized consulting services and training for incident response teams to help them develop the skills and knowledge needed to effectively respond to security incidents. In addition, Microsoft provides guidance on detecting, investigating, and responding to security incidents. Microsoft also offers a range of tools and services to help incident response teams investigate and analyze security incidents. These tools and services include digital forensics, threat intelligence, and advanced analytics.

Incident response is primarily a reactive practice in the security operations (SecOps) discipline, and it consists of investigating and remediating active attacks on your organization.

As a measure of how well security operations can reduce organizational risk, the incident response directly impacts the mean time to acknowledge (MTTA) and mean time to remediate (MTTR). For incident response teams to reduce risk, good working relationships between threat hunters, intelligence, and incident management teams (if present) are crucial.

In SecOps, the system's security assurances are maintained and restored when live adversaries attack it. The NIST CSF describes how to detect, respond, and recover well.

- The SecOps team must detect adversaries in the network, who are often incentivized to remain hidden, enabling them to achieve their objectives unhindered. In the enterprise activity logs, this can be done proactively or in response to an alert of suspicious activity.

- As soon as SecOps detects a potential adversary action or campaign, they should investigate whether an actual attack is underway (a true positive) or a false alarm (a false positive). They should also enumerate the purpose and scope of the adversary operation.

- SecOps is ultimately responsible for preserving and restoring business services (confidence, integrity, and availability) following an attack.

The biggest security risk is from human attack operators (of varying skill levels) for most organizations. Anti-malware products built with signature and machine learning approaches have significantly reduced the risk of automated/repeated attacks for most organizations. Despite this, there are notable exceptions, such as WannaCrypt and NotPetya, which moved faster than these defenses.

Because of their adaptability, human attack operators are challenging to counter (instead of automated/repeated logic), but they also operate at the same rate of speed as defenders.

A security operations center (SOC) is crucial in limiting an attacker's time and access to valuable systems and data. A malicious attacker can continue conducting attack operations and gaining access to sensitive systems for as long as they remain in the environment.

Microsoft and General Data Protection Regulation

General Data Protection Regulation (GDPR) is a regulation in the European Union that requires organizations to protect the personal data of their customers and employees.

The GDPR Advisory Board comprises experts from law, technology, and data protection who can provide guidance and advice on how to best comply with the GDPR.

What Is GDPR?   Privacy and security laws are stricter in the EU under the GDPR than elsewhere. Even though it was drafted and passed by the EU, it imposes obligations on any organization that targets or collects information about European citizens. GDPR came into effect on May 25, 2018. If a company violates its privacy and security standards, harsh fines will be imposed, reaching millions.

The GDPR Toolkit is designed to give customers the information they need to understand their data protection obligations. At the same time, the training and certification programs offer customers the skills to manage their data effectively in compliance with the GDPR. The GDPR Advisory Board is there to provide an expert, impartial perspective on the GDPR. At the same time, the Toolkit and training programs are designed to ensure customers are fully informed and equipped to comply with the regulations. This combination of expert insights and practical, hands-on education gives customers the information and skills they need to manage their data in line with the GDPR properly.

Microsoft has ensured its products and services comply with GDPR standards. It has implemented various measures, such as data encryption, to protect personal data. Microsoft has also provided tools to help organizations understand and manage their data. It has also established a data protection officer role to monitor compliance with GDPR. Microsoft has also conducted audits to ensure its products and services meet GDPR requirements. They have also proactively guided customers on how to comply with GDPR. Finally, Microsoft has set up a GDPR Compliant Center to help customers with GDPR compliance.

Microsoft also offers a GDPR Assessment Toolkit to help organizations assess and prepare for GDPR. It has also launched a GDPR Compliance Toolkit to help customers understand how to manage their data in compliance with the GDPR.

Microsoft Compliance Manager

The Microsoft Compliance Manager helps organizations ensure their operations comply with applicable laws, regulations, and industry standards. It provides an integrated platform for managing and monitoring compliance processes and tools for helping organizations detect and respond to potential compliance risks. Compliance Manager also offers real-time reporting and analytics capabilities to help organizations identify gaps in their compliance posture. It can also be integrated with other Microsoft solutions, such as Office 365 and Dynamics 365.

On the Compliance Manager overview page, you can see your current compliance score, what needs improvement, and take action to improve it (see Figure 3-11). As you complete improvement actions to comply with regulations, standards, or policies, Compliance Manager awards you points that are combined into an overall compliance score. Your score is affected differently by each action based on its potential risks, and you can prioritize which actions to focus on based on your compliance score.

Microsoft 365 Compliance Manager calculates your initial score based on the Microsoft 365 data protection baseline. The baseline includes key regulations and standards for data protection.

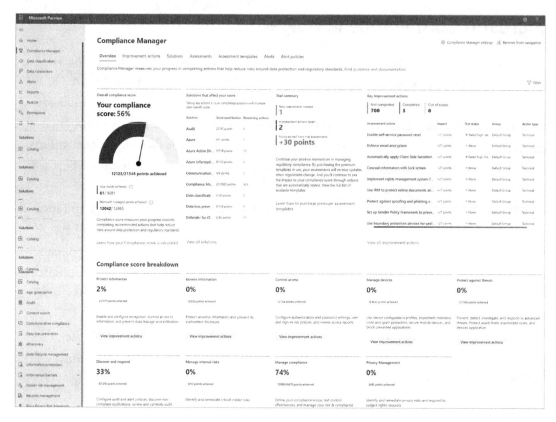

Figure 3-11. *Compliance Manager*

Azure Policy

Azure Policy helps organizations to define and enforce standards and practices at scale. It enables customers to define policy rules that are applied to Azure resources to ensure compliance with company standards and service level agreements. It also provides visibility into their cloud environment and helps to detect and remediate noncompliant resources. Azure Policy also helps organizations to quickly identify and respond to security threats in their cloud environment. It helps to enforce security best practices and ensure that resources are compliant with industry regulations.

Additionally, Azure Policy helps to reduce operational costs and helps organizations to optimize their cloud usage. Azure Policy helps to automate the process of ensuring compliance and security, allowing organizations to focus on other tasks and projects. It also provides organizations with the ability to audit and monitor their cloud resources in real-time. This visibility into their environment allows organizations to quickly identify any gaps in security or compliance, as well as potential areas of improvement. This makes it easier to take corrective action and mitigate any potential risks. It also enables organizations to automate the process of responding to any risks, ensuring that their cloud environment stays secure and compliant. This helps to reduce the time and effort required for managing their cloud environment, freeing up valuable resources for other projects.

Additionally, organizations can take advantage of the scalability of the cloud to quickly respond to changing business needs and optimize their cloud environment for cost efficiency. This helps to ensure that organizations are able to maximize the value of their cloud investments. Automated cloud management tools can help organizations to achieve these goals by automating and optimizing cloud operations, providing visibility into their cloud usage, and enabling organizations to manage their cloud costs more effectively.

Risk Assessment (ID.RA)

In general, risk assessment evaluates the potential risks associated with a particular activity or project. It involves identifying and analyzing potential risks, determining the likelihood of their occurrence, and developing strategies to manage or mitigate them. Risk assessment helps organizations make informed decisions by understanding the risks associated with a certain activity or project. It also helps organizations develop strategies to reduce risks and ensure that the activity or project is conducted safely and efficiently. This allows organizations to save time and money by avoiding potential risks and problems before they occur. Risk assessment also helps organizations better understand their operations and the environment they operate in. This, in turn, allows organizations to make informed decisions and take proactive steps to identify and mitigate potential risks. Risk assessment also helps organizations build a strong safety culture and promote a safe working environment for employees. This also helps organizations to stay compliant with safety regulations, build trust with stakeholders, and improve their reputation in the marketplace.

Risk Assessment for Microsoft Azure

A risk assessment includes an analysis of the security, compliance, and privacy controls used by Microsoft Azure. The evaluation also includes a review of the architecture, operational processes, and customer-specific configurations. Finally, it evaluates the effectiveness of the security controls and recommends any necessary changes. Microsoft Azure also provides security recommendations to customers based on the assessment. Customers can use these recommendations to improve the security of their cloud environment. The evaluation also gives customers visibility into their security posture and compliance with industry standards. This gives customers confidence that their cloud environment is secure and compliant. It also allows customers to adjust and ensure that their security controls are up to date. This helps customers reduce the risk of a security breach and data loss, as well as protect their and customers' data. Ultimately, this allows customers to gain trust and maintain a good reputation.

Let's now explore the Azure NIST Identify mapping for risk assessment and Microsoft's outlined responsibility classification among Microsoft and customers, which is in line with the cloud security shared responsibility models.

Figure 3-12 depicts the NIST Identify category for risk assessment.

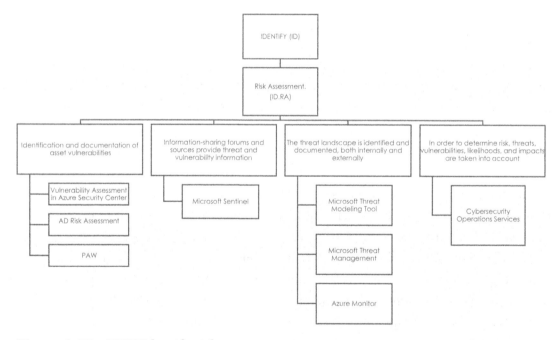

Figure 3-12. *NIST Identify risk assessment*

As part of the Azure cloud shared responsibility model, the NIST CSF security functions are provided in Table 3-4 with respect to ID.RA)

Table 3-4. *ID.RA Responsibility Matrix*

Category	Subcategory	Informative References	Responsibility	Customer Responsibility	Microsoft Azure Responsibility
Risk Assessment (ID.RA): Organizations know the cybersecurity risks to their operations (including mission, functions, image, and reputation), assets, and personnel.	ID.RA-1: The vulnerability of assets is identified and documented	NIST SP 800-53 Rev. 4 CA-2, CA-7, CA-8, RA-3, RA-5, SA-5, SA-11, SI-2, SI-4, SI-5	Shared	As a customer, you are responsible for continuously analyzing your system assets (e.g., customer applications, databases, and operating systems) for vulnerabilities. It is the customer's responsibility to document vulnerabilities once they are identified.	Microsoft Azure documents reflect any security issues or vulnerabilities identified or remediated as part of continuous monitoring. Using the vulnerability scanning processes, Microsoft Azure tracks vulnerabilities through closure. In addition to maintaining, securing, managing, and storing information system and asset documentation, Microsoft Azure service teams also keep a detailed record of known vulnerabilities.

(continued)

Table 3-4. (*continued*)

Category	Subcategory	Informative References	Responsibility	Customer Responsibility	Microsoft Azure Responsibility
	ID.RA-2: Information on cyber threats and vulnerabilities is obtained from information sharing forums and sources	NIST SP 800-53 Rev. 4 PM-15, PM-16, SI-5	Shared	The National Vulnerability Database (NVD), an updated database of vulnerabilities maintained by the National Institute of Standards and Technology (NIST), is one example of cyber threat intelligence.	Several external communications, including the United States Computer Emergency Readiness Team (US-CERT) and the National Information Security Agency (NVD), provide Microsoft Azure with cyber threat intelligence and vulnerabilities for all asset types. Microsoft Azure's Management Portal or a 24-hour dedicated phone line is available for reporting security incidents at any time. In addition, Azure disseminates alerts received from vendor websites and other third-party services (Internet Security System, US-CERT advisories, and alerts) throughout the organization. In addition to addressing notifications and disseminating security alerts (e.g., emails, RSS feeds) received directly from external organizations (US-CERT) other than the Services Operation Center or Microsoft Support, Microsoft Azure Security also addresses notifications received directly from external organizations (US-CERT).

| ID.RA-3: It is necessary to identify and document internal as well as external threats | NIST SP 800-53 Rev. 4 RA-3, SI-5, PM-12, PM-16 | Shared | Internal and external threats must be identified and documented by the customer. | Microsoft conducts and documents internal and external threats to Microsoft Azure and the information it processes, stores, or transmits to mitigate threats to Microsoft Azure. The probability and magnitude of harm resulting from unauthorized access, use, disclosure, disruption, modification, or destruction are included. |
| ID.RA-4: A business impact and likelihood analysis is conducted | NIST SP 800-53 Rev. 4 RA-2, RA-3, PM-9, PM-11, SA-14 | Customer | Customers must identify and document the potential business impact and likelihood of such events. | N/A |

(continued)

211

Table 3-4. (*continued*)

Category	Subcategory	Informative References	Responsibility	Customer Responsibility	Microsoft Azure Responsibility
	ID.RA-5: A threat's vulnerability, its likelihood, and its impact are used to determine a risk's level	NIST SP 800-53 Rev. 4 RA-2, RA-3, PM-16	Shared	Based on the identified vulnerabilities, threats, and business impacts, the customer determines risk.	Microsoft Azure determines risk by periodically assessing its environment and updating its policies and procedures. This is necessary to ensure compliance with changing regulations, contractual requirements, business processes, technical requirements, and operational requirements. Threats, vulnerabilities, likelihoods, and impacts influence risk. These factors include, but are not limited to, the likelihood and magnitude of harm that could occur if Microsoft Azure and the information it processes, stores, or transmits were accessed, used, disclosed, disrupted, modified, or destroyed by an unauthorized party. The risk of failure is assessed annually or as necessary.

| ID.RA-6: Identifying and prioritizing risk responses | NIST SP 800-53 Rev. 4 PM-4, PM-9 | Shared | Risks are identified and prioritized by the customer based on organizationally-defined risk tolerances. | Azure's Cloud+Enterprise (C+E) Security team prioritizes responses to identified risks. Security-related information generated by assessments and monitoring, such as vulnerability scan results and recurring control testing, is correlated and analyzed by the Microsoft Azure Continuous Monitoring team, which scans the Microsoft Azure environment monthly and analyzes it. Depending on the risk level, Azure prioritizes and mitigates all vulnerabilities based on actionability (i.e., requiring remediation), risk reduction, false positivity, or risk acceptance. |

Vulnerability Assessments in Microsoft Defender for Cloud

Vulnerability assessments identify and assess security weaknesses in an organization's information systems. These assessments help organizations prioritize their security efforts and identify areas to reduce risk.

Vulnerability assessments should be conducted regularly to keep up with the changing security landscape and new threats. Organizations should also implement measures to mitigate the risks identified in the assessments. Furthermore, organizations should develop a plan of action for addressing the identified weaknesses and regularly track their progress to ensure that the vulnerabilities are addressed effectively. Regular reviews should also be conducted to identify and address any new vulnerabilities.

Security breaches should be reported to the relevant authorities, and the organization should ensure that similar incidents do not happen. Security policies should be updated regularly to reflect the latest trends and technologies. Regular training should be provided to employees to ensure they know the organization's security policies. Employees should also be encouraged to report suspicious activity or security threats. Additionally, organizations should regularly monitor their systems to identify any security vulnerabilities. Security systems should also be tested periodically to ensure they are working correctly.

Qualys Integration with Defender for Cloud   Qualys powers the vulnerability scanner included with Microsoft Defender for Cloud. Qualys' scanner is one of the leading tools for the real-time identification of vulnerabilities, and it's available only with Microsoft Defender for Servers. You don't need a Qualys license or even a Qualys account; everything is handled seamlessly inside Defender for Cloud.

Organizations should also invest in the latest security technologies to protect their systems from cyber threats and should develop a disaster recovery plan to quickly and effectively respond to any security incidents.

Microsoft Defender for Cloud's vulnerability assessment is a security tool that helps protect your cloud infrastructure from cyber threats. It scans for vulnerabilities and provides detailed reports so you can identify and fix any potential security issues.

It helps to keep your data safe and secure. It also helps to identify malicious activities and suspicious behavior on your network. It can be used to monitor and detect any unauthorized access to your cloud infrastructure.

Figure 3-13 depicts the Microsoft Defender vulnerability management capabilities.

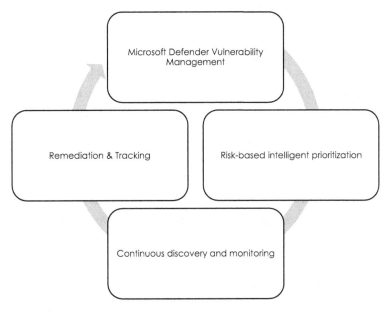

Figure 3-13. *Microsoft Defender vulnerability management capabilities*

Additionally, Microsoft Defender continuously monitors your cloud infrastructure for security threats. It detects any suspicious activities, such as data exfiltration, and can help to prevent data breaches. Microsoft Defender also provides visibility into the activities of privileged users, allowing administrators to monitor and detect any malicious or suspicious activity. In addition, it provides a secure platform for data storage and retrieval, ensuring data integrity and privacy. It also provides detailed insights into your cloud infrastructure, allowing you to identify any weak points and take preventive measures.

Microsoft Defender enables administrators to set granular access control policies for privileged users, ensuring that only authorized users can access sensitive data. Furthermore, its advanced analytics capabilities allow administrators to detect abnormal activities and take corrective measures quickly. Its secure data storage and retrieval capabilities also help protect data from unauthorized access and maintain its integrity. Moreover, Microsoft Defender offers automated patching for applications and systems, ensuring that all security vulnerabilities are addressed promptly. This helps to ensure that the system is secure from potential threats.

Microsoft Defender also provides real-time threat detection and response capabilities. This helps identify and immediately respond to potential security threats, ensuring that data and systems remain secure. Additionally, automated patching helps to ensure that any new security vulnerabilities are addressed quickly and effectively before malicious actors can exploit them.

Microsoft Defender also has various features to protect user data, such as data encryption, secure password storage, and two-factor authentication. These features ensure user data is kept safe, even if a threat successfully penetrates the system's defenses. Additionally, the automated patching feature helps to ensure that any newly discovered security vulnerabilities are addressed quickly and effectively before malicious actors can exploit them.

While devices are not connected to the corporate network, Defender vulnerability management's built-in agentless scanners continuously monitor and detect risk.

With consolidated inventories, you can monitor and assess your organization's assets, including software applications, digital certificates, hardware and firmware, and browser extensions, in real time.

You can assess your cyber exposure using advanced vulnerability and configuration assessment tools, including the following:

- *Assessment of security baselines*: Create customizable baseline profiles for measuring risk compliance against established benchmarks, such as the Center for Internet Security (CIS) and Security Technical Implementation Guides (STIG).

- *Visibility into software and vulnerabilities*: You can get an overview of the organization's software inventory and software changes such as installations, uninstallations, and patches.

- *Network Share Assessment*: A network share assessment provides actionable recommendations for securing vulnerable internal network shares.

- *Authenticated scan for Windows*: You can scan unmanaged Windows devices regularly for software vulnerabilities using Microsoft Defender Vulnerability Management credentials to access the devices remotely.

- *Threat analytics and event timelines*: An understanding and prioritization of vulnerabilities can be achieved through threat analytics and event timelines.

- *Browser extensions assessment*: You can assess the browser extensions installed on different browsers in your organization. You can view information on each extension's permissions and level of risk.

- *Digital certificates assessment*: You can check the digital certificates installed across your organization on a central certificate inventory page. You can identify certificates before they expire and identify potential vulnerabilities due to weak signature algorithms.

- *Hardware and firmware assessment*: You can view a list of available hardware and firmware in your organization organized by system models, processors, and BIOS. Each view includes details such as the vendor's name, the number of weaknesses, threats insights, and the number of exposed devices.

By leveraging Microsoft's threat intelligence, breach likelihood predictions, business contexts, and device assessments, Defender Vulnerability Management can quickly prioritize your organization's greatest vulnerabilities. You can quickly resolve the most critical vulnerabilities by providing a single view of prioritized recommendations from multiple security feeds, along with necessary details such as related CVEs and exposed devices. Prioritization that is based on risk does the following:

- *Focuses on emerging threats*: It dynamically prioritizes security recommendations based on vulnerabilities currently exploited in the wild and emerging threats that pose the greatest threat to organizations.

- *Identify active breaches*: It correlates vulnerability management and EDR insights to prioritize vulnerabilities exploited during active breaches.

- *High-value assets are protected*: Exposed devices with business-critical applications, confidential data, or high-value users are identified.

AD Risk Management

AD risk management focuses on understanding, managing, and mitigating the risks associated with digital assets. It involves identifying, assessing, and controlling risks to prevent potential losses and maximize the return on investments. It also includes developing strategies to handle cyber security threats. This is done using a combination of technical, administrative, and physical measures. It is also essential to review and update risk management policies regularly.

Continuous monitoring of digital assets is also essential to ensure the organization's security. This helps to identify potential risks and vulnerabilities and take the necessary steps to remediate them promptly. Through these strategies, organizations can control access to their data, detect suspicious activities, and respond quickly in case of a breach. Additionally, staff members must maintain awareness and education to protect the organization's data and assets. It also helps to ensure that the organization's risk management strategies are practical and up-to-date. Regular risk assessments are essential to ensure the security of the organization. Implementing the latest technology and solutions is necessary to protect the organization's data and assets. Regular data backups should also be performed to ensure data is not lost during a data breach. Security policies should be reviewed and updated regularly to ensure they align with current best practices.

Necessary security measures should also be implemented to protect the organization's data and assets. Finally, staff members should be trained to recognize and respond to security threats. This will help to reduce the risk of a data breach, as the organization will have an up-to-date copy of its data. Regularly reviewing and updating security policies will also ensure they align with the latest security measures and industry standards. Training staff members to recognize and respond to potential security threats will also help further protect the organization's data and assets.

Design and Implementation of Active Directory

Users and administrators can find and use directory information using Active Directory's structured data store, which uses a hierarchical logical structure to organize directory information.

Network objects are stored in hierarchical directories, which are hierarchical structures. Directory services, such as Active Directory Domain Services (AD DS), provide methods for storing directory data and making it accessible to network administrators and users. Data about user accounts, such as names, passwords, telephone numbers, etc., is stored by AD DS and can be accessed by other authorized users on the same network.

Administrators and users can easily find and use information about network objects with Active Directory. The directory information is organized logically and hierarchically based on a structured data store.

Typically, Active Directory objects consist of servers, volumes, printers, and user and computer accounts that can be shared across networks.

Authentication and access control to Active Directory objects are integrated into security. Network administrators can manage directory data and organization across their network with a single network logon, and authorized users can access network resources anywhere. Even the most complex networks can be managed easily using policy-based administration.

You can use Windows Server AD DS in your environment by deploying a centralized, delegated administrative model and enabling SSO. To create an AD DS deployment strategy that meets your organization's needs, you must identify the deployment tasks and the current environment of your organization. Once the tasks and environment are identified, you can create a customized plan to deploy AD DS successfully. This plan should include a timeline and steps to ensure a successful deployment. Finally, the plan should be tested and evaluated before being implemented. After the plan is implemented, it should be monitored and adjusted as needed. Regular maintenance and troubleshooting should be completed to ensure continued success. Finally, user training should be provided to ensure the successful use of the new system.

A scalable, secure, and manageable infrastructure can be created with AD DS in Windows Server, simplifying user and resource management. Managing your network infrastructure, including branch offices, Microsoft Exchange Server, and multiple forests, is possible with AD DS.

The AD DS deployment process involves three phases: the design phase, the deployment phase, and the operation phase. As part of the design phase, the design team creates the logical structure for AD DS that best meets the needs of each department within the organization that will use the directory service. Following approval of the design, the deployment team tests it in a lab environment and then implements it in a production environment. The deployment team performs testing during deployment, which may impact the design phase. Once the deployment is complete, the operations team maintains the directory service.

Microsoft Sentinel

Microsoft Sentinel is a cloud-native security information and event management (SIEM) platform from Microsoft. It provides real-time monitoring, threat detection, and response capabilities. Sentinel enables organizations to quickly detect, investigate and respond to advanced threats. It uses machine learning to detect organizational threats and provides visualizations that help analysts quickly prioritize and analyze threats. The Microsoft Sentinel service is a paid subscription.

Microsoft Sentinel also provides automated response capabilities to help organizations respond quickly to incidents. Sentinel also offers APIs to integrate with existing security tools, making it easier to leverage existing investments. It also provides detailed logging and reporting to help organizations detect emerging threats and optimize their security posture. Sentinel's AI-driven analytics engine helps organizations detect and respond to threats faster and more effectively, reducing the time and effort required to investigate and respond to incidents. This allows organizations to focus more on their core competencies and helps ensure their systems' security.

Microsoft Sentinel's automated threat detection and response capabilities help organizations stay ahead of the ever-evolving cyber threats and protect their data and systems. It also helps organizations improve their visibility into their security posture and compliance with security regulations. This can save organizations time and money, as they don't have to dedicate resources to manual threat detection and response.

Sentinel's AI-driven security solutions are also highly intuitive and can be quickly and easily deployed. This helps to reduce the time and costs associated with training and onboarding, allowing organizations to focus on the more essential aspects of their security posture. In addition, Sentinel's AI-driven security solutions are designed to scale with an organization's changing needs, providing the flexibility they need to stay ahead of threats. This allows organizations to quickly adapt to new threats and rapidly respond to evolving security needs. Sentinel's AI-driven security solutions are reliable and cost-effective, making them the perfect choice for any organization looking to protect its assets.

Connecting your data sources is the first step in onboarding Microsoft Sentinel.

Sentinel provides real-time integration with Microsoft solutions out of the box with many connectors available. Some of these connectors include the following:

- You can use Microsoft Defender for Cloud, Microsoft Defender for IoT, as well as Microsoft 365 Defender.

- You can get Azure services such as Azure Active Directory, Azure Activity, Azure Storage, Azure Key Vault, and Azure Kubernetes.

Using Microsoft Sentinel, you can connect your data sources via common event format, Syslog, or REST-API, as well as the broader security and application ecosystem.

You can use data connectors to start ingesting data into Microsoft Sentinel once you have onboarded it into your workspace. You can integrate Microsoft services in real-time using Microsoft Sentinel's out-of-the-box connectors. For example, the Microsoft 365 Defender connector integrates data from Office 365, Azure Active Directory (Azure AD), Microsoft Defender for Identify, and Microsoft Defender for Cloud Apps as a service-to-service connector.

How to Enable It

You enable Microsoft Sentinel and configure data connectors to monitor and protect your environment. In addition to connecting your data sources using data connectors, you can select from a gallery of expertly designed workbooks that surface insights based on your data. You can easily customize these workbooks according to your needs.

Microsoft products have many connectors, such as the Microsoft 365 Defender service-to-service connector. You can also set up built-in connectors for non-Microsoft products, such as Syslog or Common Event Format (CEF).

The Microsoft Sentinel service is a paid service that requires an active Azure subscription and a Log Analytics workspace. You will need to complete the following steps in order to turn on Microsoft Sentinel.

1. Log in to the Azure Portal.

2. Under search services and locate the Microsoft Sentinel services.

3. Choose Add Workspace.

4. You can use multiple workspaces for Microsoft Sentinel, but the data is isolated to one. You can select a workspace to use or create a new one. Installing Microsoft Sentinel on the default workspaces created by Microsoft Defender for Cloud is impossible.

5. Choose Add Sentinel.

Microsoft Threat Modeling Tool

The Threat Modeling Tool is a crucial Microsoft Security Development Lifecycle (SDL) element. Software architects can significantly reduce the total development cost by identifying and resolving potential security issues early. In addition, Microsoft designed the tool to make threat modeling easier for nonsecurity experts by providing clear guidance on creating and analyzing threat models. Using the Threat Modeling Tool, engineers can quickly identify and address security issues, reducing the risk of compromise and the impact of any potential attack. This allows developers to create more secure software while reducing development costs.

The Threat Modeling Tool is a powerful tool that protects user data, guards against cyber attacks, and promotes secure software development. It is an essential tool for any software development team looking to keep their applications secure. It can help developers identify potential security risks, quickly identify and fix security vulnerabilities, and ensure their applications meet security standards.

Furthermore, it can be done in an efficient, cost-effective manner. The Threat Modeling Tool provides a systematic approach to security testing tailored to the specific application being developed. It allows developers to review the security architecture of their applications and identify potential threats and vulnerabilities. It also guides mitigating those risks and provides best practices on secure coding. Additionally, it allows teams to quickly identify and address security issues before they become costly problems. The tool also helps ensure the application complies with industry regulations and standards. It is an invaluable tool for any development team building secure applications.

Anyone who knows how their system works and is familiar with information security can use threat modeling.

Using this technique, you can create a data-flow diagram and analyze it for potential threats in four different phases.

- *Design*: The design of your system begins with capturing all of the requirements. It is the design phase where you gather the most data about what you will build and what you will use to make it.

- *Break*: You can analyze the data-flow diagram and find potential security issues using a threat-modeling framework. The break phase involves using the data-flow diagram to identify potential threats against your system. A threat-modeling framework is then used to find the most common threats and ways to defend against them.

- *Fix*: You can choose the proper security controls for each issue. STRIDE threats are mapped to different security controls with different functions and types, and in this stage, their fate is decided.

- *Verify*: Verify requirements are met, issues are found, and security controls are in place. It ensures that assumptions are validated, requirements are met, and security controls are implemented before the system is deployed as part of the threat-modeling process.

Identifying vulnerabilities and recommending strategies to reduce risk early in the development life cycle is an effective way to secure systems, applications, networks, and services.

Microsoft Threat Management

Microsoft Threat Management is a comprehensive security solution that enables organizations to detect, investigate, and respond to threats. It helps to protect against malware, phishing attacks, and other malicious activities. It also offers data loss prevention and protection from advanced persistent threats.

Microsoft Threat Management provides an end-to-end security solution that enables organizations to respond quickly to threats. It also helps to reduce costs associated with security breaches and provides peace of mind for organizations. It also helps to increase employee productivity by allowing them to work securely from any device or location. It is also designed to be easy to use and manage, allowing organizations to deploy and maintain a secure environment quickly. It also offers real-time visibility into security threats so organizations can quickly identify and respond to them. The solution also enables organizations to comply with industry regulations and standards. It also provides cost savings by reducing the need for hardware and software and simplifying IT management.

Protect devices, identities, apps, emails, data, and cloud workloads with unified threat protection.

By providing the right tools and intelligence to the right people, Microsoft empowers your organization's defenders. With our cloud-native SIEM, Microsoft Sentinel, you can gain insights across your entire organization while securing your digital estate. With Microsoft Defender for Cloud and Microsoft 365 Defender, you can protect your end users using integrated, automated XDR.

Azure Monitor

Microsoft Azure Monitor is a comprehensive monitoring service for applications and infrastructure hosted on the Azure cloud platform. It provides a centralized view of the performance and health of cloud resources, allowing users to detect and diagnose performance issues, track changes, and make proactive decisions to optimize the performance of their applications.

Azure Monitor also provides intelligent analytics and insights to help users troubleshoot and diagnose problems. It also enables users to set up alerts to be notified of any changes in resource performance or availability. Azure Monitor also helps users ensure their applications are secure and compliant with industry standards. It also provides detailed reports, enabling users to gain insights into their cloud infrastructure and act accordingly.

Azure Monitor is a powerful tool that can help organizations ensure their applications' success. It can help to detect and fix any issues quickly, maximize uptime, and provide detailed insights for better decision-making.

The Azure Monitor platform includes metrics, logs, traces, and changes based on a common monitoring data platform.

With Azure Monitor, you can use a common set of tools to analyze data from multiple resources simultaneously. Some resources may write to other locations before they are collected into Logs or Metrics, and monitoring data may also be sent to different locations to support certain scenarios.

Figure 3-14 depicts Azure Monitor.

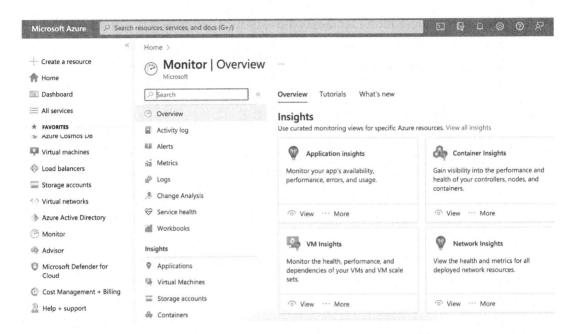

Figure 3-14. *Azure Monitor*

Azure Monitor also enables users to optimize their cloud resources to reduce costs and increase efficiency. It also provides detailed cost analysis, allowing users to monitor and control their cloud spending. Azure Monitor can also detect and alert users of potential security threats or incidents. It monitors the performance of applications in real-time and can detect anomalies that might indicate a security breach or malicious activity. It also provides detailed compliance reports to ensure users meet industry standards, helping them avoid potential penalties or other repercussions. Finally, Azure Monitor provides detailed insights into applications' usage and performance, assisting users in optimizing their resources and maximizing their cloud efficiency.

As part of your monitoring strategy, you will want to minimize costs. While some data collection and features in Azure Monitor are free, others are charged based on their configurations, amount of data collected, or frequency of use. As you plan your implementation for cost optimization, you should be familiar with Azure Monitor pricing, as the articles in this scenario identify any recommendations that include a cost.

As part of your monitoring strategy, you should identify the goals and requirements of your plan before you design and implement a monitoring solution. To maximize the performance and reliability of your applications, the strategy describes your specific requirements, the configuration that meets those requirements, and the processes to leverage the monitoring environment. It would be best to choose Azure Monitor configuration options consistent with your strategy.

Cybersecurity Operations Services

Microsoft Cybersecurity Operations Services provides comprehensive solutions to help companies protect their data, networks, and systems from cyber threats. The services include threat detection, incident response, remediation, security operations center automation, and more. They also offer various training programs to help organizations stay updated with cybersecurity best practices. Microsoft also provides 24/7 monitoring and support to help organizations promptly address security issues. Furthermore, they provide risk assessment and compliance services to ensure organizations meet industry regulations. They also offer a suite of tools to help organizations manage their security posture and a library of best practices that can be used to help improve their security posture.

Additionally, Microsoft offers a threat intelligence platform to help organizations stay abreast of emerging threats. Microsoft's security services are designed to help organizations reduce their risk of cyber attacks, protect their data, and maintain regulatory compliance. The company also provides consulting services to help organizations implement security strategies.

Microsoft's security services are tailored to the specific needs of each organization, allowing them to tailor their security strategy to their particular industry, size, and risk profile. These services also help organizations stay updated with the latest cybersecurity trends, ensuring their systems remain secure against emerging threats. Organizations can also leverage Microsoft's security expertise to audit their existing security protocols and identify areas for improvement. The consultants can then provide guidance and resources to help the organization address any identified weaknesses.

This allows companies to be proactive in their security efforts rather than reactive. As a result, organizations can reduce the risk of data breaches and other malicious attacks and ensure their data and systems are protected.

In Azure Policy, resources and actions are compared to business rules by comparing their properties to those rules. These business rules are described in JSON format as policy definitions. A policy initiative (called a *policySet*) combines several business rules to simplify management. Once you have defined your business rules, you can assign a policy definition or initiative to any scope of Azure resources that supports it, including management groups, subscriptions, resource groups, and individual resources. A Resource Manager assignment applies to all resources within its scope, and subscopes can be excluded if necessary.

Azure Policy uses a JSON format to form the logic used to determine whether a resource is compliant or not. Defining a rule includes metadata and the policy rule. Functions, parameters, logical operators, conditions, and property aliases can be used to match precisely the scenario you want. Policy rules determine which resources are evaluated based on the scope of the assignment.

Summary

In this chapter, you read about methods to design and deploy a strategy for identify security services in line with the NIST CSF mapping of Azure and in line with Asset Management (ID.AM), Business Environment (ID.BE), Governance (ID. GV), and Risk Assessment (ID.RA).

In the next chapter of the book, you will read about designing and deploying a Detect solution in alignment with the NIST framework.

CHAPTER 4

Design and Deploy a Protect Solution: Part 1

Organizations should establish a comprehensive cloud security strategy that includes authentication, authorization, and encryption to protect their cloud resources. Regular monitoring of cloud resources should also be implemented to detect any potential security threats. Finally, regular backups should be taken to ensure that data is not lost in the event of a security breach.

Cloud security protection is essential because it helps organizations protect their data and assets in the cloud from various cyber threats and attacks. Cloud security protection is essential for organizations that use cloud services to store data and applications. It helps organizations protect their assets, ensure compliance, maintain availability, reduce costs, and scale security as needed.

The National Institute of Standards and Technology (NIST) Cybersecurity Framework (CSF) helps organizations manage and reduce cybersecurity risk. Microsoft Cybersecurity NIST Protect is a set of cybersecurity solutions offered by Microsoft that aligns with the NIST CSF.

Microsoft Cybersecurity NIST Protect provides several tools and services to help organizations protect their cloud-based infrastructure, applications, and data. This chapter provides the fundamentals of cybersecurity, key terminologies, and the foundation needed to understand how Azure and the NIST CSF's Protect module can work together.

Microsoft Azure offers a wide variety of protect services aligning to the NIST CSF; it's so much that the coverage of designing and deploying a protect solution is broadly classified into two chapters.

© Puthiyavan Udayakumar 2023
P. Udayakumar, *Design and Deploy a Secure Azure Environment*,
https://doi.org/10.1007/978-1-4842-9678-3_4

By the end of this chapter, you should understand the following:

- Azure protect security services

- PR.AC: Identify Management, Authentication and Access Control

- PR.AT: Awareness and Training

Introduction to NIST Protect

NIST has developed the CSF to manage cybersecurity-related risk; it complements risk management processes and cybersecurity programs. The framework consists of guidelines, standards, and best practices that organizations can use to assess and improve their cybersecurity posture.

The Protect function of the NIST CSF is one of five functions and focuses on identifying and implementing safeguards to protect against potential cybersecurity threats. The Protect function is broken down into several categories.

- *Access control*: Limiting access to sensitive information and systems to only authorized personnel

- *Awareness and training*: Ensuring that all employees are aware of cybersecurity risks and are trained on how to prevent and respond to them

- *Data security*: Implementing measures to protect sensitive data, such as encryption and backup procedures

- *Information protection processes and procedures*: Developing policies and procedures to protect information and systems from unauthorized access, modification, or destruction

- *Maintenance*: Ensuring that all hardware and software are maintained and updated to address known vulnerabilities

- *Protective Technology*: Implementing technology solutions such as firewalls, intrusion detection systems, and other tools to protect against cyber threats

Organizations can enhance their cybersecurity posture and decrease the risk of cybersecurity incidents by following the guidelines and best practices outlined in the NIST CSF Protect function. Figure 4-1 shows the five categories of the NIST CSF Protect function.

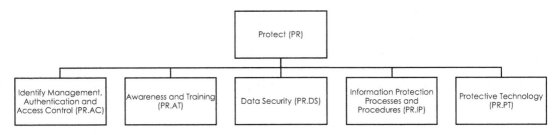

Figure 4-1. *NIST Protect categories*

NIST CSF Identify Management Authentication and Access Control (PR.AC) is classified further into six subcategories, as depicted in Figure 4-2.

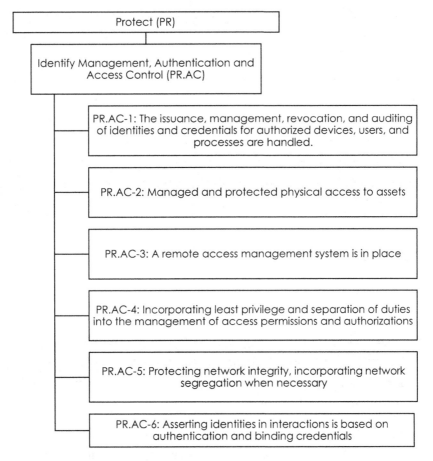

Figure 4-2. *NIST Protect subcategories*

Identify Management, Authentication, and Access Control (PR.AC)

Identify management, authentication, and access control are essential components of cybersecurity. They help protect systems and sensitive information from unauthorized access and ensure that only authorized individuals can access critical resources.

Identify management (IDM) refers to managing user identities and their access to resources within an organization. It involves creating, managing, and deleting user accounts; granting and revoking access privileges; and ensuring user access is consistent with organizational policies. IDM controls digital identities and user access permissions within an organization's network or system. It involves establishing and maintaining user identities, providing user authentication, and managing access to digital resources, such as applications, systems, data, and networks. IDM solutions typically include user account management, identify provisioning and de-provisioning, authentication and authorization services, password management, and access control. IDM can enforce policies, such as password complexity rules, multifactor authentication, and role-based access control. IDM also ensures that only authorized individuals can access sensitive information or systems while minimizing the risk of unauthorized access, data breaches, and other cybersecurity threats. IDM is critical in protecting organizations from cyber-attacks, identify theft, and other security risks.

Key Aspects of IDM

Here are some key aspects of identify management:

- *Identify provisioning*: IDM solutions provide tools for creating and managing user accounts and assigning roles and permissions to each user. This ensures that each user has the right access to the resources they need to perform their job without giving them access to information they don't need.

- *Authentication and authorization*: IDM solutions provide mechanisms for authenticating users, including password-based authentication, multifactor authentication (MFA), or biometric authentication. Once a user is authenticated, IDM solutions offer mechanisms to authorize access to specific resources based on their role and permissions.

- *Access control*: IDM solutions provide tools for controlling access to specific resources, such as applications, data, and networks. This can include role-based access control (RBAC), which assigns access permissions based on a user's job function, or attribute-based access control (ABAC), which assigns access permissions based on specific attributes of the user or resource.

- *Password management*: IDM solutions provide tools for managing user passwords, including password policies, expiration, and password complexity requirements. This helps to prevent password-related security breaches, such as password guessing or brute-force attacks.

- *Identify verification*: IDM solutions can include tools for verifying a user's identify, such as digital certificates or smart cards. These technologies can provide an additional layer of security by requiring the user to provide physical proof of their identify.

- *Single sign-on (SSO)*: IDM solutions can enable SSO, allowing users to access multiple applications and systems with a single set of credentials. Passwords that are reused or weak are less likely to cause security breaches.

- *Federation*: IDM solutions can support federation, allowing users to access resources across different organizations or systems without needing to maintain separate credentials. Federation can be particularly useful for large organizations or those that frequently collaborate with other organizations.

- *Identify governance and administration (IGA)*: IDM solutions can include IGA tools, which provide governance and administration capabilities for managing user identities and access permissions across an organization. IGA tools can help to ensure that access permissions are up-to-date, compliant with regulations, and aligned with business needs.

- *Audit and compliance*: IDM solutions can provide audit and compliance capabilities, which allow organizations to track and monitor user activity and access to resources. Security breaches or incidents can be detected and handled quickly, demonstrating compliance with regulations or industry standards.

IDM solutions are critical for protecting sensitive information and preventing unauthorized access to resources within an organization. An IDM solution minimizes the risk of data breaches and other cyberattacks by ensuring that each user has the right level of access and permissions and by providing strong authentication and access control mechanisms.

Methods of Authentication

Authenticating an individual or system before granting access to a resource involves verifying their identify. Authentication mechanisms include passwords, biometric factors such as fingerprints or facial recognition, smart cards, and digital certificates.

Authentication is a critical component of IT security because it helps ensure that only authorized users are granted access to sensitive information and resources while minimizing the risk of unauthorized access and data breaches. Authentication is verifying the identify of a user, device, or system attempting to access a resource, such as an application, network, or data. Authentication is critical to cybersecurity because it ensures that only authorized users are granted access to sensitive information or resources while minimizing the risk of unauthorized access and data breaches. The following are the various method of authentication that exist:

- *Password-based authentication*: Password-based authentication is the most common form of authentication, where a user must provide a username and password to access a resource. The system checks the username and password against a database to verify the user's identify.

- *Multifactor authentication*: This is a more secure form of authentication that requires the user to provide multiple forms of identification, such as a password and a fingerprint, a password and a unique code sent directly to their phone, or a password and a security token. MFA makes it much harder for attackers to gain unauthorized access, even if they know the user's password.

- *Biometric authentication*: This uses a physical characteristic of the user to verify their identify, such as a fingerprint, facial recognition, or voice recognition. Biometric authentication can be very secure but requires specialized hardware and software.

- *Certificate-based authentication*: This involves the use of digital certificates to verify a user's identify. The user must have a valid certificate that a trusted authority has issued.

- *Token-based authentication*: This involves using a token, such as a smart card or USB key, to authenticate the user. The token contains a digital certificate or another form of identification that is used to verify the user's identify.

- *Risk-based authentication*: This form of authentication assesses the risk level of a login attempt and adjusts the authentication requirements accordingly. For example, additional authentication factors may be required if a login attempt is deemed high-risk based on certain factors, such as an unfamiliar location or device.

- *Adaptive authentication*: This form of authentication uses machine learning algorithms to analyze user behavior and adjust the authentication requirements accordingly. For example, if a user's behavior changes, such as attempting to access a resource at an unusual time, additional authentication factors may be required.

Azure Mapping for PR.AC

Microsoft Azure asset management capabilities via various services and products enables organizations to manage their assets and resources more efficiently. It provides a centralized platform to track, monitor, and manage assets, as well as insights into their performance. It also helps to reduce costs and maximize productivity.

A key component of asset management is the implementation of controls for securing Azure resources, including recommendations about permissions for security personnel, access to asset inventory, and managing approvals for services and resources (inventory, tracking, and correcting).

A security posture can be accurately assessed only by identifying a system's assets and value. Assets include tangible elements such as information or equipment and abstract ones such as reputation. It is essential to quantify the impact of these assets. Every organization must identify its digital assets and determine what level of protection they require.

Discover all your cloud resources by querying your asset inventory. Tagging and grouping your assets according to their service nature, location, or other characteristics will help you organize them logically. Maintain a continuously updated asset inventory for your security organization. By aggregating security insights and risks centrally, you can ensure your security organization can monitor risks to cloud assets.

Audit and restrict user access to cloud services to ensure only approved cloud services can be used. Maintain security attributes and configurations of assets throughout their life cycles.

Your cloud assets should be protected from accidental or malicious modifications by limiting access to asset management features. Create an allow list and block unauthorized software from executing in your environment by ensuring that only authorized software is executed.

We'll now explore the Azure NIST identify mapping for asset management and Microsoft's outlined responsibility classification among Microsoft and customers, which is with inline cloud security shared responsibility models.

Figure 4-3 depicts the subcategories of Azure mapping against the Protect module of the NIST CSF.

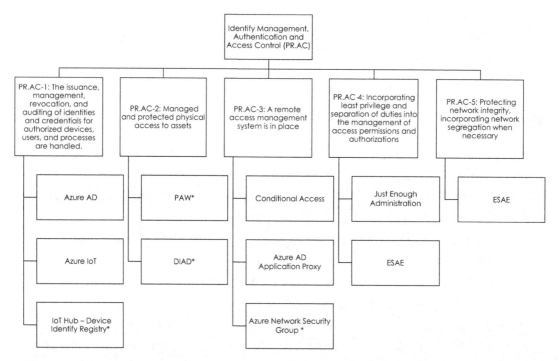

Figure 4-3. *NIST PR.AC subcategories mapping with Azure protect capabilities*

As part of the Azure Cloud shared responsibility model, the NIST CSF security functions are provided in Table 4-1 with respect to PR.AC.

Table 4-1. *PR.AC Management Responsibility Matrix*

Category	Subcategory	Informative References	Responsibility	Customer Responsibility	Microsoft Azure Responsibility
Physical and logical assets are protected using identify management and access control (PR. AC) to limit access to authorized users, processes, and devices.	PR.AC-1: The issuance, management, revocation, and auditing of identities and credentials for authorized devices, users, and processes are handled.	NIST SP 800-53 Rev. 4 AC-2, IA Family	Shared	The customer is responsible for properly identifying and authenticating users for authorized devices, users, and processes.	As part of Microsoft Azure, Active Directory manages, issues, revokes, and audits identities and credentials for authorized devices, users, and processes.

(continued)

Table 4-1. (*continued*)

Category	Subcategory	Informative References	Responsibility	Customer Responsibility	Microsoft Azure Responsibility
	PR.AC-2: Managed and protected physical access to assets.	NIST SP 800-53 Rev. 4 PE-2, PE-3, PE-4, PE-5, PE-6, PE-9	Microsoft Azure	N/A	Physical security perimeters are used to manage and control physical access to assets in Microsoft Azure. Microsoft data centers are certified by SSAE16/ISAE 3402 and ISO 27001. Microsoft data centers are physically constructed, managed, and monitored 24 hours a day in nondescript buildings to protect data and services from unauthorized access and environmental threats. Pre-approved deliveries are received in a secure loading bay and monitored by authorized personnel. Badge-controlled gates restrict access to data centers. A physical barrier separates loading bays from information processing facilities. Access to data centers and information systems is monitored with CCTV. Facilities are monitored through cameras at perimeter doors, entrances and exits, interior aisles, caged areas, high-security areas, shipping and receiving, parking lots, and other external areas.

			Microsoft buildings are controlled, and entry into data centers is restricted to those with a card reader (swiping the card reader with an authorized ID badge) or biometrics. Employees and contractors without ID cards must be positively identified at the front desk. A Microsoft employee must wear an identify badge at all times, and they must challenge or report anyone without a badge. In addition, Microsoft employees must accompany guests.
PR.AC-3: A remote access management system is in place.	NIST SP 800-53 Rev. 4 AC-17, AC-19, AC-20	Shared	Application and data management within tenant storage is the responsibility of the customer. A PIN-based authentication method and Microsoft Smart Card certificates are required for remote access to the Microsoft intranet. Microsoft Azure users must follow the standard operating procedure for remote access. With Microsoft Azure, two-factor authentication, security groups, access control certificates, and limited entry points for Microsoft employees are enforced for remote connections to the information system. The defined security groups implement usage restrictions.

(continued)

239

Table 4-1. (*continued*)

Category	Subcategory	Informative References	Responsibility	Customer Responsibility	Microsoft Azure Responsibility
	PR.AC-4: Incorporating least privilege and separation of duties into the management of access permissions and authorizations.	NIST SP 800-53 Rev. 4 AC-2, AC-3, AC-5, AC-6, AC-16	Shared	The customer ensures segregation of duties and least privilege by providing appropriate access levels for each user based on their job function.	Microsoft Azure's access permissions and authorization management incorporate the least privilege principles and duties separation. Microsoft Azure operations teams are segregated and defined with different levels of access and privileges determined by asset owners/custodians.
	PR.AC-5: Protecting network integrity, incorporating network segregation when necessary.	NIST SP 800-53 Rev. 4 AC-4, SC-7	Shared	Application hosting in Microsoft Azure is the customer's responsibility, who must ensure network integrity by using network segmentation, firewalls, antivirus, and intrusion detection, as appropriate.	Microsoft Azure employs multiple levels of network segregation to protect network integrity, and network segregation is incorporated when necessary. Microsoft Azure clusters are logically segregated by Virtual Local Area Networks (VLANs) to separate customer traffic from other Microsoft network traffic. The Microsoft Azure network is accessible from outside the cluster only through NAT-based restrictions, and Azure services are implemented on physical nodes in the data center VLAN.

ACLs on routers and load balancers are also used for firewalling external customer traffic. Only specific known protocols are permitted, and most internal traffic is filtered via ACLs on routers and layer 3 switches.

PR.AC-6: Asserting identities in interactions is based on authentication and binding credentials.	NIST SP 800-53: AC-2, AC-3, AC-5, AC-6, AC-16, AC-19, AC-24, IA-2, IA-4, IA-5, IA-8, PE-2, PS-3	Shared	The customer's responsibilities are identify proofing, tying credentials to identities, and asserting identities in appropriate interactions.

Personnel at Microsoft Azure must wear identify badges at all times to ensure their identities are verified and bound to their credentials. They must challenge or report individuals who are not wearing badges. Employees at Microsoft Azure are expected to assert their identify badges when appropriate, such as when entering a building. Microsoft Azure personnel use multifactor authentication to access the production environment, including a Microsoft Active Directory username, password, PIN, smartcard, and, in some cases, biometrics.

Azure AD

Azure AD is a cloud-based identify and access management service from Microsoft. It enables organizations to securely manage user access to applications, resources, and networks in the cloud and on the premises. It also provides single sign-on to thousands of SaaS applications. Azure AD helps streamline user authentication and authorization process, making it easier for organizations to manage user access. It also provides features such as multifactor authentication, identify protection, and Conditional Access to applications and resources, making it more secure than traditional user management solutions.

Azure AD also supports self-service password reset and single sign-on, allowing users to access applications with fewer steps. It is also highly scalable and can be integrated with existing authentication systems, making it an ideal choice for organizations of any size. Azure AD also provides access control and security features, such as multifactor authentication, data encryption, and user behavior monitoring. It is also easy to set up and manage, making it an excellent solution for small businesses. Furthermore, Azure AD is highly cost-effective, with no additional costs associated with setup and maintenance. It also offers a variety of support options to customers, such as online tutorials, technical support, and community forums.

Azure AD offers several capabilities to help organizations protect their identities and resources, including the following:

- *Identify and access management*: Azure AD provides a secure and scalable way to manage identities and access to resources in the cloud and on-premises.

- *SSO*: Azure AD allows users to sign in once and access all the cloud and on-premises applications they are authorized to use.

- *MFA*: Azure AD offers MFA to enhance security by requiring users to provide an additional form of authentication before accessing resources.

- *Application management*: Azure AD offers a centralized application management solution that enables administrators to manage and secure access to all the applications used within an organization.

- *Conditional Access*: Azure AD allows administrators to define policies that control resource access based on various conditions, such as location, device, user, and risk.

- *Identify Protection*: Azure AD Identify Protection helps protect organizations from identify-based risks, such as account compromise, by leveraging machine learning to detect and mitigate threats in real time.

- *PIM*: Azure AD PIM allows organizations to manage and monitor privileged access to resources by assigning just-in-time access, requiring approval workflows, and providing audit logs.

- *Group Management*: Azure AD enables administrators to create and manage groups to simplify the management of users and resources.

- *Self-Service Password Reset*: Azure AD offers self-service password reset to enable users to reset their passwords without administrator intervention.

- *Azure AD Connect*: Azure AD Connect is a tool that helps synchronize on-premises directories with Azure AD, enabling organizations to manage identities and access for their users.

- *Access Reviews*: Azure AD Access Reviews allows administrators to regularly review access rights to resources, ensuring that only the right people can access the right resources at the right time.

The NIST CSF Protect function also provides a framework for identifying, assessing, and managing cybersecurity risks to protect against unauthorized access, theft, and destruction of assets. It includes guidelines for implementing access controls, monitoring activities, and detecting and responding to cybersecurity incidents.

How It Works

Azure AD is a Microsoft cloud-based identify and access management (IAM) solution. It provides a way to manage identities and access to resources in the cloud and on-premises. Here is a high-level overview of how Azure AD works:

- *Identify creation and synchronization*: The first step is to create user identities in Azure AD or synchronize existing on-premises identities to Azure AD using Azure AD Connect. This allows users to authenticate and access resources in Azure AD.

- *Authentication*: When users try to access a resource, Azure AD authenticates them by verifying their identify through a username and password or other authentication methods like MFA. This process can also include validating the device, location, and other factors using Azure AD's Conditional Access policies.

- *Authorization*: Once a user is authenticated, Azure AD checks if the user is authorized to access the resource they are requesting. This is done by checking the user's group membership, role assignments, or other policies set by the administrator.

Azure AD supports various authentication and authorization methods, such as password-based authentication, MFA, and OAuth, to ensure that only authorized users can access resources.

- *Application integration*: Azure AD can integrate with various applications and services, including Microsoft and third-party applications, to enable seamless single sign-on (SSO) for users. This reduces the number of passwords users need to remember and improves the user experience.

- *Identify protection*: In real-time, Azure AD Identify Protection leverages machine learning to detect and mitigate identify-based risks, such as account compromise and suspicious sign-in activities. Azure AD Identify Protection uses machine learning algorithms to detect and prevent identify-based attacks such as brute-force attacks, password spray attacks, and anomalous sign-ins.

- *Audit and monitoring*: Azure AD provide audit and monitoring capabilities, including logs and reporting, to help administrators track user and application activity, monitor security events, and detect potential security issues.

- *Compliance*: Azure AD supports compliance with various regulatory and industry standards such as GDPR, HIPAA, and FedRAMP by providing features such as auditing, reporting, and policy enforcement.

By leveraging Azure AD's access management, authentication and authorization, identify protection, threat intelligence, and compliance features, organizations can better protect their resources and comply with the NIST CSF Protect function.

Design Considerations

Here are the design considerations:

- *Plan for scalability*: Azure AD can scale to support thousands of users and applications. However, designing your Azure AD deployment to scale efficiently is important. This includes using the appropriate tier of Azure AD, designing for redundancy and failover, and planning for future growth.

- *Use MFA*: Enabling MFA for Azure AD can significantly improve security by requiring users to provide additional authentication factors beyond just a password. Consider implementing MFA for all users, especially those with privileged access.

- *Implement RBAC)*: RBAC allows you to assign permissions to users and groups based on their roles and responsibilities. This helps ensure that users have access to Azure resources appropriately.

- *Monitor Azure AD logs*: Azure AD logs provide valuable information about user and application activity. Enable Azure AD auditing and monitor logs regularly to identify any suspicious activity.

- *Use Azure AD Connect for hybrid environments*: If you have a hybrid environment with on-premises Active Directory, use Azure AD Connect to synchronize user identities between on-premises and Azure AD. This allows for a consistent user experience and enables SSO for hybrid environments.

- *Enable Conditional Access*: Conditional Access policies allow you to control access to Azure AD based on specific conditions such as location, device, or user group. This helps improve security by ensuring that only authorized users can access resources.

- *Configure Azure AD for high availability*: Ensure that your Azure AD deployment is configured to minimize downtime and ensure your users and applications can access Azure AD resources when needed.

- *Use Azure AD Password Protection*: Azure AD Password Protection allows you to enforce custom password policies and prevent weak passwords. It can also detect and block password spray attacks.

- *Monitor Azure AD logs*: Azure AD logs provide valuable information about user and application activity. Enable Azure AD auditing and monitor logs regularly to identify any suspicious activity.

By following these best practices, you can design an Azure AD deployment that is scalable, is secure, and provides the functionality required to meet your organization's needs.

How To Enable It

Azure AD includes several features and capabilities that align with the NIST CSF Protect function. To use Azure AD, you will need the following prerequisites to deploy:

- *Microsoft Azure subscription*: You need a Microsoft Azure subscription to use Azure AD. You can sign up for a free Azure trial or purchase an Azure subscription from the Azure Portal.

- *Azure AD tenant*: After signing up for an Azure subscription, you need to create an Azure AD tenant. An Azure AD tenant is a dedicated instance of Azure AD that represents your organization's IAM system.

- *Internet connection*: To access and use Azure AD services, you must have a stable Internet connection.

- *Supported web browser*: You will need a supported web browser to access Azure AD services through the Azure Portal. Microsoft recommends using Microsoft Edge, Google Chrome, or Mozilla Firefox.

- *User accounts*: To use Azure AD, you will need user accounts that can be used to authenticate and access resources. You can create new user accounts in Azure AD or synchronize existing accounts from an on-premises Active Directory using Azure AD Connect.

- *Application integration*: If you plan to integrate Azure AD with applications, you will need to ensure that the applications are supported by Azure AD and can be integrated with Azure AD using appropriate methods such as SAML, OAuth, or OpenID Connect.

By meeting these prerequisites, you can set up and use Azure AD to manage identities and access to resources in the cloud and on-premises.

Azure AD Subscription Types?   There are three main subscription types for Azure AD, each with its features and capabilities.

Free: This subscription includes an Azure subscription and provides basic identify and access management capabilities such as user and group management, single sign-on for cloud applications, and self-service password reset. The free subscription is best suited for small organizations that need basic identify management features.

Basic: This subscription type includes all the features of the Free subscription and adds more advanced features such as group-based access management, MFA, and Azure AD Application Proxy. The Basic subscription is ideal for small to medium-sized organizations that require more advanced security features.

Premium: This subscription type includes all the features of the Basic subscription and adds more advanced features such as identify protection, PIM, Conditional Access, and Microsoft Cloud App Security. The Premium subscription suits large organizations with complex security requirements and needs advanced threat protection capabilities.

In addition to these subscription types, Azure AD offers add-ons for specific scenarios, such as Azure AD B2C for customer identify and access management and Azure AD Domain Services for hybrid scenarios. Organizations can choose the subscription type that best fits their needs and upgrade or downgrade their subscription as needed.

Deploying Azure AD involves setting up and configuring your Azure AD tenant, users, and applications. Here is a high-level overview of the steps involved:

1. *Log in*: Log in to the Azure Portal.

2. *Create an Azure AD tenant*: After signing up for an Azure subscription, create an Azure AD tenant representing your organization's identify and access management system.

3. *Add users to Azure AD*: Create user accounts in Azure AD or synchronize existing accounts from an on-premises Active Directory using Azure AD Connect.

4. *Set up authentication*: Configure authentication methods such as password-based authentication, MFA, or Azure AD Conditional Access policies to secure user authentication.

5. *Register and configure applications*: Register and configure applications in Azure AD for SSO or integrate them with Azure AD using appropriate methods such as SAML, OAuth, or OpenID Connect.

6. *Set up identify protection*: Configure Azure AD Identify Protection to monitor and protect user identities from security risks.

7. *Set up access management*: Configure Azure AD access management features such as group-based access management, Conditional Access, and PIM to control resource access.

8. *Monitor and manage Azure AD*: Use Azure AD monitoring and management tools such as Azure AD logs and Azure AD Connect Health to monitor and manage your Azure AD tenant.

In a nutshell, deploying Azure AD involves setting up and configuring various features and components to provide secure identify and access management for your organization's resources in the cloud and on-premises.

Azure IoT

Azure IoT is a cloud-based platform provided by Microsoft for building, deploying, and managing Internet of Things (IoT) solutions. It provides a wide range of tools and services that help organizations securely connect, monitor, and manage their IoT devices, and analyze data generated by these devices. Azure IoT enables organizations to collect data from a variety of sources such as sensors, devices, and applications, and then use this data to gain insights, improve operational efficiency, and make informed business decisions. The following are some of the key features and capabilities of Azure IoT:

- *Device management*: Azure IoT provides device management capabilities that enable organizations to remotely manage and monitor their IoT devices, including device registration, configuration, and firmware updates.

- *Data processing*: Azure IoT provides services such as Azure Stream Analytics and Azure Functions that allow organizations to process and analyze data generated by their IoT devices in real time.

- *Integration*: Azure IoT integrates with a wide range of Azure services, including Azure Event Grid, Azure Logic Apps, and Azure Machine Learning, to provide a comprehensive IoT solution.

- *Security*: Among the robust security features in Azure IoT are role-based access control, secure device connectivity, and encryption of data in transit and at rest.

- *Scalability*: Azure IoT is designed to support large-scale IoT deployments, allowing organizations to easily scale their IoT solutions as needed.

Azure IoT provides several features and capabilities that align with the NIST CSF Protect function. Here are some of the ways Azure IoT supports the NIST CSF Protect function:

- *Device management*: Azure IoT provides device management capabilities such as remote device monitoring, management, and firmware updates to ensure devices are secure and up-to-date.

- *Authentication and authorization*: Azure IoT supports authentication and authorization methods such as certificate-based authentication, token-based authentication, and Azure AD integration to ensure that only authorized devices and users can access IoT resources.

- *Data encryption*: Azure IoT provides end-to-end data encryption capabilities to ensure data is secure at rest and in transit.

- *Threat detection and prevention*: Azure IoT integrates with Azure Security Center to provide detection and prevention capabilities such as anomaly detection, threat intelligence, and incident response.

- *Compliance*: With Azure IoT, you can audit, report, and enforce policies that support compliance with regulatory and industry standards, such as GDPR, HIPAA, and FedRAMP.

Organizations can better protect their IoT resources and comply with NIST CSF Protect function by leveraging Azure IoT's device management, authentication and authorization, data encryption, threat detection and prevention, and compliance features.

Design Considerations

Here are some design considerations:

- *Use a layered architecture*: A layered architecture can help you design a scalable and secure IoT solution. It can help you separate concerns and modularize your solution, making it easier to manage and maintain.

- *Use secure communication protocols*: Choose protocols such as HTTPS, MQTT over SSL, and AMQP over SSL for transmitting data between IoT devices and the cloud. This helps ensure that data is encrypted in transit and can help prevent data breaches.

- *Implement security at every level*: Security should be implemented at every level, including the device, network, and cloud. Implementing security features such as authentication, authorization, and access control can help ensure that IoT devices and data are secure.

- *Use Azure IoT Hub*: Azure IoT Hub is a cloud service that enables bidirectional communication between IoT devices and the cloud. It provides device management, data routing, and device-to-cloud telemetry features. Using Azure IoT Hub can help you manage your IoT solution more efficiently and securely.

- *Use Azure Stream Analytics*: Azure Stream Analytics is a real-time stream processing service that allows you to analyze and process data from IoT devices in real time. It can help you gain insights and take action on IoT data more quickly.

- *Implement device management*: These features, such as firmware updates, device configuration, and remote management can help you manage your IoT devices more efficiently and securely.

- *Monitor your IoT solution*: Monitoring your IoT solution can help you identify and resolve issues quickly. Azure provides monitoring and diagnostic tools such as Azure Monitor and Azure Log Analytics that can help you monitor your IoT solution and gain insights into device behavior.

By following these design best practices, you can design an Azure IoT solution that is secure, scalable, and efficient.

How To Enable It

Deploying an Azure IoT solution involves several steps, including setting up the IoT hub, registering devices, configuring security, and processing data. Here is a high-level overview of the steps involved in deploying an Azure IoT solution:

1. *Create an IoT hub*: The first step in deploying an Azure IoT solution is to create an IoT Hub in the Azure Portal. The IoT Hub is the central component of the solution and provides a secure and scalable cloud-hosted service for managing and communicating with IoT devices.

2. *Register devices*: Once the IoT Hub is set up, you can register IoT devices with the hub. This involves creating a device identify within the IoT Hub and configuring the device to connect to the hub.

3. *Configure security*: It is essential to secure your IoT solution to prevent unauthorized access and data breaches. Azure IoT provides various security features such as device authentication, device-to-cloud and cloud-to-device message encryption, and access control.

4. *Process data*: With your devices registered and secured, you can start processing data generated by your devices. Azure IoT provides various tools and services for processing IoT data, such as Azure Stream Analytics and Azure Functions.

5. *Visualize data*: Once data is processed, you can visualize it using various tools such as Azure Time Series Insights, Power BI, or custom dashboards built using Azure Web Apps.

6. *Monitor and manage*: Finally, monitoring and managing your Azure IoT solution is essential. Azure IoT provides various tools and services to monitor and manage your solution, such as Azure IoT Central, Azure IoT Hub Device Explorer, and Azure Monitor.

Azure IOT Subscription Types   You can choose from several Azure IoT subscription types depending on your specific needs. Here are some of the main subscription types:

Free: The free subscription is a basic plan that allows you to experiment with Azure IoT services. You can connect up to five devices to IoT Hub and send up to 8,000 messages daily.

Using the basic tier, you can communicate unidirectionally with the cloud, while using the standard tier, you can communicate bidirectionally with the cloud.

Basic 1 and Standard tier 1: The basic subscription is a paid plan that offers more features and capacity than the free subscription. It allows you to send up to 400,000 messages daily.

Basic 2 and Standard tier 2: The subscription is a more advanced paid plan offering additional features and capacity. It allows you to send up to 6 million messages daily.

Basic 3 and Standard tier 3: The subscription is for high deployment plan offering sophisticated features and capacity. It allows you to send up to 30 million messages daily.

Each subscription type has different pricing and features, so evaluating your specific needs and choosing the type that best meets your requirements is important.

Conditional Access

An organization's security perimeter now includes user and device identify, and access control decisions can be based on identify-driven signals. As part of the new identify-driven control plane, Azure AD Conditional Access brings signals together to make decisions and enforce organizational policies. When using a Conditional Access policy, the user must complete an action if the end users want to access a resource. For instance, if a payroll manager wants to access the payroll application, the manager must do multifactor authentication.

A primary goal for administrators is to enhance productivity wherever and whenever users need it and ensure the security of the organization's assets.

When necessary, implement Conditional Access policies to protect your organization's resources from cyberattacks. Azure AD uses various signals to determine whether an access request is authorized. Here are some of the common signals that Azure AD uses:

- *User sign-in*: Azure AD monitors user sign-in events to determine if they are attempting to access a resource. This includes tracking the user's identify, IP address, and device information.

- *Device health*: Azure AD can evaluate the health of the device attempting to access a resource, including its operating system version, antivirus status, and other security configurations.

- *Location*: Azure AD can determine the location of the user or device attempting to access a resource using IP address and other location-based data.

- *User behavior*: Azure AD can monitor user behavior to detect anomalies, such as unusual sign-in patterns or access attempts from unfamiliar locations.

- *Risk*: Azure AD can evaluate the risk associated with a particular access request based on various factors, including the user's previous sign-in behavior, the device used to access the resource, and the location of the access attempt.

- *Device management*: Azure AD can check if the device is registered with Microsoft Intune or any other MDM solution, which enforces the policies set by the organization.

By analyzing these signals and applying the access policies set by the organization, Azure AD can help ensure that only authorized users with trusted devices and locations can access organizational resources.

Azure AD Conditional Access allows administrators to enforce organizational policies and security requirements on users accessing Azure resources. With Azure AD Conditional Access, administrators can create policies requiring users to meet certain conditions, such as using multifactor authentication or being on a trusted network, before accessing certain resources. This helps ensure that only authorized users can access sensitive data and applications, reducing the risk of unauthorized access and data breaches.

For example, an administrator could create a policy that requires all users attempting to access a specific application to use multifactor authentication, and only allow access from trusted locations. If a user attempts to access the application without meeting these conditions, they will be denied access. Azure AD Conditional Access can be used to protect various Azure resources, including Azure Active Directory, Azure Portal, Azure AD-connected apps, and other cloud services.

These are key benefits of Azure Conditional Access:

- *Improved security*: With Conditional Access, organizations can enforce more stringent security policies and access controls to help protect sensitive resources.

- *Enhanced user experience*: Conditional Access policies can be customized to provide a more seamless user experience, such as allowing access without MFA if the user is on a trusted device.

- *Greater visibility and control*: Conditional Access policies give administrators greater visibility and control over access to organizational resources, enabling them to identify and remediate potential security threats quickly.

Azure AD Conditional Access maps to several categories of the NIST CSF Protect function, which focuses on safeguarding data, systems, and assets against potential cyber threats.

- *Identify management and access control*: Azure AD Conditional Access helps organizations implement strong access controls to prevent unauthorized access to systems and data. Organizations can significantly reduce the risk of unauthorized access by enforcing policies requiring multifactor authentication, Conditional Access based on device health or location, and other conditions.

- *Awareness and training*: In addition to enforcing access controls, organizations can use Azure AD Conditional Access to provide training and awareness to users. For example, organizations can configure policies that require users to complete security training or acknowledge a security policy before accessing certain resources.

- *Data security*: Azure AD Conditional Access helps organizations protect their data by controlling who has access to it and under what conditions. By enforcing policies requiring certain authentication factors or device conditions, organizations can ensure that only authorized users can access sensitive data.

- *Information protection processes and procedures*: Azure AD Conditional Access can help organizations enforce information protection processes and procedures by requiring users to follow certain security policies before accessing certain resources. For example, organizations can configure policies that require users to use encryption or comply with certain data handling procedures before accessing sensitive data.

Azure AD Conditional Access is critical in protecting Azure resources from cybersecurity attacks by enforcing access controls and policies based on specific conditions. Here are some of the ways that Azure AD Conditional Access helps protect Azure resources:

- *MFA*: Azure AD Conditional Access can be configured to require MFA for specific users, applications, or scenarios. This adds an extra layer of security to prevent unauthorized access, even if an attacker has obtained a user's credentials.

- *Device compliance*: Azure AD Conditional Access can enforce policies requiring devices to comply with certain security requirements, such as having antivirus software installed, before allowing access to Azure resources. This helps ensure that only trusted devices are used to access sensitive resources.

- *Location-based access*: Azure AD Conditional Access can enforce policies that only allow access to Azure resources from specific locations or IP addresses. This helps prevent unauthorized access from unknown or untrusted locations.

- *Risk-based access*: Azure AD Conditional Access can evaluate the level of risk associated with a user or device and enforce policies accordingly. For example, if a user attempts to access a sensitive Azure resource from an unfamiliar location, the access request may be denied or require additional authentication steps.

- *Conditional Access app control*: This feature provides real-time monitoring and control of user sessions for cloud applications. It helps prevent unauthorized access to cloud applications and secures critical data by controlling copy, paste, and print operations within the applications.

There are several key security design best practices for Azure AD Conditional Access that organizations should consider.

- *Start with a least privilege access model*: Organizations should start with a least privilege access model, which means that users should only have access to the resources they need to do their jobs. Azure AD Conditional Access can help enforce this model by enforcing access controls based on specific conditions.

- *Use MFA everywhere*: MFA is a critical security control that helps prevent unauthorized access to sensitive resources. Organizations should consider using MFA for all users, applications, and scenarios, including those protected by Azure AD Conditional Access.

- *Use risk-based access controls*: Azure AD Conditional Access can evaluate the risk associated with a particular access request and enforce policies accordingly. Organizations should consider using risk-based access controls to dynamically adjust security policies based on the level of risk associated with a particular user or device.

- *Implement device compliance policies*: Organizations should consider implementing device compliance policies that require devices to meet certain security requirements, such as having antivirus software installed or being encrypted.

- *Monitor user and device sign-in events*: Azure AD provides detailed sign-in and audit logs that can help organizations monitor user and device sign-in events. Organizations should regularly review these logs to detect potential security threats.

- *Regularly review and update policies*: Azure AD Conditional Access policies should be regularly reviewed and updated according to organizational security policies.

- *Enable Conditional Access App Control*: Enabling Conditional Access App Control provides real-time monitoring and control of user sessions for cloud applications. It helps prevent unauthorized access to data in cloud applications and secures critical data by controlling copy, paste, and print operations within the applications.

By following these best practices, organizations can help ensure that Azure AD Conditional Access is implemented in a way that effectively protects their Azure resources from cybersecurity attacks.

How To Enable It

To achieve your organization's application and resource access NIST CSF protect strategy, you must carefully plan your Azure AD Conditional Access deployment. Azure AD Conditional Access policies provide great configuration flexibility, but you must plan carefully to prevent undesirable outcomes.

Conditions for accessing resources in Azure AD are automated based on user, device, and location signals. Organizations can use Azure AD Conditional Access policies to create security controls that block access, require MFA, or restrict user sessions when needed and stay out of the user's way when not.

The following is a high-level process to turn on Azure AD Conditional Access:

1. *Acquire the necessary licenses*: As mentioned earlier, Azure AD Conditional Access requires an Azure AD Premium P1 or P2 license. If an organization still needs to get these licenses, it must acquire them.

2. *Configure Azure AD Connect*: If an organization wants to apply Azure AD Conditional Access policies to on-premises applications, it will need to configure Azure AD Connect to synchronize on-premises identities with Azure AD.

3. *Enable Cloud App Discovery*: Organizations should enable Cloud App Discovery to understand better the cloud applications used within their environment.

4. *Configure Azure AD Identify Protection*: Organizations should enable Azure AD Identify Protection to help detect and remediate identify-based risks.

5. *Define Azure AD Conditional Access policies*: Organizations can define Azure AD Conditional Access policies in the Azure Portal, which specify the conditions that must be met before access is granted to specific resources. These conditions can include user, device, location, and application factors.

6. *Test the policies*: Before enforcing Azure AD Conditional Access policies, organizations should test them to ensure they work as expected.

7. *Enforce the policies*: Once the policies have been tested and validated, organizations can enforce them to help protect their resources.

The following is an example of turning on the MFA Conditional Access policy in Azure AD:

1. Log in to the Azure Portal.

2. Search for *Azure Active Directory, Security and Conditional Access*.

3. Click New Policy.

4. Choose users or workload identities based on your plan to include or exclude users/groups.

5. When selecting cloud apps or Actions ➤ Include, ensure all are selected.

6. Choose to grant access, require multifactor authentication, and click Access Controls ➤ Grant.

7. Make sure that "Enable policy" is set to "Report-only" and confirm your settings.

8. Create your policy by clicking Create.

It's important to note that the Azure AD Conditional Access deployment process can vary depending on an organization's specific requirements and use cases.

Azure AD Conditional Access Subscription Type?   Azure AD Conditional Access is a capability offered in Azure AD, which is available in several editions. The license requirements for Azure AD Conditional Access depend on the edition of Azure AD that an organization has.

Azure AD Free: Azure AD Free includes some basic role-based authentication. However, to access more Conditional Access policies, organizations need to upgrade to a higher edition of Azure AD Premium P1 or Premium P2.

Azure AD Premium P1: Azure AD Premium P1 includes more advanced Conditional Access policies, such as location-based access and the ability to block access based on device health. It also includes features like self-service password reset, group access management, and application proxy. Azure AD Premium P1 requires a per-user license.

Azure AD Premium P2: Azure AD Premium P2 includes all the features of Azure AD Premium P1, as well as additional features like Identify Protection, Privileged Identify Management, and Access Reviews. Azure AD Premium P2 also requires a per-user license.

It's important to note that Azure AD Conditional Access policies can also be applied to specific applications or services, which may have their own licensing requirements.

In summary, the license requirements for Azure AD Conditional Access depend on the edition of Azure AD that an organization has. While some basic Azure AD Conditional Access policies are available in Azure AD Free, more advanced policies require a higher edition of Azure AD, such as Azure AD Premium P1 or P2.

Azure AD's Application Proxy

Azure AD Application Proxy is a cloud-based service that enables remote access to on-premises applications without requiring organizations to expose their applications to the public Internet. This helps to enhance the security of on-premises applications by reducing the attack surface.

Azure AD Application Proxy establishes a secure connection between the user's device and the Azure AD Application Proxy service. When a user attempts to access an on-premises application published through Azure AD Application Proxy, the request is sent to the Azure AD Application Proxy service, which forwards the request to the on-premises application. The response from the application is then securely relayed back to the user's device through the Azure AD Application Proxy service. Azure AD Application Proxy also provides additional security features such as MFA and Conditional Access policies, which can be used to enforce granular access controls based on the user's identify, device, location, and other factors.

A single sign-on to Azure Active Directory allows users to access cloud and on-premises applications via an external URL or internal application portal, enabling secure remote access. A single sign-on to Azure Active Directory allows users to access cloud and on-premises applications. A single sign-on to line-of-business (LOB) applications, such as Remote Desktop, SharePoint, Teams, Tableau, Qlik, and Application Proxy, can be provided by Application Proxy.

These are the key benefits of Azure AD Application Proxy:

- *Enhanced security*: Using Azure AD Application Proxy, organizations can secure their on-premises web applications and ensure that only authorized users can access them. Azure AD Application Proxy provides authentication and authorization capabilities, and requests are routed through Azure AD, which provides additional security features such as MFA.

- *Simplified access*: With Azure AD Application Proxy, external users can access on-premises web applications using a web browser or mobile app without needing a VPN connection or opening ports in a firewall. This makes it easier for organizations to provide secure remote access to their applications.

- *Reduced infrastructure complexity*: Azure AD Application Proxy eliminates the need for organizations to maintain complex infrastructure such as VPNs, web application proxies, or reverse proxies. This reduces the overall complexity of the infrastructure and helps organizations save costs.

- *Granular access control*: Azure AD Application Proxy provides granular access control capabilities, allowing organizations to define access policies based on user, device, location, and application. This ensures that only authorized users can access the published application.

- *Secure remote access*: With Azure AD Application Proxy, organizations can securely expose their on-premises web applications to users outside the corporate network without needing a VPN. This enables employees, partners, and customers to access critical applications from anywhere while maintaining security and compliance.

- *Seamless user experience*: Azure AD Application Proxy provides a seamless user experience for accessing on-premises web applications. Users can access these applications using an SSO experience without remembering different application credentials.

- *Application-level authentication and authorization*: Azure AD Application Proxy enables organizations to enforce application-level authentication and authorization policies for on-premises web applications. This will enable organizations to make sure that only authorized users are accessing these applications and that they are accessing the applications with the appropriate permissions.

- *Scalability*: Azure AD Application Proxy is a cloud-based service that can scale to meet the needs of organizations of all sizes. This makes it easy for organizations to add new applications or users as needed without worrying about capacity limitations or infrastructure requirements.

Azure AD Application Proxy maps to several functions within the NIST CSF Protect category, which focuses on implementing safeguards to ensure the delivery of critical infrastructure services. Here are a few ways Azure AD Application Proxy can support the Protect category:

- *Access control*: Azure AD Application Proxy provides access control for on-premises web applications by integrating with Azure AD. Administrators can define access policies, configure SSO, and enforce MFA for users accessing these applications.

- *Identify management and authentication*: Azure AD Application Proxy enables secure user authentication and identify management for on-premises web applications. It supports modern authentication protocols, such as OAuth and OpenID Connect, and allows users to authenticate using their corporate credentials.

- *Information protection processes and procedures*: Azure AD Application Proxy helps protect sensitive information by enabling organizations to enforce application-level authentication and authorization policies for on-premises web applications. This ensures that only authorized users are accessing these applications and accessing them with the appropriate permissions.

- *Security continuous monitoring*: Azure AD Application Proxy provides visibility into user access to on-premises web applications. Administrators can use Azure AD logs and reporting to monitor user access patterns, identify suspicious activity, and respond to security incidents.

Finally, Azure AD Application Proxy allows organizations to securely publish internal web applications to external users through a cloud-based service.

How It Works

Here are the steps:

1. *Register the application*: The on-premises web application is registered with Azure AD Application Proxy using the Azure Portal. During the registration process, a connector is installed on a server inside the organization's network. The connector is a proxy that securely forwards requests to the on-premises application.

2. *Configure access*: Access to the application is configured through Azure AD. This includes defining who can access the application and their access type, such as read-only or read-write.

3. *Authentication and authorization*: When users attempt to access the application, they are authenticated by Azure AD using their credentials. Once authenticated, Azure AD checks the user's authorization to ensure they can access the application and what level of access they have.

4. *Connect to the application*: Once the user is authorized, the Azure AD Application Proxy connector establishes a secure connection to the on-premises application using the connector. This connection is secured using SSL encryption and is initiated by the connector, so there's no need for the on-premises application to be exposed to the Internet.

5. *Application access*: The user is then presented with the on-premises web application through their web browser. The user can access the application as if running locally on their device without connecting to a VPN.

The following are the key security design best practices for Azure AD Application Proxy:

- *Secure the connector*: The Azure AD Application Proxy connector is the component that facilitates communication between the cloud service and the on-premises application. Ensure the connector is installed on a secure server within the organization's network and configured to communicate only with the Azure AD Application Proxy cloud service.

- *Enforce access policies*: Define access policies in Azure AD to ensure that only authorized users can access the on-premises application. Implement MFA to secure user access further.

- *Implement identify management best practices*: Implement best practices for identify management, such as strong password policies, and enforce account lockout policies to prevent brute-force attacks.

- *Use SSL encryption*: Ensure that all communication between the Azure AD Application Proxy cloud service and the on-premises application is encrypted using SSL/TLS. This helps protect against eavesdropping and data tampering.

- *Monitor access and activity*: Use Azure AD logs and reporting to monitor user access to on-premises applications and set up alerts for suspicious activity. This helps detect and respond to potential security incidents.

- *Keep software up-to-date*: Ensure that all components of the Azure AD Application Proxy solution, including the connector and on-premises applications, are updated with the latest security patches and updates.

- *Test and validate the solution*: Perform regular testing and validation of the Azure AD Application Proxy solution to ensure it is configured and operating correctly. This includes testing for security vulnerabilities and ensuring access policies work as expected.

By following these best practices, organizations can help ensure that Azure AD Application Proxy is configured securely and provides a strong layer of protection for on-premises applications.

How To Enable It

Azure AD Application Proxy allows you to publish applications, such as SharePoint sites, Outlook Web Access, and IIS-based apps, within your private network while providing secure access to users outside your network through Microsoft Azure Active Directory Application Proxy. Your employees can access your apps from home using their own devices and authenticate using this cloud-based proxy. Connectors are slim Windows services that install inside your networks. They maintain outbound connections from within your networks to the proxy services. When users access published applications, these connections are used to provide access.

Here are some deployment considerations for Azure AD Application Proxy:

- *Application compatibility*: Check if your applications are compatible with Azure AD Application Proxy. The application should be able to work with the proxy server and support HTTP/S protocol for access.

- *Networking and firewall configuration*: The on-premises network where the applications reside should allow traffic to and from the Azure AD Application Proxy. You may need to configure firewalls and network security groups to allow traffic through specific ports.

- *Certificate management*: Ensure that the SSL certificates used by the on-premises applications are valid and trusted by the Azure AD Application Proxy. You may need to install SSL certificates on the on-premises server and configure the proxy to use them.

- *Authentication and authorization*: Configure the authentication and authorization settings for the applications you want to publish using Azure AD Application Proxy. You can choose between Integrated Windows Authentication, Passthrough Authentication, or Azure AD Single Sign-On.

- *User and group management*: Define who can access the applications published through Azure AD Application Proxy by configuring user and group assignments in Azure AD. You can also use Conditional Access policies to restrict access based on device, location, or other factors.

- *High availability and scalability*: Azure AD Application Proxy offers high availability and scalability features that allow you to handle traffic spikes and ensure availability. Consider enabling autoscaling, load balancing, and deploying multiple instances for redundancy.

- *Monitoring and logging*: Configure monitoring and logging for Azure AD Application Proxy to track usage, detect issues, and troubleshoot problems. You can use Azure Monitor and Azure Log Analytics to see the proxy's performance and usage.

- *Licensing*: Azure AD Application Proxy requires an Azure AD Premium P1 or P2 license for each user who accesses a published application. Ensure that you have the appropriate licenses for your users and applications.

To deploy Azure AD's Application Proxy, you can follow these steps:

1. Log in to the Azure Portal with an account with global administrator or application administrator permissions.

2. In the navigation pane on the left, click Azure Active Directory.

3. Under Manage, select Application Proxy.

4. Click the Enable Application Proxy button at the top of the page.

5. On the Enable Application Proxy page, review the requirements and limitations for using the application proxy and then click Enable.

6. Once the application proxy is enabled, you can start registering and publishing on-premises applications for remote access.

7. To register an application, click the "Add an application" button and follow the prompts to provide the necessary information, such as the internal URL, pre-authentication settings, and user assignment.

8. Once the application is registered, you can publish it for remote access by clicking the Publish button and selecting the appropriate settings, such as the external URL, authentication method, and access control.

9. After the application is published, you can test the remote access by opening a browser and entering the external URL.

Microsoft Azure AD Application Proxy is easy to use, cost-effective, and secure. You can use Azure AD Application Proxy to make on-premises applications use Azure's authorization controls and security analytics. Azure AD Application Proxy will automatically disable after an expiration date.

Just Enough Administration

Just Enough Administration (JEA) is a feature of Azure that allows you to create and delegate administrative tasks to users on an as-needed basis. JEA provides a way to limit the administrative privileges granted to users, ensuring that they have access only to the specific administrative tasks they need to perform.

JEA works by creating a custom PowerShell endpoint that exposes a subset of the administrative capabilities of the system. Administrators can define specific tasks that are allowed, and JEA will restrict users to only those tasks. With JEA, administrators can define custom PowerShell cmdlets, scripts, and functions that non-administrative users can execute. These users can run these commands remotely on the JEA endpoint without having full administrative access to the system. JEA provides several benefits, including the following:

- Reduced risk of accidental or intentional system changes by nonadministrative users

- Improved security by limiting administrative privileges to specific tasks

- Simplified management of administrative tasks by delegating tasks to users on an as-needed basis

- Auditing capabilities that allow administrators to monitor and track the activities of JEA users

JEA is a powerful tool for managing access to critical systems and ensuring that administrative privileges are granted only to those who need them. It is beneficial in environments where multiple users require access to administrative tasks, but granting full administrative access is not practical or desirable. JEA is important from a cybersecurity standpoint because it provides a way to limit administrative privileges and reduce the risk of unauthorized access or malicious activities.

Here are some of the reasons why JEA is essential for cybersecurity:

- *Least privilege*: The principle of least privilege is a fundamental security concept that states that users should be granted only the minimum level of access required to perform their job. JEA helps enforce this principle by allowing administrators to limit access to only the specific administrative tasks users need.

- *Role-based access control*: JEA supports role-based access control, which means that access to specific administrative tasks can be granted based on a user's role in the organization. This helps ensure that users have access only to the resources and privileges they need to perform their job, reducing the risk of accidental or intentional misuse.

- *Auditing and logging*: JEA provides auditing and logging capabilities that allow administrators to track and monitor users' activities who are granted administrative access. This helps detect and investigate any suspicious or malicious activities.

- *Customizable permissions*: JEA allows administrators to define custom PowerShell cmdlets, scripts, and functions that nonadministrative users can execute. This enables administrators to tailor the permissions and tasks available to users based on their specific needs, further reducing the risk of unauthorized access or misuse.

- *Simplified management*: By delegating administrative tasks to users on an as-needed basis, JEA simplifies the management of administrative tasks and reduces the risk of errors or misconfigurations resulting from granting full administrative access to users.

The Protect function of the NIST CSF includes implementing safeguards to ensure the delivery of critical infrastructure services. JEA helps organizations achieve this by implementing a least-privilege access model. Here's how:

- *Access control*: JEA allows organizations to limit administrative privileges by granting access to specific administrative tasks only. This helps prevent unauthorized access and reduces the risk of errors or misconfigurations that can occur with full administrative access.

- *Customizable permissions*: JEA allows organizations to define custom PowerShell cmdlets, scripts, and functions that non-administrative users can execute. This enables organizations to tailor permissions and tasks to users based on their specific needs, reducing the risk of unauthorized access or misuse.

The following are the essential key design security best practices for JEA:

- *Least privilege*: Implement a least-privilege access model to ensure that users can only access the specific administrative tasks they need to perform their job. This reduces the risk of unauthorized access and misuse of administrative privileges.

- *RBAC*: Use RBAC to assign administrative tasks to users based on their role in the organization. This helps ensure that users have access only to the resources and privileges they need to perform their job, reducing the risk of accidental or intentional misuse.

- *Customizable permissions*: Define custom PowerShell cmdlets, scripts, and functions that non-administrative users can execute. This enables administrators to tailor the permissions and tasks available to users based on their specific needs, further reducing the risk of unauthorized access or misuse.

- *Auditing and logging*: Enable auditing and logging capabilities to monitor and track the activities of JEA users. This helps detect and investigate any suspicious or malicious activities.

- *Network segmentation*: Consider implementing network segmentation to isolate JEA endpoints from the rest of the network. This helps reduce the risk of lateral movement by attackers in case of a compromise.

- *Secure remote access*: Implement secure remote access to JEA endpoints, such as using a VPN or multifactor authentication. This helps prevent unauthorized access and reduces the risk of credential theft.

- *Regular updates and patches*: Keep JEA endpoints and systems up to date with the latest security patches and updates to prevent known vulnerabilities from being exploited.

- *Regular testing and validation*: Regularly test and validate JEA configurations and permissions to ensure they work as intended and detect any potential security issues.

By implementing these security best practices, organizations can help ensure the security and integrity of their JEA environment and reduce the risk of unauthorized access or misuse of administrative privileges.

How To Enable It

The Just Enough Administration feature in PowerShell 5.0 and higher allows nonadministrators limited access to execute the commands, scripts, and executables required for discovery. Microsoft JEA improves security by limiting nonadministrators access to discovery commands, scripts, and executables. By doing so, MID servers can collect information on Windows machines without needing full administrator privileges.

Microsoft JEA provides role-based administration through PowerShell Remoting, which manages communication and authentication using Windows Remote Management (WinRM). As a result of this framework, computers using the HTTP protocol can be managed securely and reliably. PowerShell Remoting uses two total ports (5985, 5986) for HTTP and HTTPS, which are easier to secure than multiple ports used in dynamic port mapping in WMI.

Here are the steps to enable JEA:

1. *Install the JEA toolkit*: Install the JEA toolkit on the target server(s) using PowerShell. You can download the toolkit from the PowerShell Gallery using the following command:

```
Install-Module -Name Microsoft.PowerShell.JEA
```

2. *Create a JEA endpoint configuration*: Use the New-
   PSSessionConfigurationFile cmdlet to create a JEA endpoint
   configuration file (.pssc). This file contains the PowerShell
   cmdlets and functions that JEA users will be able to access. You
   can define custom PowerShell cmdlets, scripts, and processes that
   can be executed by nonadministrative users and specify the roles
   and permissions for each user.

3. *Register the JEA endpoint configuration*: Use the Register-
   PSSessionConfiguration cmdlet to register the JEA endpoint
   configuration file with the local PowerShell session configuration.
   This makes the JEA endpoint available for use by JEA users.

4. *Grant permissions to JEA users*: Use the Set-
   PSSessionConfiguration cmdlet to grant permissions to JEA
   users based on their role in the organization. You can specify
   which cmdlets and functions each user can access and which
   parameters they can use.

5. *Test the JEA endpoint*: Use the Test-PSSessionConfiguration
   cmdlet to test the JEA endpoint configuration and ensure that it is
   working as intended.

6. *Connect to the JEA endpoint*: Using the PowerShell remoting
   feature, JEA users can connect to the JEA endpoint. They can
   run PowerShell cmdlets and functions that are available to their
   role, but they need access to the full administrative capabilities of
   the server.

By following these steps, you can enable JEA and provide users with secure, role-
based access to administrative tasks on your server(s).

What Does JEA Work On?   JEA provides RBAC functionality through Windows
PowerShell remote access for Windows Servers and Windows client operating
systems. You use Windows PowerShell remoting when you start a Windows
PowerShell remote session on one computer and then execute tasks on another.
JEA works on any Windows Server 2016 or later operating system and Windows
10 or later.

Managed and Protected Physical Access to Assets

An organization can reduce cybersecurity risks by following the guidelines in the NIST CSF. PR.AC is one of the categories in the framework, which stands for "Protect managed and protected physical access to assets."

The PR.AC category ensures that physical access to an organization's assets is managed and protected. This includes implementing physical security controls, such as access controls, security cameras, and alarm systems, to prevent unauthorized asset access. The goal is to ensure that only authorized individuals can access sensitive information, systems, and equipment and that physical security breaches can be detected and responded to quickly.

The PR.AC category also emphasizes the importance of regularly assessing physical security risks, monitoring access logs, and conducting security awareness training for employees to help them recognize and report potential physical security breaches.

The goal of the PR.AC category is that only authorized personnel have access to an organization's assets and that physical security breaches are quickly prevented, detected, and responded to. This involves implementing a range of physical security controls.

- *Access controls*: Limiting physical access to assets through security badges, keycards, biometric authentication systems, or other methods

- *Security cameras*: Monitoring physical access to assets through the use of security cameras that can capture footage of unauthorized access attempts

- *Alarms and sensors*: Installing alarms and sensors to detect and alert security personnel of unauthorized access attempts or suspicious activity

- *Physical security audits*: Conduct regular physical security audits to identify potential vulnerabilities in the system and address them before they are exploited

- *Security awareness training*: Educating employees on the importance of physical security and how to recognize and report potential physical security breaches

By implementing these physical security controls and best practices, organizations can protect their assets against physical security threats and reduce the risk of cyberattacks resulting from unauthorized physical access. This helps ensure the confidentiality, integrity, and availability of sensitive information and critical infrastructure.

Awareness and Training (PR.AT)

Cybersecurity awareness and training educate individuals, employees, and organizations on cybersecurity risks, threats, and best practices. Cybersecurity awareness and training aim to improve the knowledge and skills of individuals in recognizing and responding to cyber threats and protecting their personal and organizational data and systems from unauthorized access, theft, or damage.

NIST Protect PR.AT is a framework that focuses on awareness and training to protect an organization's information, systems, and assets. The framework is designed to help organizations develop and implement effective training programs to ensure that all employees know their roles and responsibilities in safeguarding sensitive information and systems from threats and attacks.

The following is a mapping of the PR.AT framework's components to the critical elements of awareness and training:

- *PR.AT-1: Security awareness and training program*: This component requires organizations to develop and implement a formal security awareness and training program that covers all employees, contractors, and other authorized users. The program should include periodic training sessions, communication of policies and procedures, and testing to ensure that employees understand their roles and responsibilities.

- *PR.AT-2: Threat awareness*: This component requires organizations to train employees regularly on current and emerging threats to the organization's information, systems, and assets. This training should include examples of how threats can manifest and how employees can recognize and report potential threats.

- *PR.AT-3: Training for specialized roles*: This component requires organizations to provide specialized training for employees who require additional security knowledge, such as IT staff, system administrators, and information security professionals.

- *PR.AT-4: Awareness of policy and procedures*: This component requires organizations to ensure that all employees are aware of the organization's policies and procedures related to information security. This includes policies on the acceptable use of technology, access control, incident reporting, and data classification.

- *PR.AT-5: Training on the safe use of technology*: This component requires organizations to provide employees with training on the safe and secure use of technology. This includes training on safe browsing habits, avoiding phishing attacks, and protecting mobile devices.

As part of the Azure cloud shared responsibility model, the NIST CSF security functions are provided in Table 4-2 with respect to PR.AT.

Table 4-2. PR.AT Management Responsibility Matrix

Category	Subcategory	Informative References	Responsibility	Customer Responsibility	Microsoft Azure Responsibility
Awareness and Training (PR.AT): The personnel and partners are properly trained to perform their information security-related duties and responsibilities as part of the organization's cybersecurity awareness education program.	PR.AT-1: Training and information are provided to all users.	NIST SP 800-53 Rev. 4 AT-2, PM-13	Shared	Following the job descriptions, the customer is responsible for training its employees and vendors, including basic security awareness training and role-based training, as necessary.	Staff members at Microsoft participate in Microsoft Azure-sponsored security training programs and receive periodic security awareness updates to ensure all users are informed and trained. As part of Microsoft's ongoing security education program, employees and third-party partners are trained on non-disclosure provisions, which minimizes risks.

(continued)

Table 4-2. (*continued*)

Category	Subcategory	Informative References	Responsibility	Customer Responsibility	Microsoft Azure Responsibility
	PR.AT-2: Privileged users understand their roles and responsibilities.	NIST SP 800-53 Rev. 4 AT-3, PM-13	Shared	Training is the customer's responsibility for privileged users, including basic awareness training and role-based training as appropriate per job description.	All Microsoft Azure privileged users follow a role-based training program to ensure they understand their roles and responsibilities. It is a mandatory security and awareness training program for Microsoft Azure that assists individuals in gaining a better understanding of security processes and procedures relevant to the role they have been placed in and is directly related to their job duties.
	PR.AT-3: Roles & responsibilities are understood by third parties (e.g., suppliers, customers, partners)	NIST SP 800-53 Rev. 4 PS-7, SA-9	Shared	Third-party stakeholders must be adequately informed of their roles and responsibilities by the customer.	The Microsoft Information Security Policy ensures that all stakeholders understand their security roles and responsibilities as Microsoft Azure's provider of subscribed services.

PR.AT-4: Roles and responsibilities are understood by senior executives	NIST SP 800-53 Rev. 4 AT-3, PM-13	Customer Responsibility	Customers must ensure their senior executives know their security roles and responsibilities.	N/A
PR.AT-5: Information and physical security personnel understand their roles and responsibilities	NIST SP 800-53 Rev. 4 AT-3, PM-13	Shared	Following their respective regulatory and internal policies, the customer is responsible for ensuring that information security personnel understand their roles and responsibilities.	A Microsoft Azure training program ensures that all information security and physical security personnel understand their assigned roles and responsibilities.

Azure Mapping for PR.AT

Microsoft's "Cybersecurity is for everyone" is an educational program designed to provide individuals and businesses with the knowledge and skills to protect themselves against cyber threats. The program is based on the idea that cybersecurity is everyone's responsibility and that all individuals, regardless of their job or background, can benefit from cybersecurity training. NIST Protect Awareness and Training (PR.AT) is classified into five subcategories, as depicted in Figure 4-4.

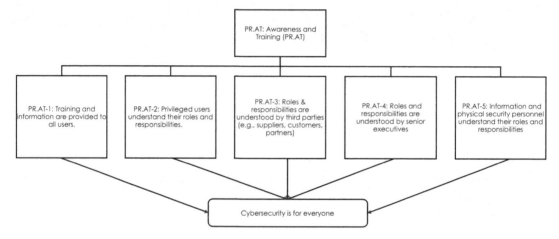

Figure 4-4. *NIST PR.AT Azure mapping*

The program covers a range of cybersecurity topics, including the following:

- Describes the basic concept of cybersecurity

- Establishes the guiding principles and core components of zero trust

- Examines ransomware and extortion-based threats

- The basics and beyond of security

The learning path consists of a series of video lectures, articles, and quizzes and is designed to be self-paced, allowing individuals to learn at their own pace. The program is free on the Microsoft Learn website and is aimed at a broad audience, including individuals, small business owners, and employees of larger organizations. See the following sites:

```
https://www.microsoft.com/en-ww/security/business/security-101/what-is-
cybersecurity?rtc=1
```

```
https://learn.microsoft.com/en-gb/users/gitasharmasheher-3612/
collections/yrrbdgy2d6158?source=docs&culture=en-us&country=us
```

The learning program is a valuable resource for anyone looking to improve their knowledge and skills in cybersecurity. By educating individuals on basic security principles and best practices, Microsoft is helping to create a culture of cybersecurity awareness and promoting a safer digital environment for everyone.

Summary

In this chapter, you read about designing and deploying a strategy for protecting security services in line with the NIST CSF mapping of Azure services including PR.AC: Identify Management, Authentication and Access Control, and PR.AT: Awareness and Training.

In the next chapter, you will read about the next part of designing and deploying a strategy for protecting security services.

CHAPTER 5

Design and Deploy a Protect Solution: Part 2

Data security is of paramount importance in today's digital age. As our lives become increasingly interconnected and dependent on technology, protecting sensitive information has become a critical concern for individuals, businesses, and governments.

Data security is particularly crucial in cloud computing because of its unique characteristics and challenges.

Cloud computing follows a shared responsibility model, where the cloud service provider (CSP) and the customer share responsibilities for data security. While the CSP is responsible for securing the underlying cloud infrastructure, the customer is responsible for ensuring their data and applications are secure within the cloud. Understanding and implementing appropriate security controls is crucial for customers to protect their data effectively.

Cloud computing involves storing and processing data on remote servers owned and maintained by CSPs. The confidentiality of sensitive data is critical to prevent unauthorized access or data breaches. Robust data encryption techniques and access control mechanisms are essential to protect data confidentiality in the cloud.

By the end of this chapter, you should be able to understand the following:

- Data Security (PR.DS)

Data Security

Data security in terms of cybersecurity refers to protecting sensitive digital information from unauthorized access, theft, destruction, and alteration. It involves implementing various security measures to ensure that data is kept safe and secure from external threats, such as hackers, cybercriminals, and other malicious actors. The data can include sensitive personal data, financial information, and proprietary business data.

281

© Puthiyavan Udayakumar 2023
P. Udayakumar, *Design and Deploy a Secure Azure Environment*,
https://doi.org/10.1007/978-1-4842-9678-3_5

Data security involves various practices and technologies to prevent and mitigate cyber threats. The following are some of the essential practices and technologies used in data security:

- *Access control*: This refers to implementing procedures to limit who can access certain data, such as using passwords, biometric authentication, and other security measures.

- *Encryption*: This involves converting plaintext data into a coded format that authorized parties can read only with the appropriate decryption key. Encryption can protect data both while it is stored and while it is in transit.

- *Data backup and recovery*: Regular data backup and recovery is a crucial aspect of data security, as it ensures that important information can be restored in case of a cyberattack, hardware failure, or another disaster.

- *Network security*: This includes firewalls, intrusion detection and prevention systems, and other technologies to protect networks from unauthorized access and cyber threats.

- *Anti-malware software*: This is designed to detect and remove viruses and other malware from computer systems. This can help prevent malware from stealing or damaging sensitive data.

- *Security audits and updates*: Regular security audits and updates are essential to ensure that data security measures are effective and up-to-date and to identify and address potential vulnerabilities before cybercriminals can exploit them.

In addition to these technical measures, data security involves human factors such as employee education and training, policy development, and risk management. Individuals, businesses, and organizations must stay updated with the latest data security threats and trends and implement appropriate security measures to protect their digital assets. A cybersecurity attack on data refers to hackers, cybercriminals, or other malicious actors attempting to gain unauthorized access to digital information. Cybersecurity attacks can come in many forms and can be aimed at stealing sensitive data, damaging or destroying digital infrastructure, or disrupting normal business operations. These are some common types of cybersecurity attacks on data:

- *Malware attacks*: Malware refers to any software designed to harm computer systems, steal data, or gain unauthorized access. Malware can include viruses, worms, Trojans, and other malicious software.

- *Phishing attacks*: Phishing is a social engineering technique that tricks users into providing sensitive information, such as usernames, passwords, and credit card numbers. Phishing attacks are often carried out through email or other communication channels.

- *Ransomware attacks*: Ransomware is malware that encrypts data on a victim's computer system, making it inaccessible. Cybercriminals then demand payment for the decryption key needed to unlock the data.

- *Denial-of-service (DoS) attacks*: DoS attacks aim to disrupt normal business operations by overwhelming a system or network with traffic, rendering it unusable.

- *Advanced persistent threats (APTs)*: APTs are long-term, targeted attacks that are designed to steal sensitive data or gain unauthorized access to a system or network. APTs often involve sophisticated techniques and can be difficult to detect and mitigate.

Organizations should implement appropriate security measures to protect against cybersecurity attacks on data, such as access controls, encryption, regular data backups, and recovery procedures, network security measures, and anti-malware software. It is also essential for individuals and organizations to stay up-to-date with the latest cybersecurity threats and trends and to take appropriate action to protect their digital assets. The NIST CSF provides guidelines, best practices, and standards for organizations to manage and reduce cybersecurity on data. One of the critical components of the NIST CSF is the Protect function, designed to help organizations safeguard their data and systems from cyber threats. The Protect function includes a set of subcategories and practices that organizations can implement to strengthen their data security measures. NIST Protect Data Security (PR.DS) is classified into eight subcategories, as depicted in Figure 5-1.

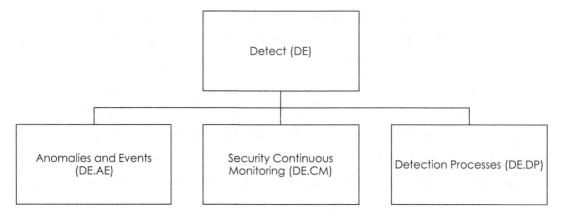

Figure 5-1. *NIST PR.DS*

By implementing the subcategories and practices under the Protect function, organizations can significantly improve their data security measures and reduce their risk of cyber threats. The NIST CSF is a valuable resource for organizations of all sizes and industries looking to enhance their cybersecurity posture.

Azure Mapping for Data Security

Azure offers a wide range of security features to help protect your data, applications, and infrastructure. Specifically regarding data security, Azure provides several features and services that align with the NIST guidelines for protecting sensitive information. Here are some ways Azure helps you meet NIST guidelines for data security:

- *Encryption*: Azure provides several options for encrypting data at rest and in transit. You can use Azure Disk Encryption to encrypt virtual machine disks, Azure Storage Service Encryption to encrypt data stored in Azure Blob Storage or Azure Files, and Azure Key Vault to manage and safeguard cryptographic keys.

- *Access controls*: Azure offers several features for controlling access to your data, including role-based access control (RBAC), Azure Active Directory, and Azure AD Privileged Identify Management. These features allow you to grant permissions to users and groups based on their roles and responsibilities and monitor and audit access to your data.

- *Threat detection*: Azure provides several tools for detecting and responding to threats, including Azure Security Center and Azure Sentinel. These tools use machine learning and AI to analyze data from multiple sources and detect anomalies and potential threats to your data.

- *Compliance*: Azure offers several compliance certifications and attestations, including SOC 1, SOC 2, ISO 27001, HIPAA, and GDPR. These certifications and attestations demonstrate that Azure meets rigorous security and privacy standards.

By leveraging these and other security features offered by Azure, you can help ensure that your data is protected from unauthorized access, theft, and other threats while meeting NIST guidelines for data security. Figure 5-2 maps PR.DS to Azure features.

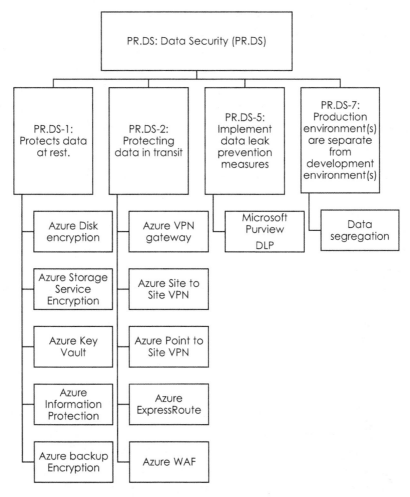

Figure 5-2. *NIST PR.DS to Azure mapping*

As part of the Azure cloud shared responsibility model, the NIST CSF security functions are provided in Table 5-1 with respect to PR.DS.

Table 5-1. PR.DS Management Responsibility Matrix

Category	Subcategory	Informative References	Responsibility	Customer Responsibility	Microsoft Azure Responsibility
Data Security (PR.DS): Information and records (data) are managed consistent with the organization's risk strategy to protect the confidentiality, integrity, and availability of information.	PR.DS-1: Protects data at rest.	NIST SP 800-53 Rev. 4 SC-28	Shared	Microsoft Azure provides the technology to use Azure Storage Account Keys (SAKs) to protect data at rest, but the customer is responsible for using those methods.	Microsoft Azure protects data at rest, but the customer must ensure encryption and data protection safeguards.
	PR.DS-2: Protecting data in transit.	NIST SP 800-53 Rev. 4 SC-8	Customer Responsibility	To enable protected communications in transit, the customer must configure their technology stack.	N/A

| PR.DS-3: Removal, transfer, and disposition of assets are formally managed. | NIST SP 800-53 Rev. 4 CM-8, MP-6, PE-16 | Microsoft Azure | N/A | Microsoft Azure datacenter colocations protect digital media assets for the lifecycle of their assets. Before disposing of Microsoft Azure assets, they are cleared, purged, or destroyed according to documented regulations, and Microsoft Azure assets are not transferred. An onsite asset destruction service is available through Microsoft Azure to destroy assets. |
| PR.DS-4: Ensuring availability through adequate capacity. | NIST SP 800-53 Rev. 4 AU-4, CP-2, SC-5 | Shared | Applications and tenant environments are monitored and planned by the customer. | For Microsoft Azure to ensure availability, capacity planning is conducted. Capacity planning involves determining the system's size, performance, and resilience. As well as how security controls influence Azure's performance, these elements also support data availability and continuity objectives as part of the overall security functionality of the system. |

(continued)

287

Table 5-1. (*continued*)

Category	Subcategory	Informative References	Responsibility	Customer Responsibility	Microsoft Azure Responsibility
	PR.DS-5: Implement data leak prevention measures.	NIST SP 800-53 Rev. 4 AC-4, AC-5, AC-6, PE-19, PS-3, PS-6, SC-7, SC-8, SC-13, SC-31, SI-4	Shared	Controlling information flow into and out of the customer's information system is the customer's responsibility.	The Microsoft Azure network is protected from data leaks by implementing technical controls. Networks are segregated through VLANs in Microsoft Azure, and access to the Microsoft Azure network from other internal Microsoft networks and the Internet is strictly controlled. Access Control Lists (ACLs) strictly control access to the Microsoft Azure network.

PR.DS-6:	NIST SP 800-53	Microsoft Azure	N/A	The change and release
Software,	Rev. 4 SI-7			management process of Microsoft
firmware, and				Azure thoroughly reviews software
information				updates for unauthorized changes
integrity are				before they enter production
verified using				environments. Code changes must
integrity-				be reviewed and approved before
checking				being deployed to the environment.
mechanisms.				If the integrity verification fails,
				deployment fails, and the process
				restarts.
				As part of Microsoft Azure's
				operating environment, network
				integrity scanning reduces the risk
				of software components or devices
				potentially being tampered with.
				Azure reassesses the integrity
				of software and information by
				monitoring events reported by
				integrity monitoring.
				Moreover, each Microsoft Azure
				controller manages the lifecycle
				of applications running in its
				cluster and the provisioning and
				monitoring of hardware.

(continued)

Table 5-1. (*continued*)

Category	Subcategory	Informative References	Responsibility	Customer Responsibility	Microsoft Azure Responsibility
	PR.DS-7: Production environment(s) are separate from development environment(s).	NIST SP 800-53 Rev. 4 CM-2	Customer Responsibility	It is the customer's responsibility to separate test and production environments.	N/A
	PR.DS-8: Hardware integrity is verified with integrity-checking mechanisms.	NIST SP 800-53: SA-10, SI-7	Microsoft Azure	N/A	Microsoft Azure controllers also manage the lifecycle of applications running in their clusters and monitor the hardware under their control.

Azure offers several options for protecting data at rest. When data is at rest, it is stored in a storage medium, such as a disk or a database, and is not actively being processed or transmitted. Here are some ways that Azure helps protect your data at rest:

- *Encryption*: Azure provides several options for encrypting data at rest, including Azure Disk Encryption, Azure Storage Service Encryption, and Azure Database Encryption. Azure Disk Encryption encrypts virtual machine disks, while Azure Storage Service Encryption encrypts data stored in Azure Blob Storage or Azure Files. Azure Database Encryption encrypts data stored in Azure SQL Database, Azure Database for PostgreSQL, and Azure Database for MySQL.

- *Azure Key Vault*: Azure Key Vault is a cloud-based service that provides a secure repository for managing cryptographic keys and secrets, including encryption keys. Azure Key Vault can encrypt data at rest, and Azure services can be integrated with Azure Key Vault to manage encryption keys.

- *Azure Backup*: Azure Backup is a cloud-based backup solution that enables you to backup and restore data in Azure. Azure Backup provides encryption for data at rest and during transmission.

- *Azure Information Protection*: Azure Information Protection (AIP) is a cloud-based solution that enables you to classify, label, and protect sensitive information. AIP provides encryption for data at rest and in transit, allowing you to define data protection policies.

By leveraging these features and services, you can ensure that your data is protected at rest, even if it is stored on a disk or in a database. Azure's security features also help you meet regulatory compliance requirements and protect your data from unauthorized access, theft, and other threats.

Azure provides several solutions for protecting data in transit, which refers to data actively being transmitted between systems or applications. Here are some ways that Azure helps protect your data in transit:

- *Transport Layer Security (TLS)*: Azure supports TLS, a protocol that provides encryption and authentication for data in transit. TLS is used to secure connections between web applications and services, and Azure uses TLS to secure connections to Azure services and resources.

- *Azure Virtual Network*: Azure Virtual Network enables you to create isolated virtual networks in Azure, which can be used to connect resources and services securely. Azure Virtual Network provides several features for securing data in transit, including virtual private network (VPN) connections and Azure ExpressRoute, which provides a dedicated, private connection between on-premises infrastructure and Azure data centers.

- *Azure Application Gateway*: Azure Application Gateway is a web traffic load balancer that provides SSL/TLS termination for web traffic. This means that traffic between clients and the application gateway is encrypted using SSL/TLS, decrypted at the gateway and forwarded to the back-end web servers.

- *Azure VPN Gateway*: Azure VPN Gateway provides secure VPN connections between on-premises infrastructure and Azure Virtual Network. Azure VPN Gateway supports several VPN protocols, including TLS and Internet Protocol Security (IPsec).

- *Azure Front Door*: Azure Front Door is a global service that provides load balancing and application delivery. Azure Front Door provides SSL/TLS termination for web traffic, which means that traffic between clients and Azure Front Door is encrypted using SSL/TLS.

By leveraging these features and services, you can protect your data in transit between systems and applications. Azure's security features also help you meet regulatory compliance requirements and protect your data from unauthorized access, theft, and other threats.

Azure offers a data loss prevention (DLP) solution to help you identify, monitor, and protect sensitive information across your organization. Here are some features and capabilities of Azure DLP:

- *Sensitive information detection*: Azure DLP can scan your data to identify sensitive information, such as credit card numbers, Social Security numbers, and other types of personally identifiable information (PII).

- *Policy-based protection*: Azure DLP allows you to define policies for protecting sensitive information. For example, you can create a policy that prevents users from sending emails that contain credit card numbers or other sensitive information.

- *Automatic classification and labeling*: Azure DLP can automatically label sensitive information based on predefined or custom classifications. This can help you enforce policies and ensure that sensitive data is properly protected.

- *Integration with Azure services*: Azure DLP can integrate with Azure services, such as Azure Information Protection and Azure Active Directory, to provide additional protection for sensitive data.

- *Compliance reporting*: Azure DLP provides compliance reporting to help you meet regulatory requirements, such as GDPR, HIPAA, etc. You can use compliance reporting to monitor and report on data protection activities, such as policy violations and sensitive data discovery.

By leveraging Azure DLP, you can help protect sensitive information and comply with regulatory requirements. Azure DLP can be used to protect data in Azure services, on-premises, and in other cloud services.

Azure Disk Encryption

Azure Disk Encryption is a service provided by Microsoft Azure that enables you to encrypt the data stored on your Azure virtual machine disks. With this service, you can ensure that your data is protected and cannot be accessed by unauthorized parties. Azure Disk Encryption provides several security controls that align with the security requirements specified by the NIST Protect mapping.

Following are the various controls for NIST Protect Mapping:

- *Access control*: Azure Disk Encryption provides access control mechanisms that allow you to control who has access to your encrypted data. You can use Azure Active Directory (Azure AD) to manage user access to your Azure resources, including Azure Key Vault and virtual machines.

- *Audit and accountability*: Azure Disk Encryption provide audit logging capabilities that allow you to track and monitor access to your encrypted data. Azure Monitor can collect and analyze log data for your Azure resources, including virtual machines and Azure Key Vault.

- *Configuration management*: Azure Disk Encryption provides configuration management controls that allow you to manage the encryption settings for your virtual machines. You can use Azure Policy to define and enforce compliance policies for your Azure resources, including virtual machines and Azure Key Vault.

- *Data protection*: Azure Disk Encryption provides data protection mechanisms that help protect your virtual machine data. The BitLocker encryption technology used by Azure Disk Encryption helps prevent unauthorized access to your data, and the integration with Azure Key Vault provides secure key storage and management.

- *Identify and authentication*: Azure Disk Encryption integrate with Azure AD to provide identify and authentication controls for your Azure resources. You can use Azure AD to manage user access to your resources and enforce multifactor authentication (MFA) for added security.

When you enable disk encryption on an Azure virtual machine, the data on the virtual machine disks is encrypted before storing it in Azure storage. This helps ensure that even if someone gains unauthorized access to your virtual machine, they cannot read the data on the disks.

Azure Disk Encryption uses the industry-standard BitLocker encryption technology to encrypt the disks. BitLocker is a full-disk encryption feature available in Windows operating systems, and it encrypts data at rest, helping to protect the confidentiality and integrity of the data. Azure Disk Encryption also allows you to bring your own encryption keys to encrypt the virtual machine disks. This helps you control your encryption keys and ensures only authorized users can access the data. Azure Disk Encryption is a security feature in Microsoft Azure that helps protect your virtual machines by encrypting the data on their disks. It provides encryption of both the operating system disk and the data disk, ensuring that sensitive data is protected.

Azure Disk Encryption uses BitLocker encryption technology to encrypt the disks. BitLocker is a full-disk encryption feature built into the Windows operating system. It encrypts the data on the disks, making it unreadable to anyone who needs the decryption key. There are two types of encryption keys used with Azure Disk Encryption: platform-managed and customer-managed keys. Platform-managed keys are automatically generated and managed by Azure. With customer-managed keys, you can bring your own encryption keys (BYOK) and manage them yourself.

When using customer-managed keys, you have complete control over your encryption keys and can revoke or rotate them as needed. This provides you with extra security and controls over your data. Azure Disk Encryption supports both Windows and Linux virtual machines. It also integrates with Azure Key Vault, a cloud-based key management service, to provide centralized and secure key storage.

Enabling Azure Disk Encryption is a straightforward process, and you can do it through the Azure Portal, Azure PowerShell, or Azure CLI. Once you have enabled disk encryption, the data on your disks are encrypted automatically. You can monitor the status of your encrypted disks through the Azure Portal or Azure CLI. Azure Disk Encryption provides several benefits for securing and protecting your virtual machine data.

The following are the key benefits of Azure Disk Encryption:

- *Enhanced data security*: Azure Disk Encryption helps protect your virtual machine disks and data by encrypting them with BitLocker. This helps guard against unauthorized access to your data, even if someone gains access to your virtual machine.

- *Flexibility in encryption key management*: With Azure Disk Encryption, you can use either platform-managed or customer-managed encryption keys. This gives you the flexibility to choose how you want to manage your encryption keys and gives you an extra layer of control over your data.

- *Seamless integration with Azure services*: Azure Disk Encryption integrates with Azure services, such as Azure Key Vault, to provide centralized key management and secure key storage. This makes it easy to manage your encryption keys and ensures they are protected and secure.

- *Support for multiple operating systems*: Azure Disk Encryption supports Windows and Linux virtual machines, providing a consistent approach to disk encryption across multiple operating systems.

- *Ease of deployment*: Azure Disk Encryption is easy to deploy and manage, with support for deployment through the Azure Portal, Azure PowerShell, or Azure CLI. This makes starting with disk encryption and managing your encrypted disks easy.

Azure Disk Encryption also supports using customer-managed keys, which allows you to bring your own encryption keys to encrypt the virtual machine disks. You can use either the AES-128 or AES-256 encryption algorithm when using customer-managed keys. The choice between AES-128 and AES-256 depends on your specific security requirements. AES-256 provides a higher level of security because it uses a larger key size than AES-128. However, AES-256 requires more processing power to encrypt and decrypt data, which can affect performance. In general, both AES-128 and AES-256 are considered robust encryption algorithms that provide a high level of security.

How It Works

Azure Disk Encryption encrypts the data on the disks of your virtual machines in several steps:

1. *Provision an Azure Key Vault*: You must first create an Azure Key Vault to store the encryption keys used for disk encryption. Azure Key Vault is a cloud-based key management service that provides secure storage and management of cryptographic keys, certificates, and secrets.

2. *Generate or import an encryption key*: Once you have provisioned an Azure Key Vault, you can generate or import an encryption key to be used for disk encryption. You can choose to use a customer-managed key or a platform-managed key. If you choose to use a customer-managed key, you must provide the key to Azure Key Vault.

3. *Enable encryption for virtual machine disks*: You can enable encryption for your virtual machine disks using the Azure Portal, Azure PowerShell, or Azure CLI. When you enable disk encryption, Azure creates a virtual machine extension that installs the BitLocker encryption software on the virtual machine.

4. *Securely encrypt virtual machine disks*: Once disk encryption is enabled, the virtual machine disks are securely encrypted with the BitLocker encryption technology. Encryption encrypts the entire disk, including the operating system and any data stored on the disk.

5. *Manage encryption keys*: Azure Disk Encryption integrates with Azure Key Vault to manage encryption keys. If you use a customer-managed key, you can rotate, revoke, or replace the key as needed. Azure Key Vault provides a secure and centralized location for storing and managing your encryption keys.

6. *Monitor disk encryption status*: You can monitor the disk encryption status of your virtual machines through the Azure Portal, Azure PowerShell, or Azure CLI. You can view the encryption status of individual disks and track the progress of encryption operations.

Design Considerations

Here are some design security best practices for using Azure Disk Encryption from a NIST Protect standpoint:

- *Limit access*: Limit access to Azure Disk Encryption keys to only those who need access. Follow the principle of least privilege and grant access only to those who require it for their job duties.

- *Use robust encryption algorithms*: Use strong encryption algorithms for encrypting your virtual machine disks. NIST recommends using AES encryption with a key size of at least 256 bits.

- *Use secure key management*: Use Azure Key Vault to store and manage your encryption keys. Use access policies and RBAC to control who can manage the keys.

- *Rotate encryption keys*: Rotate your encryption keys regularly to minimize the risk of key compromise. Use Azure Key Vault to rotate your encryption keys and update your virtual machines to use the new keys.

- *Monitor and log key usage*: Monitor and log key usage to detect unauthorized access or usage of your encryption keys.

- *Use secure boot*: Use Secure Boot to protect against boot-time malware and unauthorized access to your virtual machines.

- *Follow security best practices for virtual machines*: Follow security best practices for virtual machines, such as keeping your virtual machines up to date with security patches, using strong passwords, and limiting network access.

- *Use network security controls*: Use network security controls, such as firewalls and network security groups, to limit network traffic to and from your virtual machines.

- *Enable auditing and monitoring*: Enable auditing and monitoring for your virtual machines to detect and respond to security incidents.

- *Implement data backups*: Implement data backups for your virtual machines to ensure you can recover your data during a security incident or disaster.

Please note that these are general security best practices, and specific requirements may vary depending on your organization's security policies and regulatory requirements.

How to Enable It

Before you can enable Azure Disk Encryption for your virtual machines, you need to ensure that your environment meets the following prerequisites:

- *Supported operating system*: Azure Disk Encryption supports encryption for virtual machines running Windows or Linux operating systems. You must use a supported operating system and version for encryption to work correctly.

- *Azure Key Vault*: You must create an Azure Key Vault in the same Azure subscription and region as your virtual machine. Azure Key Vault stores and manages the encryption keys used for encrypting your virtual machine disks.

- *Encryption key*: You must have an encryption key created in Azure Key Vault to encrypt your virtual machine disks. The encryption key can be either a key explicitly created for Azure Disk Encryption or an existing key that meets the required specifications.

- *Virtual machine size*: Azure Disk Encryption is supported for virtual machines running on specific VM sizes. The supported VM sizes vary depending on the operating system and Azure region you are using.

- *User role*: You must have the necessary permissions to enable encryption for your virtual machines. You need at least a Contributor or Virtual Machine Contributor role to enable Azure Disk Encryption.

- *Azure Active Directory*: If you want to use Azure AD to authenticate to your virtual machines, you must have Azure AD configured in your Azure environment.

- *PowerShell or Azure CLI*: You can enable Azure Disk Encryption using either PowerShell or Azure CLI. You must have the appropriate PowerShell or Azure CLI version installed on your local machine to use either of these tools.

Please note that the prerequisites may vary depending on your specific scenario, so it's recommended to refer to the Azure documentation for detailed guidance on enabling encryption for your virtual machines.

To turn on Azure Disk Encryption for your virtual machines, you can follow these general steps:

1. *Prepare your environment*: Before you enable Azure Disk Encryption, ensure that your virtual machines meet the requirements for encryption, including a supported operating system and virtual machine size, and that you have the necessary permissions to enable encryption.

2. *Create an encryption key*: Create an encryption key in Azure Key Vault to encrypt your virtual machine disks. You can use an existing key or create a new one specifically for this purpose.

3. *Enable encryption for your virtual machine*: Enable encryption for your virtual machine by creating a new encrypted virtual machine from a gallery image or encrypting an existing virtual machine.

4. *Select the encryption key*: When enabling encryption, specify the encryption key you created in step 2 to encrypt the virtual machine disks.

5. *Monitor the encryption status*: After enabling encryption for your virtual machine, monitor the encryption status to ensure the encryption process is successful. You can check the encryption status of your virtual machine disks in the Azure Portal or by using PowerShell commands.

6. *Rotate encryption keys*: Rotate your encryption keys regularly to ensure your virtual machines remain secure. You can use Azure Key Vault to rotate your encryption keys and update your virtual machines to use the new keys.

Please note that the steps for enabling Azure Disk Encryption may vary depending on your specific scenario, so it's recommended to refer to the Azure documentation for detailed guidance on enabling encryption for your virtual machines.

Key Insights of Azure Disk Encryption   Azure Disk Encryption is available in all Azure regions worldwide. Azure Disk Encryption supports both Windows and Linux virtual machines. Azure Disk Encryption uses the BitLocker Drive Encryption algorithm for Windows virtual machines and DM-Crypt for Linux virtual machines, and Azure Disk Encryption integrates with Azure Key Vault for secure key management and storage. Azure Disk Encryption supports both managed disks and unmanaged disks. Azure Disk Encryption supports multiple deployment scenarios, including virtual machine scale sets, Azure Batch, and Azure Kubernetes Service.

Azure Storage Service Encryption

Azure Storage Service Encryption is a feature of Azure storage that provides data encryption at rest. With Azure Storage Service Encryption, data is automatically encrypted before it is persisted to disk and decrypted when retrieved. This provides a secure way to store data in Azure storage, ensuring that even if someone gains physical access to the disk drives where the data is stored, they cannot read it without the encryption keys.

Azure Storage Service Encryption uses Microsoft-managed keys to encrypt and decrypt the data, and the keys are automatically rotated at regular intervals to ensure maximum security. This feature is available for Azure Blob storage, Azure Files, and Azure Queue storage and can be easily enabled through the Azure Portal, Azure CLI, or Azure PowerShell. Azure Storage Service Encryption can also help organizations meet compliance requirements, as it provides encryption of data at rest, which is often required by various regulatory standards. Additionally, because Azure manages the encryption, it eliminates the need for customers to manage and protect their own encryption keys, simplifying key management and reducing the risk of key compromise.

The following are the key benefits of Azure Storage Service Encryption:

- *Easy to enable*: Azure Storage Service Encryption can be easily enabled through the Azure Portal, Azure CLI, or Azure PowerShell, with no additional coding or configuration required.

- *Strong security*: Azure Storage Service Encryption uses Advanced Encryption Standard (AES) 256-bit encryption to encrypt data at rest, providing high security. Microsoft manages the encryption keys, which are rotated automatically at regular intervals to ensure maximum security.

- *Compliance*: Azure Storage Service Encryption helps organizations meet compliance requirements that require encryption of data at rest, such as HIPAA, PCI DSS, and GDPR.

- *No performance impact*: There is no noticeable performance impact when using Azure Storage Service Encryption, as the encryption and decryption of data are done automatically and seamlessly.

- *Cost-effective*: Azure Storage Service Encryption is available at no additional cost, so you can protect your data without incurring additional expenses.

- *Seamless integration*: Azure Storage Service Encryption integrates seamlessly with other Azure services, making it easy to use and integrate into your existing workflows.

- *Centralized key management*: Azure Storage Service Encryption uses Microsoft-managed keys, eliminating the need for customers to manage and protect their own encryption keys. This simplifies key management and reduces the risk of key compromise.

How It Works

Azure Storage Service Encryption works by encrypting data at rest in Azure storage accounts. When you enable Azure Storage Service Encryption for a storage account, all data written to that storage account is encrypted with Advanced Encryption Standard (AES) 256-bit encryption. The encryption and decryption of data are done automatically and seamlessly, so there is no noticeable impact on performance.

Microsoft manages the encryption keys used by Azure Storage Service Encryption, and the keys are automatically rotated at regular intervals to ensure maximum security. The keys are stored in Azure Key Vault, a secure key management service that allows you to manage and control access to keys used by Azure services. When you read data from an Azure storage account with Azure Storage Service Encryption enabled, the data is automatically decrypted using the encryption key. The decryption process is also seamless and transparent to the user, so there is no need to change your application or data access patterns.

Azure Storage Service Encryption is available for Azure Blob storage, Azure Files, and Azure Queue storage. You can enable it through the Azure Portal, Azure CLI, or Azure PowerShell.

Design Considerations

The following are the key design security best practices for Azure Storage Service Encryption:

- *Enable encryption for all storage accounts*: Enable Azure Storage Service Encryption for all storage accounts to ensure that all data at rest is encrypted.

- *Use Azure Key Vault for key management*: Use Azure Key Vault to manage and store your encryption keys. This allows you to control access to the keys and ensure they are secure.

- *Use managed disks for virtual machines*: If you use virtual machines in Azure, use managed disks instead of unmanaged ones. Managed disks are automatically encrypted with Azure Storage Service Encryption.

- *Use Azure Blob storage for large files*: If you need to store large files, such as media files, use Azure Blob storage. Azure Blob storage supports client-side encryption, which allows you to encrypt data before it is sent to Azure.

- *Use RBAC to control access*: Use RBAC to control access to your storage accounts and encryption keys. This allows you to restrict access to only those who need it.

- *Use virtual networks to isolate storage accounts*: Use virtual networks to isolate your storage accounts and limit access to them. This helps to prevent unauthorized access to your data.

- *Regularly rotate encryption keys*: Regularly rotate your keys to ensure maximum security. Azure Storage Service Encryption automatically rotates keys, but you can also manually rotate keys if necessary.

How to Enable It

Azure Storage Service Encryption is a feature that provides encryption of data at rest for Azure Blob storage, Azure Files, and Azure Queue storage. It is designed to help protect against unauthorized access to data by providing data encryption at the storage level. When enabled, Azure Storage Service Encryption encrypts all new data written to the storage account and any existing data that is modified or overwritten. A Microsoft-managed encryption key encrypts and decrypts the data automatically when accessed. This provides a seamless way to encrypt data without requiring changes to applications or data access patterns. Azure Storage Service Encryption uses Advanced Encryption Standard (AES) 256-bit encryption to encrypt the data. AES is a widely used and trusted encryption algorithm, and a key size of 256 bits provides high security.

To enable Azure Storage Service Encryption, you need to enable the feature in the Azure Portal, Azure CLI, or Azure PowerShell. Once enabled, all data stored in the storage account is automatically encrypted at rest. Azure Storage Service Encryption can help organizations meet compliance requirements, such as those requiring data encryption at rest. It also provides an additional layer of security to help protect against unauthorized access to data and can help reduce the risk of data breaches. It's important to note that Azure Storage Service Encryption encrypts only data at rest and does not provide encryption of data in transit. To encrypt data in transit, you should use a protocol such as HTTPS or SSL/TLS. Additionally, Azure Storage Service Encryption does not protect against unauthorized access to data by users with valid credentials, so it's important to follow security best practices for access control and authentication.

The following are some prerequisites that must be met before you can enable Azure Storage Service Encryption:

- *Azure Storage Account*: You must have an Azure Storage Account to enable Azure Storage Service Encryption.

- *Supported Storage Service*: Currently, only Azure Blob Storage and Azure Files support Azure Storage Service Encryption.

- *Service-Managed or Customer-Managed Key*: You must choose between service-managed keys or customer-managed keys. Service-managed keys are simpler to manage but offer less control, while customer-managed keys provide more control over the encryption process.

- *Azure Key Vault*: If you choose customer-managed keys, you must have an Azure Key Vault to store your encryption keys.

- *RBAC Access*: You must have the necessary permissions to manage encryption settings for the storage account. This can be granted through RBAC in Azure.

- *Data Encryption Standard (DES) Enabled*: If you want to use customer-managed keys, DES must be enabled for your Azure Key Vault.

You can successfully enable Azure Storage Service Encryption for your storage accounts by ensuring that these prerequisites are met.

You can turn on Azure Storage Service Encryption for a storage account using the Azure Portal, Azure PowerShell, or Azure CLI.

Here are the general steps using Azure Portal:

1. Sign in to the Azure Portal and navigate to the storage account you want to enable encryption for.

2. In the menu on the left, select Encryption.

3. On the Encryption page, toggle the "Service-managed encryption" option to Enabled.

4. Click Save to enable encryption.

Here are the general steps using Azure PowerShell:

1. Open a PowerShell command prompt and sign in to your Azure account.

2. Use the `Get-AzStorageAccount` cmdlet to retrieve the storage account object.

3. Use the `Set-AzStorageAccount` cmdlet to enable encryption for the storage account, specifying the `EnableEncryptionService` parameter as `True`.

Here are the general steps using Azure CLI:

1. Open a command prompt and sign in to your Azure account.

2. Use the `az storage account update` command to enable encryption for the storage account, specifying the `--encryption-services blob` parameter.

Key Insights of Azure Storage Service Encryption   Azure Storage Service Encryption is available in all Azure regions worldwide. The service encrypts data at rest in Azure Blob storage, Azure Files, and Azure Queue storage using industry-standard encryption algorithms such as AES-256. Azure Storage Service Encryption supports Microsoft and customer-managed keys stored in Azure Key Vault. Azure Storage Service Encryption can be enabled per storage account, allowing you to choose which storage accounts require encryption. Azure Storage Service Encryption has no additional cost and is included in the price of the underlying storage service. Azure Storage Service Encryption is a recommended security best practice for protecting data at rest in Azure storage accounts.

Azure Key Vault

Azure Key Vault is a cloud-based service offered by Microsoft Azure that provides a secure way to store and manage cryptographic keys, secrets, and certificates. It allows you to safeguard sensitive data such as encryption keys, passwords, and other secrets used by your applications, services, and systems. Azure Key Vault also provides centralized access control and auditing capabilities to ensure the security and compliance of your keys and secrets.

The following are some key features of Azure Key Vault:

-   *Centralized key management*: Azure Key Vault provides a central location to manage your keys and secrets, allowing you to control access and permissions for your applications and users quickly.

-   *Secure storage*: Azure Key Vault uses hardware security modules (HSMs) to provide secure storage and management of your keys and secrets. This protects your data from theft, unauthorized access, and other security threats.

- *Key life-cycle management*: Azure Key Vault supports the entire life cycle of your cryptographic keys, from creation and rotation to backup and recovery. This helps you maintain the security and availability of your keys and secrets over time.

- *Integration with other Azure services*: Azure Key Vault integrates with other Azure services such as Azure Active Directory, Azure Virtual Machines, and Azure Storage, allowing you to easily secure and manage your applications and services across your Azure environment.

The following are the key benefits of Azure Key Vault:

- *Secure key management*: Azure Key Vault allows you to securely store and manage cryptographic keys, secrets, and certificates in a centralized location. It uses hardware security modules (HSMs) to protect your keys and secrets, safeguarding them from unauthorized access, theft, and other security threats.

- *Simplified key management*: Azure Key Vault simplifies key management by providing a single location to store and manage your keys and secrets. It also offers APIs and SDKs to quickly integrate your applications, services, and systems.

- *Compliance*: Azure Key Vault helps you comply with regulatory requirements such as HIPAA, GDPR, etc. It provides features such as audit logs, access control, and key rotation to help you maintain the security and compliance of your keys and secrets.

- *Cost-effective*: Azure Key Vault is a cost-effective solution for key management. It eliminates the need for costly hardware and software investments, reducing the overall cost of key management.

- *Integration*: Azure Key Vault integrates with other Azure services such as Azure Virtual Machines, Azure App Service, and Azure Functions, making it easy to secure and manage your applications and services across your Azure environment.

- *High availability and disaster recovery*: Azure Key Vault provides high availability and disaster recovery options to ensure your keys and secrets are always available when needed. It also includes backup and restore capabilities to protect against data loss.

How to Enable It

Azure Key Vault provides a secure and central repository for storing and managing cryptographic keys, certificates, and secrets used to secure applications and services in the cloud.

In the real world, developers, IT professionals, and security teams can use Azure Key Vault to manage cryptographic keys and secrets to protect sensitive data and resources. For example, a development team might use Azure Key Vault to store and manage encryption keys that are used to encrypt and decrypt data at rest in a cloud-based application.

Azure Key Vault can also manage SSL/TLS certificates to secure websites and other services. In this case, the certificates can be stored in Azure Key Vault and automatically renewed, eliminating the need for manual certificate management. Another common use case for Azure Key Vault is storing API keys and other secrets used to access third-party services, such as authentication or payment APIs. By using Azure Key Vault to store and manage these secrets, you can reduce the risk of accidentally exposing them in source code or configuration files.

The following are some prerequisites for using Azure Key Vault:

- *Azure subscription*: You must have an active Azure subscription to create and manage Azure Key Vault instances.

- *Resource group*: You must have a resource group in which to create the Azure Key Vault instance. A resource group is a logical container for Azure resources that enables you to manage and organize them.

- *Azure AD tenant*: You must have an Azure AD tenant to create and manage Azure Key Vault instances. An Azure AD tenant is a dedicated instance of Azure AD that an organization owns and uses to manage its users and applications.

- *Permissions*: You must have the appropriate permissions to create and manage Azure Key Vault instances. This includes permissions to create and manage resources in the resource group, and permissions to manage Azure AD users and groups.

- *Virtual network (optional)*: To use private endpoints for Azure Key Vault, you must have a virtual network configured in Azure.

- *Firewall and network security group (optional)*: If you want to restrict network access to the Azure Key Vault instance, you can configure a firewall and network security group to limit traffic to specific IP addresses or ranges.

These prerequisites provide the foundation for creating and managing Azure Key Vault instances and ensuring their security and integrity.

Azure Key Vault is a fully managed service in Azure, so you do not need to turn it on. However, to start using Azure Key Vault, you must create a Key Vault instance and configure access policies and authentication settings.

Here are the high-level steps to create an Azure Key Vault instance:

1. Log in to the Azure Portal.

2. Click "Create a resource" in the menu on the left.

3. Search for *Key Vault* in the search bar and select Key Vault from the results.

4. Click Create.

5. Fill out the required fields, such as subscription, resource group, and name.

6. Choose the desired pricing tier and region.

7. Configure the access policies to define who can access the keys, certificates, and secrets in the Key Vault instance.

8. Configure authentication settings, such as enabling Azure AD authentication and setting up access policies for Azure AD users and groups.

9. Click Create to create the Key Vault instance.

Once the Key Vault instance is created, you can use the Azure Key Vault APIs or Azure Key Vault cmdlets to manage keys, certificates, and secrets in the Key Vault instance.

Key Insights of Azure Storage Service Encryption   Azure Key Vault is available in all Azure regions worldwide. Azure Key Vault can be used to store and manage cryptographic keys used for Azure Disk Encryption, Azure Storage Service Encryption, and Azure Virtual Machines. Azure Key Vault can be accessed programmatically using Azure SDKs, REST APIs, and PowerShell, providing flexible integration options for applications and services. Azure Key Vault can be used to store and manage secrets, such as connection strings and passwords, used by applications and services running in Azure. Azure Key Vault provides access controls and audit logs for key management operations, enabling organizations to meet compliance and regulatory requirements. Azure Key Vault integrates with Azure Active Directory to provide secure authentication and authorization for access to keys, secrets, and certificates. Azure Key Vault supports both software- and hardware-based security modules, including FIPS 140-2 Level 2 validated hardware security modules. Azure Key Vault supports compliance with regulatory and industry standards, including HIPAA, HITRUST, PCI DSS, and ISO 27001.

Azure Information Protection

Azure Information Protection (AIP) is a cloud-based solution from Microsoft that helps organizations classify, label, and protect sensitive data. AIP allows organizations to control and safeguard their sensitive data, whether stored in the cloud or on-premises, by applying encryption, rights management, and access policies. With AIP, organizations can classify their data based on its sensitivity and then apply labels and protection policies to control access to the data. This helps ensure that only authorized personnel can access the data, even if it is shared or stored outside the organization's boundaries.

AIP integrates with other Microsoft cloud services, such as Office 365 and SharePoint, as well as on-premises file servers and other third-party applications. AIP also provides a unified policy and reporting interface to manage and monitor data protection across the organization. With AIP, organizations can apply labels to documents and emails based on the content, such as the sensitivity of the information or the regulatory requirements, and automatically apply encryption, watermarks, and other protection measures to those documents and emails. AIP also integrates with Microsoft Cloud App Security, allowing organizations to extend their protection policies to cloud services, such as OneDrive, SharePoint, and Exchange Online.

In summary, Azure Information Protection helps organizations do the following:

- Classify and label sensitive data based on content and context

- Apply persistent protection policies that travel with the data

- Control access to sensitive information both inside and outside the organization

- Monitor and track the usage of protected data

- Extend protection policies to cloud services.

The following are the key benefits of AIP:

- *Comprehensive protection*: AIP provides a complete set of tools to classify, label, and protect sensitive data, both inside and outside the organization. With AIP, organizations can apply persistent protection policies that travel with the data, regardless of its location, ensuring that sensitive data is always protected.

- *Easy to use*: AIP integrates with Microsoft Office applications, such as Word, Excel, and PowerPoint, making it easy for users to apply protection labels and policies to their documents and emails. AIP also offers automation and integration options to simplify and streamline the protection process.

- *Regulatory compliance*: AIP provides a range of built-in classification and protection options that comply with many regulatory standards, such as GDPR, HIPAA, and PCI DSS. Organizations can also create custom policies to meet their specific compliance requirements.

- *Increased security*: AIP helps to increase the security of sensitive data by providing encryption, watermarks, and other protection measures. Additionally, AIP offers integration with Microsoft Cloud App Security, enabling organizations to extend their protection policies to cloud services.

- *Monitoring and tracking*: AIP provide organizations with visibility into how their sensitive data is being used, allowing them to monitor and track access to protected data and detect any suspicious activity.

To manage and reduce cybersecurity risk, organizations can use the NIST CSF. The Protect function within the NIST CSF focuses on implementing safeguards to ensure delivery of critical infrastructure services. AIP can help organizations meet the goals of the Protect function by providing several security measures, as follows:

- *Access control*: AIP allows organizations to control access to sensitive data both inside and outside the organization. Organizations can apply protection labels and policies to documents and emails, preventing unauthorized access.

- *Data protection*: AIP provides encryption, watermarks, and other protection measures to sensitive data, ensuring that it remains confidential and secure.

- *Risk management*: AIP provides a range of built-in classification and protection options that comply with regulatory standards, such as GDPR, HIPAA, and PCI DSS. Organizations can also create custom policies to meet their specific compliance requirements.

- *Monitoring and awareness*: AIP provide organizations with visibility into how their sensitive data is being used, allowing them to monitor and track access to protected data and detect any suspicious activity.

In a nutshell, AIP provides several security measures that align with the goals of the Protect function within the NIST CSF. By using AIP, organizations can implement safeguards to protect their sensitive data, reduce cybersecurity risk, and ensure the delivery of critical infrastructure services.

How It Works

AIP provides organizations with comprehensive tools to classify, label, and protect their sensitive data, as well as monitor it and integrate it with other tools.

- *Classification*: AIP allows organizations to classify sensitive data based on content and context. This can include the sensitivity of the information, regulatory requirements, and other factors. AIP provides built-in and customizable classification labels to help organizations categorize their data.

- *Labeling*: Once data is classified, AIP allows organizations to apply protection labels to their documents and emails. These labels define the protection policies that will be applied to the data, such as encryption, watermarks, and access controls.

- *Protection*: AIP applies protection policies to the labeled data, ensuring it remains secure and confidential. Protection policies can include encryption to prevent unauthorized access, watermarks to track the use of the data, and access controls to limit who can access the data.

- *Monitoring*: AIP provides organizations with visibility into how their sensitive data is being used. This includes tracking who has accessed the data, when it was accessed, and from where. Organizations can use this information to detect suspicious activity and ensure their sensitive data remains secure.

- *Integration*: AIP integrates with Microsoft Office applications, such as Word, Excel, and PowerPoint, and with other cloud services, such as OneDrive, SharePoint, and Exchange Online. This allows organizations to apply protection policies to their data no matter where it is located.

Design Considerations

These are the essential best practices for designing security in AIP:

- *Implement a strong access control policy*: Limit access to sensitive data and ensure that only authorized users can access it. Use Azure AD to enforce authentication and authorization policies.

- *Use classification labels*: AIP provides a way to classify data based on sensitivity and set policies to control its access. Use classification labels to protect sensitive data according to its sensitivity level.

- *Use encryption*: AIP uses encryption to protect data both in transit and at rest. Use encryption to protect your data from unauthorized access.

- *Monitor and log access*: Implement a logging and monitoring system to track access to sensitive data. Use Azure Log Analytics to monitor and alert on suspicious activity.

- *Enforce DLP policies*: Use AIP to enforce DLP policies that prevent sensitive data from being shared outside your organization.

- *Train your users*: Educate your users on how to use AIP and protect sensitive data. Implement regular training sessions to keep users up-to-date with the latest security best practices.

- *Use AIP scanner*: The AIP scanner can help you discover and classify sensitive data stored in your organization's file shares and repositories.

- *Implement AIP policies*: Use AIP policies to classify and protect sensitive data automatically. AIP policies can be based on content, location, user, or device.

- *Use MFA*: Implement MFA to provide an additional layer of security for your AIP environment.

- *Regularly review and update security policies*: Regularly review and update your security policies to ensure they remain effective against evolving threats.

How to Enable It

AIP is part of Microsoft Purview Information Protection (formerly Microsoft Information Protection). With Microsoft Purview Information Protection, sensitive information can be found, classified, protected, and governed wherever it goes.

Here are some example use cases for AIP:

- *Protecting sensitive data*: AIP can protect sensitive data such as financial information, intellectual property, and personal data. It enables you to classify data based on sensitivity and apply labels controlling access and usage.

- *Compliance*: AIP can help organizations meet compliance requirements such as GDPR, HIPAA, and ISO 27001. It supports many compliance standards and enables organizations to classify and protect data based on compliance requirements.

- *Collaboration*: AIP can facilitate secure collaboration between teams within an organization or with external partners. It enables users to share data securely and control access based on policies.

- *Email protection*: AIP can encrypt emails, prevent forwarding, and control access. It enables users to send secure emails to external recipients and protects emails containing sensitive data.

- *Regulatory requirements*: AIP can be used to meet regulatory requirements for data protection, such as HIPAA and PCI-DSS. It supports many regulatory requirements and enables organizations to classify and protect data based on regulatory requirements.

- *DLP*: AIP can be integrated with DLP solutions to identify and protect sensitive data. It enables organizations to apply protection policies to data in real time and prevent data loss or leakage.

- *Cloud migration*: AIP can be used to protect data during cloud migration. It enables organizations to classify and protect data before migrating it to the cloud, ensuring it remains secure throughout migration.

- *DRM*: AIP can be used for digital rights management, enabling organizations to control access to protected documents, prevent unauthorized sharing, and revoke access as needed.

The following are the prerequisites for AIP:

- *Azure subscription*: You need an Azure subscription to use AIP.

- *Azure Active Directory*: Azure AD is used for authentication and authorization in AIP. It would be best if you had an Azure AD tenant to use AIP.

- *Azure Rights Management (Azure RMS)*: AIP uses Azure RMS to protect and manage data. It would be best to have Azure RMS set up before using AIP.

- *Office 365 subscription*: If you want to use AIP with Office documents, you must have an Office 365 subscription.

- *Windows Server Active Directory*: If you want to use AIP with on-premises applications and services, you must set up Windows Server Active Directory.

- *Client applications*: AIP supports various client applications, including Office 365 apps, Adobe Acrobat, and Windows Explorer. Ensure that the client applications used in your organization are compatible with AIP.

- *User training*: AIP is a security tool that requires proper user training to be effective. Ensure your users are trained on using AIP and the importance of protecting sensitive data.

- *Network connectivity*: Ensure your network has the necessary connectivity to use AIP. AIP requires Internet access for authentication and authorization with Azure AD and Azure RMS.

- *Compliance requirements*: Ensure your organization's compliance requirements are met before implementing AIP. AIP can help you meet compliance requirements, but it is essential to understand your organization's specific requirements.

- *Planning and design*: Proper planning and design are essential for a successful AIP implementation. Consider your organization's specific needs, such as data classification, policies, and user access, when planning your AIP implementation.

The following are the steps to turn on AIP:

1. *Sign in to the Azure Portal*: Go to the Azure Portal and sign in with your Azure account.

2. *Create an Azure Information Protection tenant*: If you don't already have an Azure Information Protection tenant, you can create one by clicking the "Create a resource" button and searching for Azure Information Protection.

3. *Assign licenses*: To use Azure Information Protection, you must assign licenses to your users. You can do this through the Azure Portal or PowerShell.

4. *Configure policies*: Using Azure Information Protection, you can configure policies to classify and protect your data. You can configure policies based on content, location, user, or device.

5. *Install the Azure Information Protection client*: The Azure Information Protection client labels and protects data on client devices. You can download and install the client from the Microsoft Download Center.

6. *Test your configuration*: Before rolling out Azure Information Protection to your organization, test your configuration to ensure it works as expected.

Note that the steps to turn on Azure Information Protection may vary depending on your organization's requirements and the specific configuration you choose. Microsoft offers detailed documentation and support resources to help you implement Azure Information Protection effectively.

Key Insights of Azure Information Protection   Azure Information Protection can be accessed using the Azure Portal, PowerShell, and REST APIs, providing flexible integration options for applications and services. Azure Information Protection provides access controls and audit logs for data protection operations, enabling organizations to meet compliance and regulatory requirements. Azure Information

Protection integrates with Azure Active Directory to provide secure authentication and authorization for access to protected data. Azure Information Protection can be integrated with Microsoft Office applications, such as Word, Excel, and PowerPoint, to classify and label documents automatically.

Azure Backup Encryption

Azure Backup Encryption is a feature of Azure Backup that provides additional security for backup data stored in Azure. With Azure Backup Encryption, backup data is encrypted using customer-managed keys, providing an additional layer of security beyond the built-in encryption provided by Azure Storage. When Azure Backup Encryption is enabled, backup data is encrypted before it leaves the source machine and is stored in Azure in an encrypted format. This encryption ensures that the data is protected both in transit and at rest, preventing unauthorized access and ensuring the confidentiality of the data.

Customers can use their own keys to encrypt backup data, giving them complete control over the encryption keys and ensuring that only authorized parties can access the data. Azure Backup Encryption also supports key rotation, enabling customers to change encryption keys periodically to enhance security further. Azure Backup Encryption provides an additional layer of security for backup data stored in Azure, helping customers meet compliance requirements and ensure the confidentiality and integrity of their data.

Azure Backup Encryption provides several key benefits to customers who are looking to secure their backup data in Azure.

- *Enhanced security*: Azure Backup Encryption provides an additional layer of security for backup data by encrypting it using customer-managed keys. This ensures that only authorized parties have access to the data, even if it is intercepted by a third party.

- *Compliance*: Azure Backup Encryption helps organizations meet compliance requirements by providing enhanced security for backup data. Customers can use their own encryption keys, stored in Azure Key Vault, to ensure that their data is encrypted in accordance with regulatory requirements.

- *Protection against ransomware*: Azure Backup Encryption helps protect against ransomware attacks by preventing attackers from accessing backup data even if they gain access to the backup storage account.

- *Key management*: Azure Backup Encryption provides customers with complete control over the encryption keys used to encrypt and decrypt their backup data. It enables customers to manage their encryption keys securely and compliantly, ensuring they are accessible only to authorized parties.

- *Key rotation*: Azure Backup Encryption supports key rotation, allowing customers to change encryption keys periodically to further enhance security.

- *Simple configuration*: Enabling Azure Backup Encryption is a straightforward process and can be done through the Azure Portal or using PowerShell scripts. Customers can quickly and easily enable encryption for their backup data without requiring any additional infrastructure.

Azure Backup Encryption aligns with several NIST CSF categories related to protecting data, including the following:

- *Identify (ID)*: Azure Backup Encryption allows organizations to identify sensitive data that needs to be protected by providing encryption options for data backups. Organizations can better protect sensitive data from unauthorized access or theft by encrypting sensitive data.

- *Protect (PR)*: Azure Backup Encryption provides encryption options for data backups, which helps protect data from unauthorized access, theft, or loss. Additionally, Azure Backup Encryption allows organizations to implement access controls and policies for data backups to protect sensitive data further.

- *Detect (DE)*: Azure Backup Encryption allows organizations to detect any unauthorized access or tampering with data backups. This can help organizations quickly identify and respond to potential security incidents.

- *Respond (RS)*: Azure Backup Encryption allows organizations to respond quickly to security incidents related to data backups. By providing encryption options, access controls, and policies for data backups, organizations can better protect sensitive data and quickly respond to any security incidents.

- *Recover (RC)*: Azure Backup Encryption allows organizations to recover data backups quickly and securely. By providing encryption options, access controls, and policies for data backups, organizations can better protect sensitive data and ensure that it can be recovered during a security incident or disaster.

How It Works

Azure Backup Encryption provides encryption options for data backups in Azure, which helps protect sensitive data from unauthorized access or theft.

- *Backup data encryption*: When you enable Azure backup encryption, the data is encrypted using AES 256-bit encryption at the source before it's sent to Azure for storage. This means that the data is encrypted before it leaves the customer's environment, so only encrypted data is transmitted over the Internet to Azure.

- *Key management*: Azure Backup Encryption uses Azure Key Vault to manage and store encryption keys. Encryption keys are managed by the customer and not shared with Azure Backup. Customers can bring their keys to Key Vault or use the service-managed keys. Azure Backup Encryption also supports key rotation, where new keys can be generated and used for future backups, making it harder for attackers to access sensitive data even if they get access to a previously used encryption key.

- *Access control*: Azure Backup Encryption also provides access controls and policies for data backups. You can specify who has access to backups and how they can access them. For example, you can specify that only specific users or roles can access the backups, or you can restrict access to specific IP addresses or locations.

- *Recovery*: To restore data from an encrypted backup, encryption keys are required to decrypt the data. Customers can restore data directly from Azure Backup or use Azure Site Recovery to recover entire workloads.

Design Considerations

The following are critical design security best practices for Azure Backup Encryption:

- *Use strong passwords*: Create strong passwords that are difficult to guess or crack. Passwords should be at least eight characters long and include a mix of uppercase and lowercase letters, numbers, and symbols.

- *Enable MFA*: Use MFA to add an extra layer of security to your backup data. This will ensure that only authorized users can access and manage your backups.

- *Encrypt backup data*: Use Azure Backup Encryption to encrypt your backup data at rest and in transit. This will help protect your data from unauthorized access and ensure its confidentiality.

- *Implement RBAC*: Use RBAC to control access to your backup data. Only grant access to users who need it, and restrict access to sensitive data.

- *Use network security groups (NSGs)*: Use NSGs to control traffic flow to and from your backup infrastructure. This will help protect your data from malicious attacks and ensure its integrity.

- *Implement DLP*: Use DLP policies to prevent sensitive data from being backed up to Azure. This will help protect your data from accidental or intentional leaks.

- *Enable auditing and monitoring*: Enable auditing and monitoring to track user activity and detect unauthorized access or data breaches. This will help you quickly identify and respond to security incidents.

- *Keep your backup software up-to-date*: Regularly update it to ensure it is free of vulnerabilities and security flaws. This will help you keep your data secure and prevent data breaches.

- *Perform regular backups and testing*: Perform regular backups and test your backups to ensure they are working properly. This will help you recover your data during a disaster or data loss.

How to Enable It

Azure Backup Encryption supports encryption using either RSA or AES keys. Customers can use their own encryption keys, stored in Azure Key Vault, to encrypt backup data, ensuring that only authorized parties can access the data. Azure Backup Encryption also supports key rotation, allowing customers to change encryption keys periodically to enhance security. Azure Backup Encryption protects against ransomware attacks by preventing attackers from accessing backup data even if they gain access to the backup storage account.

Enabling Azure Backup Encryption is a straightforward process and can be done through the Azure Portal or PowerShell scripts. Once it's enabled, customers can monitor backup activity and view backup reports to ensure their data is backed up securely.

The following are key security deployment considerations to keep in mind when deploying Azure Backup Encryption:

- *Encryption key management*: Proper management of encryption keys is crucial for the security of your backups. Decide whether you want to use Microsoft-managed keys or customer-managed keys. If you choose customer-managed keys, you must manage them carefully and ensure they are protected from unauthorized access.

- *Authentication and authorization*: Ensure only authorized users can access Azure Backup resources. Implement strong authentication mechanisms, such as MFA, and use RBAC to control access to your backup data.

- *Network security*: Implement network security controls such as NSGs and VPNs to protect your backup data from unauthorized access and malicious attacks.

- *Monitoring and alerting*: Implement monitoring and alerting mechanisms to detect any suspicious activity and security incidents. Configure Azure Monitor to collect and analyze logs, and set up alerts to notify you of any security events.

- *Compliance*: Ensure that your Azure Backup deployment complies with security and privacy regulations, such as GDPR, HIPAA, and PCI DSS. Azure Backup offers compliance certifications, such as SOC 1/2/3, ISO 27001, and HIPAA, to help you meet your compliance requirements.

- *Backup retention and disposal*: Establish policies for backup retention and disposal to ensure that backup data is retained for only as long as necessary and securely disposed of when no longer needed. This helps to reduce the risk of data breaches and minimize the impact of a security incident.

By considering these key security deployment considerations, you can help ensure that your Azure Backup Encryption deployment is secure and compliant with industry best practices and standards.

To turn on Azure Backup Encryption, you need to follow these steps:

1. Navigate to the Azure Portal and sign in with your account credentials.

2. In the search bar, select Backup and Site Recovery from the list of available services.

3. Select the backup policy for which you want to enable encryption.

4. Click the Backup Configuration tab and click Encryption.

5. Toggle the Encryption option to On.

6. Choose the encryption key type you want to use: Microsoft-managed key or customer-managed key. If you choose to use a customer-managed key, you must provide the Key Vault URL and key name.

7. Save the changes.

Once encryption is turned on, Azure Backup will automatically encrypt all backup data at rest and in transit using the specified encryption key. This will help protect your data from unauthorized access and ensure its confidentiality.

Key Insights of Azure Backup   Azure Backup supports backup and recovery for various workloads, including virtual machines, SQL Server, SharePoint, and Exchange. Azure Backup provides flexible backup scheduling and retention policies, enabling organizations to tailor their backup strategy to their needs. Azure Backup supports backup to the cloud and on-premises, providing a hybrid data protection solution for organizations with diverse IT environments. Azure Backup integrates with Azure Site Recovery to provide disaster recovery capabilities for workloads protected by Azure Backup. Azure Backup supports compliance with regulatory and industry standards, including HIPAA, HITRUST, PCI DSS, and ISO 27001. Azure Backup provides access controls and audit logs for backup and recovery operations, enabling organizations to meet compliance and regulatory requirements. Azure Backup can be accessed using the Azure Portal, PowerShell, and REST APIs, providing flexible integration options for applications and services.

Azure VPN Gateway

Azure VPN Gateway is a cloud-based service that provides secure and reliable connectivity between on-premises networks and Azure resources. It allows you to create site-to-site VPN connections to connect your on-premises infrastructure to Azure resources such as virtual machines, networks, and other services.

Azure VPN Gateway supports multiple protocols such as Internet Protocol Security (IPsec) and Secure Sockets Layer (SSL) VPN. It offers various VPN types, including Point-to-Site, Site-to-Site, and ExpressRoute. Azure VPN Gateway can create a secure hybrid network by extending your on-premises network to Azure. This enables you to leverage the scalability and flexibility of the cloud while maintaining the security and control of your on-premises infrastructure.

Azure VPN Gateway also provides high availability and automatic failover, ensuring that your VPN connection remains available and reliable even during an outage or failure. Additionally, it integrates with Azure Monitor to provide real-time monitoring and logging, enabling you to detect and diagnose issues with your VPN connection quickly.

Azure VPN Gateway offers several key benefits.

- *Secure connectivity*: Azure VPN Gateway provides secure connectivity between your on-premises infrastructure and Azure resources using industry-standard protocols such as IPsec and SSL VPN. This ensures that your data is transmitted securely over the Internet and is protected from unauthorized access.

- *Hybrid network*: Azure VPN Gateway enables you to create a hybrid network by extending your on-premises network to Azure. This allows you to leverage the scalability and flexibility of the cloud while maintaining the security and control of your on-premises infrastructure.

- *Multiple VPN types*: Azure VPN Gateway supports multiple VPN types, including Point-to-Site VPN, Site-to-Site VPN, and ExpressRoute. This lets you choose the VPN type that best fits your connectivity needs.

- *High availability*: Azure VPN Gateway provides high availability and automatic failover, ensuring that your VPN connection remains available and reliable even during an outage or failure.

- *Real-time monitoring and logging*: Azure VPN Gateway integrates with Azure Monitor to provide real-time monitoring and logging of your VPN connection. This enables you to detect and diagnose issues with your VPN connection quickly.

- *Scalability*: Azure VPN Gateway is highly scalable and can support thousands of concurrent connections. This makes it suitable for large-scale deployments.

- *Cost-effective*: Azure VPN Gateway offers a cost-effective solution for connecting your on-premises infrastructure to Azure resources. You only pay for the VPN Gateway hours you use and the data transferred over the VPN connection.

Azure VPN Gateway maps to the NIST SP 800-53 Rev. 5 controls:

- *Access control (AC)*: Azure VPN Gateway provides access control mechanisms through Azure RBAC, allowing you to grant users only the necessary permissions to manage the VPN Gateway resources.

- *Identification and authentication (IA)*: Azure VPN Gateway supports various authentication methods such as pre-shared keys (PSK), certificates, and Azure AD for user authentication.

- *Audit and accountability (AU)*: Azure VPN Gateway logs all the network traffic and security events related to the VPN connection, which can be analyzed and audited using Azure Monitor.

- *Configuration management (CM)*: Azure VPN Gateway offers centralized management and configuration through Azure Portal, Azure CLI, and Azure PowerShell.

- *Contingency planning (CP)*: Azure VPN Gateway provides high availability and automatic failover capabilities to ensure continuity of service in case of a failure.

- *Incident response (IR)*: Azure VPN Gateway enables you to detect and respond to security incidents through Azure Monitor, which provides real-time monitoring and alerting.

- *Media protection (MP)*: Azure VPN Gateway encrypts all the network traffic and supports advanced encryption protocols such as AES256 and SHA-2, to protect the data in transit.

By mapping Azure VPN Gateway to the NIST SP 800-53 Rev. 5 controls, you can ensure that your VPN Gateway deployment meets the required security and privacy standards.

Design Considerations

The following are the key design security best practices for Azure VPN Gateway:

- *Use the latest VPN Gateway SKU*: Microsoft recommends using the latest VPN Gateway SKU as it provides the best performance and security features.

- *Use point-to-site VPN with Azure Active Directory authentication*: This ensures secure access to resources and prevents unauthorized access.

- *Use site-to-site VPN with route-based VPNs*: This ensures secure connectivity between on-premises and Azure resources.

- *Enable forced tunneling for site-to-site VPN*: This ensures that all traffic from the on-premises network is routed through the VPN tunnel, providing an additional layer of security.

- *Use network security groups*: Network security groups provide a way to filter network traffic to and from the VPN Gateway.

- *Use virtual network peering instead of VPN Gateway peering*: Virtual network peering is more secure than VPN Gateway peering because it does not rely on the Internet for communication.

- *Use Azure Firewall or a third-party firewall*: This provides an additional layer of security by filtering traffic to and from the VPN Gateway.

- *Use Azure Monitor for logging and monitoring*: Azure Monitor provides visibility into the VPN Gateway and can help identify security threats.

- *Use strong authentication methods*: Strong authentication methods, such as multi-factor authentication, should be used to prevent unauthorized access.

- *Regularly review and update security settings*: It is important to regularly review and update security settings to ensure that the VPN Gateway remains secure.

How to Enable It

Azure VPN Gateway is a virtual network gateway that provides a secure connection between an Azure virtual network and an on-premises or another virtual network. It establishes secure tunnels using industry-standard protocols such as IPsec and SSL/TLS. The Azure VPN Gateway can be used for both point-to-site VPN (connecting individual devices to the virtual network) and site-to-site VPN (connecting an entire on-premises network to the virtual network). It also provides high availability through active-active and active-passive configurations and supports features such as forced tunneling and custom IPsec/IKE policies.

When using Azure VPN Gateway, you need to ensure that you have the following prerequisites in place:

- *Azure subscription*: You need an active Azure subscription to create an Azure VPN Gateway.

- *Virtual network*: You must create a virtual network you want to connect to the Azure VPN Gateway. This can be done using Azure Portal, Azure PowerShell, Azure CLI, or any other deployment method supported by Azure.

- *Subnets*: You must create at least one subnet in the virtual network that you want to connect to the Azure VPN Gateway.

- *Public IP address*: You need a public IP address for the VPN Gateway. This can be an Azure public IP address or a public IP address you own.

- *VPN device*: You need to have a VPN device that is compatible with the Azure VPN Gateway. This can be a physical or virtual VPN device running on a virtual machine.

- *VPN client configuration*: If you plan to use a point-to-site VPN, you need to have the VPN client configuration files for your operating system. Azure provides VPN client configuration files for Windows, Mac, Linux, and iOS.

- *Gateway subnet*: You need to create a subnet for the VPN Gateway. This subnet is used by the VPN Gateway to host its virtual network interface.

- *Routing*: You need to configure routing between the on-premises and virtual networks you want to connect to the Azure VPN Gateway.

Once you have these prerequisites, you can create an Azure VPN Gateway and configure the necessary settings for your VPN connection.

The following are the key security best practices for Azure VPN Gateway:

- *Strong authentication*: Use strong authentication mechanisms such as MFA for all VPN connections to prevent unauthorized access.

- *Encryption*: Use encryption to protect the data transmitted over the VPN connection. Use a minimum of 128-bit encryption for data confidentiality.

- *Network security*: Implement network security controls such as NSGs and VPNs to protect your VPN Gateway from unauthorized access and malicious attacks.

- *Certificate management*: Use digital certificates to authenticate VPN connections. Ensure that the certificates are valid and have not expired.

- *Access control*: Implement RBAC to control access to your VPN Gateway resources. Ensure that only authorized users have access to your VPN Gateway resources.

- *Monitoring and alerting*: Implement monitoring and alerting mechanisms to detect suspicious activity and security incidents. Configure Azure Monitor to collect and analyze logs and set up alerts to notify you of any security events.

- *Compliance*: Ensure that your Azure VPN Gateway deployment complies with security and privacy regulations, such as GDPR, HIPAA, and PCI DSS. Azure VPN Gateway offers compliance certifications, such as SOC 1/2/3, ISO 27001, and HIPAA, to help you meet your compliance requirements.

By implementing these security best practices, you can help ensure that your Azure VPN Gateway deployment is secure and compliant with industry best practices and standards.

Azure Site-to-Site VPN

Azure Site-to-Site VPN is a VPN connection that allows you to securely connect an on-premises network to an Azure virtual network over the Internet. It enables you to extend your on-premises network to the cloud and access resources hosted in Azure as if they were on your local network.

With Azure Site-to-Site VPN, you can connect multiple on-premises sites to the same Azure virtual network or connect various Azure virtual networks. The connection is established using industry-standard IPsec/IKE protocols and can be configured to use custom IPsec/IKE policies to meet specific security requirements.

Azure Site-to-Site VPN requires a VPN gateway in Azure and a compatible VPN device on-premises. Once the VPN connection is established, traffic between the on-premises network and the Azure virtual network is encrypted and transmitted securely over the Internet.

The following are the key benefits of Azure Site-to-Site VPN:

- *Secure connectivity*: Azure Site-to-Site VPN uses industry-standard IPsec/IKE protocols to establish a secure, encrypted connection between on-premises and Azure virtual networks. This ensures that all network traffic is transmitted securely over the Internet.

- *Extends your network*: Site-to-Site VPN allows you to extend your on-premises network to the cloud, giving you access to Azure resources as if they were on your local network. This allows you to take advantage of the scalability and flexibility of the cloud without sacrificing the security of your on-premises network.

- *Multiple connections*: Azure Site-to-Site VPN supports multiple VPN connections to the same Azure virtual network, providing high availability and load balancing of VPN traffic.

- *Customizable*: You can customize the IPsec/IKE policies to meet specific security requirements and control traffic routing between the on-premises and Azure virtual networks.

- *Cost-effective*: Site-to-Site VPN is a cost-effective solution for connecting on-premises networks to Azure. It uses the Internet as the underlying transport instead of dedicated leased lines or MPLS circuits.

- *Easy to configure*: Setting up a Site-to-Site VPN connection is straightforward and can be done using Azure Portal, Azure PowerShell, or Azure CLI. This makes it easy to deploy and manage VPN connections across multiple sites.

- *High performance*: Azure Site-to-Site VPN supports both basic and standard VPN gateway SKUs, allowing you to choose the right performance and feature set for your needs. The standard SKU provides higher throughput and more features, such as active-active and active-passive high availability configurations.

Here's how Azure Site-to-Site VPN maps to the Protect function of the NIST CSF:

- *Access control*: Azure Site-to-Site VPN provides access control to the Azure virtual network by requiring authentication and authorization before allowing VPN connections.

- *Data security*: Site-to-Site VPN uses IPsec/IKE protocols to encrypt all traffic between the on-premises and Azure virtual networks. This ensures that data transmitted over the VPN connection is secure and protected against interception.

- *Information protection processes and procedures*: Azure Site-to-Site VPN provides configurable IPsec/IKE policies that can be customized to meet specific security requirements. Azure virtual network gateways also support custom routing tables and network security groups, allowing you to control traffic flows and apply security rules.

- *Maintenance*: Azure Site-to-Site VPN is a managed service, which means that Microsoft is responsible for maintaining and updating the VPN gateway infrastructure. You can also use Azure Monitor and Azure Security Center to monitor VPN connections and identify potential security issues.

- *Protective technology*: Azure Site-to-Site VPN uses industry-standard IPsec/IKE protocols to establish a secure VPN connection between the on-premises and Azure virtual networks. The VPN gateway infrastructure is hosted in Azure data centers and is protected by various security controls and processes.

Design Considerations

The following are the key security design best practices for Azure Site-to-Site VPN:

- *Use strong authentication*: Use strong authentication mechanisms, such as Azure AD or RADIUS, to authenticate VPN users and devices.

- *Configure custom IPsec/IKE policies*: Customize IPsec/IKE policies to meet your specific security requirements, such as encryption algorithms, key strengths, and hashing algorithms.

- *Implement network segmentation*: Use segmentation to limit access to resources on the Azure virtual network and apply network security groups to control traffic flow between subnets.

- *Monitor VPN connections*: Use Azure Monitor to monitor VPN connections and identify potential security issues, such as failed authentication attempts, abnormal traffic patterns, or policy violations.

- *Use Azure Firewall*: Implement Azure Firewall to protect the Azure virtual network from unauthorized access and threats and enable logging and auditing to track network activity.

- *Apply security updates*: Apply security updates to VPN gateways and virtual machines on the Azure virtual network to address known security vulnerabilities.

- *Follow the least privilege principle*: Apply the least privilege principle to access control, granting users and devices only the permissions required to perform their specific tasks.

- *Use Azure Security Center*: Use Azure Security Center to monitor and manage security across your Azure environment, including Site-to-Site VPN connections.

- *Implement MFA*: Implement MFA for VPN users and administrators to increase security and reduce the risk of unauthorized access.

- *Regularly review logs and audit trails*: Review logs and audit trails regularly to identify potential security issues and investigate any suspicious activity.

How to Enable It

Azure Site-to-Site VPN is a way to establish a secure, encrypted connection between an Azure virtual network and an on-premises network. This allows you to extend your on-premises network to the cloud, giving you access to Azure resources as if they were on your local network.

To set up a site-to-site VPN, you must create a VPN gateway in Azure and configure it to connect to your on-premises VPN device. The VPN gateway can be a basic or a standard SKU, depending on your performance and feature requirements. You'll also need to configure your on-premises VPN device to connect to the Azure VPN gateway.

The connection between the Azure VPN gateway and the on-premises VPN device is established using industry-standard IPsec/IKE protocols, which provide strong encryption and secure communication. You can use custom IPsec/IKE policies to meet specific security requirements. Once the VPN connection is established, traffic between the on-premises network and the Azure virtual network is encrypted and transmitted securely over the Internet. You can control traffic routing between the networks and configure security rules using network security groups in Azure. Azure Site-to-Site VPN also supports multiple VPN connections to the same Azure virtual network, providing high availability and load balancing of VPN traffic. Additionally, you can configure forced tunneling to ensure that all Internet-bound traffic from the on-premises network is routed through the VPN tunnel for enhanced security.

Here are the critical prerequisites for setting up Azure Site-to-Site VPN:

- *Azure subscription*: You need an Azure subscription to deploy Site-to-Site VPN.

- *Azure virtual network*: Create an Azure virtual network in the region of your choice. The virtual network should have at least one subnet and no overlapping IP addresses with your on-premises network.

- *On-premises VPN device*: You need an on-premises VPN device that supports IKEv1 or IKEv2 and IPsec and can connect to Azure using Site-to-Site VPN. Supported VPN devices include Cisco ASA, Juniper SRX, and Check Point Security Gateway.

- *Public IP address*: You need a public IP address for the VPN device on your on-premises network.

- *IP address space*: You need to ensure that the IP address space used by your on-premises network does not overlap with the IP address space used by the Azure virtual network.

- *DNS settings*: Configure DNS settings for the Azure virtual and on-premises networks to ensure that name resolution works correctly.

- *Firewall rules*: Configure firewall rules on your on-premises network to allow traffic to and from the Azure virtual network.

- *Permissions*: Ensure you have the necessary permissions to create and manage VPN gateways and virtual machines on the Azure virtual network.

By meeting these prerequisites, you can ensure that your site-to-site VPN deployment goes smoothly and is optimized for your organization's connectivity requirements.

The following are key deployment considerations for Azure Site-to-Site VPN:

- *Connectivity requirements*: Before deploying Azure Site-to-Site VPN, determine the connectivity requirements for your organization, such as the number of on-premises sites, the amount of traffic to be transmitted, and the types of applications and services to be accessed.

- *Network topology*: Consider the network topology of your on-premises network and the Azure virtual network, and ensure that they can be connected using Azure Site-to-Site VPN. You may need to configure network address translation (NAT) or routing to enable connectivity.

- *Gateway SKU*: Choose the appropriate gateway SKU for your site-to-site VPN deployment based on your connectivity requirements and bandwidth needs. For example, the Basic gateway SKU is suitable for small-scale deployments, while the VpnGw1-5 gateway SKUs are designed for large-scale deployments.

- *Gateway subnet*: Create a dedicated gateway subnet for your site-to-site VPN deployment to ensure that the VPN gateway can be deployed without interfering with other resources on the Azure virtual network.

- *Public IP address*: Assign a public IP address to the VPN gateway to enable external connectivity and ensure that the gateway can be accessed from your on-premises network.

- *VPN devices*: Ensure that your on-premises VPN devices are compatible with Azure Site-to-Site VPN and support the required protocols and encryption algorithms.

- *Security considerations*: Implement security controls, such as authentication, authorization, and encryption, to ensure that the Azure Site-to-Site VPN connections are secure and protected against unauthorized access and threats.

- *Monitoring and management*: Implement monitoring and management tools, such as Azure Monitor and Azure Security Center, to monitor site-to-site VPN connections, identify potential security issues, and manage VPN gateways and virtual machines on the Azure virtual network.

By considering these deployment considerations, you can ensure that your site-to-site VPN deployment is optimized for your organization's connectivity requirements and security needs.

To turn on Azure Site-to-Site VPN, you can follow these general steps:

1. *Create an Azure virtual network*: Create an Azure virtual network in the region of your choice, and configure the address space and subnets according to your requirements.

2. *Create a VPN gateway*: Create a VPN gateway in the virtual network using the Azure Portal or Azure CLI. It would be best to choose the appropriate gateway SKU based on your connectivity requirements and bandwidth needs.

3. *Configure the VPN gateway*: Configure the VPN gateway settings, such as the VPN type (IKEv1 or IKEv2), the public IP address for the gateway, and the routing settings.

4. *Configure the on-premises VPN device*: Configure the device with the appropriate settings, such as the VPN type, public IP address of the VPN gateway, and shared key.

5.   *Verify connectivity*: Test the connectivity between the on-premises network and the Azure virtual network using tools such as ping or traceroute.

6.   *Configure routing*: Configure the routing settings on both the on-premises VPN device and the Azure virtual network to ensure that traffic can be routed correctly between the two networks.

7.   *Implement security controls*: Implement security controls, such as authentication, authorization, and encryption, to ensure that site-to-site VPN connections are secure and protected against unauthorized access and threats.

These are general steps to turn on Azure Site-to-Site VPN. The specific steps and settings may vary depending on the VPN device and Azure configuration that you are using. Microsoft provides detailed documentation and guides to help you set up Azure Site-to-Site VPN correctly.

Azure Point-to-Site VPN

Azure Point-to-Site VPN is a VPN connection that enables you to securely connect individual computers or devices to an Azure virtual network over the public Internet. Unlike Azure Site-to-Site VPN, which connects entire networks, Azure Point-to-Site VPN connects individual client devices to an Azure virtual network.

With Azure Point-to-Site VPN, you can create secure connections between your on-premises computers or devices and the Azure virtual network without needing a VPN gateway or dedicated VPN hardware. This can be useful for remote workers who need access to corporate resources or for development and testing scenarios where you need to connect to an Azure virtual network from a local computer.

The Azure Point-to-Site VPN uses the Secure Sockets Tunneling Protocol (SSTP) to provide a secure connection between the client device and the Azure virtual network. The SSTP protocol uses the HTTPS protocol and TCP port 443 to establish a secure tunnel, which ensures that the data transmitted between the client device and the virtual network is encrypted and secure. To use Azure Point-to-Site VPN, you need to install a VPN client on the client device, such as the Azure VPN client, which is available for Windows, macOS, and Linux. The client device must also have a valid digital certificate, which is used for authentication when connecting to the Azure virtual network.

Azure Point-to-Site (P2S) VPN provides a secure connection between on-premises resources and Azure virtual networks over the Internet. The following are some of the key benefits of Azure P2S VPN:

- *Secure connectivity*: Azure P2S VPN uses industry-standard protocols such as IKEv2 and SSTP to provide a secure and encrypted connection between on-premises resources and Azure virtual networks. This helps to ensure that the data transmitted over the Internet is secure and protected from unauthorized access.

- *Remote access*: Azure P2S VPN allows remote workers to securely access on-premises resources from any location with an Internet connection. This can improve productivity by enabling employees to work from home or on the go.

- *Scalability*: Azure P2S VPN can easily scale to support many remote workers or devices. This makes it an ideal solution for organizations that must provide secure remote access to many employees or contractors.

- *Easy setup*: Azure P2S VPN can be set up quickly and easily using the Azure Portal or PowerShell. This makes it a convenient solution for organizations that need to deploy remote access quickly.

- *Integration with other Azure services*: Azure P2S VPN can be integrated with other Azure services such as Azure Active Directory, Azure Virtual Network, and Azure Load Balancer. This allows organizations to leverage the full power of Azure to build secure, scalable, and highly available solutions.

How It Works

P2S is a VPN connection that securely connects remote workers or devices to Azure virtual networks over the Internet.

1. The first step is to create a virtual network in Azure. Your resources, such as virtual machines, databases, and web apps, reside in this network.

2. Next, you create a VPN gateway in the virtual network. The VPN gateway is a virtual machine that provides the endpoint for the VPN connection.

3. You then configure the Point-to-Site VPN connection. This involves defining the address space for the virtual network and the VPN client address pool.

4. After the configuration, the remote worker or device can download and install the VPN client software on their computer. The VPN client establishes a secure connection with the VPN gateway in the virtual network.

5. Once the connection is established, the remote worker or device can access resources in the virtual network as if they were on the same network.

6. All traffic between the remote worker or device and the virtual network is encrypted and secured with industry-standard protocols such as IKEv2 and SSTP.

Azure P2S VPN can also be integrated with other Azure services, such as Azure Active Directory for authentication and authorization, Azure Information Protection for data classification and protection, and Azure Traffic Manager for load balancing and high availability.

Design Considerations

The following are the key design security best practices for P2S VPN:

-   *Use MFA*: Require remote workers to use MFA to authenticate to the P2S VPN. This helps to prevent unauthorized access to the virtual network.

-   *Use certificate-based authentication*: Configure the P2S VPN to use certificate-based authentication instead of username and password. This provides an additional layer of security by ensuring that only trusted devices can connect to the VPN.

- *Use a dedicated subnet for VPN clients*: Create a dedicated subnet in the virtual network for VPN clients. This allows you to apply NSG rules to restrict traffic to and from the VPN clients.

- *Use a separate virtual network for P2S VPN*: Consider using a different virtual network for P2S VPN to isolate VPN traffic from other resources in the virtual network.

- *Use Azure Firewall*: Use Azure Firewall to secure inbound and outbound traffic to and from the virtual network. You can create a firewall rule to allow VPN traffic to the virtual network.

- *Enable logging and monitoring*: Enable logging and monitoring of the P2S VPN traffic using Azure Monitor or Azure Log Analytics. This allows you to detect and respond to security incidents in real time.

- *Limit access to VPN gateway*: Limit access to the VPN gateway by using NSGs to restrict traffic to and from the VPN gateway. Only allow traffic from trusted IP addresses or ranges.

- *Use Azure Active Directory for authentication and authorization*: Use Azure Active Directory to manage authentication and authorization for P2S VPN clients. This allows you to control access to the virtual network based on user identify.

- *Rotate certificates and keys*: Rotate the certificates and keys used for P2S VPN regularly to reduce the risk of unauthorized access.

- *Follow security best practices for remote workers*: Ensure that remote workers follow security best practices such as using strong passwords, keeping software up to date, and avoiding public Wi-Fi networks.

How to Enable It

P2S VPN is typically used when remote workers need to access resources in an Azure virtual network, such as virtual machines, databases, and web apps. It is also commonly used for site-to-site connectivity where a site-to-site VPN is impossible, such as when remote workers are mobile or work from home.

To establish a P2S VPN connection, a virtual network gateway is created in the Azure virtual network, which acts as the VPN endpoint. The VPN gateway can be configured to use industry-standard protocols such as IKEv2, SSTP, or OpenVPN to encrypt and secure the traffic between the remote device and the virtual network.

To connect to the P2S VPN, the remote worker or device must install the VPN client software. The VPN client software is available for various operating systems, including Windows, MacOS, iOS, and Android. Once the VPN client is installed, the remote worker can establish a secure connection to the virtual network by providing their credentials and initiating the connection.

The following are the key deployment considerations for Azure Point-to-Site (P2S) VPN:

- *VPN Gateway SKU*: Azure provides different VPN Gateway SKUs based on the required features and capabilities. Select the appropriate SKU based on the required throughput, number of connections, and supported VPN protocols.

- *VPN protocol*: Azure P2S VPN supports multiple VPN protocols, including IKEv2, SSTP, and OpenVPN. Select the appropriate VPN protocol based on the client platform and security requirements.

- *Client operating systems*: P2S VPN supports many client operating systems, including Windows, macOS, iOS, and Android. Consider the supported operating systems and version compatibility while selecting the VPN client.

- *VPN client configuration*: Configure the VPN client with the required settings, including VPN protocol, authentication method, and gateway settings. Use scripts or Group Policy Objects (GPOs) to deploy and manage VPN client settings at scale.

- *Certificate management*: P2S VPN supports certificate-based authentication. Use Azure Key Vault or other certificate management tools to manage and rotate the certificates used for VPN authentication.

- *NSG*: Use NSG to restrict inbound and outbound traffic to the VPN clients and VPN gateway. Define rules based on the required protocols, ports, and source/destination IP addresses.

- *DNS configuration*: Configure DNS settings for the virtual network to ensure that the VPN clients can resolve the required resources in the virtual network.

- *Routing configuration*: Configure routing tables and user-defined routes to ensure that the VPN clients can access the required resources in the virtual network.

- *Azure Firewall integration*: Use Azure Firewall to secure inbound and outbound traffic to and from the virtual network. Define the required rules to allow VPN traffic to the virtual network.

- *MFA*: Use MFA to add a layer of security to P2S VPN authentication. Integrate P2S VPN with Azure Active Directory and configure MFA settings for VPN clients.

- *Monitoring and logging*: Enable logging and monitoring of P2S VPN traffic to detect and respond to security incidents in real time. Use Azure Monitor or Log Analytics to monitor VPN gateway and client activities.

- *High availability*: Consider deploying multiple VPN gateways in an active-standby or active-active configuration to ensure high availability and business continuity. Configure gateway SKUs and connection resilience settings based on the required availability and redundancy levels.

The following are the key prerequisites for Azure Point-to-Site (P2S) VPN:

- *Azure subscription*: You need an active Azure subscription to create and configure the virtual network and VPN gateway required for P2S VPN.

- *Virtual network*: You must create a virtual network in Azure before you can configure P2S VPN. The virtual network must have a subnet with enough IP address space to accommodate the VPN clients.

- *VPN gateway*: You must create a VPN gateway in the virtual network to enable P2S VPN connectivity. The VPN gateway must be configured with the appropriate settings, such as VPN protocol, routing, and security settings.

- *VPN client*: You must install a VPN client on the remote device to connect to the VPN gateway. The VPN client must be compatible with the selected protocol and operating system.

- *Authentication certificate*: You need a root certificate or an intermediate certificate authority (CA) issued by a trusted public CA or an internal CA. This certificate is used to authenticate the VPN client and the VPN gateway.

- *Public IP address*: You need to have a public IP address assigned to the VPN gateway to enable P2S VPN connectivity from the Internet.

- *NSG*: You need to have a NSG associated with the virtual network and VPN gateway to allow inbound and outbound traffic to the VPN clients and VPN gateway.

- *DNS configuration*: You need to configure DNS settings for the virtual network to ensure that the VPN clients can resolve the required resources in the virtual network.

- *Routing configuration*: You must configure routing tables and user-defined routes to ensure that the VPN clients can access the required resources in the virtual network.

It's important to note that several deployment considerations and best practices should be followed when configuring Azure Point-to-Site VPN to ensure security, scalability, and performance. These include selecting the appropriate VPN gateway SKU, VPN protocol, and client operating systems, configuring certificate management, network security group rules, routing, and integrating with other Azure services such as Azure Firewall and Azure Active Directory.

To turn on Azure P2S VPN, you need to follow these steps:

1. *Create a virtual network*: You need to create a virtual one in Azure if you still need to. This can be done using the Azure Portal, Azure CLI, or Azure PowerShell.

2. *Create a VPN gateway*: Once the virtual network is created, you need to create a VPN gateway in the virtual network. You can use the Azure Portal, Azure CLI, or Azure PowerShell. Select the appropriate SKU, VPN protocol, and other required settings when creating the VPN gateway.

3. *Configure the VPN gateway*: Once the VPN gateway is created, you need to configure it with the required settings, such as IP address space, routing, and security settings. You can configure the VPN gateway using the Azure Portal, Azure CLI, or Azure PowerShell.

4. *Create a root certificate*: You must create a root certificate for authentication between the VPN client and the VPN gateway. You can create a root certificate using a tool like OpenSSL.

5. *Upload the root certificate*: Once the root certificate is created, you need to upload it to the Azure Portal and configure the VPN gateway to use it for authentication.

6. *Configure the VPN client*: You need to configure the VPN client on each remote device that needs to connect to the VPN gateway. This involves installing the VPN client software and configuring the required settings, such as the VPN protocol, authentication method, and gateway settings.

7. *Connect to the VPN gateway*: Once the VPN client is configured, you can connect to the VPN gateway by providing your credentials and initiating the connection. The VPN client will establish a secure connection to the VPN gateway, and the remote device can access resources in the virtual network.

It's important to note that several deployment considerations and best practices should be followed when configuring Azure Point-to-Site VPN to ensure security, scalability, and performance. These include selecting the appropriate VPN gateway SKU, VPN protocol, and client operating systems, configuring certificate management, network security group rules, routing, and integrating with other Azure services such as Azure Firewall and Azure Active Directory.

Azure ExpressRoute

Azure ExpressRoute is a service provided by Microsoft Azure that enables organizations to establish private, dedicated, and high-bandwidth connections between their on-premises infrastructure and Azure data centers. It provides a more reliable, secure, and predictable connection than a traditional Internet-based connection. With ExpressRoute, you can create private connections between your on-premises infrastructure, such as your data center or colocation facility, and Azure. These private connections are established using a dedicated connection through a connectivity provider, such as a telecommunications provider or a connectivity partner. The connection can be established via a dedicated physical circuit, such as a T1 line or a fiber-optic cable, or a virtual circuit, such as MPLS.

There are two main types of Azure ExpressRoute:

- *Private*: This ExpressRoute connection is dedicated to a single customer and is not shared with other customers. It provides a private and secure connection between the customer's on-premises infrastructure and Azure. Private ExpressRoute circuits can be configured with various bandwidth options, ranging from 50 Mbps to 100 Gbps.

- *Public*: This type of ExpressRoute connection allows customers to connect to Azure services that are exposed publicly over the Internet, such as Microsoft 365 or Azure Storage. Public ExpressRoute circuits can establish a dedicated, private, and high-bandwidth connection to these services, improving performance and security.

Additionally, Microsoft offers two deployment models for ExpressRoute.

- The classic deployment model uses a separate resource manager for ExpressRoute, based on Azure Service Manager (ASM). This model is now deprecated and is not recommended for new deployments.

- The Resource Manager deployment model is based on the Azure Resource Manager (ARM), the recommended deployment model for ExpressRoute. It provides a unified deployment and management experience for all Azure resources, including ExpressRoute.

In addition to these types and models, Microsoft offers various ExpressRoute peering options, enabling customers to peer with different Microsoft services and partners. These include Microsoft peering, which enables customers to connect to Microsoft cloud services such as Azure, Dynamics 365, and Office 365, and partner peering, which enables customers to connect to cloud services offered by Microsoft partners.

There are several benefits to using Azure ExpressRoute, including the following:

- *High performance*: ExpressRoute provides a dedicated, high-bandwidth connection that can be configured up to 100 Gbps. This ensures low-latency connectivity with consistent and reliable network performance.

- *Enhanced security*: ExpressRoute provides a private connection that does not traverse the public Internet, making it less susceptible to security threats like DDoS attacks and malware. ExpressRoute supports private peering, allowing you to connect directly to Azure services without going through the public Internet.

- *Better reliability*: ExpressRoute provides a dedicated, redundant, resilient connection with a service level agreement (SLA) of 99.9 percent, ensuring high availability and business continuity.

- *Cost savings*: ExpressRoute can help reduce your network costs by eliminating the need for expensive dedicated circuits, reducing data transfer costs, and providing predictable network performance.

How It Works

Azure ExpressRoute establishes a dedicated, private, high-bandwidth connection between your on-premises infrastructure and Azure data centers. This connection is established through a connectivity provider, such as a telecommunications provider or a connectivity partner, using a dedicated physical or virtual circuit.

The following is a high-level overview of how Azure ExpressRoute works:

1. *Choose a connectivity provider*: You must select one offering ExpressRoute connectivity. Microsoft has partnered with several telecommunications providers and connectivity partners worldwide to offer ExpressRoute connectivity.

2. *Configure your network*: You must configure your on-premises network to establish a private connection to Azure. This may involve configuring routers, switches, firewalls, and other network devices to support ExpressRoute connectivity.

3. *Create an ExpressRoute circuit*: You must create an ExpressRoute circuit in Azure and configure it with the appropriate settings, such as the connectivity provider, bandwidth, and routing settings.

4. *Connect to Azure*: You must connect your on-premises network and Azure using the ExpressRoute circuit. This may involve setting up a cross-connect, configuring the virtual network gateway, and establishing routing.

5. *Exchange traffic*: Once the connection is established, you can exchange traffic between your on-premises infrastructure and Azure. This traffic can be sent over the ExpressRoute circuit, which provides a dedicated, private, and high-bandwidth connection that does not traverse the public Internet.

6. *Monitor and manage the connection*: You need to monitor and manage the ExpressRoute connection to ensure it performs as expected. This may involve configuring network security and monitoring, integrating with other Azure services such as Azure Virtual Network and Azure Firewall, and managing circuit capacity and billing.

Azure ExpressRoute provides several benefits, including high performance, enhanced security, better reliability, and cost savings. It is commonly used for hybrid cloud connectivity, disaster recovery, data migration, and big data analytics.

Azure ExpressRoute is a service offered by Microsoft Azure that provides a dedicated, private connection between an organization's on-premises infrastructure and Azure data centers. This connection is crucial for ensuring secure and reliable communication between the two environments.

Design Considerations

Here are some key design security best practices for Azure ExpressRoute:

- *Use private peering*: Azure ExpressRoute supports two types of peering: private and public. Private peering is a more secure option as it creates a private, dedicated connection between the on-premises infrastructure and the Azure virtual network. This ensures that traffic between the two environments is not exposed to the public Internet.

- *Implement NSGs*: NSGs are a key security feature in Azure that allows you to filter network traffic to and from Azure resources. They can be applied to virtual network subnets, individual virtual machines, and network interfaces. NSGs can help protect your Azure resources from malicious traffic and restrict access to resources only to authorized users and applications.

- *Use ExpressRoute with Azure Private Link*: Azure Private Link allows you to access Azure services (such as Azure Storage, Azure SQL Database, and Azure Cosmos DB) over a private, dedicated connection instead of over the public Internet. Using ExpressRoute with Azure Private Link, you can ensure that your organization's data stays within your private network and is not exposed to the public Internet.

- *Implement firewall rules*: Firewall rules can be used to restrict inbound and outbound traffic to your Azure resources. You can use them to allow traffic only from trusted sources, block specific IP addresses or ranges, and restrict access to specific ports or protocols. This can help prevent unauthorized access to your Azure resources.

- *Use ExpressRoute with VPN Gateway*: You can use ExpressRoute with VPN Gateway to provide an additional layer of security for your on-premises infrastructure. VPN Gateway allows you to create a secure, encrypted tunnel between your on-premises infrastructure and Azure virtual networks. This can help protect your data from interception or eavesdropping by unauthorized parties.

- *Use ExpressRoute Direct for high-security scenarios*: ExpressRoute Direct is a premium offering that provides a dedicated, private connection with higher bandwidth and lower latencies than the standard ExpressRoute. It is designed for high-security scenarios requiring the highest network performance, reliability, and security.

How to Enable It

Azure ExpressRoute is ideal for organizations that require a private, dedicated, and high-bandwidth connection between their on-premises network and Azure. Here are some use cases for Azure ExpressRoute deployment:

- *Hybrid cloud deployment*: Many organizations use a hybrid cloud model, where some applications and services are hosted in the cloud, and others are hosted on-premises. Azure ExpressRoute can be used to create a private and dedicated connection between the two environments, allowing for seamless integration and data transfer.

- *Big data and analytics*: Organizations that use big data and analytics tools, such as Hadoop or Spark, may require large amounts of data transfer between their on-premises network and Azure. Azure ExpressRoute provides a dedicated, high-bandwidth connection that can significantly reduce data transfer times and improve performance.

- *Disaster recovery and business continuity*: Azure ExpressRoute can be used as part of a disaster recovery or business continuity plan. By creating a private and dedicated connection between your on-premises network and Azure, you can ensure that critical applications and services remain available during a disaster or outage.

- *High-security environments*: Organizations that require high levels of security and compliance, such as government agencies or healthcare providers, may require a private and dedicated connection to Azure. Azure ExpressRoute provides a secure and reliable connection that can meet these requirements.

- *High-performance computing*: Organizations that use high-performance computing (HPC) applications, such as simulations or modeling, may require a dedicated and high-bandwidth connection to Azure. Azure ExpressRoute can provide the necessary connectivity and performance to support these applications.

To enable Azure ExpressRoute, there are several prerequisites that you need to meet.

- *An Azure subscription*: You need an active Azure subscription to use Azure ExpressRoute.

- *A supported Azure region*: Azure ExpressRoute is available in several Azure regions. It would be best to choose a region your connectivity provider supports.

- *A connectivity provider*: You need to have an active connection with an Azure ExpressRoute connectivity provider. You can choose from several providers, including telecom, cloud exchange, and colocation.

- *A physical connection*: You need to establish a physical connection between your on-premises network and the connectivity provider's network. This can be done through a dedicated private line, an Ethernet connection, or a VPN connection.

- *Network hardware*: You need the appropriate network hardware to support the Azure ExpressRoute connection. This includes routers, switches, and other networking equipment.

- *Network configuration*: You must configure your on-premises network to support the Azure ExpressRoute connection. This includes configuring routing, security, and other network settings.

- *Virtual network in Azure*: You need to have a virtual network set up in Azure that will be connected to your on-premises network through the ExpressRoute circuit.

- *Public IP addresses*: You must have public IP addresses available to configure the ExpressRoute circuit and virtual network gateway.

- *Administrative access*: You need administrative access to your on-premises network and Azure to configure and manage the ExpressRoute connection.

- *Understanding of billing and pricing*: You need to understand the billing and pricing for Azure ExpressRoute, including the charges for data transfer, circuit uptime, and other services.

Meeting these prerequisites is essential to successfully enabling Azure ExpressRoute and ensuring your Azure environment is secure and reliable.

Enabling Azure ExpressRoute involves several steps, including creating an ExpressRoute circuit, configuring the appropriate settings in Azure, and connecting to the circuit from your on-premises network. Here is an overview of the steps involved in enabling Azure ExpressRoute:

1. *Choose an ExpressRoute connectivity provider*: Azure ExpressRoute can be enabled through several connectivity providers, including telecom providers, cloud exchange providers, and colocation providers. It would be best if you chose a provider that best meets your organization's needs.

2. *Create an ExpressRoute circuit*: After choosing a connectivity provider, you must create an ExpressRoute circuit in the Azure Portal. This involves specifying the connectivity provider, the location of the circuit, the bandwidth requirements, and other settings.

3. *Configure Azure settings*: After creating the ExpressRoute circuit, you must configure the appropriate settings in Azure, including creating a virtual network gateway and configuring peering settings. You must also configure routing and security settings to ensure traffic is appropriately directed between your on-premises network and Azure.

4. *Connect to the circuit*: Once you have configured the appropriate settings in Azure, you can connect to the ExpressRoute circuit from your on-premises network. This involves setting up a physical connection between your on-premises network and the

connectivity provider's network, configuring routing settings on your network, and testing the connection to ensure it is working properly.

5. *Verify connectivity and performance*: After enabling Azure ExpressRoute, you should verify that you have connectivity to Azure resources and that performance is acceptable. You can use tools like Azure Network Watcher to monitor network traffic and troubleshoot any issues that may arise.

Enabling Azure ExpressRoute can be a complex process that requires careful planning and configuration. The following best practices and working with an experienced connectivity provider is essential to ensure your Azure environment is secure and reliable.

Key Insights of Azure ExpressRoute   Azure ExpressRoute is available in more than 100 locations worldwide, including North America, Europe, Asia, and Australia. According to a Microsoft report, ExpressRoute offers up to 99.9 percent reliability for Azure services, which can be higher than the reliability offered by a typical Internet connection. Microsoft partners with more than 70 global network service providers to offer ExpressRoute connectivity, providing customers with a wide range of connectivity options. According to a Microsoft report, ExpressRoute provides higher throughput and lower latencies than traditional Internet connections, which can improve application performance. Microsoft offers a free trial of Azure ExpressRoute, allowing customers to test the service before committing to a paid plan.

Azure WAF

Azure Web Application Firewall (WAF) is a cloud-based security service offered by Microsoft Azure that provides centralized protection to web applications from common exploits and vulnerabilities, such as SQL injection, cross-site scripting, and application-layer DDoS attacks. Azure WAF helps ensure web application security and availability by inspecting incoming web traffic and filtering out malicious requests.

Azure WAF works by deploying a web application gateway (WAG) before your web application. The WAG acts as a reverse proxy that intercepts incoming traffic and routes it to the web application. Before traffic is passed on to the web application, it is inspected by the WAF for malicious content and behavior. The WAF uses a set of rules and policies to identify and block attacks, such as the OWASP Top 10, a widely recognized list of the top 10 web application security risks.

Azure WAF provides several benefits to organizations, including the following:

- *Easy deployment and management*: Azure WAF is a cloud-based service easily deployed and managed through the Azure Portal. This makes setting up and configuring the WAF for your web applications easy.

- *Protection against common attacks*: Azure WAF protects against common exploits and vulnerabilities, such as SQL injection, cross-site scripting, and application-layer DDoS attacks.

- *Customizable rules and policies*: Azure WAF allows you to customize the rules and policies that are used to identify and block attacks. This allows you to tailor the WAF to the specific needs of your web application.

- *Real-time monitoring and logging*: Azure WAF provides real-time monitoring and logging of web traffic, allowing you to identify and respond to attacks as they happen.

- *Scalability*: Azure WAF is a scalable service that can handle high volumes of web traffic, making it suitable for large-scale web applications.

Azure WAF can help organizations meet the Protect function of the NIST CSF by providing centralized protection for web applications from common exploits and vulnerabilities. Here are some examples of how Azure WAF maps to the Protect function of the NIST CSF:

- *Access control*: Azure WAF provides access control capabilities that can help organizations enforce policies and prevent unauthorized access to web applications. This includes blocking or allowing traffic based on IP addresses, countries, and other criteria.

- *Data protection*: Azure WAF can help protect sensitive data by filtering out malicious requests that contain SQL injection or cross-site scripting attacks, among others. It can also encrypt data in transit using HTTPS.

- *Monitoring and logging*: Azure WAF provides real-time monitoring and logging of web traffic, which can help organizations detect and respond to attacks as they happen. The logs generated by Azure WAF can be used for forensic analysis and to identify trends and patterns in web traffic.

- *Incident response*: Azure WAF can be part of an incident response plan to block traffic quickly and mitigate attacks. It can also be integrated with other Azure security services, such as Azure Security Center, to provide a more comprehensive incident response plan.

How It Works

Azure WAF is a cloud-based security service that protects web applications from common exploits and vulnerabilities. Here is an overview of how Azure WAF works:

- *Deploy a WAG*: To use Azure WAF, you must first deploy a WAG before your web application. The WAG acts as a reverse proxy that intercepts incoming traffic and routes it to the web application.

- *Traffic inspection*: Before traffic is passed on to the web application, it is inspected by the Azure WAF for malicious content and behavior. The WAF uses a set of rules and policies to identify and block attacks, such as the OWASP Top 10, a widely recognized list of the top 10 web application security risks.

- *Customizable rules and policies*: Azure WAF allows you to customize the rules and policies used to identify and block attacks. You can create custom rules specific to your web application and adjust the sensitivity of the WAF to match your security needs.

- *Real-time monitoring and logging*: Azure WAF provides real-time monitoring and logging of web traffic, allowing you to identify and respond to attacks as they happen. The WAF generates detailed reports on web traffic and security events, which can be used to troubleshoot issues and improve your security posture.

- *Integration with Azure Security Center*: Azure WAF integrates with Azure Security Center, which provides a centralized location for managing and monitoring the security of your Azure resources. Azure Security Center provides recommendations for improving your security posture and configuring Azure WAF.

Design Considerations

Here are some security design best practices for Azure Web WAF:

- *Keep the WAF updated*: Azure WAF rules and policies are updated regularly to protect against new threats and vulnerabilities. It is important to keep the WAF updated to ensure it effectively blocks the latest attacks.

- *Use the OWASP rule set*: The OWASP rule set is a set of rules that can be used with Azure WAF to block common web application attacks. The OWASP rule set is widely used and well-maintained, making it a good choice for most organizations.

- *Use custom rules*: Besides the OWASP rule set, organizations should create rules specific to their web applications. This can help ensure that the WAF can detect and block attacks unique to the organization's environment.

- *Use managed rules*: Azure WAF provides a set of managed rules that can be used to block common attacks. Microsoft developed and maintained these managed rules and can help organizations quickly implement adequate protection against common threats.

- *Monitor and analyze logs*: Azure WAF generates logs that can be used to monitor web traffic and detect attacks. Organizations should monitor these logs regularly and analyze them for trends and patterns that may indicate an attack.

- *Use Azure Security Center*: Azure Security Center can provide additional protection and visibility into web application security. It can help organizations identify vulnerabilities and misconfigurations in their Azure environment and provide recommendations for improving security.

- *Test the WAF regularly*: It is essential to test the Azure WAF regularly to ensure it is effective at blocking attacks. This can be done using tools such as penetration testing and vulnerability scanning.

How to Enable It

Azure WAF is a security feature of Azure Application Gateway, a cloud-based load-balancing solution. Azure WAF provides centralized protection for web applications against common exploits and vulnerabilities. It uses a rules-based engine to inspect web traffic and block attacks identified by the rules.

Azure WAF offers the following features:

- *OWASP rule set*: Azure WAF includes the Open Web Application Security Project (OWASP) rule set, a widely used set of rules for blocking common web application attacks.

- *Managed rules*: Azure WAF provides a set of managed rules that are developed and maintained by Microsoft. These rules can be used to block common attacks, such as SQL injection and cross-site scripting.

- *Custom rules*: Organizations can create custom rules to block attacks specific to their web applications.

- *Real-time monitoring and logging*: Azure WAF provide real-time monitoring and logging of web traffic. This can help organizations detect and respond to attacks as they happen.

- *SSL/TLS encryption*: Azure WAF can encrypt web traffic using SSL/TLS encryption.

- *Access control*: Azure WAF provides access control capabilities that can be used to enforce policies and prevent unauthorized access to web applications.

- *Integration with Azure Security Center*: Azure WAF can be integrated with Azure Security Center to provide additional protection and visibility into web application security.

The following are the essential prerequisites for Azure Web Application Firewall (WAF):

- *Azure subscription*: To use Azure WAF, you need an active Azure subscription. You can sign up for a free trial if you don't have one.

- *Azure resources*: You must create or have existing Azure resources, such as a virtual network, a public IP address, and an application gateway.

- *Application Gateway*: Azure WAF is a feature of Azure Application Gateway. You will need to create an application gateway to use WAF.

- *Back-end pool*: The application gateway must have a back-end pool configured with one or more servers running your web application.

- *SSL certificate*: If your web application uses SSL/TLS encryption, you will need an SSL certificate to configure HTTPS.

- *WAF policy*: You must create a WAF policy to configure the rules and settings for Azure WAF.

- *NSG*: If you want to restrict access to your web application, you can use a NSG to define inbound and outbound traffic rules.

- *DNS record*: You must create a DNS record to point your domain name to the public IP address associated with your application gateway.

- *Access control*: You may want to configure access control rules to restrict access to your web application based on IP addresses or other criteria.

To enable Azure Web Application Firewall (WAF), you can follow these steps:

1. *Create an Azure Application Gateway*: Azure WAF is a feature of Azure Application Gateway, so you need to create an application gateway first. You can create an application gateway through Azure Portal, Azure CLI, or PowerShell.

2. *Configure a back-end pool*: The application gateway must have a back-end pool configured with one or more servers running your web application. You can add back-end pools through Azure Portal, Azure CLI, or PowerShell.

3. *Configure a listener*: You need to configure a listener for the application gateway to listen to incoming traffic. You can configure a listener through the Azure Portal, Azure CLI, or PowerShell.

4. *Enable WAF*: Once you have created an application gateway, you can enable WAF by creating a WAF policy and associating it with the application gateway. You can create a WAF policy through the Azure Portal or using Azure CLI or PowerShell.

5. *Configure WAF policy*: You can configure the WAF policy with the rules and settings that you want to apply to your web application. You can use the default rule set or create custom rules. You can configure the WAF policy through the Azure Portal, Azure CLI, or PowerShell.

6. *Associate the WAF policy with the listener*: You need to associate the WAF policy with the listener to enable WAF for incoming traffic. You can associate the WAF policy with the listener through the Azure Portal or by using Azure CLI or PowerShell.

7. *Test and monitor*: Once you have enabled WAF, you should test your web application to ensure it functions properly. You should also monitor the traffic to your web application to detect and respond to any attacks that WAF blocks.

These steps can help you enable Azure WAF and configure it to protect your web application from common exploits and vulnerabilities.

Microsoft Purview DLP

A company's financial data, proprietary data, credit card numbers, health records, or Social Security numbers are among the sensitive information they control. The practice of data loss prevention prevents users from inappropriately sharing this sensitive data with people who should not have access to it. This practice can help protect sensitive data and reduce risk.

Defining DLP policies in Microsoft Purview enables you to identify, monitor, and automatically protect sensitive data across the following:

- OneDrive, Teams, Exchange, and SharePoint are Microsoft 365 services

- Applications such as Word, Excel, and PowerPoint are included in the Office suite

- Endpoints running Windows 10, Windows 11, and macOS (three of the latest versions released)

- Non-Microsoft cloud applications

- File shares and SharePoint on-premises

DLP uses deep content analysis to detect sensitive items, not just a simple text scan. In addition to primary data matches to keywords, regular expression evaluation, internal function validation, and secondary data matches close to primary data matches, content is analyzed for secondary data matches. As well as machine learning algorithms, DLP detects content that matches your DLP policies using other methods.

Microsoft Purview DLP is a feature of Microsoft Purview, a unified data governance service that helps organizations discover, understand, and manage their data. Purview DLP allows organizations to protect sensitive data by identifying and classifying sensitive information in their data estate and applying policies to prevent unauthorized access, usage, or sharing of this data. With Microsoft Purview, you can define DLP policies that identify sensitive data and apply data protection rules to prevent unauthorized access or disclosure. Purview supports a range of data protection capabilities, including masking, encryption, and access control. You can use Purview to discover and classify sensitive data assets and then use DLP policies to protect that data from being accessed or disclosed inappropriately.

With Purview DLP, organizations can create custom data classification labels and policies that align with their specific regulatory and compliance requirements. The service scans data sources such as SQL Server, Azure Data Lake Storage, and SharePoint Online to discover and classify sensitive data such as personally identifiable information (PII), financial information, and intellectual property. It then provides actionable insights into how sensitive data is being used and shared within the organization and helps enforce policies to prevent data leakage or loss. Purview DLP also integrates with Microsoft Information Protection to provide advanced data protection capabilities such as encryption and access controls. Additionally, it provides a centralized dashboard that allows organizations to monitor and manage their data governance policies across their entire data estate.

Microsoft Purview DLP is a powerful tool for organizations looking to secure their sensitive data and comply with data protection regulations.

How It Works

Microsoft Purview DLP provides a comprehensive approach to discovering, classifying, protecting, and monitoring sensitive data within an organization's data estate. Here are the critical steps involved in how it works:

1. *Data discovery*: Purview DLP scans data sources such as SQL Server, Azure Data Lake Storage, and SharePoint Online to discover sensitive data such as personally identifiable information (PII), financial information, and intellectual property.

2. *Data classification*: The service automatically classifies the data based on pre-configured or custom data classification policies. These policies can be based on regulatory or compliance requirements, such as GDPR, CCPA, or HIPAA. Purview DLP also allows organizations to create custom data classification labels and policies aligning with their needs.

3. *Policy enforcement*: Purview DLP applies policies to enforce data protection rules once the data is classified. Policies can block access to sensitive data or notify administrators of potential data breaches.

4. *Monitoring and reporting*: Purview DLP provides a centralized dashboard that allows organizations to monitor and manage their data governance policies across their entire data estate. The dashboard provides insights into how sensitive data is being used and shared within the organization and helps enforce policies to prevent data leakage or loss.

5. *Integration with Microsoft Information Protection*: Purview DLP
    integrates with Microsoft Information Protection to provide
    advanced data protection capabilities such as encryption and
    access controls. This integration ensures that sensitive data is
    protected throughout its life cycle.

Microsoft Purview DLP can be mapped to the NIST CSF Protect category, which
focuses on developing and implementing appropriate safeguards to ensure the delivery
of critical infrastructure services. Here are some examples of how Purview DLP can help
organizations meet the Protect category's objectives:

- *Asset management*: Purview DLP helps organizations discover,
  classify, and manage sensitive data assets. It enables organizations
  to identify critical data assets and apply appropriate safeguards to
  protect them from cyber threats.

- *Access control*: Purview DLP provides access controls to ensure
  that only authorized personnel can access sensitive data. It helps
  organizations enforce policies to prevent unauthorized access, usage,
  or sharing of sensitive data.

- *Data security*: Purview DLP provides encryption, masking, and
  redaction capabilities to protect sensitive data. It helps organizations
  comply with data protection regulations and prevent data leakage
  or loss.

- *Security awareness training*: Purview DLP provides insights into how
  sensitive data is used and shared within the organization. It enables
  organizations to develop and implement security awareness training
  programs to educate employees about data protection policies and
  best practices.

Design Considerations

The following are the key security design best practices for Microsoft Purview DLP:

- *Follow the principle of least privilege*: Limit access to sensitive data to
  only those who need it—grant permissions to data assets based on a
  need-to-know basis.

- *Implement strong access controls*: Use role-based access controls and MFA to ensure only authorized users can access sensitive data.

- *Use encryption*: Purview DLP provides data encryption capabilities that can be used to protect sensitive data at rest and in transit. Use encryption to protect sensitive data, even if it is stolen or intercepted.

- *Implement data classification policies*: Develop and implement data classification policies to help identify and protect sensitive data. Classify data according to its sensitivity and apply appropriate security controls to protect it.

- *Monitor and audit*: Purview DLP provides monitoring and audit capabilities that can be used to track and report on user activity. Use these capabilities to detect and respond to suspicious activity.

- *Regularly update and patch*: Keep Purview DLP up-to-date with the latest patches and updates to protect it against the latest threats.

- *Train employees*: Educate employees on data protection policies and best practices. Ensure they understand the importance of protecting sensitive data and know the risks associated with data breaches.

- *Test and validate*: Regularly test and validate the effectiveness of your security controls to ensure that they are working as intended. Conduct regular penetration testing and vulnerability assessments to identify and address weaknesses in your security posture.

These security design best practices can help organizations protect their sensitive data and comply with data protection regulations.

How to Enable It

Each organization's DLP plan and implementation will be different due to its business needs, goals, resources, and situation. All successful DLP implementations share some elements, however. Rather than scanning text for sensitive items, DLP uses deep content analysis. Content analysis involves the evaluation of regular expressions, the evaluation of internal functions, and the analysis of secondary data matches close with the primary data match.

DLP also utilizes machine learning algorithms and other methods to detect content that matches your DLP policies. Here are the essential prerequisites for Microsoft Purview DLP:

- *Purview account*: To use Purview DLP, you must have a Purview account. If you don't have a Purview account, you can create one by following the instructions on the Azure Portal.

- *Azure subscription*: To use Purview DLP, you must have an Azure subscription. If you don't have an Azure subscription, you can sign up for a free trial or purchase a subscription.

- *Permissions*: Ensure that you have the necessary permissions to configure and manage Purview DLP policies. You must have the Data Protection Administrator role in Azure AD to create and manage Purview DLP policies.

These key prerequisites can help organizations ensure they have the resources and permissions to deploy and manage Purview DLP effectively. The following are key deployment considerations for Microsoft Purview DLP:

- *Data sources*: Consider which data sources you want to scan for sensitive data. Purview DLP supports scanning data sources such as Azure Data Lake Storage, SQL Server, and SharePoint Online. Ensure that the data sources you want to scan are compatible with Purview DLP.

- *Data classification*: Consider how you want to classify sensitive data. Purview DLP provides predefined and custom classification labels that can be used to identify sensitive data. Determine which classification labels are relevant to your organization and how you want to apply them.

- *Policy actions*: Consider what actions you want to take when sensitive data is detected. Purview DLP provides actions such as alerting, blocking access, and redacting data. Determine which policy actions are appropriate for your organization and how you want to configure them.

- *Performance*: Consider the performance impact of Purview DLP on your data sources. Scanning large volumes of data for sensitive information can impact performance, so you may need to adjust scanning schedules and thresholds to minimize performance impact.

- *Integration with other security tools*: Consider how Purview DLP integrates with other security tools in your organization. Purview DLP can integrate with Azure Sentinel, Azure Active Directory, and Azure Security Center. Determine how you want to integrate Purview DLP with your existing security tools.

- *Compliance requirements*: Consider compliance requirements such as GDPR, CCPA, and HIPAA when deploying Purview DLP. Purview DLP provides data classification, encryption, and audit logging features that can help organizations meet compliance requirements.

These key deployment considerations can help organizations successfully deploy Purview DLP and protect their sensitive data.

To turn on Microsoft Purview DLP, and follow these steps:

1. Sign in to the Azure Portal.

2. Navigate to the Purview account that you want to enable DLP for.

3. Click the Data Protection option in the menu on the left.

4. Click the "Add policy" button on the Data Protection page.

5. On the Create a Data Protection Policy page, enter a name and define the policy.

6. Select the data sources that you want to scan for sensitive data. You can select data sources such as Azure Data Lake Storage, SQL Server, and SharePoint Online.

7. Configure the data classification settings. You can use predefined or custom classification labels to identify sensitive data.

8. Set up policy actions. You can configure actions such as alerting, blocking access, or redacting data based on policy violations.

9. Review and save the policy.

Once the policy is created, Purview DLP will scan the selected data sources for sensitive data and enforce the policy rules. You can monitor policy violations and take corrective actions as needed.

Data Segregation

Azure data Segregation is a security practice that separates data in Azure services based on sensitivity or criticality. This practice helps organizations protect their sensitive data and reduce the risk of unauthorized access, disclosure, or modification.

Azure data Segregation can be achieved through a variety of mechanisms, including the following:

- *Azure resource groups*: Grouping related Azure resources, such as virtual machines and storage accounts, together in a resource group can help organizations logically separate their data and control access based on the resource group.

- *Azure virtual networks*: Creating virtual networks in Azure can help organizations isolate their data and control traffic flow between resources within the virtual network.

- *Azure Active Directory*: Using Azure Active Directory to manage access to Azure resources can help organizations control who has access to their data.

- *RBAC*: Using RBAC to assign roles to users and groups can help organizations control their actions on Azure resources.

- *Encryption*: Encrypting data at rest and in transit can help organizations protect their data from unauthorized access.

Azure data segregation is a critical security practice for organizations that store sensitive data in Azure services. Organizations can reduce the risk of data breaches and other security incidents by separating data based on its sensitivity or criticality.

Summary

In this chapter, you read about methods to design and deploy a strategy for protecting security services in line with the NIST CSF mapping about data security.

In the book's next chapter, you will read about designing and deploying a strategy for protecting security services with regard to Information Protection Processes and Procedures (PR.IP) and Protective Technology (PR.PT).

CHAPTER 6

Design and Deploy a Protect Solution: Part 3

Cybersecurity is essential to protect an organization's data from malicious attacks. These processes and procedures involve using firewalls, encryption, and authentication technologies to secure the system. Regular review and updates of these processes and procedures are necessary to ensure the system is up-to-date and secure.

This is because cybercriminals are constantly creating new methods to breach a system, and the security measures implemented must be able to detect and prevent these threats. Additionally, regular reviews and updates of these processes and procedures help ensure that employees follow the best practices and that the system can respond quickly to any new threats.

Cybersecurity technologies are essential for preventing cyberattacks and protecting valuable data. Organizations should ensure they have the right tools to protect their networks and data.

By the end of this chapter, you will understand the following:

- Information Protection Processes and Procedures
- Protective Technology

© Puthiyavan Udayakumar 2023
P. Udayakumar, *Design and Deploy a Secure Azure Environment*,
https://doi.org/10.1007/978-1-4842-9678-3_6

Information Protection Processes and Procedures (PR.IP)

PR.IP refers to a set of security controls and practices designed to protect an organization's information assets from unauthorized access, modification, disclosure, or destruction.

PR.IP controls typically include policies, procedures, and technical measures to safeguard sensitive information and ensure its confidentiality, integrity, and availability. These controls are designed to reduce the risk of security incidents, such as data breaches, cyberattacks, and insider threats.

Examples of PR.IP controls include the following:

- Developing policies and procedures for classifying and handling sensitive information

- Implementing access controls to restrict access to sensitive information

- Conducting periodic vulnerability assessments and penetration testing

- Monitoring and analyzing system logs to detect and respond to potential security incidents

- Implementing data backup and recovery procedures

- Training employees on information security best practices

The PR.IP security controls within the NIST Cybersecurity Framework (CSF) focus on protecting an organization's information assets.

Specifically, the PR.IP category includes security controls related to developing, implementing, and maintaining information protection processes and procedures. These controls are designed to protect sensitive information against unauthorized access, theft, modification, or destruction.

Here are some examples of controls within the PR.IP category:

- Developing policies and procedures to define how sensitive information should be classified, handled, and protected

- Deploying access controls to restrict access to sensitive information to only authorized personnel

- Conducting periodic vulnerability assessments and penetration testing to identify potential weaknesses in the organization's information protection processes

- Monitoring and analyzing system logs to detect and respond to potential security incidents

- Implementing data backup and recovery procedures to ensure that critical data can be restored in case of a system failure or data loss

There are several benefits of implementing PR.IP in cybersecurity, including the following:

- *Improved data security*: PR.IP controls protect sensitive information from unauthorized access, modification, and theft. By implementing these controls, organizations can enhance the security of their data and reduce the risk of data breaches.

- *Increased compliance*: Many industries and organizations are subject to regulations and standards that require them to protect sensitive information by implementing PR.IP controls; organizations can demonstrate compliance with these regulations and avoid potential penalties for noncompliance.

- *Better risk management*: PR.IP controls help organizations identify potential risks and vulnerabilities in their information systems. By implementing controls to mitigate these risks, organizations can better manage their overall cybersecurity posture and reduce the likelihood of security incidents.

- *Enhanced business continuity*: PR.IP controls include procedures for backing up and restoring critical data, which can help organizations recover from data loss or system failure more quickly. This can help minimize downtime and maintain business continuity during a cyberattack or other security incident.

- *Improved reputation*: Data breaches and other security incidents can damage an organization's reputation and erode customer trust by implementing PR.IP controls; organizations can demonstrate their commitment to protecting sensitive information and safeguarding the privacy of their customers and stakeholders.

Implementing PR.IP can help organizations improve their cybersecurity posture, reduce the risk of security incidents, and protect sensitive information from unauthorized access or disclosure.

Azure Mapping for PR.IP

The NIST CSF focuses on implementing safeguards to protect an organization's information assets. Several Azure services can be used to implement PR.IP controls and achieve compliance with the NIST CSF. Here are some examples:

- *Azure Information Protection (AIP)*: AIP is a cloud-based solution that provides tools to classify, label, and protect sensitive data based on its sensitivity. AIP can be used to implement PR.IP controls that are related to data classification, access control, and data protection.

- *Azure Key Vault*: Azure Key Vault is a cloud-based service that securely stores cryptographic keys, certificates, and secrets. It can be used to implement PR.IP controls related to cryptographic key management and secure storage of sensitive information.

- *Azure Active Directory (Azure AD)*: Azure AD is a cloud-based identify and access management (IAM) service that provides authentication and authorization services for Azure resources. It can be used to implement PR.IP controls related to access control and identify management.

- *Azure Security Center*: Azure Security Center is a cloud-based security management service that provides centralized security management and threat protection for Azure resources. It can be used to implement PR.IP controls related to threat detection and response, vulnerability management, and compliance monitoring.

- *Azure Sentinel*: Azure Sentinel is a cloud-based security information and event management (SIEM) service that provides real-time threat detection and response capabilities for Azure resources. It can be used to implement PR.IP controls related to threat detection and response.

- *Azure Virtual Network*: Azure Virtual Network is a cloud-based service that provides a virtualized network infrastructure for Azure resources. It can be used to implement PR.IP controls related to network security, segmentation, and isolation.

- *Azure Firewall*: Azure Firewall is a cloud-based network security service that provides centralized firewall management and threat protection for Azure resources. It can be used to implement PR.IP controls related to network security and access control.

- *Azure Bastion*: Azure Bastion is a cloud-based service that provides secure remote access to Azure resources using a browser-based interface. It can be used to implement PR.IP controls related to secure remote access and identify management.

- *Azure Policy*: Azure Policy is a cloud-based service that provides policy-based management for Azure resources. It can be used to implement PR.IP controls related to compliance monitoring and enforcement.

- *Azure DevOps*: Azure DevOps is a cloud-based service providing tools for continuous integration and delivery (CI/CD) of applications and services. It can be used to implement PR.IP controls related to software development security, code review, and vulnerability management.

Figure 6-1 depicts the NIST Protect information processes and procedure against Azure services.

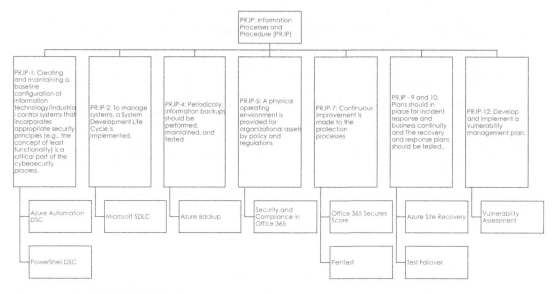

Figure 6-1. *NIST PR.IP to Azure mapping*

As part of the Azure cloud shared responsibility model, the NIST CSF security functions are provided in Table 6-1 with respect to PR.IP.

Table 6-1. PR.IP Management Responsibility Matrix

Category	Subcategory	Informative References	Responsibility	Customer Responsibility	Microsoft Azure Responsibility
PR.IP: Security policies (that address purpose, scope, roles, responsibilities, management commitment, and coordination among organizational entities), processes, and procedures are maintained and used to manage protection of information systems and assets.	PR.IP-1: Creating and maintaining a baseline configuration of information technology/industrial control systems that incorporates appropriate security principles (e.g., the concept of least functionality) is a critical part of the cybersecurity process.	NIST SP 800-53 Rev. 4 CM-2, CM-3, CM-4, CM-5, CM-6, CM-7, CM-9, SA-10	Shared	Configuration control and baseline configuration for the information systems employed should be developed, documented, and maintained by the customer. To ensure the security of these controls and baselines, appropriate security principles must be incorporated.	Hardware, software, and network devices are reviewed and updated annually by Microsoft Azure. A development and test environment is used to develop, test, and approve changes before entering a production environment.

(continued)

Table 6-1. (*continued*)

Category	Subcategory	Informative References	Responsibility	Customer Responsibility	Microsoft Azure Responsibility
	PR.IP-2: To manage systems, a System Development Life Cycle is implemented.	NIST SP 800-53 Rev. 4 SA-3, SA-4, SA-8, SA-10, SA-11, SA-12, SA-15, SA-17, PL-8	Shared	System development lifecycle processes should be implemented and adhered to by the customer.	All engineering and development projects at Microsoft follow the System Development Lifecycle (SDL). For all system development projects, a security requirements analysis must be performed. During the development phases, this document acts as a framework to identify potential risks and mitigation strategies that can be implemented and tested during the development process. The system development life cycle includes critical security reviews and approvals.

PR.IP-3:Efforts	NIST SP	Customer	Before implementing	N/A
Should made to maintain configuration change control	800-53 Rev. 4 CM-3, CM-4, SA-10	Responsibility	changes to the information system, the customer must determine which changes are configuration controlled. Before implementing changes, the customer must analyze changes to the information system to determine potential security impacts. The customer is responsible for reviewing configuration-controlled modifications to the information system and approving or disapproving them based on a security impact analysis. Configuration change decisions must be documented, and the requested change and the decided-upon change must be recorded.	

(continued)

Table 6-1. (*continued*)

Category	Subcategory	Informative References	Responsibility	Customer Responsibility	Microsoft Azure Responsibility
	PR.IP-4: Periodically, information backups should be performed, maintained, and tested	NIST SP 800-53 Rev. 4 CP-4, CP-6, CP-9	Shared	In order to restore from backups, customers must enable geo-replicated backups in their subscriptions.	Using complex algorithms, Microsoft Azure Storage replicates user-level data synchronously locally, providing three copies of redundancy. Asynchronous replication of data can be done to remote regions in some instances.
	PR.IP-5: A physical operating environment is provided for organizational assets by policy and regulations	NIST SP 800-53 Rev. 4 PE-10, PE-12, PE-13, PE-14, PE-15, PE-18	Microsoft Azure	N/A	To align the system with business goals and objectives, Microsoft Azure's formal technology strategy is updated and maintained annually. To reduce the impact on organizational operations, organizational assets, individuals, and Microsoft Azure customers, Microsoft Azure plans and coordinates security-related activities such as upgrading the application and infrastructure, performing security audits and testing, and conducting continuity planning exercises affecting the information system with Azure C+E Security management before performing such activities.

Subcategory	NIST SP Reference	Responsibility	Customer	Microsoft Azure
PR.IP-6: Policy dictates how data is destroyed.	NIST SP 800-53 Rev. 4 MP-6	Microsoft Azure	N/A	To be reused in a Microsoft Azure data center, Microsoft Azure digital media must be cleaned/purged using Microsoft Azure-approved tools that comply with NIST SP 800-88. The data center environment of Microsoft Azure does not use nondigital media.
PR.IP-7:Continuous improvement is made to the protection processes	NIST SP 800-53 Rev. 4 CA-2, CA-7, CP-2, IR-8, PL-2, PM-6	Shared	Processes for protecting data must be continuously reviewed and improved by the customer.	Microsoft Azure continuously reviews and improves its protection processes through internal review processes, audits, continuous monitoring, and other methods.
PR.IP-8: It is essential to share the effectiveness of protection technologies with the appropriate parties.	NIST SP 800-53 Rev. 4 AC-21, CA-7, SI-4	Customer Responsibility	Protection technologies should be shared with the appropriate parties by the customer.	N/A

(continued)

377

Table 6-1. (*continued*)

Category	Subcategory	Informative References	Responsibility	Customer Responsibility	Microsoft Azure Responsibility
	PR.IP-9: Plans should in place for incident response and business continuity.	NIST SP 800-53 Rev. 4 CP-2, IR-8	Customer Responsibility	Incident and business continuity plans, as well as disaster recovery plans, are the responsibility of the customer. The customer must review and improve all response and recovery plans to address relevant changes and any problems encountered.	N/A
	PR.IP-10:The recovery and response plans should be tested.	NIST SP 800-53 Rev. 4 CP-4, IR-3, PM-14	Customer Responsibility	The customer must test all customer response and recovery plans.	N/A

| PR.IP-11: Cybersecurity is vital in human resources practices, such as deprovisioning and personnel screening. | NIST SP 800-53 Rev. 4 PS Family | Customer Responsibility | Creating, reviewing, and updating human resources practices should include appropriate cybersecurity processes. According to the customer's internal policies and procedures, all Customer positions requiring access to Microsoft Azure must be assigned risk designations consistent with those policies and procedures. In addition, the customer must establish screening criteria for individuals seeking access to Microsoft Azure. Customers are responsible for screening individuals before authorizing access to the Microsoft Azure environment and disabling access to the Microsoft Azure system for terminated employees within the contractually agreed timeframe. | N/A |

(continued)

Table 6-1. (*continued*)

Category	Subcategory	Informative References	Responsibility	Customer Responsibility	Microsoft Azure Responsibility
	PR.IP-12:Develop and implement a vulnerability management plan.	NIST SP 800-53 Rev. 4 RA-3, RA-5, SI-2	Shared	The customer must develop and implement a vulnerability management plan to analyze and report on their applications for flaws.As part of this vulnerability management plan, the customer's applications and databases should also be scanned and corrected for vulnerabilities. Those customers using an operating system image not provided by Microsoft Azure will be responsible for scanning for vulnerabilities in the operating system. The customer is responsible for ensuring that vulnerability scanning tools enumerate components, flaws, and improper configurations according to established standards. Besides formatting checklists and test procedures, these tools should also measure vulnerability impacts.	Servers, network devices, web applications, and databases are authenticated vulnerability scans as part of Microsoft Azure's inventory. Remediation of flaws is implemented by the Azure security team.

Azure Automation Desired State Configuration

Azure Automation Desired State Configuration (DSC) is a cloud-based service provided by Microsoft Azure that enables the deployment, configuration, and management of resources in an automated and scalable manner. It is a configuration management tool that allows administrators to define the desired state of a set of resources and ensure they remain in that state over time.

With Azure Automation DSC, administrators can define a configuration as a PowerShell script, DSC configuration file, or DSC module. The configuration defines the desired state of a set of resources, such as virtual machines, databases, and network settings. Azure Automation DSC then applies the configuration to the resources and ensures that they remain desired.

Azure Automation DSC provides a centralized location for managing configurations, which can be applied to multiple resources across multiple environments. It also provides versioning and rollback capabilities, allowing administrators to manage configuration changes easily.

Azure Automation DSC integrates with other Azure services, such as Azure Monitor, which enables administrators to monitor and alert on configuration drift, and Azure Log Analytics, which provides a central location for analyzing logs and diagnosing issues.

The following are the key benefits of using Azure Automation DSC:

- *Consistency*: Azure Automation DSC ensures that your resources remain desired, enabling consistency across your environment. This reduces the risk of configuration drift and helps ensure your environment remains secure and stable.

- *Automation*: Azure Automation DSC configures your resources, allowing you to deploy and manage your infrastructure more efficiently. This reduces manual effort and enables you to scale your environment more easily.

- *Versioning and rollback*: Azure Automation DSC provides versioning and rollback capabilities, enabling you to manage configuration changes easily. This helps ensure that you can quickly revert to a previous version of your configuration if necessary.

- *Integration*: Azure Automation DSC integrates with other Azure services, such as Azure Monitor and Azure Log Analytics, enabling you to monitor and analyze your configurations more easily. This provides you with greater visibility and control over your environment.

- *Customization*: Azure Automation DSC provides flexibility and customization options, allowing you to tailor your configurations to your needs. This enables you to configure your resources to meet your business requirements best.

In a nutshell, Azure Automation DSC provides a powerful and flexible tool for managing and automating the configuration of your resources in the Azure cloud. It can help you to achieve greater consistency, efficiency, and control over your environment.

How It Works

Azure Automation DSC enables administrators to define a configuration that describes the desired state of a set of resources in Azure. This configuration is written in PowerShell, DSC configuration files, or DSC modules.

Once the configuration is defined, Azure Automation DSC applies it to the targeted resources. It uses a pull model, where the target resources periodically request the configuration from the Azure Automation DSC service. Azure Automation DSC monitors the resources when the configuration is applied to ensure they remain in the desired state. If a resource drifts from the desired state, Azure Automation DSC can automatically remediate the issue to bring the resource back to the desired state.

Azure Automation DSC provides versioning and rollback capabilities, enabling administrators to manage configuration changes. This allows them to easily track changes to their configurations and revert back to previous versions if necessary. Azure Automation DSC also integrates with other Azure services, such as Azure Monitor and Log Analytics. This enables administrators to monitor their configurations and identify issues or configuration drift quickly.

The following are key deployment considerations for Azure Automation DSC:

- *Use source control*: Store your DSC configurations in source control (e.g., Git) to manage changes and collaborate. This also allows you to roll back changes if needed easily.

- *Test configurations*: Test your configurations on a small scale before applying them to a larger environment. This can help you catch any issues before they affect your entire environment.

- *Use parameters*: Use parameters in your DSC configurations to make them more flexible and reusable. This allows you to define different configurations for different environments or scenarios.

- *Use modules*: Use PowerShell modules in your DSC configurations to make them more modular and reusable. This can reduce code duplication and simplify your configurations.

- *Monitor and alert*: Monitor your DSC configurations for compliance and errors using Azure Monitor and set up alerts for critical events. This helps you stay informed and respond quickly to any issues.

- *Use versioning*: Use versioning in your DSC configurations to manage changes and ensure that your resources remain in a known and secure state. This also allows you to roll back changes if needed.

- *Use runbooks*: Use Azure Automation runbooks to automate everyday tasks, such as deploying new configurations or remedying configuration drift. This can reduce manual effort and improve your efficiency.

By following these tips, you can work more effectively with Azure Automation DSC and ensure your resources remain secure and compliant.

Design Considerations

The following are essential security design best practices for Azure Automation DSC:

- *Secure credentials*: When configuring automation account credentials, ensure they are secured properly. You can use Azure Key Vault to store and manage credentials securely.

- *Role-based access control (RBAC)*: Use RBAC to control access to automation accounts and associated resources. This ensures that only authorized users can manage and access automation resources.

- *Network security*: Ensure that automation accounts and associated resources are located within secure network segments and that network traffic is restricted using network security groups (NSGs).

- *Encryption*: Use encryption to protect sensitive data, such as configuration data or credentials, when in transit or at rest.

- *Regular auditing*: Regularly audit automation accounts and associated resources to ensure that they are being used as intended and that no unauthorized changes have been made.

- *Secure communications*: Use secure protocols such as TLS when communicating with Azure Automation DSC services.

- *Version control*: Use version control to manage configuration changes and ensure they can be rolled back if necessary.

- *Secure baselines*: Use secure baselines for configuration management to ensure that all resources are configured securely and consistently.

- *Regular Updates*: Regularly update Azure Automation DSC services to protect them against known vulnerabilities.

In a nutshell, following these security design best practices can ensure that your Azure Automation DSC implementation is secure and meets your organization's compliance requirements.

How to Enable It

Azure Automation DSC can be adopted for the following use cases:

- *Consistent configuration management*: Azure Automation DSC enables you to define and enforce a compatible configuration across your environment. This helps to reduce configuration drift and ensures that your resources remain in a known and secure state.

- *Automated configuration management*: Azure Automation DSC allows you to automate the configuration of your resources. This reduces the manual effort required to manage your environment and improves your ability to respond to environmental changes.

- *Compliance management*: Azure Automation DSC enables you to maintain compliance with various regulatory requirements, such as HIPAA, PCI DSS, and SOX. You can use Azure Automation DSC to enforce configuration policies and generate compliance reports.

- *Scale and flexibility*: Azure Automation DSC can manage resources at scale, whether you have a few resources or thousands. Azure Automation DSC is flexible, allowing you to define and manage configurations using PowerShell scripts, DSC configuration files, or third-party tools.

The following are the prerequisites for using Azure Automation DSC:

- *An Azure subscription*: You will need an Azure subscription to create an automation account and other associated resources.

- *Azure Automation account*: You must create an Azure Automation account to use Azure Automation DSC.

- *Nodes to manage*: You will need nodes (e.g., virtual machines) to manage. These can be located on-premises or in the cloud.

- *PowerShell DSC modules*: You must install the appropriate PowerShell DSC modules on the nodes you want to manage.

- *Azure virtual machine (VM) extension*: You must install the Azure VM extension on the nodes you want to manage. This extension enables the nodes to communicate with the Azure Automation service.

- *Network connectivity*: The nodes you want to manage must be able to communicate with the Azure Automation service. This may require configuring network settings or firewall rules.

- *RBAC permissions*: You must have the appropriate RBAC permissions to create and manage automation resources in your subscription.

These are the main prerequisites for using Azure Automation DSC. You can find more detailed information in the Azure documentation.

The following are high-level steps to turn on Azure Automation DSC:

1. *Create an automation account*: Create an Azure Automation account, which provides the framework for managing your automation resources.

2. *Add nodes*: Add the resources you want to manage to your automation account. This can be done manually or through an orchestration tool such as Azure Virtual Machine Scale Sets.

3. *Define configurations*: Create configurations for the resources you want to manage. These configurations define the desired state of the resources and can be written in PowerShell or DSC configuration files.

4. *Assign configurations*: Assign the configurations to the nodes you want to manage. This can be done manually or through automation using Azure Resource Manager templates.

5. *Monitor and remediate*: Monitor the resources to ensure they remain in the desired state, and remediate any issues. You can use tools such as Azure Monitor and Azure Log Analytics to help with monitoring and remediation.

6. *Update and maintain*: As your environment evolves, update and maintain your configurations to ensure they remain up-to-date and compliant.

These are the basic steps for turning on Azure Automation DSC. More detailed instructions can be found in the Azure documentation.

PowerShell Desired State Configuration

PowerShell DSC is a configuration management platform in Windows PowerShell that enables the deployment and management of software and system configurations. It allows administrators to define the desired state of their systems using a declarative syntax and then continuously monitor and enforce that state.

DSC can manage various aspects of Windows systems, including registry settings, file system permissions, services, software installations, and more. It works by using configuration files, which define the desired state of a system, and then applying those configurations to the target systems. DSC can also be integrated with other management tools, such as System Center Configuration Manager (SCCM) and Azure Automation, to provide a comprehensive configuration management solution.

DSC is a powerful tool for managing the configuration of Windows systems. DSC is built on top of Windows PowerShell and uses a declarative syntax to define the desired state of a system. This makes it easy to manage and automate the configuration of multiple systems at scale, ensuring consistency and reducing the risk of manual errors.

DSC allows administrators to define configuration files containing a list of resources and their desired state. Resources are the building blocks of DSC configurations, representing a system's components, such as a file, a user, or a service. Each resource defines a specific configuration setting, such as a file's contents or a service's state. DSC provides various built-in resources for managing common configuration tasks, such as managing Windows services, configuring the registry, and managing user accounts. In addition, DSC can be extended with custom resources, which enable administrators to manage almost any aspect of a Windows system.

DSC can be used to configure both Windows Server and Windows client systems and can also be used to configure Azure virtual machines. DSC configurations can be applied to individual systems, groups of systems, or even entire data centers, making it easy to manage configurations at scale.

In addition, DSC provides a reporting feature that enables administrators to monitor the compliance of their systems with their desired state configuration. This makes it easy to identify any systems out of compliance and take corrective action if necessary.

The following are the key benefits of PowerShell DSC:

- *Automation*: DSC provides a way to automate the configuration of Windows systems, reducing the need for manual intervention and minimizing the risk of human errors.

- *Consistency*: DSC ensures that configurations are applied consistently across systems, reducing the risk of configuration drift and improving overall system stability.

- *Scalability*: DSC enables administrators to manage configurations at scale, with the ability to apply configurations to individual systems, groups of systems, or entire data centers.

- *Reusability*: DSC configurations are reusable and can be easily applied to multiple systems or environments, saving time and effort in managing configurations.

- *Version control*: DSC configurations can be stored in version control systems, enabling administrators to track changes and roll back to previous configurations if necessary.

- *Reporting*: DSC provides reporting features that enable administrators to monitor the compliance of their systems with their desired state configuration and identify any systems that are out of compliance.

- *Customization*: DSC enables administrators to create custom resources to manage almost any aspect of a Windows system, making it a highly flexible tool for configuration management.

- *Integration*: DSC can be integrated with other management tools, such as SCCM and Azure Automation, providing a comprehensive configuration management solution.

PowerShell DSC is a powerful tool that simplifies configuration management, reduces errors, and provides greater consistency and scalability in managing Windows systems.

How It Works

PowerShell DSC defines the desired state of a Windows system and then applies that configuration to the system using a set of resources. Here are the key steps for how DSC works:

- *Define the configuration*: The first step is to define the system's desired state in a configuration file using a declarative syntax. This includes specifying which resources should be applied and their desired state.

- *Compile the configuration*: The configuration file is compiled into a MOF file, which is a management object format file containing the information needed to configure the system.

- *Apply the configuration*: The MOF file is applied to the target system using the DSC engine, a Windows PowerShell component. The DSC engine compares the system's current state to the desired state specified in the MOF file and applies any necessary changes to bring the system into compliance with the desired state.

- *Monitor and maintain the configuration*: Once the configuration has been applied, the DSC engine monitors the system to ensure it complies with the desired state. If any changes are made to the system that takes it out of compliance, the DSC engine will take corrective action to bring the system back into compliance.

- *Reporting and troubleshooting*: DSC provides reporting features that enable administrators to monitor the compliance of their systems with the desired state configuration. Administrators can troubleshoot the issue if any systems are out of compliance and take corrective action if necessary.

In a nutshell, PowerShell DSC provides a declarative, automated approach to configuring Windows systems, making it easier to manage configurations at scale, ensure consistency, and minimize the risk of human errors.

How to Enable It

To turn on PowerShell DSC on a Windows system, follow these steps:

1. *Install Windows Management Framework 4.0 or later*: DSC is included in Windows Management Framework 4.0 or later, so you must ensure it's installed on your system. You can download Windows Management Framework from the Microsoft Download Center.

2. *Configure the Local Configuration Manager*: The Local Configuration Manager (LCM) is a DSC component that manages the local system's configuration. You'll need to configure the LCM to tell it how to apply configurations. You can do this by running the `Set-DscLocalConfigurationManager` cmdlet in PowerShell.

3. *Create a configuration file*: You'll need to create a DSC configuration file that specifies the system's desired state. This includes defining which resources should be applied and their desired state.

4. *Compile the configuration file*: Once you've created it, you must compile it into a MOF file using the `Start-DscConfiguration` cmdlet.

5. *Apply the configuration*: Finally, you'll need to apply the configuration to the system using the `Start-DscConfiguration` cmdlet. The DSC engine will compare the system's current state to the desired state specified in the MOF file and apply any necessary changes to bring the system into compliance with the desired state.

Once you've turned on DSC and applied your first configuration, the LCM will continue to monitor the system and ensure it remains compliant with the desired state. You can also create and apply additional configurations as needed to manage other aspects of the system.

Microsoft SDL

The Microsoft Software Development Lifecycle (SDL) is a comprehensive approach to software development used by Microsoft and its partners to develop high-quality software products. The Microsoft SDL is a process that encompasses all stages of the software development life cycle, from planning and requirements gathering to design, development, testing, deployment, and maintenance.

The Microsoft SDL includes the following stages:

- *Planning and requirements gathering*: In this stage, the software development team works with stakeholders to define the business requirements and objectives for the software product.

- *Design*: In this stage, the software development team creates a detailed design for the software product, including architecture, data modeling, and user interface design.

- *Development*: In this stage, the software development team writes the code for the software product using programming languages such as C++, C#, and Java.

- *Testing*: In this stage, the software development team performs testing to ensure that the software product functions as intended and meets the defined requirements.

- *Deployment*: In this stage, the software product is deployed to production environments, and the necessary infrastructure and support are implemented.

- *Maintenance*: In this stage, the software development team maintains the software product, addressing bugs and making updates as needed.

The Microsoft SDL emphasizes the importance of collaboration and communication throughout the software development process and incorporates agile development methodologies to enable greater flexibility and adaptability to change requirements. The Microsoft SDL also incorporates security and quality assurance best practices to ensure that software products are secure, reliable, and of high quality.

Here are some of the key elements of the Microsoft SDL:

- *Agile development methodologies*: The Microsoft SDL incorporates agile development methodologies such as Scrum and Kanban, which enable greater flexibility and adaptability to changing requirements. Agile development emphasizes collaboration and communication between team members, continuous delivery of working software, and the ability to respond quickly to changes in customer needs.

- *Collaboration and communication*: The Microsoft SDL emphasizes the importance of collaboration and communication throughout the software development process. This includes involving stakeholders in the planning and requirements-gathering stages and working closely with team members to ensure that the software product meets the defined requirements and is of high quality.

- *Continuous integration and delivery*: The Microsoft SDL emphasizes the importance of continuous integration and delivery, which involves continuously integrating new code changes into the main codebase and delivering working software to customers regularly. This enables faster feedback and helps to ensure that the software product meets customer needs.

- *Quality assurance and testing*: The Microsoft SDL incorporates quality assurance and testing best practices to ensure that software products are secure, reliable, and of high quality. This includes automated testing, manual testing, and code reviews.

- *Security*: The Microsoft SDL incorporates security best practices to ensure that software products are secure and resilient to attacks. This includes threat modeling, code analysis, and regular security testing.

- *Tools and technologies*: The Microsoft SDL includes a variety of tools and technologies to help manage the software development process, including project management tools, collaboration tools, and software development tools such as Visual Studio.

The Microsoft SDL provides a comprehensive approach to software development that emphasizes collaboration, communication, quality, and security, and incorporates agile development methodologies and the latest tools and technologies.

How to Enable It

Through the implementation of the SDL, security and privacy are integrated throughout all phases of the development process, reducing the number and severity of vulnerabilities in software.

Three core concepts are at the heart of the Microsoft SDL: education, continuous process improvement, and accountability. Investing in knowledge transfer helps organizations respond appropriately to technological changes and threats. It is crucial to educate and train technical job roles within a software development group continuously. Because security risks aren't static, the SDL heavily emphasizes knowledge of security risk better to understand the causes and effects of security vulnerabilities. A new technology advancement or a new threat must be incorporated into SDL processes, which require regular evaluation and change. Using data, we can assess training effectiveness, confirm process compliance, and make future changes based on post-release metrics. Additionally, the SDL requires the archival of all data necessary to service an application in a crisis. The organization can provide concise and cogent guidance to all stakeholders when coupled with detailed security response and communication plans.

The Microsoft SDL consists of practices supporting security assurance and compliance requirements. By integrating security and privacy considerations into every phase of the software development life cycle, the SDL helps ensure that software products are developed in a way that meets security and compliance requirements. This is particularly important for heavily regulated industries, such as healthcare, finance, and government. The SDL practices help organizations meet regulatory requirements, such as HIPAA, PCI-DSS, and GDPR, and demonstrate due diligence in managing security risks associated with software products.

The Microsoft Security Development Lifecycle (SDL) consists of 12 practices, as shown here:

1. *Security training*: Ensure that all developers receive security training regularly, including secure coding practices and common vulnerabilities.

2. *Define security requirements*: Identify and document security and privacy requirements for the software product.

3. *Define metrics and compliance reporting*: Describe how engineers will be held accountable to meet minimum security standards.

4. *Perform threat modeling*: Identify potential security threats and vulnerabilities.

5. *Design requirements*: Use threat modeling techniques to identify potential security threats and vulnerabilities and design security features for the product.

6. *Define and use cryptography standards*: Protect data using appropriate cryptographic solutions.

7. *Manage the security risk of using third-party components*: Assess reported vulnerabilities and maintain an inventory of third-party components.

8. *Use approved tools*: Establish and publish a list of approved tools and their associated security checks.

9. *Perform static analysis security testing (SAST)*: Validate secure coding policies by analyzing source code before it is compiled.

10. *Perform dynamic analysis security testing (DAST)*: Verify running and fully integrated software security at runtime.

11. *Penetration testing*: Conduct security testing, such as penetration testing and vulnerability scanning, to identify and address vulnerabilities.

12. *Establish incident response*: Have the plan to respond to security incidents and vulnerabilities, including security patches and updates.

Security and Compliance in Office 365

Security and compliance are critical aspects of Office 365, Microsoft's cloud-based productivity suite. Office 365 includes built-in security and compliance features to help organizations protect their data and meet regulatory requirements.

Some of the critical security features of Office 365 are as follows:

- *MFA*: This feature requires users to provide additional authentication factors, such as a fingerprint or a code sent to their mobile phone, in addition to their password, to access Office 365 services.

- *Data loss prevention*: This feature helps prevent sensitive data from being shared outside the organization by automatically detecting and blocking data leaks.

- *Encryption*: Office 365 encrypts data both in transit and at rest to protect it from unauthorized access.

- *Advanced threat protection*: This feature uses machine learning and other techniques to protect against advanced threats like phishing attacks and malware.

- *Mobile device management*: This feature allows organizations to manage and secure mobile devices used to access Office 365 services.

Office 365 also includes various compliance features designed to help organizations meet regulatory requirements. Some of these features include the following:

- *Compliance Manager*: This tool helps organizations understand and manage their compliance posture by providing a dashboard of compliance controls and a risk assessment tool.

- *eDiscovery*: This feature allows organizations to search and export data across Office 365 services for legal and compliance purposes.

- *Audit Logs*: Office 365 keeps detailed logs of user activity, which can be used to demonstrate compliance with regulatory requirements.

- *Information Protection*: This feature allows organizations to classify and protect sensitive data across Office 365 services.

By incorporating these security and compliance features into Office 365, Microsoft helps organizations protect their data and meet regulatory requirements.

Microsoft Office 365 includes a range of capabilities that align with the NIST Protect function, one of the five core functions of the NIST CSF.

Some of the key capabilities of Office 365 that align with the NIST Protect function include the following:

- *Identify and access management*: Office 365 includes strong identify and access management controls, such as MFA and RBAC, to prevent unauthorized access to sensitive data.

- *Encryption*: Office 365 encrypts data in transit and at rest using industry-standard encryption protocols to protect against unauthorized access.

- *Data loss prevention*: Office 365 includes built-in DLP policies that help prevent sensitive data from being shared outside the organization by automatically detecting and blocking data leaks.

- *Compliance controls*: Office 365 includes a range of built-in compliance controls, such as eDiscovery and audit logging, to help organizations meet regulatory requirements.

- *Threat protection*: Office 365 includes advanced threat protection features, such as anti-phishing and anti-malware, to protect against advanced threats and phishing attacks.

- *Mobile device management*: Office 365 includes mobile device management (MDM) features that allow organizations to manage and secure mobile devices to access Office 365 services.

By leveraging these capabilities in Office 365, organizations can help improve their cybersecurity posture and align with the NIST Protect function. Additionally, organizations can customize and extend these capabilities through third-party tools and services to enhance their security and compliance posture.

Security and compliance in Office 365 work by implementing a range of built-in features and controls to protect data and meet regulatory requirements. Some of the critical aspects of how security and compliance works in Office 365 are as follows:

- *Incident response*: Office 365 provides tools for incident response, including alerts and reporting, to help organizations detect and respond to security incidents.

By leveraging these built-in security and compliance features and controls, organizations can help protect their data and meet regulatory requirements when using Office 365. Additionally, organizations can customize and extend these features through third-party tools and services to enhance security and compliance posture.

There are several key design considerations for security and compliance in Office 365, which include the following:

- *Data classification*: Before migrating to Office 365, it's essential to classify data according to its sensitivity level. This helps ensure that appropriate security and compliance measures are applied to each data type.

- *Identify and access management*: It's important to implement strong identify and access management controls in Office 365, such as MFA and RBAC, to prevent unauthorized access to sensitive data.

- *Encryption*: Office 365 encrypts data in transit and at rest, but ensuring that encryption is properly configured and enforced for all data is essential.

- *Compliance controls*: Office 365 includes a range of built-in compliance controls, such as eDiscovery and audit logging, that should be properly configured and monitored to ensure compliance with regulatory requirements.

- *Incident response*: Organizations should have a plan in place for responding to security incidents in Office 365, such as data breaches or unauthorized access, to minimize the impact of these events.

- *Third-party integrations*: Many organizations use third-party tools to extend the functionality of Office 365, such as email security or archiving tools. It's important to ensure these tools are properly integrated with Office 365 and not introduce additional security or compliance risks.

By considering these design considerations, organizations can help ensure that their use of Office 365 meets their security and compliance requirements.

How to Enable It

Security and compliance features are already built-in and enabled by default in Office 365. However, some features may require additional configuration or customization to meet specific organizational needs. Here are some general steps to ensure that security and compliance features are fully enabled in Office 365:

1. Sign in to the Office 365 admin center with your administrator credentials.

2. Click the Settings icon in the navigation menu on the left, and then click Security & Compliance.

3. Review the security and compliance dashboard to ensure all features are enabled and configured as needed. You may need to enable specific features, such as data loss prevention or threat protection, or customize policies to meet organizational needs.

4. Review any alerts or notifications related to security or compliance issues, and take appropriate action as needed.

5. Consider implementing additional security and compliance tools or services from third-party vendors to enhance your security posture further.

It's important to note that security and compliance is an ongoing process. Organizations should regularly review and update their security and compliance settings to ensure that they are adequately protected against evolving threats and regulatory requirements.

Office 365 Secure Score

Office 365 Secure Score is a security analytics tool that evaluates an organization's Office 365 environment and provides a score based on the organization's security posture. The score is calculated based on a series of security control recommendations, and it reflects the extent to which an organization has adopted and implemented these controls.

Secure Score objectively measures an organization's security posture and helps identify areas where security improvements can be made. The tool provides recommendations on improving the security posture, such as enabling multi-factor authentication or configuring data loss prevention policies. The recommendations are prioritized based on their potential impact on security, and the tool guides how to implement them.

In addition to providing a score, Secure Score provides detailed reports on the security posture of an organization's Office 365 environment. The reports include about Information on the organization's security controls, The current state of each control and Recommendations for improving each control.

Secure Score is designed to help organizations improve their overall security posture by identifying and addressing vulnerabilities and risks in their Office 365 environment. Organizations can reduce their risk of data breaches, malware attacks, and other security incidents by implementing the recommended security controls.

Office 365 Secure Score provides several The following are the key benefits for organizations:

- *Objective security posture measurement*: Secure Score accurately measures an organization's security posture by evaluating its Office 365 environment against a set of security control recommendations. This helps organizations understand how well they are protecting their data and systems and identify areas for improvement.

- *Prioritized recommendations*: Secure Score provides recommendations for improving an organization's security posture, prioritized based on their potential impact on security. This helps organizations focus on the most important and impactful security controls.

- *Customizable scoring*: Secure Score allows organizations to customize their scoring based on specific security needs and priorities. This enables organizations to focus on the security controls that are most relevant and important to their business.

- *Gamification*: Secure Score includes gamification features encouraging users to improve their security posture. Users can earn points for implementing security controls, and organizations can use leaderboards and other features to create friendly competition and motivate employees to improve security.

- *Detailed reporting*: Secure Score provides detailed reports on an organization's security posture, including information on the current state of each security control and recommendations for improving each control. This helps organizations track their progress over time and identify areas for ongoing improvement.

In a nutshell, Office 365 Secure Score provides organizations a powerful tool for improving their security posture and reducing the risk of data breaches and other security incidents. Organizations can better protect their data and systems from cyber threats by implementing the recommended security controls and continuously monitoring their security posture.

Office 365 Secure Score maps to the Protect function of the NIST CSF by providing security control recommendations that help protect an organization's Office 365 environment. Some of the critical areas where Office 365 Secure Score maps to the NIST Protect function include the following:

- *Access control*: Office 365 Secure Score recommends implementing strong access controls, such as MFA, to protect against unauthorized access to sensitive data.

- *Data protection*: Office 365 Secure Score includes recommendations for protecting data in transit and at rest, such as enabling encryption and implementing data loss prevention policies.

- *Threat detection and response*: Office 365 Secure Score recommends implementing threat detection and response capabilities, such as enabling auditing, logging, and configuring security alerts.

- *Incident response*: Office 365 Secure Score includes recommendations for developing and testing incident response plans, including backup and recovery procedures and communication plans.

Design Considerations

These are essential design best practices to consider when using Office 365 Secure Score:

- *Define your security priorities*: Before using Office 365 Secure Score, defining your security priorities and goals is essential. This will help you prioritize which security controls to implement first and focus your efforts on the highest-risk areas.

- *Establish a baseline*: It's essential to establish a baseline for your current security posture before using Office 365 Secure Score. This will help you track your progress and measure the effectiveness of your security improvements over time.

- *Customize your scoring*: Office 365 Secure Score allows you to customize the scoring of the security controls based on your specific business needs and priorities. Make sure to adjust the scoring to match your security objectives.

- *Prioritize recommendations*: Office 365 Secure Score recommends improving your security posture. Prioritize the recommendations based on their potential impact on security and feasibility of implementation.

- *Implement continuous monitoring*: Monitoring your security posture is critical to maintaining an effective security posture. Use Office 365 Secure Score to evaluate your environment and identify areas for improvement regularly.

- *Leverage automation*: Office 365 Secure Score supports automation using PowerShell scripts and other tools. Automating security tasks can save time and reduce the risk of human error.

- *Foster a security culture*: Building a security culture within your organization is critical to maintaining an effective security posture. Use Office 365 Secure Score to help educate and engage employees on the importance of security.

How to Enable It

Office 365 Secure Score is a feature built into the Office 365 Security & Compliance Center. Here are the steps to turn on Office 365 Secure Score:

1. Sign in to the Office 365 Security & Compliance Center using your Office 365 administrator credentials.

2. Click Secure Score under the Threat Management section in the navigation pane on the left.

3. If this is your first time using Office 365 Secure Score, you will be prompted to enable it. Click Enable to turn on Office 365 Secure Score.

4. Once you have enabled Office 365 Secure Score, you can view your organization's current score, recommendations for improving your score, and a history of your score over time.

5. You can also customize your scoring by adjusting the weights assigned to each security control based on your organization's priorities.

6. To implement the recommended security controls, click the Action button next to each recommendation and follow the provided steps.

7. Use the Secure Score Analyzer tool to track your progress over time and identify areas for further improvement.

As you can see, turning on Office 365 Secure Score is a straightforward process that can help you improve your organization's security posture and reduce the risk of cyber threats.

Azure Site Recovery

Azure Site Recovery (ASR) is a cloud-based disaster recovery as a service (DRaaS) provided by Microsoft Azure. It enables you to protect and recover your on-premises applications and workloads by replicating them to a secondary site or Azure.

Specifically, with Azure Site Recovery, businesses can replicate their on-premises virtual machines and workloads to a secondary location or Azure, ensuring they are always available during an unexpected outage or disaster. It provides automated replication and recovery of workloads, simplifying the disaster recovery process and minimizing the recovery time objective (RTO) and recovery point objective (RPO).

With ASR, you can create a disaster recovery plan to protect your business-critical applications from unexpected outages, natural disasters, and other disruptive events. ASR automates the replication and recovery of your workloads, ensuring that they are up-to-date and readily available in case of failure.

Here are some key features and benefits of Azure Site Recovery:

- *Replication*: ASR continuously replicates your virtual machines, applications, and data to a secondary site or Azure. This ensures that your data is up-to-date and readily available during a disaster.

- *Automated disaster recovery*: Azure Site Recovery automates the replication and recovery of workloads to ensure business continuity during a disaster.

- *Orchestration*: ASR automates the recovery process by orchestrating the failover and failback of your workloads. This ensures that your applications are brought back online quickly and efficiently.

- *Multiplatform support*: ASR supports various platforms, including Windows and Linux virtual machines, Hyper-V and VMware virtual machines, and physical servers.

- *Application awareness*: ASR is application-aware and can help ensure the consistent recovery of your applications, including multitier applications.

- *Customizable recovery plans*: ASR allows you to create customized recovery plans based on your business needs and priorities. This includes specifying the order in which virtual machines are recovered and the time interval between each recovery step.

- *Cost-effective*: ASR is a cost-effective disaster recovery solution that eliminates the need for expensive secondary data centers and reduces the cost of maintaining a disaster recovery infrastructure.

- *Testing and validation*: Azure Site Recovery allow testing and validating disaster recovery plans without impacting the production environment.

In a nutshell, Azure Site Recovery is a robust disaster recovery solution that provides automated replication and recovery of your workloads, ensuring that your business-critical applications are up-to-date and readily available during a failure.

ASR can be used to help organizations meet many of the security and compliance requirements set out in the NIST CSF under the Protect function.

Here are some ways in which ASR maps to NIST Protect:

- *Data backup and recovery*: ASR provides a robust data backup and recovery solution, helping organizations ensure the availability and integrity of their critical data in the event of a disaster or data loss.

- *Disaster recovery planning*: ASR enables organizations to create a disaster recovery plan that includes the replication and recovery of critical workloads, minimizing the impact of a disaster on business operations.

- *Multiplatform support*: ASR supports various platforms, including Windows and Linux virtual machines, Hyper-V and VMware virtual machines, and physical servers, enabling organizations to protect their entire IT environment.

- *Customizable recovery plans*: ASR allows organizations to create customized recovery plans based on their business needs and priorities, ensuring that workloads are recovered in the correct order and within the required time frame.

- *Compliance reporting*: ASR provides compliance reporting capabilities, enabling organizations to demonstrate compliance with various regulatory requirements and standards.

Design Considerations

Here are some essential design best practices for implementing ASR in your organization:

- *Assess your disaster recovery requirements*: Before implementing ASR, it's essential to assess your organization's disaster recovery requirements, such as RPOs and RTOs. This will help you determine which workloads must be replicated and how frequently.

- *Choose the right replication method*: ASR offers multiple replication methods, such as replication to a secondary data center or to Azure. Choose the replication method that best suits your organization's needs.

- *Use Azure Virtual Network*: To ensure secure and efficient replication of data and virtual machines to Azure, use Azure Virtual Network. This will enable you to configure a secure connection between your on-premises environment and Azure.

- *Plan for network bandwidth*: Replicating data and virtual machines to a secondary location or Azure requires network bandwidth. Plan for the necessary bandwidth to ensure that replication is completed within the desired time frame.

- *Test and validate your disaster recovery plan*: Once it is in place, test and validate it regularly. This will help you identify issues and ensure your organization is ready to respond to a disaster.

- *Monitor and maintain ASR*: Monitor ASR continuously to ensure that replication is working as expected. Also, ensure that ASR is updated and maintained with the latest security patches and updates.

Implementing these best practices can help ensure that ASR is configured correctly and meets your organization's disaster recovery requirements.

How to Enable It

To turn on Azure Site Recovery, you will need to follow these steps:

1. *Sign in to the Azure Portal*: Go to the Azure Portal and sign in with your Azure account credentials.

2. *Create a Recovery Services vault*: In the Azure Portal, navigate to the "Recovery Services vaults" section and click Add. Follow the prompts to create a new vault, including choosing a subscription, resource group, and a unique name for the vault.

3. *Select the replication source*: Once the vault is created, select Site Recovery from the menu on the left and click "Prepare infrastructure." Select the replication source: a VMware virtual machine, a Hyper-V virtual machine, or a physical server.

4. *Create a replication policy*: Next, you will need to create a replication policy. This policy will determine how often data is replicated and how long it is retained.

5. *Configure replication settings*: After creating the replication policy, you will need to configure replication settings. This includes choosing the target location for replication, configuring network settings, and specifying storage accounts.

6. *Install and configure the ASR agent*: To enable replication, you must install the ASR agent on the source machine. Follow the prompts to download and install the agent.

7. *Enable replication*: Once the ASR agent is installed and configured, you can enable replication. Navigate to the "Replicate application" section in the Azure Portal, select the source machine, and click Enable replication. Follow the prompts to complete the process.

After enabling replication, Azure Site Recovery will automatically replicate data and virtual machines according to the replication policy you have configured. You can monitor the replication status and manage your disaster recovery plan through the Azure Portal.

Key Insights of Azure Site Recovery   Azure Site Recovery is available in more than 50 regions worldwide, providing global coverage for disaster recovery scenarios. Azure Site Recovery is designed to support a wide range of workloads, including VMware, Hyper-V, and physical servers, providing a comprehensive disaster recovery solution for organizations with diverse IT environments. Azure Site Recovery supports both one-click failover and planned failover, allowing organizations to respond to disasters quickly or to perform planned maintenance activities without downtime. Microsoft offers a service level agreement (SLA) for Azure Site Recovery, guaranteeing an RPO of 15 minutes or less for all protected virtual machines. Azure Site Recovery is tightly integrated with other Azure services, such as Azure Backup and Azure Virtual Networks, providing a comprehensive solution for backup, recovery, and networking needs. Microsoft offers a free trial of Azure Site Recovery, allowing customers to test the service before committing to a paid plan.

Vulnerabilities Assessment

Microsoft Defender for Cloud is a cloud-native security solution designed to help organizations protect their cloud-based assets and workloads from various threats, including vulnerabilities. One of its key features is its ability to perform continuous vulnerability assessments of cloud environments. Microsoft Defender for Cloud uses a combination of machine learning and human expertise to identify potential vulnerabilities in an organization's cloud environment. It can scan cloud resources such as virtual machines, containers, and applications and assess their security posture based on various factors such as misconfigurations, software vulnerabilities, and security policy compliance.

The solution provides real-time alerts and detailed reports on vulnerabilities, enabling organizations to remediate any issues and maintain a strong security posture quickly. It also offers guidance on addressing vulnerabilities, with recommendations for mitigations and remediation steps. Microsoft Defender for Cloud integrates with other Microsoft security solutions, such as Azure Sentinel and Microsoft 365 Defender, to provide a comprehensive security platform for the entire cloud environment. It also supports third-party integrations through open APIs, enabling organizations to extend and integrate their capabilities into their security workflows.

Microsoft Defender for Cloud Vulnerability Assessment provides several key benefits, including the following:

- *Comprehensive scanning*: Microsoft Defender for Cloud Vulnerability Assessment scans your cloud environment thoroughly to identify vulnerabilities in your virtual machines, network security groups, storage accounts, and more. This helps you understand your cloud environment's risk posture and take necessary actions to mitigate those risks.

- *Automated vulnerability management*: The tool provides automatic scanning and prioritization of vulnerabilities based on severity and offers recommended actions for remediation. This helps you to quickly identify and address vulnerabilities in your environment, reducing the time and effort required to manage security risks.

- *Integration with other security tools*: Microsoft Defender for Cloud Vulnerability Assessment integrates with other Microsoft security tools, including Microsoft Defender for Endpoint and Azure Security Center, to provide a holistic approach to cloud security management. This integration ensures that you have a complete view of your security posture and can take a coordinated approach to manage vulnerabilities.

- *Real-time monitoring*: The tool provides real-time monitoring and alerts for new vulnerabilities that may arise in your environment. This helps you stay on top of new threats and vulnerabilities and proactively address them.

- *Compliance reporting*: Microsoft Defender for Cloud Vulnerability Assessment provides compliance reporting capabilities that enable you to assess and report on the compliance status of your cloud environment. This helps you to meet regulatory requirements and demonstrate compliance with auditors and other stakeholders.

When deploying Microsoft Defender for Cloud Vulnerability Assessment, several key considerations must be remembered. These include the following:

- *Supported platforms*: Ensure that the cloud environment and platforms you use are supported by Microsoft Defender for Cloud Vulnerability Assessment. This includes Azure, AWS, and Google Cloud Platform.

- *Permissions*: Ensure the necessary permissions are granted for the tool to scan your cloud environment. This includes permissions to access virtual machines, network security groups, storage accounts, and other resources.

- *Integration*: Consider integrating Microsoft Defender for Cloud Vulnerability Assessment with other Microsoft security tools, including Microsoft Defender for Endpoint and Azure Security Center. This provides a coordinated approach to managing security threats in your cloud environment.

- *Scanning frequency*: Consider the frequency you want to scan your cloud environment for vulnerabilities. This will depend on factors such as the size of your environment and the criticality of your assets.

- *Remediation*: Consider how you will remediate identified vulnerabilities. Microsoft Defender for Cloud Vulnerability Assessment recommends remediation actions, but you will need to have a process to address these vulnerabilities.

- *Reporting*: Consider how you will report on vulnerabilities and compliance to stakeholders such as auditors and management. Microsoft Defender for Cloud Vulnerability Assessment provides compliance reporting capabilities to help with this.

- *Performance impact*: Consider the impact of scanning on the performance of your cloud environment. Microsoft Defender for Cloud Vulnerability Assessment provides options for minimizing the impact of scanning, such as scheduling scans during off-peak hours.

- *Training and support*: Ensure that your IT staff is trained on using Microsoft Defender for Cloud Vulnerability Assessment and that you have access to support resources from Microsoft. This will help you get the most out of the tool and address any issues.

How to Enable It

To turn on Microsoft Defender for Cloud Vulnerability Assessment, follow these steps:

1. Log in to the Azure Portal.

2. Go to the Azure Defender Security Center by clicking the Security Center icon in the navigation menu on the left.

3. Select Azure Defender from the menu on the left of the Security Center dashboard.

4. Select the subscription and resource group you want to protect with Azure Defender.

5. Click the Vulnerability Assessment tab.

6. If you have not yet enabled the Vulnerability Assessment, click "Set up vulnerability assessment."

7. Choose the virtual machines and storage accounts you want to scan for vulnerabilities.

8. Choose the scanning frequency and time window that works best for your environment.

9. Click the Create button to start the vulnerability assessment process.

10. Wait for the initial scan to complete. Once the scan is finished, you can view the vulnerabilities detected in the Azure Defender Security Center dashboard.

Microsoft Defender for Cloud Vulnerability Assessment is available as part of Azure Defender, which requires a paid subscription. If you do not have Azure Defender enabled, you must subscribe to it before you can turn on Microsoft Defender for Cloud Vulnerability Assessment.

Protective Technology (PR.PT)

Protective technology refers to cybersecurity technologies designed to protect systems and data from cyberattacks. Protective technologies are a critical component of any cybersecurity strategy, and they are designed to prevent attacks from occurring and detect and respond to attacks when they do occur.

Some common types of protective technologies include the following:

- *Firewalls*: Firewalls are protective technology used to monitor and control traffic to and from a network. Firewalls can be either hardware or software-based, designed to prevent unauthorized access to a network.

    - A network firewall is a security device designed to monitor and control incoming and outgoing network traffic based on predetermined security rules. Its primary function is to block unauthorized access to a network and prevent malicious traffic from entering or leaving the network.

- Network firewalls can be hardware-based or software-based and are typically located at the perimeter of a network, where they act as the first line of defense against cyber threats. They analyze network traffic and compare it against predefined rules to determine whether to allow or block the traffic. These rules can be based on various criteria, such as the source and destination IP addresses, ports, protocols, and application types.

- Firewalls can be configured to allow or block traffic based on several factors, such as the following:

  - *Packet filtering*: This is the most basic form of firewall filtering, which examines individual packets of data as they pass through the firewall and blocks packets that do not meet the predefined security rules.

  - *Stateful inspection*: This is a more advanced form of firewall filtering that examines the context of each packet, including the source and destination IP addresses, ports, and protocol, and compares it against known traffic patterns to determine whether to allow or block the traffic.

  - *Application-level gateway*: This type of firewall filters traffic at the application layer, allowing administrators to control access to specific applications or services.

  - *Next-generation firewall (NGFW)*: This is a type of firewall that incorporates additional security features, such as intrusion detection and prevention, deep packet inspection, and malware filtering, to provide a more comprehensive security solution.

- In summary, a network firewall is a critical component of network security, as it helps to protect networks from cyber threats by controlling access to the network and filtering out malicious traffic.

- *Intrusion prevention systems (IPSs)*: IPS technology is designed to detect and prevent intrusions by monitoring network traffic for signs of malicious activity. IPSs can be network- or host-based, protecting both physical and virtual environments.

- *Anti-malware*: Anti-malware technology prevents and removes malicious software from systems. Anti-malware solutions can be either signature-based or behavior-based, designed to protect against viruses, worms, trojans, and other types of malware.

- *Encryption*: Encryption technology is used to protect data by encoding it in a way that makes it unreadable without a decryption key. Encryption can be used to protect data at rest or in transit, which is an effective way to prevent data theft.

- *Access control*: Access control technologies restrict access to systems and data to authorized users only. Access control can be achieved through passwords, biometrics, and multi-factor authentication.

- *Backup and disaster recovery*: Backup and disaster recovery technologies ensure that systems and data can be recovered during a cyberattack or other disasters. Backup solutions can be either on-premise or cloud-based, and they are designed to provide a rapid recovery time in the event of an outage or data loss.

In the context of the NIST CSF, *protective technology* refers to the cybersecurity control category implemented to limit or contain the impact of a cybersecurity event. The NIST CSF defines it as safeguards and countermeasures to protect organizational assets, including hardware, software, networks, and data, from cyber threats. Protective technology controls can be divided into several subcategories.

- *Access control*: Access control technologies limit access to organizational assets to authorized users only.

- *Awareness and training*: Education and training programs can help employees to identify and prevent cyber threats.

- *Data security*: Data security technologies, such as encryption, protect sensitive data from unauthorized access or disclosure.

- *Information protection processes and procedures*: Policies and procedures can help ensure that information is protected and managed securely.

- *Maintenance*: Regular maintenance and updating of hardware and software can ensure that security vulnerabilities are identified and addressed promptly.

- *Protective technology*: The implementation of protective technologies, such as firewalls, intrusion detection/prevention systems, and anti-malware, can help to prevent and detect cyber threats.

In summary, protective technology is a critical component of the NIST CSF, including the cybersecurity controls implemented to protect organizational assets from cyber threats.

Azure Mapping for PR.PT

Azure provides various services that can help organizations implement PR.PT controls by the NIST CSF to protect their assets. Some of the Azure services that can be used for this purpose include the following:

- *Azure Firewall*: This is a network security service that provides a fully stateful firewall as a service with built-in high availability and unrestricted cloud scalability.

- *Azure DDoS Protection*: This service protects against distributed denial-of-service (DDoS) attacks on Azure resources.

- *Azure Security Center*: This is a unified security management and advanced threat protection service that helps organizations to prevent, detect, and respond to cybersecurity threats.

- *Azure Key Vault*: This cloud-based service provides secure storage and management of cryptographic keys, certificates, and secrets.

- *Azure Advanced Threat Protection (ATP)*: This cloud-based security solution helps detect and investigate advanced attacks and insider threats across on-premises and cloud environments.

- *Azure Information Protection*: This is a cloud-based service that helps organizations classify, label, and protect sensitive data, regardless of where it is stored or how it is shared.

- *Azure Virtual Machines*: This service provides virtual machines in the cloud, which can be used to host applications and services securely.

- *Azure Active Directory*: This is a cloud-based identify and access management service that provides single sign-on and multi-factor authentication capabilities and access control for applications and resources.

In summary, Azure provides a range of services that can help organizations implement PR.PT controls per the NIST CSF to protect their assets against cyber threats, as shown in Figure 6-2.

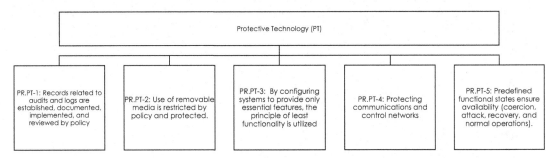

Figure 6-2. *NIST PR.PT to Azure mapping*

As part of the Azure cloud shared responsibility model, the NIST CSF security functions are provided in Figure 6-3 with respect to PR.PT.

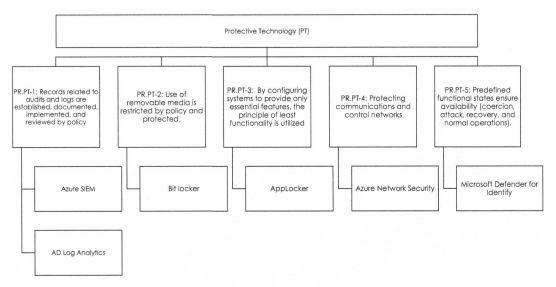

Figure 6-3. *NIST PR.PT Azure service subcategory mapping*

As part of the Azure Cloud shared responsibility model, the NIST CSF security functions are provided in Table 6-2 with respect to PR.PT.

Table 6-2. *PR.PT Management Responsibility Matrix*

Category	Subcategory	Informative References	Responsibility	Customer Responsibility	Microsoft Azure Responsibility
Protective Technology (PR.PT): Technical security solutions are managed to ensure the security and resilience of systems and assets, consistent with related policies, procedures, and agreements.	PR.PT-1: Records related to audits and logs are established, documented, implemented, and reviewed by policy	NIST SP 800-53 Rev. 4 AU Family	Shared	Customer's responsibility to determine which events their software application must be able to audit and what auditable events beyond the required events should be auditable for the customer's needs. The customer will also document, implement, and review these logs by policy.	As part of ongoing system risk assessments, which include identified vulnerabilities, business requirements, and Azure security standards, the Azure security team has developed a broad set of auditable events specific to Microsoft Azure. In Microsoft Azure security configuration baselines, audit log events are defined by audit policies. Microsoft Azure Security reviews the general event set when a system is changed significantly to ensure auditable events address any vulnerabilities. Security assessments, bulletins, etc.) identify new events when a new service is released or a vulnerability or threat is identified. Change management procedures are used to make changes to the service as necessary, and risk assessments are also part of the change management process.

| PR.PT-2: Use of removable media is restricted by policy and protected. | · NIST SP 800-53 Rev. 4 MP-2, MP-4, MP-5, MP-7 | Microsoft Azure | N/A | In order to restrict physical access to all Microsoft Azure media, the data center access process requires individuals to have a legitimate business reason for accessing the data. Asset owners must assign their assets with an asset classification; this requirement does not apply to any asset. In order to protect the confidentiality, integrity, and availability of information assets in Microsoft Azure data centers, the Asset Protection Standard defines the safeguards needed. A Microsoft Azure data center secures digital media assets, including server assets and network devices used for backup. Information stored in Microsoft Azure data centers is not stored on nondigital media, and Microsoft Azure digital media assets are physically and securely stored there. Microsoft Azure data centers are protected by physical access controls (access badges, biometrics, etc.) and video surveillance. |

(continued)

Table 6-2. (*continued*)

Category	Subcategory	Informative References	Responsibility	Customer Responsibility	Microsoft Azure Responsibility
	PR.PT-3: By configuring systems to provide only essential features, the principle of least functionality is utilized	· NIST SP 800-53 Rev. 4 AC-3, CM-7	Shared	Customers configure information systems only to provide essential capabilities. This can involve using USGCB guidance and CIS Benchmarks to ensure that only essential functions are provided.	Each base operating system image, configuration script, and configuration file deployed within Microsoft Azure considers the USGCB and CIS Benchmarks. These baselines ensure that only the essential functions, ports, protocols, and services are enabled for each server role. To configure network devices, the Azure Networking Standards and Architecture team uses recommended configurations based on each hardware vendor and updates the baseline standards periodically based on vendor recommendations. Configuration baselines enable only essential functions, ports, protocols, and services.

PR.PT-4: Protecting communications and control networks	· NIST SP 800-53 Rev. 4 AC-4, AC-17, AC-18, CP-8, SC-7	Shared	The customer's network and communications protect the information flow between the customer's applications and external systems. The customer is responsible for documenting usage restrictions, configuration and connection requirements, and implementation guidance for accessing the customer's application.	Microsoft Azure implements boundary protection by implementing controlled devices at the network boundary and at critical points in the Microsoft Azure infrastructure. The overarching principle within Microsoft Azure is to allow only connection and communication that is necessary for systems to function, blocking all other ports, protocols, and connections by default. Through a combination of virtual local area network (VLAN) isolation, software load balancers, filters, firewalls, and access control lists, Microsoft Azure enforces approved authorizations for controlling the flow of information within and between interconnected systems.
PR.PT-5: Predefined functional states ensure availability (coercion, attack, recovery, and normal operations).	· NIST SP 800-53: CP-7, CP-8, CP-11, CP-13, PL-8, SA-14, SC-6	Microsoft Azure	N/A	Microsoft Azure has set up several alternate processing sites (identically replicated and backed up), allowing critical missions and business functions to resume operations if the primary processing site cannot be restored. Using Microsoft Azure's backup and recovery procedures, operations can be resumed within the contingency plan defined for data replication and geo replication.

Azure Security Information and Event Management

Azure SIEM is a cloud-based security solution provided by Microsoft Azure that helps organizations to identify, monitor, and respond to security threats and compliance violations in real-time. It combines security information management (SIM) and security event management (SEM) capabilities, providing a centralized platform for managing security logs and alerts.

Azure SIEM collects security data from various sources, such as network devices, servers, applications, and cloud services, and uses advanced analytics and machine learning algorithms to detect and respond to security threats. It provides a unified view of security events and incidents, enabling security teams to investigate and respond to security incidents quickly and effectively.

Some of the key features of Azure SIEM include real-time threat detection and alerts, automated incident response, threat intelligence integration, and compliance management. Azure SIEM integrates with other Azure security services, such as Azure Security Center, to provide a comprehensive security solution for Azure cloud environments. Azure Sentinel is a cloud-native SIEM and SOAR solution provided by Microsoft Azure. It helps organizations collect, detect, investigate, and respond to security threats across their entire IT infrastructure in real-time.

Azure Sentinel is designed to be highly scalable, leveraging the power of Azure to process vast amounts of data from various sources, including logs, telemetry, and other security-related events. It uses advanced analytics and machine learning to detect anomalous behavior, suspicious activities, and potential threats and provides actionable insights and alerts to security analysts. Azure Sentinel also provides built-in automation and orchestration capabilities to help security teams respond to security incidents quickly and effectively. It allows security analysts to create custom workflows and playbooks to automate repetitive tasks and orchestrate response actions across different security tools and systems.

Some of the key features of Azure Sentinel include advanced analytics, threat intelligence integration, machine learning, security automation and orchestration, and customizable dashboards and reports. Azure Sentinel also integrates with other Azure security services, such as Azure Security Center, to provide a comprehensive security solution for Azure cloud environments.

The following are The following are the key benefits of using Azure Sentinel:

- *Cloud-native*: Azure Sentinel is built natively on Azure, which provides highly scalable and elastic cloud computing resources, so you can quickly scale up or down based on your security needs.

- *Integrated security*: Azure Sentinel integrates with various Microsoft security solutions, such as Microsoft 365 Defender and Azure Security Center, as well as third-party solutions, to provide a comprehensive security solution for your entire IT infrastructure.

- *Advanced analytics*: Azure Sentinel uses advanced analytics and machine learning to detect security threats in real time, helping to reduce false positives and improve the accuracy of security alerts.

- *Automated incident response*: Azure Sentinel provides built-in automation and orchestration capabilities to help security teams respond to security incidents quickly and effectively, reducing manual intervention and response times.

- *Customizable dashboards and reports*: Azure Sentinel provides customizable dashboards and reports, allowing you to easily visualize and analyze your security data and identify potential threats.

- *Threat intelligence integration*: Azure Sentinel integrates with various threat intelligence sources to provide up-to-date and relevant threat intelligence, helping you to stay ahead of emerging threats.

- *Cost-effective*: Azure Sentinel offers a predictable, per-gigabyte pricing model, which allows you to pay only for the amount of data processed, making it a cost-effective solution for managing security events and incidents.

In a nutshell, Azure Sentinel provides a powerful, cloud-native security solution that helps organizations to detect, investigate, and respond to security threats across their entire IT infrastructure in real time.

The NIST CSF provides guidelines and best practices for improving cybersecurity across various industries and organizations. Azure Sentinel can be mapped to the Protect category of the NIST CSF as follows:

- *Identify*: In this phase; organizations identify the information, systems, and assets that need protection. Azure Sentinel provides a centralized platform for managing security logs and alerts, which can help organizations identify potential threats and vulnerabilities in their IT infrastructure.

- *Protect*: This phase involves implementing safeguards to protect against potential cyber threats. Azure Sentinel helps organizations protect their IT infrastructure by providing real-time threat detection and automated incident response capabilities. It also integrates with various Microsoft security solutions, such as Microsoft 365 Defender and Azure Security Center, to provide a comprehensive security solution for the organization.

- *Detect*: In this phase; organizations detect security threats in real time by monitoring their IT infrastructure for suspicious activities and anomalies. Azure Sentinel uses advanced analytics and machine learning to detect security threats and provides actionable insights and alerts to security analysts.

- *Respond*: In this phase, organizations respond to security incidents quickly and effectively. Azure Sentinel provides built-in automation and orchestration capabilities to help security teams respond to security incidents quickly and reduce response times.

- *Recover*: This phase involves restoring normal operations after a security incident. Azure Sentinel provides visibility into security incidents, allowing organizations to analyze and learn from past incidents and improve their security posture.

Here are some design best practices for Azure Sentinel:

- *Define your data sources*: Before you start ingesting data into Azure Sentinel, it is essential to define your data sources. This includes identifying which logs and data types you must collect from your on-premises and cloud environments.

- *Leverage Azure Monitor*: Azure Sentinel is built on Azure Monitor, which provides a unified platform for collecting, analyzing, and acting on telemetry from your applications and infrastructure. By leveraging Azure Monitor, you can easily collect data from various sources, including Azure services, third-party services, and custom applications.

- *Use Log Analytics workspaces*: Azure Sentinel requires a Log Analytics workspace to store and analyze your data. Creating a dedicated workspace for Azure Sentinel is recommended to ensure that your data is separated from other workloads and to optimize performance.

- *Plan for data retention*: Azure Sentinel allows you to retain data for up to two years, but this comes at a cost. It is essential to plan for data retention to ensure you are not storing unnecessary data and incurring unnecessary costs.

- *Configure data connectors*: Azure Sentinel provides a wide range of data connectors to integrate with different data sources. It is important to configure data connectors properly to ensure that you are collecting all the necessary data and minimizing the risk of missing important events.

- *Define your security rules*: Azure Sentinel uses security rules to identify security events and trigger automated responses. It is important to define your security rules carefully to ensure you detect relevant threats and minimize false positives.

- *Automate responses*: Azure Sentinel allows you to automate responses to security events using Logic Apps or Azure Functions. It is recommended to automate responses to minimize the time it takes to respond to threats and to reduce the risk of human error.

- *Test your Azure Sentinel deployment*: It is important to thoroughly test your Azure Sentinel deployment before going live. This includes testing your data sources, security rules, and automated responses to ensure they work as expected.

- *Monitor Azure Sentinel performance*: Azure Sentinel provides a range of performance metrics and logs to monitor the health and performance of your deployment. Monitoring these metrics to identify and resolve issues before they impact your security posture is important.

- *Implement RBAC*: Azure Sentinel provides RBAC to control access to your deployment. It is essential to implement RBAC to ensure that only authorized personnel have access to sensitive data and security controls.

How to Enable It

To turn on Azure Sentinel, follow these steps:

1. Log in to the Azure Portal.

2. In the menu on the left, select "Create a resource."

3. Search for *Azure Sentinel* in the search bar and select it from the results.

4. Click the Create button to create a new Azure Sentinel instance.

5. Fill in the required fields, such as subscription, resource group, and workspace, and click the "Review + create" button.

6. Review the settings and click the Create button to start the deployment process.

7. Once the deployment is complete, you can access Azure Sentinel by selecting it from the "All services" menu in the Azure Portal.

After turning on Azure Sentinel, you must configure data connectors to ingest data into your deployment. You can also configure security rules and automated responses to start detecting and responding to security threats. It is essential to regularly monitor your Azure Sentinel deployment to ensure that it is working as expected and to make any necessary adjustments.

AD Log Analytics

Azure Log Analytics is a service provided by Microsoft Azure that allows organizations to collect, analyze, and visualize log data from various sources in the cloud or on-premises. It provides a centralized location for collecting and querying log data, making it easier for organizations to monitor and troubleshoot their applications and infrastructure.

Azure Log Analytics uses a query language called Kusto Query Language (KQL) to analyze and visualize log data. This language provides a robust set of operators and functions that allow users to extract and manipulate data from various sources. It also allows users to create custom queries and alerts to monitor specific events or performance metrics.

Some of the key features of Azure Log Analytics include the following:

- *Log collection*: Azure Log Analytics can collect data from various sources such as Azure resources, Windows and Linux servers, and custom applications.

- *Log analysis*: Azure Log Analytics provides a powerful query language and visualization tools to help users analyze and gain insights from their log data.

- *Alerting*: Users can create custom alerts based on specific events or performance metrics to ensure they are notified of any issues or potential problems.

- *Integration with other Azure services*: Azure Log Analytics can be integrated with other Azure services such as Azure Monitor, Azure Sentinel, and Azure Automation to provide a comprehensive monitoring and management solution.

Azure Log Analytics is a powerful tool that can help organizations monitor and manage their applications and infrastructure more effectively, reducing downtime and improving performance.

AD log analysis refers to analyzing the event logs generated by Microsoft Active Directory to gain insights into the behavior and activities of users and systems within an Azure AD environment. Azure AD is a popular directory service that organizations use to manage user accounts, permissions, and resources. It generates logs that record various events, such as user authentication, group policy changes, and account management activities.

By analyzing Azure AD logs, administrators can gain valuable insights into the security and performance of their Azure AD environment, identify potential security threats, troubleshoot issues, and ensure compliance with regulatory requirements. AD log analysis involves collecting and consolidating Azure AD logs from various sources, parsing and interpreting the log data, and analyzing the data using correlation, trend analysis, and anomaly detection techniques.

Here are some examples of how Azure Log Analytics can be used for Azure AD:

- *Authentication monitoring*: Azure Log Analytics can collect logs related to Azure AD authentication events, including successful and failed logins, password changes, and multi-factor authentication events. Administrators can use this data to monitor user access to their Azure AD resources and detect potential security threats.

- *Application usage analysis*: Azure Log Analytics can collect logs related to Azure AD application usage, including user sign-ins and consent grants. This data can be used to monitor application usage trends and identify potential issues with application performance or user adoption.

- *Access control monitoring*: Azure Log Analytics can collect logs related to Azure AD access control activities, including group membership changes and permission assignments. This data can be used to monitor changes to access control policies and identify potential security risks.

- *Compliance reporting*: Azure Log Analytics can generate compliance reports for Azure AD activities, such as user account activity and access control changes. These reports can be used to meet regulatory requirements and audit Azure AD usage.

Azure Log Analytics can be used to implement access control for Azure Active Directory (Azure AD) in several ways. Here are some examples of how Azure Log Analytics can help organizations implement access control for Azure AD and map to the Protect function of the NIST CSF:

- *Identify protection*: Azure Log Analytics can monitor Azure AD authentication logs for suspicious activity and configure alerts to notify security teams of anomalies. This helps organizations protect their identities and limit access to their Azure AD resources.

- *RBAC*: Azure Log Analytics can monitor changes to Azure AD role assignments and identify any unauthorized changes. This helps organizations implement a role-based access control model and limit access to their Azure AD resources.

- *MFA*: Azure Log Analytics can monitor Azure AD MFA logs and identify any failed attempts or anomalies. This helps organizations implement a multi-factor authentication model and protect their identities from unauthorized access.

- *User and group management*: Azure Log Analytics can monitor changes to Azure AD user and group memberships and identify any unauthorized changes. This helps organizations implement a user and group management model and limit access to their Azure AD resources.

By implementing these access control measures using Azure Log Analytics, organizations can better protect their Azure AD resources and align with the Protect function of the NIST CSF.

Design Considerations

The following are the key design best practices for Azure Log Analytics for Azure AD:

- *Define data collection requirements*: Before implementing Azure Log Analytics for Azure AD, it's essential to define the data collection requirements. This includes identifying the Azure AD activities that need to be monitored, the data sources to collect logs from, and the log retention requirements.

- *Configure data collection*: Once the data collection requirements are defined, it's essential to configure data collection in Azure Log Analytics. This includes configuring log sources, defining log queries, and configuring alerts for important events.

- *Define access controls*: It's essential to define access controls for Azure Log Analytics to ensure that only authorized personnel can log data. This includes defining RBAC for Azure Log Analytics and configuring access policies for Azure AD logs.

- *Implement retention policies*: Azure Log Analytics limits the amount of data that can be stored, so it's essential to implement retention policies to manage log data. This includes defining retention periods and configuring data archiving or deletion policies.

- *Monitor performance*: It's essential to monitor the performance of Azure Log Analytics for Azure AD to ensure that log data is being collected and processed efficiently. This includes monitoring data ingestion rates, query performance, and alert processing times.

- *Integrate with other Azure services*: Azure Log Analytics can be integrated with other Azure services, such as Azure Sentinel and Azure Monitor, to provide a more comprehensive monitoring and management solution for Azure AD. Considering these integrations is important when designing the Azure Log Analytics solution for Azure AD.

- *Monitor for security threats*: Finally, it's essential to monitor for security threats using Azure Log Analytics for Azure AD. This includes configuring alerts for suspicious activity, such as failed login attempts, and monitoring for unauthorized access to Azure AD resources.

How to Enable It

To enable Azure Log Analytics for Azure Active Directory (Azure AD), follow these steps:

1. *Create an Azure Log Analytics workspace*: If you haven't already, create an Azure Log Analytics workspace in your Azure subscription. This workspace will be used to collect and store Azure AD logs.

2. *Enable Azure AD diagnostics logging*: In the Azure Portal, navigate to your Azure AD tenant and enable diagnostics logging for Azure AD. This will allow Azure AD to send logs to your Azure Log Analytics workspace.

3. *Configure log collection*: Once diagnostics logging is enabled, configure log collection in your Azure Log Analytics workspace. You can do this by creating a new data source for Azure AD and specifying the Azure AD log types you want to collect.

4. *Configure log alerts*: After log collection is configured, create alerts in Azure Log Analytics for important Azure AD events. This will notify you when specific events occur in Azure AD, such as failed login attempts or changes to access control policies.

5. *Analyze log data*: Once log collection and alerts are configured, you can analyze the log data in Azure Log Analytics. This can be done using log queries, allowing you to search and filter data based on specific criteria.

6. *Integrate with other Azure services*: Azure Log Analytics can be integrated with other Azure services, such as Azure Sentinel and Azure Monitor, to provide a more comprehensive monitoring and management solution for Azure AD. Consider these integrations when enabling Azure Log Analytics for Azure AD.

In a nutshell, enabling Azure Log Analytics for Azure AD involves configuring diagnostics logging in Azure AD, configuring log collection in Azure Log Analytics, and setting up alerts and log queries to monitor Azure AD activity.

Here are some key deployment considerations for Azure Log Analytics for Azure Active Directory (Azure AD):

- *Data volume*: The amount of data generated by Azure AD can be significant, especially in large organizations with many users and applications. It's essential to consider the data volume when deploying Azure Log Analytics for Azure AD and ensure that the log analytics workspace has sufficient capacity to handle the data.

- *Data retention*: The data retention requirements for Azure AD logs can vary depending on compliance and regulatory requirements. It's important to consider the retention requirements when deploying Azure Log Analytics for Azure AD and ensure that logs are stored for the required duration.

- *Compliance*: Organizations may need to comply with various regulations and standards such as HIPAA, PCI DSS, and GDPR. It's important to ensure that Azure Log Analytics for Azure AD meets the organization's compliance requirements.

- *Access controls*: Access to Azure AD logs should be restricted to authorized personnel to ensure data privacy and security. Defining RBAC and access policies to restrict access to Azure AD logs is essential.

- *Performance*: Azure Log Analytics for Azure AD should be designed to handle the organization's performance requirements. This includes optimizing log queries and alerts to minimize resource utilization and ensure the timely processing of logs.

- *Alerting*: It's essential to configure alerts in Azure Log Analytics for Azure AD to notify administrators of important events such as failed login attempts, suspicious activity, and changes to access control policies.

- *Integration with other services*: Azure Log Analytics for Azure AD can be integrated with other Azure services, such as Azure Sentinel and Azure Monitor, to provide a more comprehensive monitoring and management solution. Consider integrating these services based on the needs of the organization.

Microsoft BitLocker

Microsoft BitLocker is a full-disk encryption feature included with Microsoft Windows operating systems. It is designed to protect data by encrypting entire disk volumes, including the Windows operating system and all user data, and protecting them with a password or a smart card.

Microsoft BitLocker uses Advanced Encryption Standard (AES) encryption with either 128-bit or 256-bit keys to encrypt data on the disk. It also provides additional security features, such as a Trusted Platform Module (TPM), which can be used to store encryption keys and protect them from unauthorized access.

Microsoft BitLocker is available in various editions of Windows, including Windows 10 Pro, Enterprise, and Education, as well as Windows Server 2008 and later versions. It can be managed through Group Policy or Microsoft SCCM. It can provide a more secure computing environment with other security features, such as Windows Hello for Business.

Microsoft BitLocker provides several key benefits.

- *Data protection*: BitLocker encrypts the entire contents of a disk, including the operating system and user files, helping to protect sensitive data from unauthorized access in case of theft or loss of the device.

- *Ease of use*: BitLocker is integrated with Windows operating systems and can be easily enabled through the Control Panel or Group Policy, making it easy to use and manage.

- *Centralized management*: BitLocker can be managed centrally using Group Policy, Microsoft SCCM, or other third-party tools, allowing administrators to configure and enforce encryption policies across many devices.

- *Compatibility*: BitLocker is compatible with various storage devices, including hard drives, solid-state drives (SSDs), and USB flash drives, making it versatile and flexible.

- *Integration with other security features*: BitLocker can be used with other security features, such as Windows Hello for Business, to provide an even more secure computing environment.

- *Compliance*: BitLocker can help organizations comply with various regulatory requirements, such as HIPAA and GDPR, by ensuring that sensitive data is encrypted and protected from unauthorized access.

Microsoft BitLocker aligns with the NIST CSF function of Protect in the following ways:

- *Asset management*: BitLocker helps protect the confidentiality and integrity of data assets by encrypting the entire disk, including the operating system and user data.

- *Access control*: BitLocker can be configured to require a password or smart card authentication to access encrypted data, providing strong access control.

- *Awareness and training*: BitLocker can be part of an organization's security awareness and training program, with employees being trained to enable and use it to protect sensitive data.

- *Data security*: BitLocker helps protect data at rest, preventing unauthorized access in case of loss or theft of the device.

- *Information protection processes and procedures*: BitLocker can be centrally managed through Group Policy, SCCM, or other tools, allowing for consistent implementation and enforcement of encryption policies.

- *Maintenance*: BitLocker requires regular maintenance, such as updating encryption keys and ensuring compatibility with new hardware and software, to ensure the ongoing protection of data.

- *Protective technology*: BitLocker provides strong encryption using Advanced Encryption Standard (AES) and can be integrated with other protective technologies, such as TPM, to enhance security.

Microsoft BitLocker helps organizations protect their data assets and aligns with the NIST CSF Protect function by providing encryption, access control, awareness and training, central management, maintenance, and integration with other protective technologies.

Design Considerations

The following are the key design best practices for Microsoft BitLocker:

- *Use a strong password*: When enabling BitLocker, use a strong password or passphrase to protect the encryption key. The password should be at least eight characters long and include a mix of uppercase and lowercase letters, numbers, and symbols.

- *Use TPM or other hardware-based protection*: BitLocker can use a TPM or other hardware-based protection to store encryption keys and protect them from unauthorized access. TPM can provide enhanced security and help prevent tampering with the encryption key.

- *Enable pre-boot authentication*: BitLocker can be configured to require preboot authentication, which requires a password or smart card to be entered before the operating system boots. This can provide an additional layer of security.

- *Use Group Policy to configure BitLocker*: Use Group Policy to configure BitLocker on multiple devices, allowing centralized management and consistent configuration across the organization.

- *Use a recovery key*: Create a recovery key when enabling BitLocker, which can be used to unlock the drive in case the password or smart card is lost, or the TPM fails.

- *Use BitLocker network unlock*: BitLocker Network Unlock allows a BitLocker-protected device to automatically unlock the drive when connected to a specific network, which can streamline the authentication process.

- *Perform regular audits*: Regularly audit BitLocker-protected devices to ensure encryption is enabled and properly configured. This can help identify and address potential security issues.

Overall, following these best practices can help ensure that BitLocker is properly configured and provides maximum protection for your organization's data.

How to Enable It

Microsoft BitLocker can be enabled in Azure using the following steps:

1. *Provision an Azure VM*: Provision a Windows VM in Azure.

2. *Enable encryption for OS Disk*: Once the VM is provisioned, navigate to the Azure Portal and select the VM. Under the Disks section, select the OS disk and click "Disk encryption."

3. *Create a Key Vault*: If you haven't already, create a Key Vault in Azure to store the encryption keys. You can do this by navigating to Key Vaults in the Azure Portal and clicking Add.

4. *Configure Key Vault*: Once the Key Vault is created, navigate back to the VM and click "Disk encryption." Select the Key Vault and provide the necessary permissions.

5. *Enable BitLocker*: Under the "Disk encryption" section, click Enable to enable BitLocker for the OS disk.

6. *Monitor the progress*: The encryption process can take some time to complete. You can monitor progress by checking the Activity log in the Azure Portal.

Once BitLocker is enabled, you can manage it through the Azure Portal, PowerShell, or other management tools.

Here are the steps to enable Microsoft BitLocker in Windows OS:

1. *Open the Control Panel*: Click the Start menu and select Control Panel.

2. *Go to System and Security*: In the Control Panel, click System and Security and then select BitLocker Drive Encryption.

3. *Choose the drive to encrypt*: Select the drive you want to encrypt and click Turn On BitLocker. Note that BitLocker is available for only specific editions of Windows, such as Windows 10 Pro or Enterprise.

4. *Choose a password or smart card*: Choose a password or insert a smart card to protect the encryption key. You can also choose to require a PIN for added security.

5. *Choose the encryption method*: Select the encryption method you want to use. BitLocker supports either AES-128 or AES-256 encryption.

6. *Save the recovery key*: Create a recovery key that can be used to unlock the drive in case the password or smart card is lost or the TPM fails.

7. *Start encryption*: Once configuring the necessary settings, click Start Encrypting to begin the encryption process.

8. *Monitor the progress*: The encryption process can take some time to complete, depending on the size of the drive and the speed of your computer. You can monitor progress by checking the BitLocker status in the Control Panel.

Once BitLocker is enabled, you can manage it through the Control Panel or other management tools. It is important to note that allowing BitLocker may impact the performance of the VM, so you should test thoroughly before deploying to production. Additionally, proper key management practices should be followed to ensure the security of the encrypted data.

The following are the critical deployment considerations for Microsoft BitLocker:

- *Hardware requirements*: BitLocker requires a TPM version 1.2 or later or a USB flash drive to store the encryption key. Ensure that your hardware meets the TPM requirement before deploying BitLocker.

- *OS requirements*: BitLocker is available only on specific editions of Windows, such as Windows 10 Pro or Enterprise. Ensure that the operating system version is compatible with BitLocker.

- *Encryption method*: BitLocker supports either AES-128 or AES-256 encryption. Choose an encryption method that is appropriate for your organization's security requirements.

- *Key management*: Proper key management practices should be followed to ensure the security of the encrypted data. The recovery key should be stored securely, and access to it should be restricted.

- *Performance impact*: Enabling BitLocker may impact the performance of the computer. Test thoroughly before deploying to production machines, and monitor performance after deployment.

- *Configuration*: BitLocker can be configured using Group Policy or the command prompt. Ensure that the configuration settings are appropriate for your organization's security requirements.

- *Training*: End users should be trained on how to use BitLocker and what to do in case of an issue or if the recovery key is needed.

- *Compliance*: If your organization is subject to compliance regulations, ensure that BitLocker meets the compliance requirements before deploying it.

By considering these key deployment considerations, you can ensure that BitLocker is properly deployed and configured for your organization's security requirements.

Microsoft AppLocker

Microsoft AppLocker is a security feature available in Windows operating systems that allows administrators to control which applications can run on a computer or network. AppLocker helps organizations enforce security policies by restricting the execution of unauthorized or malicious software while allowing authorized applications to run. It is designed to help organizations enhance security and reduce the risk of malware or other types of unauthorized software being introduced into the network. AppLocker can be managed through Group Policy or PowerShell, allowing administrators to define application rules based on file paths, digital signatures, or publisher names.

Microsoft AppLocker has four types of rules that can be created.

- *Executable rules*: These rules are used to control the execution of executable files, including EXE, COM, and BAT files.

- *Windows Installer rules*: These rules are used to control the installation of applications that use Windows Installer technology (MSI files).

- *Script rules*: These rules control the execution of scripts, including PowerShell, VBScript, and JavaScript files.

- *DLL rules*: These rules are used to control the loading of dynamic link libraries (DLLs), which are files that contain code that can be used by multiple applications simultaneously.

By creating rules for these types of files, administrators can control which applications are allowed to run on a computer or network, helping to enhance security and reduce the risk of security threats.

The following are the key benefits of Microsoft AppLocker:

- *Enhanced security*: AppLocker helps organizations improve security by controlling which applications can run on their computers or network. AppLocker can reduce the risk of malware or other security threats by blocking unauthorized or malicious software.

- *Centralized management*: AppLocker can be managed centrally through Group Policy or PowerShell, allowing administrators to define rules for applications based on file paths, digital signatures, or publisher names.

- *Granular control*: AppLocker provides granular control over which applications are allowed to run. Administrators can create rules that allow or block specific applications or groups based on file type, publisher, or other criteria.

- *Flexibility*: AppLocker supports various file types and applications, including executable files, scripts, DLLs, and Windows Store apps.

- *Easy deployment*: AppLocker is included with Windows operating systems, making it easy to deploy and use without additional software or licensing costs.

- *Reporting*: AppLocker provides reporting capabilities, allowing administrators to monitor and analyze application usage and compliance with security policies.

Overall, AppLocker provides powerful features for controlling which applications can run on Windows computers and networks, helping organizations enhance security and reduce the risk of security threats.

Here is the NIST CSF Protect mapping for Microsoft AppLocker:

- *Identify (ID)*: AppLocker can help organizations identify which applications can run on their network and enforce security policies to prevent unauthorized software from running.

- *Protect (PR)*: AppLocker provides granular control over which applications are allowed to run, helping protect the network from malware and other security threats.

- *Detect (DE)*: AppLocker provides reporting capabilities, allowing administrators to detect and analyze application usage and compliance with security policies.

- *Respond (RS)*: AppLocker can respond to security incidents by blocking the execution of malicious software or other unauthorized applications.

- *Recover (RC)*: AppLocker does not directly contribute to the recovery function of the NIST CSF. However, by helping to prevent security incidents and reduce the risk of malware or other types of unauthorized software being introduced into the network, AppLocker can indirectly contribute to the recovery function by reducing the impact of security incidents on the organization.

Design Considerations

Here are some design best practices for Microsoft AppLocker:

- *Define a clear application control policy*: Before implementing AppLocker, it is essential to define a clear application control policy that outlines which applications are allowed to run on the network and which are not. This policy should be based on business requirements and security best practices.

- *Test rule sets in a controlled environment*: It is essential to test rule sets in a controlled environment before implementing them on production systems. This will help identify any issues or conflicts that may arise and ensure that the rule sets effectively achieve their intended goals.

- *Use publisher rules where possible*: Publisher rules are generally the easiest and most effective way to create AppLocker rules, as they allow administrators to create rules based on the digital signature of an application. This can help to prevent unauthorized or malicious software from running on the network.

- *Consider creating multiple rule sets*: Depending on the organization's needs, it may be beneficial to create multiple rule sets to control the execution of different types of applications. For example, one rule set could be made for executables, while another could be created for scripts.

- *Regularly review and update rule sets*: Application control policies and rule sets should be reviewed and updated to ensure they are still effective and in line with business requirements and security best practices.

- *Ensure proper testing of new applications*: When new applications are introduced into the network, they should be properly tested to ensure they are compatible with AppLocker rule sets and do not cause conflicts or security issues.

- *Monitor AppLocker events*: AppLocker events should be regularly monitored to identify security issues or policy violations. This can help to detect and respond to security incidents promptly.

How to Enable It

AppLocker is a feature that is only available in Windows operating systems, it is possible to configure AppLocker policies on Windows VMs running in Azure. To configure AppLocker policies on Windows VMs in Azure, you can follow these steps:

1. Log in to the Windows VM on which you want to configure AppLocker policies.

2. Open the Local Group Policy Editor by entering **gpedit.msc** in the Start menu.

3. In the Local Group Policy Editor, navigate to Computer Configuration ➤ Windows Settings ➤ Security Settings ➤ Application Control Policies ➤ AppLocker.

4. Configure the AppLocker policies as desired, such as creating executable, script, or DLL rules.

5. Once the AppLocker policies have been configured, they will be enforced on the Windows VM.

Note that AppLocker is available in only specific editions of Windows, such as Windows 10 Enterprise and Windows Server 2016. Additionally, AppLocker policies can be centrally managed using Group Policy or Microsoft Endpoint Manager (formerly Microsoft System Center Configuration Manager).

AppLocker policies can be configured and managed using Microsoft Intune. Microsoft Intune is a cloud-based endpoint management solution that allows administrators to manage devices and applications from a single console.

To configure AppLocker policies using Microsoft Intune, you can follow these steps:

1. Sign in to the Microsoft Endpoint Manager admin center.

2. Create an AppLocker policy by going to Devices ➤ Configuration profiles ➤ Create profile ➤ Windows 10 and later ➤ Endpoint protection.

3. Under the Endpoint protection settings, select AppLocker and configure the rules for executables, scripts, and DLLs as desired.

4. Assign the policy to the appropriate groups of users or devices.

5. Once the policy is assigned, it will be enforced on the devices targeted by the policy.

Note that the availability of AppLocker policies in Intune may vary depending on the edition of Intune that you are using. AppLocker policies can also be centrally managed using Group Policy or other management solutions such as Microsoft System Center Configuration Manager.

Here are some key deployment considerations for AppLocker:

- *Application compatibility*: Before deploying AppLocker, it is essential to test and ensure that the applications that are used in your organization are compatible with the AppLocker policies. Some applications may have dependencies on specific files or executables that may be blocked by AppLocker policies.

- *User education and training*: It is essential to provide training and education to users about the AppLocker policies and how they can impact their ability to run specific applications. Users should be made aware of any changes in the application approval process and how they can request policy exceptions if needed.

- *Testing and validation*: It is essential to thoroughly test and validate the AppLocker policies before deploying them to production systems. This helps identify any issues or conflicts that may arise and allows for adjustments to be made before impacting users.

- *Rule creation and maintenance*: AppLocker policies are based on rules defining which applications can run on a system. It is essential to regularly review and update these rules to ensure that they are practical and up-to-date.

- *Centralized management*: AppLocker policies can be centrally managed using Group Policy, Microsoft Endpoint Manager, or other management solutions. It is essential to have a centralized management approach to ensure consistency and ease of management.

- *Monitoring and auditing*: AppLocker policies should be regularly monitored and audited to ensure that they are adequately enforced and prevent unauthorized applications from running on systems. This can also help to identify any policy violations or attempts to circumvent the policies.

- *Backup and recovery*: It is essential to have a backup and recovery plan in place for AppLocker policies to ensure that they can be restored in the event of data loss or corruption. This can minimize downtime and ensure the continued effectiveness of the policies.

Azure Network Security Services

Azure Network Security refers to the security measures and technologies used to protect and secure the network infrastructure and assets in a Microsoft cloud environment. It involves implementing security controls to protect cloud-based resources, such as virtual machines, virtual networks, databases, and applications, from various threats and attacks.

Azure Network Security differs from traditional on-premises network security because it relies on shared responsibility between the cloud service provider and the customer. Cloud service providers like Microsoft Azure offer various security services and features to protect their cloud infrastructure. Still, customers are responsible for securing their own applications and data in the cloud.

Azure Network Security refers to the security measures and technologies used to protect and secure the network infrastructure and assets in the Azure cloud. This includes protecting virtual machines, virtual networks, and other Azure services against various threats, such as malware, unauthorized access, and data breaches.

Azure Network Security includes a range of security features and services, such as the following:

- *Network isolation*: Azure Network Security involves using virtual private networks (VPNs), firewalls, and access controls to isolate cloud-based resources and limit access to authorized users and applications.

- *Virtual network security*: Azure Virtual Network provides isolation and segmentation of virtual machines and services within a virtual network. NSGs can be used to control inbound and outbound traffic, while VPNs and ExpressRoute connections can provide secure connectivity to on-premises networks.

- *Firewall services*: Azure Firewall is a managed, cloud-based firewall service that provides network-level protection for Azure Virtual Network resources. It offers application and network-level protection, including stateful and stateless packet filtering and network address translation (NAT) for outbound traffic.

- *DDoS protection*: Azure DDoS Protection protects against DDoS attacks by automatically detecting and mitigating attacks. It offers standard and advanced protection, providing more granular control and visibility into traffic flows.

- *Security Center*: Azure Security Center provides a central location for managing security across Azure services, including Azure Virtual Network. It offers continuous monitoring, threat detection, and security recommendations to help organizations identify and remediate security vulnerabilities and threats.

- *Third-party security solutions*: Azure also offers integration with third-party security solutions, such as virtual appliances and security services from leading vendors, to provide additional security and protection for Azure Virtual Network resources.

Securing and protecting Azure networks is essential for several reasons:

- *Data protection*: Azure networks often host sensitive and critical data, such as customer information, financial data, and intellectual property. If this data is not secured correctly, it can be vulnerable to theft, misuse, or compromise, leading to severe financial and reputational damage.

- *Compliance requirements*: Many organizations have requirements that mandate data protection and systems, such as HIPAA, PCI DSS, and GDPR. Securing Azure networks helps ensure these requirements are met, and organizations can avoid costly fines and legal repercussions.

- *Availability*: Azure networks are critical for many organizations, and any disruptions or downtime can have serious consequences. Securing Azure networks can help ensure that systems and data are available and accessible when needed and can help mitigate the risks of cyberattacks and other security incidents.

- *Reputation*: Security incidents can damage an organization's reputation and erode customer trust. By securing Azure networks, organizations can demonstrate their commitment to protecting customer data and can help build trust and confidence with stakeholders.

- *Business continuity*: Azure networks are often essential for business continuity, and disruptions or failures can significantly impact operations. Securing Azure networks can help ensure that systems and data are protected against threats and risks and can help minimize the impacts of security incidents and other disruptions.

These are the Azure VNet security services that exist in the Microsoft cloud:

- *NSGs*: NSGs are an essential network security feature that allows you to control traffic flow in and out of a virtual network in Azure. NSGs can create inbound and outbound security rules to allow or deny traffic based on source and destination IP address, port, and protocol.

- *Azure Firewall*: Azure Firewall is a managed network security service that provides advanced firewall capabilities for your virtual network. It can filter traffic based on application and network-level rules and provides threat intelligence-based filtering to block known malicious traffic.

- *Azure DDoS protection*: Azure DDoS Protection protects against DDoS attacks on your virtual network. It uses Azure's global network to mitigate DDoS attacks and provides real-time monitoring and alerting.

- *Azure private link*: Azure Private Link is a service that allows you to securely access services over a private endpoint within your virtual network. It provides a private and secure connection between your virtual network and Azure services such as Azure Storage, Azure SQL Database, and Azure Kubernetes Service (AKS).

- *Azure VPN Gateway*: Azure VPN Gateway is a service that provides secure and reliable cross-premises connectivity between your on-premises network and Azure virtual networks. It can be used to connect to on-premises resources or other Azure virtual networks.

- *Azure ExpressRoute*: Azure ExpressRoute is a service that provides a dedicated, private connection between your on-premises infrastructure and Azure data centers. It offers higher reliability, faster speeds, and lower latencies than a traditional Internet connection.

- *Azure Bastion*: Azure Bastion is a service that provides secure and seamless RDP and SSH connectivity to your virtual machines directly from the Azure Portal without needing a VPN connection. It provides an additional layer of security by removing the need for public IP addresses or opening inbound ports on your virtual machines.

These are just some of the Azure Virtual Network security services available in the Microsoft cloud, and many others can be used to secure your virtual network.

Design Considerations

These are essential security design best practices for Azure Network Security:

- *Implement network segmentation*: Divide your Azure network into smaller, isolated subnets to limit the spread of attacks and contain potential breaches.

- *Use NSGs*: NSGs filter inbound and outbound traffic to Azure resources, providing an additional layer of security for your Azure network.

- *Enable Azure Firewall*: Azure Firewall is a managed, cloud-based firewall service that contains centralized network security across your Azure VNet resources. It allows you to create, enforce, and log application and network connectivity policies across subscriptions and virtual networks.

- *Use Azure DDoS Protection*: Azure DDoS Protection helps protect your Azure Virtual Network resources from DDoS attacks by automatically detecting and mitigating attacks.

- *Use Azure Bastion*: Azure Bastion is a managed PaaS service that provides secure and seamless RDP/SSH connectivity to your virtual machines directly from the Azure Portal over TLS.

- *Implement IAM*: Use Azure AD to manage user access and authentication across your Azure resources.

- *Use Azure Security Center*: Azure Security Center is a unified security management solution that provides threat protection across your hybrid cloud workloads. It provides continuous monitoring and alerts and allows you to assess and improve your Azure Network security posture.

- *Use Azure ExpressRoute*: Azure ExpressRoute provides a private, dedicated connection between your on-premises infrastructure and Azure data centers, reducing exposure to public networks and improving security.

- *Implement encryption*: Use Azure Disk Encryption to encrypt data at rest for virtual machines running in Azure. Use Azure VPN Gateway to encrypt data in transit between on-premises infrastructure and Azure resources.

- *Monitor and audit your Azure Network*: Use Azure Monitor and Azure Log Analytics to collect and analyze logs and metrics from your Azure resources, providing visibility into your Azure Network security posture and helping you identify potential security threats and vulnerabilities.

How to Enable It

To enable security for networks in the Microsoft Azure cloud, you can follow these steps:

1. *Implement network segmentation*: Divide your Azure Network into smaller, isolated subnets to limit the spread of attacks and contain potential breaches.

    1. You can create an Azure virtual network to achieve network segmentation by following these steps:

        1. Open the Azure Portal and select "Create a resource" from the menu on the left.

        2. Search for *Virtual network* and select "Virtual network" from the results.

        3. Click the + Add button to create a new virtual network.

        4. Give your virtual network a name and choose the region where it will be located. You can also create a new resource group or use an existing one.

        5. In the "Address space" section, specify the IP address range for your virtual network.

        6. In the Subnet section, click + Add subnet to create a new subnet.

        7. Give your subnet a name and specify the IP address range for the subnet.

8. Repeat steps 6–7 to create additional subnets for your network segmentation.

9. Click "Review + create" to review your virtual network configuration.

10. Click Create to create your virtual network.

2. Once your virtual network is created, you can configure NSGs and routing to control traffic between subnets and to and from the Internet. You can also connect your virtual network to other networks using virtual network peering, site-to-site VPN, or ExpressRoute.

2. *Use NSGs*: NSGs filter inbound and outbound traffic to Azure resources, providing an additional layer of security for your Azure Network. To configure NSGs, go to the Azure Portal, select your virtual network, and then select "Network security groups" from the left-hand menu.

1. You can enable NSGs in Azure by following these steps:

1. Open the Azure Portal and select the resource group that contains the virtual network you want to secure.

2. Navigate to the virtual network and select "Network security group" from the menu on the left.

3. Click the + Add button to create a new NSG.

4. Give your NSG a name, choose the region where it will be located, and click Create.

5. Once your NSG is created, you can add inbound and outbound security rules to allow or deny traffic based on source and destination IP addresses, ports, and protocols.

6. To apply your NSG to a subnet, navigate to the subnet and select Subnet from the menu on the left. In the "Network security group" section, choose your NSG from the drop-down menu.

7. Click Save to apply your changes.

2. It's important to note that NSGs are just one part of securing your Azure network. It would help if you also considered implementing other security measures such as Azure Firewall, Azure DDoS Protection, and Azure VPN Gateway.

3. *Enable Azure Firewall*: Azure Firewall is a managed, cloud-based firewall service that manages centralized network security across your Azure Virtual Network resources. To enable Azure Firewall, go to the Azure Portal, select your virtual network, and select Firewalls from the menu on the left.

   1. You can enable Azure Firewall in the Azure Portal by following these steps:

      1. Open the Azure Portal and select "Create a resource" from the menu on the left.

      2. Search for *Azure Firewall* and select Azure Firewall from the results.

      3. Click the + Add button to create a new Azure Firewall instance.

      4. Give your firewall a name and choose the region where it will be located. You can also create a new resource group or use an existing one.

      5. In the "Firewall settings" section, configure the following settings:

         1. *Public IP address*: Choose an existing public IP address or create a new one.

         2. *Virtual network*: Choose the virtual network where you want to deploy the Azure Firewall.

         3. *Subnets*: Choose one or more subnets where you want to deploy the Azure Firewall.

      6. In the "Firewall policy" section, choose the firewall policy you want to apply to your Azure Firewall. You can create a new policy or use an existing one.

7. Click "Review + create" to review your Azure Firewall configuration.

8. Click Create to create your Azure Firewall.

2. Once your Azure Firewall is created, you can configure rules to control inbound and outbound traffic to and from your virtual network. You can also monitor traffic and configure logging and analytics to detect and respond to security threats.

4. *Use Azure DDoS Protection*: Azure DDoS Protection helps protect your Azure Virtual Network resources from DDoS attacks by automatically detecting and mitigating attacks. To enable Azure DDoS Protection, go to the Azure Portal, select your virtual network, and select "Distributed denial of service (DDoS) protection" from the menu on the left.

1. You can enable Azure DDoS Protection on your virtual network in the Azure Portal by following these steps:

   1. Open the Azure Portal and navigate to the virtual network you want to protect.

   2. Select "Distributed denial of service (DDoS) protection" in the virtual network menu.

   3. On the DDoS protection pane, click On to enable DDoS protection.

   4. Choose the protection plan that you want to use. You can choose the Basic plan, which provides automatic protection for all virtual networks in your subscription, or the Standard plan, which offers advanced protection features such as traffic analytics and custom policies.

   5. Choose the mitigation settings that you want to use. You can choose to use the default settings or customize the settings based on your specific needs.

   6. Click Save to enable DDoS protection on your virtual network.

2. Once DDoS protection is enabled on your virtual network, Azure will automatically detect and mitigate DDoS attacks targeting your network. You can monitor the DDoS protection status and review mitigation reports in the Azure Portal.

5. *Use Azure Bastion*: Azure Bastion is a managed PaaS service that provides secure and seamless RDP/SSH connectivity to your virtual machines directly from the Azure Portal over TLS. To enable Azure Bastion, go to the Azure Portal, select your virtual machine, and select Bastion from the menu on the left.

1. You can enable Azure Bastion on your Azure virtual machines using the Azure Portal by following these steps:

1. Open the Azure Portal and navigate to the virtual machine you want to connect to using Azure Bastion.

2. Click Connect in the virtual machine menu.

3. On the Connect pane, select Bastion as the type of connection.

4. On the Bastion pane, configure the following settings:

1. *Virtual network*: Select the virtual network to which the virtual machine is connected.

2. *Subnet*: Select the subnet within the virtual network you want to use for Bastion.

3. *Public IP address*: Choose whether to use an existing public IP address or create a new one.

4. *Authentication type*: Choose whether to use password authentication or SSH key authentication.

5. Click Create to create the Azure Bastion resource.

6. Once the Azure Bastion resource is created, you can connect to the virtual machine by clicking the Connect button in the virtual machine menu and selecting Bastion as the type of connection.

2. Note that Azure Bastion is a paid service, so you will be charged for its users based on the time you use it. Review the pricing details before enabling Azure Bastion on your virtual machines.

6. *Monitor and audit your Azure Network*: Use Azure Monitor and Azure Log Analytics to collect and analyze logs and metrics from your Azure resources, providing visibility into your Azure Network security posture and helping you identify potential security threats and vulnerabilities. To enable Azure Monitor and Azure Log Analytics, go to the Azure Portal, select your subscription, and then select Monitor from the menu on the left.

1. To monitor and audit your Azure Network, you can use Azure Network Watcher, a monitoring and diagnostic service for Azure networking. Here are the steps to get started:

    1. Create a Network Watcher resource in the Azure Portal.

    2. Configure Network Watcher to monitor your Azure network. You can enable the following features:

        1. *Network Performance Monitor*: Monitors connectivity and performance between Azure virtual machines, on-premises resources, and Internet-facing endpoints.

        2. *Connection Monitor*: Monitors network connectivity between Azure virtual machines and Internet-facing endpoints.

        3. *IP Flow Verify*: Verifies if traffic is allowed or denied based on your network security group rules.

        4. *Next Hop*: Determines the next hop type and IP address of the traffic flow.

        5. *VPN Diagnostics*: Helps diagnose and troubleshoot VPN connections between Azure and on-premises networks.

        6. *Firewall Diagnostics*: Helps diagnose and troubleshoot Azure Firewall configuration and traffic issues.

3. Use Azure Monitor to monitor your Azure Network Watcher resources. Azure Monitor is a platform service that provides a centralized monitoring and logging solution for Azure resources.

4. Use Azure Log Analytics to collect and analyze log data from Network Watcher resources. Azure Log Analytics is a service that collects and analyzes log and performance data from Azure resources and other sources.

2. Using these tools, you can monitor and audit your Azure Network to identify issues, troubleshoot problems, and optimize performance.

Microsoft Defender for Identify

Microsoft Defender for Identify (formerly known as Azure Advanced Threat Protection or Azure ATP) is a cloud-based security solution from Microsoft that helps organizations protect their on-premises Active Directory environments from advanced threats. It provides real-time monitoring, detection, and response to security threats.

Microsoft Defender for Identify collects and analyzes data from various sources, including network traffic, events from Active Directory, and other sources, to identify potential threats. It uses machine learning algorithms and other advanced techniques to detect suspicious activity and anomalies in the environment.

Microsoft Defender for Identify provides a range of security features, including the following:

- *Advanced threat detection*: Detects advanced attacks and insider threats in real time

- *Behavioral analytics*: Uses machine learning algorithms to analyze user and device behavior to detect anomalies and suspicious activity

- *Threat intelligence*: Incorporates Microsoft's extensive threat intelligence to detect known and emerging threats

- *Automated response*: Responds to incidents automatically or provides recommendations to security teams for remediation

- *User and entity behavior analytics (UEBA)*: Uses UEBA to identify unusual activity or behavior across the environment

Microsoft Defender for Identify provides organizations with a powerful tool to protect their on-premises Active Directory environments from advanced security threats. The following are the key benefits of Microsoft Defender for Identify:

- *Advanced threat detection*: Microsoft Defender for Identify uses machine learning and behavioral analytics to detect advanced attacks and insider threats in real time, including credential theft, lateral movement, and privilege escalation.

- *Comprehensive coverage*: Microsoft Defender for Identify covers on-premises Active Directory environments, including domain controllers, domain-joined servers, and workstations.

- *Threat intelligence*: Microsoft Defender for Identify incorporates Microsoft's extensive threat intelligence to detect known and emerging threats.

- *UEBA*: UEBA is used to identify unusual activity or behavior across the environment, such as anomalous logon activity, use of compromised credentials, and unusual network traffic.

- *Automated response*: Microsoft Defender for Identify provides automated responses to security incidents or recommendations for remediation to help security teams quickly mitigate threats.

- *Integration with other security solutions*: Microsoft Defender for Identify integrates with other Microsoft security solutions, such as Microsoft Defender for Endpoint, Microsoft Cloud App Security, and Azure Sentinel, to provide a comprehensive security posture for organizations.

- *Visibility and insights*: Microsoft Defender for Identify provides visibility into the activity of users, devices, and applications across the environment and generates actionable insights to help organizations improve their security posture.

- *Easy deployment*: Microsoft Defender for Identify can be easily deployed and managed through the Azure Portal without additional infrastructure or software.

Here are some mappings between the NIST CSF and Microsoft Defender for Identify:

- *Identify*: Microsoft Defender for Identify helps organizations identify potential security risks and anomalies by continuously monitoring user, device, and application activity across on-premises Active Directory environments.

- *Protect*: Microsoft Defender for Identify helps protect against advanced attacks and insider threats by leveraging machine learning and behavioral analytics to detect and alert on suspicious activity and by providing automated responses to security incidents.

- *Detect*: Microsoft Defender for Identify detects anomalous activity and behavior using UEBA, threat intelligence, and other advanced techniques and provides alerts and recommendations for remediation.

- *Respond*: Microsoft Defender for Identify provides automated responses to security incidents, such as disabling compromised accounts or blocking suspicious activity, and generates recommendations for remediation.

- *Recover*: Microsoft Defender for Identify helps organizations recover from security incidents by providing visibility and insights into the activity of users, devices, and applications and by generating reports and analytics to help improve security posture.

Microsoft Defender for Identify helps organizations implement a comprehensive security posture that aligns with the NIST CSF by providing advanced threat detection, automated response, and actionable insights.

Design Considerations

Microsoft Defender for Identify is a comprehensive security solution for identifying and detecting threats in a network. Here are some design best practices for Microsoft Defender for Identify:

- *Plan your deployment*: Before deploying Microsoft Defender for Identify, carefully design the deployment based on your organization's needs and requirements.

- *Ensure Active Directory synchronization*: Ensure that Active Directory is synchronized with Azure AD to enable Microsoft Defender for Identify to identify and analyze the security risks across on-premises and cloud environments.

- *Enable all available security features*: Enable all available security features in Microsoft Defender for Identify to ensure maximum protection against potential threats.

- *Set up alerts*: Set up alerts for specific events or suspicious activity to be notified immediately in case of security breaches.

- *Regularly review alerts*: Review alerts generated by Microsoft Defender for Identify to identify potential risks and take necessary action.

- *Configure threat intelligence*: Leverage the latest information and updates to detect and respond to new and emerging threats.

- *Configure automatic response actions*: Configure automatic response actions to respond quickly to security events and minimize the impact of potential security incidents.

- *Configure network traffic monitoring*: Configure network traffic monitoring to identify suspicious network activity and take necessary action.

- *Conduct regular vulnerability assessments*: Conduct regular vulnerability assessments to identify potential security risks and take necessary steps to mitigate them.

- *Train employees*: Educate employees on cybersecurity best practices to prevent common threats such as phishing, social engineering, and other forms of cyberattacks.

How to Enable It

To enable Microsoft Defender for Identify, you need to follow these steps:

1. Sign in to the Microsoft Defender for Identify portal using your Azure AD credentials.

2. Go to the Configuration page in the portal and select the "Sensor setup" tab.

3. Download the installation package for the sensor, a lightweight agent that needs to be installed on each domain controller in your network.

4. Install the sensor on each domain controller using the installation package downloaded in the previous step.

5. After the sensor is installed, it will send security events to the Microsoft Defender for Identify portal, where you can see alerts and take necessary actions.

6. To enable advanced threat protection features, you need to configure the appropriate settings in the portal. These features include automatic investigation and remediation of threats, threat intelligence, and more.

7. Once configured the appropriate settings, you can monitor and manage security events from the Microsoft Defender for Identify portal.

Note   Before enabling Microsoft Defender for Identify, ensure that your Active Directory environment is synchronized with Azure AD and that you have appropriate permissions and licenses to use the service.

Here are some deployment considerations to keep in mind when implementing Microsoft Defender for Identify:

- *Network architecture*: Consider your network architecture to ensure the Microsoft Defender for Identify sensor can communicate with the cloud service. Make sure that there are no firewall or proxy settings that may block communication.

- *Infrastructure requirements*: Ensure that the hardware and software infrastructure meets the minimum requirements for deploying Microsoft Defender for Identify.

- *User and group considerations*: Consider the user and group permissions required for deploying Microsoft Defender for Identify. Ensure that users and groups are granted appropriate permissions to access and use the service.

- *Deployment plan*: Plan your deployment strategy based on your organization's needs and requirements. Consider the number of domain controllers, location, and other factors affecting deployment.

- *Active Directory synchronization*: Ensure that Active Directory is synchronized with Azure AD to enable the Microsoft Defender for Identify to identify and analyze the security risks across on-premises and cloud environments.

- *Licensing and pricing*: Understand the licensing and pricing options for Microsoft Defender for Identify to determine the most cost-effective deployment option for your organization.

- *Data protection*: Ensure that data protection and privacy policies are in place to comply with industry standards and regulations.

- *Deployment testing*: Before deploying Microsoft Defender for Identify, perform testing to ensure that the service works as expected and does not interfere with other services or applications.

- *Training*: Provide training to IT staff and end-users on using Microsoft Defender for Identify and responding to security events.

- *Maintenance and support*: Develop a maintenance plan and ensure that support is available to resolve any issues that may arise quickly.

Key Insights of Azure Network Services   Azure Virtual Network is available
in more than 60 regions worldwide, providing global cloud networking coverage.
Azure ExpressRoute is available in more than 100 locations worldwide, providing
private connectivity to Azure services for organizations around the globe. Microsoft
Azure provides a range of network security features, including Azure Firewall,
NSGs, Azure DDoS Protection, and Azure Private Link, to help organizations protect
their cloud-based networks from cyber threats. Azure Private Link provides private
connectivity between Azure services and virtual networks, assisting organizations
in securing their network traffic and reducing exposure to the public Internet.
Microsoft Azure offers a range of compliance certifications and regulatory
compliance, including SOC 1, SOC 2, HIPAA, and PCI DSS, demonstrating the
platform's commitment to network security and compliance.

Summary

In this chapter, you read about methods to design and deploy a strategy for protecting
security services in line with NIST CSF mapping of Azure services with regard to PR.IP.

In the book's next chapter, you will read about designing and deploying detect
solutions in alignment with the NIST CSF.

CHAPTER 7

Design and Deploy a Detect Solution

The National Institute of Standards and Technology (NIST) Cybersecurity Framework (CSF) Detect is one of the five functions of the NIST CSF. It is a set of activities and techniques that help organizations identify cybersecurity events and anomalous activities in their networks, systems, and applications in a timely and effective manner. The Detect function is designed to provide visibility into potential cybersecurity threats and to enable a timely response to mitigate or prevent their impact.

Anomalies in cybersecurity are unusual or unexpected patterns or events that deviate from the normal behavior or expected activity in an organization's network, system, or application. These anomalies can signal a security threat or attack and are often used as an indicator of compromise (IOC) by security analysts.

Detecting and analyzing anomalies in cybersecurity is critical to maintaining a strong cybersecurity posture. Security analysts use various techniques to identify anomalies, including log analysis, network traffic analysis, and machine learning algorithms that can identify patterns of behavior and activity that may indicate a security threat. Responding to anomalies promptly and effectively is essential to minimize the impact of cybersecurity incidents. This requires security teams to have a well-defined incident response plan that outlines the steps to take in the event of an anomaly or security incident. The incident response plan should also include procedures for containing the incident, investigating the cause, and restoring normal operations.

Microsoft provides several cybersecurity-related tools and services to help organizations detect cyberattacks against cloud-based infrastructure, applications, and data. This chapter provides the fundamentals of NIST CSF's Detect module and the Azure services that relate to it.

© Puthiyavan Udayakumar 2023
P. Udayakumar, *Design and Deploy a Secure Azure Environment*,
https://doi.org/10.1007/978-1-4842-9678-3_7

By the end of this chapter, you will understand the following:

- Azure detect security services

- Anomalies and Events (DE.AE)

- Security Continuous Monitoring (DE.CM)

- Detection Processes (DE. DP)

Incident Detection in Cybersecurity

Incident detection in cybersecurity refers to the process of identifying and recognizing potential security incidents or breaches within a computer network or information system. It involves using various technologies, tools, and techniques to monitor network traffic, system logs, and other data sources to identify IOCs or suspicious activities that could indicate a security incident.

The primary goal of incident detection is to identify security incidents as early as possible, allowing organizations to respond promptly and effectively to mitigate the impact and minimize potential damage. Organizations can prevent or limit unauthorized access, data breaches, service disruptions, and other malicious activities by detecting and investigating incidents promptly. The following are why you need a detection solution:

- *Increased visibility*: The right tools can provide deeper visibility into an organization's network, systems, and applications. This increased visibility enables security teams to identify anomalies and events that may indicate a potential security incident.

- *Early detection*: Early detection of cybersecurity incidents is essential to mitigating the impact of those incidents. With the right tools, security teams can detect incidents early, allowing them to respond quickly and prevent the incident from spreading.

- *Proactive threat hunting*: The right tools can also enable proactive threat hunting, where security teams actively search for potential security incidents rather than waiting for them to be detected by an alert.

- *Improved incident response*: When an incident is detected, the right tools can improve the incident response process by providing more detailed information, allowing the security team to respond more effectively.

- *Compliance requirements*: Many regulatory compliance requirements mandate the use of specific tools for detecting security incidents. Using the right tools can help organizations meet these requirements and avoid penalties for noncompliance.

The right tools to detect anomalies and events in cybersecurity are critical for organizations because they provide the ability to identify and respond to potential security incidents before they become significant problems. Here are some standard cybersecurity detection tools and mechanisms:

- *Security information and event management (SIEM) systems*: SIEM systems collect and analyze security-related data from multiple sources to identify and respond to security incidents.

- *Intrusion detection systems (IDSs) and intrusion prevention systems (IPSs)*: These systems monitor network traffic for signs of suspicious activity and can automatically block or prevent attacks.

- *Endpoint detection and response (EDR) systems*: These systems monitor and analyze activity on endpoint devices, such as laptops or servers, to identify and respond to potential security incidents.

- *Network traffic analysis (NTA) tools*: These tools analyze network traffic to identify and respond to potential security incidents, including anomalies and threats.

- *User behavior analytics (UBA) tools*: These tools use machine learning and other advanced techniques to identify user behavior patterns that may indicate a potential security threat.

- *Malware detection tools*: These tools identify and block or remove malware from a system, including viruses, Trojans, and other malicious software.

- *Vulnerability scanning tools*: These tools scan systems and applications for known vulnerabilities that attackers could exploit.

- *Penetration testing tools*: These tools simulate attacks against a system or application to identify weaknesses and vulnerabilities.

- *File integrity monitoring (FIM) systems*: These systems monitor files and system settings for changes that may indicate a potential security threat.

- *Cloud security posture management (CSPM) tools*: These tools monitor cloud environments for potential security threats and vulnerabilities, including misconfigurations and compliance violations.

These are just a few examples of the many cybersecurity detection tools and mechanisms available. The most effective approach is often to use a combination of tools and techniques to create a comprehensive and layered cybersecurity defense.

Here are some examples of corporations that have detected cybersecurity attacks using Microsoft Azure Security tools:

- *Travelex*: Travelex, a foreign currency exchange company, used Azure Sentinel to detect and respond to a ransomware attack in 2020 that resulted in the encryption of its IT systems and a ransom demand of $6 million.

- *Coats*: Coats, a global thread and yarn manufacturer, used Azure Sentinel to detect and respond to a cyberattack in 2020 that resulted in employee data theft.

- *Marriott International*: Marriott International used Azure Sentinel to detect and respond to a data breach in 2018 that affected up to 500 million customers, including passport numbers and payment card information.

Introduction to NIST Detect

The NIST CSF Detect category focuses on developing and implementing strategies to detect cybersecurity events promptly.

The Detect function is broken down into several subcategories, including the following:

- Anomalies and Events (DE.AE) is focused on identifying and analyzing anomalies and events that may indicate a cybersecurity issue. This includes techniques such as network monitoring, log analysis, and threat intelligence. Organizations can detect and investigate potential security incidents by monitoring network activity and system logs, such as unauthorized access attempts or unusual user activity.

- Security Continuous Monitoring (DE.CM) emphasizes continuously monitoring systems and networks to detect potential threats in real-time. This subcategory includes strategies for implementing automated monitoring tools, establishing thresholds for abnormal activity, and implementing incident response procedures.

- Detection Processes (DE. DP) refers to the processes and activities that organizations can use to detect cybersecurity events and potential incidents.

Together, DE.AE, DE.CM, and DE.DP help organizations develop effective detection strategies that promptly identify and respond to potential cybersecurity incidents before they cause significant damage or data loss.

Organizations can enhance their cybersecurity posture and decrease the risk of cybersecurity incidents by following the guidelines and best practices outlined in the NIST CSF Detect function, shown in Figure 7-1.

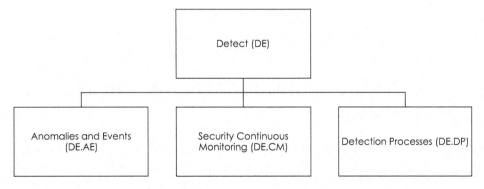

Figure 7-1. *NIST Detect categories*

Value of Azure NIST CSF Detect   Adopting the NIST CSF Detect capabilities can bring numerous benefits to an organization including improved detection of security threats. By adopting the NIST CSF Detect capabilities, organizations can establish more advanced threat detection and response mechanisms. They can use the NIST guidelines to develop an effective cybersecurity posture capable of detecting and mitigating a wide range of security threats.

Anomalies and Events (DE.AE)

DE.AE deals with identifying and responding to unusual activities, events, or behaviors that may indicate a security breach or potential threat to an organization's systems, network, or data. *Anomalies* refer to deviations from standard patterns of activity, which may include unusual network traffic, unauthorized access attempts, abnormal system or user behavior, unexpected changes in system configurations, and other similar events. These anomalies can be detected using various tools and techniques, such as intrusion detection systems, SIEM solutions, and data analytics.

On the other hand, *events* refer to specific incidents or occurrences that require investigation and response from the organization's security team. Events may include successful or failed login attempts, system crashes, malware infections, data breaches, and other security incidents that can impact the organization's security posture.

DE.AE is critical in ensuring organizations can quickly detect and respond to security incidents and prevent potential damage or loss to their systems and data. By monitoring and analyzing anomalies and events, security teams can proactively identify potential threats and take appropriate measures to mitigate them. Let's review a couple of examples to help illustrate the concept of DE.AE in cybersecurity.

Example 1: Cybersecurity Security Professional at Midsize Client

Suppose you work for a company that manages an extensive network of servers and workstations. One day, you notice that there is an unusual spike in network traffic, and the server logs indicate that there have been several failed logins attempts from an unknown IP address. These events could be considered anomalies since they deviate from the normal patterns of activity that you would expect to see on your network.

As a security professional, you know these anomalies could be a sign of a potential security breach, so you decide to investigate further. You use your SIEM solution to correlate anomalous events with other data sources, such as firewall logs and antivirus alerts, to identify any other potential indicators of compromise.

Your investigation reveals that the unknown IP address was attempting to access a sensitive database containing confidential customer information. Fortunately, your organization has implemented robust security controls, such as multifactor authentication (MFA) and network segmentation, that prevent the attacker from gaining access to the database. However, you decide to investigate the incident further to determine how the attacker could bypass your initial security measures and what steps you can take to prevent similar attacks in the future.

In this example, DE.AE played a crucial role in identifying potential security threats, investigating anomalies, and responding to events promptly and effectively. By monitoring and analyzing network traffic, logs, and other data sources, security professionals can proactively detect potential threats and take appropriate measures to mitigate them before they cause significant damage or loss.

Example 2: Cybersecurity Analyst Working for a Financial Institution

Let's say you're a cybersecurity analyst working for a financial institution. Your organization processes a high volume of transactions daily, and it's critical to ensure that the systems and networks used to process these transactions are secure and protected from unauthorized access.

One day, you notice that there's been an unusual increase in failed login attempts to one of your critical servers. This could be considered an anomaly since it deviates from the normal pattern of activity, which typically involves successful login attempts from authorized users.

As a DE.AE expert, this anomaly could indicate a potential security threat. So you investigate the event and discover that an attacker has been attempting to gain unauthorized access to the server using stolen credentials.

You then use your SIEM solution to analyze logs and network traffic to determine the scope of the attack and identify any other potential indicators of compromise. This helps you discover that the attacker was also attempting to exfiltrate sensitive customer data.

You quickly act to contain the attack, change the affected user credentials, and implement additional security controls to prevent similar attacks in the future.

Azure Mapping to Anomalies and Events (DE.AE)

Azure provides a range of cybersecurity capabilities that help organizations monitor, detect, and respond to potential security threats, including DE.AE.

Azure Sentinel is a cloud-native SIEM solution that uses machine learning and analytics to detect and respond to security threats. Sentinel enables organizations to collect security data from various sources, including Azure services, third-party solutions, and on-premises systems. With Sentinel, organizations can detect and investigate potential security threats in real time, with automated response capabilities that can help mitigate threats before they cause significant damage.

Azure Monitor is another Azure service that provides monitoring capabilities for applications and infrastructure deployed in Azure. With Azure Monitor, organizations can collect and analyze metrics, logs, and performance data from Azure services and third-party solutions. This data can be used to identify potential security threats and anomalies in real time, enabling organizations to respond quickly and effectively.

Azure Security Center is a centralized security management solution that provides unified visibility and control over security across Azure and hybrid environments. Security Center enables organizations to assess their security posture, identify potential vulnerabilities, and implement appropriate security controls to protect against threats.

Azure Active Directory (Azure AD) is a cloud-based identify and access management solution that provides authentication and authorization services for Azure and other Microsoft services. Azure AD enables organizations to implement MFA, Conditional Access policies, and other security controls to protect against unauthorized access to their systems and data.

There are several critical benefits of DE.AE in the cybersecurity world, including the following:

- *Early detection of potential threats*: DE.AE enables security teams to identify and investigate anomalies and events that may indicate a potential security breach or threat. This early detection allows organizations to respond quickly and effectively to mitigate potential damage or loss.

- *Proactive security monitoring*: DE.AE involves continuously monitoring systems, networks, and data sources to identify and investigate potential security incidents before they can cause significant harm. This proactive approach helps organizations stay one step ahead of potential attackers.

- *Improved incident response*: DE.AE enables security teams to respond quickly and effectively to security incidents by providing real-time alerts and actionable insights. This helps organizations minimize the impact of security incidents and prevent them from escalating into significant breaches.

- *Enhanced visibility and situational awareness*: DE.AE provide organizations with enhanced visibility into their systems, networks, and data sources, allowing them to identify potential security gaps and vulnerabilities. This improved situational awareness helps organizations make informed decisions about their security posture and implement appropriate security controls.

- *Compliance and regulatory requirements*: DE.AE help organizations meet compliance and regulatory requirements by providing the tools and capabilities to monitor and analyze security-related data. This allows organizations to demonstrate to auditors and regulators that they have implemented appropriate security controls to protect their systems and data.

Figure 7-2 shows the categories of DE.AE.

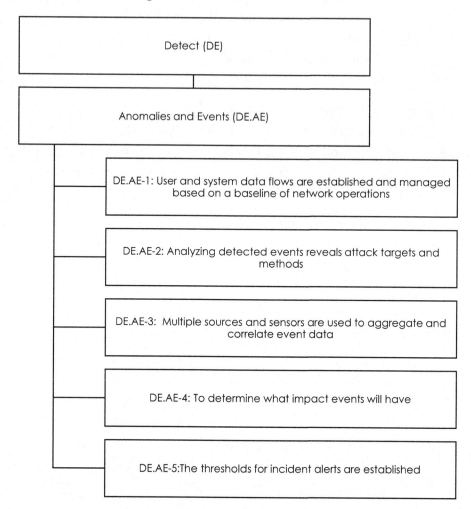

Figure 7-2. *NIST CSF DE.AE*

Figure 7-3 shows the NIST CSF DE.AE to Azure mapping.

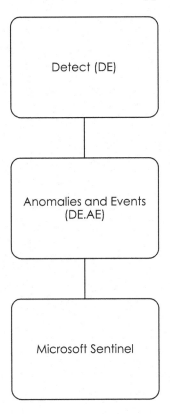

Figure 7-3. *Azure mapping to the Detect module of the NIST CSF*

As part of the Azure cloud shared responsibility model, the NIST CSF security functions are provided in Table 7-1 with respect to DE.AE.

Table 7-1. DE.AE Responsibility Matrix

Category	Subcategory	Informative References	Responsibility	Customer Responsibility	Microsoft Azure Responsibility
Anomalies and Events (DE.AE): Timely detection of abnormal activity is made, and the potential impact of events is understood.	DE.AE-1:User and system data flows are established and managed based on a baseline of network operations	NIST SP 800-53 Rev. 4 AC-4, CA-3, CM-2, SI-4	Customer Responsibility	The customer must establish and manage network operations and expected data flows for users and systems.	N/A
	DE.AE-2: Analyzing detected events reveals attack targets and methods	NIST SP 800-53 Rev. 4 AU-6, CA-7, IR-4, SI-4	Shared	To detect inappropriate or unusual activity, the customer must review and analyze the audit records of the information system. The customer must develop a continuous monitoring strategy following the requirements. To demonstrate the ongoing security of the system, the customer should document what information is essential for them to monitor and why that information is sufficient.	Multiple stages are involved in Microsoft Azure's incident management process. Preparing, detecting, analyzing, containing, eradicating, and recovering after an incident are all steps in incident management.

DE.AE-3: Multiple sources and sensors are used to aggregate and correlate event data	NIST SP 800-53 Rev. 4 AU-6, CA-7, IR-4, IR-5, IR-8, SI-4	Shared	Multiple sources of security-related information must be correlated and analyzed by the customer. The customer should employ automated mechanisms to track security incidents and collect and analyze incident information.	A central repository aggregate logs from Microsoft Azure Infrastructure devices for analysis.
DE.AE-4:It is determined what impact events will have	NIST SP 800-53 Rev. 4 CP-2, IR-4, RA-3, SI -4	Customer Responsibility	Among other tasks, the customer is responsible for assessing the impact of information gathered from multiple sources related to security, including periodic assessments and ongoing monitoring.	N/A
DE.AE-5:The thresholds for incident alerts are established	NIST SP 800-53 Rev. 4 IR-4, IR-5, IR-8	Customer Responsibility	As a result of the incident analysis, the customer is responsible for responding appropriately. The customer should establish appropriate thresholds for incident alerts based on proper monitoring data and industry inputs.	N/A

Azure Sentinel

As mentioned, Azure Sentinel is a cloud-native SIEM solution that enables organizations to collect, analyze, and respond to security events in real time. It is a scalable, flexible, and cost-effective solution that provides unified visibility across an organization's entire IT environment, including on-premises, cloud, and hybrid environments.

Key features of Azure Sentinel include the following:

- *Data ingestion*: Sentinel can collect security data from various sources, including Azure services, third-party solutions, and on-premises systems.

- *Threat detection*: Sentinel uses machine learning and behavioral analytics to detect potential security threats in real time. This includes identifying anomalies in user behavior, network traffic, and application activity.

- *Incident response*: Sentinel provides a range of incident response capabilities, including the ability to investigate and triage security incidents, automate response actions, and create customized security playbooks.

- *Integration with Microsoft services*: Sentinel is tightly integrated with other Microsoft services, including Azure Security Center, Azure Active Directory, and Azure Functions.

- *Customization*: Sentinel is highly customizable and can be tailored to meet the specific security needs of an organization. This includes the ability to create custom queries, alerts, and workflows.

- *Compliance*: Sentinel provides built-in compliance dashboards and reports that enable organizations to meet regulatory requirements and industry standards.

Azure Sentinel also offers a range of detection capabilities for the Azure cloud that enable organizations to monitor, detect, and respond to potential security threats. These capabilities include the following:

- *Integration with Azure services*: Sentinel integrates with a wide range of Azure services, including Azure Active Directory, Azure Virtual Machines, Azure SQL Database, and Azure Kubernetes Service. This enables organizations to collect and analyze security data from these services and identify potential security threats.

- *Azure Resource Graph*: Sentinel leverages Azure Resource Graph to query and analyze data from Azure resources. This includes searching for specific resources, analyzing resource metadata, and identifying potential security threats.

- *Azure Security Center integration*: Sentinel integrates with Azure Security Center to provide unified visibility and control over security across Azure and hybrid environments. This includes assessing security posture, identifying potential vulnerabilities, and implementing appropriate security controls to protect against threats.

- *Azure Monitor integration*: Sentinel integrates with Azure Monitor to collect and analyze metrics, logs, and performance data from Azure services and third-party solutions. This data can be used to identify potential security threats and anomalies in real time.

- *Azure Functions*: Sentinel integrates with Azure Functions, enabling organizations to automate security tasks and processes. This includes triggering automated responses to potential security threats, such as blocking IP addresses or isolating compromised resources.

- *Machine learning*: Sentinel uses machine learning to analyze security data and identify potential threats. This includes automatically classifying and prioritizing security incidents based on their severity and potential impact.

Azure Sentinel works to detect anomalies and events through a combination of data ingestion, analytics, and alerting.

- *Data ingestion*: Azure Sentinel ingests data from various sources such as Azure Activity Logs, Azure Security Center alerts, Azure Firewall logs, or any third-party sources. This data is then normalized and stored in a central location for further analysis.

- *Analytics*: Azure Sentinel uses machine learning, behavioral analytics, and other detection techniques to identify anomalous behavior and events. It provides a rich set of out-of-the-box detection rules for common scenarios, such as detecting failed logins, suspicious PowerShell commands, or brute-force attacks. Organizations can also create custom detection rules or queries based on their needs.

- *Alerting*: Azure Sentinel generates an alert when an anomaly or event is detected. Organizations can configure alert workflows to ensure that alerts are triaged and responded to promptly and efficiently. This includes defining who receives alerts, how they are handled, and the priority level.

In addition to data ingestion, analytics, and alerting, Azure Sentinel provides tools for investigating and triaging incidents. Organizations can also define playbooks to automate the response to a specific type of security incident.

Azure Sentinel works by ingesting data from various sources, analyzing it using machine learning and behavioral analytics, and alerting organizations to potential security threats. Using Azure Sentinel, organizations can improve their security posture and quickly respond to potential security incidents.

Azure Sentinel provides various detection capabilities to help organizations detect and respond to potential security threats. These capabilities include the following:

- *Behavioral analytics*: Sentinel uses machine learning and behavioral analytics to identify abnormal behavior in systems and networks that may indicate a security threat. This includes user behavior, network traffic, and application activity.

- *Threat intelligence*: Sentinel integrates with threat intelligence feeds to identify known threats and IOCs in real time. This helps organizations detect and respond to potential security threats before they can cause significant harm.

- *Anomaly detection*: Sentinel uses statistical analysis to detect system and network behavior anomalies that may indicate a security threat. This includes anomalies in user behavior, network traffic, and system activity.

- *Log correlation*: Sentinel collects and analyzes logs from various sources, including Azure services, third-party solutions, and on-premises systems. By correlating this data, Sentinel can identify potential security threats and provide actionable insights to security teams.

- *Hunting queries*: Sentinel allows security teams to perform ad hoc queries and searches to investigate potential security incidents. This includes the ability to search for specific events, patterns, or IOCs.

- *Machine learning*: Sentinel uses machine learning to analyze security data and identify potential threats. This includes automatically classifying and prioritizing security incidents based on their severity and potential impact.

- *Security playbooks*: Sentinel includes a library of pre-built security playbooks that provide step-by-step guidance on responding to potential security threats. These playbooks can be customized to meet the specific needs of an organization.

Azure Sentinel offers a variety of ways to detect anomalies and events in real time. Here are some tips to detect anomalies and events using Azure Sentinel:

- *Configure data sources*: Configure data sources such as Azure Activity Logs, Azure Security Center alerts, Azure Firewall logs, or any third-party sources to send logs to Azure Sentinel.

- *Create detection rules*: Create detection rules or queries to detect anomalies and events. Azure Sentinel provides a rich set of out-of-the-box rules for common scenarios, such as detecting failed logins, suspicious PowerShell commands, or brute-force attacks. You can also create custom detection rules or queries based on your organization's needs.

- *Set alert thresholds*: Set alert thresholds to define the severity of an anomaly or event. You can define thresholds for various parameters such as event count, frequency, or specific conditions like specific IP addresses or unusual login activity.

- *Customize alert workflows*: Customize alert workflows to determine how alerts are handled. You can define how alerts are sent, who receives them, and the priority level.

- *Investigate and respond*: Investigate alerts and events to determine if a security incident has occurred. Azure Sentinel provides tools for investigating incidents and triaging them. You can also define playbooks to automate the response to a specific type of security incident.

- *Monitor and improve*: Monitor your detection rules and alert thresholds and refine them over time to improve your security posture.

Design Considerations

The following are the key best practices for designing a Azure Sentinel solution to detect anomalies and events:

- *Define security goals*: Define your organization's security goals and priorities. This will help you identify the key data sources and detection rules that must be configured to meet your security needs.

- *Identify data sources*: Identify the data sources relevant to your security goals and configure them to send logs to Azure Sentinel. This includes Azure Activity Logs, Azure Security Center alerts, Azure Firewall logs, or third-party sources.

- *Use prebuilt detection rules*: Azure Sentinel provides a rich set of prebuilt detection rules for common scenarios such as detecting brute-force attacks, anomalous login activity, or suspicious PowerShell commands. Use these rules as a starting point and customize them based on your organization's specific needs.

- *Create custom detection rules*: Create custom detection rules or queries based on your organization's security goals and requirements. Ensure that these rules are tuned to minimize false positives and are prioritized based on severity.

- *Set alert thresholds*: Define alert thresholds based on your organization's specific security goals for your detection rules. Ensure that alert thresholds are set appropriately to minimize noise while detecting potential security threats.

- *Configure custom alert workflows*: Define custom alert workflows to ensure that alerts are triaged and responded to promptly and efficiently. This includes defining who receives alerts, how they are handled, and the priority level.

- *Define incident response playbooks*: Define incident response playbooks to automate the response to specific security incidents. Ensure these playbooks are regularly reviewed and updated based on changing security requirements.

- *Monitor and refine*: Continuously monitor your detection rules and alert thresholds and refine them based on your organization's evolving security needs.

How to Enable It

Enabling Azure Sentinel to detect anomalies and events involves the following steps:

1. *Connect data sources*: Connect data sources to Azure Sentinel by configuring them to send logs to the solution. This includes Azure Activity Logs, Azure Security Center alerts, Azure Firewall logs, or third-party sources.

2. *Configure analytics rules*: Configure analytics rules or queries to detect anomalies and events. Azure Sentinel provides a rich set of out-of-the-box rules for common scenarios, such as detecting failed logins, suspicious PowerShell commands, or brute-force attacks. You can also create custom detection rules or queries based on your organization's needs.

3. *Set alert thresholds*: Set alert thresholds to define the severity of an anomaly or event. You can define thresholds for various parameters such as event count, frequency, or specific conditions like specific IP addresses or unusual login activity.

4. *Configure alert workflows*: Configure alert workflows to determine how alerts are handled. You can define how alerts are sent, who receives them, and the priority level.

5. *Investigate and respond*: Investigate alerts and events to determine if a security incident has occurred. Azure Sentinel provides tools for investigating incidents and triaging them. You can also define playbooks to automate the response to a specific type of security incident.

6. *Monitor and improve*: Monitor your detection rules and alert thresholds and refine them over time to improve your security posture.

To enable Azure Sentinel to detect anomalies and events, it is essential to ensure data sources are properly connected and that analytics rules are configured appropriately. It is also necessary to define alert workflows and incident response playbooks to ensure that alerts are handled effectively. By following these steps, organizations can improve their security posture and quickly respond to potential security threats.

Key Insights of Azure Sentinel   Azure Sentinel processes more than 5 trillion daily signals from various sources such as Azure, Microsoft 365, and third-party integrations. Azure Sentinel has more than 100 built-in connectors for popular cloud services and security solutions, making collecting and analyzing data from multiple sources more accessible. Sentinel can perform threat hunting and investigations with AI and machine learning capabilities to identify malicious activity in real time. When writing this book, the average time to detect a security threat with Azure Sentinel is less than 30 seconds, while the average time to respond and mitigate the threat is less than 5 minutes.

Security Continuous Monitoring (DE.CM)

DE.SCM is an essential practice in cybersecurity that involves the ongoing collection, analysis, and evaluation of security-related data to maintain an up-to-date understanding of the security posture of an organization's information systems. SCM helps identify and address potential vulnerabilities, threats, and security incidents in real time, allowing organizations to respond promptly and effectively.

Let's get started with DevSecOps, before a deep dive into SCM.

Getting Started with DevSecOps

DevSecOps is a software development methodology that integrates security into every stage of the software development life cycle, from planning to deployment and maintenance. It aims to break down the silos between development, security, and operations teams and create a culture of shared responsibility for security.

Traditionally, security has been seen as a separate function responsible for identifying and mitigating security risks. This approach has resulted in security being treated as an afterthought, with developers focusing on functionality and performance rather than security. DevSecOps aims to change this by shifting security left in the software development process. This means that security is integrated into the development process from the beginning, with security controls and testing built into the development pipeline.

The DevSecOps methodology is built on the principles of continuous integration, continuous delivery, and continuous deployment. These principles enable developers to quickly build, test, and deploy software securely and automatically.

Continuous integration involves regularly merging code changes into a shared repository and running automated tests to ensure the code functions as expected. Continuous delivery involves automating and deploying code changes to a production environment. Continuous deployment takes this further by automatically deploying code changes to production without human intervention.

The DevSecOps methodology also involves using various tools and technologies to enable continuous monitoring, testing, and analysis of code and infrastructure. This includes static and dynamic code analysis tools, vulnerability scanning, penetration testing, and automated security testing. It enables organizations to detect and respond to security threats more quickly. By integrating security into the development process, security issues can be identified and remediated earlier, reducing the risk of a security breach.

DevSecOps also helps to improve collaboration between development, security, and operations teams. By breaking down the silos between these teams, organizations can create a culture of shared responsibility for security, which results in a more secure and resilient application or infrastructure.

To implement DevSecOps successfully, organizations need to adopt several best practices.

- *Shift security left*: Integrate security into the development process, and ensure developers are trained on secure coding practices.

- *Use automation*: Automate security testing and monitoring to enable continuous feedback and analysis of code and infrastructure.

- *Collaborate*: Break down silos between development, security, and operations teams, and create a culture of shared responsibility for security.

- *Use best-of-breed tools*: Use the best tools and technologies available for security testing and monitoring and integrate them into the development pipeline.

- *Prioritize security*: Make security a top priority and ensure it is built into every aspect of the development process.

DevSecOps Continuous Monitoring

DevSecOps continuous monitoring is a security practice that involves continuously monitoring an application or infrastructure to identify security vulnerabilities and threats in real time. It is a critical aspect of the DevSecOps methodology, which focuses on integrating security into the software development process.

Continuous monitoring involves gathering and analyzing security-related data using various tools and techniques. This data includes information about the infrastructure, application code, network traffic, user behavior, and system logs. Continuous monitoring is designed to identify potential security threats such as malicious activity, vulnerabilities, misconfigurations, and compliance violations.

DevSecOps continuous monitoring requires collaboration between the development, security, and operations teams. It involves automating security checks throughout the software development life cycle, from code development to deployment and maintenance. The goal is to ensure that security is integrated into every stage of the development process, resulting in a more secure and resilient application or infrastructure.

Consider a hypothetical example of a software development team working on a web application. The group follows a DevSecOps methodology and has integrated security into every stage of the software development life cycle.

As part of the continuous monitoring process, the team has set up several automated security checks that run regularly to identify potential security vulnerabilities or threats. These checks include the following:

- *Static code analysis*: The team uses a static code analysis tool to scan the code for potential security issues. The tool checks for common security vulnerabilities such as SQL injection, cross-site scripting (XSS), and buffer overflow.

- *Dynamic code analysis*: The team also uses an active code analysis tool to test the application in a simulated production environment. This tool checks for vulnerabilities such as weak authentication, access control issues, and insecure configuration.

- *Infrastructure monitoring*: The team uses a tool to monitor the application's infrastructure. This tool checks for open ports, outdated software, and misconfigured firewall rules.

- *User behavior monitoring*: The team also monitors user behavior to identify potential security threats. This includes monitoring user logins, access to sensitive data, and unusual activity.

The team is notified immediately if any automated checks detect a potential security issue. They can then take action to remediate the issue before it becomes a security threat.

For example, if the static code analysis tool detects a potential SQL injection vulnerability, the team can review the code and make the necessary changes to fix the issue. They can then rerun the automated tests to ensure the issue is resolved.

479

Continuous monitoring enables the team to quickly identify and remediate security issues, reducing the risk of a security breach. It also helps to ensure that security is integrated into every aspect of the development process, creating a more secure and resilient application.

Azure Mapping to Security Continuous Monitoring (DE.CM)

Azure offers several services that can be used for DE.CM, including the following:

- *Azure Security Center*: This service provides a central hub for monitoring and managing the security of Azure resources. It continuously monitors security configurations and vulnerabilities, threat detection using advanced analytics, and security recommendations.

- *Azure Sentinel*: This service provides intelligent security analytics and threat intelligence across the enterprise. It monitors security events, alerts, and incidents from various sources, including Azure resources, on-premises infrastructure, and other cloud platforms.

- *Azure Monitor*: This service provides monitoring and alerting capabilities for Azure resources and applications. It offers continuous monitoring of performance metrics, logs, and diagnostics data and can be used to detect security events and anomalies.

- *Azure Network Watcher*: This service provides network monitoring and diagnostics capabilities for Azure resources. It offers continuous network traffic and connectivity monitoring, packet capture and analysis for troubleshooting, and security analysis.

- *Azure AD*: This service provides identify and access management capabilities for Azure resources and applications. It monitors user activity, access permissions, and authentication events to detect potential security threats and anomalies.

- *Azure Policy*: This service provides a way to enforce compliance and
  security policies across Azure resources and applications. It offers
  continuous monitoring of resource configurations and can be used to
  detect noncompliant or insecure configurations.

By using these Azure services for DE.CM, organizations can proactively detect and
respond to security threats and vulnerabilities, ensuring the security and compliance of
their Azure environments.

Figure 7-4 depicts the subcategories of DE.CM in relation to the Detect module of the
NIST CSF.

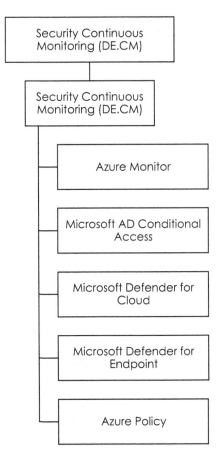

Figure 7-4. *Azure services for DE.CM*

As part of the Azure cloud shared responsibility model, the NIST CSF security
functions are provided in Table 7-2 with respect to DE.CM.

Table 7-2. DE.CM Responsibility Matrix

Category	Subcategory	Informative References	Responsibility	Customer Responsibility	Microsoft Azure Responsibility
Security Continuous Monitoring (DE.CM): The information system and assets are monitored at discrete intervals to identify cybersecurity events and verify the effectiveness of protective measures.	DE.CM-1: The network is monitored to detect potential cybersecurity events	NIST SP 800-53 Rev. 4 AC-2, AU-12, CA-7, CM-3, SC-5, SC-7, SI-4	Shared	Customers who use a non-Microsoft Azure-provided operating system image are responsible for scanning for vulnerabilities within that operating system.	Microsoft Azure logs security-relevant events on its servers, which act as monitoring devices. Azure monitors all hosts in the environment and sends alarms to security team members and contingent workers.
	DE.CM-2: The physical environment is monitored to detect potential cybersecurity events	NIST SP 800-53 Rev. 4 CA-7, PE-3, PE-6, PE-20	Microsoft Azure	N/A	Security events within a Microsoft Azure datacenter are documented by the security team, which is responsible for capturing the details of the events to capture the details as accurately as possible.

DE.CM-3: Personnel activity is monitored to detect potential cybersecurity events	NIST SP 800-53 Rev. 4 AC-2, AU-12, AU-13, CA-7, CM-10, CM-11	Shared	The customer is responsible for monitoring employee access to the environment for potential security incidents.	Microsoft Azure monitors all personnel activity for the detection of potential cybersecurity events. This includes monitoring physical and logical access, in addition to monitoring the potential of social engineering threats.

Moreover, these reports include an investigative analysis documenting how a security event was investigated and attempts were made to identify its root cause. For the improvement of security procedures across the Azure data center security program, any remediation actions or lessons learned are also included in the report.

(continued)

Table 7-2. (*continued*)

Category	Subcategory	Informative References	Responsibility	Customer Responsibility	Microsoft Azure Responsibility
	DE.CM-4: Malicious code is detected	NIST SP 800-53 Rev. 4 SI-3	Shared	The customer must use malicious code detection mechanisms.	Malicious code is detected using antivirus software in Microsoft Azure. These tools use signature-based detection mechanisms and behavior monitoring, network inspection, and heuristics to detect malicious code that signature-based detection may miss.
	DE.CM-5: Unauthorized mobile code is detected	NIST SP 800-53 Rev. 4 SC-18, SI-4. SC-44	Shared	Customer must decide which mobile code technologies are acceptable or unacceptable within the system. Customer must scan for and detect any unauthorized mobile code (code downloaded and executed by the client machine rather than the remote host).	Microsoft Azure authorizes, monitors, and controls the use of mobile code developed by the service teams, including peer review and security code review, to detect the presence of unauthorized mobile code. Code may not be released without following these processes.

DE.CM-6: External service provider activity is monitored to detect potential cybersecurity events	NIST SP 800-53 Rev. 4 CA-7, PS-7, SA-4, SA-9, SI-4	Customer Responsibility	Security functional requirements must be included in acquisition contracts, and personnel security requirements must be established for third parties.	N/A
DE.CM-7: Monitoring for unauthorized personnel, connections, devices, and software is performed	NIST SP 800-53 Rev. 4 AU-12, CA-7, CM-3, CM-8, PE-3, PE-6, PE-20, SI-4	Shared	The customer is responsible for monitoring its system for unauthorized personnel, connections, devices, and software.	A security incident management team incident response procedure for unauthorized access to the Microsoft Azure Infrastructure environment is followed.

(continued)

485

Table 7-2. (*continued*)

Category	Subcategory	Informative References	Responsibility	Customer Responsibility	Microsoft Azure Responsibility
	DE.CM-8: Vulnerability scans are performed	NIST SP 800-53 Rev. 4 RA-5	Shared	Customers who use an operating system image other than the one provided by Microsoft Azure are responsible for scanning for vulnerabilities in the operating system. Customers are responsible for ensuring that vulnerability scanning tools enumerate components, flaws, and improper configurations, format checklists, and test procedures, and assess vulnerability impacts according to standards.	Security-related information collected from assessments and monitoring, such as vulnerability scan results, updates to findings, and recurring control testing, is correlated and analyzed by Microsoft Azure's continuous monitoring. As a result of the vulnerability assessment, it is determined if it is actionable (requiring remediation), risk reduced, false positive, or accepted. If applicable, the results are summarized into reports that are used to track findings. Azure mitigates all high-risk vulnerabilities within 30 days of discovery and moderate-risk vulnerabilities within 90 days of discovery.

Azure Monitor

Azure Monitor is a monitoring solution provided by Microsoft Azure, designed to collect and analyze telemetry data from various sources, including applications, infrastructure, and network services.

In terms of cybersecurity incident detection, Azure Monitor provides a range of features and capabilities that can help security teams detect and respond to security incidents.

For example, Azure Monitor can collect and analyze logs and events from Azure resources, such as virtual machines, databases, storage accounts, and on-premises resources, using agents and connectors. It also integrates with Azure Security Center, a unified security management solution, to provide additional security insights and recommendations.

Azure Monitor also includes features like alerting and notifications, which can be used to trigger automated responses or manual investigations when specific events or conditions are detected. This can help security teams quickly identify and respond to potential security incidents.

Overall, Azure Monitor is a powerful tool for monitoring and detecting security incidents in Azure and hybrid environments, providing visibility and insights into the security posture of an organization's infrastructure and applications.

Here are some key benefits of Azure Monitor in terms of cloud security:

- *Centralized monitoring*: Azure Monitor provides a centralized platform for monitoring and analyzing security-related events and logs across all Azure services and resources.

- *Real-time alerts*: Azure Monitor can detect security incidents in real-time and trigger alerts or notifications to the security team, enabling them to respond quickly to potential threats.

- *Automated responses*: Azure Monitor can be integrated with Azure Logic Apps or Azure Functions to automate responses to security incidents, such as shutting down a compromised resource or initiating an investigation.

- *Advanced analytics*: Azure Monitor includes powerful analytics capabilities that help security teams identify patterns and trends in security events, providing insights into potential threats and vulnerabilities.

- *Integration with Azure Security Center*: Azure Monitor integrates with Azure Security Center, which provides a unified dashboard for monitoring and managing security across all Azure services and resources.

- *Multi-cloud support*: Azure Monitor supports monitoring of both Azure and non-Azure resources, enabling security teams to monitor and analyze security-related events in multi-cloud environments.

- *Cost-effective*: Azure Monitor offers a pay-as-you-go pricing model, making it a cost-effective solution for monitoring cloud security.

Azure Monitor can help organizations implement and improve their cybersecurity posture by supporting the CSF's Detect capabilities, which include the following functions:

- *Anomalies and events*: Azure Monitor can detect and analyze anomalies and events in real time, providing insights into potential security threats or suspicious activities.

- *Continuous monitoring*: Azure Monitor provides continuous monitoring of Azure resources and services, enabling security teams to identify potential threats and vulnerabilities as they emerge.

- *Detection processes*: Azure Monitor includes features like alerting and notifications, which can trigger automated responses or manual investigations when specific events or conditions are detected.

- *Monitoring strategies*: Azure Monitor can be customized to support different monitoring strategies, such as proactive monitoring or event-driven monitoring, depending on an organization's specific needs and requirements.

- *Improvements*: Azure Monitor provides analytics and reporting capabilities to help organizations track and improve their detection capabilities by analyzing trends and patterns in security-related events and incidents.

Design Considerations

Here are some Azure Monitor security design best practices for the Detect category:

- *Identify critical assets and services*: Identify critical assets and services that need to be monitored and configure Azure Monitor to collect telemetry data from those resources.

- *Establish baseline behavior*: Using historical data or other sources to identify anomalies and potential security threats, establish a baseline for normal behavior for each asset or service.

- *Define alerting thresholds*: Define alerting thresholds based on the established baseline behavior and configure Azure Monitor to trigger alerts or notifications when those thresholds are exceeded.

- *Implement automated responses*: Implement automated responses to security incidents, such as shutting down a compromised resource, using Azure Logic Apps or Azure Functions.

- *Integrate with Azure Security Center*: Integrate Azure Monitor with Azure Security Center to gain additional security insights and recommendations and to enable unified monitoring and management of security across all Azure services and resources.

- *Use advanced analytics*: Use Azure Monitor's advanced analytics capabilities, such as machine learning and anomaly detection, to identify patterns and trends in security events and to proactively detect potential threats.

- *Monitor non-Azure resources*: Configure Azure Monitor to monitor non-Azure resources using agents or connectors, such as on-premises servers or third-party cloud services.

- *Regularly review and update*: Regularly review and update your monitoring strategy and alerting thresholds to ensure they are aligned with your organization's evolving security needs and requirements.

How to Enable It

To enable Azure Monitor to detect security incidents, follow these general steps:

1. *Configure logging and diagnostics*: Configure Azure services and resources to send logs and diagnostics data to Azure Monitor. This includes enabling diagnostic settings, configuring log sources, and setting log retention policies.

2. *Create alert rules*: Create alert rules in Azure Monitor to detect security-related events and anomalies based on specific conditions, such as failed logins, suspicious IP addresses, or unusual user behavior.

3. *Configure notifications*: Configure notifications for alerts to be sent to security teams or other stakeholders via email, SMS, or webhook.

4. *Implement automated responses*: Implement automated responses to security incidents, such as triggering a runbook or shutting down a compromised resource, using Azure Logic Apps or Azure Functions.

5. *Integrate Azure Security Center*: Integrate Azure Monitor with Azure Security Center to gain additional security insights and recommendations and enable unified monitoring and management of security across all Azure services and resources.

6. *Regularly review and update*: Regularly review and update your alert rules and notifications to ensure they are aligned with your organization's evolving security needs and requirements.

In addition to these steps, it's essential to regularly review and analyze security-related data and events in Azure Monitor to identify potential threats and vulnerabilities and to implement security measures to prevent or mitigate them proactively. By following these steps and best practices, organizations can enable Azure Monitor to detect and respond to security incidents effectively.

Azure Monitor deployment helps in security detection by providing a centralized platform for collecting, analyzing, and responding to security-related telemetry data from Azure services and resources. Here are some ways that Azure Monitor deployment can help in security detection:

- *Log collection and analysis*: Azure Monitor can collect and analyze logs from Azure services and resources, including operating system logs, application logs, and Azure service logs. This enables security teams to identify potential security threats and anomalies, such as failed logins, unusual user behavior, or suspicious network traffic.

- *Metrics and performance monitoring*: Azure Monitor can monitor performance metrics for Azure services and resources, including CPU usage, memory usage, and network traffic. This can help detect abnormal activity that may indicate a security incident, such as high CPU usage or network traffic spikes.

- *Alerting and notifications*: Azure Monitor can be configured to generate alerts and notifications based on specific conditions or events, such as failed login attempts, malware detections, or suspicious network traffic. This enables security teams to respond quickly to potential security incidents and take appropriate action.

- *Automated responses*: Azure Monitor can trigger automated responses to security incidents, such as shutting down a compromised resource, using Azure Logic Apps or Azure Functions. This can help contain security incidents and prevent further damage.

- *Integration with Azure Security Center*: Azure Monitor can be integrated with Azure Security Center to gain additional security insights and recommendations and to enable unified monitoring and management of security across all Azure services and resources.

By deploying Azure Monitor for security detection, organizations can gain a comprehensive view of their Azure environment and detect potential security threats and incidents promptly and effectively.

Key Insights of Azure Monitor   When writing this book, Azure Monitor processes more than 5 trillion data points per day. Azure Monitor is integrated with more than 100 Azure services. Azure Monitor provides insights into more than 20 different Azure resource types. Azure Monitor has more than 50 prebuilt monitoring solutions, such as Azure Active Directory, Azure SQL Database, and Azure Kubernetes Service. Azure Monitor supports more than 10 data sources, including log data, metrics data, and application insights. Azure Monitor can trigger alerts based on metrics, logs, and custom queries. Azure Monitor provides real-time dashboards that can be customized to show the most critical data to the user. Azure Monitor supports integration with third-party tools and services like PagerDuty, ServiceNow, and Slack. Azure Monitor provides built-in analytics capabilities like log search, alerts, and queries. Azure Monitor is scalable and can monitor resources in small to large-scale enterprise environments.

Azure AD Conditional Access

Azure Active Directory AD Conditional Access is a feature that allows administrators to set policies that determine who can access specific resources in the organization. It helps organizations control access to their resources by enforcing particular rules. This feature enables administrators to define conditions that must be met before a user can access a resource. These conditions can include the user's location, the device they are using, and the application they are trying to access. With Azure AD Conditional Access, organizations can ensure that only authorized users are accessing their resources, which helps to prevent data breaches and other security incidents.

Conditional Access policies can help detect cybersecurity incidents by requiring additional authentication or blocking access based on unusual or risky behavior. For example, suppose a unique login attempt is detected from a location that the user has not accessed before or from a device that has not been previously registered. In that case, the policy can require MFA or deny access entirely. Conditional Access policies can also be configured to alert administrators when specific conditions are met, such as when a user attempts to access a resource from a blacklisted IP address or when an unusual amount of data is being downloaded from a particular account. This can help IT teams to quickly investigate and respond to potential security incidents.

Azure AD Conditional Access can help organizations meet the Detect function of the NIST CSF by providing capabilities to detect cybersecurity incidents and abnormal behavior.

Here are some ways in which Azure AD Conditional Access can help with the Detect function:

- *User and entity behavior analytics (UEBA)*: Azure AD Conditional Access can be configured to use UEBA to analyze user behavior and detect anomalous activity. For example, it can detect login attempts from unknown devices or locations or attempts to access sensitive data outside of normal business hours.

- *Risk-based access controls*: Azure AD Conditional Access enables organizations to implement risk-based access controls to identify and block risky behavior. This can include blocking access attempts from IP addresses associated with known threats or requiring additional authentication for high-risk activities.

- *Real-time alerts*: Azure AD Conditional Access can be configured to generate real-time alerts when policy violations occur. These alerts can help organizations quickly detect and respond to potential security incidents.

- *Integration with SIEM solutions*: Azure AD Conditional Access can integrate with SIEM solutions to enable central monitoring and analysis of policy violations and user activity. This can help organizations to detect and respond to cybersecurity incidents more effectively.

Azure AD Conditional Access evaluates an organization's policies to determine whether to allow or deny access to resources in the cloud. The policies can be based on various factors such as user identify, device type, location, application, and risk level. When a user attempts to access a resource, Azure AD Conditional Access evaluates the policies against the user's current context, including their identify, device, and location. If the user meets the requirements specified in the policy, the access is granted, and if not, the access is denied or prompted for additional verification.

How It Works

The user attempts to access a resource, and the user requests a cloud resource, such as an application, file, or email. Then the following steps happen:

1. *Policies are evaluated*: Azure AD Conditional Access evaluates the policies the organization defines based on the user's identify, device, location, application, and risk level.

2. *Access is granted or denied*: If the user meets the requirements specified in the policy, access is granted; otherwise, access is denied or prompted for additional verification, such as MFA.

3. *Actions are taken based on policy*: Azure AD Conditional Access can be configured to take specific actions based on the policy, such as requiring MFA or blocking access entirely.

Design Considerations

Here are some design best practices for implementing Azure AD Conditional Access:

- *Use risk-based policies*: Implement policies that use risk-based access controls, such as requiring additional authentication for high-risk activities or blocking access attempts from IP addresses associated with known threats.

- *Use MFA*: Require MFA for all access attempts, particularly for privileged accounts or sensitive data.

- *Use Azure AD Identify Protection*: Enable Azure AD Identify Protection to detect and respond to potential identify-based attacks, such as password spray or brute-force attacks.

- *Implement policies for noncompliant devices*: Implement policies to control access from noncompliant devices, such as requiring device compliance or blocking access entirely.

- *Use geolocation policies*: Implement geolocation policies to control access based on the user or device's location, particularly for high-risk or sensitive resources.

- *Monitor policy violations*: Monitor policy violations and generate alerts for potential security incidents. This can help organizations to detect and respond to potential threats more effectively.

- *Test policies in a nonproduction environment*: Test policies in a nonproduction environment before deploying them to a production environment to ensure they are working as intended.

- *Limit the number of policies*: Limit the number of policies to avoid policy conflicts or unintended consequences. This can also make it easier to manage and monitor policies.

- *Use audit logging*: Enable audit logging for Azure AD Conditional Access to track policy changes and violations. This can help with compliance requirements and incident response.

How to Enable It

Azure AD can be used for various identify and access management (IAM) scenarios. Here are some common use cases for Azure AD:

- *Single sign-on (SSO)*: Azure AD can provide SSO to multiple cloud applications and services, allowing users to authenticate once and access all their authorized resources without needing additional authentication.

- *Identify and access management*: Azure AD provides comprehensive identify and access management capabilities, such as user provisioning and deprovisioning, role-based access control, and self-service password reset.

- *Federation and external collaboration*: Azure AD support federation with other identify providers, enabling external users to securely access resources in your organization. This can be used to allow for collaboration with partners, vendors, or contractors.

- *MFA*: Azure AD supports MFA, which can be used to provide an additional layer of security for accessing sensitive resources. MFA can be enforced based on user or group, location, device, or other factors.

- *Device management*: Azure AD provides device management capabilities, such as managing device registration, configuration, and compliance. This can be used to ensure that only authorized and compliant devices can access organizational resources.

- *Application access management*: Azure AD can be used to manage access to cloud-based and on-premises applications. This includes enforcing access policies and controlling application access based on user and group membership.

- *Reporting and monitoring*: Azure AD provide rich reporting and monitoring capabilities, allowing administrators to track usage and identify potential security threats.

Overall, Azure AD is a robust identify and access management solution that can secure cloud and hybrid environments, streamline access management, and provide users with a seamless authentication experience. To enable Azure AD Conditional Access, follow these steps:

1. Sign in to the Azure Portal with your Azure AD credentials.

2. Navigate to Azure Active Directory from the menu on the left.

3. Click Conditional Access in the Security section in the Azure Active Directory menu.

4. Click the New Policy button to create a new policy.

5. Configure the policy settings based on the access requirements and risk level. This includes specifying the conditions for access, such as user identify, device type, location, and application, and the actions to take based on those conditions, such as requiring MFA or blocking access entirely.

6. Click the Create button to save the policy.

7. Assign the policy to the appropriate user or group by selecting the policy from the Conditional Access pane and clicking the Assignments button.

8. Select the user or group to which the policy will be applied.

9.   Click the "Enable policy" toggle to enable the policy.

10.   Once the policy is enabled, it will be enforced for the specified users and applications. You can create multiple policies for different scenarios and applications as needed.

Azure AD Premium or Enterprise Mobility + Security licenses may be required to use some Azure AD Conditional Access features. Also, it is essential to thoroughly test policies in a nonproduction environment before deploying them to a production environment to ensure they are working as intended.

Key Insights of Azure Active Directory AD Conditional Access   To help protect and secure identities, applications, and data in the cloud, Azure AD Security provides several features that enable organizations to secure their cloud-based resources, including MFA, Conditional Access, IAM, identify protection, PIM, and Azure AD Connect. According to Microsoft, using Azure AD Conditional Access can reduce the risk of account compromise by 99.9 percent. Microsoft reports that more than 80 percent of data breaches are caused by compromised credentials and Azure AD Conditional Access can help prevent these types of attacks. Azure AD Conditional Access policies are used to protect more than 8 million applications.

Microsoft Defender for Cloud

Microsoft Defender for Cloud is a cloud-native security solution that provides advanced threat protection for cloud workloads and services across various cloud platforms, including Azure, AWS, and Google Cloud Platform. It is a unified solution integrating multiple security services, such as Azure Security Center, Azure Defender, and Microsoft 365 Defender, to view security threats across cloud environments comprehensively.

Microsoft Defender for Cloud uses advanced machine learning and behavioral analytics to detect security incidents across cloud environments. It provides continuous monitoring and detection to help organizations avoid potential security threats. It also provides security recommendations and actionable insights to help organizations improve their security posture.

Some key features of Microsoft Defender for Cloud include the following:

- *Threat protection*: Microsoft Defender for Cloud provides advanced threat protection for cloud workloads and services, including protection against malware, viruses, and other malicious code.

- *Compliance management*: Microsoft Defender for Cloud helps organizations meet regulatory compliance requirements by providing visibility into compliance status and recommendations for improving compliance.

- *Identify and access management*: Microsoft Defender for Cloud provides identify and access management capabilities, such as MFA and Conditional Access policies, to help organizations secure access to cloud resources.

- *Network security*: Microsoft Defender for Cloud provides network security capabilities, such as virtual network segmentation and traffic filtering, to help organizations secure their cloud network.

- *Incident response*: Microsoft Defender for Cloud provides incident response capabilities, such as security alerts and notifications, to help organizations quickly detect and respond to security incidents.

Here are some ways Microsoft Defender for Cloud can help organizations meet the NIST CSF Detect function:

- *Continuous monitoring*: Microsoft Defender for Cloud provides continuous monitoring of cloud workloads and services, using advanced machine learning and behavioral analytics to detect user and system behavior anomalies that may indicate a security threat.

- *Threat intelligence*: Microsoft Defender for Cloud integrates with threat intelligence sources to identify known threats and IOCs. This includes using Microsoft's global threat intelligence network to identify and block known malicious IP addresses, URLs, and domains.

- *Security analytics*: Microsoft Defender for Cloud provides advanced analytics to help organizations detect security incidents and threats. This includes using behavioral analysis to identify unusual user and system behavior patterns and signature-based detection to identify known malware and other malicious code.

- *Integration with other security solutions*: Microsoft Defender for Cloud integrates with other security solutions, such as Azure Sentinel and Microsoft 365 Defender, to provide a more comprehensive view of security threats across cloud environments.

- *Security alerts and notifications*: Microsoft Defender for Cloud generates security alerts and information when a security incident is detected. This includes providing details on the nature of the threat, the severity of the threat, and recommendations for mitigating the threat.

It is a unified solution integrating multiple security services, such as Azure Security Center, Azure Defender, and Microsoft 365 Defender, to comprehensively view security threats across cloud environments. Microsoft Defender for Cloud uses advanced machine learning and behavioral analytics to detect security incidents across cloud environments. Here are some of the ways it detects security incidents:

- *Behavioral analysis*: Microsoft Defender for Cloud uses behavioral analysis to detect user and system behavior anomalies that may indicate a security threat. This includes monitoring for unusual login patterns, file access patterns, and other activities that may indicate a breach.

- *Signature-based detection*: Microsoft Defender for Cloud uses signature-based detection to identify and block known malware and malicious code. This includes using signature-based detection to identify known malware variants, such as viruses and Trojans.

- *Integration with other security solutions*: Microsoft Defender for Cloud integrates with other security solutions, such as Azure Sentinel and Microsoft 365 Defender, to provide a more comprehensive view of security threats across cloud environments.

- *Security alerts and notifications*: Microsoft Defender for Cloud generates security alerts and notifications when a security incident is detected. This includes providing details on the nature of the threat, the severity of the threat, and recommendations for mitigating the threat.

Overall, Microsoft Defender for Cloud provides robust security capabilities for detecting security incidents across cloud environments. It is designed to provide continuous monitoring and detection to help organizations avoid potential security threats.

Design Considerations

Here are some design security practices for Microsoft Defender for Cloud:

- *Enable security features*: Microsoft Defender for Cloud provides a range of security features, such as anti-malware, network security groups, and virtual network segmentation. Ensure all relevant security features are enabled and configured correctly to provide comprehensive threat protection.

- *Use RBAC*: Use RBAC to control access to Microsoft Defender for Cloud resources. This ensures that only authorized users can access sensitive information and configuration settings.

- *Regularly review security alerts*: Regularly review security alerts generated by Microsoft Defender for Cloud to identify potential security threats and take appropriate action.

- *Enable logging and monitoring*: Enable logging and monitoring to track user and system activity and detect anomalies in behavior that may indicate a security threat.

- *Regularly review security policies*: Regularly review security policies to ensure they align with current security best practices and compliance requirements.

- *Perform regular vulnerability assessments*: To identify potential security weaknesses in the cloud environment and take appropriate remediation action.

- *Follow security best practices*: Follow security best practices for securing cloud environments, such as implementing strong passwords, enabling MFA, and regularly patching and updating software and systems.

How to Enable It

Microsoft Defender for Cloud provides a range of use cases to help organizations secure their cloud environments. Some of the critical use cases include:

- *Threat detection and response*: Microsoft Defender for Cloud uses advanced analytics and threat intelligence to detect and respond to security threats in real time.

- *Vulnerability management*: Microsoft Defender for Cloud helps organizations identify and remediate vulnerabilities in their cloud environment to reduce the risk of security incidents.

- *Compliance management*: Microsoft Defender for Cloud helps organizations achieve and maintain compliance with regulatory standards such as GDPR, HIPAA, and PCI DSS by providing audit logs, compliance reports, and other features.

- *Identify and access management*: Microsoft Defender for Cloud helps organizations manage and secure user identities and access to cloud resources, including privileged access management and MFA.

- *Cloud workload protection*: Microsoft Defender for Cloud protects cloud workloads, including virtual machines, containers, and serverless functions, to help organizations protect their critical applications and services.

- *Cloud security posture management*: Microsoft Defender for Cloud provides visibility into an organization's cloud security posture and provides recommendations to improve security and reduce risk.

- *Security information and event management*: Microsoft Defender for Cloud provides centralized SIEM capabilities to help organizations identify security incidents and respond quickly to potential threats.

By providing these use cases, Microsoft Defender for Cloud helps organizations improve the security of their cloud environment and reduce the risk of security incidents and breaches.

Microsoft Defender for Cloud is designed to automatically detect security incidents and threats in your cloud environment. However, to ensure that it is detecting incidents effectively, there are some steps you can take to configure and fine-tune its settings:

1. *Enable Microsoft Defender for Cloud*: To enable Microsoft Defender for Cloud, you must have an Azure subscription and a Microsoft Defender for Cloud license. Once you have both, you can allow Microsoft to Defender for Cloud by following the instructions in the Microsoft documentation.

2. *Configure data sources*: Microsoft Defender for Cloud integrates with other cloud services, such as Azure Security Center, to gather and analyze data for potential security threats. You should ensure all relevant data sources are configured and integrated with Microsoft Defender for Cloud.

3. *Review security recommendations*: Microsoft Defender for Cloud provides security recommendations to help you identify potential security risks in your cloud environment. Review these recommendations regularly and take appropriate action to remediate any issues identified.

4. *Fine-tune policies*: Microsoft Defender for Cloud provides a range of policies that can be used to detect security incidents and threats. Fine-tune these policies to align with your organization's security requirements and risk profile.

5. *Review security alerts*: Microsoft Defender for Cloud generates alerts when a security incident or threat is detected. Review these alerts regularly and take appropriate action to mitigate the threat.

6. *Use security analytics*: Microsoft Defender for Cloud provides security analytics that can be used to identify security incidents and threats based on behavioral analysis and other advanced techniques. Use these analytics to gain insights into potential threats and take appropriate action to mitigate them.

By following these steps, you can configure Microsoft Defender for Cloud to detect security incidents and threats in your cloud environment effectively.

Key Insights of Microsoft Defender for Cloud   Microsoft Defender for Cloud is a powerful security solution that offers advanced threat protection, visibility and control, and automation and orchestration capabilities. Its integration with other Microsoft products makes it a comprehensive security solution that can help organizations stay protected against sophisticated threats. It also provides a range of capabilities, including vulnerability management and compliance assessment. Microsoft Defender for Cloud's threat detection and response is a set of capabilities that help detect, investigate, and remediate threats across your organization's cloud environments. It provides a unified view of security across your cloud resources, enabling you to quickly identify potential security incidents and take appropriate action to mitigate them.

Microsoft Defender for Endpoint

Microsoft Cloud for Endpoint (formerly known as Microsoft Defender for Endpoint) is a cloud-based endpoint security solution designed to help organizations protect their devices and endpoints from cyber threats. It combines endpoint protection, detection, investigation, and response capabilities into a single solution.

Microsoft Cloud for Endpoint provides real-time protection against malware, ransomware, and other cyber threats that can compromise endpoints. It also includes endpoint detection and response (EDR) capabilities, which enable organizations to detect and investigate suspicious activities on endpoints in real time. Microsoft Cloud for Endpoint also includes automation and orchestration capabilities, which enable organizations to respond to security incidents faster and more efficiently. Microsoft Cloud for Endpoint leverages Microsoft's threat intelligence capabilities to provide organizations with insights into emerging threats and trends. It also integrates with other Microsoft security solutions, such as Azure Sentinel and Microsoft Defender for Office 365, to provide comprehensive protection across an organization's entire digital estate. Microsoft Cloud for Endpoint helps organizations improve their endpoint security posture and reduce the risk of cyber threats and attacks on their devices and endpoints.

From a cybersecurity perspective, Microsoft Cloud for Endpoint helps organizations in several ways.

- *Endpoint protection*: Microsoft Cloud for Endpoint provides real-time protection against malware, ransomware, and other cyber threats that can compromise endpoints.

- *EDR*: Microsoft Cloud for Endpoint includes EDR capabilities, which enable organizations to detect and investigate suspicious activities on endpoints in real time.

- *Automated investigation and response*: Microsoft Cloud for Endpoint includes automation and orchestration capabilities, which enable organizations to respond to security incidents faster and more efficiently.

- *Threat intelligence*: Microsoft Cloud for Endpoint leverages Microsoft's threat intelligence capabilities to provide organizations with insights into emerging threats and trends.

- *Integration with other Microsoft security solutions*: Microsoft Cloud for Endpoint integrates with other Microsoft security solutions, such as Azure Sentinel and Microsoft Defender for Office 365, to provide comprehensive protection across an organization's entire digital estate.

- *Risk-based vulnerability management*: Microsoft Cloud for Endpoint provides risk-based vulnerability management capabilities, enabling organizations to prioritize and remediate vulnerabilities based on their potential impact.

Microsoft Cloud for Endpoint helps organizations improve their endpoint security posture and reduce the risk of cyber threats and attacks on their devices and endpoints. Microsoft Cloud for Endpoint can help organizations achieve the Detect function of the NIST CSF in several ways.

- *EDR*: This can help organizations identify potential security incidents and respond to them quickly.

- *Automated investigation and response*: Microsoft Cloud for Endpoint includes automation and orchestration capabilities to help organizations respond to security incidents faster and more efficiently. This can help organizations reduce the time and effort required to investigate and remediate incidents.

- *Threat intelligence*: Microsoft Cloud for Endpoint leverages Microsoft's threat intelligence capabilities to provide organizations with insights into emerging threats and trends. This can help organizations stay up-to-date on the latest threats and adjust their security strategies accordingly.

- *Risk-based vulnerability management*: Microsoft Cloud for Endpoint provides risk-based vulnerability management capabilities that enable organizations to prioritize and remediate vulnerabilities based on their potential impact on the organization. This can help organizations reduce the likelihood of a successful cyberattack.

- *Integration with other Microsoft security solutions*: Microsoft Cloud for Endpoint integrates with other Microsoft security solutions, such as Azure Sentinel and Microsoft Defender for Office 365, to provide comprehensive protection across an organization's entire digital estate. This can help organizations detect and respond to security incidents across multiple platforms and services.

In summary, Microsoft Cloud for Endpoint can help organizations achieve the Detect function of the NIST CSF by providing real-time detection and response capabilities, threat intelligence, risk-based vulnerability management, and integration with other Microsoft security solutions.

Design Considerations

Here are some design security practices for Microsoft Defender for Endpoint:

- *Enable automatic updates*: Ensure that automatic updates are enabled for Microsoft Defender for Endpoint to ensure the solution is always up-to-date with the latest threat intelligence and security patches.

- *Implement strong access controls*: Ensure access to Microsoft Defender for Endpoint is restricted to authorized personnel only. This includes implementing strong authentication and authorization controls, such as MFA and role-based access control.

- *Monitor for suspicious activity*: Monitor Microsoft Defender for Endpoint for any suspicious activity, such as failed login attempts or unusual network traffic patterns. This can help detect potential security incidents early.

- *Implement secure configurations*: Ensure that Microsoft Defender for Endpoint is configured securely according to industry best practices and vendor recommendations. This includes configuring policies, settings, and configurations to meet organizational security requirements.

- *Regularly review and update policies*: Regularly review and update Microsoft Defender for Endpoint policies to ensure that they are aligned with organizational security requirements and industry best practices.

- *Perform regular vulnerability assessments*: Perform regular vulnerability assessments on Microsoft Defender for Endpoint to identify potential vulnerabilities and address them before attackers can exploit them.

- *Monitor for compliance*: Monitor Microsoft Defender for Endpoint for compliance with regulatory requirements and industry standards, such as PCI DSS and ISO 27001.

- *Enable integration with other security solutions*: Integrate Microsoft Defender for Endpoint and other security solutions, such as SIEM solutions or threat intelligence platforms, to provide comprehensive protection across the organization's digital estate.

How to Enable It

Here are some everyday use cases for Microsoft Defender for Endpoint:

- *Threat detection and response*: Microsoft Defender for Endpoint includes advanced threat detection and response capabilities that enable organizations to detect and respond to cyber threats in real time. The solution uses behavioral analysis, machine learning, and other advanced techniques to identify suspicious activity on endpoints and provide detailed insights into the nature and scope of potential security incidents.

- *Endpoint protection*: Microsoft Defender for Endpoint provides various endpoint protection capabilities, including antivirus, firewall, and intrusion detection and prevention. The solution is designed to protect against various cyber threats, including malware, ransomware, and advanced persistent threats (APTs).

- *Vulnerability management*: Microsoft Defender for Endpoint includes risk-based vulnerability management capabilities that enable organizations to prioritize and remediate vulnerabilities based on their potential impact on the organization. The solution provides detailed insights into the nature and severity of vulnerabilities and recommends remediation actions based on organizational risk tolerance.

- *Compliance monitoring*: Microsoft Defender for Endpoint includes compliance monitoring capabilities that enable organizations to monitor endpoint activity for compliance with regulatory requirements and industry standards. The solution can be configured to monitor specific compliance requirements, such as PCI DSS, HIPAA, and GDPR.

- *Incident investigation and remediation*: Microsoft Defender for Endpoint includes advanced incident investigation and remediation capabilities that enable organizations to investigate and remediate security incidents quickly and efficiently. The solution provides detailed insights into the nature and scope of security incidents and recommends remediation actions based on organizational risk tolerance.

To enable Microsoft Defender for Endpoint to detect security incidents, organizations should follow these steps:

1. *Deploy Microsoft Defender for Endpoint*: Organizations should deploy Microsoft Defender for Endpoint on all endpoints, including desktops, laptops, and servers. This can be done using Microsoft Endpoint Manager or another endpoint management solution.

2. *Configure policies*: Organizations should configure Microsoft Defender for Endpoint policies to meet organizational security requirements. This includes configuring policies for antivirus, firewall, and other endpoint protection capabilities.

3. *Monitor for suspicious activity*: Organizations should monitor Microsoft Defender for Endpoint for any suspicious activity, such as failed login attempts or unusual network traffic patterns. This can be done using the Microsoft Defender Security Center.

4. *Investigate and remediate incidents*: If a security incident is detected, organizations should investigate and remediate the incident quickly and efficiently. Microsoft Defender for Endpoint includes advanced incident investigation and remediation capabilities that can help organizations identify the root cause of an incident and take appropriate remediation actions.

5. *Review and update policies*: Organizations should regularly review and update Microsoft Defender for Endpoint policies to ensure that they are aligned with organizational security requirements and industry best practices.

6. *Perform vulnerability assessments*: Organizations should regularly perform vulnerability assessments on Microsoft Defender for Endpoint to identify and address potential vulnerabilities before attackers can exploit them.

7. *Enable integration with other security solutions*: Organizations should integrate Microsoft Defender for Endpoint and other security solutions, such as SIEM solutions or threat intelligence platforms, to provide comprehensive protection across the organization's digital estate.

By following these steps, organizations can enable Microsoft Defender for Endpoint to detect security incidents quickly and efficiently and take appropriate remediation actions to protect against cyber threats.

Key Insights of Microsoft Defender for Endpoint   Microsoft Defender for Endpoint is a comprehensive security solution that protects endpoints from various security threats, including malware, phishing, ransomware, and other attacks. Deploying and using Microsoft Defender for Endpoint requires a comprehensive approach that includes endpoint protection, real-time monitoring, threat intelligence, integration with other security solutions, incident response, user education and awareness, and compliance.

Azure Policy

Azure Policy is a service in Microsoft Azure that allows organizations to create, assign, and manage policies to enforce compliance with organizational standards and regulatory requirements. It provides a centralized, scalable, and flexible way to apply governance across Azure resources, ensuring that they meet specific requirements related to security, compliance, and operational best practices.

These are the key features of Azure Policy:

- *Centralized management*: Azure Policy provides a centralized location to create, manage, and assign policies across an entire Azure environment.

- *Customizable policies*: Azure Policy allows organizations to create custom policies using various tools, including Azure Resource Manager templates, PowerShell, and the Azure Policy service.

- *Policy enforcement*: Azure Policy enforces policies by evaluating Azure resources against defined policies and taking appropriate actions, such as blocking resource creation or modifying resource configurations.

- *Automated compliance reporting*: Azure Policy provides automated compliance reporting, allowing organizations to monitor policy compliance across their entire Azure environment and generate reports for audit and compliance purposes.

- *Integration with other Azure services*: Azure Policy integrates with other Azure services, such as Azure Resource Manager, Azure Security Center, and Azure DevOps, to provide a comprehensive governance solution for Azure resources.

To implement policies aligned with the NIST CSF using Azure Policy, organizations should follow these steps:

1. *Identify policy requirements*: Organizations should identify policy requirements related to the NIST CSF, such as tagging, naming conventions, and security configurations.

2. *Create policies*: Organizations should create policies using the Azure Policy service or other tools, such as Azure Resource Manager templates or PowerShell scripts, to enforce the identified policy requirements.

3. *Assign policies*: Organizations should assign policies to Azure resources, such as resource groups or subscriptions, to ensure they are enforced across the entire Azure environment.

4. *Monitor policy compliance*: Organizations should monitor policy compliance using the Azure Policy service or other tools, such as Azure Security Center, to ensure policies are being enforced and remediate noncompliant resources.

5. *Review and update policies*: Organizations should regularly review and update policies to ensure they align with organizational security requirements and regulatory frameworks, such as the NIST CSF.

By implementing Azure Policy and enforcing policies aligned with the NIST CSF, organizations can ensure that their Azure resources meet specific security, compliance, and operational requirements, reducing the risk of cyber threats and improving overall governance across their Azure environment.

Designing Azure Policy from a cybersecurity standpoint is crucial to ensure the security of an organization's Azure resources. The following are some design best practices for Azure Policy:

- *Start with a clear policy goal*: Before creating an Azure Policy, starting with a clear goal is essential. Define the specific objective, the resources you want to apply the policy, and the rules you want to enforce.

- *Use built-in Azure Policy definitions*: Azure Policy provides pre-built policy definitions for common compliance requirements such as PCI DSS, HIPAA, and ISO 27001. Using these prebuilt policy definitions is recommended as they are regularly updated to match new compliance standards.

- *Keep policies simple*: Overcomplicated policies can lead to unintended consequences and confuse users. Keep policies simple and easy to understand.

- *Assign policies at the appropriate scope*: Assign policies in the proper scope to ensure they are applied to the correct resources. For example, a policy that applies to all resources in a subscription should be assigned to the subscription level. In contrast, a policy that applies to a specific resource group should be assigned to that resource group.

- *Use policy exemptions with caution*: Policy exemptions can be helpful, but they should be used cautiously. It is recommended to avoid exemptions if possible and only use them if necessary.

- *Test policies in a nonproduction environment*: Before implementing a policy in a production environment, testing it in a nonproduction environment is essential to ensure it works as expected.

- *Monitor policy compliance*: Azure Policy provides a compliance dashboard to monitor policy compliance. It is recommended to regularly monitor policy compliance to ensure policies are being enforced correctly.

The following are examples:

- *Enforce resource naming conventions*: Implement a policy that enforces a specific naming convention for Azure resources. For example, all virtual machines should be named VM-<BusinessUnit>-<Environment>-<SequenceNumber>.

- *Enforce encryption*: Implement a policy that ensures all storage accounts are encrypted. The procedure can require encryption keys or Azure Key Vault to manage encryption.

- *Restrict network access*: Implement a policy that restricts network access to resources. For example, a policy can restrict access to resources only from approved IP addresses or virtual networks.

- *Enforce MFA*: Implement a policy that requires MFA for Azure Active Directory users. This policy can help prevent unauthorized access to Azure resources.

- *Monitor activity logs*: Implement a policy that monitors Azure activity logs for suspicious activity. The policy can send alerts or trigger automated actions when suspicious activity is detected.

How to Enable It

Here are some use cases for Azure Policy:

- *Enforce compliance*: Organizations can use Azure Policy to enforce compliance with industry standards or regulatory requirements. For example, a policy can be created to ensure all resources are deployed in specific regions that comply with data sovereignty regulations.

- *Resource tagging*: Azure Policy can be used to enforce resource tagging. Resource tagging can be used for billing, resource management, and security purposes. For example, a policy can be created to ensure all resources are tagged with a specific owner or department.

- *Security*: Azure Policy can be used to enforce security best practices. For example, a policy can be created to ensure all resources are encrypted using a specific encryption mechanism. Policies can also be used to ensure that all resources have specific access controls configured.

- *Cost management*: Azure Policy can be used to enforce cost management best practices. For example, a policy can be created to ensure all resources are deployed in specific regions offering the lowest cost.

To enable Azure Policy, follow these steps:

1. Navigate to the Azure Policy service in the Azure Portal.

2. Click Assignments and then click "Assign policy."

3. Select the scope for the policy assignment (i.e., subscription, resource group, or resource).

4. Select the policy definition that you want to enforce.

5. Configure the policy effect (i.e., audit or deny).

6. Click Review + Create to create the policy assignment.

Azure Policy is a powerful tool for enforcing compliance, security, cost management, and resource management policies in Azure. By following best practices and enabling policies that align with organizational goals, organizations can ensure that their Azure resources are being used to maximize efficiency, compliance, and security.

Key Insights of Azure Policy   Azure Policy is a service in Microsoft Azure that enables organizations to create, assign, and manage policies to enforce compliance and governance across their Azure resources. It ensures that resources deployed in Azure comply with organizational standards, industry regulations, and government compliance requirements. Azure Policy enables administrators to define policies that govern different aspects of their Azure infrastructure, including resource types, locations, and tags. With Azure Policy, administrators can create policies that enforce security requirements, such as requiring multifactor authentication or blocking weak passwords. They can also create policies that ensure compliance with regulatory requirements, such as requiring encryption or auditing all resource changes. Policies can be created using Azure Policy's built-in definitions or custom policies.

Detection Processes (DE.DP)

Detection is a crucial component of any cybersecurity incident management process. It is the process of identifying potential security incidents, and it plays a critical role in minimizing the impact of those incidents. Effective detection processes allow organizations to detect and respond to incidents quickly, reducing the risk of data breaches, data loss, and other cyberattacks. There are various detection processes that organizations can use as part of their incident management strategy. Here are some of the most common detection processes:

- *IDSs*: An IDS is a software or hardware system that monitors network traffic for suspicious activity. The system can detect unusual patterns of traffic that may indicate an attack, such as a sudden increase in traffic or a high number of failed login attempts.

- *Log analysis*: Logs are a record of events that occur on a system or network. Log analysis involves examining these logs for unusual events or patterns of activity that may indicate a security incident. For example, log analysis can detect unauthorized access attempts or data exfiltration.

- *EDR*: EDR solutions are designed to detect and respond to endpoint threats like laptops and servers. EDR solutions can detect malicious activity, such as creating new files or modifying existing ones, that may indicate an attack.

- *Threat intelligence*: Threat intelligence involves gathering and analyzing information about potential threats to an organization. This can include information about known vulnerabilities, malware, and other threats. Threat intelligence can be used to detect and prevent security incidents proactively.

- *UBA*: UBA solutions analyze user behavior on a network to detect suspicious activity. This can include failed login attempts, attempts to access unauthorized resources, and unusual activity patterns.

Let's look at an example to understand better how detection processes work in the real world.

Suppose a financial institution has implemented an IDS to detect potential security incidents. The IDS is configured to monitor network traffic for unusual activity, such as attempts to access unauthorized resources or exfiltrate data. One day, the IDS alerts the security team to a potential security incident. The security team investigates the alert and discovers that an attacker has gained unauthorized access to a database containing sensitive customer information. The security team can respond quickly to the incident, preventing the attacker from exfiltrating any data and minimizing the impact of the incident.

In this example, the IDS detected the potential security incident, allowing the organization to respond quickly and effectively. Without the IDS, the organization may not have discovered the incident until much later, potentially allowing the attacker to exfiltrate sensitive customer data and causing significant damage to the organization.

Effective detection processes are essential for any organization's cybersecurity incident management strategy. By implementing a range of detection processes, organizations can quickly detect and respond to security incidents, minimizing the impact of those incidents and protecting sensitive data and resources.

The NIST CSFT Detect processes (DE.DP) guides how organizations can identify and quickly respond to potential cybersecurity incidents.

DE.DP has five subcategories, which are as follows:

- *DE.DP-1: Anomalies and Events*: This subcategory identifies potential cybersecurity events and anomalies that could indicate a security breach. This can be achieved by collecting and analyzing data from various sources, such as security logs, network traffic, and user activity. For example, an organization could use intrusion detection systems to monitor network traffic for unusual patterns or suspicious activities.

- *DE.DP-2: Impact Assessment*: Once a potential cybersecurity incident has been identified, the organization must assess its potential impact. This involves determining the scope and severity of the incident, the potential damage to assets, and the potential impact on business operations. This assessment will help the organization prioritize its response efforts and allocate resources accordingly.

- *DE.DP-3: Continuous Monitoring*: Continuous monitoring involves collecting and analyzing cybersecurity-related data to identify potential incidents. This subcategory focuses on the importance of regular monitoring and how it can help detect potential threats before they can cause significant harm. For example, an organization could use automated tools to continuously monitor system logs and network traffic to identify potential threats.

- *DE.DP-4: Detection Processes*: This subcategory focuses on developing and implementing specific detection processes and procedures to identify potential incidents. This involves defining the roles and responsibilities of personnel, establishing reporting procedures, and identifying the tools and technologies needed to support detection efforts. For example, an organization could establish a Security Operations Center (SOC) to monitor and respond to potential incidents.

- *DE.DP-5: Response Planning*: Once a potential incident has been identified, the organization must develop and implement a response plan. This involves defining the steps that need to be taken to contain and mitigate the incident and the roles and responsibilities of personnel involved in the response effort. This subcategory emphasizes the importance of developing and testing response plans to ensure they are effective and efficient.

The DE.DP category adds value to enterprise cybersecurity by providing a framework for detecting potential cybersecurity incidents and responding to them promptly and effectively. By following the guidance provided in the framework, organizations can develop robust detection and response capabilities, which can help minimize the impact of security breaches and protect critical assets.

In summary, the DE.DP category of the NIST CSF guides how organizations can detect potential cybersecurity incidents and respond to them promptly and effectively. By following the guidance in this category, organizations can develop robust detection and response capabilities, which can help protect against cybersecurity threats and minimize the impact of security breaches.

Azure Mapping to DE.DP

Cybersecurity detection refers to the set of activities and technologies organizations use to detect potential security threats and vulnerabilities in their digital systems and networks. The process involves identifying and analyzing IOCs, signs of malicious activity, or unauthorized access to digital resources. The detection process aims to identify threats as early as possible so that organizations can respond quickly and mitigate the potential impact of an attack.

The detection process adds significant value to an organization's cybersecurity posture by helping them to do the following:

- *Identify potential threats*: By continuously monitoring digital systems and networks, organizations can quickly identify any signs of malicious activity or unauthorized access.

- *Respond quickly to threats*: When a threat is detected, organizations can respond quickly to minimize the attack's potential impact. This may involve implementing remediation measures, such as isolating affected systems or patching vulnerabilities.

- *Enhance overall security posture*: By implementing a robust detection process, organizations can proactively identify vulnerabilities and take steps to prevent future attacks. This helps improve the organization's overall security posture, making it more resilient to cyber threats.

- *Comply with regulatory requirements*: Many regulatory frameworks, such as GDPR and HIPAA, require organizations to implement robust detection processes to protect sensitive data and personal information.

The cybersecurity detection process is critical to an organization's cybersecurity strategy. By continuously monitoring digital systems and networks, organizations can identify potential threats and respond promptly, which can help minimize the impact of an attack and enhance overall security posture.

Microsoft offers several Azure services to support detection processes in the cybersecurity domain. Here are some critical Azure services that can help organizations detect and respond to security threats:

- *Azure Security Center*: This service provides continuous monitoring and threat protection for Azure resources. It uses advanced analytics and machine learning to identify potential security threats and provides recommendations for remediation.

- *Azure Sentinel*: This cloud-native SIEM solution provides intelligent security analytics and threat intelligence across your enterprise. It uses machine learning and advanced analytics to detect real-time security threats.

- *Azure Advanced Threat Protection*: This service helps detect and investigate advanced attacks and insider threats across on-premises, cloud, and hybrid environments. It uses machine learning to analyze behavior and identify suspicious activity.

- *Azure Firewall*: This service provides network security to protect your Azure resources. It includes threat intelligence-based filtering, network traffic analytics, and intrusion detection.

- *Azure DDoS Protection*: This service provides DDoS protection for Azure resources. It includes traffic monitoring, anomaly detection, and automatic mitigation.

- *Azure Monitor*: This service provides a centralized platform for monitoring the performance and availability of Azure resources. It includes features such as log analytics, metrics analysis, and alerts.

Overall, these Azure services can help organizations implement robust detection processes that enable them to detect and respond to security threats promptly and efficiently. By leveraging these services, organizations can improve their cybersecurity posture and protect their valuable digital assets.

Here are some ways in which Azure services can map to the NIST CSF DE. DP category:

- *Continuous monitoring*: Azure Security Center monitors your Azure environment, analyzing data from various sources such as network traffic, Azure activity logs, and threat intelligence feeds to identify potential security threats.

- *Analysis*: Azure Sentinel is a cloud-native SIEM solution that provides intelligent security analytics and threat intelligence across your entire enterprise. It uses machine learning algorithms and advanced analytics to detect real-time security threats.

- *Event correlation*: Azure Sentinel can correlate events from multiple sources to identify complex security threats that other security tools may miss.

- *Threat intelligence*: Azure Sentinel integrates with Microsoft Threat Intelligence, a service that provides real-time threat intelligence and analysis to help identify potential security threats.

- *Automated response*: Azure Security Center can automatically respond to security threats by applying policies to block traffic, isolate compromised resources, and trigger alerts to security teams.

- *Incident management*: Azure Sentinel provides incident management capabilities, allowing security teams to track and investigate security incidents from a single pane of glass.

- *Reporting*: Azure Security Center provides customizable dashboards and reports that allow security teams to track compliance with security policies and identify areas that may require additional attention.

Overall, by leveraging these Azure services, organizations can implement robust detection processes that enable them to detect and respond to security threats promptly and efficiently.

Figure 7-5 depicts the subcategories of DE. DP, against the Detect module of the NIST CSF.

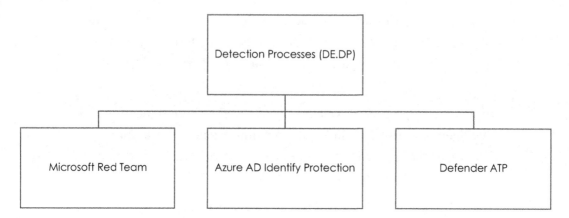

Figure 7-5. *DE.DP*

As part of the Azure cloud shared responsibility model, the NIST CSF security functions are provided in Table 7-3 with respect to DE. DP.

Table 7-3. *DE. DP Responsibility Matrix*

Category	Subcategory	Informative References	Responsibility	Customer Responsibility	Microsoft Azure Responsibility
Detection Processes (DE.DP): Detection processes and procedures are maintained and tested to ensure timely and adequate awareness of anomalous events.	DE.DP-1: Roles and responsibilities for detection are well defined to ensure accountability	NIST SP 800-53 Rev. 4 CA-2, CA-7, PM-14	Customer Responsibility	A well-defined and documented process for defining and documenting roles and responsibilities for detection is the customer's responsibility.	N/A
	DE.DP-2: Detection activities comply with all applicable requirements	NIST SP 800-53 Rev. 4 CA-2, CA-7, PM-14, SI-4	Shared	In order to meet the customer's requirements, the customer must develop a detection process.	A Third Party Assessment Organization (3PAO) developed a Security Assessment Plan as part of the Azure assessment performed by Microsoft. Microsoft has evaluated and continues to assess compliance with applicable requirements for all detection activities.

(continued)

521

Table 7-3. (*continued*)

Category	Subcategory	Informative References	Responsibility	Customer Responsibility	Microsoft Azure Responsibility
	DE.DP-3: Detection processes are tested	NIST SP 800-53 Rev. 4 CA-2, CA-7, PE-3, PM-14, SI-3, SI-4	Shared	Customers are responsible for testing their event detection processes.	Microsoft Azure reviews and updates the detection settings for anomalous events annually. Changes to the detection settings are developed, tested, and approved before entering the production environment.
	DE.DP-4: Event detection information is communicated to appropriate parties	NIST SP 800-53 Rev. 4 AU-6, CA-2, CA-7, RA-5, SI-4	Shared	The customer is responsible for informing appropriate parties internally and externally of event detection, including establishing a point of contact and escalation plan so Microsoft can provide updates.	According to federal regulatory requirements for incident management and investigation, Microsoft Azure Security has defined a set of log events and alerts in consultation with legal and corporate affairs. By using this structure, Microsoft Azure services can be identified as suspicious and misused, and abused. The service teams define event collection and notification processes to comply with applicable regulations.

DE.DP-5: Detection processes are continuously improved	NIST SP 800-53 Rev. 4, CA-2, CA-7, PL-2, RA-5, SI-4, PM-14	Shared	The customer is responsible for continuously updating detection processes and portions of the security assessment plan.	Microsoft Azure conducts a continuous review of detection settings and baseline configurations of hardware, software, and network devices every year. When there is an increase in risk, Microsoft Azure Security notifies service teams and adjusts monitoring accordingly.

Azure AD Identify Protection

Azure AD Identify Protection is a cloud-based service provided by Microsoft that helps organizations detect and respond to potential security threats that involve user identities in Azure AD. Azure AD Identify Protection provides real-time threat detection and remediation, which helps organizations protect against a wide range of identify-based attacks, including phishing, credential stuffing, and password spray attacks.

The key features of Azure AD Identify Protection include the following:

- *Risk-based Conditional Access*: Azure AD Identify Protection uses machine learning algorithms to analyze user behavior and detect anomalies that may indicate a compromised account. Based on the risk level associated with the anomaly, the service can dynamically adjust access controls to ensure that only trusted users can access sensitive resources.

- *Identify analytics*: Azure AD Identify Protection provides detailed analytics on user activity, which can help organizations identify suspicious behavior and prevent potential security threats. The service uses advanced machine learning algorithms to analyze user behavior, detect anomalies, and identify potential security risks.

- *Automated remediation*: Azure AD Identify Protection provides automated remediation capabilities, enabling organizations to respond quickly to potential security threats. For example, the service can automatically block suspicious IP addresses or force users to reset their passwords if their accounts are compromised.

- *Risk-based sign-in*: Azure AD Identify Protection provides risk-based sign-in capabilities, which can help organizations prevent unauthorized access to sensitive resources. Based on the risk level associated with the sign-in attempt, the service can prompt users for additional authentication or deny access altogether.

- *Threat intelligence*: Azure AD Identify Protection integrates with Microsoft's threat intelligence services, including Microsoft Intelligent Security Graph, which provides real-time threat intelligence to help organizations identify and respond to potential security threats.

To better understand how Azure AD Identify Protection works, let's consider an example scenario.

Suppose a user attempts to sign in to an Azure AD account using a password compromised in a data breach. Azure AD Identify Protection would detect the use of a compromised password and raise the risk level associated with the sign-in attempt. Based on the risk level, the service may prompt the user for additional authentication, such as MFA, to verify their identify.

Alternatively, suppose a user attempts to sign in to an Azure AD account from a new IP address that has not been associated with their account in the past. Azure AD Identify Protection would detect the anomalous sign-in attempt and raise the risk level associated with the activity. The service may require additional authentication or deny access based on the risk level. Here is a brief overview of how Azure AD Identify Protection works:

- *Risk detection*: Azure AD Identify Protection monitors all authentication events and user activity across your organization's Azure AD environment. It uses machine learning algorithms and threat intelligence to detect suspicious behavior and potential security risks.

- *Risk assessment*: When a potential risk is detected, Azure AD Identify Protection calculates a risk score based on various factors, such as the user's location, device, and activity history. The risk score helps determine the severity of the potential risk and the appropriate response.

- *Risk-based Conditional Access*: Azure AD Identify Protection can enforce Conditional Access policies based on the risk score. For example, if a user's risk score is high, they may be required to use MFA or be blocked from accessing certain resources.

- *Remediation recommendations*: Azure AD Identify Protection provides guidance on how to remediate potential risks, such as resetting a user's password or blocking a user's account. These recommendations are based on Microsoft's security intelligence and best practices.

- *Reporting and insights*: Azure AD Identify Protection provides detailed reporting and insights into potential risks, including the number of risky sign-in attempts, the users and devices involved, and the remediation actions are taken.

For example, let's say a user attempts to sign in to their Azure AD account from a new device in a foreign country. This activity may trigger a risk event in Azure AD Identify Protection, as it's an unusual sign-in location for the user.

Azure AD Identify Protection will calculate a risk score based on various factors, such as the user's activity history, the location of the sign-in attempt, and the device used. If the risk score is high, Azure AD Identify Protection can enforce a Conditional Access policy, such as requiring MFA for the user.

In addition, Azure AD Identify Protection will provide recommendations on how to remediate the potential risk, such as blocking the user's account or requiring a password reset. This helps organizations proactively protect their critical data and resources from unauthorized access.

Here are some examples of how Azure AD Identify Protection can map to the NIST CSF Detect function:

- *Continuous monitoring*: Azure AD Identify Protection monitors users, devices, and applications in an organization's environment for potential identify-related risks. It identifies anomalies such as sign-in attempts from unfamiliar locations, devices, or IP addresses and alerts the security team to investigate these events.

- *Alerting and reporting*: Azure AD Identify Protection provides real-time alerts and reports to security teams when suspicious activities are detected. These alerts can be customized to suit the organization's specific needs, and they can help security teams respond to potential security incidents promptly and efficiently.

- *Risk-based Conditional Access*: Azure AD Identify Protection uses risk-based Conditional Access policies to block or grant application access based on the user's risk level. This can help to prevent unauthorized access to sensitive applications and data.

- *MFA*: Azure AD Identify Protection supports MFA (MFA), which can help to prevent unauthorized access to user accounts. It can be configured to require MFA when a user attempts to access sensitive data or applications from an unfamiliar device or location.

- *Investigative capabilities*: Azure AD Identify Protection provides investigative capabilities to security teams to help them identify the root cause of security incidents. It provides a detailed audit trail of all user activities, including sign-in attempts, access requests, and application usage, which can be used to investigate security incidents and identify potential threats.

Design Considerations

Here are some security design practices for Azure AD Identify Protection:

- *Enable MFA*: MFA can significantly enhance security by requiring users to provide an additional authentication factor beyond their passwords, such as a one-time passcode or biometric factor.

- *Implement Conditional Access policies*: Azure AD Identify Protection can leverage Conditional Access policies to enforce specific access rules based on the user's risk level or location.

- *Enable risk-based policies*: Azure AD Identify Protection has built-in risk detection capabilities that can identify risky user behaviors. Administrators can configure policies to block or require additional authentication based on detected risks automatically.

- *Monitor sign-in logs*: Regular monitoring of sign-in logs can help detect and prevent unauthorized access attempts, as well as enable the identification of compromised accounts.

- *Implement just-in-time access*: Just-in-Time access allows administrators to grant temporary access to resources for a specified period, reducing the risk of unauthorized access and maintaining the least privilege.

- *Use identify governance tools*: Identify governance tools can help organizations manage access to resources by ensuring that only the appropriate users can access sensitive data.

- *Enforce password policies*: Password policies should be enforced to ensure users create strong passwords and change them regularly.

- *Implement RBAC*: RBAC can help organizations maintain the least privilege by granting users access only to the resources required to perform their job functions.

- *Regularly review and update policies*: Regularly reviewing and updating policies ensures they remain relevant and effective against emerging threats.

- *Enable Azure AD PIM*: Azure AD PIM enables organizations to manage and monitor access to privileged roles, ensuring that only authorized users can access sensitive resources.

These are just a few security design practices that can be implemented when using Azure AD Identify Protection. Organizations should also consider industry-specific regulations and compliance requirements when designing security practices.

How to Enable It

Azure AD Identify Protection provides several use cases to protect identities and detect potential security risks. The following are some of the use cases of Azure AD Identify Protection:

- *Risk-based Conditional Access*: Azure AD Identify Protection helps protect sensitive apps and data using risk-based Conditional Access policies. It can detect and block risky sign-ins based on various risk factors such as user location, device platform, IP address, etc. This helps in preventing unauthorized access to your organization's resources.

- *Fraud detection*: Azure AD Identify Protection uses machine learning algorithms to detect fraudulent activities, such as fake accounts, sign-ins from known malicious IP addresses, and brute-force attacks. This helps in preventing identify theft and credential stuffing attacks.

- *Password protection*: Azure AD Identify Protection offers password protection policies that can detect weak or compromised passwords and force users to reset them. It also helps in detecting leaked credentials and alerting administrators to act.

- *User risk policy*: Azure AD Identify Protection can analyze user behavior and detect potential risks, such as logins from unfamiliar locations or devices. Based on this analysis, it can apply user risk policies that require users to go through additional authentication steps or block access entirely.

To enable Azure AD Identify Protection, follow these steps:

1. Sign in to the Azure Portal.

2. Navigate to Azure Active Directory ➤ Identify Protection.

3. Click the Getting Started button and follow the prompts to set up Azure AD Identify Protection.

4. Once the setup is complete, you can configure policies and settings to protect your organization's identities and detect potential security risks.

To enable specific use cases, such as risk-based Conditional Access or password protection, you can configure the relevant policies within Azure AD Identify Protection. This can be done by creating a new policy and defining the conditions and actions for that policy. For example, you can create a risk-based Conditional Access policy that blocks access to certain applications if a user is signing in from a high-risk location.

In addition, Azure AD Identify Protection integrates with other Microsoft security solutions, such as Microsoft Defender for Identify and Microsoft Cloud App Security, to provide a comprehensive security solution for your organization's identities.

Key Insights of Azure Identify Protection   Azure Identify Protection is a cloud-based security service that uses Azure AD signals to detect potential security threats in real time. It helps organizations to protect their identities, applications, and data by providing insights into suspicious activities and enabling remediation actions to be taken promptly. Azure Identify Protection can help organizations to detect and respond to security incidents by providing real-time insights into potential threats and enabling remediation actions to be handled promptly.

Microsoft Defender ATP

Microsoft Defender Advanced Threat Protection (ATP) is a security platform designed to help enterprises prevent, detect, investigate, and respond to advanced threats and vulnerabilities across their network. It provides endpoint protection for Windows 10 devices, servers, and macOS. The solution leverages machine learning and behavioral analytics to detect and block known and unknown threats and helps identify suspicious behavior and potential attacks. Microsoft Defender ATP integrates with other Microsoft security solutions, such as Azure ATP and Office 365 ATP, to provide a comprehensive security solution for enterprise environments.

Here are some key benefits of Microsoft Defender ATP:

- *Advanced threat protection*: Microsoft Defender ATP uses a combination of machine learning and behavioral analytics to detect and block known and unknown threats, including malware, ransomware, and other forms of malicious software.

- *Endpoint protection*: The solution provides endpoint protection for Windows 10 devices, servers, and macOS, ensuring that all devices are protected against cyber threats.

- *Centralized management*: The solution provides a centralized management console that allows security teams to monitor and manage security alerts, incidents, and responses.

- *Real-time visibility*: Microsoft Defender ATP provides real-time visibility into security incidents and potential threats, allowing security teams to respond quickly and effectively.

- *Integration with other Microsoft security solutions*: The solution integrates with other Microsoft security solutions, such as Azure ATP and Office 365 ATP, to provide a comprehensive security solution for enterprise environments.

- *Automated investigation and response*: Microsoft Defender ATP uses automation and machine learning to investigate security incidents and respond to threats, reducing the time and resources needed for manual investigations.

- *Threat intelligence*: The solution leverages Microsoft's global threat intelligence network to provide up-to-date threat intelligence and protect against emerging threats.

- *Customizable alerts and reports*: Microsoft Defender ATP allows security teams to customize them based on their specific needs and requirements, providing greater flexibility and control over the security environment.

- *Cloud-based solution*: Microsoft Defender ATP is a cloud-based solution that can be easily deployed and managed across multiple locations and devices.

- *Easy to use*: Microsoft Defender ATP is designed to be user-friendly and intuitive, with a simple and easy-to-use interface that makes it easy for security teams to manage and monitor their security environment.

The following are some of the key elements of Microsoft Defender ATP:

- *Endpoint protection*: Microsoft Defender ATP offers advanced protection against various threats, including malware, viruses, and ransomware.

- *Behavior-based detection*: This feature uses machine learning algorithms to identify abnormal behavior on endpoints that could indicate an attack.

- *Threat intelligence*: Microsoft Defender ATP incorporates threat intelligence from various sources to provide up-to-date information about emerging threats.

- *Cloud-based management*: Microsoft Defender ATP is a cloud-based solution allowing organizations to manage and monitor their endpoint security from a centralized console.

- *Automated investigation and response*: Microsoft Defender ATP automate the investigation and remediation of security incidents, reducing the time and resources required to respond to threats.

- *Vulnerability management*: Microsoft Defender ATP includes a vulnerability management feature that helps organizations identify and remediate vulnerabilities in their endpoints.

- *Security posture dashboard*: The security posture dashboard provides a comprehensive view of an organization's security posture, highlighting areas that may require attention.

- *Integration with other Microsoft security solutions*: Microsoft Defender ATP integrates with other Microsoft security solutions, such as Azure AD Identify Protection and Microsoft Cloud App Security, to provide a comprehensive security solution for organizations.

- *Advanced hunting*: Microsoft Defender ATP includes an advanced hunting feature that allows security teams to search for threats across their endpoints using a powerful query language.

- *Threat analytics*: Microsoft Defender ATP includes threat analytics that helps security teams understand the nature and scope of threats, allowing them to take appropriate action to protect their organization.

These features make Microsoft Defender ATP a comprehensive endpoint security solution that can help organizations detect, investigate, and respond to cyber threats.

How It Works

Here's how Microsoft Defender ATP works:

- *Endpoint agents*: Microsoft Defender ATP uses lightweight agents installed on each endpoint device. These agents continuously monitor the system for any suspicious behavior, such as the execution of malicious files or the modification of critical system files.

- *Endpoint detection and response*: The agents use behavioral analysis to detect and respond to advanced threats that might have evaded traditional antivirus solutions. They analyze system activity, network traffic, and file behavior to identify suspicious patterns and IOCs.

- *Cloud-powered protection*: Microsoft Defender ATP is powered by Microsoft's cloud infrastructure, which provides global threat intelligence and machine learning models to identify and block known and emerging threats.

- *Threat analytics*: The solution provides threat analytics and insights that help security teams prioritize and investigate alerts, identify the root cause of incidents, and take corrective actions.

- *Integration with Microsoft 365*: Microsoft Defender ATP is tightly integrated with Microsoft 365, which enables it to leverage Microsoft's cloud services and applications, such as Microsoft Intune for device management and Microsoft Cloud App Security for cloud app protection.

- *Automated response*: The solution provides automated response capabilities that enable security teams to quickly isolate infected devices, block malicious processes, and remediate vulnerabilities.

Microsoft Defender ATP aligns with the NIST CSF Detect function by providing a range of capabilities that help organizations detect potential security incidents. Some of the key capabilities of Microsoft Defender ATP, which map to the NIST CSF Detect function, are as follows:

- *EDR*: Microsoft Defender ATP provides real-time visibility into endpoint activity and alerts security teams to potential threats. It uses machine learning and behavioral analytics to detect and respond to advanced threats that may go undetected by traditional antivirus solutions.

- *Threat intelligence*: Microsoft Defender ATP uses threat intelligence from Microsoft's global network of sensors to provide real-time insights into emerging threats. It also integrates with third-party threat intelligence feeds to provide additional context and insights into potential threats.

- *Automated investigation and response*: Microsoft Defender ATP includes automated investigation and response capabilities to help security teams quickly triage and respond to potential threats. It uses machine learning to identify and prioritize potential threats and can automatically contain and remediate threats as they are detected.

- *Advanced hunting*: Microsoft Defender ATP includes advanced hunting capabilities that proactively enable security teams to search for potential threats across their environment. It uses advanced queries and machine learning to identify potential threats and provides tools to help security teams investigate and respond to them.

- *Integration with other security solutions*: Microsoft Defender ATP integrates with a wide range of other security solutions, including Azure Security Center, Microsoft Cloud App Security, and Microsoft Information Protection, to provide a comprehensive security solution that covers all aspects of an organization's environment.

In summary, Microsoft Defender ATP provides a range of capabilities that align with the NIST CSF Detect function, including endpoint detection and response, threat intelligence, automated investigation and response, advanced hunting, and integration with other security solutions. These capabilities help organizations detect and respond to potential security incidents quickly and effectively, reducing the risk of data breaches and other security incidents.

Design Considerations

Here are some security design best practices for Microsoft Defender ATP:

- *Enable real-time protection*: Real-time protection ensures your devices are continuously monitored for potential threats. Enable real-time protection in Microsoft Defender ATP to detect and mitigate any potential security issues quickly.

- *Use machine learning and AI*: Microsoft Defender ATP uses advanced machine learning and AI technologies to identify potential threats and anomalous behavior. Utilize these technologies to detect and respond to threats in real time.

- *Enable cloud-based protection*: With cloud-based protection, Microsoft Defender ATP can leverage the power of the cloud to identify and mitigate potential threats quickly. Enable cloud-based protection to ensure that your devices are protected even when offline.

- *Utilize threat intelligence*: Microsoft Defender ATP utilizes threat intelligence from various sources to identify potential threats. Incorporate threat intelligence feeds into your security strategy to stay ahead of emerging threats.

- *Implement security baselines*: Implementing security baselines ensures that your devices are configured securely. Use Microsoft Defender ATP security baselines to ensure your devices are secure and compliant with industry standards.

- *Use automated response capabilities*: Microsoft Defender ATP provides automated response capabilities that allow you to respond to potential threats quickly. Utilize these capabilities to automate your incident response process and reduce the time to remediate security incidents.

- *Conduct regular security assessments*: Regular security assessments allow you to identify potential security gaps and weaknesses in your environment. Use Microsoft Defender ATP to conduct regular security assessments and ensure your environment is secure.

- *Monitor and analyze security data*: Monitoring and analyzing security data allows you to identify potential environmental threats and anomalies. Use Microsoft Defender ATP to monitor and analyze security data and quickly respond to potential threats.

- *Implement least privilege access*: Implementing least privilege access ensures that users only have access to the resources they need to do their job. Use Microsoft Defender ATP to monitor and enforce least privilege access policies to reduce the risk of security incidents.

- *Utilize MFA*: MFA adds an extra layer of security to your environment by requiring users to provide additional authentication factors. Use Microsoft Defender ATP to enforce MFA policies and reduce the risk of unauthorized access.

How to Enable It

Here are some use cases for Microsoft Defender ATP:

- *Endpoint protection*: Microsoft Defender ATP provides comprehensive protection for all endpoints across the organization, including Windows, macOS, Linux (RHEL 7.2+, CentOS Linux 7.2+, Ubuntu 16 LTS, or higher LTS, SLES 12+, Debian 9+ and Oracle Linux 7.2), and Android devices. It uses various threat intelligence sources and machine learning algorithms to detect and block known and unknown threats.

- *Threat intelligence*: Microsoft Defender ATP collects and analyzes vast amounts of threat intelligence data from various sources, such as Microsoft's cloud services, third-party security vendors, and security research communities. It uses this data to provide real-time threat intelligence updates to organizations, enabling them to defend against emerging threats proactively.

- *EDR*: Microsoft Defender ATP provides powerful EDR capabilities that enable organizations to detect and investigate threats in real-time. It uses advanced behavior-based detection techniques and machine learning algorithms to identify suspicious activities, such as fileless attacks, lateral movement, and privilege escalation.

- *Incident response*: Microsoft Defender ATP provides a centralized incident response console that enables security teams to investigate and respond to security incidents quickly and efficiently. It provides a timeline view of events and enables security teams to take remediation actions, such as isolating devices, blocking malicious files, and quarantining email messages.

To enable Microsoft Defender ATP to detect security incidents, organizations need to follow these steps:

1. *Deploy Microsoft Defender ATP*: Organizations need to deploy Microsoft Defender ATP agents on all endpoints across the organization to enable real-time threat detection and response.

2. *Configure policies*: Organizations need to configure policies to define the security posture of the endpoints. This includes defining antivirus and firewall settings, defining threat protection settings, and configuring advanced features such as exploit protection and device control.

3. *Monitor endpoints*: Organizations must monitor endpoints continuously for any suspicious activities and alerts generated by Microsoft Defender ATP.

4. *Investigate and remediate*: In a security incident, organizations must investigate the incident and take remediation actions using the incident response console provided by Microsoft Defender ATP.

Key Insights of Defender ATP   The Microsoft Defender ATP security solution provides advanced threat protection to resources in Azure, on-premises, and other cloud platforms. Your organization can use it to identify and block malicious activity, such as malware, viruses, and other malicious actions, before they can harm its assets. With Microsoft Defender ATP, you can protect your organization's IT assets across multiple environments from threats. By leveraging advanced threat detection and response capabilities, integrated security features, and customizable policies, you can improve your security posture and reduce the risk of security incidents.

Microsoft Red Team

Microsoft Red Team is a group of cybersecurity professionals hired to test and evaluate the security posture of an organization's network and systems. The goal of a red team is to simulate real-world attacks on an organization's systems and infrastructure to identify vulnerabilities and improve overall security.

The Microsoft Red Team provides several services to help organizations improve their security posture:

- *Red team assessments*: The Microsoft Red Team simulates real-world attacks against an organization's network and systems in a Red Team Assessment. The team uses various techniques, tools, and methodologies to identify and exploit vulnerabilities to gain access to sensitive data or systems. The assessment results are used to identify weaknesses in the organization's security posture and develop strategies to address them.

- *Penetration testing*: Penetration testing evaluates an organization's security by attempting to exploit vulnerabilities in its network and systems. The Microsoft Red Team provides penetration testing services to identify weaknesses in an organization's security defenses.

- *Social engineering*: Social engineering is using psychological manipulation to trick individuals into revealing sensitive information or granting access to systems or networks. The Microsoft Red Team provides social engineering services to test an organization's security awareness and identify areas for improvement.

- *Incident response*: The Microsoft Red Team provides incident response services to help organizations respond to and recover from cybersecurity incidents. The team works closely with the organization's security and IT staff to identify the source of the incident, contain the damage, and restore systems and data.

- *Training and awareness*: The Microsoft Red Team provides training and awareness services to educate employees on best practices for cybersecurity. The team provides training on password hygiene, email security, and phishing awareness.

In addition to these services, the Microsoft Red Team provides ongoing support to organizations to help them maintain a strong security posture. This includes regular security assessments, vulnerability scans, and ongoing monitoring and analysis of the organization's network and systems.

To ensure the effectiveness of its services, the Microsoft Red Team employs various tools and techniques, including custom-built tools and frameworks, open-source tools, and commercial security products. The team also works closely with other security teams within Microsoft, including the Microsoft Security Response Center, to stay up-to-date on the latest threats and vulnerabilities.

The Microsoft Red Team is a valuable resource for organizations looking to improve their security posture and protect against cyber threats. Its services help organizations identify vulnerabilities, develop strategies to address them and maintain a strong security posture over time.

Microsoft does not officially offer a Red Team service as a part of its standard products or services. However, Microsoft employs its own internal Red Team to help identify and mitigate security risks in its products and services. Additionally, Microsoft offers services and tools organizations can use to establish their own red teams. Some of these offerings include the following:

- *Microsoft 365 Defender*: Microsoft 365 Defender is a cloud-based security solution that provides a unified view of an organization's security posture. It includes multiple services that help detect and respond to security threats, such as Microsoft Defender for Endpoint, Microsoft Defender for Office 365, Microsoft Cloud App Security, and Azure Defender.

- *Azure Sentinel*: Azure Sentinel is a cloud-native SIEM solution that helps organizations collect, analyze, and act on security data from across their enterprise. It uses machine learning algorithms to detect and respond to threats in real-time and provides a centralized dashboard for monitoring security alerts.

- *Microsoft Threat Intelligence Center*: MSTIC is a team of cybersecurity experts within Microsoft that provides threat intelligence to Microsoft's own Red Team, as well as external customers. MSTIC analyzes large volumes of data to identify emerging threats and provides insights to help organizations improve their security posture.

- *Azure Security Center*: Azure Security Center is a cloud-based security management solution that provides unified visibility and control over an organization's security posture across Azure, on-premises, and other cloud environments. It provides continuous security assessments, recommendations, and advanced threat detection and response capabilities.

- *Attack Surface Analyzer*: Attack Surface Analyzer is a free tool from Microsoft that helps organizations identify security risks by analyzing changes to system configurations, files, and registry settings. It provides a detailed report of potential security issues and mitigation recommendations.

Organizations can leverage these offerings to establish their own red teams or enhance their existing red team capabilities. By using Microsoft's tools and services, organizations can more effectively identify and respond to security threats and proactively identify and mitigate security risks.

Summary

In this chapter, you read about methods to design and deploy a strategy for detect security services in line with NIST CSF's mapping of Azure services in with regard to DE.AE, DE.CM, and DE. DP.

In the next chapter of the book, you will read about designing and deploying a respond solution in alignment with the NIST CSF.

CHAPTER 8

Design and Deploy a Respond Solution

The National Institute of Standards and Technology (NIST) Cybersecurity Framework (CSF) Respond category refers to the actions taken by an organization to respond to a detected cybersecurity incident. The goal of the Respond category is to contain the impact of the incident, ensure business continuity, and prevent future incidents from occurring. Several key activities are included in the NIST CSF's Respond category, such as response planning, communications, analysis, mitigation, and improvements.

Organizations can minimize the impact of cybersecurity incidents on their business operations by following these activities. The NIST CSF provides a framework for organizations to develop and implement effective incident response capabilities.

Responding to a security incident involves preparation, identification, containment, analysis, eradication, recovery, and lessons learned. Following a well-defined incident response plan based on the NIST CSF guidelines can help organizations improve their incident response capabilities and minimize the impact of security incidents.

By the end of this chapter, you will understand the following:

- Azure respond security services

- Response Planning (RS.RP)

- Communications (RS.CO)

- Analysis (RS.AN)

- Mitigation (RS.MI)

© Puthiyavan Udayakumar 2023
P. Udayakumar, *Design and Deploy a Secure Azure Environment*,
https://doi.org/10.1007/978-1-4842-9678-3_8

Incident Response in Cybersecurity

Incident response in cybersecurity refers to managing and mitigating security incidents within an organization's information technology infrastructure. It involves detecting, analyzing, and responding to incidents to minimize the damage caused and restore normal operations as quickly as possible. The primary goal of incident response is to handle security incidents effectively and efficiently, thereby minimizing the impact on the organization's systems, data, and reputation. It involves a coordinated approach that combines people, processes, and technology to address and manage the incident.

The goal of the Respond category is to contain the impact of the incident, ensure business continuity, and prevent future incidents from occurring. Incident response in cybersecurity outlines several key activities within the Respond category, including the following:

- *Response planning*: Organizations should have a documented response plan for a cybersecurity incident. This plan should include roles and responsibilities, communication procedures, and steps for containing and mitigating the incident.

- *Communications*: It is essential to have clear and effective communication channels for reporting, managing, and resolving a cybersecurity incident. This includes internal communications among stakeholders and external communication with partners, customers, and regulatory bodies.

Throughout the incident, continuous communication is essential. Regular updates should be provided to internal stakeholders, keeping them informed about the progress of the incident response and any additional actions being taken. External stakeholders should also receive timely updates on addressing the breach and protecting their accounts.

Remember, communication during a password breach incident should prioritize transparency, accuracy, and empathy. Users and customers affected by the breach should receive clear guidance on changing passwords, monitoring accounts, and protecting their personal information.

- *Analysis*: Organizations should thoroughly analyze the incident to understand the scope, impact, and root cause. This includes collecting and preserving evidence, identifying affected systems and data, and conducting a forensic investigation.

- *Mitigation*: Once the incident has been analyzed, organizations should take steps to contain and mitigate the incident. This may include isolating affected systems, deploying patches or updates, and resetting compromised passwords.

- *Improvements*: Finally, organizations should improve their incident response capabilities based on lessons learned from the incident. This includes updating response plans, improving communication procedures, and conducting employee training and awareness programs.

By following these activities, organizations can effectively respond to cybersecurity incidents and minimize their impact on business operations.

As mentioned, responding to a security incident involves a set of actions that organizations take to minimize the damage caused by the incident, contain the impact, investigate the cause, and prevent future occurrences.

- *Preparation*: This involves developing an incident response plan and assembling a team to execute the plan. The plan should include roles, responsibilities, communication protocols, incident severity classification, and incident response procedures. The team should include members from IT, security, legal, public relations, and other relevant departments.

- *Identification*: The first step in responding to an incident is to identify that an incident has occurred. This could be through automated detection systems or by personnel reporting unusual activities or events. During a cybersecurity incident, effective communication is crucial to minimize damage, coordinate response efforts, and keep stakeholders informed. It's essential to have an incident triage process in place to assess the severity of the incident and allocate resources accordingly.

- *Containment*: Once an incident has been identified, the next step is to contain it to prevent it from spreading further. This could involve disconnecting affected systems from the network, blocking communication with external entities, or disabling user accounts.

- *Analysis*: After containing the incident, the next step is to analyze to determine the scope and impact of the incident. This involves collecting and analyzing data from affected systems, identifying the incident's root cause, and identifying any exploited vulnerabilities.

- *Eradication*: Once the analysis is complete, the next step is to eradicate the incident. This could involve removing malware, patching vulnerabilities, or restoring affected systems from backups.

- *Recovery*: After the incident has been eradicated, the next step is to recover normal operations. This could involve restoring data and systems, verifying the integrity of the restored data, and ensuring that all systems are functioning correctly.

- *Lessons learned*: The final step in the incident response process is to conduct a post-incident review to identify lessons learned and improve the incident response plan for future incidents.

Microsoft recommends a four-step process to respond to a cybersecurity incident.

1. *Assess the situation*: Assess the severity and scope of the incident, and identify affected systems and data. Determine if the incident is ongoing and, if so, contain the threat to prevent further damage.

2. *Notify stakeholders*: Notify relevant stakeholders, such as IT staff, business leaders, and customers, about the incident and the steps being taken to address it. Provide regular updates as the situation evolves.

3. *Investigate the incident*: Conduct a thorough investigation to determine the root cause, identify affected data, and assess the impact of the incident. Preserve evidence for possible legal action.

4. *Remediate and recover*: Act to remediate the incident, such as restoring data from backups, patching vulnerabilities, or implementing additional security controls. Develop a plan to monitor for other threats and vulnerabilities and ensure the incident does not happen again.

Throughout the incident response process, it is essential to document all actions taken and to continuously review and improve incident response plans to better prepare for future incidents.

Introduction to NIST Respond

The Respond function of the NIST CSF is focused on developing and implementing the appropriate actions to take when a cybersecurity incident occurs. The goal of this function is to ensure that an organization can quickly and effectively respond to a cybersecurity incident, minimize the impact of the incident, and restore normal operations as soon as possible.

The Adopt Improvements custom category focuses on improving the organization's incident response capabilities through ongoing evaluation and testing. It involves reviewing the incident response plan, identifying areas for improvement, and updating the plan based on lessons learned from past incidents.

The Respond function of the NIST CSF is essential for any organization that wants to manage cybersecurity risks effectively. By developing and implementing a comprehensive incident response plan and following the guidelines outlined in the NIST CSF, organizations can minimize the impact of a cybersecurity incident and quickly restore normal operations. Additionally, the Respond function can help organizations improve their incident response capabilities by providing a framework for ongoing evaluation and testing. Figure 8-1 shows the NIST CSF Respond module categorization.

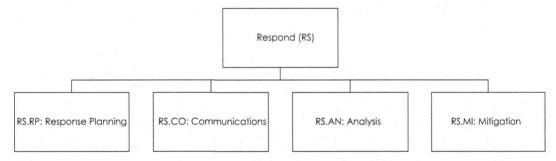

Figure 8-1. *NIST Respond categories*

By implementing the NIST CSF Respond module, organizations can achieve the following:

- *Improve incident response capabilities*: The NIST CSF provides a structured approach to incident response, allowing organizations to develop and implement an effective incident response plan. This helps organizations to improve their incident response capabilities and reduce the impact of cyberattacks.

- *Enhance communication and collaboration*: The NIST CSF response module emphasizes the importance of communication and collaboration between different teams during incident response. This helps organizations respond to incidents more effectively and minimize the impact of cyberattacks.

- *Reduce response time*: The NIST CSF response module provides a structured approach to incident response, which helps organizations to respond to incidents more quickly and effectively. This reduces the response time and minimizes the impact of cyberattacks.

- *Reduce costs*: By implementing the NIST CSF response module, organizations can reduce the costs associated with incident response. This is achieved by reducing the impact of cyberattacks and minimizing the time and resources required to respond to incidents.

- *Improve overall cybersecurity posture*: Since the NIST CSF Respond module is part of a comprehensive cybersecurity framework that helps organizations improve their overall cybersecurity posture, by implementing the Respond module, organizations can improve their incident response capabilities and reduce the risk of cyberattacks.

Value of Azure NIST CSF Respond   Adopting the NIST CSF Respond capabilities can bring numerous benefits to an organization including Improved response to security threats. The value of the NIST CSF Respond module lies in its ability to provide organizations with a structured approach to incident response. This framework helps organizations develop and implement an effective incident response plan to protect their systems and data from cyberattacks.

Response Planning (RS.RP)

RS.RP is a category in the cybersecurity world that deals with responding to unusual activities, events, or behaviors that may indicate a security breach or potential threat to an organization's systems, network, or data.

Response planning is a crucial component of any effective cybersecurity program. It helps organizations prepare for, detect, respond to, and recover from incidents that could harm their business operations, reputation, and assets.

Response planning involves several key steps, including the following:

- *Develop an incident response plan (IRP)*: An IRP is a documented plan that outlines the steps an organization will take during a cybersecurity incident. The plan should include the roles and responsibilities of key stakeholders, procedures for responding to incidents, communication protocols, and guidance for managing the incident from start to finish.

- *Define incident scenarios*: Incident scenarios are hypothetical situations that may occur and can help organizations identify potential threats and risks. Organizations should create a range of incident scenarios based on their specific business needs and risk profile. These scenarios can include cyberattacks, data breaches, insider threats, and other incidents that could impact the organization.

- *Establish incident response team (IRT)*: An IRT is a group of stakeholders responsible for managing the response to a cybersecurity incident. The team should include members from different departments and areas of expertise, such as IT, legal, human resources, and public relations. Each member should have a clearly defined role and responsibilities within the team.

- *Conduct tabletop exercises*: Tabletop exercises are simulations of potential incident scenarios and are designed to test the effectiveness of the organization's IRP and IRT. The exercises help identifies gaps and weaknesses in the plan and allow the team to practice responding to incidents in a safe, controlled environment.

- *Continuous improvement*: Response planning is an ongoing process that requires regular review and updates. Organizations should review their IRPs and incident scenarios regularly to ensure they are up-to-date and effective. The IRT should also conduct post-incident reviews to identify areas for improvement and adjust their processes accordingly.

By implementing response planning, organizations can improve their overall cybersecurity posture by doing the following:

- *Being better prepared*: Response planning helps organizations to be better prepared for potential cybersecurity incidents. By creating an IRP, defining incident scenarios, and establishing an IRT, organizations can be more proactive in their approach to incident management.

- *Reducing incident impact*: Response planning can help reduce a cybersecurity incident's impact. Organizations can quickly detect and respond to incidents by having a well-defined plan in place, reducing the time it takes to recover from the incident and minimizing the impact on business operations and assets.

- *Meeting compliance requirements*: Many compliance frameworks require organizations to have an incident response plan. Organizations can meet these requirements by implementing response planning and avoiding potential legal or regulatory consequences.

- *Enhancing stakeholder confidence*: Effective response planning can enhance stakeholder confidence in the organization's ability to manage cybersecurity incidents. Organizations can demonstrate their commitment to cybersecurity and ability to respond to incidents effectively by having a well-defined plan.

In summary, NIST CSF response planning is critical to any effective cybersecurity program. By developing an incident response plan, defining incident scenarios, establishing an IRT, conducting tabletop exercises, and continuously improving their processes, organizations can improve their overall cybersecurity posture, reduce the impact of incidents, meet compliance requirements, and enhance stakeholder confidence.

Example: NIST CSF Response Plan

Let's look at an example to help illustrate the NIST CSF response plan concept.

Suppose a large financial institution has detected a potential security breach in its network. They suspect that an attacker may have gained unauthorized access to sensitive financial data and need to respond quickly to prevent further damage.

The first step in responding to the security incident is to activate the incident response plan. This plan outlines the specific actions that the organization needs to take to contain and mitigate the breach. The response plan is a critical component of the NIST CSF, as it ensures that the organization is prepared to respond to incidents promptly and effectively.

In this example, the response plan would include the following steps:

1. *Isolate the affected system*: The first step is isolating the affected system from the network to prevent the attacker from accessing additional data. This step involves identifying the systems that have been compromised and disconnecting them from the network.

2. *Investigate the incident*: Once the affected systems have been isolated, the incident response team needs to investigate the incident to determine the extent of the breach. This step involves gathering information about the attack, such as the type of attack, the systems that have been affected, and the data that has been compromised.

3. *Notify stakeholders*: The next step is to notify stakeholders about the incident. This includes internal stakeholders, such as senior management and the board of directors, and external stakeholders, such as customers and regulators. The notification should include a description of the incident, the steps the organization is taking to respond to the incident, and any potential impact on stakeholders.

4. *Contain the breach*: Once the investigation is complete, the incident response team must contain the breach to prevent further damage. This involves identifying the root cause of the breach and taking steps to prevent the attacker from accessing any additional data.

5. *Remediate the affected systems*: The next step is to remediate the affected systems. This involves restoring the systems to a known good state and implementing security measures to prevent similar attacks in the future.

6. *Review the incident response plan*: Finally, the incident response team should review the incident response plan to identify any areas that need to be improved. This includes reviewing the response plan's effectiveness, identifying gaps in the organization's security posture, and making recommendations for future improvements.

The financial institution can effectively respond to the security incident and mitigate any potential damage by following these steps. The incident response plan is a critical component of the NIST CSF, as it ensures that the organization is prepared to respond to incidents promptly and effectively.

Azure Mapping to Response Planning (RS.RP)

Azure provides a range of cybersecurity capabilities that help organizations monitor, detect, and respond to potential security threats, including RS.RP. Microsoft has designed its services and tools to help organizations meet the NIST CSF response plan requirements. Microsoft provides various services that can assist organizations in identifying, protecting, detecting, responding to, and recovering from cybersecurity incidents.

Microsoft's services can help organizations identify their assets and dependencies, implement safeguards to ensure their assets' confidentiality, integrity, and availability; detect cybersecurity events in real time; respond to cybersecurity incidents quickly and effectively; and recover from cybersecurity incidents by restoring data and applications from backups.

The NIST CSF response plan guides organizations to develop and implement response activities during a cybersecurity incident. Azure, Microsoft's cloud computing platform, offers various services that can help organizations meet the requirements of the response plan.

Preparation

The preparation part of the response plan involves the development of policies, procedures, and other documentation to guide the response to cybersecurity incidents. Azure offers several services that can support this function, including the following:

- *Azure Policy*: This service allows organizations to create and enforce policies for their Azure resources. This can help ensure that resources are configured correctly to prevent security incidents.

- *Azure Security Center*: This unified security management solution provides visibility into the security state of resources across an organization's Azure environment. This can help organizations identify potential security issues and take action to address them.

- *Azure Monitor*: This service provides monitoring and alerting capabilities for Azure resources. This can help organizations detect and respond to security incidents promptly.

Detection and Analysis

The detection and analysis parts of the response plan involve identifying and analyzing cybersecurity events to determine whether they are actual security incidents. Azure offers several services that can support this function, including the following:

- *Azure Sentinel*: This cloud-native security information and event management (SIEM) solution provides advanced threat detection and response capabilities. It uses machine learning and other techniques to identify and prioritize security events and can help organizations investigate and remediate security incidents.

- *Azure Advanced Threat Protection*: This service helps organizations detect and investigate advanced attacks on their on-premises and cloud resources. It uses machine learning and behavioral analytics to identify suspicious activity and provides detailed reports and alerts to help organizations respond to security incidents.

- *Azure Security Center*: Besides supporting the preparation function, Azure Security Center also provides threat detection capabilities. It uses machine learning and other techniques to analyze resource configurations and activity and provides recommendations for improving security.

Containment, Eradication, and Recovery

The containment, eradication, and recovery function of the response plan involves the following:

- Containing the spread of a security incident

- Removing any malicious activity

- Restoring affected systems to a normal state

Azure offers several services that can support this function, including the following:

- *Azure Site Recovery*: This service provides disaster recovery capabilities for Azure VMs and on-premises physical servers. It can help organizations quickly recover from a security incident by restoring affected systems to their previous state.

- *Azure Backup*: This service provides backup and recovery capabilities for Azure resources, including VMs, databases, and files. It can help organizations recover data that may have been lost or corrupted due to a security incident.

- *Azure Security Center*: Besides supporting the preparation, detection, and analysis functions, Azure Security Center also provides response capabilities. It recommends containing and eradicating security incidents and provides detailed reports and alerts to help organizations recover from security incidents.

Post-Incident Activity

The post-incident activity function of the response plan involves reviewing the response to a security incident and identifying areas for improvement. Azure offers several services that can support this function, including the following:

- *Azure Monitor*: Besides supporting the preparation function, Azure Monitor also provides insights into the performance and availability of Azure resources. This can help organizations identify areas where they may need to improve their security posture.

- *Azure Security Center*: Besides supporting the preparation, detection and analysis, and containment, eradication, and recovery functions, Azure Security Center also provides ongoing security monitoring and management capabilities. It can help organizations continually improve their security posture and respond to emerging threats.

Figure 8-2 shows the categories of RS.RP.

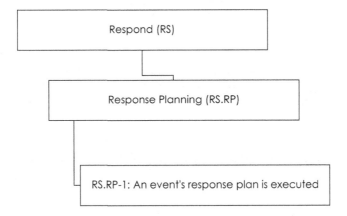

Figure 8-2. *RS.RP*

Azure provides several security capabilities that align with the NIST CSF Respond (RS) category. Azure Security Center offers incident response capabilities to help organizations investigate and respond to security incidents. It provides incident management and tracking features, allowing security teams to manage and coordinate their response efforts centrally. It also offers built-in integration with popular SIEM solutions for streamlined incident response workflows.

Figure 8-3 depicts the subcategories of mapping Azure services to the Respond module of the NIST CSF.

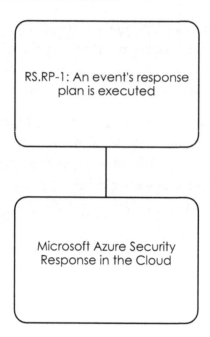

Figure 8-3. *Azure mapping of NIST CSF RS.RP*

As part of the Azure cloud shared responsibility model, the NIST CSF security functions are provided in Table 8-1 with respect to Response Planning RS.RP.

Table 8-1. RS.RP Responsibility Matrix

Category	Subcategory	Informative References	Responsibility	Customer Responsibility	Microsoft Azure Responsibility
Response Planning (RS. RP): Response processes and procedures are executed and maintained, to ensure timely response to detected cybersecurity events.	RS.RP-1: Response plan is executed during or after an event	NIST SP 800-53 Rev. 4 CP-2, CP-10, IR-4, IR-8	Customer Responsibility	After or during an incident, the customer implements incident response plans. The customer must consider any shared touchpoints included within the customer's authorization boundary and any customer applications that use the provider's infrastructure. Additionally, unless the incident is caused by Microsoft or as a result of a Microsoft action, the customer is responsible for response planning for customer applications. Microsoft will inform the customer during an incident if the customer provides Microsoft with a point of contact and an escalation plan.	N/A

Microsoft Azure Security Response in the Cloud

Security is critical for Azure customers, as they must protect their data and applications from cyberattacks and other security threats. Azure provides a range of security controls to help customers protect their data and applications, including an Incident Response control. The Incident Response control is designed to help customers detect, investigate, and respond to security incidents on the Azure cloud.

What Is Azure Security Control: Incident Response?

Azure Security Control: Incident Response is a set of tools and procedures that help customers detect and respond to security incidents on the Azure cloud. The Incident Response control is designed to help customers minimize the impact of security incidents by quickly detecting and containing them before they can cause significant damage. The control includes investigating their root cause and implementing remediation steps to prevent similar incidents from occurring in the future.

Key Features of Azure Security Control: Incident Response

The Incident Response control includes various features that help customers detect and respond to security incidents on the Azure cloud. Some of the key features are as follows:

- *Automated threat detection*: Azure's Security Center includes various tools for automatically detecting potential security threats. These tools use machine learning algorithms and behavioral analytics to detect anomalous behavior that may indicate a security threat. When a potential threat is detected, Security Center sends an alert to the customer, providing them with details of the potential threat.

- *Incident management*: The incident management feature of the Azure Security Center provides a set of tools for managing security incidents. This feature allows customers to assign incidents to specific team members, track the progress of the incident investigation, and manage the overall incident response process.

- *Remediation steps*: Once a security incident has been detected and investigated, the Incident Response control provides customers with remediation steps to help prevent similar incidents from occurring in the future. These remediation steps may include applying patches or updates to software, changing access controls, or implementing other security measures.

- *Integration with third-party tools*: The Incident Response control integrates with various third-party tools and services, allowing customers to leverage their existing security infrastructure to detect and respond to security incidents on the Azure cloud.

Benefits of Azure Security Control: Incident Response

The Incident Response control provides customers with a range of benefits, including the following:

- *Quick detection and response*: The Incident Response control helps customers quickly detect and respond to security incidents on the Azure cloud. This helps minimize the impact of security incidents and reduce the risk of data loss or system downtime.

- *Improved incident management*: The incident management feature of the Azure Security Center helps customers manage security incidents more effectively. This helps ensure that incidents are addressed promptly and efficiently, minimizing the risk of further damage.

- *Reduced risk of future incidents*: The remediation steps provided by the Incident Response control help customers reduce the risk of future security incidents. By implementing these steps, customers can address the root cause of security incidents and prevent similar incidents.

- *Integration with existing security infrastructure*: The Incident Response control integrates with various third-party tools and services, allowing customers to leverage their existing security infrastructure to detect and respond to security incidents on the Azure cloud. This helps customers maximize their investment in security infrastructure and improve their overall security posture.

Azure's cybersecurity incident response plan is designed to help customers identify and respond to security incidents that may impact their cloud-based infrastructure. The plan includes a series of steps that customers can take to detect and mitigate security incidents and a set of best practices that can help prevent future incidents.

Here are the key steps involved in the Azure cybersecurity incident response plan:

- *Preparation and planning*: The first step in any incident response plan is to prepare and plan for potential security incidents. Azure provides a range of tools and resources to help customers assess their current security posture and develop a comprehensive security plan. This includes tools for vulnerability scanning, threat detection, risk assessment, and documentation on best practices for securing Azure resources.

- *Detection*: The next step is to detect security incidents as they occur. Azure provides various tools to help customers monitor their cloud-based infrastructure for potential security threats. This includes tools for monitoring network traffic, application logs, and system activity, as well as automated alerts and notifications when potential security incidents are detected.

- *Containment*: Once a security incident has been detected, the next step is to contain the incident to prevent further damage. Azure provides various tools to help customers isolate and contain potential security threats. This includes tools for network segmentation, virtual machine isolation, access control, and the ability to disable compromised accounts and revoke access privileges.

- *Analysis and investigation*: Once the incident has been contained, the next step is to analyze and investigate the incident to determine the scope and severity of the attack. Azure provides various tools to help customers analyze and investigate potential security threats. This includes tools for forensic analysis, malware detection, threat intelligence, and access to Microsoft's global security research and incident response team.

- *Remediation and recovery*: The next step is to remediate and recover once the incident has been analyzed and investigated. Azure provides various tools to help customers remediate and recover from potential security threats. This includes tools for restoring data from backups, patching vulnerabilities, and reconfiguring compromised resources, as well as the ability to conduct post-incident reviews and implement lessons learned.

In addition to these key steps, Azure also provides a range of best practices and recommendations to help customers prevent security incidents from occurring in the first place. This includes guidance on implementing strong access controls, securing data in transit and at rest, and regularly patching and updating software and systems.

How to Build the Response Plan

Microsoft provides guidance on security incident response planning that follows a five-phase approach.

Figure 8-4 depicts the five-phase approach to security incident response planning.

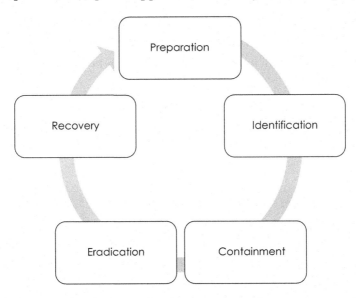

Figure 8-4. *The five-phase approach to security incident response planning*

Here is a brief overview.:

- *Preparation*: In this phase, organizations should establish an incident response team, develop an incident response plan, and perform regular training and testing.

- *Identification*: This phase involves detecting potential security incidents and gathering information to determine whether an incident has occurred.

- *Containment*: In this phase, organizations should take steps to limit the impact of the incident and prevent it from spreading.

- *Eradication*: In this phase, organizations should eliminate the cause of the incident and ensure that all affected systems are clean and secure.

- *Recovery*: This phase involves restoring normal operations and ensuring all affected systems are fully functional.

Microsoft recommends that organizations follow the NIST CSF to guide their incident response planning and execution. Additionally, Microsoft provides various tools and services to assist organizations with incident response, including the Microsoft Intelligent Security Graph, which provides threat intelligence and real-time insights into security incidents.

Table 8-2 can be used as a checklist to prepare your security operations center (SOC) to respond to cybersecurity incidents using Microsoft security incident planning.

Table 8-2. *Level 0 Incident Response Planning Phase and Tasks*

Incident Response Planning Phase	Tasks

Preparation:

Consider conducting periodic tabletop exercises of foreseeable business-impacting cyber incidents that force your organization's management to examine difficult risk-based decisions.

Microsoft recommends that organizations take the following steps to prepare for security incidents:

1. *Establish an incident response team:* Establish a dedicated team with clear roles and responsibilities. This team should include representatives from IT, security, legal, and other key areas of the organization.

2. *Develop an incident response plan:* Develop a comprehensive incident response plan that covers all phases of incident response, from detection and containment to eradication and recovery. The plan should be reviewed and updated regularly to remain relevant and effective.

3. *Perform regular training and testing:* Provide regular training to incident response team members to ensure they know their roles and responsibilities. Conduct regular tabletop exercises to test the incident response plan and identify areas for improvement.

4. *Establish communication and escalation procedures:* Establish clear communication and escalation procedures for incident response. This includes identifying key stakeholders, establishing lines of communication, and defining escalation procedures in the event of a major incident.

5. *Implement security controls:* Implement security controls, such as access controls, firewalls, and intrusion detection systems (IDSs), to prevent security incidents from occurring in the first place. Regularly review and update these controls to ensure that they remain effective.

By following these steps, organizations can prepare themselves to respond effectively to security incidents. Adequate preparation is a critical part of incident response and can help organizations minimize the impact of security incidents and quickly return to normal operations.

(continued)

Table 8-2. (*continued*)

Incident Response Planning Phase	Tasks
Establish an incident response team	Identify members, roles, and responsibilities. Establish escalation procedures.
Develop an incident response plan	Create a plan that covers all phases of incident response. Review and update the plan regularly.
Perform regular training and testing	Train incident response team members on their roles and responsibilities. Conduct tabletop exercises to test the incident response plan.

Identification:

Microsoft recommends that organizations take the following steps to identify potential security incidents:

1. *Implement monitoring tools*: Implement monitoring tools, such as IDSs, SIEM solutions, and endpoint detection and response (EDR) software, to detect and alert on potential security incidents.

2. *Establish alert thresholds*: Establish alert thresholds for the monitoring tools to detect potential incidents promptly. The thresholds should be set based on the organization's risk profile and the specific threats.

3. *Conduct regular security assessments*: Conduct regular security assessments to identify vulnerabilities and potential attack vectors. These assessments can involve vulnerability scans, penetration testing, and other techniques to identify weaknesses in the organization's security posture.

4. *Analyze system logs*: Analyze system logs and other data sources to detect unusual activity that may indicate a security incident. This can involve reviewing logs from firewalls, servers, network devices, and other sources to identify anomalies or suspicious activity.

5. *Use threat intelligence*: Use threat intelligence to identify potential threats and understand the tactics, techniques, and procedures (TTPs) used by attackers. This can involve commercial threat intelligence services, open-source intelligence (OSINT), and internal threat intelligence sources.

(*continued*)

Table 8-2. (*continued*)

Incident Response Planning Phase	Tasks
By following these steps, organizations can improve their ability to detect and identify potential security incidents. Effective identification is critical to incident response and can help organizations respond more quickly and effectively to security incidents.	
Detect potential security incidents	Use monitoring tools to detect anomalies, unusual behavior, and suspicious activity. Establish thresholds and alerts for unusual events.
Gather information	Collect and analyze data from multiple sources to determine if an incident has occurred. Use tools such as log analysis, network traffic analysis, and EDR solutions.

Containment:

Microsoft recommends that organizations take the following steps to contain security incidents:

1. *Isolate affected systems*: Immediately isolate affected systems from the network to prevent the incident from spreading. This can be done by disconnecting the affected system from the network or by configuring firewalls and access controls to restrict network traffic to and from the affected system.

2. *Implement network segmentation*: Implement network segmentation to limit the attacker's movement within the network. This involves dividing the network into smaller, isolated segments and restricting access between them. This can help prevent the attacker from moving laterally and accessing other network parts.

3. *Apply access controls*: Apply access controls to restrict access to sensitive data and systems. This can involve implementing two-factor authentication, role-based access controls, and other security measures to ensure only authorized users can access sensitive data and systems.

(*continued*)

Table 8-2. *(continued)*

Incident Response Planning Phase	Tasks

4. *Deploy endpoint protection solutions:* Deploy endpoint protection solutions, such as EDR software, to detect and block malicious activity on endpoints. These solutions can help detect and stop malware, ransomware, and other threats before they can cause damage to the system or spread to other endpoints on the network.

5. *Monitor for further activity:* Continuously monitor the affected systems and network for different activities related to the incident. This can involve using IDS, SIEM solutions, and other monitoring tools to detect and alert any further malicious activity.

By following these steps, organizations can prevent security incidents from spreading to other parts of the network or causing further damage. Effective containment is a critical part of incident response and can help minimize the impact of security incidents on the organization.

Limit the impact of the incident	Take immediate steps to isolate affected systems and prevent the incident from spreading. Implement network segmentation and access controls to restrict the attacker's movement.

Eradication:

Microsoft recommends that organizations take the following steps to eradicate security incidents:

1. *Identify and remove malware:* Identify and remove any malware that may be present on the affected system or network. This can involve using anti-malware software, manual removal techniques, or a combination of both.

2. *Patch vulnerabilities:* Patch any vulnerabilities the attacker exploited to access the system or network. This can involve applying software updates, configuring access controls, or other techniques to address the incident's root cause.

(continued)

Table 8-2. (*continued*)

Incident Response Planning Phase	Tasks

3. *Reset credentials*: Reset any compromised credentials, such as passwords or access tokens; the attacker may have used that to access the system or network. This can involve forcing users to reset their passwords, revoking access tokens, or other techniques to prevent further unauthorized access.

4. *Conduct forensic analysis*: Conduct a forensic analysis of the affected system or network to identify the scope of the incident and any other systems or data that may have been compromised. This can involve reviewing logs, analyzing memory dumps, and other techniques to identify the attacker's actions and determine the extent of the damage.

5. *Verify system integrity*: Verify the integrity of the affected system or network to ensure that all malicious code has been removed and the system is secure. This can involve running anti-malware scans, reviewing logs, and conducting other tests to ensure the system is free from further compromise.

By following these steps, organizations can eradicate security incidents and ensure their systems and data are secure. Effective eradication is a critical part of incident response and can help prevent further damage from occurring.

Eliminate the cause of the incident	Identify and remove any malware, backdoors, or other malicious software. Use antivirus software, threat hunting tools, and malware analysis techniques to identify and eradicate the threat.
Ensure all affected systems are clean and secure	Verify that all systems are free of malware and have the latest security updates and patches installed. Conduct vulnerability scans to identify and remediate any weaknesses.

(continued)

Table 8-2. (*continued*)

Incident Response Planning Phase	Tasks

Recovery:

Microsoft recommends that organizations take the following steps to recover from security incidents:

1. *Restore data and systems:* Restore any data or systems affected by the incident. This can involve using backups, snapshots, or other techniques to restore data to its pre-incident state.

2. *Monitor systems:* Monitor systems and data to ensure the incident has been fully resolved and no further damage has occurred. This can involve monitoring tools, such as IDS and SIEM solutions, to detect further incidents.

3. *Conduct post-incident review:* Conduct a post-incident review to identify the incident's root cause and any areas for improvement. This can involve reviewing logs, conducting interviews with stakeholders, and analyzing other data sources to determine the cause of the incident.

4. *Update incident response plan:* Update the incident response plan based on the lessons learned from the incident. This can involve updating procedures, adding new tools or technologies, or making other changes to improve the organization's ability to respond to future incidents.

5. *Communicate with stakeholders:* Communicate with stakeholders, such as customers, partners, and employees, to inform them of the incident and the steps taken to address it. This can involve providing regular updates, answering questions, and addressing stakeholders' concerns.

By following these steps, organizations can recover from security incidents and ensure their systems and data are secure. Effective recovery is a critical part of incident response and can help organizations minimize the impact of incidents on their business operations and reputation.

(*continued*)

Table 8-2. (*continued*)

Incident Response Planning Phase	Tasks
Restore normal operations	Gradually bring systems back online and verify that they are functioning as expected. Reconfigure any settings or policies that were changed during the incident.
Ensure all affected systems are fully functional	Conduct post-incident testing to ensure that all systems are functioning properly and there are no residual effects of the incident. Review and update incident response plan and procedures based on lessons learned.

Microsoft provides several recommendations and best practices for building a cybersecurity incident response plan. These recommendations are designed to help organizations prepare for and respond to security incidents promptly and effectively.

- *Develop an incident response plan*: The first step in building a cybersecurity incident response plan is to develop a comprehensive plan that outlines the steps to be taken during a security incident. The plan should include clear guidelines for detecting, reporting, and responding to security incidents and procedures for containing and recovering from the incident. The plan should also identify the roles and responsibilities of key stakeholders, including incident response team members, IT staff, and executive management.

- *Identify key risks and threats*: To ensure that the incident response plan is effective, it is essential to identify the key risks and threats most likely to impact the organization. This can be done through a risk assessment process, which involves identifying potential vulnerabilities and threats and evaluating each risk's likelihood and potential impact. Organizations can develop targeted incident response plans tailored to their specific needs by identifying key risks and threats.

- *Establish an incident response team*: An incident response team manages security incidents and implements the incident response plan. The team should comprise individuals with various technical and business skills, including IT staff, legal counsel, and executive management. The team should also have a designated leader responsible for coordinating the response effort and ensuring all team members work together effectively.

- *Conduct regular training and testing*: To ensure that the incident response plan is effective, it is essential to conduct regular training and testing. This helps to ensure that all team members are familiar with the incident response plan and are prepared to respond to security incidents promptly and effectively. Testing should be conducted regularly to identify any weaknesses in the plan and to ensure that the plan is updated as needed.

- *Implement security controls*: To prevent security incidents from occurring in the first place, it is essential to implement a range of security controls, such as firewalls, intrusion detection systems, and antivirus software. These controls can help detect and prevent security threats before they can cause significant damage and can also help minimize the impact of security incidents when they occur.

- *Implement monitoring and logging*: Monitoring and logging are critical components of any incident response plan. These tools help to detect security incidents in real time and can provide valuable information about the incident, including the scope and impact of the attack. By implementing monitoring and logging tools, organizations can quickly detect and respond to security incidents and use the information collected to improve their incident response plans over time.

- *Engage with third-party providers*: Finally, engaging with third-party providers, such as cloud service providers and security vendors, is essential to ensure an effective incident response plan. These providers can offer valuable expertise and resources that can help organizations detect and respond to security incidents promptly and effectively. By working closely with third-party providers, organizations can ensure that their incident response plans are up-to-date and effective and can also benefit from the latest security best practices and technologies.

A comprehensive incident response plan is critical to protecting an organization's data and infrastructure from security threats. By following these best practices and recommendations from Microsoft, organizations can develop effective incident response plans tailored to their specific needs and help minimize the impact of security incidents when they occur.

Microsoft Incident Response Plan   It provides a framework for responding to cyber incidents in a structured and effective manner. It is a preplanned set of actions and procedures that guide incident responders through the various stages of an incident, from initial detection and assessment to containment, remediation, and recovery. The plan is designed to be flexible and adaptable to different types of incidents and can be customized to fit an organization's specific needs. The Microsoft incident response plan is also designed to work with other Microsoft security solutions, such as Azure Sentinel and Microsoft Defender for Endpoint, to provide a comprehensive incident response and recovery solution. Organizations can reduce the time and impact of a security incident and minimize the risk of data loss or business disruption by having a well-defined and tested incident response plan in place.

Communications (RS.CO)

RS.CO Communications is one of the subcategories within the NIST CSF Respond category. (RS.CO also stands for Response Coordination, so here we'll be specific by using "RS.CO Communications.") It is focused on establishing communication plans and processes that enable effective communication and coordination among stakeholders during and after a cybersecurity incident. This subcategory includes the development of communication protocols, procedures, and contact lists, as well as regular communication drills and exercises to ensure that stakeholders are familiar with their roles and responsibilities in the event of a cybersecurity incident.

Effective communication during a cybersecurity incident is critical to minimizing damage and restoring normal operations as quickly as possible. Communication plans should be designed to ensure that all necessary parties are informed about the incident promptly and accurately, including incident response teams, senior management, employees, customers, partners, and relevant authorities.

The RS.CO Communications process typically involves the following key steps:

1. *Identify the communication needs*: Determine the communication needs of the project or organization. This includes identifying the target audience, the information that needs to be communicated, and the frequency of communication.

2. *Develop a communication plan*: Develop a plan for how communication will occur, including who will communicate, what will be communicated, how often, and through what channels.

3. *Implement the communication plan*: Put the communication plan into action, including ensuring all stakeholders know the plan, communicating the necessary information, and responding to any questions or concerns.

4. *Monitor and control communication*: Monitor the communication process to ensure it is effective and adjust as needed. Control the communication process to prevent misinformation or misunderstandings.

5. *Evaluate communication effectiveness*: Evaluate the effectiveness of the communication process to determine whether the communication plan achieved its objectives and identify areas for improvement.

6. *Document*: Document all communication activities to ensure stakeholders have a clear record of what was communicated and when.

7. *Monitor*: Effective communication is essential for project success and should be planned, implemented, and monitored carefully throughout the project lifecycle.

The following are the key best practices for RS.CO Communications:

- *Tailor communication to the audience*: Understand the communication needs of your target audience and tailor your messages to meet those needs. Different stakeholders may require different types or levels of communication.

- *Use a variety of communication channels*: Utilize a range of communication channels such as email, meetings, presentations, reports, and social media to reach a broader audience and ensure that messages are conveyed effectively.

- *Be clear and concise*: Communicate information in a clear, concise, and easy-to-understand manner to prevent confusion and ensure that the message is received correctly.

- *Communicate regularly*: Ensure regular communication with stakeholders to keep them informed about project progress, changes, and issues. This helps build trust and maintain stakeholder engagement.

- *Listen actively*: Actively listen to stakeholder feedback, questions, and concerns, and respond promptly and appropriately. This demonstrates that you value their input and are committed to open communication.

- *Document communication*: Keep a record of all communication activities to facilitate communication tracking, monitoring, and reporting. This helps to ensure accountability and transparency throughout the project.

- By following these best practices, you can improve the effectiveness of your communication efforts, build stronger stakeholder relationships, and increase the likelihood of project success.

By leveraging these Azure services, organizations can implement effective communication practices while maintaining the security and compliance of their communications.

Azure Mapping to Response Communication (RS.CO)

Azure Mapping to Response Communication (RS.CO) is a framework developed by Microsoft Azure to help organizations prepare for and respond to cybersecurity incidents. The framework guides how to identify, assess, and respond to security incidents in a structured and effective manner.

The RS.CO framework consists of four phases: Prepare, Detect, Respond, and Recover. Each phase includes specific steps and activities organizations can take to improve their security posture and enhance their incident response capabilities. Organizations establish the foundation for effective incident response in the Prepare phase by defining policies, procedures, and communication plans. They also conduct risk assessments and identify critical assets and data that must be protected.

Organizations implement monitoring and alerting systems in the Detect phase to detect potential security incidents. They also establish incident response teams and procedures for investigating and responding to incidents. In the Respond phase, organizations take immediate action to contain and mitigate the impact of the incident. This includes investigating the incident, identifying the root cause, and preventing further damage. In the Recover phase, organizations restore normal operations and assess the effectiveness of their incident response process. They also take steps to improve their security posture and prevent similar incidents from occurring in the future.

Effective incident response requires coordination and collaboration between internal and external stakeholders, including law enforcement agencies. Microsoft Azure's incident response process includes procedures for working with law enforcement agencies to investigate and respond to security incidents.

In this context, law enforcement agencies can provide valuable support and expertise in investigating and prosecuting cybercriminals. They can also help to identify and mitigate potential threats to public safety and critical infrastructure. The process of coordinating with law enforcement agencies typically begins during the preparation phase of the incident response process. During this phase, organizations establish communication plans and protocols for working with external stakeholders, including law enforcement agencies.

One of the key considerations in this phase is to identify the appropriate law enforcement agency to work with, based on the type and severity of the incident. For example, in the case of a cyberattack involving financial fraud, organizations may work with the Federal Bureau of Investigation (FBI) or the Secret Service. In the case of a national security threat, organizations may work with the Department of Homeland Security (DHS) or the National Security Agency (NSA).

Once the appropriate law enforcement agency has been identified, organizations can begin to establish communication channels and protocols for working with them. This typically involves identifying key points of contact within the law enforcement agency and establishing procedures for sharing information and coordinating response activities.

During the detection and response phases of the incident response process, organizations may work closely with law enforcement agencies to investigate and respond to security incidents. This may involve sharing information about the incident, providing access to systems and data for forensic analysis, and coordinating response activities to prevent further damage.

In some cases, law enforcement agencies may take the lead in investigating the incident and prosecuting the perpetrators. In these cases, organizations may need to work closely with the law enforcement agency to provide evidence and support their investigation.

It's important to note that organizations should exercise caution when working with law enforcement agencies and ensure that they comply with all legal and regulatory requirements. This includes obtaining appropriate legal counsel and ensuring that all communication and coordination with law enforcement agencies is conducted in a manner that is consistent with applicable laws and regulations.

In addition to working with law enforcement agencies, organizations may need to coordinate with other external stakeholders, such as regulators, industry associations, and other organizations that the incident may impact. This may involve sharing information about the incident, coordinating response activities, and collaborating on strategies to mitigate the impact of the incident.

Coordination with law enforcement agencies is an essential aspect of effective incident response. By establishing communication plans and protocols for working with law enforcement agencies, organizations can improve their ability to investigate and respond to security incidents and protect their critical assets and data.

Several Azure services can be used to help achieve effective communication during a cybersecurity incident. These include the following:

- *Azure Monitor*: Azure Monitor is a platform for collecting and analyzing telemetry data from Azure resources and applications. It provides real-time monitoring and alerting capabilities to help organizations quickly detect and respond to security incidents.

- *Azure Sentinel*: Azure Sentinel is a cloud-native SIEM solution that provides a centralized platform for managing security incidents. It uses machine learning and artificial intelligence (AI) to detect and respond to threats in real time.

- *Azure Security Center*: Azure Security Center is a unified security management system that provides continuous monitoring and security assessments for Azure resources. It can help organizations identify and remediate security issues and vulnerabilities quickly.

- *Azure Active Directory (AD)*: Azure AD is a cloud-based IAM solution that provides secure authentication and authorization for Azure resources and applications. It can help organizations control access to sensitive data and resources during a security incident.

- *Azure Site Recovery*: Azure Site Recovery is a disaster recovery and business continuity solution that can help organizations recover quickly from a cybersecurity incident. It provides replication and failover capabilities for Azure VMs and physical servers, ensuring that critical applications and data are available during an incident.

- *Azure Virtual Network*: Azure Virtual Network is a cloud-based networking solution that enables organizations to create isolated virtual networks in the Azure cloud. It can help organizations secure network traffic and prevent unauthorized access to sensitive data.

- *Azure ExpressRoute*: Azure ExpressRoute is a dedicated private connection between an organization's on-premises infrastructure and Azure data centers. It provides a secure and reliable connection to help organizations manage network traffic during a security incident.

These Azure services can be combined to create a comprehensive incident response plan with effective communication and stakeholder collaboration. By leveraging these services, organizations can improve their ability to detect, respond to, and recover from cybersecurity incidents, ultimately helping to protect their critical assets and data.

As part of the Azure Cloud shared responsibility model, NIST Cybersecurity Framework security functions are provided in Table 8-3 with respect to RS.CO Communications.

Table 8-3. *RS.CO Responsibility Matrix*

Category	Subcategory	Informative References	Responsibility	Customer Responsibility	Microsoft Azure Responsibility
Communications (RS.CO): Response activities are coordinated with internal and external stakeholders, as appropriate, to include external support from law enforcement agencies.	RS.CO-1: Employees know their roles and the order of operations in case of an emergency	NIST SP 800-53 Rev. 4 CP-2, CP-3, IR-3, IR-8	Shared	During incident response, customers are responsible for training personnel regarding their roles and the appropriate order of operations.	To ensure personnel knows their roles and the order of operations, Microsoft Azure personnel receive training in the incident response process.
	RS.CO-2: Events are reported by established criteria	NIST SP 800-53 Rev. 4 AU-6, IR-6, IR-8	Shared	Customers are also responsible for taking appropriate action when Microsoft Azure's security team reports an issue.	According to Microsoft Azure's event reporting criteria, business continuity and incident response managers are required to register events with internal and external stakeholders. As appropriate, Microsoft must also seek external support from law enforcement agencies.

(continued)

Table 8-3. (*continued*)

Category	Subcategory	Informative References	Responsibility	Customer Responsibility	Microsoft Azure Responsibility
	RS.CO-3: Planned sharing of information	NIST SP 800-53 Rev. 4 CA-2, CA-7, CP-2, IR-4, IR-8, PE-6, RA-5, SI-4	Shared	Reporting events to internal and external stakeholders, per established criteria, and external support to law enforcement agencies is required.	A Microsoft Azure Incident Response Plan outlines procedures for sharing information in the event of an anomaly or incident. Suppose an incident requires reporting to a government agency. In that case, the Azure Security and SIM teams support the reporting guidelines in the US CERT - Federal Incident Reporting Guidelines (`http://www.us-cert.gov/government-users/reporting-requirements.html`) according to the Azure Incident Response Plan.

	NIST SP 800-53		
RS.CO-4: Responding to stakeholders' following plans	NIST SP 800-53 Rev. 4 CP-2, IR-4, IR-8	Customer Responsibility	The customer is responsible for sharing information, as outlined in incident response plans, with internal and external stakeholders, including law enforcement agencies.	N/A
RS.CO-5: Information is shared voluntarily with external stakeholders to enhance cybersecurity situational awareness	NIST SP 800-53 Rev. 4 PM-15, SI-5	Customer Responsibility	To achieve broader cybersecurity situational awareness, customers must determine which information is shared voluntarily with internal and external stakeholders.	N/A

Communications in the Real World

Cybersecurity incident communication management is effectively communicating information about a cybersecurity incident to relevant stakeholders. This includes internal stakeholders such as employees and executives and external stakeholders such as customers, partners, and regulatory bodies.

The goal of cybersecurity incident communication management is to ensure that all relevant stakeholders are informed about the incident in a timely and accurate manner and that they are provided with clear and concise information about the nature of the incident, the potential impact on their data, and systems, and the steps being taken to mitigate the risk.

Effective communication is critical during a cybersecurity incident, as it can help reduce the incident's impact, prevent further damage, and build trust with stakeholders. On the other hand, poor communication can lead to confusion, panic, and distrust, which can exacerbate the impact of the incident and damage the reputation of the affected organization.

The following are key components of effective cybersecurity incident communication management:

- *Incident response plan*: A well-defined incident response plan is essential for effective communication management during a cybersecurity incident. The plan should outline the roles and responsibilities of each team member, the communication channels and protocols to be used, and the steps to mitigate the risk and restore systems and data.

- *Establish a communication team*: A dedicated communication team should be established to manage all aspects of communication during a cybersecurity incident. This team should include members from different IT, legal, public relations, and marketing departments. The team should be trained on the incident response plan and communication protocols.

- *Identify and prioritize stakeholders*: All stakeholders affected by the incident should be identified and prioritized based on their level of involvement and impact. Stakeholders may include employees, customers, partners, suppliers, regulators, and law enforcement agencies.

- *Clear and concise messaging*: Clear and concise messaging is critical for effective communication during a cybersecurity incident. The messaging should be tailored to each stakeholder group's specific needs and concerns and should include information about the nature and scope of the incident, the potential impact on their data and systems, and the steps being taken to mitigate the risk.

- *Timely and frequent updates*: Timely and frequent updates are essential for keeping stakeholders informed about the incident and the progress being made in mitigating the risk. Updates should be provided through multiple channels, such as email, social media, and a dedicated incident response website, to ensure all stakeholders are reached.

- *Consistent messaging*: Consistency is critical for effective communication management during a cybersecurity incident. All messaging should be consistent across all communication channels and stakeholders to avoid confusion and ensure all stakeholders receive the same information.

- *Transparency and honesty*: Transparency and honesty are essential for building trust with stakeholders during a cybersecurity incident. Organizations should be transparent about the nature and scope of the incident and honest about the steps to mitigate the risk and restore systems and data.

- *Preparedness training*: Preparedness training ensures that all team members are prepared to communicate effectively during a cybersecurity incident. Training should include crisis communication protocols, messaging templates, and best practices for communicating with stakeholders.

- *Conduct post-incident analysis*: After the incident has been resolved, a post-incident analysis should be conducted to evaluate the effectiveness of the incident response plan and communication management. Lessons learned should be documented and incorporated into future incident response plans.

In summary, effective cybersecurity incident communication management is critical for reducing the impact of a cybersecurity incident, preventing further damage, and building trust with stakeholders. This requires a well-defined incident response plan, clear and concise messaging, timely and frequent updates, consistency, transparency and honesty, and preparedness training. By following these best practices, organizations can effectively manage communication during a cybersecurity incident and minimize the damage caused.

Analysis (RS.AN)

As you know, the NIST CSF module Respond is focused on activities that address a cybersecurity incident, including detection, analysis, containment, and recovery. Practical analysis is essential to the success of these activities, as it helps to identify the incident's root cause, assess the impact, and develop an appropriate response plan. This section will discuss using Azure tools, services, and cloud security products for cybersecurity analysis as part of the Respond module of the NIST CSF.

The NIST Analysis component of the Respond module focuses on understanding the nature and scope of a cybersecurity incident, including its impact on organizational assets and operations. It involves analyzing the data collected during the Detect phase to identify the incident's cause, assess the damage's extent, and develop a response plan. To effectively use the NIST Analysis component for cybersecurity response, organizations should follow the following steps:

1. *Identify and prioritize assets*: The first step is identifying the critical assets at risk during a cybersecurity incident. These assets may include sensitive data, key systems, and infrastructure. These assets can be prioritized based on their criticality to the organization and the potential impact of an incident.

2. *Collect and analyze data*: The next step is to collect and analyze data to understand the scope and nature of the incident. This data may include logs, network traffic, system data, and other relevant information. The data can be analyzed using various tools and techniques, including machine learning and behavioral analytics, to identify patterns and anomalies that may indicate a cybersecurity incident.

3. *Determine the cause of the incident*: Once the data has been analyzed, the next step is to determine the cause of the incident. This may involve examining the systems and applications involved, as well as any relevant network activity. The goal is to identify the incident's root cause and any vulnerabilities the attacker may have exploited.

4. *Assess the impact of the incident*: The next step is to assess the impact on the organization's assets and operations. This includes understanding the extent of the damage caused by the incident and the potential impact on business operations and continuity. This information can be used to prioritize response activities and allocate resources effectively.

5. *Develop a response plan*: Finally, organizations should develop a response plan based on the analysis conducted. This plan should include the specific steps that need to be taken to contain and mitigate the incident, as well as the communication and reporting requirements. The response plan should be tested and updated regularly to ensure its effectiveness during a cybersecurity incident.

Azure Mapping to Response Communication (RS.AN)

The Respond module of the NIST CSF is focused on activities that address a cybersecurity incident, including detection, analysis, containment, and recovery. Effective analysis is crucial to the success of these activities, as it helps to identify the incident's root cause, assess the impact, and develop an appropriate response plan.

Azure provides a range of tools and services that can support cybersecurity analysis. These include the following:

- *Azure Security Center*: Azure Security Center is a unified security management system that provides a centralized view of security across all Azure resources. It can help detect and mitigate potential security risks by providing security recommendations and threat intelligence. It provides continuous monitoring and security assessments to detect and respond to potential security incidents.

- *Azure Sentinel*: Azure Sentinel is a cloud-native SIEM solution that provides real-time analysis of security data from various sources, including Azure resources, third-party products, and custom applications. It uses advanced analytics and machine learning to detect and respond to potential security incidents, including data breaches, malware infections, and other cyberattacks.

- *Azure Advanced Threat Protection (ATP)*: Azure ATP is a cloud-based security solution that provides advanced threat detection and response for on-premises resources, including Active Directory. It uses machine learning and behavioral analytics to detect potential security threats, including credential theft, lateral movement, and privilege escalation.

- *Azure DDoS Protection*: Azure DDoS Protection is This service provides advanced protection against distributed denial-of-service (DDoS) attacks. It uses a combination of network-level and application-level controls to detect and mitigate potential DDoS attacks in real-time.

- *Azure network security groups*: Azure network security groups are network security rules that control traffic flow to and from Azure resources. They can be used to filter traffic based on source and destination IP address, protocol, and port. They can also be used to enforce network segmentation to prevent the lateral movement of attackers within the network.

- *Azure Firewall*: Azure Firewall is a cloud-based firewall service that provides network-level security for Azure resources. It can be used to filter traffic based on application, network, and user identify. It also provides threat intelligence to block known malicious IP addresses and domains.

- *Azure Application Gateway*: Azure Application Gateway is a web application firewall (WAF) service that provides application-level security for web applications. It can be used to filter traffic based on HTTP headers and cookies. It also provides protection against common web application attacks, including SQL injection and cross-site scripting (XSS).

Here are some examples of how these Azure tools and services can be used for cybersecurity analysis as part of the Respond module of the NIST CSF:

- *Detection of potential security incidents*: Azure Security Center, Azure Sentinel, and Azure ATP can be used to detect potential security incidents in real time. They use advanced analytics and machine learning to analyze security data from various sources, including network traffic, logs, and endpoints. They can also provide alerts and notifications to security teams when potential security incidents are detected.

- *Conducting forensic analysis*: Azure Security Center and Azure Sentinel can be used to analyze security incidents. They can provide a complete timeline of the incident, including the source and scope of the attack. They can also provide detailed logs and telemetry data to help identify the incident's root cause.

- *Assessing the impact of the incident*: Azure Security Center and Azure Sentinel can be used to assess the impact of the incident on the organization. They can provide a complete inventory of affected resources, including virtual machines, storage accounts, and databases.

Analyzing cybersecurity incidents in Azure Cloud involves a systematic process that leverages various Azure tools and services to promptly identify and respond to incidents. The following are the key steps for analyzing cybersecurity incidents in the Azure cloud:

1. *Incident detection*: The first step in analyzing a cybersecurity incident is to detect it. Azure provides various security tools, such as Azure Security Center, Azure Sentinel, and Azure Advanced Threat Protection (ATP), which can detect security incidents automatically. These tools can help identify any unusual activities and behaviors within the Azure environment, including failed login attempts, access from unknown sources, and malicious activity.

2. *Incident classification*: Once the incident has been detected, the next step is to classify it. The incident classification helps to determine the type of incident, its severity, and the appropriate

response plan. Azure Security Center uses threat intelligence and machine learning to classify incidents based on their severity level and provides response recommendations.

3. *Incident investigation*: The next step is to investigate the incident to identify its root cause and scope. Azure Sentinel provides a centralized platform for security investigation and analysis. It uses machine learning and artificial intelligence to correlate security data from different sources, including Azure logs and third-party security solutions, to provide a comprehensive view of the incident.

4. *Incident containment*: Once the incident has been investigated, the next step is to contain it to prevent further damage. Azure Security Center provides recommendations on how to contain the incident effectively. For example, it can guide isolating compromised virtual machines or blocking suspicious IP addresses.

5. *Incident eradication*: After containing the incident, the next step is fully eradicating the threat. Azure ATP can help identify any compromised accounts or systems and provide guidance on how to remediate them. Additionally, Azure Security Center provides recommendations on how to patch systems to prevent similar incidents in the future.

6. *Incident recovery*: The final step is to recover from the incident. Azure provides various backup and disaster recovery solutions that can be used to recover data and systems affected by the incident. Azure Site Recovery can be used to replicate critical systems to another location to ensure business continuity.

Incident detection is a crucial part of any cybersecurity incident response plan. In Microsoft Azure cloud, incident detection involves using various tools and services to identify security incidents and potential threats. Azure provides several security tools and services to help organizations detect security incidents automatically. The following are some of the Azure tools and services that can be used for incident detection:

- *Azure Security Center*: Azure Security Center is a unified security management system that provides continuous monitoring and threat detection for Azure resources. It uses machine learning and advanced analytics to identify security risks and provide recommendations on remediating them. It also provides a centralized dashboard for security monitoring and reporting.

- *Azure Sentinel*: Azure Sentinel is a cloud-native SIEM system that provides real-time threat detection and response. It uses AI and machine learning to analyze large amounts of data from different sources, including Azure logs and third-party solutions, to detect threats and anomalies. It also provides automated threat response and remediation workflows.

- *Azure ATP*: Azure ATP is a cloud-based security solution that provides advanced threat detection and protection for on-premises and cloud environments. It uses machine learning and behavioral analytics to identify suspicious activities and detect advanced threats, such as APTs. It also provides automated response and remediation workflows.

- *Azure NSGs*: Azure NSGs is a security feature that provides network-level security for Azure resources. NSGs can be used to restrict inbound and outbound traffic based on source and destination IP addresses, ports, and protocols. They can also be used to create security rules to allow or deny specific types of traffic.

- *Azure Firewall*: Azure Firewall is a cloud-native firewall service that provides network-level security for Azure resources. It uses a combination of rules and policies to allow or deny traffic based on source and destination IP addresses, ports, and protocols. It also provides application-level protection for outbound traffic to prevent data exfiltration.

- *Azure DDoS Protection*: Azure DDoS Protection is a service that protects against DDoS attacks. It uses a combination of network and application-level protection to detect and mitigate DDoS attacks in real time.

Figure 8-5 shows the RS.AN categories.

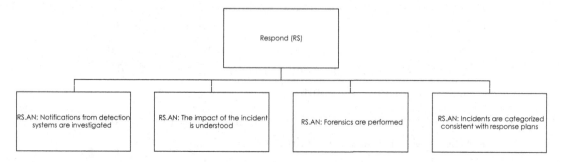

Figure 8-5. *NIST Respond subcategories analysis*

As part of the Azure Cloud shared responsibility model, the NIST CSF security functions are provided in Table 8-4 with respect to RS.AN.

Table 8-4. *RS.AN Responsibility Matrix*

Category	Subcategory	Informative References	Responsibility	Customer Responsibility	Microsoft Azure Responsibility
Analysis (RS. AN): Analysis is conducted to ensure adequate response and support recovery activities.	RS.AN-1: Notifications from detection systems are investigated	NIST SP 800-53 Rev. 4 AU-6, CA-7, IR-4, IR-5, PE-6, SI-4	Shared	A customer is responsible for analyzing and investigating detection system notifications to ensure adequate recovery support is provided.	As a monitoring device, Microsoft Azure's system components alert employees to suspicious events, aggregate logs, and generate reports. Logs are aggregated, and reports are generated. Logs from Microsoft Azure infrastructure devices are stored in a central repository, aggregating them for analysis. Upon analysis, notifications are investigated where appropriate.
	RS.AN-2: The impact of the incident is understood	NIST SP 800-53 Rev. 4 CP-2, IR-4	Shared	Microsoft Azure's security team should be informed of any incident that may negatively impact Microsoft Azure assets in any way. The customer must assess and communicate the impact of any incident.	All of Microsoft Azure's service teams contribute to analyzing the impact of an incident within the infrastructure of Microsoft Azure, according to the incident recovery plans.

(continued)

Table 8-4. (*continued*)

Category	Subcategory	Informative References	Responsibility	Customer Responsibility	Microsoft Azure Responsibility
	RS.AN-3: Forensics are performed	NIST SP 800-53 Rev. 4 AU-7, IR-4	Shared	The customer should perform forensic investigations to ensure adequate response and support for recovery activities. The results of the forensic study should inform any lessons learned.	Microsoft Azure performs necessary forensics whenever a contractually agreed upon service is implicated.
	RS.AN-4: Incidents are categorized consistent with response plans	NIST SP 800-53 Rev. 4 CP-2, IR-4, IR-5, IR-8	Customer Responsibility	To the customer's response plan, incidents must be assessed and categorized.	N/A

Microsoft Incident Response

Microsoft Incident Response from Azure Cloud is a comprehensive set of services and tools designed to help organizations quickly detect and respond to security incidents in their Azure environment. Keeping organizations secure is a constantly changing and increasingly complex task. Many companies need more resources, time, and expertise to build incident response programs.

Microsoft Incident Response offers an integrated approach to the incident response that can help you remediate a complex breach (or prevent one altogether). Over 1,000 years of combined incident response experience have enabled us to resolve attacks from ransomware criminals to nation-state threat actors worldwide. Now that the Microsoft Incident Response Retainer is generally available, Microsoft Security is expanding its incident response presence.

The Microsoft Incident Response Retainer service is a proactive and collaborative support model offered by Microsoft that helps organizations prepare for, respond to, and recover from cybersecurity incidents. It is designed to provide access to Microsoft's cybersecurity experts and resources, including Microsoft's Detection and Response Team (DART), to help customers improve their incident response capabilities.

The Incident Response Retainer service is a subscription-based service that provides access to a dedicated team of Microsoft security experts who can provide guidance and support during a cybersecurity incident. The service includes a range of benefits, such as the following:

- *Rapid response*: The Microsoft Incident Response Retainer service provides rapid response to cybersecurity incidents, with Microsoft's security experts available 24/7 to help customers assess and mitigate potential security threats.

- *Proactive support*: The Incident Response Retainer service also includes proactive support to help customers improve their incident response capabilities. Microsoft security experts work with customers to identify potential security risks and develop strategies to mitigate those risks.

- *Access to expertise*: The service provides access to Microsoft's cybersecurity experts, including the DART team, who can guide incident response best practices, threat intelligence, and remediation strategies.

589

- *Continuous improvement*: The Incident Response Retainer service also includes continuous improvement initiatives, such as tabletop exercises and incident response simulations, to help customers refine their incident response plans and capabilities.

- *Customized solutions*: Microsoft's Incident Response Retainer service is customizable to meet each organization's unique needs. Microsoft security experts work with customers to develop a customized incident response plan and provide ongoing support and guidance to ensure the plan is effective.

The Microsoft Incident Response Retainer service is designed to help organizations of all sizes and industries prepare for and respond to cybersecurity incidents. The service particularly benefits organizations with limited in-house incident response expertise or requiring additional support to manage complex security incidents.

In this section, we'll dive deeper into the details of these services and explore how they can help organizations protect their cloud resources from cyber threats.

Threat Intelligence

One of the key features of Microsoft Incident Response from Azure Cloud is threat intelligence. Azure Security Center provides threat intelligence feeds from Microsoft's global security intelligence network, enabling organizations to identify and respond to potential security threats proactively. The threat intelligence feeds provide real-time information about new and emerging threats, including malware campaigns, phishing attacks, and other malicious activities.

By leveraging threat intelligence, organizations can proactively identify and respond to security threats before they can cause damage. For example, if a new malware campaign is detected, organizations can quickly identify and block the malicious traffic, preventing it from spreading across their Azure environment.

Advanced Threat Detection

Another essential feature of Microsoft Incident Response from Azure Cloud is advanced threat detection. Azure Security Center uses machine learning algorithms to detect advanced real-time threats, including suspicious network activity, malware, and abnormal user behavior.

The machine learning algorithms analyze vast amounts of data from Azure resources to identify potential security threats. This data includes network traffic, system logs, and user activity information. By analyzing this data, machine learning algorithms can identify patterns and anomalies that may indicate a security threat.

Once a potential threat is detected, Azure Security Center can automatically alert security teams, enabling them to investigate and respond to the incident quickly. This can help organizations reduce the time required to detect and respond to security incidents, minimizing the impact of the incident on their business operations.

Security Incident and Event Management

Azure Security Center also integrates with leading SIEM solutions to provide centralized logging and monitoring for Azure resources. This enables organizations to quickly identify and respond to security incidents across their Azure environment.

By integrating Azure Security Center with their existing SIEM solution, organizations can get a unified view of their security posture across their entire IT environment. This can help them identify potential security threats and respond more effectively to security incidents.

Security Automation and Orchestration

Another essential feature of Microsoft Incident Response from Azure Cloud is security automation and orchestration. Azure Security Center includes automation and orchestration capabilities that enable organizations to automate incident response processes and reduce the time required to remediate security incidents.

For example, if a security incident is detected, Azure Security Center can automatically launch a playbook that contains predefined response steps. These response steps may include blocking the source IP address, isolating the affected resource, or deploying additional security measures to prevent the incident.

By automating incident response processes, organizations can reduce the time required to remediate security incidents, minimizing the impact of the incident on their business operations.

Incident Response Playbooks

Finally, Microsoft Incident Response from Azure Cloud provides pre-defined incident response playbooks that enable organizations to respond to common security incidents quickly. These playbooks include step-by-step instructions for detecting, investigating, and responding to security incidents.

The incident response playbooks provided by Azure Security Center are based on industry best practices and are designed to help organizations respond to security incidents more effectively. They include detailed instructions for identifying potential threats, investigating, and responding to security incidents.

Microsoft Incident Response from Azure Cloud is a robust set of services and tools that can help organizations quickly detect and respond to security incidents in their Azure environment. Organizations can better protect their cloud resources from cyber threats by leveraging threat intelligence, advanced threat detection, SIEM, security automation, and incident response playbooks.

By taking advantage of these services and tools, organizations can proactively identify and respond to potential security threats before they cause damage.

Microsoft Incident Response Services   This service provides a comprehensive and proactive approach to incident response and recovery, designed to help organizations prepare for, detect, and respond to cyber threats in real time. It leverages advanced tools and technologies such as Microsoft Azure Sentinel and Microsoft Defender for Endpoint to provide real-time threat detection and response. It also includes a team of experienced incident responders available 24/7 to provide guidance and support in the event of a security incident. Microsoft Incident Response services are also designed to work with other Microsoft security solutions, such as Azure Security Center and Microsoft 365 Defender, to provide a comprehensive security solution for your organization.

Mitigation (RS.MI)

RS.MI is an essential component of the NIST Cybersecurity Framework module Respond. It refers to the activities performed to prevent an event's expansion, mitigate its effects, and eradicate the incident. The goal of mitigation is to limit the damage and recover the system to a secure state as soon as possible.

Mitigation is a critical phase in the incident response process, involving several steps. These steps include identifying the scope of the incident, containing the impact, eliminating the cause of the incident, and implementing security measures to prevent future incidents. The mitigation phase is essential because it helps to prevent further damage to the organization's systems, data, and reputation.

The Mitigation category of the Respond module focuses on the action's organizations should take to prevent the expansion of an event, mitigate its effects, and eradicate the incident.

The Mitigation category includes the following subcategories:

- *RS.MI-1*: A response plan is executed during or after an incident.

- *RS.MI-2*: Communications are coordinated among internal stakeholders and external partners (e.g., information-sharing forums, sector coordinating councils, ISACs, regulators) as appropriate.

- *RS.MI-3*: Mitigation activities are prioritized based on their likely effectiveness in reducing risk, severity, and likelihood of harm.

- *RS.MI-4*: Continuity plans are implemented in parallel with incident response to maintain critical services, products, and operations.

- *RS.MI-5*: Technologies and processes are implemented to restore systems, services, and data affected by the incident to normal operations.

- *RS.MI-6*: System and network configurations are modified to prevent future incidents.

Let's look at these subcategories and how they can be implemented using the NIST CSF and Azure tools and services.

RS.MI-1: A response plan is executed during or after an incident

The first step in responding to a cybersecurity incident is to have a well-defined incident response plan. This plan should outline the roles and responsibilities of each incident response team member, the procedures for detecting and reporting an incident, and the steps to take to contain, eradicate, and recover from the incident.

Azure provides several tools and services to help organizations create and execute incident response plans. For example, Azure Security Center can help organizations detect and respond to threats with its advanced threat protection capabilities, which include behavioral analysis, machine learning, and security intelligence. Azure Sentinel is a cloud-native SIEM solution that can help organizations detect and investigate security incidents across their hybrid environment. Additionally, Azure Advisor provides best practices and guidance for securing Azure resources.

RS.MI-2: Communications are coordinated among internal stakeholders and external partners (e.g., information-sharing forums, sector coordinating councils, ISACs, regulators) as appropriate

Effective communication is critical during a cybersecurity incident. It's important to establish clear lines of communication among internal stakeholders, such as IT teams, legal teams, senior management, and external partners, such as law enforcement agencies, regulators, and industry groups.

Azure provides several tools and services to facilitate communication during a cybersecurity incident. For example, Azure Notification Hubs can be used to send targeted push notifications to users across various platforms, such as iOS, Android, and Windows. Azure Event Grid provides a simple way to route events between Azure services and other applications, while Azure Service Bus provides reliable message delivery between distributed applications.

RS.MI-3: Mitigation activities are prioritized based on their likely effectiveness in reducing risk, severity, and likelihood of harm

During a cybersecurity incident, it's essential to prioritize mitigation activities based on their likely effectiveness in reducing risk, severity, and likelihood of harm. This involves analyzing the incident, identifying the root cause, and implementing the appropriate mitigation measures.

Azure provides several tools and services that can help organizations prioritize mitigation activities. For example, Azure Security Center provides a prioritized list of security recommendations based on the severity of the issue, the impact on the environment, and the likelihood of exploitation. Azure Monitor provides detailed insights into the performance and health of Azure resources, while Azure Log Analytics provides advanced analytics and search capabilities for logs and metrics.

Design Considerations

There are several best practices that organizations can follow to ensure that their mitigation efforts are practical, including the following:

- *Establish a mitigation plan*: Organizations should develop a mitigation plan that outlines the steps to be taken in the event of a security incident. The plan should include containment, analysis, eradication, and recovery procedures, as well as contact information for key stakeholders.

- *Prioritize critical systems*: Organizations should prioritize critical systems and data for mitigation efforts, as attackers will likely target these systems.

- *Automate response*: Organizations should use automation tools to speed up response times and reduce the impact of an incident. This can include using automated alerts and notifications and automated response actions.

- *Monitor and analyze system logs*: Organizations should monitor and analyze system logs and network traffic to detect potential threats and anomalies. This can help to identify security incidents early and reduce the impact of an attack.

- *Conduct regular training and awareness programs*: Organizations should conduct regular training and awareness programs for employees to educate them on the risks of cybersecurity threats and the steps they can take to mitigate them.

Microsoft provides tools, services, and cloud security products to help organizations mitigate cybersecurity incidents. These include the following:

- *Azure Security Center*: Azure Security Center provides a centralized location for monitoring the security of Azure resources. It provides alerts, recommendations, and insights into the security of the organization's cloud environment. Azure Security Center can help organizations identify and mitigate security risks and implement security best practices.

- *Microsoft Defender for Endpoint*: Microsoft Defender for Endpoint is a cloud-based endpoint protection platform that provides advanced threat protection and device management capabilities. It helps organizations identify and respond to advanced threats, including malware, exploits, and vulnerabilities.

- *Azure Sentinel*: Azure Sentinel is a cloud-native SIEM solution that provides intelligent security analytics and threat intelligence across the enterprise. It can help organizations to detect and respond to cybersecurity incidents in real time.

- *Azure Backup*: Azure Backup is a cloud-based backup and recovery solution that provides automatic backups of Azure VMs, databases, and files. It can help organizations to recover data and systems in the event of a cybersecurity incident.

- *Azure Site Recovery*: Azure Site Recovery is a disaster recovery solution that replicates and recovers on-premises and cloud-based systems. It can help organizations recover systems and data in a cybersecurity incident or other disaster.

- *Azure Key Vault*: Azure Key Vault provides a secure storage location for cryptographic keys, certificates, and other secrets. It allows you to manage and control access to these secrets, which can help prevent the misuse of sensitive data.

- *Azure Firewall*: Azure Firewall is a managed firewall service that provides network-level protection for Azure resources. It uses rules and policies to allow or deny traffic to and from Azure resources and provides centralized management and monitoring.

- *Azure DDoS Protection*: Azure DDoS Protection is a service that protects against DDoS attacks. It combines network-level and application-level protection to detect and mitigate DDoS attacks.

- *Azure Virtual Network*: Azure Virtual Network provides isolation and segmentation for Azure resources. It allows you to create private networks and control traffic flow between them, which can help prevent the spread of a cybersecurity incident.

- *Azure Active Directory*: Azure Active Directory provides identify and access management for Azure resources. It allows you to control access to Azure resources based on user roles and permissions and provides multi-factor authentication and other security features to prevent unauthorized access.

Figure 8-6 shows the NIST CSF RS.MI subcategories.

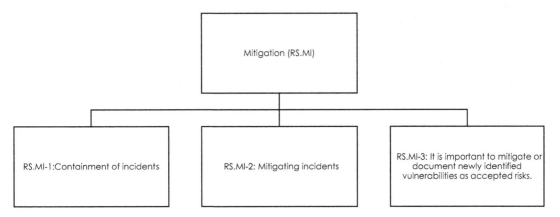

Figure 8-6. *NIST Respond subcategories of RS.MI*

As part of the Azure cloud shared responsibility model, the NIST CSF security functions are provided in Table 8-5 with respect to RS.MI.

Table 8-5. *RS.MI Responsibility Matrix*

Category	Subcategory	Informative References	Responsibility	Customer Responsibility	Microsoft Azure Responsibility
Mitigation (RS. MI): Activities are performed to prevent expansion of an event, mitigate its effects, and eradicate the incident.	RS.MI-1: Containment of incidents	NIST SP 800-53 Rev. 4 IR-4	Shared	It is the customer's responsibility to contain incidents and alert Microsoft Azure's security team if incidents threaten Microsoft Azure assets.	An incident triage team will evaluate the severity of an incident and initiate appropriate containment plans during Microsoft Azure's incident management assessment stage.
	RS.MI-2: Mitigating incidents	NIST SP 800-53 Rev. 4 IR-4	Shared	To prevent the spread of an incident, it is the customer's responsibility to mitigate all incidents.	The Microsoft Azure incident management team uses a management process for handling incidents, which includes preparation, detection, analysis, containment, eradication, recovery, and post-incidents.

RS.MI-3: It is important to mitigate or document newly identified vulnerabilities as accepted risks.	NIST SP 800-53 Rev. 4 CA-7, RA-3, RA-5 Shared	Microsoft Azure Customer Responsibility Matrix identifies the shared touch points that need to be reviewed and risk assessed by the customer. Microsoft Azure virtual machines or storage solutions customers purchase must be scanned for applications. Through the Microsoft Azure Trust Center, customers can obtain detailed information about threat-mitigating security practices implemented by them.	As part of Microsoft Azure, the Microsoft user assigned the incident ticket will resolve the incident and provide mitigation (what was done to resolve the incident). For optional correlation of incidents within the incident management system, service teams can also provide root cause information.

Azure Security Center

Azure Security Center is a cloud-native security management solution that provides unified security management and advanced threat protection across hybrid cloud workloads. It provides a centralized view of the security posture of Azure resources and helps organizations identify and address security vulnerabilities and misconfigurations promptly.

Azure Security Center monitors Azure resources and provides security recommendations based on industry-standard best practices and compliance requirements. These recommendations include suggestions for configuring security features, such as firewalls and access controls, and identifying vulnerabilities that need to be addressed.

In addition to providing security recommendations, Azure Security Center also provides advanced threat detection capabilities. It uses machine learning and analytics to detect suspicious activity and identify potential security threats, such as malware and phishing attacks. It also provides real-time threat intelligence feeds from Microsoft's global security teams and partners.

Azure Security Center provides several features that can help organizations mitigate cybersecurity incidents. These include the following:

- *Continuous monitoring*: Azure Security Center provides continuous monitoring of Azure resources, allowing organizations to detect security threats and vulnerabilities promptly.

- *Security recommendations*: Azure Security Center provides security recommendations based on industry-standard best practices and compliance requirements, helping organizations to proactively address security vulnerabilities and misconfigurations.

- *Advanced threat detection*: Azure Security Center uses machine learning and analytics to detect suspicious activity and identify potential security threats.

- *Threat intelligence*: Azure Security Center provides real-time threat intelligence feeds from Microsoft's global security teams and partners, helping organizations stay updated with the latest threats.

- *Integration with third-party security tools*: Azure Security Center can be integrated with third-party security tools and services, allowing organizations to leverage their security investments.

By using Azure Security Center, organizations can better protect their Azure resources from cybersecurity threats and mitigate the impact of security incidents.

Azure Security Center has been renamed to Microsoft Defender for Cloud, and it is now a part of Microsoft Defender for Endpoint, a cloud-native application protection platform (CNAPP).

Microsoft Defender for Cloud (formerly Azure Security Center) is a unified infrastructure security management system for protecting workloads running in Azure, on-premises, and other clouds. It provides integrated and adaptive threat protection across hybrid cloud workloads and helps organizations prevent, detect, and respond to cybersecurity threats.

Microsoft Defender for Cloud includes several key features that help organizations to protect their cloud resources:

- *Continuous monitoring*: Microsoft Defender for Cloud continuously monitors the security posture of Azure resources, providing real-time alerts and insights into potential security threats.

- *Threat protection*: Microsoft Defender for Cloud uses machine learning and artificial intelligence to detect and prevent cyberattacks, such as malware, phishing, and ransomware.

- *Compliance*: Microsoft Defender for Cloud helps organizations to comply with industry standards and regulations by providing built-in compliance assessments, policy management, and audit reports.

- *Secure score*: Microsoft Defender for Cloud provides a secure score to measure an organization's security posture and identify areas for improvement.

- *Integration*: Microsoft Defender for Cloud integrates with other Microsoft security solutions, such as Microsoft Defender for Endpoint and Microsoft Cloud App Security, to provide a comprehensive security solution for organizations.

Microsoft Defender for Cloud is a powerful tool for organizations that want to protect their cloud resources from cybersecurity threats. This platform allows organizations to gain visibility into their security posture, detect and respond to threats in real time, and ensure compliance with industry standards and regulations. Microsoft Defender for Cloud (formerly Azure Security Center) provides several capabilities that can help organizations respond to a cybersecurity incident:

- *Automated incident response*: Microsoft Defender for Cloud provides automated incident response capabilities, allowing organizations to investigate and remediate security incidents quickly. When a potential security threat is detected, Microsoft Defender for Cloud can automatically quarantine affected resources, apply security patches, and initiate other remediation actions.

- *Threat intelligence*: Microsoft Defender for Cloud uses machine learning and artificial intelligence to detect and prevent cyberattacks, such as malware, phishing, and ransomware. It also provides threat intelligence feeds that allow organizations to stay up-to-date on the latest threats and take proactive measures to prevent them.

- *Alert management*: Microsoft Defender for Cloud provides centralized alert management, allowing organizations to view and respond to security alerts from multiple sources in a single dashboard. This can help organizations to identify and respond to potential security threats quickly.

- *Integration with other security tools*: Microsoft Defender for Cloud integrates with other Microsoft security tools, such as Microsoft Defender for Endpoint and Microsoft Cloud App Security, as well as third-party security tools, allowing organizations to have a unified view of their security posture and respond to incidents more effectively.

- *Continuous monitoring and detection*: Microsoft Defender for Cloud provides continuous monitoring and detection of security threats, allowing organizations to detect and respond to incidents quickly. It also provides real-time threat intelligence and proactive guidance to help organizations prevent future incidents.

In summary, Microsoft Defender for Cloud provides organizations with the tools and capabilities to detect and respond to cybersecurity incidents quickly. By delivering automated incident response, threat intelligence, alert management, integration with other security tools, and continuous monitoring and detection, Microsoft Defender for Cloud helps organizations stay ahead of emerging threats and respond to incidents more effectively.

How to Enable It

Microsoft Defender for Cloud provides several features and tools to help you respond to and mitigate cybersecurity incidents. Here are some of the ways that you can use Microsoft Defender for Cloud to respond to and mitigate cybersecurity incidents:

- *Incident investigation*: Microsoft Defender for Cloud provides detailed information about security incidents, including alerts, recommendations, and a timeline of events. You can use this information to investigate the incident and determine the scope and impact of the attack.

- *Threat detection and response*: Microsoft Defender for Cloud uses machine learning and behavioral analysis to detect and respond to advanced threats. It can automatically block malicious activity, quarantine infected devices, and alert security teams to suspicious activity.

- *Vulnerability management*: Microsoft Defender for Cloud can help you identify and prioritize vulnerabilities in your environment and provide guidance on how to remediate them. It can also automatically deploy patches and updates to help protect your environment from known vulnerabilities.

- *Security posture assessment*: Microsoft Defender for Cloud can assess your security posture against industry standards and best practices and provide recommendations for improving your security posture.

- *Threat intelligence*: Microsoft Defender for Cloud provides intelligence feeds that can help you stay informed about the latest threats and vulnerabilities. You can use this information to proactively monitor your environment and act to protect against emerging threats.

- *Integration with other security tools*: Microsoft Defender for Cloud integrates with other Microsoft security tools and third-party security solutions, allowing you to create a comprehensive security solution that spans your entire environment.

Using these features and tools, you can leverage Microsoft Defender for Cloud to respond to and mitigate cybersecurity incidents promptly and effectively.

To use Microsoft Defender for Cloud, you must have an Azure subscription and the following prerequisites:

- *An Azure AD tenant*: You must have an Azure AD tenant to authenticate and manage access to Microsoft Defender for Cloud.

- *Subscription permissions*: You must have the necessary permissions to enable and configure Microsoft Defender for Cloud. These permissions are typically assigned to the owner or contributor role for the Azure subscription.

- *Supported operating systems*: Microsoft Defender for Cloud supports various operating systems, including Windows, Linux, and macOS. You must have supported operating systems deployed in your environment to use Microsoft Defender for Cloud.

- *Microsoft Defender for Endpoint*: If you want to use Microsoft Defender for Cloud to protect your endpoints, you must also have Microsoft Defender for Endpoint deployed in your environment.

- *Connectivity to Azure*: To use Microsoft Defender for Cloud, your environment must be able to connect to Azure services over the internet. You may need to configure network settings or firewalls to enable connectivity.

Once you have met these prerequisites, you can enable and configure Microsoft Defender for Cloud to protect your environment against cyber threats.

To enable Microsoft Defender for Cloud, follow these steps:

1. Sign in to the Azure Portal.

2. In the menu on the left, click Security Center.

3. If this is your first-time using Security Center, you must click "Get started" and choose the subscription you want to use for Security Center.

4. Once you select a subscription, click Enable Security Center.

5. After enabling the Security Center, you will be directed to the dashboard. From here, you can start exploring the different features and settings available.

Note that Microsoft Defender for Cloud is a premium feature of Azure Security Center, so you may need to upgrade to a paid plan to access this functionality. Once you have enabled Microsoft Defender for Cloud, you can start configuring its settings and integrating it with other Microsoft security tools and third-party security solutions to enhance your organization's cybersecurity posture.

Note   Microsoft Defender for Cloud is a cloud-native platform that provides unified security management and advanced threat protection across your hybrid cloud workloads, including those running in Azure, on-premises, and other clouds. It uses advanced machine learning and behavioral analytics to detect and respond to threats in real time. It provides actionable insights and remediation guidance to help you better protect your environment. Microsoft Defender for Cloud is also designed to integrate with other Microsoft security services, such as Azure Sentinel and Azure Security Center, to provide a comprehensive security solution for your organization.

Summary

In this chapter, you read about methods to design and deploy a strategy for responding to security services in line with the NIST CSF mapping of Azure services in line with RS.RP, RS.CO, RS.AN, and RS.MI.

In the book's final chapter, you will read about designing and deploying recovery solutions aligning to NIST CSF and see a list of best practices to consider in recovering and securing from day-two operations.

CHAPTER 9

Design and Deploy a Recovery Solution

NIST cybersecurity incident recovery guidelines provide a framework for organizations to prepare, detect, respond to, and recover from cybersecurity incidents. The policies are designed to be flexible and adaptable to various organizations, regardless of size or industry. They provide a structured approach to incident response and recovery that can help organizations effectively manage cybersecurity incidents and minimize the impact of these incidents on their operations and reputation.

Microsoft offers several cybersecurity incident recovery solutions and tools that organizations can use to detect, respond to, and recover from cybersecurity incidents. Some of the essential Microsoft cybersecurity incident recovery tools and solutions are Microsoft Defender for Endpoint, Microsoft 365 Defender, Azure Sentinel, Azure Backup, and Azure Site Recovery.

By the end of this chapter, you will understand the following:

- NIST recovery
- Azure Recovery services mapping
- Azure Backup
- Azure Site Recovery

Cybersecurity Incident Recovery

Cloud recovery solutions offer several advantages over traditional on-premises recovery options. For example, they typically provide greater scalability, flexibility, and cost-effectiveness. In addition, cloud-based solutions can be accessed from anywhere, which is particularly useful in a physical disaster or outage that prevents access to on-premises resources.

© Puthiyavan Udayakumar 2023
P. Udayakumar, *Design and Deploy a Secure Azure Environment*,
https://doi.org/10.1007/978-1-4842-9678-3_9

Furthermore, cloud-based recovery solutions can provide additional security and protection against cyberattacks. By storing data in multiple locations and utilizing advanced encryption and access controls, cloud providers can help to safeguard against data loss and unauthorized access. Additionally, many cloud providers offer built-in tools for monitoring and responding to security threats, which can help organizations to identify and mitigate cyberattacks quickly.

Building a recovery solution from a cybersecurity incident involves systematically preparing, responding, and restoring systems and data. Here are some critical steps to consider:

- *Incident response planning*: Develop a comprehensive incident response plan that outlines the steps to be taken during and after a cybersecurity incident. This plan should define roles and responsibilities, establish communication protocols, and include predefined containment, investigation, and recovery procedures.

- *Backup and recovery strategy*: Implement a robust backup strategy to back up critical systems and data regularly. Determine the frequency of backups based on the importance and volatility of the data. Consider using a combination of local and remote backups, including cloud-based backup solutions, for added redundancy and accessibility.

- *Segmentation and isolation*: Implement network segmentation to isolate critical systems and sensitive data from the rest of the network. This helps prevent lateral movement by attackers and limits the impact of a breach. By dividing the network into smaller segments, you can control access and contain the incident more effectively.

- *Monitoring and detection*: Deploy security monitoring tools and solutions to detect and alert you of potential security breaches or suspicious activities. This includes intrusion detection and prevention systems (IDPs), security information and event management (SIEM) systems, and endpoint detection and response (EDR) solutions. Continuous monitoring helps identify incidents early and allows for a prompt response.

- *Incident containment and investigation*: In the event of a cybersecurity incident, isolate affected systems to prevent further damage or unauthorized access. Engage cybersecurity experts or incident response teams to investigate the incident, identify the cause, and determine the extent of the breach. Collect relevant evidence for legal and forensic purposes.

- *Recovery and remediation*: Based on the investigation findings, develop a plan to restore affected systems and data. This may involve rebuilding compromised systems, applying patches and updates, and removing malware or unauthorized access. Consider leveraging cloud-based recovery solutions to expedite restoration and ensure business continuity.

- *Testing and validation*: Regularly test and validate the effectiveness of your recovery solution through tabletop exercises and simulated incident scenarios. Identify any gaps or weaknesses in the recovery process and make necessary improvements. This proactive approach helps ensure that your recovery solution is reliable and can effectively restore operations during a real incident.

- *Continuous improvement*: Cybersecurity threats are constantly evolving, so staying updated on emerging risks and new mitigation techniques is crucial. Regularly review and update your recovery solution to align with the evolving threat landscape. Engage in industry forums, attend conferences, and leverage the expertise of cybersecurity professionals to enhance your recovery capabilities.

Introduction to NIST Recovery

The NIST CSF Recovery module is one of the five functions that guide organizations to improve their cybersecurity posture and effectively respond to security incidents. The Recovery module focuses on developing and implementing strategies to recover from cybersecurity incidents, including restoring systems, data, and business operations. The Recovery module is essential for organizations to ensure business continuity, reduce the impact of security incidents, and restore normal operations as quickly as possible.

The NIST CSF Recovery Module is divided into three categories: Recovery Planning, Improvements, and Communications. Here's a breakdown of each category:

- *Recovery Planning*: The Recovery Planning category involves developing and implementing strategies and procedures to recover from security incidents. It includes the following subcategories:

  - *Recovery Planning*: Developing and implementing plans to restore systems, applications, and data in the event of a security incident. This includes identifying critical assets and prioritizing their recovery.

  - *Recovery Coordination*: Coordinating recovery efforts among various teams and stakeholders within the organization. This involves establishing clear lines of communication and roles and responsibilities for incident response.

- *Communications and Information Sharing*: This includes establishing procedures for communicating with internal and external stakeholders during and after a security incident. This includes sharing information about the incident, its impact, and the organization's response efforts.

  - *Improvements*: The Improvements category involves implementing processes to improve recovery capabilities over time. It includes the following subcategories:

  - *Improvements*: Conduct regular assessments of recovery capabilities and identify areas for improvement. This involves analyzing the effectiveness of recovery plans, procedures, and processes and making necessary adjustments.

  - *Lessons Learned*: Conduct post-incident reviews to identify areas for improvement and incorporate those lessons into recovery planning and procedures. This includes identifying the incident's root cause and making necessary changes to prevent similar incidents from occurring in the future.

- *Coordination Among Entities*: Coordinating with external entities, such as industry groups, government agencies, and other organizations, to share information and best practices for recovery planning and processes.

- *Communications*: The Communications category involves establishing clear lines of communication with internal and external stakeholders during and after a security incident. It includes the following subcategories:

  - *Public Relations and Reputation*: Establishing procedures for managing public relations and reputational damage in the event of a security incident. This includes communicating with customers, partners, and the media about the incident and the organization's response efforts.

  - *Risk Management*: Assessing the impact of security incidents on the organization's overall risk profile and making necessary adjustments to risk management strategies.

  - *Information Sharing*: Establishing procedures for sharing information about security incidents with internal and external stakeholders. This includes sharing information about the incident, its impact, and the organization's response efforts.

Example: Data Breach

A real-world example of the NIST CSF Recovery module in action is the Equifax data breach in 2017. The breach affected more than 143 million people and exposed sensitive personal and financial information, including Social Security numbers, birth dates, and addresses. Equifax responded to the breach by following the NIST CSF Recovery module, which helped them recover from the incident and minimize the impact on their business.

Specifically, Equifax developed and implemented a recovery plan that prioritized restoring critical systems and data. They also established clear lines of communication with internal and external stakeholders, including customers, partners, and regulatory agencies. Equifax conducted post-incident reviews to identify areas for improvement and made necessary changes to their recovery planning and processes.

Additionally, Equifax improved its recovery capabilities by conducting regular assessments and incorporating lessons learned into its recovery planning and procedures. They also coordinated with external entities, such as industry groups and government agencies, to share information and best practices for recovery planning and processes.

Considering recovery options is crucial for organizations for several reasons:

- *Minimize downtime*: Cybersecurity incidents can cause significant disruptions to business operations, leading to downtime that can result in financial losses and damage to reputation. Organizations can minimize downtime and quickly restore their systems and services by having recovery options in place, enabling them to resume normal operations more rapidly.

- *Business continuity*: Recovery options ensure the continuity of critical business functions and services. They allow organizations to maintain essential operations, serve customers, and meet their obligations even in the face of a cybersecurity incident. This helps prevent long-term disruptions and ensures that the organization can operate smoothly.

- *Mitigate financial losses*: The financial impact of cybersecurity incidents can be substantial. Recovery options help organizations reduce financial losses by enabling them to recover data, systems, and services efficiently. This minimizes the impact on revenue, customer trust, and potential legal liabilities associated with the incident.

- *Protect data and intellectual property*: Data is a valuable asset for organizations, and cybersecurity incidents can result in data loss, theft, or unauthorized access. Recovery options, such as data backups and restoration processes, ensure that organizations can recover their data, protecting sensitive information and intellectual property from being permanently compromised or lost.

- *Maintain customer trust*: Cybersecurity incidents can erode customer trust and loyalty. By demonstrating a robust recovery capability, organizations can reassure customers that they take security seriously and can recover from incidents. This helps maintain customer confidence and protects the organization's reputation in the long run.

- *Regulatory compliance*: Many industries have specific regulatory requirements for incident response and recovery. By considering recovery options, organizations can ensure compliance with applicable regulations, demonstrating their commitment to protecting sensitive information and meeting legal obligations.

- *Improve incident response*: Recovery options are integral to the overall incident response process. By considering recovery options, organizations enhance their incident response capabilities, making them more resilient and better prepared to handle future incidents. This includes developing recovery plans, establishing communication protocols, and identifying the necessary resources and tools for efficient recovery.

- *Enhance organizational resilience*: Cybersecurity incidents are inevitable, and organizations must be prepared to respond effectively. By considering recovery options, organizations build resilience to cyber threats. They develop the ability to bounce back from incidents, adapt to new challenges, and continuously improve their security posture.

Overview of the NIST CSF Recovery Module

The Recover module of the NIST CSF focuses on developing and implementing strategies to restore services, systems, and data after a cybersecurity incident. Its primary goal is to ensure timely recovery and restoration of operations, minimize the impact of incidents, and improve organizational resilience. The Recovery module consists of several key components and activities, including the following:

- *Recovery planning*: Developing and maintaining a recovery plan that outlines the processes, procedures, and resources required for effective response and restoration

- *Improvements*: Continuously identifying lessons learned from incidents and implementing necessary changes and improvements to enhance future recovery efforts

- *Communications*: Establishing communication channels and protocols to ensure effective and timely information sharing with stakeholders, including employees, customers, partners, and regulators

- *Coordination*: Coordinating recovery activities across different teams and departments to facilitate efficient and organized response efforts

- *Service continuity*: Ensuring the availability and continuity of critical services by implementing backup and redundancy mechanisms and leveraging alternate infrastructure or cloud services

- *Information integrity*: Verifying the integrity of restored systems and data to ensure they have not been compromised or altered during recovery

- *External engagement*: Collaborating with external entities, such as incident response teams, law enforcement agencies, and industry partners, to leverage their expertise and support in recovery efforts

Example: Recovering from a Ransomware Attack

Let's consider a real-world example of a company recovering from a ransomware attack to illustrate the application of the NIST CSF Recovery module.

ABC Manufacturing is a midsize manufacturing company that experienced a ransomware attack, which encrypted its critical systems and data. The attack caused significant disruption to their operations, leading to production downtime and potential financial losses.

- *Recovery planning*: ABC Manufacturing had already developed a comprehensive incident response plan for its cybersecurity program. This plan outlined the steps to be taken during a cybersecurity incident, including specific procedures for ransomware attacks. The project included backup and recovery strategies, contact information for relevant stakeholders, and predefined roles and responsibilities of the incident response team.

- *Improvements*: During the recovery process, ABC Manufacturing assessed the incident's impact and conducted a detailed analysis of the attack vectors and vulnerabilities exploited. They identified gaps in their security controls and made improvements, such as implementing stricter access controls, enhancing network segmentation, and strengthening endpoint security.

- *Communications*: ABC Manufacturing established a communication plan to inform employees, customers, and partners about the incident and its impact on operations. They provided regular updates on the progress of recovery efforts, steps taken to mitigate the attack, and guidance on potential risks or actions to be taken by stakeholders.

- *Coordination*: The incident response team at ABC Manufacturing coordinated with various internal groups, including IT, security, operations, and legal, to ensure a cohesive and organized recovery process. They scheduled regular meetings and established clear lines of communication to address any challenges, share updates, and make critical decisions.

- *Service continuity*: ABC Manufacturing leveraged its backup and recovery mechanisms to restore critical services. They implemented regular data backups stored in separate locations to prevent data loss. By working closely with their cloud service provider, they rapidly restored their systems and data from the most recent backup, minimizing the downtime and impact on production.

- *Information integrity*: Manufacturing ensured the integrity of the restored systems and data by conducting thorough checks and validations. They performed integrity verification processes, including comparing restored data with known good copies, running malware scans, and conducting data integrity tests. This ensured that the recovered systems and data were free from any lingering malware or unauthorized modifications.

- *External engagement*: ABC Manufacturing engaged external entities to assist with their recovery efforts. They collaborated with a reputable incident response firm that specialized in ransomware incidents. The external experts helped analyze the attack, identify the root cause, and provide guidance on effective recovery strategies. Additionally, ABC Manufacturing worked closely with law enforcement agencies to report the incident, share relevant information, and potentially aid in the investigation.

Throughout the recovery process, ABC Manufacturing documented all actions, decisions, and lessons learned. This information was used to improve their incident response and recovery capabilities, ensuring a more resilient and prepared cybersecurity posture.

By following the NIST CSF Recovery module and leveraging best practices, ABC Manufacturing successfully restored its operations after the ransomware attack. They minimized the impact on production, mitigated financial losses, and enhanced their overall cybersecurity posture through the lessons learned.

It's important to note that each recovery scenario is unique, and the specific steps and actions taken will vary based on the incident, the organization's resources, and available technologies.

Value of Azure NIST CSF Recovery   Within the Recover function, several categories and subcategories address specific aspects of recovery, such as Recovery Planning (RC.RP), Improvements (RC.IM), Communications (RC.CO), and Service Continuity (RC.SC).

Organizations can effectively plan for and execute recovery activities following a cybersecurity incident by addressing these categories and their associated subcategories.

Azure Mapping to NIST Recovery

Azure Recovery Services is a cloud-based service offered by Microsoft Azure that provides businesses backup and disaster recovery solutions. It allows organizations to protect their critical data and applications by creating backups and replicating them to Azure, ensuring data availability and minimizing downtime in case of an outage or disaster.

The following are the key components of Azure Recovery Services:

- *Azure Backup*: Azure Backup is the core component of Azure Recovery Services. It provides a scalable, secure, cost-effective backup solution for various workloads, including virtual machines, files and folders, databases, and Azure infrastructure services. Azure Backup offers features such as incremental backups, backup scheduling, retention policies, and backup encryption to protect data in transit and at rest.

  - *Azure VM Backup*: Azure VM Backup is a specialized backup solution for Azure virtual machines. It enables the creation of recovery points to protect Azure VMs and leverages the Azure Backup service for storage and management. Azure VM Backup supports both Windows and Linux VMs, and it offers features like backup policies, application-consistent backups, and item-level recovery for files and folders.

  - *Azure Disk Backup*: Azure Disk Backup is a feature of Azure Backup that provides backup and restore capabilities for Azure-managed disks. It enables the creation of point-in-time backups for managed disks attached to virtual machines. These backups can be used for data recovery or disk-level restore operations. Azure Disk Backup offers incremental backups, retention policies, and encryption to secure the data.

  - *Azure Site Recovery*: Azure Site Recovery (ASR) is a disaster recovery solution that helps replicate and orchestrate the recovery of on-premises workloads, virtual machines, and Azure VMs to another Azure region or an on-premises location. ASR supports physical and virtual machines running on various platforms, including Windows, Linux, Hyper-V, and VMware. It provides automated replication, continuous health monitoring, and recovery plans to streamline the failover and failback processes.

Benefits of Azure Recovery Services

The following are the benefits:

- *Scalability and flexibility*: Azure Recovery Services is a cloud-based solution offering the flexibility to scale backup and recovery resources per the organization's needs. It eliminates the need for managing on-premises infrastructure, allowing businesses to focus on core operations.

- *Cost-effectiveness*: Azure Recovery Services follows a pay-as-you-go model, reducing the upfront capital expenditure on infrastructure. The costs are based on usage, enabling organizations to optimize their backup and recovery expenses.

- *Reliability and availability*: Azure Recovery Services leverages Microsoft's robust global infrastructure, ensuring high availability and data durability. It provides geo-redundancy and replication options to protect against regional failures, ensuring that backups and replicas are stored in multiple data centers.

- *Centralized management*: Azure provides a unified management portal for managing and monitoring backups, replication, and recovery operations. This centralized approach simplifies the administration and reduces complexity.

- *Security and compliance*: Azure Recovery Services incorporates several security measures to protect data, including encryption in transit and at rest, role-based access control (RBAC), and compliance with various industry standards and regulations.

- *Automated disaster recovery*: Azure Site Recovery automates the failover and failback processes, reducing recovery time objectives (RTO) and recovery point objectives (RPO). It provides orchestrated recovery plans and continuous monitoring to ensure a smooth recovery experience.

Azure Backup and Recovery Best Practices   Performing, validating, and protecting data and configuration backups at each service tier falls under backup and recovery.

Figure 9-1 shows the Azure Recovery Services categories.

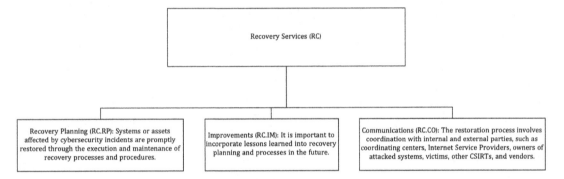

Figure 9-1. *RS.RP*

As part of the Azure cloud shared responsibility model, the NIST CSF security functions are provided in Table 9-1 with respect to RS.RP.

Table 9-1. RS.RP Responsibility Matrix

Category	Subcategory	Informative References	Responsibility	Customer Responsibility	Microsoft Azure Responsibility
Recovery Planning (RC. RP): Systems or assets affected by cybersecurity incidents are promptly restored through the execution and maintenance of recovery processes and procedures.	RC.RP-1: When an event occurs, a recovery plan is executed	NIST SP 800-53 Rev. 4 CP-10, IR-4, IR-8	Shared	The development and execution of incident response plans during or after an event are the customer's responsibility. This includes considering shared touchpoints within the customer's authorization boundary and any customer applications that rely on the provider's infrastructure. Unless caused by Microsoft or a result of Microsoft's action, the customer is accountable for incident handling concerning their applications. Furthermore, the customer is expected to provide a point of contact and an escalation plan, enabling Microsoft to keep them informed during incidents.	When customers enable geo-replicated backups and alternative site processing, Microsoft Azure executes recovery processes on their behalf. After a disruption, compromise, or failure, Microsoft Azure's business continuity plan details how each system can be recovered and reconstituted to its known state. The business continuity plan specifies how each Microsoft Azure system will be recovered. Microsoft Azure has developed a model for implementing incident-handling controls. Multiple incident handling methodologies contribute to this framework, which includes NIST SP 800-61 Rev. 2, Computer Security Incident Handling Guide, ISO/IEC 27035:2011, and SANS Institute publication Computer Security Incident Handling.

| Improvements (RC.IM): It is important to incorporate lessons learned into recovery planning and processes in the future. | RC.IM-1: Lessons learned are incorporated into recovery plans | NIST SP 800-53 Rev. 4 CP-2, IR-4, IR-8 | Shared | Recovery plans should incorporate lessons learned, and those changes should be communicated to stakeholders by the customer. | In Microsoft Azure's recovery process, recovery plans are reviewed and updated based on lessons learned. |
| | RC.IM-2: A new recovery strategy is in place | NIST SP 800-53 Rev. 4 CP-2, IR-4, IR-8 | Shared | Lessons learned must be incorporated into recovery strategies as frequently as necessary by the customer. | The recovery procedure in Microsoft Azure involves conducting an annual review and update cycle of recovery plans, incorporating valuable insights and lessons learned. |

(*continued*)

Table 9-1. (*continued*)

Category	Subcategory	Informative References	Responsibility	Customer Responsibility	Microsoft Azure Responsibility
Communications (RC.CO): The restoration process involves coordination with internal and external parties, such as coordinating centers, Internet Service Providers, owners of attacked systems, victims, other CSIRTs, and vendors.	RC.CO-3: Internal stakeholders and executive and management teams are notified of recovery activities	NIST SP 800-53 Rev. 4 CP-2, IR-4	Shared	The customer's responsibility is to communicate recovery activities to internal stakeholders, including executive and management teams. Stakeholders within the customer's organization should also be informed of incident management service level agreement findings.	Microsoft Azure ensures the maintenance of an incident response plan through contractual service level agreements and effectively communicates recovery activities to customers.

Azure Backup

Azure Backup is a cloud-based backup and restore service provided by Microsoft Azure. It enables organizations to protect their data and applications by creating backups of their on-premises or cloud-based systems. Azure Backup helps in data recovery during a cybersecurity incident by providing the following features:

- *Data protection*: Azure Backup allows you to back up various data types, including files, folders, virtual machines, databases, and system states. It ensures that your critical data is securely stored in Azure.

- *Incremental backups*: Azure Backup performs incremental backups, which means that after the initial full backup, it backs up only the changes made since the last backup. This reduces the time and storage required for backups.

- *Automatic backup scheduling*: You can define backup schedules based on your requirements. Azure Backup supports daily, weekly, monthly, and yearly backup frequencies. It also provides flexible retention policies, allowing you to retain backups for extended periods.

- *Off-site data storage*: Azure Backup stores your backups in Azure, which provides geographically distributed data centers with redundancy and durability. Storing backups off-site ensures that your data is protected even if your on-premises infrastructure is compromised.

- *Data encryption*: Azure Backup encrypts your data at rest and in transit. It uses Azure Storage Service Encryption to secure your backups. Additionally, you can enable customer-managed keys for enhanced control over data encryption.

- *Rapid recovery*: In a cybersecurity incident, you can quickly restore your data and applications from Azure Backup. You can perform a full restore or recover specific files, folders, virtual machines, or databases.

- *Cross-region replication*: Azure Backup can replicate backups across Azure regions. This helps in creating additional copies of your backups in different geographic locations, providing further protection against regional disasters or attacks.

- *Monitoring and reporting*: Azure Backup provides monitoring and reporting features to track the health and status of your backups. You can receive notifications, view backup reports, and monitor backup job completion to ensure the reliability of your data protection strategy.

By leveraging Azure Backup, organizations can enhance their cybersecurity incident recovery plans by having a reliable and scalable backup solution that helps protect critical data, facilitates rapid recovery, and ensures business continuity in the face of cyber threats or data loss incidents.

Key Components of Azure Backup

Azure Recovery Services Vault and Backup Vault are two components of the Azure Backup service. While they serve similar purposes, there are some differences in their functionalities and use cases. Let's explore each of them in detail:

- *Azure Recovery Services vault*: Azure Recovery Services vault is a cloud-based management entity that provides a unified interface for managing backup and recovery operations. It is a container for storing and organizing backup data, policies, and recovery points. Some key features of Azure Recovery Services vault include the following:

  - *Centralized management*: It enables centralized management of backup operations for various workloads across different Azure subscriptions and regions. You can create and manage multiple vaults as per your organizational requirements.

  - *Backup policy management*: Azure Recovery Services vault allows you to define and manage backup policies. Backup policies specify the backup frequency, retention period, and other settings for the protected resources. You can apply these policies to specific workloads or groups of resources.

- *Recovery point management*: The vault stores recovery points, which are the snapshots or copies of data at specific points in time. It provides capabilities to manage and configure the retention period for recovery points. You can restore data from these recovery points based on your recovery needs.

- *Cross-region replication*: Azure Recovery Services vault supports cross-region replication, allowing you to replicate your backup data to a secondary region for additional data protection and disaster recovery purposes. This ensures your backups are available even if a specific region or data center is affected.

- *Integration with Azure Site Recovery*: The Recovery Services vault integrates with Azure Site Recovery, enabling disaster recovery scenarios. You can replicate virtual machines or physical servers to a secondary site or Azure for business continuity and data protection.

- *Azure Backup multiuser authorization (MUA)*: MUA enhances the protection of critical operations on your Recovery Services vaults. Azure Backup uses another Azure resource called the Resource Guard to ensure critical operations are only performed with appropriate authorization.

- *Backup Vault*: Backup Vault is a specific type of Recovery Services vault explicitly designed for managing Azure VM backups. It provides a dedicated interface for configuring, monitoring, and managing backup operations for Azure virtual machines. Some key features of Backup Vault include the following:

  - *Azure VM backup*: Backup Vault protects Azure VMs by providing seamless integration with the Azure platform. It simplifies configuring backup policies and managing backups for Azure virtual machines.

  - *Application-consistent backups*: Backup Vault ensures application-consistent backups of Azure VMs, ensuring that the backup captures the state of the applications and databases running on the VMs at a specific time. This allows for reliable restores of VMs and their associated applications.

- *Item-level recovery*: Backup Vault allows for item-level recovery of files and folders within Azure VMs. You can selectively restore specific files or folders without restoring the entire virtual machine.

- *Instant file recovery*: It provides the ability to perform instant file recovery for Azure VM backups. This feature allows you to access and recover individual files from the backup without restoring the entire VM or volume.

- *VM restore*: Backup Vault facilitates restoring entire Azure VMs, including the VM configuration, disks, and associated resources. You can restore VMs to the same location or different Azure regions.

- *Integration with Azure Backup*: Backup Vault integrates with other Azure Backup features, such as long-term retention, backup policies, and cross-region replication.

In summary, Azure Recovery Services Vault and Backup Vault are components of Azure Backup. The Recovery Services vault provides centralized management and control over backup operations for various workloads, while the Backup Vault focuses specifically on managing Azure VM backups with features tailored to Azure virtual machines.

Overview of Supported Elements

Azure Backup can back up various types of data sources and workloads. Here are some examples of what you can back up using Azure Backup:

- *Files and folders*: You can back up individual files and folders from your on-premises servers, Azure virtual machines (VMs), or Azure file shares. This allows you to protect important documents, configurations, and other file-level data.

- *Virtual machines*: Azure Backup supports backing up Azure VMs and on-premises VMs running on Hyper-V or VMware. It provides comprehensive protection for the VMs, including the operating system, applications, and data. This ensures that your entire VM infrastructure is backed up and recoverable.

- *Databases*: Azure Backup supports backing up databases running on various platforms, including Microsoft SQL Server, SAP HANA, Azure Database for PostgreSQL, Azure Database for MySQL, and Azure Cosmos DB. It allows you to perform application-consistent backups, ensuring data integrity and recoverability.

- *System states*: Azure Backup can back up the system state of your Windows servers, including critical components like Active Directory, registry, and system files. This enables you to restore the entire server to a specific point in time, including its configuration and system-level settings.

- *Azure files*: Azure Backup allows you to protect Azure file shares, ensuring that your file data stored in Azure is backed up and recoverable. This includes both general-purpose and premium file shares.

- *Azure virtual network*: Azure Backup supports backing up and restoring Azure virtual networks (VNets). This includes VNet configurations, subnets, virtual network gateways, and other network resources. It helps in ensuring the availability and recoverability of your network infrastructure.

- *Azure Kubernetes Service (AKS) clusters*: Azure Backup protects Azure AKS clusters. It allows you to back up and restore your AKS cluster resources, including node pools, pods, and configurations.

- *Azure Blob Storage*: Azure Backup offers the ability to back up Azure Blob Storage accounts. This includes block and append blobs, allowing you to protect your object storage data.

These are just a few examples of what you can back up using Azure Backup. The service is designed to support a wide range of data sources, workloads, and platforms, providing comprehensive data protection and recovery capabilities for your organization's critical assets.

The Azure Backup service provides support for different components through its matrix component. The matrix component defines the capabilities and limitations of Azure Backup for additional data sources, operating systems, and workload types. Let's explore the additional support provided by Azure Backup through its matrix component:

- *Operating systems*: Azure Backup supports a wide range of operating systems for data protection, including Windows, Linux, and macOS. It covers various versions of these operating systems, ensuring compatibility with different environments.

- *Data sources*: Azure Backup allows you to protect various types of data sources. This includes file and folder backups, where you can back up specific files and directories on your system. It also supports volume-level backups, enabling you to protect entire volumes or disks.

  - For virtual machines, Azure Backup provides comprehensive support for Azure VMs and on-premises VMs running on Hyper-V or VMware. You can protect the VMs, operating systems, applications, and data.

  - Azure Backup also protects Azure file shares, Azure Database for PostgreSQL, Azure Database for MySQL, and Azure Cosmos DB. These data sources can be backed up and restored using Azure Backup.

- *Workloads*: Azure Backup is designed to support a wide range of workloads. It provides specific solutions for various workload types, ensuring optimal backup and restore operations. Some of the supported workloads include:

  - *Azure VMs*: Azure Backup integrates with Azure VMs to provide consistent and application-consistent backups for Windows and Linux VMs. This ensures that the VMs are properly quiesced during the backup process, resulting in reliable restore points.

  - *SQL Server*: Azure Backup supports backing up SQL Server databases running on Azure VMs or on-premises servers. It enables transactionally consistent backups, allowing you to recover individual databases or perform point-in-time restores.

- *SAP HANA*: Azure Backup supports backing up SAP HANA databases running on Azure VMs. It ensures data consistency and can restore the databases to a specific point in time.

- *Azure files*: Azure Backup allows you to protect Azure file shares, ensuring that your file data is backed up and recoverable in case of accidental deletions or corruptions.

- *Backup features*: Azure Backup provides several essential backup features to ensure reliable data protection:

  - *Incremental backups*: Azure Backup performs incremental backups after the initial full backup by capturing only the changes made since the last backup. This approach minimizes the backup time and reduces the storage consumption.

  - *Backup scheduling and retention policies*: You can define backup schedules based on your requirements. Azure Backup supports daily, weekly, monthly, and yearly backup frequencies. It also allows you to define retention policies, specifying how long to retain the backups.

  - *Compression and encryption*: Azure Backup compresses the backup data to minimize storage consumption and optimize data transfer. It also encrypts the data at rest and in transit to ensure security.

  - *Backup monitoring and reporting*: Azure Backup provides monitoring and reporting capabilities, allowing you to track the health and status of your backups. You can receive notifications, view backup reports, and monitor backup job completion.

- *Recovery Options*: Azure Backup offers multiple recovery options to restore your data and applications:

  - *File and folder restore*: You can perform granular file and folder restores from backups, enabling you to recover specific files or directories without restoring the entire backup.

  - *Virtual machine restore*: For VM backups, Azure Backup allows you to restore entire VMs or individual disks. You can restore VMs to the exact location or different locations within Azure.

- *Application restore*: Azure Backup provides application-consistent backups for workloads like SQL Server and SAP HANA, enabling you to restore databases and applications to a specific point in time.

- *Long-term retention*: Azure Backup can store backups for extended periods, ensuring compliance with regulatory requirements. You can configure long-term retention policies to retain backups for years.

In conclusion, Azure Backup provides extensive support for different components through its matrix component. It covers various operating systems, data sources, and workload types, ensuring that organizations can protect and recover their critical data and applications effectively.

Protect Against Ransomware

Azure Backup provides several features and best practices to help protect against ransomware attacks and mitigate their impact. Here's how Azure Backup can help in protecting your data from ransomware:

- *Off-site data storage*: Azure Backup stores your backups in the cloud, which ensures that your backup data is physically separated from your primary infrastructure. This isolation reduces the risk of ransomware infecting both the primary data and the backup copies.

- *Immutable backups*: Azure Backup offers the option to enable immutability for backup data. Immutable backups prevent any modification, deletion, or encryption of backup data for a specified retention period. This feature adds a layer of protection against ransomware attacks by making backup data tamper-proof.

- *RBAC*: Azure Backup utilizes RBAC to provide granular access control to backup data. You can limit access to backup resources by implementing proper RBAC policies and preventing unauthorized modifications or deletions.

- *Monitoring and alerts*: Azure Backup provides monitoring and alerting capabilities to detect any suspicious activities or anomalies. You can set up alerts for backup failures, unusual backup patterns, or unauthorized access attempts. Timely detecting such events can help you respond quickly to ransomware attacks.

- *Backup isolation*: Azure Backup allows you to create separate backup vaults or Recovery Services vaults for different workloads or departments. This isolation helps contain the impact of a ransomware attack by limiting its spread to specific backup sets and minimizing the risk of cross-contamination.

- *Recovery points and versioning*: Azure Backup maintains multiple recovery points for your data. In case of a ransomware attack, you can restore your data to a previous clean state by selecting a recovery point from before the attack. Having multiple recovery points and versioning enables you to choose the most suitable restore point based on the integrity of the data.

- *Data encryption*: Azure Backup encrypts your data at rest and in transit. It uses Azure Storage Service Encryption to secure your backups. Encrypting the backup data ensures that even if attackers gain access to the backup files, they won't be able to read the data without the encryption keys.

- *Backup monitoring and testing*: Monitoring and testing your backup and restore processes is crucial for ransomware protection. Azure Backup provides monitoring capabilities to track the health and status of backup jobs. Performing periodic test restores helps validate the backup data integrity and ensures you can recover your data effectively if needed.

Azure Backup Key Insights   Azure Backup provides robust protection against ransomware, it is also essential to follow security best practices such as implementing strong access controls, keeping software and systems up-to-date, and educating users about phishing and social engineering techniques. A comprehensive defense strategy involves a combination of preventive measures, backup solutions, and incident response plans to mitigate the risks associated with ransomware attacks.

Azure Backup Security Features Overview

Azure Backup provides several security features to protect data during backup and restore operations. There are no infrastructure requirements for Azure Backup, which offers secure, cost-effective, and simple data protection for all your Azure data assets. This solution is Azure's built-in data protection solution for most workloads. In the cloud, your mission-critical workloads will be fully protected with backups available and managed at scale across your entire backup estate. These security features help safeguard data against unauthorized access, breaches, and other security risks. Here is an in-depth overview of the security features in Azure Backup:

Encryption at rest:

- Azure Backup automatically encrypts data at rest using Azure Storage Service Encryption (SSE).

- SSE ensures that data is encrypted before being stored on the underlying storage media, providing data confidentiality and protection against unauthorized access.

Encryption in transit:

- Azure Backup uses secure transport protocols, such as SSL/TLS, to encrypt data during transit.

- This ensures that data transferred between the source system and Azure Backup remains encrypted, protecting it from interception and tampering.

RBAC:

- Azure Backup integrates with Azure Active Directory (Azure AD) and follows RBAC principles.

- RBAC allows you to assign specific roles and permissions to users or groups, controlling their access to Azure Backup resources and operations.

- This helps enforce the principle of least privilege and ensures that only authorized individuals can perform backup and restore tasks.

Authentication and authorization:

- Azure Backup authenticates and authorizes access to backup resources and operations.

- It utilizes Azure AD authentication to verify the identify of users or applications attempting to access backup data.

- Multi-factor authentication (MFA) can be enabled to add an extra layer of security for user authentication.

Backup data isolation:

- Azure Backup ensures data isolation by segregating backup data from other customer data within the Azure infrastructure.

- Backup data is stored in dedicated storage accounts, ensuring it is logically separated and protected against unauthorized access.

Compliance and certifications:

- Azure Backup adheres to various compliance standards and certifications, including ISO 27001, SOC 1, SOC 2, and HIPAA.

- These compliance measures ensure that Azure Backup meets stringent security requirements and undergoes regular data protection and privacy audits.

Monitoring and auditing:

- Azure Backup integrates with Azure Monitor and Azure Security Center for monitoring and auditing backup operations.

- Monitoring provides real-time visibility into backup activities, while auditing helps track and analyze backup-related events and activities for compliance and security analysis.

Geo-redundancy:

- Azure Backup allows you to store backup data in geo-redundant storage, replicating data across multiple Azure regions.

- Geo-redundancy helps ensure data availability and resilience in case of regional failures or disasters.

By leveraging these security features, Azure Backup helps protect your data during backup and restore operations, ensuring that your data remains confidential, available, and protected against security threats.

Azure VM Backup

Azure VM Backup is a feature provided by Azure Backup that allows you to protect and restore Azure VMs in case of data loss or disaster recovery scenarios. It enables you to create backups of entire VMs, including the operating system, applications, and data and provides a reliable and efficient way to protect your VM infrastructure. Here are some key aspects of Azure VM Backup:

- *Full VM backup*: Azure VM Backup captures the entire state of an Azure VM, including the VM configuration, operating system, applications, and data. It creates a snapshot of the VM at a specific time, ensuring that all the components required for a complete restore are included.

- *Incremental backups*: Azure VM Backup uses incremental backups, meaning that only the changes made to the VM are captured in subsequent backups after the initial full backup. This reduces the backup time and storage requirements.

- *Application-consistent backups*: Azure VM Backup ensures application-consistent backups by leveraging the Volume Shadow Copy Service (VSS) snapshot technology. This ensures that the backups are taken in a state where all applications and data are consistent, preserving data integrity and enabling reliable restores.

- *Backup policies*: You can define backup policies in Azure Backup to specify the backup frequency, retention settings, and other backup parameters for your Azure VMs. Backup policies allow you to automate and manage the backup process across multiple VMs.

- *Restore options*: Azure VM Backup provides various restore options to meet your recovery needs. You can restore the entire VM or specific disks from a backup. You can also perform file-level recovery to restore individual files and folders within the VM backup.

- *Cross-region replication*: Azure VM Backup supports cross-region replication, allowing you to replicate your VM backups to a different Azure region. This provides additional protection and ensures business continuity in a regional outage.

- *Long-term retention*: Azure VM Backup allows you to define long-term retention policies for your VM backups. This enables you to retain backups for an extended period, meeting compliance requirements or providing archival storage.

- *Integration with Azure Site Recovery*: Azure VM Backup integrates with Azure Site Recovery, which provides disaster recovery capabilities for VMs. You can replicate VM backups to a secondary Azure region and orchestrate failover and failback processes in the event of a disaster.

By utilizing Azure VM Backup, you can protect your Azure VMs and ensure their availability and recoverability. It provides a robust backup solution integrated with the Azure platform, simplifying backup management and providing peace of mind in case of data loss or unexpected incidents.

How to Backup, Restore, and Manage Azure VM Using Azure Backup

To backup, restore, and manage Azure VMs using Azure Backup, you can follow these steps. First, to create an Azure Recovery Services vault, follow these steps:

1. Go to the Azure Portal and search for *Recovery Services vault* in the search bar.

2. Click "Recovery Services vault" from the results and then click Add to create a new vault.

3. Provide a unique name, and select your subscription, resource group, and desired region.

4. Click Review + Create and Create to create the vault.

To enable Backup for Azure VMs, follow these steps:

1. Open the newly created Recovery Services vault and click Backup in the menu on the left.

2. Click + Backup to start the backup wizard.

3. In the "Backup goal" section, select Azure Virtual Machine as the workload type.

4. In the "Backup target" section, select the Azure VMs you want to back up.

5. Configure the backup policy by selecting the backup frequency, retention settings, and other options.

6. Review the settings and click "Enable backup" to start the backup process.

To perform a VM backup, follow these steps:

1. Once the backup is enabled, Azure Backup will automatically create backup snapshots based on the configured backup policy.

2. You can monitor the backup progress and status from the Backup Items section of the Recovery Services vault.

To restore an Azure VM, go to the Recovery Services vault and click "Backup items" in the menu on the left.

1. Select the desired Azure VM from the list of backup items.

2. In the Restore tab, you can restore the VM to the same location or a different Azure region.

3. Specify the restore point by selecting a recovery date and time.

4. Configure the restore settings, such as virtual network, storage account, and resource group.

5. Review the settings and click Restore to start the VM restore process.

In the Recovery Services vault, you can manage various aspects of Azure VM backups.

- You can view the backup job status, monitor backup health, and set up alerts for backup failures or issues.

- Configure backup policies to define the backup frequency, retention settings, and other backup parameters.

- Perform restore operations, including full VM, file, or item-level restore.

It's important to note that Azure Backup also provides additional features and options for managing and protecting Azure VMs, such as application-consistent backups, backup retention policies, cross-region replication, and long-term retention.

Azure Disk Backup

Azure Disk Backup is a feature of Azure Backup that allows you to protect and recover data stored on Azure-managed disks or Azure Data Disks. It provides a reliable and efficient way to back up your disk data, ensuring data protection and enabling quick restores in case of data loss or disaster recovery scenarios. Here are some key aspects of Azure Disk Backup:

- *Disk-level backup*: Azure Disk Backup allows you to back up individual Azure-managed disks or Azure Data Disks attached to Azure virtual machines. It captures the disks' state at a specific time, including the data, configuration, and operating system.

- *Incremental backups*: Azure Disk Backup utilizes incremental backups, meaning only the changes made since the last backup are captured. This minimizes the backup time and storage requirements.

- *Application-consistent backups*: Azure Disk Backup ensures application-consistent backups by leveraging the VSS snapshot technology. Application-consistent backups guarantee that the backed-up data is consistent, preserving data integrity and enabling reliable restores.

- *Backup policies*: You can define backup policies in Azure Backup to specify your disk backups' frequency and retention settings. Backup policies allow you to automate and manage the backup process across multiple disks and virtual machines.

- *Backup retention*: Azure Disk Backup provides flexible retention options, allowing you to choose the duration for which backups should be retained. You can configure short-term retention for regular restores and long-term retention for compliance or archival purposes.

- *Restore options*: Azure Disk Backup enables various restore options to meet your recovery requirements. You can restore individual disks or entire virtual machines using the backup data. You can also perform item-level recovery to restore specific files or folders from the backup.

- *Integration with Azure Backup*: Azure Disk Backup seamlessly integrates with other Azure Backup features and services. This includes centralized management through the Azure Portal, monitoring and alerting capabilities, cross-region replication for additional data protection, and integration with Azure Site Recovery for disaster recovery scenarios.

- *Security and compliance*: Azure Disk Backup ensures the security and compliance of your backup data. It encrypts your backups at rest using Azure Storage Service Encryption and provides secure transmission during backup and restores operations. It also helps meet regulatory requirements by enabling data retention policies and supporting backup encryption.

By utilizing Azure Disk Backup, you can protect your critical disk data in Azure and ensure its availability and recoverability. It provides a reliable backup solution integrated with the Azure platform, simplifying backup management and offering peace of mind in case of data loss or unexpected incidents.

How to Backup, Restore, and Manage Azure Disk Backup using Azure Backup

To backup, restore, and manage Azure Disk Backup, you can follow the steps in this section.

To enable Azure Disk Backup, follow these steps:

1. Open the Azure Portal and navigate to the desired Recovery Services vault.

2. In the menu on the left, click Backup Items and + Backup to start the backup configuration.

3. Select the desired Azure VM that has the disks you want to back up.

4. In the Backup Goal section, choose Azure Disk Backup as the workload type.

5. Select the disks you want to back up and click Enable Backup to start the backup process.

To perform a disk backup, follow these steps:

- Once the backup is enabled, Azure Disk Backup will automatically create incremental backups of the selected disks according to the configured backup policy.

- You can monitor the backup progress and status from the Backup Items section of the Recovery Services vault.

To restore Azure disks, go to the Recovery Services vault and click Backup Items in the menu on the left. Then follow these steps:

1. Select the desired disk or disks that you want to restore.

2. In the Restore tab, choose the restore point by selecting a specific recovery date and time.

3. Specify the restore settings, such as the target resource group, virtual machine, or create a new disk.

4. Review the settings and click Restore to initiate the disk restore process.

In the Recovery Services vault, you can manage various aspects of Azure Disk Backup.

- Monitor backup health and status, view backup job history, and track backup storage usage.

- Set up alerts for backup failures or issues using Azure Monitor or Azure Backup's built-in alerting capabilities.

- Configure backup policies to define the backup frequency, retention settings, and other backup parameters.

- Perform disk-level restores or item-level recovery for specific files or folders within the backup data.

It's important to note that Azure Disk Backup is integrated with Azure Backup and leverages the capabilities provided by Azure Backup. This includes centralized management, monitoring, alerting, cross-region replication, and integration with Azure Site Recovery for disaster recovery scenarios. Following the previous steps, you can effectively back up, restore, and manage your Azure Disk Backup data, ensuring data protection and quick recovery when needed.

Azure Blob Backup

Azure Blob Backup refers to backing up and protecting data stored in Azure Blob storage. Azure Blob Storage is a scalable and cost-effective object storage service offered by Microsoft Azure, commonly used to store unstructured data such as files, images, videos, and documents. To ensure data resiliency and availability, Azure provides various mechanisms for backing up and protecting data stored in Azure Blob. Here are some key aspects of Azure Blob Backup.

Azure Blob versioning:

- Azure Blob storage supports versioning, which allows you to preserve and access different versions of an object over time.

- With versioning enabled, each modification to a blob creates a new version, providing a historical record of changes.

- Versioning helps protect against accidental deletions, corruptions, or overwrites of data.

Azure Blob soft delete:

- Azure Blob storage provides a soft delete feature that helps safeguard against accidental deletions.

- When soft delete is enabled, deleted blobs are retained for a specified retention period, allowing you to recover them if needed.

- Soft delete provides an additional layer of data protection and recovery options.

Azure Blob replication:

- Azure Blob storage offers different replication options, including Locally Redundant Storage (LRS), Zone-Redundant Storage (ZRS), Geo-Redundant Storage (GRS), and Read-Access Geo-Redundant Storage (RA-GRS).

- Replication ensures that data is stored redundantly across multiple Azure data centers, protecting against regional failures and improving data availability.

Azure Blob snapshot:

- Azure Blob storage supports the creation of snapshots, which are point-in-time copies of blobs.

- Snapshots allow you to capture the state of a blob at a specific time, providing an easy way to restore previous versions of the data.

- Snapshots are read-only, preserving the data integrity and immutability of the snapshot.

Azure Backup for Azure Blob storage:

- While Azure Blob storage provides data redundancy and durability, you can further enhance data protection by leveraging Azure Backup.

- Azure Backup offers backup capabilities for Azure virtual machines and file shares, and you can utilize it to back up data stored in Azure Blob storage through these services.

Third-party backup solutions:

- Additionally, third-party backup solutions in the Azure Marketplace specifically focus on backing up and protecting data stored in Azure Blob storage.

- These solutions offer automated backups, customizable retention policies, cross-region replication, and advanced data management capabilities.

Choosing the appropriate combination of Azure Blob storage features, data replication options, and backup solutions is important based on your specific data protection requirements, compliance needs, and recovery objectives. Consider evaluating your data's criticality and designing a comprehensive backup strategy to ensure the safety and availability of your Azure Blob data.

How to Back Up and Restore Azure Blob Storage Using Azure Backup

Azure Blob storage offers built-in replication and data resiliency features, but there is no direct mechanism within Azure Backup to enable Blob-specific backups.

To ensure data protection and backup for Azure Blob storage, you can consider the following approaches.

Replication options:

- Azure Blob storage offers different replication options, such as LRS, ZRS, GRS, and RA-GRS.

- Choose the appropriate replication option based on your availability and durability requirements for Blob data.

Snapshot-based backups:

- Azure Blob storage supports snapshots, allowing you to create read-only, point-in-time copies of your Blobs.

- You can manually create snapshots or use automation tools like Azure PowerShell or Azure CLI to schedule snapshot creation at regular intervals.

Third-party backup solutions:

- Explore third-party backup solutions available in the Azure Marketplace that specifically target Azure Blob storage.

- These solutions provide automated backups, customizable retention policies, cross-region replication, and advanced data management capabilities.

Application-level backups:

- Focus on application-level backups if your Blob storage is used to store critical data for your applications.

- Implement backup mechanisms within your application code or use third-party backup libraries or tools to regularly back up the data stored in Azure Blobs.

It's important to note that Microsoft Azure regularly updates its services, and new features and capabilities may become available after my knowledge cutoff. We recommend referring to the official Azure documentation and Azure Portal for the latest information on Blob backup options and features supported by Azure Backup.

Azure File Share Backup

Azure File Share Backup is a feature provided by Azure Backup that allows you to protect and restore data stored in Azure File Shares. Azure File shares provide cloud-based network file storage that can be accessed using the standard Server Message Block

(SMB) protocol. Azure File Share Backup offers a convenient and reliable way to back up your file share data, ensuring data protection and enabling quick restores in case of data loss or unexpected incidents. Here are some key aspects of Azure File Share Backup:

- *Automated backups*: Azure File Share Backup automates backing up your Azure File shares. It creates regular backups of the file share data according to the configured backup policy, eliminating the need for manual backups.

- *Incremental backups*: Azure File Share Backup uses incremental backups, meaning that only the changes made to the file share are captured in subsequent backups after the initial full backup. This reduces backup time and storage requirements.

- *Snapshot-based backups*: Azure File Share Backup uses Azure snapshots as the underlying mechanism for capturing backups. Snapshots provide a read-only, point-in-time copy of the file share, ensuring data integrity and consistency.

- *Backup retention*: Azure File Share Backup allows you to define retention policies to specify how long backups should be retained. You can configure short-term retention for regular restores and long-term retention for compliance or archival purposes.

- *Item-level recovery*: Azure File Share Backup enables item-level recovery, allowing you to restore specific files or folders from the backup. This gives you granular control over the restore process, minimizing data loss and improving recovery efficiency.

- *Cross-region replication*: Azure File Share Backup supports cross-region replication, allowing you to replicate your file share backups to a different Azure region. This provides additional protection and ensures business continuity in a regional outage.

- *Integration with Azure Backup*: Azure File Share Backup seamlessly integrates with other Azure Backup features and services. This includes centralized management through the Azure Portal, monitoring and alerting capabilities, and integration with Azure Site Recovery for disaster recovery scenarios.

- *Security and compliance*: Azure File Share Backup ensures the security and compliance of your backup data. It encrypts your backups at rest using Azure Storage Service Encryption and provides secure transmission during backup and restores operations. It also helps meet regulatory requirements by enabling data retention policies and supporting backup encryption.

By utilizing Azure File Share Backup, you can protect your Azure File shares and ensure the availability and recoverability of your file share data. It provides a reliable backup solution integrated with the Azure platform, simplifying backup management and offering peace of mind in case of data loss or unexpected incidents.

How to Back Up and Restore Azure File Share Using Azure Backup

To backup and restore Azure File shares using Azure File Share Backup, you can follow the steps in this section.

To create an Azure Recovery Services vault, follow these steps:

1. Open the Azure Portal and navigate to the desired subscription and resource group.

2. Click "+ Create a resource" and search for *Recovery Services vault*.

3. Click "Recovery Services vault" and then click Create.

4. Provide a unique name, select the appropriate subscription and resource group, and choose the desired region for the vault.

5. Click Review + Create and Create to create the vault.

Register the Azure File Share resource with the Recovery Services vault by following these steps:

1. Open the Azure Portal and navigate to the newly created Recovery Services vault.

2. In the menu on the left, click Backup and then click the + Backup button.

3. In the "Backup goal" section, select "Azure file share" as the workload.

4. Select the appropriate Azure subscription and resource group in the "Where is your workload running?" section.

5. Select the Azure File Share you want to back up and click OK.

6. Review the settings and click "Enable backup" to register the Azure File Share with the Recovery Services vault.

Configure backup settings by following these steps:

1. After the Azure File Share is registered, click Backup in the menu on the left of the Recovery Services vault.

2. Select the Azure File Share that you want to configure backup settings for.

3. Click "Backup settings" and set the backup schedule, retention policy, and backup storage redundancy as per your requirements.

4. Click Save to apply the backup settings.

To perform a backup, follow these steps:

1. Once the backup settings are configured, Azure File Share Backup automatically performs backups based on the defined schedule.

2. The backups are stored in the Recovery Services vault and can be used for restore operations.

To perform a restore, follow these steps:

1. To restore data from a backup, navigate to the Recovery Services vault in the Azure Portal.

2. Click Backup in the menu on the left and select the Azure File Share.

3. In the Backup Items tab, choose the desired backup from the available recovery points.

4. Click Restore and select the restore type (e.g., original or alternate location).

5. Follow the prompts to complete the restore operation.

Azure File Share Backup supports item-level recovery, allowing you to restore specific files or folders from the backup. You can select the desired files/folders during the restore process.

By following these steps, you can back up and restore Azure File shares using Azure File Share Backup, simplifying the process of protecting and recovering your file share data in Azure.

Azure Backup for Database

Azure Backup offers several options for backing up and protecting databases in the Azure environment. This section highlights some of the key offerings.

Azure SQL Database Backup:

- Azure SQL Database has built-in backup capabilities that allow you to create automatic backups of your databases.

- You can configure long-term retention policies to retain backups for an extended period.

- Azure SQL Database backups are stored in Azure Blob storage, providing durability and easy restore options.

Azure SQL Managed Instance Backup:

- Azure SQL Managed Instance offers similar backup capabilities as Azure SQL Database.

- You can enable automated backups, configure retention policies, and perform point-in-time restores.

- Managed Instance backups are stored in Azure Blob storage, ensuring data durability and availability.

Azure Backup for Azure Virtual Machines (IaaS):

- If you have databases running on Azure Virtual Machines (IaaS), you can use Azure Backup to protect them.

- Azure Backup provides application-consistent backups for both Windows and Linux virtual machines.

- You can restore individual databases or entire VMs to a specific point in time.

Azure Database for PostgreSQL and Azure Database for MySQL:

- Azure Backup provides automatic backups for PostgreSQL and Azure Database for MySQL.

- You can configure backup retention and perform point-in-time restore operations.

- Backups are stored in Azure Blob storage, ensuring data durability and availability.

Azure Backup for Azure Files:

- If you are using Azure Files to store database files, Azure Backup offers backup capabilities for Azure Files shares.

- You can schedule regular backups and restore individual files or the entire file share.

Azure Backup for Azure Cosmos DB:

- Azure Backup does not provide direct backup capabilities for Azure Cosmos DB. However, Azure Cosmos DB offers built-in backup and restore capabilities.

- Azure Cosmos DB backups are managed through the Azure Portal or programmatically using Azure Cosmos DB APIs.

Azure Backup for Azure Data Lake Storage:

- Azure Backup does not provide direct backup capabilities for Azure Data Lake Storage. However, Azure Data Lake Storage offers built-in backup and restore features.

- You can create snapshots or use Data Lake Storage versioning to protect your data.

It's essential to review the specific documentation and guidelines provided by Microsoft Azure for each database service to understand the backup options and best practices available for your particular database needs.

Azure Backup for Azure Kubernetes Service

Azure Kubernetes Service (AKS) is a managed container orchestration service provided by Microsoft Azure. It simplifies containerized applications' deployment, management, and scaling using Kubernetes, an open-source container orchestration platform. While Azure Backup does not directly support backing up AKS clusters, you can utilize other mechanisms and services to ensure data protection and recoverability within an AKS environment. This section covers some considerations.

Application-level backups:

- In a containerized environment like AKS, it's essential to focus on backing up the application data rather than the infrastructure itself.

- Ensure that your applications running in AKS follow best practices for data persistence, such as using persistent volumes (PVs) and persistent volume claims (PVCs) to store critical data outside the container.

- Take regular backups of the data stored in these volumes using application-level backup mechanisms specific to your stack.

Distributed version control systems (Git):

- To protect your application deployment configurations and associated code, it's recommended to utilize distributed version control systems such as Git.

- Store your application code and deployment configurations in a Git repository to enable versioning, history tracking, and easy restore in case of accidental changes or data loss.

Infrastructure-as-code (IaC) practices:

- Apply IaC principles to your AKS environment using tools like Azure Resource Manager (ARM) templates or Azure DevOps pipelines.

- Store your infrastructure definitions and configurations in version control repositories alongside your application code.

- By maintaining infrastructure as code, you can easily recreate or restore your AKS cluster in case of a disaster or infrastructure failure.

Disaster recovery (DR):

- Implement a disaster recovery strategy for your AKS environment by leveraging Azure Site Recovery (ASR).

- ASR provides capabilities to replicate and recover your AKS infrastructure to a secondary Azure region, ensuring business continuity in case of a regional outage or disaster.

Monitoring and alerting:

- Use Azure Monitor to collect and analyze telemetry data from your AKS cluster, including container logs, performance metrics, and health checks.

- Configure alerts and notifications based on predefined thresholds or custom conditions to proactively identify issues and respond accordingly.

Remember, while Azure Backup does not offer direct AKS cluster backup support, focusing on application-level backups and following best practices for data persistence and infrastructure management is crucial. Additionally, leverage Azure services like Git, ASR, and Azure Monitor to ensure comprehensive data protection, disaster recovery, and monitoring capabilities within your AKS environment.

Azure Offline Backup

Azure offline backup refers to a backup strategy where data is backed up from an Azure environment to an offline or off-site location. It involves taking a physical copy or snapshot of the data and storing it on a separate storage device or location not directly connected to the Azure infrastructure.

Here are some key aspects of Azure offline backup:

- *Data transfer*: In an offline backup scenario, data is typically transferred using physical storage devices like hard drives or tapes. The data is extracted from the Azure environment onto the storage device, then transported to the offline location.

- *Security*: Offline backups provide an additional layer of protection as the data is physically separated from the Azure environment.

This can be advantageous when data needs to be protected from online threats like cyberattacks or unauthorized access.

- *Data protection*: By storing data offline, organizations can safeguard against accidental data loss, corruption, or disruptions in the Azure environment. During a disaster or data loss, offline backups can restore critical data and resume operations.

- *Compliance and regulatory requirements*: Offline backups can help organizations meet compliance and regulatory requirements by providing an independent copy of data stored in a separate location. This ensures data availability and integrity in case of audits or legal requirements.

- *RTO and RPO*: Using offline backups can impact the recovery time and recovery point objectives. Since offline backups require physical retrieval and restoration, the process may take longer than online or cloud-based backup and restore options.

- *Hybrid backup solutions*: Azure provides hybrid backup solutions that combine online and offline backup strategies. These solutions allow organizations to back data directly to Azure and create offline backups for additional data protection and redundancy.

It's important to note that Azure Backup primarily focuses on online backup and restore options, utilizing cloud-based storage and services within the Azure ecosystem. While offline backup can be part of an overall data protection strategy, it may require additional tools, processes, and considerations beyond the scope of Azure Backup itself.

Azure Backup Key Insights   Azure Backup has some limitations to consider for design and deployment.

There is a limit of 500 Recovery Services vaults per subscription per supported region of Azure Backup. If you require more vaults, you must purchase an additional subscription.

Azure Virtual Machines can be registered up to 1,000 per vault, MARS agents can be registered up to 50 per vault using the Microsoft Azure Backup Agent, and MABS servers can be registered up to 50 per vault.

You can protect up to 2,000 data sources/items across all workloads (such as IaaS VM, SQL, AFS) in a vault.

You can register up to 1000 Azure Virtual machines per vault. You can register up to 50 MARS agents per vault using the Microsoft Azure Backup Agent. And you can register 50 MABS servers/DPM servers to a vault.

Azure Site Recovery

Azure Site Recovery (ASR) is a cloud-based disaster recovery service provided by Microsoft Azure. It enables businesses to protect and recover their on-premises virtual machines (VMs), physical servers, and Azure VMs by orchestrating replication, failover, and failback processes.

The following are the key features and capabilities of Azure Site Recovery:

- *Replication*: ASR replicates workloads from a primary site (on-premises or another Azure region) to a secondary location for data protection and disaster recovery. It supports various replication methods, such as continuous replication, replication frequency customization, and replication policies.

- *Site-to-site disaster recovery*: ASR allows businesses to replicate and failover their entire on-premises infrastructure to Azure. This includes virtual machines, physical servers, and even entire data centers. In the event of a disaster or outage at the primary site, ASR facilitates failover to the secondary site in Azure, minimizing downtime and ensuring business continuity.

- *Azure VM disaster recovery*: ASR provides disaster recovery for Azure VMs within the same Azure region or across different regions. It replicates Azure VMs to a secondary region and allows for failover and failback operations. This ensures high availability and resilience for Azure VM workloads.

- *Cross-platform support*: ASR supports various operating systems, including Windows and Linux, and can replicate workloads running on hypervisors like Hyper-V and VMware. This cross-platform support enables businesses to protect heterogeneous IT environments.

- *Automated recovery plans*: ASR allows you to create recovery plans that define the order and dependencies of the failover process. These plans automate the recovery steps, ensuring consistency and simplifying the failover and failback processes. You can customize recovery plans based on your specific application requirements.

- *Monitoring and orchestration*: ASR provides monitoring capabilities to track the health and status of replication and recovery operations. It also offers centralized management and monitoring through the Azure Portal, where you can view replication status, set up alerts, and perform troubleshooting tasks.

- *Testing and nondisruptive recovery*: ASR enables businesses to test nondisruptive recovery plans to validate their disaster recovery strategies without impacting production workloads. This helps ensure the reliability and effectiveness of the recovery process.

- *Integration with Azure Services*: ASR seamlessly integrates with other Azure services, such as Azure Virtual Network, Azure Automation, and Azure Traffic Manager, to provide comprehensive disaster recovery solutions. It leverages Azure's global infrastructure and capabilities for enhanced resilience and scalability.

By leveraging Azure Site Recovery, businesses can achieve robust disaster recovery capabilities, reduce downtime, and ensure business continuity. ASR simplifies the replication, failover, and failback processes across on-premises and Azure environments, offering a scalable and cost-effective solution for disaster recovery.

Key Features of Azure Site Recovery

Azure Site Recovery offers several features that enable businesses to protect their workloads and ensure business continuity during a disaster.

- Replication and disaster recovery:

  - ASR facilitates the replication of on-premises VMs, physical servers, and Azure VMs to a secondary location, either within Azure or to another site.

  - It supports continuous replication or replication at customizable intervals to ensure data consistency and minimize data loss in the event of a failover.

- Application consistency:

  - ASR ensures application consistency by orchestrating the replication and failover process at the application level rather than just replicating the VMs.

  - It coordinates the replication of multi-tier applications, ensuring all components and dependencies are replicated and recovered.

- Site-to-site disaster recovery:

  - ASR enables businesses to replicate and failover their entire on-premises infrastructure to Azure, including VMs, physical servers, and data centers.

  - In the event of a disaster or outage at the primary site, ASR facilitates failover to the secondary site in Azure, minimizing downtime and ensuring business continuity.

- Azure VM disaster recovery:

  - ASR provides disaster recovery for Azure VMs within the same Azure region or across different regions.

  - It replicates Azure VMs to a secondary region and allows for failover and failback operations, ensuring high availability and resilience for Azure VM workloads.

- Cross-platform support:

  - ASR supports various operating systems, including Windows and Linux, and can replicate workloads running on hypervisors like Hyper-V and VMware.

  - This cross-platform support enables businesses to protect heterogeneous IT environments and achieve consistency in their disaster recovery strategy.

- Automated recovery plans:

  - ASR allows you to create recovery plans that define the order and dependencies of the failover process.

  - These plans automate the recovery steps, ensuring consistency and simplifying the failover and failback processes. You can customize recovery plans based on your specific application requirements.

- Monitoring and orchestration:

  - ASR provides monitoring capabilities to track the health and status of replication and recovery operations.

  - It offers centralized management and monitoring through the Azure Portal, where you can view replication status, set up alerts, and perform troubleshooting tasks.

- Testing and nondisruptive recovery:

  - ASR enables businesses to perform non-disruptive recovery plan testing to validate disaster recovery strategies without impacting production workloads.

  - This feature helps ensure the reliability and effectiveness of the recovery process.

- Integration with Azure Services:

  - ASR integrates with other Azure services, such as Azure Virtual Network, Azure Automation, and Azure Traffic Manager, to provide comprehensive disaster recovery solutions.

  - It leverages Azure's global infrastructure and capabilities for enhanced resilience and scalability.

By leveraging these features, Azure Site Recovery offers businesses a comprehensive and scalable solution for disaster recovery, enabling them to protect their workloads, minimize downtime, and ensure business continuity in the face of disruptions or disasters.

Site Recovery Services

There are several replication methods are supported by Azure Site Recovery, including Site Recovery for Azure VMs replicating between Azure regions, replication from Azure Public Multi-Access Edge Compute (MEC) to the region, replication between two Azure Public MECs and On-premises VMs, Azure Stack VMs, and physical servers. The following are the services offered by Azure Site Recovery:

- *Simple BCDR solution*: The Azure Portal makes it easy to manage replication, failover, and failback from a central location.

- *Azure VM replication*: You can replicate Azure VMs between regions, or from one Azure Public MEC to another Azure Public MEC in the same region, or from one Azure Public MEC to another Azure Public MEC in the same region.

- *VMware VM replication*: Azure Site Recovery replication appliances offer improved security and resilience over the configuration server when replicating VMware VMs to Azure.

- *On-premises VM replication*: A secondary data center on-premises or Azure can replicate on-premises VMs and physical servers. The cost and complexity of maintaining a secondary data center are eliminated with replication to Azure.

- *Workload replication*: ASR is supported for Azure virtual machines, Hyper-V and VMware virtual machines on-premises, and Windows/Linux physical servers.

- *Data resilience*: Azure Site Recovery orchestrates replication without intercepting application data. When you replicate to Azure, data is stored in Azure storage, which provides resilience. When failover occurs, Azure VMs are created using the replicated data. The same applies to Azure Site Recovery scenarios between Public MECs and Azure regions. During Azure Public MEC to Public MEC Azure Site Recovery (ASR functionality is in preview), data is stored in the Public MEC.

- *RTO and RPO targets*: Keep RTOs and RPOs within organizational limits. Azure VMs and VMware VMs can be continuously replicated with Site Recovery, while Hyper-V VMs can be replicated as often as 30 seconds. By integrating with Azure Traffic Manager, you can further reduce RTO.

- *Keep apps consistent over failover*: Recovery points capture to disk, memory, and transaction data to replicate application-consistent snapshots.

- *Testing without disruption*: Disaster recovery drills can be easily performed without affecting ongoing replication.

- *Flexible failovers*: You won't lose any data if you've planned a failover for an expected outage. If you've had an unplanned failover, you'll lose minimal data. If your primary site is once again available, you can easily return to it.

- *Customized recovery plans*: Multitier applications running on multiple VMs can be customized and sequenced using recovery plans. In recovery plans, machines are grouped together, and scripts and manual actions can be added. Azure Automation runbooks can be integrated with recovery plans.

Note   This functionality is currently supported for region-to-region replication and will be available on Azure Public MEC soon.

- *BCDR integration*: You can use Site Recovery to manage the failover of availability groups, with native support for SQL Server Always On, and protect the SQL Server backend of corporate workloads.

- *Azure automation integration*: In Azure Automation, you can download application-specific scripts ready for production and integrate them with Site Recovery.

- *Network integration*: In addition to reserving IP addresses, configuring load balancers, and using Azure Traffic Manager for efficient network switchovers, Site Recovery integrates with Azure for application network management.

Azure Site Recovery in the Event of a Cybersecurity Incident

Azure Site Recovery plays a crucial role in a cybersecurity incident by providing disaster recovery capabilities and helping organizations recover their workloads and data. Here's how Azure Site Recovery can assist in such situations:

- *Data protection and replication*: ASR replicates data from on-premises environments or Azure VMs to a secondary location, such as another Azure region. This ensures that a copy of critical data is stored securely, separate from the immediate environment. In a cybersecurity incident, this replicated data can be used for recovery.

- *Rapid recovery*: ASR enables organizations to quickly recover their workloads and applications to a secondary site or Azure. It automates the failover process, allowing near-instantaneous recovery to minimize downtime and service disruption. This helps organizations mitigate the impact of a cybersecurity incident and restore operations swiftly.

- *Application consistency*: ASR ensures application consistency during the replication and failover process. It coordinates the replication of multi-tier applications, including their dependencies, to maintain the integrity and consistency of the entire application stack. This ensures that applications can be recovered and resumed in a consistent state.

- *Point-in-time recovery*: ASR provides the ability to perform point-in-time recovery, allowing organizations to restore their workloads to a specific moment before the cybersecurity incident occurred. This feature helps recover data that might have been compromised or lost due to the incident, ensuring data integrity and minimizing data loss.

- *Network and security configuration*: ASR preserves network and security configurations during failover, ensuring the recovered environment remains secure and compliant. This includes preserving network settings, firewall rules, and access controls, which helps organizations maintain their security posture even in a cybersecurity incident.

- *Testing and planning*: ASR enables organizations to regularly test their disaster recovery plans and procedures without impacting production environments. This allows organizations to validate their readiness to recover from cybersecurity incidents and fine-tune their recovery strategies based on the test results.

- *Compliance and audit*: ASR helps organizations meet compliance requirements by providing the necessary controls and processes for disaster recovery. This includes maintaining data backups, replicating data to a secondary site, and documenting recovery plans. ASR's compliance capabilities can help organizations demonstrate their ability to recover from cybersecurity incidents during audits and regulatory assessments.

Overall, Azure Site Recovery is critical to an organization's cybersecurity incident response strategy. It ensures data protection, enables rapid recovery, maintains application consistency, and supports testing and compliance requirements. By leveraging ASR, organizations can enhance their resilience against cybersecurity incidents and reduce the impact on their operations and data.

Recovery Plans

Recovery plans in Azure Site Recovery are critical to disaster recovery and play a crucial role in recovering from a cybersecurity incident. A recovery plan defines the actions and steps required to recover your workloads and applications during a disruption. Here's a detailed explanation of recovery plans using Azure Site Recovery in the event of a cybersecurity incident:

- *Defining a recovery plan*: In the Azure Portal, you can create a recovery plan that specifies the order in which your VMs and resources should be recovered during a cybersecurity incident. You can group VMs based on their dependencies, application tiers, or any other logical grouping that suits your recovery requirements.

- *Preparing for recovery*: Within the recovery plan, you can specify pre-scripts executed before the recovery process begins. These scripts can perform tasks such as stopping certain services, shutting down specific VMs, or executing custom commands to prepare the environment for recovery.

- *Recovery groups*: Recovery groups are subsets of VMs within a recovery plan that share dependencies or require coordinated recovery. For example, if an application relies on a database server, you can group the application VM and the database VM in the same recovery group. This ensures that the database VM is recovered first before recovering the application VM.

- *VM start order*: Within a recovery group, you can define the start order of the VMs. This ensures that critical components of your application stack are recovered in the correct sequence, considering dependencies between different VMs. By defining the start order, you can ensure the proper functioning of your application after recovery.

- *Customization and script execution*: Recovery plans in Azure Site Recovery allow for customization and execution of post-scripts. These scripts can be used to perform additional configuration tasks or validations after the VMs have been recovered. For example, you can execute scripts to verify the integrity of the recovered VMs or to restore specific application settings.

- *Manual or automatic execution*: Recovery plans can be executed manually or automatically. In a cybersecurity incident, you can manually trigger the execution of a recovery plan. Alternatively, you can set up automation rules or integrate them with monitoring systems to automatically trigger the execution of a recovery plan when specific conditions or alerts are met.

- *Failover testing*: It is crucial to regularly test the recovery plans to ensure their effectiveness and validity. Azure Site Recovery allows you to perform non-disruptive failover testing, enabling you to validate the recovery process without impacting your production environment. This testing helps identify any issues or gaps in the recovery plan and allows for necessary adjustments to be made.

- *Monitoring and reporting*: Azure Site Recovery provides monitoring
  and reporting capabilities to track the execution of recovery plans.
  You can monitor the progress of VM recovery, view detailed logs, and
  receive notifications about the status of recovery operations. This
  helps ensure that the recovery plan is progressing as expected and
  provides visibility into the recovery process.

Organizations can streamline and automate the recovery process during a
cybersecurity incident by utilizing recovery plans in Azure Site Recovery. The ability
to define the recovery order, execute pre- and post-scripts, and customize the recovery
process helps ensure a systematic and efficient recovery of critical workloads and
applications. Regular testing and monitoring of recovery plans are crucial to maintain
the readiness and effectiveness of the recovery process.

The Modernization of Disaster Recovery Failovers/ Failbacks On-Premises

In Azure, on-premises disaster recovery failover/failback can be modernized by
leveraging Azure Site Recovery and Azure services.

Here's how on-premises disaster recovery failover/failback can be modernized
in Azure:

- *Replication to Azure*: Azure Site Recovery allows you to replicate your
  on-premises virtual machines, physical servers, and even VMware
  virtual machines to Azure. This replication process ensures that
  your data and workloads are continuously synchronized with Azure,
  minimizing the potential for data loss during a disaster.

- *Virtual machine conversion*: Azure Site Recovery provides tools and
  processes to convert your on-premises virtual machines into Azure
  virtual machines. This conversion enables seamless failover and
  failback operations between your on-premises environment and Azure.

- *Azure Virtual Networks*: Azure Site Recovery integrates with Azure
  Virtual Networks, allowing you to create a virtual network in Azure
  that mirrors your on-premises network configuration. This enables a
  smooth transition of your applications during failover, maintaining
  connectivity and network configurations.

- *Failover and failback automation*: Azure Site Recovery provides automation capabilities to orchestrate failover and failback processes. You can define recovery plans that specify the order in which virtual machines are failed over and define custom scripts or actions to be executed during the process. This automation minimizes downtime and ensures consistency in the failover/failback operations.

- *Testing and validation*: Azure Site Recovery offers non-disruptive testing capabilities, allowing you to validate your failover and failback processes without impacting production workloads. You can perform scheduled or ad-hoc tests to ensure the effectiveness and reliability of your disaster recovery plans.

- *Integration with Azure services*: Azure Site Recovery can integrate with other Azure services, such as Azure Backup and Azure Monitor, to enhance the overall disaster recovery capabilities. Azure Backup can be used to protect and restore data within Azure, while Azure Monitor helps monitor and manage the health and performance of your disaster recovery environment.

By leveraging Azure Site Recovery and other Azure services, organizations can modernize their on-premises disaster recovery failover/failback processes, benefit from the scalability and flexibility of the cloud, and ensure business continuity in the event of a disaster.

Azure Traffic Manager and Azure Site Recovery

Azure Traffic Manager and Azure Site Recovery are two distinct services from Microsoft Azure that serve different purposes. However, they can be used together to enhance the overall disaster recovery capabilities and improve the availability of applications during a disaster event.

Azure Traffic Manager is a DNS-based traffic load balancer that distributes incoming traffic across multiple endpoints, such as Azure regions, data centers, or on-premises locations. It helps optimize the availability and responsiveness of applications by routing users to the most appropriate endpoint based on various routing methods and health probes.

On the other hand, Azure Site Recovery is a disaster recovery service that enables the replication and recovery of on-premises virtual machines, physical servers, and VMware virtual machines to Azure. It helps organizations protect their workloads and applications by providing failover and failback capabilities in case of a disaster or disruption.

When used together, Azure Traffic Manager can be configured to monitor the health of Azure Site Recovery endpoints and dynamically route traffic to the most appropriate endpoint based on their availability and responsiveness. This integration allows for enhanced disaster recovery and high-availability scenarios.

Here's how Azure Traffic Manager can be used with Azure Site Recovery:

- *Routing methods*: Azure Traffic Manager offers various routing methods, including Performance, Priority, Weighted, Geographic, and Subnet. These routing methods can be configured to distribute traffic across different Azure regions or data centers where Azure Site Recovery endpoints are deployed. By utilizing these routing methods, traffic can be automatically rerouted to healthy endpoints in a disaster.

- *Health probes*: Azure Traffic Manager continuously monitors the health of Azure Site Recovery endpoints by sending periodic health probes. The health probes check the availability and responsiveness of the endpoints and determine their health status. If an endpoint becomes unhealthy, Azure Traffic Manager can automatically reroute traffic to other healthy endpoints, ensuring continuous availability and minimal disruption to users.

- *Failover scenarios*: In a disaster recovery scenario, Azure Site Recovery can initiate the failover process to the secondary data center or Azure region when a primary data center or location becomes unavailable. Azure Traffic Manager can be configured to detect the change in endpoint health status and automatically reroute traffic to the new healthy endpoints in the secondary location.

- *Failback scenarios*: Azure Site Recovery can initiate the failback process to restore workloads and applications once the primary data center or location becomes available after a disaster. Azure Traffic Manager can detect the restored endpoint's health and reroute traffic to the primary location, ensuring a smooth transition and resuming normal operations.

Organizations can achieve improved disaster recovery capabilities and application availability by combining Azure Traffic Manager with Azure Site Recovery. The dynamic traffic routing capabilities of Azure Traffic Manager ensure that users are directed to healthy endpoints, minimizing downtime and maximizing the availability of applications during and after a disaster event.

Azure ExpressRoute with Azure Site Recovery

Azure ExpressRoute and Azure Site Recovery are two services offered by Microsoft Azure that serve different purposes. Azure ExpressRoute provides a dedicated and private connection between on-premises networks and Azure, while Azure Site Recovery is a disaster recovery service that replicates and recovers workloads to Azure.

Although they have distinct functionalities, Azure ExpressRoute can be leveraged to enhance Azure Site Recovery deployments' performance, security, and reliability. Here's how Azure ExpressRoute can be used with Azure Site Recovery:

- *Dedicated connectivity*: Azure ExpressRoute establishes a private and dedicated connection between your on-premises network and Azure. This connection bypasses the public internet, providing a more secure and reliable pathway for data transfer between your on-premises infrastructure and Azure. By utilizing Azure ExpressRoute, the replication traffic from Azure Site Recovery can traverse this dedicated connection, ensuring optimal network performance and reducing latency.

- *Increased bandwidth*: Azure ExpressRoute offers high-bandwidth connectivity options, ranging from 50 Mbps to 100 Gbps. This increased bandwidth allows faster data replication from on-premises to Azure, enabling more efficient disaster recovery operations. With higher throughput, you can reduce the time it takes to replicate and recover workloads to Azure, minimizing the RTO and ensuring minimal data loss.

- *Private network connection*: Azure ExpressRoute enables a private and isolated network connection between your on-premises infrastructure and Azure. This private connectivity ensures that your data remains within a secure and controlled environment, enhancing the overall security of your disaster recovery infrastructure. It also helps meet regulatory compliance requirements by keeping sensitive data off the public internet.

- *Reliable network performance*: Azure ExpressRoute provides service level agreements (SLAs) for network availability and performance. By utilizing ExpressRoute for Azure Site Recovery, you can use these SLAs to ensure reliable and consistent network connectivity between your on-premises environment and Azure. This reliability is crucial for disaster recovery scenarios where consistent network connectivity is essential for replication, failover, and failback operations.

- *Integration with Azure Virtual Network*: Azure ExpressRoute can be integrated with Azure Virtual Network, allowing you to extend your on-premises network into Azure. This integration enables seamless connectivity and communication between your on-premises infrastructure and Azure resources, including Azure Site Recovery. It ensures that the replicated workloads in Azure can seamlessly connect to other Azure services and resources, facilitating a smooth failover/failback process.

By combining Azure ExpressRoute with Azure Site Recovery, organizations can leverage dedicated and secure connectivity to improve their disaster recovery deployments' performance, reliability, and security. The private and high-bandwidth connection provided by Azure ExpressRoute enhances the replication process, reduces latency, and ensures the availability of critical workloads in Azure during a disaster event.

Azure Virtual Machine Recovery with Azure Site Recovery

Azure Site Recovery enables the replication and recovery of VMs and physical servers to Azure. It helps organizations protect their workloads and applications by providing failover and failback capabilities in case of a disaster or disruption. With ASR, you can replicate your on-premises VMs to Azure or replicate Azure VMs between Azure regions for additional protection.

Here's an overview of how Azure VM recovery works with Azure Site Recovery:

- *Replication*: Azure Site Recovery replicates your on-premises VMs or Azure VMs to Azure. This replication process creates and maintains a copy of your VMs in Azure, ensuring that the data and configuration are continuously synchronized.

- *Recovery plans*: With Azure Site Recovery, you define recovery plans that specify the steps and order for recovering your VMs in case of a disaster. These recovery plans include starting the VMs, setting up networking, and executing custom scripts. Recovery plans can be customized based on your requirements and dependencies between VMs.

- *Failover*: In a disaster or disruption, you can initiate the failover process in Azure Site Recovery. Failover involves the recovery of your VMs from the replicated data in Azure. During the failover, Azure Site Recovery provisions the VMs in Azure based on the configuration defined in the recovery plan.

- *Failback*: Once the primary site or environment becomes available, you can perform the failback process to restore your VMs to the original location. Azure Site Recovery synchronizes the changes made in Azure back to the on-premises environment or the original Azure region. Failback ensures that your applications and workloads are seamlessly transitioned back to the primary site.

- *Testing and validation*: Azure Site Recovery allows you to test your disaster recovery plans without impacting your production environment. You can perform non-disruptive tests to validate the recovery process and ensure the readiness of your VMs in Azure. This testing helps identify and address any issues before an actual disaster occurs.

- *Monitoring and reporting*: Azure Site Recovery provides monitoring capabilities and generates reports on the health and performance of your replication and recovery processes. You can monitor the replication status, track the recovery progress, and receive notifications about any issues or failures.

By leveraging Azure Site Recovery, organizations can ensure business continuity and minimize downtime during a disaster. It simplifies the VM recovery process by automating failover and failback operations, providing reliable replication, and enabling testing and monitoring capabilities.

Overall Security Integration Component with Azure Site Recovery

Security is a crucial aspect of Azure Site Recovery, and Microsoft has implemented several measures to ensure the security and confidentiality of customer data. Here's an overview of the security features and practices in Azure Site Recovery:

- *Encryption*: Azure Site Recovery uses encryption to protect data in transit and at rest. Data replication from on-premises to Azure is encrypted using SSL/TLS protocols, ensuring secure transmission over the network. Data at rest in Azure is encrypted using Azure Storage Service Encryption (SSE), which employs industry-standard AES-256 encryption.

- *Network isolation*: Azure Site Recovery employs network isolation mechanisms to protect customer data. The replication traffic flows over a dedicated network channel, separate from public internet traffic. This isolation helps prevent unauthorized access and data breaches.

- *Azure Active Directory integration*: Azure Site Recovery integrates with Azure Active Directory (Azure AD) for authentication and access control. Azure AD provides identify and access management capabilities, including multi-factor authentication (MFA), role-based access control (RBAC), and Conditional Access policies, ensuring secure access to Azure Site Recovery resources.

- *RBAC*: Azure Site Recovery utilizes RBAC to provide granular access control to resources. Administrators can assign specific roles and permissions to individuals or groups, allowing them to perform only the necessary actions within Azure Site Recovery. RBAC helps ensure that users have the appropriate level of access and reduces the risk of unauthorized access.

- *Data residency*: Azure Site Recovery supports regional and geographic data redundancy. Customers can choose the Azure regions where their replicated data is stored, providing control over data residency and compliance requirements.

- *Compliance and certifications*: Azure Site Recovery meets various compliance standards and undergoes regular audits. It complies with industry standards such as ISO 27001, HIPAA, GDPR, etc. Microsoft Azure has comprehensive compliance offerings, and Azure Site Recovery inherits those certifications and attestations.

- *Security monitoring and threat detection*: Azure Site Recovery benefits from the security monitoring and threat detection capabilities provided by Azure Security Center. It helps detect and respond to security threats and provides insights into potential vulnerabilities in the ASR environment.

- *Disaster recovery testing*: Azure Site Recovery allows for non-disruptive testing of disaster recovery plans. This testing enables organizations to validate their recovery processes and ensure their systems are secure and functional during a disaster.

Microsoft Azure has a shared responsibility model for security, where Microsoft is responsible for the security of the underlying infrastructure. At the same time, customers are responsible for securing their applications and data within Azure Site Recovery. By following security best practices, configuring access controls, and implementing additional security measures, customers can enhance the security of their Azure Site Recovery deployments.

How to Set Up Disaster Recovery for an Azure VM to a Secondary Azure Region

To set up disaster recovery for an Azure VM to a secondary Azure region using the Azure Portal, you can follow these steps:

1. Sign in to the Azure Portal using your Azure account credentials.

2. Navigate to the Azure VM that you want to enable disaster recovery for.

3. In the menu on the left, under Operations, click Disaster recovery.

4. On the "Disaster recovery" page, click the "Set up disaster recovery" button.

5. On the "Set up disaster recovery" page, you will be presented with different options for disaster recovery solutions. Choose "Between Azure regions" to enable disaster recovery to a secondary Azure region.

6. In the Source section, select the source region where your VM is currently deployed.

7. In the Target section, select the target region where you want to replicate your VM for disaster recovery.

8. Specify the "Target resource group" and the "Target virtual network" in the selected target region where the replicated VM will be created during failover.

9. Configure the "Replication settings" according to your requirements. This includes the replication frequency, retention window, and application-consistent snapshot settings.

10. Review the summary of your configuration settings, and then click the OK button to start the replication setup.

11. Once the setup is complete, you will be redirected to your Azure VM's Disaster recovery page. Here, you can monitor the replication status, perform test failovers, and manage failover and failback operations.

Value of Integration Component with Azure Site Recovery   Enabling disaster recovery for an Azure VM to a secondary region may incur additional costs for the replicated resources. Make sure to review the pricing details and understand the associated costs.

It's important to note that setting up disaster recovery for an Azure VM involves additional steps beyond the ones mentioned here, such as configuring networking and storage accounts and ensuring VM compatibility. It's recommended to consult the Azure documentation or contact Microsoft Azure support for detailed guidance specific to your environment and requirements.

Azure Security Baselines for Azure Site Recovery

Azure Security Baselines provide a set of recommended security configurations and best practices for various Azure services, including Azure Site Recovery. These baselines help organizations implement a strong security posture and protect their Azure resources from common security threats. Here's an explanation of the Azure security baseline for Azure Site Recovery:

- *Security recommendations*: The Azure Security Baseline for Azure Site Recovery includes specific security recommendations and best practices that should be implemented to enhance the security of ASR deployments. These recommendations cover various areas, such as network security, access control, encryption, and monitoring.

- *Network security*: The baseline may include recommendations to ensure proper network security for ASR. This could involve implementing NSGs to control inbound and outbound traffic, setting up virtual network service endpoints for ASR, and utilizing Azure ExpressRoute for private and dedicated connectivity.

- *Access control*: The baseline guides access control mechanisms for Azure Site Recovery. This may include recommendations to implement Azure AD authentication for ASR management, enforce multifactor authentication (MFA) for user accounts, and apply the principle of least privilege by granting appropriate permissions to ASR resources.

- *Encryption*: The baseline emphasizes using encryption to protect data in transit and at rest. It may recommend enabling SSL/TLS encryption for replication traffic between on-premises and Azure, Azure SSE for data at rest, and Azure Key Vault for managing encryption keys.

- *Monitoring and logging*: The baseline may include recommendations for implementing monitoring and logging solutions to detect and respond to security incidents in ASR deployments. This could involve enabling Azure Monitor to collect and analyze logs, set up alerts for suspicious activities, and integrate with Azure Security Center for threat detection and security insights.

- *Backup and recovery*: The baseline may cover best practices for backup and recovery in Azure Site Recovery. This could include recommendations for configuring backup retention policies, testing recovery plans, and regularly reviewing and updating recovery procedures.

- *Compliance and auditing*: The Azure Security Baseline for Azure Site Recovery may align with relevant compliance standards and regulatory requirements. It may guide configuring ASR to meet specific compliance requirements, such as GDPR, HIPAA, or ISO 27001.

It's important to note that Azure Security Baselines are not static and may evolve to address emerging security threats and incorporate new best practices. Organizations should regularly review and update their Azure Site Recovery deployments based on the latest security recommendations from Azure Security Baselines and other relevant security resources provided by Microsoft.

Backup and Restore Plan to Protect Against Ransomware

Creating a backup and restore plan is crucial for protecting against ransomware in a Microsoft Azure cloud environment. Here's a more detailed and illustrative explanation of how you can set up such a plan using Azure cloud services:

- *Identify critical data and assets*: Start by identifying the critical data, applications, and assets in your Azure environment that must be protected against ransomware. This could include virtual machines, databases, storage accounts, and file shares.

- *Azure Backup*: Utilize Azure Backup, a cloud-based backup solution, to create backups of your Azure resources. Azure Backup supports various Azure services like virtual machines, databases, and file shares. It offers features such as incremental backups, encryption, and retention policies.

- *Recovery Services vault*: Create a Recovery Services vault in Azure to centralize and manage your backup data. The vault serves as a container for storing backup data securely. Configure the appropriate settings, such as retention period and backup frequency, based on your recovery objectives and compliance requirements.

- *Backup policies*: Define backup policies within the Recovery Services vault to specify which resources should be backed up, the frequency of backups, and the retention period. You can create separate policies for different types of resources or applications based on their criticality and RPOs.

- *Backup schedules*: Configure backup schedules within the backup policies to determine when backups should be taken. You can choose daily, weekly, or custom schedules based on your needs. Ensure backup schedules do not overlap with known maintenance or peak usage periods.

- *Application-consistent backups*: Enable application-consistent backups whenever possible. This ensures that the backup consistently captures a snapshot of the application and its data. Azure Backup provides integration with various Azure services to achieve application-consistent backups.

- *Data retention*: Determine the appropriate data retention period for your backups. Consider factors such as compliance requirements, business needs, and the potential impact of ransomware attacks. Azure Backup allows you to set retention policies to manage backup data retention automatically.

- *Offline backup copies*: Consider creating offline backup copies to protect against ransomware targeting your primary backups. Azure

Backup allows offline backup copies by exporting backups to another Azure region or downloading them to an on-premises location.

- *Test restores*: Periodically perform test restores from your backups to validate their integrity and verify that the restoration process works as expected. Testing restores helps ensure that you can recover your critical data during a ransomware attack.

- *Monitoring and alerts*: Enable monitoring and configure alerts to be notified of any backup failures or anomalies. Azure provides monitoring capabilities through Azure Monitor, which can generate alerts based on predefined thresholds or custom criteria.

- *Security and access control*: Implement strong security measures to protect your backup data. Utilize features like encryption at rest, RBAC, and Azure AD authentication to secure your backups from unauthorized access.

Remember that a backup and restore plan is insufficient to protect against ransomware. It should complement other security measures, such as implementing network security controls, enabling threat detection and monitoring, and educating users about phishing and social engineering risks.

Regularly review and update your backup and restore plan based on changes in your Azure environment, the evolving threat landscape, and new capabilities offered by Azure services.

Azure Site Recovery   As part of your business continuity and disaster recovery (BCDR) strategy, Site Recovery orchestrates and automates the replication of Azure virtual machines, on-premises machines to Azure, and servers to secondary data centers. Because of Azure's inability to support persistent MAC addresses, software with MAC-based license models can't be used for migration to Azure and disaster recovery. Organizations can automate Site Recovery workflows using the REST API, PowerShell, or the Azure SDK.

Summary

In this chapter, you read about designing and deploying recovery solutions aligned to the NIST CSF and saw a list of best practices to consider in recovering and securing from day-two operations.

Thank you for choosing to read this book. Good luck on your Azure security future.

Index

A

© Puthiyavan Udayakumar 2023
P. Udayakumar, *Design and Deploy a Secure Azure Environment*,
https://doi.org/10.1007/978-1-4842-9678-3

S

W, X, Y

Z

Printed in the United States
by Baker & Taylor Publisher Services